Lecture Notes in Computer Science

Janusz Górski (Ed.)

Computer Safety, Reliability, and Security

25th International Conference, SAFECOMP 2006
Gdansk, Poland, September 27-29, 2006
Proceedings

Volume Editor

Janusz Górski
Gdansk University of Technology
Department of Software Engineering
ul. Narutowicza 11/12, 80-952 Gdansk, Poland
E-mail: jango@pg.gda.pl

Library of Congress Control Number: 2006932795

CR Subject Classification (1998): D.1-4, E.4, C.3, F.3, K.6.5

LNCS Sublibrary: SL 2 – Programming and Software Engineering

ISSN 0302-9743
ISBN-10 3-540-45762-3 Springer Berlin Heidelberg New York
ISBN-13 978-3-540-45762-6 Springer Berlin Heidelberg New York

Springer is a part of Springer Science+Business Media

springer.com

Printed in Germany

Typesetting: Camera-ready by author, data conversion by Scientific Publishing Services, Chennai, India
Printed on acid-free paper SPIN: 11875567 06/3142 5 4 3 2 1 0

Preface

Welcome to SAFECOMP 2006, the 25th International Conference on Computer Safety, Security and Reliability, held in Gdansk, Poland. Since it was established in 1979 by the European Workshop on Industrial Computer Systems, Technical Committee 7 on Safety, Reliability and Security (EWICS TC7), SAFECOMP has continuously contributed to the progress in high integrity applications of information technologies. The conference focuses on the state of the art, experience and new trends in the areas of safety, security and reliability of critical IT systems and applications and serves as a platform for knowledge and technology transfer for researchers, industry (suppliers, operators, users), regulators and certifiers of such systems. SAFECOMP provides ample opportunity to exchange insights and experiences on emerging methods, approaches and practical solutions to safety, security and reliability problems across the borders of different application domains and technologies.

The SAFECOMP 2006 program reflected in this book included 32 papers selected from 101 submissions of full texts. The submissions came from authors representing 26 different countries from Europe, Asia, and North and South America. The 32 accepted papers were prepared by experts representing 14 different countries. The above data confirm the broad and increasing interest in SAFECOMP and the topics addressed.

The program was supplemented by three keynote presentations by outstanding invited experts (not included in this book). The keynotes focused on interdisciplinary aspects of dependability of computer systems, practical aspects of application of safety standards and new challenges of information security research and development.

Preparation of the SAFECOMP 2006 program was a long and intensive process. Its success is the result of the hard work, involvement and support of the International Program Committee, the external reviewers, the keynote speakers, and most of all, the authors who submitted numerous excellent contributions. Selecting from them was by no means an easy task and in many cases some very good papers could not be accepted because of the program constraints.

I would like to thank all those who contributed to the preparation of the SAFECOMP 2006 program for their competence, dedication and sustainable support. I would also like to thank my colleagues from the Information Assurance Group of the Department of Software Engineering of Gdansk University of Technology for their organizational support. Special thanks are due to the National Organizing Committee, for its involvement in the preparation of the conference.

The next conference, SAFECOMP 2007, will take place in Nuremberg, Germany, and in the name of the organizers I am extending to you the invitation to contribute to and attend this important event in the field of Computer Safety, Reliability and Security.

July 2006 Janusz Górski

Organization

Program Chair

Janusz Górski, Poland

EWICS Chair

Udo Voges, Germany

Organizing Committee

Janusz Górski (Co-chair)
Aleksander Jarzębowicz (Co-chair)
Janusz Czaja
Grzegorz Gołaszewski
Alfreda Kortas
Jakub Miler
Marcin Olszewski

International Program Committee

Stuart Anderson, UK
Ramesh Bharadwaj, USA
Andrzej Białas, Poland
Robin Bloomfield, UK
Sandro Bologna, Italy
Andrea Bondavalli, Italy
Bettina Buth, Germany
Tadeusz Cichocki, Poland
Peter Daniel, UK
Erland Jonsson, Sweden
Wolfgang Ehrenberger, Germany
Massimo Felici, UK
Robert Genser, Austria
Chris Goring, UK
Bjørn Axel Gran, Norway
Wolfgang Grieskamp, USA
Wolfgang Halang, Germany
Monika Heiner, Germany
Maritta Heisel, Germany
Connie Heitmeyer, USA
Ming-Yuh Huang, USA
Chris Johnson, UK
Mohamed Kaâniche, France
Karama Kanoun, France
Floor Koornneef, Netherlands
Peter Ladkin, Germany
Jan Magott, Poland
Marcelo Masera, Italy
Meine van der Meulen, UK
Odd Nordland, Norway
Simone Pozzi, Italy
Gerd Rabe, Germany
Felix Redmill, UK
Krzysztof Sacha, Poland
Francesca Saglietti, Germany
Erwin Schoitsch, Austria
Nicolas Sklavos, Greece
Jeanine Souquières, France

Werner Stephan, Germany
Mark Sujan, UK
Atoosa P.-J. Thunem, Norway
Jos Trienekens, Netherlands
Adolfo Villafiorita, Italy
Udo Voges, Germany
Andrzej Wardziński, Poland
Albrecht Weinert, Germany
Marc Wilikens, Italy
Rune Winther, Norway
Stefan Wittmann, Belgium
Eric Wong, USA
Zdzisław Żurakowski, Poland

External Reviewers

Lei Bu
Lassaad Cheikhrouhou
Silvano Chiaradonna
Sergio Contini
Lorenzo Falai
Igor Nai Fovino
Felicita Di Giandomenico
Jeremie Guiochet
Paweł Głuchowski
Tom Heijer
Hai Hu
Martin Gilje Jaatun
Bin Lei
Paolo Lollini
Thea Peacock
Yu Qi
Georg Rock
Marco Roveri
Peter Ryan
Holger Schmidt
Martin Skambraks
Paweł Skrobanek
Alberto Stefanini
Avinanta Tarigan
Roberto Tiella
I. Made Wiryana
Wei Zhang

Sponsoring Organizations

Organizing Institutions

Scientific Sponsors

European
Network of
Clubs for
REliability and
Safety of
Software

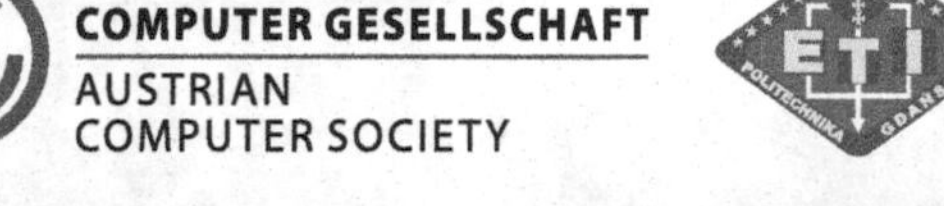

DECOS

Industrial Sponsors

Assurance & Trust Cases
tckon.eu

Table of Contents

Systems of Systems

Security and Survivability Analysis

Nuclear Safety and Application of Standards

Formal Approaches

Networks Dependability

Coping with Change and Mobility

Safety Analysis and Assessment

Poster Session

6th FP Integrated Project DECOS

Modelling

System of Systems Hazard Analysis Using Simulation and Machine Learning

Robert Alexander, Dimitar Kazakov, and Tim Kelly

Department of Computer Science
University of York, York, YO10 5DD, UK
{robert.alexander, dimitar.kazakov, tim.kelly}@cs.york.ac.uk

Abstract. In the operation of safety-critical systems, the sequences by which failures can lead to accidents can be many and complex. This is particularly true for the emerging class of systems known as systems of systems, as they are composed of many distributed, heterogenous and autonomous components. Performing hazard analysis on such systems is challenging, in part because it is difficult to know in advance which of the many observable or measurable features of the system are important for maintaining system safety. Hence there is a need for effective techniques to find causal relationships within these systems. This paper explores the use of machine learning techniques to extract potential causal relationships from simulation models. This is illustrated with a case study of a military system of systems.

1 Introduction

Large-scale military and transport Systems of Systems (SoS) present many challenges for safety. The term 'SoS' is somewhat controversial — attempts at definitions can be found in [1] and [2]. It is easy, however, to identify uncontroversial examples, Air Traffic Control and Network Centric Warfare being the most prominent. These examples feature mobile components distributed over large areas, such as regions, counties or entire continents. Their components frequently interact with each other in an ad-hoc fashion, and have the potential to cause large-scale destruction and injury.

It follows that for SoS that are being designed and procured now, safety has a high priority. This is particularly true for SoS incorporating new kinds of autonomous component systems, such as Unmanned Aerial Vehicles (UAVs).

This paper is concerned with one aspect of the safety process for SoS, specifically hazard analysis. This is an important first step in any risk-based safety process. Unfortunately, performing hazard analysis on SoS is not easy. Quite apart from the novelty of these systems, and the commensurate lack of examples to work from, the characteristics of SoS raise serious difficulties. For example, ad hoc communications mean that information errors can propagate through the system by many, and unpredictable, routes.

The following section describes the problems faced in SoS hazard analysis, then section 3 proposes multi-agent simulation as a possible solution. An approach to performing hazard analysis, using simulation combined with machine learning, is outlined

J. Górski (Ed.): SAFECOMP 2006, LNCS 4166, pp. 1–14, 2006.

in section 4, and the results of a case study are presented in section 5. Section 6 compares the work with existing applications of simulation in safety and section 7 discusses the issue of model fidelity.

2 The Problem of SoS Hazard Analysis

A definition of the term 'SoS hazard' was given by the authors in [3] as *"Condition of an SoS configuration, physical or otherwise, that can lead to an accident."* It follows that SoS hazard analysis is the process of finding those conditions that can lead to accidents.

The problems faced by safety analysts when attempting to perform hazard analysis on SoS fall into two key categories: the immediate issue of failure effect propagation, and the more pernicious category of 'System Accidents'. It has been noted by Kelly and Wilkinson, in [4], that these problems are present in conventional systems, too, but the characteristics of SoS exacerbate them.

2.1 Deriving the Effects of a Failure

In a conventional system, such as a single vehicle or a chemical plant, the system boundary is well-defined and the components within that boundary can be enumerated. When a safety analyst postulates some failure of a component, the effect of that failure can be propagated through the system to reveal whether or not the failure results in a hazard. This is not always easy, because of the complexity of possible interactions and variability of system state, hence the need for systematic analysis techniques, automated analysis tools, and system designs that minimise possible interactions. To make the task more tractable, most existing hazard analysis techniques (such as FFA and HAZOP) deal with only a single failure at a time; coincident failures are rarely considered.

In an SoS, this problem is considerably worse. The system boundary is not well defined, and the set of entities within that boundary can vary over time, either as part of normal operation (a new aircraft enters a controlled airspace region) or as part of evolutionary development (a military unit receives a new air-defence system). Conventional tactics to minimise interactions may be ineffective, because the system consists of component entities that are individually mobile. In some cases, particularly military systems, the entities may be designed (for performance purposes) to form ad-hoc groupings amongst themselves. Conventional techniques may be inadequate for determining whether or not some failure in some entity is hazardous in the context of the SoS as a whole.

2.2 System Accidents

Perrow, in [5], discusses what he calls 'normal accidents' in the context of complex systems. His 'Normal Accident Theory' holds that any complex, tightly-coupled system has the potential for catastrophic failure stemming from simultaneous minor failures. Similarly, Leveson, in [6] notes that many accidents have multiple necessary causes. In such cases it follows that an investigation of any one cause *prior to the accident* (i.e. without the benefit of hindsight) would not have shown the accident to be plausible.

An SoS can certainly be described as a 'complex, tightly-coupled system', and as such is likely to experience such accidents. This line of reasoning can be taken slightly further, however, to note that a 'normal accident' could result from actions by each of two entities that were safe in themselves, but that are hazardous in combination with each other and the wider SoS context.

This latter issue is more immediate when we consider that many SoS will incorporate systems drawn from multiple manufacturers, developed at different times, and operated by multiple organisations. The evolutionary and dynamic nature of SoS structures means that a system designer will not necessarily ever have a clear picture of the entire SoS context.

2.3 Dealing with These Problems

It follows from the above that in order to perform effective hazard analysis for SoS, there is a need for a hazard analysis approach that can find the hazards in a system containing multiple autonomous entities that interact in complex and continually changing ways.

To some extent, this situation is comparable to that faced by the military modelling and simulation community when they attempted to build models that incorporated explicit modelling of entity behaviour rather than only high-level mathematical abstractions. Their solution was the development of multi-agent simulation, which is discussed in the next section.

3 Multi-agent Simulation

Ferber, in [7] provides the following definition of multi-agent simulation: *"Multi-agent simulation is based on the idea that it is possible to represent in computerised form the behaviour of entities which are active in the world, and that it is possible to represent a phenomenon as the fruit of the interactions of an assembly of agents with their own operational autonomy."*

Similarly, Ilachinski, in [8] offers *"[Multi-agent simulations] consist of a discrete heterogenous set of spatially distributed individual agents, each of which has its own characteristic properties and rules of behaviour."*

Typically, the value of multi-agent simulation is asserted in comparison to the mathematical models that have traditionally been used in biology, economics and military analysis. Ferber notes that agent-based models allow the integration of quantitative variables, differential equations and symbolic rules into agent behaviour, thereby providing a means to exploit qualitative observations as well as quantitative information [7]. He also notes that such 'micro-worlds' allow analysts to experiment by modifying agent behaviour and adding new agent types, which is not possible with high-level mathematical models. Most significantly for our purposes, Ferber comments that such simulations *"make it possible to model complex situations whose overall structures emerge from interactions between individuals"*.

Ilachinski, in [8] makes a similar point: in a multi-agent simulation, different levels of behaviour can be observed. Analysts can examine both the top-level emergent behaviour and the low-level interactions between individual agents. That is, the simulations can both predict overall behaviour and explain *why* it occurs.

4 Hazard Analysis Method

The approach described in this paper combines simulation and machine learning. The SoS to be analysed is represented by a model in which each major component of the system (such as an aircraft or radar station) is represented by an agent. Each agent is described in terms of its physical capabilities (such as the ability to fly at a certain speed) and its rules of behaviour. The simulated system is then placed in a simulated environment (containing, for example, terrain and hostile forces) and given orders and objectives for an appropriate military mission.

The resulting simulation model will have dynamics that are too complex to understand merely by watching it run. It is therefore necessary to derive other models that characterise its behaviour and that *are* simple enough for humans to read and understand.

This derivation is achieved by defining a set of deviations over the simulation model, and exploring the set of combinations of these deviations. Machine learning allows an automated analysis of the resulting output data, resulting in a set of comprehensible rules that relate deviations to accidents occurring in the simulation. The intention is that these rules will guide analysts towards identifying some hazards in the system that they otherwise would have missed.

The five steps of the method are described in the following five sections.

4.1 Build Model

The approach is potentially open to multiple modelling approaches, but the effectiveness of the analysis process will hinge on the type of model used. Models that are used for traditional performance analysis can focus heavily on capturing the overall *functionality* of the system. Models for hazard analysis need to capture much of the *mechanism* of the system's operation. This is for two reasons:

- The system needs to be manipulated in ways which the original designers might not expect (particularly in ways which relate to implementation rather than to functional specification), and the model has to respond appropriately.
- Deviations will be derived by studying how the system works and applying a set of heuristics. Mechanical detail that is not modelled cannot be used in this process.

Inter-agent mechanisms (communications protocols, operating procedures, roles) are more important than intra-agent mechanisms (since the internal behaviour of agents will already be well understood). In order to capture the necessary inter-agent mechanisms, agent actions and communication must be made explicit. Also, as discussed by Hall-May in [9], an important aspect of the system model is that of 'policy' or 'operational doctrine', the set of rules or procedures that attempt to constrain the global behaviour of the system.

Further discussion of modelling approaches is outside the scope of this paper. The important issue of model fidelity, however, is addressed in section 7.

4.2 Specify Deviations for Model

Given the model specified in the previous step, a set of possible deviations must be derived. There are many ways to do this, but the one that is used in this paper is to identify the *channels* over which *interactions* can occur between entities. Examples of channels include network wires, radio transmissions or simply being located in the same airspace. A set of *guide words* is then used to hypothesise some *failure modes* of these channels. Each combination of some entity exhibiting some failure mode on some channel provides a single distinct 'deviation'.

The use of guide words for deriving deviations is based on their usage in HAZOP [10]. By combining the words used in HAZOP with those from the computer-system analysis method SHARD [11] we can derive the set shown in Table 1.

Table 1. Channel deviation guide words

Guide Word	Interpretation
Omission	The interaction does not occur
Commission	The interaction occurs when not expected
Early	The interaction occurs too early
Late	The interaction occurs too late
Too much	A parameter associated with the interaction is increased
Too little	A parameter associated with the interaction is decreased
Conflicting	The interaction conflicts with another interaction on the channel

4.3 Run Simulation to Explore the Effects of Deviations

Given a model and set of possible deviations, the simulation must now be run and the results recorded. In an ideal world, a run would be performed for every possible combination of deviations, but this is not realistic because of the number of such combinations entailed by even a small deviation set. An efficient approach is to work through the low-order subsets of the deviation set. Given a priori knowledge of the probability of each deviation, it will be possible to show that the higher-order subsets represent wildly improbable circumstances.

4.4 Learn Rules

The task of machine learning can be viewed as one of function approximation from a set of *training instances* expressed as input-output pairs; given a function specification (a set of named input parameters (the 'features' used for learning) and a particular form of output value), the algorithm learns the relationship between combinations of parameter values and the output of the target function for those values.

For our purposes, the features represent causes and the output values are the consequences within the simulation. All the features used in the current work are explicit parameters that are given to the model, and the target function is the set of accidents that occurs during the simulation run. For example, in an air traffic scenario, the analysis might determine that when the parameter "collision warning distance" is reduced below 8km, it becomes possible for the accident "mid-air collision" to occur.

Many machine learning algorithms are described in the literature; a summary is provided by Mitchell in [12]. Machine learning is used here to produce *descriptive* rather than *predictive* models, i.e. models are learned, but they are not then used to classify any new instances; rather, they are studied by human analysts who wish to understand how the system behaves under various failure conditions. Learning approaches that produce 'black box' outcome models (i.e. models that are not very amenable to human comprehension), such as Bayesian Learners or conventional Neural Networks, are therefore not very helpful for this purposes of this work..

Learning approaches that *do* produce comprehensible models are more valuable in that they allow the engineer or analyst to inspect the learned model to discover *why* it considers a particular parameter combination to be hazardous. This is analogous to the analyst observing the hazardous result produced by the original (simulation) model and then inspecting the event log, or watching the run via visualisation, in order to determine why the model produced the result that it did.

4.5 Investigate Rules

Once some set of rules has been learned from a system model, safety analysts need to study and make use of them. This is a two stage process:

In the first stage, the analysts must try to understand the rules, and how they relate to the modelled system (rather than the model itself). Important questions at this stage include "Why did the algorithm learn this rule?", "Is this realistic, or is it merely a simulation artifact?", "Why (in terms of the mechanisms of the model) are these particular features/causes so important?"

The output of this first stage includes a revised set of rules, which have been manually filtered (to remove rules that have no apparent correspondence to the real system) and augmented with explanations and references to particular simulation runs which express the behaviour well.

In the second stage, analysts must consider the implications of the identified hazards for the real system. Key questions are "Is this hazard serious and plausible enough to warrant our attention?" and "What are we going to do about it?".

5 Example

Our hypothesis is that the machine learning algorithm will learn rules that cover all the hazards that were identified by manual analysis. The learning tool that has been used here is a decision tree learner using the C4.5 algorithm as described by Quinlan in [13]. The algorithm was chosen because it is fast, stable implementations are readily available, and the resulting rules are human-comprehensible. The implementation used was that provided by the data mining tool WEKA (described by Witten and Frank in [14]) under the name of 'J48'.

The example uses a simulation model of a military unit engaged in anti-guerilla operations. An overview of the elements in the system is shown in figure 1. Notionally, it contains four types of entities: Unmanned Air Vehicles (UAVs), Unmanned Self-Propelled Guns (UGVs), transport helicopters and infantry sections. As the infantry move only by air, a helicopter with troops on board is represented by a single entity. Infantry sections never appear on the map on their own.

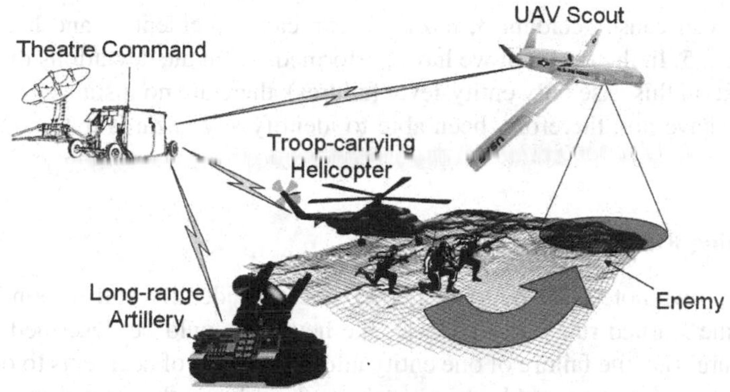

Fig. 1. The System

A single scenario has been implemented for this model, in which the units in the system must detect and neutralise a number of static enemy positions. The UAVs move on pre-defined search paths, and when they detect an enemy presence they contribute this to a shared picture which is available to all friendly entities. Responding to this shared picture, the artillery entities fire on the enemy until the UAVs report that it is adequately weakened. Once such weakened enemies are identified, the helicopters move in to take control of the areas on the ground. It is at this stage that the safety risk manifests, as the manned helicopters move across the terrain and engage the enemy.

5.1 Hazards in the Model

For a given system it is relatively easy to determine the types of accidents that can occur, since the set of entity types is finite and there are only a few ways in which an entity can be involved in an accident. Simple examination of our model reveals that the following accidents are possible:

- Accident 1 — Helicopter collides with another helicopter
- Accident 2 — Helicopter collides with a UAV
- Accident 3 — Landed helicopter is hit by artillery fire
- Accident 4 — UAV collides with a UAV
- Accident 5 — Helicopter hit by enemy fire

By running the model with all combinations of the possible entity-failure pairs (some 260000 in number), and studying the results manually, we have been able to identify the following hazards in the system:

- Hazard 1 — Friendly forces in field of fire of inaccurate artillery

- Hazard 2 — A UAV is in shared airspace with no ability to detect other airborne entities
- Hazard 3 — A helicopter moves into anti-aircraft range of a strong enemy unit

Hazard 1 can cause accident 3, hazard 2 can cause accident 4, and hazard 3 can cause accident 5. In the runs that we have performed, given the deviations that we have implemented (in this case only entity-level failures), there are no instances of accidents 1 and 2. We have not, therefore, been able to identify any hazards that would lead to them.

5.2 Learning Rules from the Model

In section 4.5, we noted that heuristics can be used to identify and respond to issues implicit in the learned rules. In this case, the heuristic could be described as 'single point of failure' (i.e. the failure of one entity allows a variety of accidents to occur), and an appropriate response would be to re-evaluate the roles in the system to redistribute some of the functionality of the entity, or to insulate other systems from the effects of its failures.

The model has approximately a quarter of a million combinations of possible deviations. For this simple model we can learn from the complete set of runs, but this will not be practical for larger examples, so it would be misleading to do so here. Therefore, only the first 8000 runs were performed. Most of these include only small numbers of failures, which is appropriate given that larger numbers of failures become increasingly improbable.

As noted above, it was possible to determine by examination the accidents that were possible. These then provided learning 'targets'; for each such target, a decision-tree model was learned to predict the combinations of failures that would cause that accident to occur. The failures that provide the learning features for the decision tree were expressed as entity-failure pairs; one example would be "UAV4 has suffered the failure loss_of_communications". The list of the accidents that were used as learning targets, together with the labels used for them in the learning tool, was as shown in Table 2.

Table 2. Possible accidents

Accident	Label
Helicopter X hit by enemy fire	ehX
Helicopter X hit by friendly artillery fire	ghX
UAV X collides with UAV Y	cuXuY
Helicopter X collides with UAV Y	chXuY

Enumerating these combinations gave 36 targets to learn models for. In practice, many of these accidents were not manifest in the available runs and so no rules were generated for them. For each accident, the 8000-run input set was processed into a table with boolean values for each of the 18 entity-failure pairs and a label of either 'safe' or the code for the target accident. Those runs that contained accidents, but not the current target accident, were discarded. This ensured that the data set contained positive and negative examples. The data set was then given to the learner, which was told to learn a decision tree for predicting the label from the parameters.

As a simple example, consider the accident 'cu1u4' i.e. where UAV 1 collided with UAV 4. Of the 8000 runs, 192 were safe and another 2048 contained cu1u4. These runs were labelled appropriately while the rest were discarded, and the resulting data set was given to the tree learner.

The resulting decision tree is shown in figure 2. The rule expressed here is that if UAV 4 exhibits the failure 'noairsensors' then this collision will occur, otherwise it will not. This learned rule is 100% accurate with respect to the training data; it perfectly captures the implicit model that was fed to it. Whether this is the optimal *inductive* inference will require further testing effort; see below.

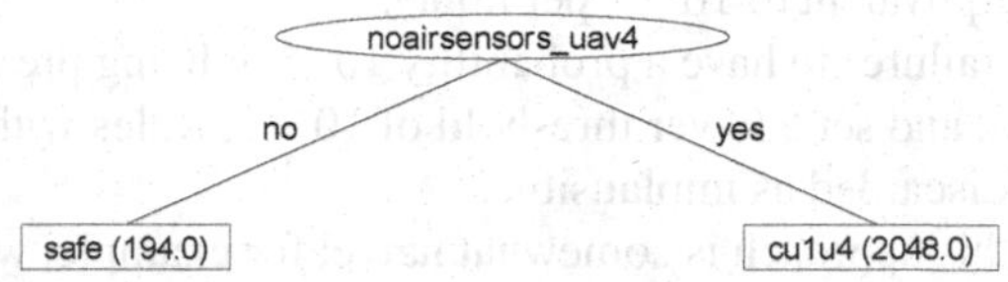

Fig. 2. Decision tree learned for accident 'cu1u4'

A more complex model is that for the accident 'gh1' (One of the UGVs hits helicopter 1). The learned tree is shown in figure 3.

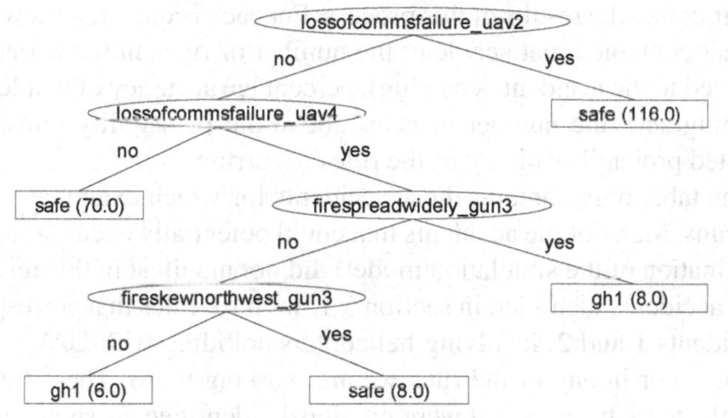

Fig. 3. Decision tree learned for accident 'gh1'

Although the tree notation is attractive for simple models, it becomes increasingly unwieldy as models become larger. As noted by Quinlan in [13], a decision tree can be 'flattened' into a set of production rules. The tree for figure 3 has five leaf nodes and therefore corresponds to the following five rules:

1. $\neg lossofcommsfailure\_uav2 \wedge \neg lossofcommsfailure\_uav4 \rightarrow safe$

2. $\neg lossofcommsfailure\_uav2 \wedge lossofcommsfailure\_uav4 \wedge \neg firespreadwidely\_gun3 \wedge \neg fireskewnorthwest\_gun3 \rightarrow accident$
3. $\neg lossofcommsfailure\_uav2 \wedge lossofcommsfailure\_uav4 \wedge \neg firespreadwidely\_gun3 \wedge fireskewnorthwest\_gun3 \rightarrow safe$
4. $\neg lossofcommsfailure\_uav2 \wedge lossofcommsfailure\_uav4 \wedge firespreadwidely\_gun3 \rightarrow accident$
5. $lossofcommsfailure\_uav2 \rightarrow safe$

In order to assess the importance of each rule, we can assess the probability of it occurring in practice by applying a priori probabilities to the individual failures and setting a 'threshold of concern' beyond which a rule will be considered too improbable to be worthwhile investigating. This is similar to the 'incredibility of failure' concept used in the nuclear industry; the probability that is used for this is given in [15] as 10^{-7} per year of operation (equivalent to 10^{-11} per hour).

We will consider all failures to have a probability 10^{-3} of being present in any given instance of the scenario, and set a lower threshold of 10^{-11}. Rules with a lower probability than that will be discarded as implausible.

It can be noted that this approach is somewhat naïve; for example, we have assumed complete independence between the failures. As the authors noted in [3], the nature of systems of systems is such that many apparently independent failures have common causes. It can also be noted that, within an entity, one failure may cause (or indeed mitigate the effects of) another. We have assumed a simple flat probability for each individual failure; these probabilities would much better justified if they came from entity-level safety analyses. For the context of this paper, however, these assumptions suffice for illustration.

Table 3 summarises the results of this process. For each accident, it shows the number of instances that contained that accident, the number of rules in the learned model (in total/rules that led to the accident occurring), percentage accuracy of that learned model (over the training set), the number of rules above the plausibility threshold and the highest estimated probability of any of the rules occurring.

Note that the table only contains those accidents for which examples were found in the first 8000 runs. Many of the accidents that could potentially occur (as apparent from a simple examination of the simulation model) did not manifest in this result set.

For the five accidents identified in section 5.1, we have rules that correspond to three of them. (Accidents 1 and 2, involving helicopters colliding with UAVs or other helicopters, do not occur in any of the runs we are working with). These three accidents correspond to the three hazards that were previously identified, as shown in Table 4.

At the beginning of this section, we gave our experimental hypothesis as "the machine learning algorithm will learn rules that cover all the hazards that were identified by manual analysis". It can be seen that the example supports this hypothesis, in that we have at least one rule that describes a way to cause the accidents corresponding to each hazard.

The question remaining is whether a safety engineer studying this simulation and the learning results would be lead directly to discovering the hazards (as opposed to merely noting that the accidents could happen). It is certainly plausible that the engineer would discover the hazards, but to give a more affirmative answer in practice (with

Table 3. Summary of the learned rules

Accident	#runs	#rules	#plausible rules	highest prob	% accuracy
eh1	6657	54/33	19	9.98×10^{-4}	96.7
eh2	6966	42/28	14	1×10^{-3}	99.3
eh3	6738	56/35	21	1×10^{-3}	99.1
eh4	6842	56/35	21	1×10^{-3}	99.2
gh1	14	5/2	2	9.97×10^{-4}	99.5
gh3	14	5/2	2	9.97×10^{-4}	99.5
cu1u4	2048	2/1	1	1×10^{-3}	100
cu4u3	3904	2/1	1	1×10^{-3}	100
(other)	0				

Table 4. Accidents found and the corresponding hazards

Label	Accident	Hazard
gh1, gh3	3	1
eh1-4	5	3
cu1u4, cu4u3	4	2

systems of realistic complexity) will require the application of the approach to larger scale industrial case studies.

5.3 Investigating These Rules

The preceding discussion has looked at the experimental results from the perspective of function approximation from failures to accidents. We can also look at how these rules relate to the behaviour of the system as observed through visualisation of the simulation runs. This is a necessary step in any case because these rules have only been learned in terms of explicit simulation parameters, rather than in terms of the actual mechanisms of the simulated system; they tell us (as simulation operators) how we can cause an accident to manifest, but they don't tell us what events within the simulation model lead to that accident. This requires additional analysis, but the analyst has an advantage in that he is aware of these learned rules and can look first at those runs that implement the rule preconditions, knowing in advance what overall result he expects to see.

In the current example, we have derived a number of rules from the simulation that describe how accidents can occur. For purposes of illustration we will follow up the accident 'gh1' (UGV fires on helicopter 1). The rules for this are given in section 5.2 and are shown in figure 3 as a decision tree. The rules specify that the necessary conditions for this accident are that UAV 4 has lost all communications and that UAV 2 has *not* suffered any loss of communications. Furthermore, UGV 3 must either be (a) firing accurately (i.e. not skewed) or (b) have its aim spread widely.

Observing some of the runs in which this accident does occur, it is apparent that removing UAV 4 from the data fusion loop (through communications loss) has an effect on the order in which enemy positions are detected, and that this affects both the order in which the guns target the enemy positions and the order in which the helicopters fly out to them. In order for this to be dangerous UAV 2 must be functioning normally; if UAV 2 has suffered a communications failure then this changes the ordering of target selection, and the corresponding outcome of airspace deconfliction actions, such that the result is a safe state. (The failures specified for UGV 3 merely mean that it must be able to hit the square it aims at).

Given this interpretation of the rules, is it plausible that this could occur in the real world, or are we merely seeing a simulation artefact? Superficially, it would seem to involve a rather unlikely combination of events (the helicopters being in just the right position at just the right time) but it can be observed that the fire from the UGVs and the movement of the helicopters are concentrated around specific locations (those occupied by the enemy positions) and specific times (when the enemy are first revealed as valid targets).

Finally, what changes can we propose to prevent this accident occurring in the future? One apparent issue is that this accident depends heavily on a failure of UAV 4. We studied the assigned flight path for UAV 4, and it was apparent that UAV 4 is particularly significant in this context in that it covers a large number of enemy positions. One viable option would be to change the UAV roles to ensure a more even distribution of coverage, perhaps by introducing an additional UAV.

6 Existing Applications of Simulation in Safety

In that the current work uses simulation for safety-related analysis, it is similar to the work of Blom *et al.* in airspace system safety [16] and Johnson in hospital evacuation [17]. Both of those, however, use Monte Carlo techniques to acquire quantitative statistical measures of the overall safety of a system under specified conditions. By contrast, the work described in this paper attempts to determine the relationship of simulation parameters to distinct (undesirable) modes of behaviour of the system; the aim is to acquire a *qualitative* understanding of system behaviour.

Computer system simulation approaches (such as the DEPEND tool described by Goswami *et al.* in [18]) generally focus on the interaction of software processes running on networked processors. Our work is distinct from that in that it explicitly deals with mobile physical entities interacting in physical space.

Perhaps the closest work described in the literature is that of Platts *et al.* in [19], in which rules are learned which relate the behaviour of an unmanned aircraft to success in a particular mission. The approach described in this paper is similar in that it involves learning rules which relate entity behaviour to unwanted hazardous consequences.

7 Model Fidelity

In this work, the aim of the simulation is to identify ways in which hazards (and hence accidents) could reasonably occur; in this respect, it is comparable to existing hazard analysis techniques. Any hazards that are identified through simulation will require further manual investigation — the simulation result is valuable in that it has drawn the analyst's attention to the hazard and 'made a case' for its plausibility by means of the recorded event trace.

A standard objection to the use of simulation for analysis is to question the fidelity of the model with respect to the real system that it purports to represent. In this context, it is important to note that almost all hazard analysis is performed with respect to some model of the real system; it cannot be said to be performed on the system itself. This is partly because the complexity of a real system is unmanageable (and much of it irrelevant) but also because hazard analysis is important very early in the safety life cycle, before the detail of the final system design is available.

Whilst there will always be concerns with the fidelity of the models we use, the use of models and approximations remains an inevitable part of real-world hazard analysis. One difference when using models for simulation, rather than for manual analysis, is that in manual analysis there is great opportunity for pragmatic human interpretation, thereby covering a multitude of deficiencies in any modelling approach adopted.

The use of simulation in our work is for what Dewar *et al.* describe in [20] as 'weak prediction'. They note that *"subjective judgement is unavoidable in assessing credibility"* and that when such a simulation produces an unexpected result *"it has created an interesting hypothesis that can (and must) be tested by other means"*. In other words, when a simulation reveals a plausible system hazard, other, more conventional analyses must be carried out to determine whether it is credible in the real system. Therefore, the role of the simulation analysis is to narrow down a huge analysis space into one that is manually tractable.

8 Summary and Future Work

This paper demonstrates an approach to performing hazard analysis for complex systems of systems using a combination of multi-agent simulation and machine learning. This was motivated by the successful use of multi-agent techniques in other fields of modelling and analysis. As illustrated in the example in this paper, we have been able to show that the approach can be used to identify hazards.

Challenges that remain to be tackled include the application of this technique to a wide variety of systems and scenarios, and combining the results of simulation and analysis across multiple scenarios and system configurations. There is also scope for further experimentation with different machine learning algorithms and different techniques for introducing deviations into simulation runs.

Acknowledgements. The work described in this paper was funded under the Defence and Aerospace Defence Partnership in High Integrity Real Time Systems (Strand 2).

References

1. Maier, M.W.: Architecting principles for systems-of-systems. In: 6th Annual Symposium of INCOSE. (1996) 567–574
2. Periorellis, P., Dobson, J.: Organisational failures in dependable collaborative enterprise systems. Journal of Object Technology **1** (2002) 107–117

3. Alexander, R., Hall-May, M., Kelly, T.: Characterisation of systems of systems failures. In: Proceedings of the 22nd International Systems Safety Conference (ISSC 2004), System Safety Society (2004) 499–508
4. Wilkinson, P.J., Kelly, T.P.: Functional hazard analysis for highly integrated aerospace systems. In: IEE Seminar on Certification of Ground / Air Systems, London, UK (1998)
5. Perrow, C.: Normal Accidents: Living with High-Risk Technologies. Basic Books, New York (1984)
6. Leveson, N.: A new accident model for engineering safer systems. In: Proceedings of the 20th International System Safety Society Conference (ISSC 2003), System Safety Society, Unionville, Virginia (2002) 476–486
7. Ferber, J.: Multi- Agent Systems: an Introduction to Distributed Artificial Intelligence. Addison-Wesley (1999)
8. Ilachinski, A.: Exploring self-organized emergence in an agent-based synthetic warfare lab. Kybernetes: The International Journal of Systems & Cybernetics **32** (2003) 38–76
9. Hall-May, M., Kelly, T.P.: Defining and decomposing safety policy for systems of systems. In: Proceedings of the 24th International Conference on Computer Safety, Reliability and Security (SAFECOMP '05). Volume 3688 of LNCS., Fredrikstad, Norway, Springer-Verlag (2005) 37–51
10. Kletz, T.: HAZOP and HAZAN: Identifying and Assessing Process Industry Hazards. 3rd edn. Institution of Chemical Engineers (1992)
11. McDermid, J.A., Nicholson, M., Pumfrey, D.J., Fenelon, P.: Experience with the application of HAZOP to computer-based systems. In: Proceedings of the Tenth Annual Conference on Computer Assurance, IEEE (1995) 37–48
12. Mitchell, T.M.: Machine Learning. McGraw-Hill (1997)
13. Quinlan, J.R.: C4.5: Programs for Machine Learning. Morgan Kauffman (1993)
14. Witten, I.H., Frank, E.: Data Mining: Practical machine learning tools and techniques. 2nd edn. Morgan Kaufmann, San Francisco (2005)
15. Ammirato, F., Bieth, M., Chapman, O.J.V., Davies, L.M., Engl, G., Faidy, C., Seldis, T., Szabo, D., Trampus, P., Kang, K.S., Zdarek, J.: Improvement of in-service inspection in nuclear power plants. Technical Report IAEA-TECDOC-1400, International Atomic Energy Agency (2004)
16. Blom, H.A.P., Stroeve, S.H., de Jong, H.H.: Safety risk assessment by Monte Carlo simulation of complex safety critical operations. In Redmill, F., Anderson, T., eds.: Proceedings of the Fourteenth Safety-critical Systems Symposium, Bristol, UK, Safety-Critical Systems Club, Springer (2006) 47–67
17. Johnson, C.: The Glasgow-hospital evacuation simulator: Using computer simulations to support a risk-based approach to hospital evacuation. Technical report, University of Glasgow (2005) Submitted to the Journal of Risk and Reliability.
18. Goswami, K.K., Iyer, R.K., Young, L.: DEPEND: A simulation-based environment for system level dependability analysis. IEEE Trans. Comput. **46** (1997) 60–74
19. Platts, J.T., Peeling, E., Thie, C., Lock, Z., Smith, P.R., Howell, S.E.: Increasing UAV intelligence through learning. In: AIAA Unmanned Unlimited, Chicago IL (2004)
20. Dewar, J.A., Bankes, S.C., Hodges, J.S., Lucas, T., Saunders-Newton, D.K., Vye, P.: Credible uses of the distributed interactive simulation (DIS) system. Technical Report MR-607-A, RAND (1996)

Through the Description of Attacks: A Multidimensional View

Igor Nai Fovino and Marcelo Masera

Institute for the Protection and the Security of the Citizen
Joint Research Centre, via E. Fermi 1,
I-20... Ispra -Va-, Italy
masera@jrc.it
igor.nai@jrc.it

Abstract. Cyber attacks are the core of any security assessment of ICT-based systems. One of the more promising research fields in this context is related to the representation of the attack patterns. Several are the models proposed to represent them; these models usually provide a generic representation of attacks. Conversely, the experience shows that attack profiles are strongly dependent upon several boundary conditions. This paper defends that from the security assessment perspective, it is necessary to integrate the knowledge contained in the attack patterns with boundary knowledge related to vulnerability of the target system and to the potential threats. In this paper, after a characterization of this boundary knowledge, we propose an n-dimensional view of the attack tree approach, integrating information on threats and vulnerabilities. Moreover, we show how to use this view to derive knowledge about the security exposure of a target system.

Keywords: Security assessment, Attack Pattern.

1 Introduction

Security threats are one of the main problems of this computer-based era. All systems making use of information and communication technologies (ICT) are prone to failures and vulnerabilities that can be exploited by malicious software and agents.

In such a scenario, it has become imperative to perform proper risk assessments, putting in evidence the main threats a system is exposed to and eventually the effectiveness of the possible countermeasures. There exist in the scientific literature some interesting approaches to the risk assessment of ICT infrastructures [7,8]. These methodologies have as core target the analysis of the system components, the interconnection between components and the set of "Security Information" (i.e. vulnerabilities, threats, attacks and countermeasures).

Although these methodologies have proved useful for zeroing in the security lacks of the analyzed systems, we believe that it is possible to improve the results of risk assessments by a more attentive and precise description of the "Security Information".

J. Górski (Ed.): SAFECOMP 2006, LNCS 4166, pp. 15–28, 2006.

In particular, in every risk assessment framework, a prominent role is played by the capacity to collect and analyze in a correct way information related to the threats, vulnerabilities and attacks that, in some way may have an undesirable effect over the analyzed system. A key point in such a task is, obviously, the description of the attack pattern which an attacker may put in act in order to realize a threat. As we describe in the section 3, there are several models proposed to represent them; these models usually provide a generic representation of attacks in term of steps needed in order to realize a, possibly malicious, goal.

However, even if such models have prove useful in the task of attack documentation gathering and sharing, the information they represent is too general and abstract to be used with real advantages in a risk assessment analysis. In the real world, the attacks profiles are strongly context dependent [1][2][3]. Therefore, a traditional attack tree can be used as an "Arianna Thread", which shows at high level the typical steps an attacker follows to realize a particular goal. In order to perform a risk assessment, it is necessary to map such an information on the real context represented by the system under analysis. In other words in is necessary to merge the information contained in the attack tree with the boundary knowledge related to vulnerability of the target system, to the security properties of the system and to the potential threats. In order to address this problem, we propose in this paper an n-dimensional view of the attack tree approach, integrating information on system, threats and vulnerabilities. Moreover, we show how to use this view to derive knowledge about the security exposure of a target system.

The paper is organized as follows: in section 2 we give some preliminary definition clarifying some basic concepts. In this section we give an overview of the risk assessment methodology we adopted as reference for the attack tree integration [8]. Moreover, in section 3 a State of the Art in Attack representation in given. In section 4 we introduce the "Boundary Knowledge" related to threat, vulnerabilities and system. Finally in section 5 we present in detail our n-dimensional attack tree approach.

2 Preliminary Definitions

The work presented in this paper, was conceived to make better use of attack trees in a risk assessment framework, enriching the trees with relevant information. In this section we give some preliminary definitions related to security concepts and we give an overview of the risk assessment methodology we adopted as reference.

2.1 Security Definitions

A risk assessment for ICT infrastructure, is strongly connected with some concepts traditionally derived from the field of computer security, in particular five are the elements of interest that need to be defined: the concepts of *Threat*, *Vulnerability*, *Attack*, *Risk* and *Asset*.

As defined in [5] and in the Internet RFC glossary of terms, a **Threat** is a potential for violation of security, which exists when there is a circumstance, capability, action, or event that could breach security and cause harm.

A **Vulnerability**, by definition [10][11], is a weakness in the architecture design/implementation of an application or a service.

An **Attack** can be identified as the entire process allowing a Threat Agent to exploit a system by the use of one or more Vulnerabilities.

According to the ISO/IEC 17799:2000 [6], a **Risk** may be defined as the probability that a damaging incident is happening (when a threat occurs because of a vulnerability), times the potential damage.

Finally according with [6] an **Asset** is defined as something that has value to the relevant stakeholders.

Roughly speaking we can think of these security entities as follows: an asset is (a) somewhat having a relevance for an organization that (b)is the target of a threat agent which, (c) by the use of some vulnerabilities, put in act (d) an attack in order to (e) damage the asset and indirectly the organization.

2.2 Risk Assessment Methodology Overview

As claimed in the introduction, our objective is to make the knowledge contained in an attack tree more useful for the assessment of risks. In literature there exist several security assessment methodologies conceived for the analysis of ICT infrastructure. We have chosen to adopt as reference the work of Masera & Nai [8]. In the methodology proposed by Masera & Nai, the authors present a risk assessment methodology tailored to the analysis of the ICT infrastructure of complex industrial systems. In the remainder of this section, we give a brief overview of this methodology. More in detail, this methodology foresees that in order to assess the security of a system, it is necessary firstly to provide a description of the system itself, of its components, of its assets, of the interaction and the relationships among the components, the assets and the external world. Such a description (expressed analytically by tables) could be used to identify in a systematic way the vulnerabilities affecting the whole system. These vulnerabilities are then described by some significant parameters and used to identify the threat that can be associated to the components and to the whole system. From the analysis of this information, one can derive the evaluation of the possible damages to the components, their propagation to the system and the consequent attack pattern. All these operations are quantified in some risk related indexes that are then employed to perform the evaluation of the security failure risk and the countermeasures. The approach adopted is based on five main steps. With regard to the topic of this paper, the attack assessment, information about attacks are represented by generic attack trees used to magnify if a system could be considered prone to a target attack. Even if this can be a good starting point in the evaluation of attack impact on a target system, we believe that integrating such attack trees with the other information contained in the target system description could give a great improvement to the analysis of a system.

3 State of the Art

In the scientific literature, there exist several methods/approaches used to describe security information related to attacks. Historically the first approach in that sense were related to the creation of vulnerability database. Bugtraq [12] is an example of such database. However, they are usually focused on the description of the vulnerabilities, lacking completely (but that isn't their goal)in the description of the way by which such vulnerabilities can be used in putting in act complex attacks. The most promising approach allowing to capture such characteristic is known in the scientific literature as *Graph Based Attack Models* [13]. In this category two can be considered the main "Modeling family": the *Petri Net based Models* and the *Attack and Fault Trees models.*

A good example of the first category can be considered the *Attack Net Model* introduced by McDermott [15] in which the places of a Petri Net represent the steps of an attack and the transitions are used to capture precise actions performed by the attackers. In this view, an attack is a pattern of states and results less intuitive to represent an attacks are results of multiple application of coordinated different attacks.

On the other hand, the second approach (attack trees), originated from the world of fault analysis, in which a tree representation of the dependencies among component of a system are used to identify the fault chains that potentially may affect a system and allowing then to evaluate the propagation of a fault through the system [16]. In this context, Bruce Schneier [17] proposed to use a similar techniques based on the use of expansion trees to show the different attacks that could affect a system. Attack trees can be used to capture the steps of an attack and their interdependecies. As showed in figure 1, the building blocks of attack trees are nodes. Every node is used to model the steps of an attack or attacker actions and the root node of the tree represents the goal of the attack [16][17]. Such an approach has been largely used and improved. For example Daley, Larson & Dawkins [18] have proposed to introduce a layering approach (stratified node topology)in the attack tree design, in order to separate the attack tree nodes based on functionality (Event level, State Level etc.). Moreover, in such a context, recently, Jajodia, Noel and O'Berry [4] have introduced an approach based on the concept of vulnerability topological analysis, allowing, starting from the combination of modeled attacker exploits, to discover attack paths.

However, to our knowledge, no much effort has been spent to enforce the link existing between an high level attack tree and its projection in a real case.

4 Boundary Conditions

As we claimed in the introduction, a "traditional" Attack Tree constitutes a good way to collect and share information about attacks, in term of the logical steps and requirements needed in order to realize a malicious scope. However, in a real case, an attack profile (and its exploitability) strongly depends on the particular context in which it is applied. In a risk assessment context, we need,

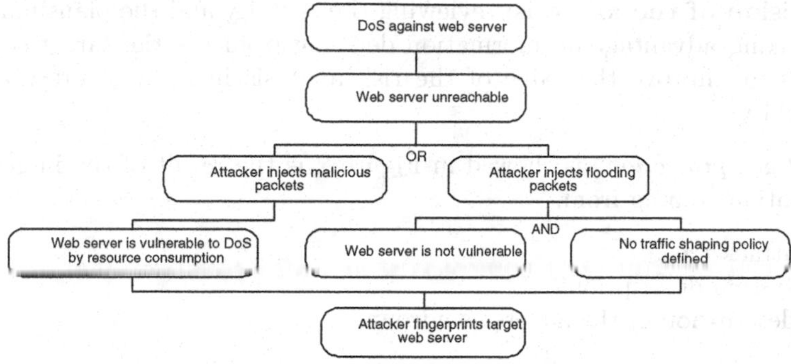

Fig. 1. Example of Schneier style Attack Tree

in order to analyze the system exposure, information about attacks, but, on the other hand, we need to evaluate the impact and the plausibility of such attacks.

Let consider the example in Figure 1. It represents the attack tree of an hypothetical Denial of Service against a web server. As it is possible to see two are the main branches of the tree: one related to a *resource consumption* scenario, in which the DoS is obtained by consuming all the resources of the webserver, and one related to a *code based vulnerability* allowing to crash the web server, making it unreachable. This is a typical attack tree description. However under a risk assessment perspective, this attack tree mainly lack in providing two relevant information:

- **Plausibility:** how plausible is the attack (in general) or, in more detail, how plausible is the exploitation of a vulnerability used in the attack or how plausible is an operation considered needed in order to perform the attack.
- **Severity:** how severe is the attack in term of potential impact.

For example, referring to the figure 1, if a firewall exists between the Internet and the Web Server and if such a firewall drops systematically every type of network scan packet (e.g. icmp packets, nmap generated packets etc.), the plausibility of the fingerprint operation has to be considered *low.* Moreover, if for example the Web Server is not affected by known *code based* vulnerability, the related branch has to be considered slightly implausible.

All available information of this type can be associated to the attack tree at the origin, evaluating for example that a particular attack configuration, for example, may generally be very improbable or that the damage caused by this attack is in average low.

When an attack tree is used in a security assessment, we need to be able to reevaluate these values; what is equivalent to make a *"projection"* of a general attack to a target, specific case. The benefits deriving from this projection are intuitively two:

1. **Pruning of the analysis input:** reassigning plausibility values on the light of a particular scenario allows, as described previously, to eliminate improbable branches, reducing then the complexity of the analysis.

2. **Precision of the analysis:** reviewing the severity and the plausibility values taking advantage of information deriving from the the target scenario, allows to improve the value of the risk analysis in term of precision and reliability.

The *attack projection*, as showed in Figure 2 is the result of the intersection of information coming from:

- The attack tree.
- The system description.
- The description of the adverse environment.

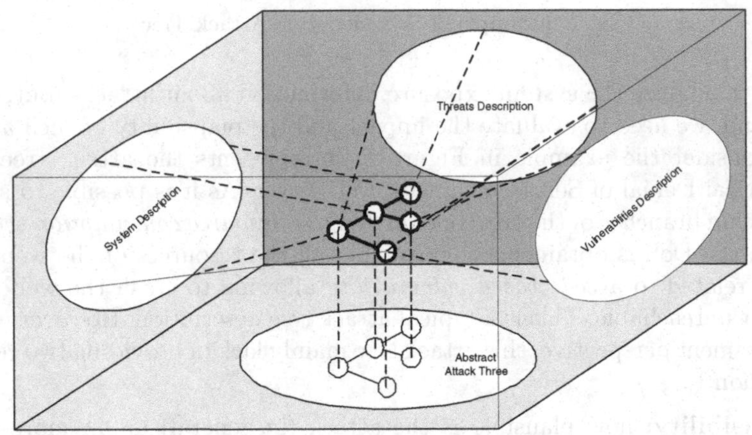

Fig. 2. Logical view of an attack tree projection

In what follows, we characterize, making use of the information coming from these sources, an "Attack Tree Projection".

4.1 System Description Information Source

Every Risk Assessment framework, departs from a system description phase. As we claimed in section 2, we adopt as reference the framework proposed by Masera et al. in [8] and the system description proposed by the same authors in [9]. In such a description, as showed in figure 3, the system is decomposed in terms of *components, subsystems, services (provided by components or subsystems), security policies, roles, stakeholders and flows between these entities.* Moreover the concept of *Asset* and *Information Asset* [19] are captured.

Under the perspective of integrating *attack trees* with information derived from the system description, three are the most relevant objects which can easily concur in the *attack projection*:

- **Components:** they host vulnerabilities and they are the target of several operations described by an attack tree. For instance, if in the example of

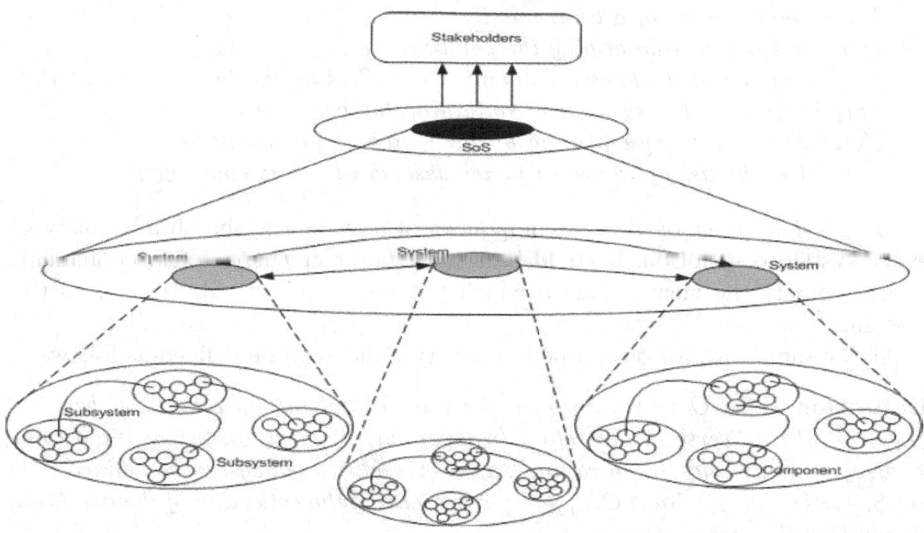

Fig. 3. Logical view of an n-dimensional attack tree

Figure 1 in the system under analysis there isn't a WebServer the attack became completely implausible. Information about the absence of a particular component in a system is a precious information allowing to prune all the branches of an attack tree that take in some way advantage of the presence of this component (see next section for more clarifications). Moreover, a component may have associated some security configurations (e.g. access rules of a firewall). Even these information may concur to the *attack projection* (let us take as example the previous one related to the network fingerprint in the WebSever DoS).

- **Services:** They are usually one of the possible final target of an attack. If some intermediate nodes of an attack tree contain a "Statement" regarding a service not provided by the target system, it is necessary to reevaluate the plausibility and the severity of the branch containing the statement
- **Security Policies:** They represent information about the operations allowed to and on a particular object (component, stakeholder, user, etc.). The knowledge of the security policies may allow to understand whether some operations described in an attack tree can be performed in a target scenario. Moreover, strong or weak policies may have an effect in the plausibility and severity evaluation of the attack tree.

In order to take advantage of this knowledge contained in the system description, it is necessary to introduce a formal representation of these objects which, as described in section 5, can be easily made compatible with the ndimensional attack tree definition.

Definition 1. *A component* c_i *is defined as a tuple* $< Name, Desc, Lov, Sb_{id}, Conf\_State, sec\_pol >$ *where:*

- *Name is the name of a component.*
- *Desc is a free text describing the component.*
- *Lov is the list of the known vulnerabilities affecting the target component.*
- Sb_{id} *is the id of the subsystem containing the component.*
- *Conf_State is the specification of the component configuration.*
- *Sec_pol is the list of security policies associated to the component*

From a logical point of view, a component of a system is the atomic entity of every system description. It could be a hardware element, a software element, or, to simplify the view, an actor which has tasks and provide services in the system.

At the same way, for our scope, a security policy can be defined as follows:

Definition 2. *let* $O = \{o_1...o_n\}$ *be the universe of the operation, let be* $C = \{c_1...c_m\}$ *the universe of the actors (component) of a system, we define a tuple* $< o_i, c_j >$ *as a "allowed operation" tuple. A security policy can be defined as a set* $S_{c_k} = \{< o_i, c_j > | o_i \in O, c_j \in C\}$ *representing the collection of the operation allowed on the component* c_k.

The previous definition is, of course, too simple to completely represent the concept of security policy, but this is out of the scope of the paper. What is relevant in this context is to emphasize the connection between this concept and the projection of the attack tree.

A service can be defined, according with [9] as follows:

Definition 3. *A service S is a tuple* $< Name, SdL, FL, value, SP >$ *where:*

- *Name identifies in a unique way a target service*
- *SdL (Services dependence list) is the list of the services concurring in the realization of the target service.*
- *FL (Function logic) is a logical expression (First order) describing the relation between the target service and the services contained in the previous lists.*
- *Value it represent the value associated to a target service.*
- *SP is the list of the security policies applied to the service.*

Information about services are extremely useful in the attack tree projection and reevaluation, for two reasons: (1) information about the associated security policies, service dependences and function logic can be used can be used to validate the feasibility of some attack steps (see next section) having then an impact on the plausibility evaluation; (2)information about service dependencies, function logic and service value can be even used to understand the real severity of a target attack in a target scenario.

4.2 Adverse Environment Information Source

For evaluating the plausibility of an attack, we need to take into consideration information about the *Adverse Environment.* In light of such knowledge, the *plausibility* of an attack tree can be reevaluated in order to obtain a more precise risk exposure evaluation. Information about the adverse environment can be usually organized in two classes:

- **Threats Information:** as claimed in Section 2, a *threat* is a potential violation of security [11]. The description of a threat, includes information about the type of threat (natural, human etc.), the description of the threat agent (e.g criminal or terroristic organizations, hackers, newbie hackers etc.), their resources etc. This type of information is very useful in the evaluation of the attack plausibility. If we know for example that at the present time there is a criminal organization having interest in damaging a particular service provided by the system under analysis we must consider more plausible all the attacks having as final scope the interruption of such service. Moreover information about their motivation, their skills and resources could improve the *plausibility evaluation*.
- **Vulnerability Information:** information about vulnerabilities associated to a target component, new tools allowing to make easier the exploitation of a particular vulnerability, has obviously a strong impact in the evaluation of the plausibility of an attack tree.

As in the case presented in the previous section, in order to take advantage of the knowledge represented by information on threats and vulnerabilities, it is necessary to introduce a formal representation of these objects which, as described in Section 5, can be easily made compatible with the ndimensional attack tree definition.

Definition 4. *A Threat Agent can be defined as a tuple* $< Name, Desc, Sk, Rs >$ *where:*

- *Name identifies the threat agent*
- *Desc contains a description of the threat agent*
- *Sk describes the skills potentially owned by the threat agent*
- *Rs describes the resources owned by the threat agent (in a qualitative manner)*

A *Threat* then can be described as follows:

Definition 5. *A Threat is defined as a tuple* $< Name, Type, TA, Mot, Category, plausibility, severity, dis\_caused >$ *where:*

- *Name identifies in a unique manner a threat*
- *Type internal, external, both*
- *TA contains a Threat Agent tuple*
- *Mot describes the motivation aiming the threat agent*
- *Category Natural (meteo, geological.), technological, human... etc.*
- *Plausibilityindex it gives a measure of the plausibility of the threat considering information in possession by the analyst*
- *Severityindex : it gives a measure of the impact the target threat may have on a certain system*
- *dis_caused: list of the disservice potentially caused, where a disservice is the negation of a service.*

In the same way we can now formally define a vulnerability.

Definition 6. *A vulnerability can be described by a tuple* $< Name, Type, Desc, Vuln\_ref, Comp\_list, Count\_list, Sev, Exp, res >$ *where:*

- *Name:identifies in a unique manner a vulnerability*
- *Type: it identifies a type of vulnerability (e.g. buffer overflow etc.).*
- *Desc: it contains information about the vulnerability as : how to take advantage of it etc..*
- *Vuln_ref: it indicates the Vulnerability Reference Number (rif. MITRE or CVE).*
- *Comp_list: list of the components affected by the vulnerability.*
- *Count_list: it contains the list of the countermeasures.*
- *Sev: it contains an index representing the severity of the vulnerability.*
- *Exp: it contains an index representing the exploitability of the vulnerability.*
- *res: a description of the resources needed to exploit the vulnerability*

In this respect, the elements of particular relevance for the "attack tree projection" context, are the exploitability of a vulnerability, the plausibility of the threat, the motivation, the resource and the skills of a threat agent (which have an impact in the plausibility evaluation of an attack) and the threat and vulnerability severity. All of them have an impact on the severity of an attack.

5 N-Dimensional Attack Tree

An attack tree is a particular graph that describes the steps of an attack process. As we explained in Sections 1, attack trees were introduced to describe and share information about attack patterns. For this reason they are not usually focused on a target scenario. On the other hand in a risk assessment perspective, in order to obtain a more precise and detailed analysis, it is useful to have attack trees focused on the target scenario. We believe that these context–relevant trees can be obtained creating a projection of the generic, abstract trees on the target scenario by the use of the "boundary knowledge" presented in Section 4. In order to do this, two relevant points need to be improved:

1. The structure of the attack tree must be enriched with information on the target system and the hypothetical threat agent allowing to characterize better the different phases of an attack. Moreover, we note that in a traditional attack tree (as presented in [17]) all nodes have the same semantic meaning from a structural point of view. This constitutes a problem in linking the proper boundary knowledges to the correct nodes.
2. The knowledge contained in the attack tree must be normalized in order to be compatible with the knowledge derived by the system description and the adverse environment description.

In what follows, we present an attack tree definition that considers the previous points.

More in details, attack tree nodes can be categorized into three main classes:

1. **Operations:** any step representing an operation made by the attacker in order to perform the attack.
2. **Vulnerabilities:** any step describing a vulnerability required in order to realize the attack.
3. **Assertions:** any step representing assumptions, results, or requirements characterizing the attack process.

All these basic steps are linked by the use of logical ports (AND, OR, and NOT).

Figure 4 gives an example of the use of these different elements.

This categorization allows to specify the different semantic meanings of the attack process steps. However, in order to improve points (1) and (2) it is necessary to define well the information associated to these object classes. Formally we can define these objects as follows:

Definition 7. *An* ***Operation*** *is a tuple* $< Name, Actor, Target, Action, Desc, Plaus, Sev >$ *where:*

- *Name identifies the operation*
- *Actor identifies who performs the action*

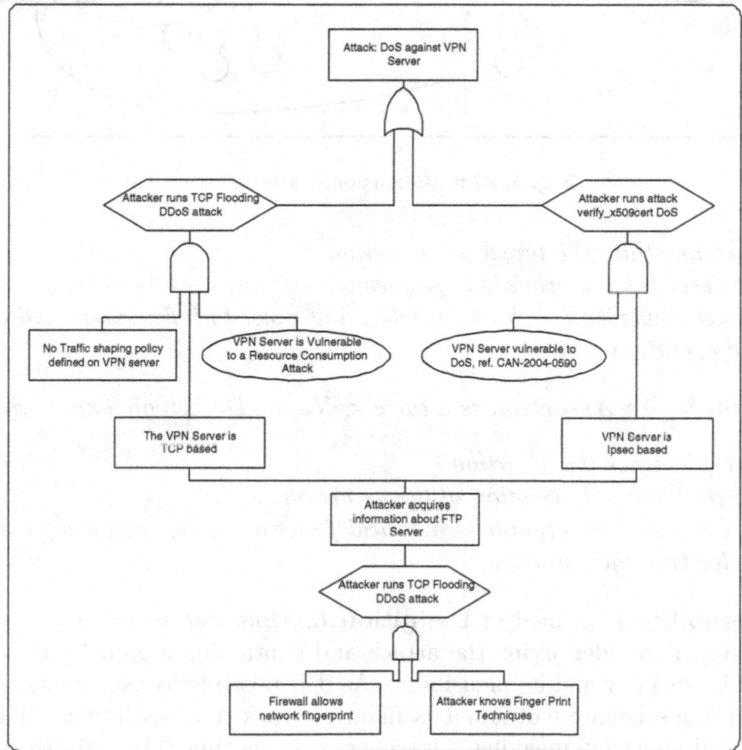

Fig. 4. An attack tree in which the squares represent *Assertions*, the circles represent *Vulnerabilities* used and the *hexagons* represents operations made by the attackers

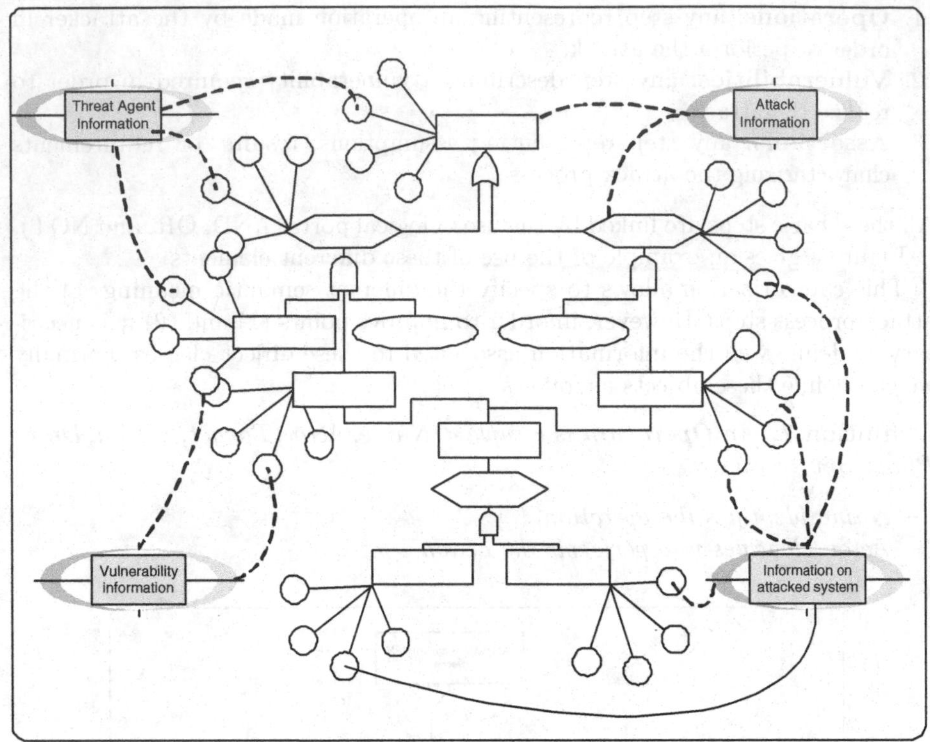

Fig. 5. Multidimensional attack tree

- *Target identifies the target of the action*
- *Desc describes the operations performed*
- *Plaus_&_Severity are the plausibility and severity index associated a priori to the operation*

Definition 8. *An **Assertion** is a tuple* $< Name, Desc, logic\_exp >$ *where*

- *Name identifies the assertion*
- *Desc contains a description of the assertion*
- *logic_exp contains eventually a logical function to be validated in order to consider true the assertion*

A **Vulnerability** is defined in **Definition 6**. Moreover, every attack tree has a special top node identifying the attack and containing a global evaluation (a priori) of its severity and its plausibility. As it is possible to see, adopting such a representation scheme we obtain a "semantic attack tree" with nodes that gains a contextual−relevant meaning. Moreover, this schema take into account the boundary knowledge described in the previous section. This schema can be then used to obtain a projection of the attack tree related to the target scenario. The projection task can be summarized as follows:

1. All the Operations of the attack tree are validated considering the configuration of the components involved, the associated security policies and the services provided by the components.
2. The Vulnerabilities used in the attack tree are validated considering the vulnerabilities associate to the respective components of the system.
3. The Assertions are validated considering the security policies, the information related to the threats (resources needed to realize vulnerabilities etc.) and the information related to the services.
4. Taking into consideration the validation results, the attack tree is pruned.
5. The values of plausibility and severity of the remaining attack tree are revised considering the associated boundary information.

The result of this process is then an attack tree which is the projection of the original and general attack-tree on a target scenario. Moreover, due to the normalization of the attack tree, it is possible to directly link the boundary information with the related nodes of the attack tree, obtaining in this way a multidimensional attack tree containing both information related to the attack, information related to the attacked system and information related to the attacker (see Figure 5).

6 Conclusion

The risk assessment evaluation of an ICT infrastructure is a extremely complex task that requires as input a complete picture of the security scenario to be analyzed. In this picture one must include the description of the attacks that realize a threat against a system. Such attacks, in the real world, are strongly context dependent. In order to develop a more realistic and precise risk assessment, we have showed how information about the boundary knowledge derived by the system and the environment description can be used in order to obtain an n-dimensional view of the attack tree projected on a target scenario. This is a first attempt, that of course needs further improvements. In particular, we plan to clarify in a formal way how the severity and the plausibility associated to the attack trees have to be modified in consideration of the boundary information. Moreover, we plan to integrate this approach into the methodology proposed in [8].

References

1. Aslam, T., Krsul, I. & Spafford, E.H.: Use of a taxonomy of security faults. In Proceedings of the Nineteenth NIST-NCSC National Information Systems Security Conference, (1996) pages 551560.
2. Kumar, S. : Classification and Detection of Computer Intrusions. PhD thesis, Department of Computer Science, Purdue University, West Lafayette, Indiana (1995).
3. Howard, J.: An Analysis of Security Incidents on the Internet, 19891995. PhD thesis, Department of Engineering and Public Policy, Carnegie Mellon University, Pittsburgh, Pennsylvania (1997).

4. S. Jajodia, S. Noel, B. O'Berry: Topological Analysis of Network Attack Vulnerability. In Managing Cyber Threats: Issues, Approaches and Challenges, V. Kumar, J. Srivastava, A. Lazarevic (eds.), Kluwer Academic Publisher (2004).
5. Jones, A., Ashenden, D.: Risk Management for Computer Security : Protecting Your Network & Information Assets. Elsevier (March 2005).
6. Code of Practice for Information Security Management. International Standard (ISO/IEC) 17799:2000.
7. Alberts, C., & Dorofee, A.: Managing Information Security Risks: The OCTAVE (SM) Approach., Addison Wesley Professional (July 2002)
8. Masera, M., Nai Fovino, I., & Sgnaolin, R.: A Framework for the Security Assessment of Remote Control Applications of Critical Infrastructure. ESReDA 29th Seminar, (2005) Ispra.
9. Masera, M., Nai Fovino, I.: Models for Security Assessment and Management. In Proceeding of the International Workshop on Complex Network and Infrastructure Protection 2006, (2006) Rome, Italy.
10. Alhazmi, O., Malaiya, Y., & Ray, I.: Security Vulnerabilities in Software Systems: A Quantitative Perspective. Lecture Notes in Computer Science, Volume 3654/2005. (2005) Publisher: Springer-Verlag GmbH.
11. Bishop, M.: Computer Security Art and Science, (November 2004) Addison Wesley.
12. Bugtraq vulnerability database. http://securityfocus.com
13. Steffan, J., Schumacher, M.: Collaborative attack modeling. In proceeding of the Symposium on Applied Computing, Madrid, Spain (2002) pp. 253 - 259
14. Tidwell, T., Larson. R., Fitch, K. & Hale, J.: Modeling Internet Attacks. Proceeding of the 2001 IEEE Workshop on Information Assurance and Security. United States Military Academy, West Point, NY (2001).
15. McDermott, J.: Attack Penetration Testing. In Proceeding of the 2000 New Security Paradigm Workshop, ACM SigSAC, ACM Press, ((2000) pp. 15-22.
16. Helmer, G., Wong, J., Slagell, M., Honavar, V., Miller, L., and Lutz, R.: A Software Fault Tree Approach to Requirements Analysis of an Intrusion Detection System. In Proceedings of the first Symposium on Requirements Engineering for Information Security (2001).
17. Schneier, B.: Modeling Security Threats, Dr. Dobb's Journal. https://www.schneier.com/paper-attacktrees-ddj-ft.html (2001).
18. Daley, K., Larson, R., & Dawkins, J.: A Structural Framework for Modeling Multi-Stage Network Attacks. Proceedings of the International Conference on Parallel Processing Workshops. ICPP Workshops (2002), pp. 5-10.
19. Masera, M. & Nai Fovino, I.: Modelling Information Assets for Security Risk Assessment in Industrial settings. 15th EICAR Annual Conference (2006).

On Certain Behavior of Scale-Free Networks Under Malicious Attacks*

Tomasz Gierszewski, Wojciech Molisz, and Jacek Rak

Gdansk University of Technology, Narutowicza 11/12
80-952 Gdansk, Poland
{tomag, womol}@eti.pg.gda.pl, jrak@pg.gda.pl

Abstract. This paper evaluates performance of scale-free networks in case of intentional removal of their nodes. The distinguishing feature of this kind of networks (Internet is an excellent example) is the power law distribution of node degrees.

An interesting behavior of scale-free networks, if node removal process is performed sufficiently long, is manifested by their migration to random networks. The main idea of our research is to quantify this process. In contrast to well explored parameters like: characteristic path length or clustering coefficient, we propose the new ones: mean maximum flow, centre of gravity of node degree distribution and other. To the best of our knowledge, these measures are proposed for the first time. Our results confirm that the migration process steps relatively fast.

1 Introduction

At present one can observe the increasing dependency of society on large-scale complex networked systems. This magnifies the consequences of failures of network elements. In the past, *failures* – caused by system deficiencies such as software errors or hardware corruptions, and *accidents* – meaning all the potentially damaging events such as natural disasters, were mostly considered. They were all assumed to be independent and random. However, many errors occur now as the result of an *attack*, often referred to as a man-made disturbance, directed toward an important network element, e.g. a node of extraordinary high degree (connected to many other nodes).

Recent wide-area networks typically utilize fiber-optic technology and Dense Wavelength Division Multiplexing (DWDM). They offer potentially unlimited capacities (tens of terabits per second), and a failure of any network element may lead to large data and revenue losses [14]. This in turn amplifies the importance of assuring the network survivability, defined as the capability of a system to fulfill its mission in a timely manner, in the presence of attacks, failures or accidents [7, 11, 13].

* This work was partially supported by the Ministry of Science and Education, Poland, under grant No 3 T11D 001 30.

J. Górski (Ed.): SAFECOMP 2006, LNCS 4166, pp. 29 – 41, 2006.

It turns out that the extent of losses after an attack strongly depends on network topology. In particular, it can be shown that an attack can be significantly harmful to networks of irregular topology, for which the degrees of network nodes deviate much from their mean value. Many recent wide-area networks have the irregular topology. What is more, their topology is often *scale-free*, meaning that the node degree distribution follows the power law. This distribution implies the existence of nodes of an extraordinary high degree, called *centers*, being seriously vulnerable to attacks. Elimination of such elements considerably degrades the overall network performance. What is important from the practical observation, networks obtain scale-free character over time because of their growth and human factor. The latter exhibits in the *rich-gets-richer* rule [1] and implies strengthen of already well connected nodes. So, many well designed networks may transform themselves into the scale-free ones in just a few steps.

The analysis of scale-free networks' behavior under attack was a subject of several research works (see e.g. [3, 4, 5]). Number of other publications considered the resemblance of Internet topology to the scale-free one [8, 15, 17]. The static properties as well as the growth process of scale-free networks were also investigated [1, 2]. However, in almost all of those papers, similar metrics like: characteristic path length or clustering coefficient were used.

Our recent works [9, 12] show, that the analysis of attacked networks should consider the dynamics of the process. Different parameters of scale-free topologies exhibit interesting properties, which allow to differentiate them from other classes of topologies. For instance, when analyzing the characteristic path length, scale-free networks seem to be rather random (having Poisson distribution of network node degrees), while the clustering coefficient parameter shows their resemblance to regular networks (of deterministic node degree distribution) [16].

This paper evaluates the network performance after an attack. An interesting behavior of scale-free networks have been noticed. We have discovered that, if node removal process is performed sufficiently long, the topology of an attacked scale-free network migrates to the random one. The main purpose of our research is to quantify this process. In contrast to well explored parameters like: characteristic path length or clustering coefficient, we propose the new ones: mean maximum flow, centre of gravity of node degree distribution and other. To the best of our knowledge, these measures are proposed for the first time. Our results confirm that the migration process steps relatively fast.

The rest of the paper is organized as follows. Section 2 briefly presents topological features of wide-area networks. It also describes in detail the circumstances that make the topologies obtain the scale-free character. Section 3 outlines the negative effects of attacks on networks of the most important types of topologies. The proposed performance measures are given in Section 4. Section 5 shows the assumptions for measuring the performance of scale-free networks under malicious attacks. Results of modeling are presented in Section 6.

2 Topological Features of Wide-Area Networks

In the past, topologies of wide-area networks were mainly ring-based. In order to provide better coverage and self-healing behavior, multiple rings were further connected together, as shown in Fig. 1. However, due to constant maturing of DWDM switching technology, mesh networks (typically of regular or random topology) are becoming more popular. It is expected that mesh topology will be the most dominant in the near future [18]. An example of a mesh wide-area network is given in Fig. 2.

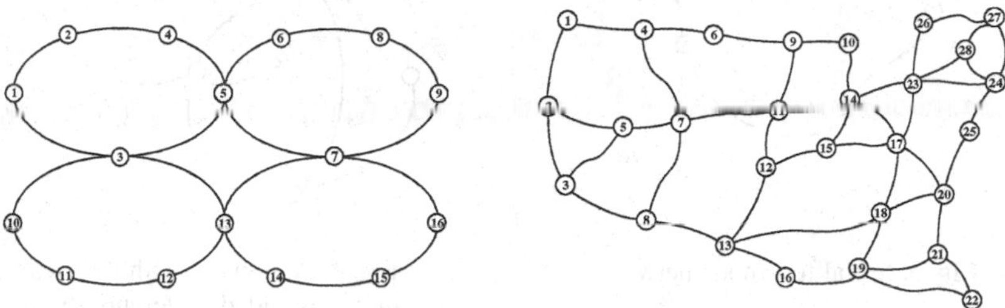

Fig. 1. Example artificial multiple ring network **Fig. 2.** U.S. Long-Distance Network

Many networks grow over time. Network growth is manifested by adding new elements (links or nodes). Since wide-area networks are frequently managed by several operators (carriers), each one having individual policy, network growth is often uncontrolled. In particular, it means that new network elements are added according to the *preferential attachment* rule. Following such a rule, also known as the *rich gets richer process*, it is more probable for a new element to become attached to the existing network element of high rather than small degree. Barabási and Albert have shown this preference to be linear and defined the probability $\Pi(n_i)$ of linking a new node to the existing network node n_i in [1] as:

$$\Pi(n_i) = \frac{\deg(n_i)}{\sum_j \deg(n_j)} \tag{1}$$

Eq. 1 states that the highly connected network nodes are more likely to obtain new neighbors during the further network growth. This process finally causes the network topology to obtain power law characteristics of node degree distribution ($P(k)\sim k^{-\gamma}$) [1]. Some nodes, referred to as *centers*, thus become highly connected, while the others tend to have a few, if any, neighbors. The power law distribution exhibits linearity in a log-log scale. Barabási and Albert called such power law networks *scale-free*, since their node degree distribution follows the power law, independent of the network size.

Figs. 3-6 show the typical example evolution of an initial regular four-node network towards a scale-free one, after preferentially adding 4, 8 and 12 nodes, respectively.

3 Topology-Dependent Impact of Attack on Networks

Elimination of central nodes in scale-free networks is recently one of the most frequently discussed issues [4]. Centers in such networks are connected to many other nodes mostly by links of high capacities and thus switch large amount of data. They are excellent goals of malicious attacks, performed to get the maximum destructive effect at minimum cost.

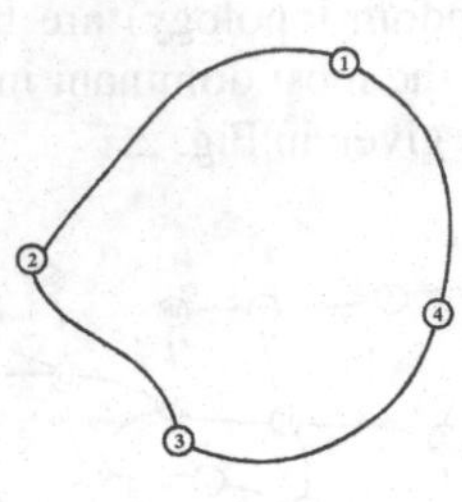

Fig. 3. Initial four-node network

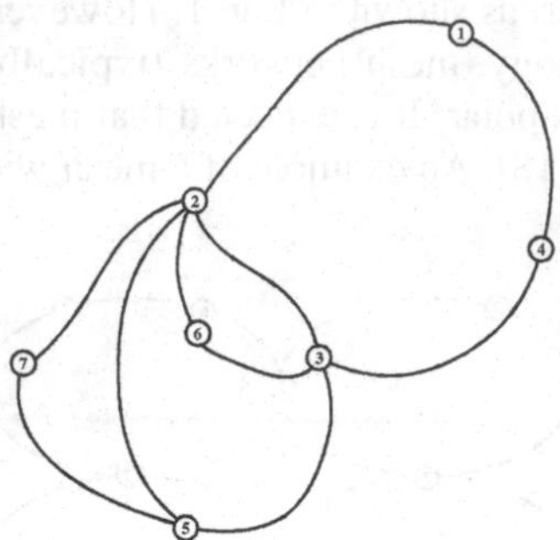

Fig. 4. A network with 8 nodes (4 nodes added preferentially)

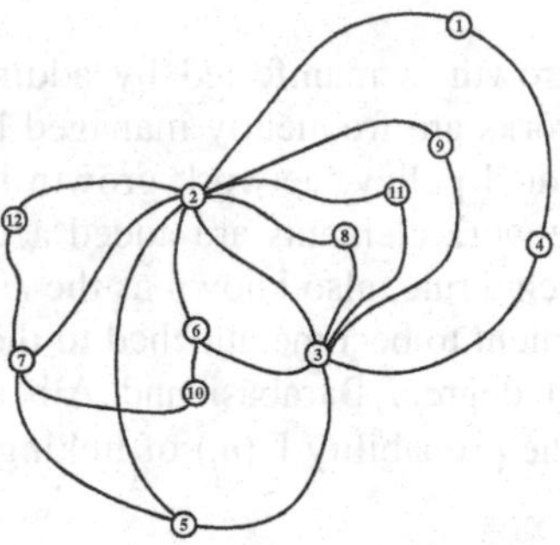

Fig. 5. A network with 12 nodes (8 nodes added preferentially)

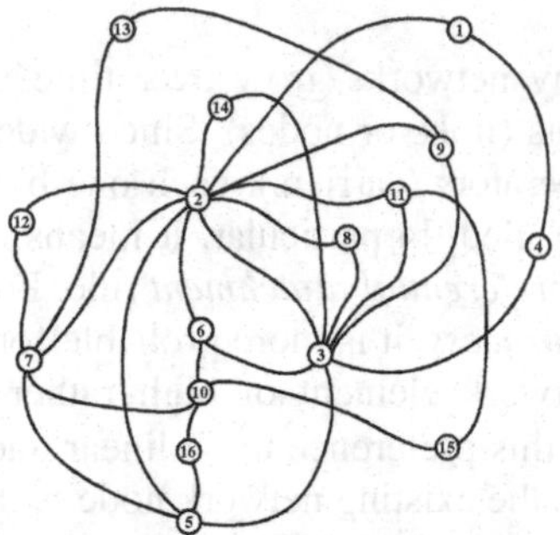

Fig. 6. A network with 16 nodes (12 nodes added preferentially)

Fig. 7 illustrates the destructive results of an attack on a scale-free network. An attack eliminating only two centers (here: nodes 2 and 3), results in disconnection of our network, complete isolation of nodes 8 and 14 and separation of remaining two subnetworks. The bigger subnetwork shown in the right part of Fig. 7 is sparse, because a failure of a node is always equivalent to the simultaneous failure of all its incident links.

However, the problem of attacks seems to be less dangerous for networks of either regular or random topology. It is because the degrees of nodes in such networks do not deviate so much from the mean value, as in the scale-free ones. Centers are hardly visible here, so attack results in such networks are less destructive, compared to scale-free networks.

Fig. 8 illustrates an attack on a network of a random topology (left part of Fig. 8), which results in a failure of two nodes (5 and 7, respectively), as given in the right part of Fig. 8. When attacking such a network, it is less likely for the remaining nodes to loose connectivity with other network elements.

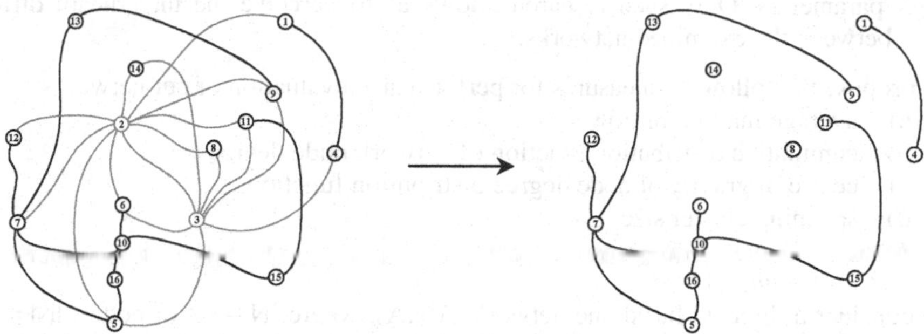

Fig. 7. A scale-free network before and after an attack (left and right part, respectively)

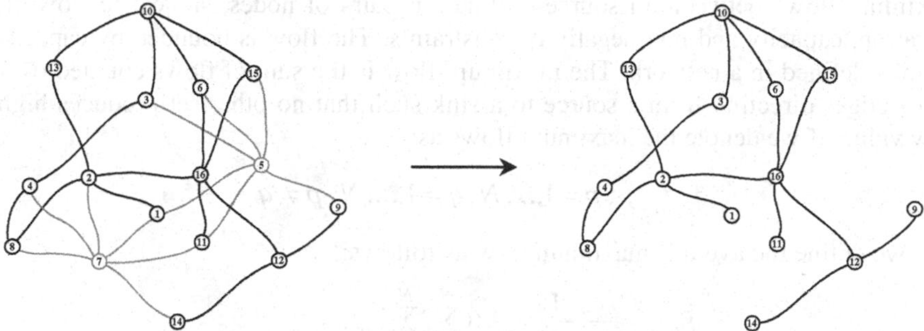

Fig. 8. A random network before and after an attack (left and right part, respectively)

Conclusion: if nodes are eliminated intentionally, scale-free networks appear to loose functionality much faster than random or regular networks.

4 Performance Measures of Scale-Free Networks Under Attacks

In order to capture the dynamics of attacked scale-free networks, a new way of network comparison is introduced. We aim at proving that when increasing the number of removed nodes, the properties of the biggest connected domain (often referred to as *spanning cluster* [4]) of remaining network are changing: it tends to migrate towards the random network.

The previous works, considering quantitative random and scale-free topologies comparison, proposed the parallel examination of both types of attacked networks, proving the differences in their behavior. In this paper, a more distinguishing way of measurement is proposed. Each time we generate a random network, with the number of nodes and edges being identical to the respective values of the spanning cluster that was obtained after attacking a scale-free network. This process is performed for each examined number of removed nodes, so that the continuous change may be observed. We are convinced that this way is more accurate, since every spanning cluster, obtained in a process of scale-free network degradation, should not be compared to the random one destroyed in the same way, but to a network with the same values of rough parameters. Only such research allows us to perceive the underneath differences between the examined networks.

We propose the following measures for performance evaluation of our networks:

a) average maximum flow
b) cumulative distribution function of network node degrees
c) centre of gravity of node degree distribution function
d) spanning cluster size.

Average Maximum Flow

We consider a directed backbone network Γ(N,A), where: N – set of nodes; |N| = N; A – set of directed arcs; |A| = M. Existing arcs are numbered in a lexicographical order. Each arc $e_m \in$ A is characterized by a set of weights like: length, cost and other.

In order to calculate the average maximum flow, one should find first the set of maximum flows between all source-destination pairs of nodes, subject to flow conservation, capacity and non-negativity constraints. The flow is bounded by capacities of links defined in a network. The maximum flow is the sum of flows counted over a set of edges directing from a source to a sink such that no other set produces higher flow value. If we denote the maximum flows as:

$$f_{p,q}^{\;*};\, p=1,\ldots,N,\, q=1,\ldots,N,\, p\neq q$$

then we define the average maximum flow as follows:

$$\overline{f}_{\max}=\frac{1}{N\times(N-1)}\times\Big(\sum_{p=1}^{N}\sum_{\substack{q=1\\q\neq p}}^{N} f_{p,q}^{\;*}\Big) \tag{2}$$

Cumulative Distribution Function (CDF) of Network Node Degrees

Definition of the cdf is based on the probability distribution. For a discrete random variable which n-th outcome (here – the degree of a node) occurs with probability P_n, it is defined as follows:

$$F(k)=\sum_{n<k} P_n \tag{3}$$

Where: k, n are node degrees; P_n is the probability of the occurrence of the degree of value n.

We also introduce the V_{CDF} parameter measuring distance between the cdf for a scale-free network and the cdf for a random network, defined as follows:

$$V_{CDF}=\sum_{k}\big((F_{RD}(k)-F_{SF}(k))\times k\big) \tag{4}$$

where $F_{SF}(k)$ and $F_{RD}(k)$ are cumulative distribution function values of scale-free and random networks, respectively.

Centre of Gravity of Node Degree Distribution Function

Centre of gravity of node degree distribution function denoted C_g is defined as follows. Treating the number of nodes of degree k as a mass (m_k) and the degree k as position, the following equation defines C_g:

$$C_g = \frac{1}{K_{total}} \sum_{k=1}^{K_{max}} m_k k \qquad (5)$$

where: P_k is a probability of the k-th node degree
K_{max} is the greatest degree of a node of the modeled network and
K_{total} is the sum of all the existing degrees of nodes.
What is more, K_{total} is not counted for every particular node, but only once if there exists a node of such degree. The mass is neglected here (singular value used) because of better results in differing network types from each other.

Spanning Cluster Size
After the repetitive node removal process, the remaining nodes are often disconnected and form isolated islands. The spanning cluster size tells how many nodes belong to the biggest cohesive cluster in a network and is denoted as *S*.

5 Modeling and Simulation Scenarios

In each single experiment we generated scale-free networks containing N=1000 nodes with a given value of mean node degree k_{mean} (which imposed a bound on the number of edges). Then networks were attacked until the number of 50 removed nodes (with granularity of 5 nodes) was obtained.

According to the simulation scenario, we assumed 6 values of $k_{mean} \in \{2.4, 2.6,\ldots, 3.4\}$. For each value of k_{mean}, 50 initial scale-free networks were generated. According to the described rules, each generated scale-free network was then attacked and the respective random network was generated. That gave the total number of 6600 scale-free and random networks examined. Each network link was assumed to have equal and unitary capacity.

All the numerical results were obtained using the environment of MATLAB and Pajek software [10].

6 Modeling Results

In the first series of experiments we observed changes in cumulative distribution function of network node degrees during continued attack. Fig. 9 illustrates the cdf functions for scale-free and random networks for $k_{mean} = 2{,}4$. Each point of each characteristic was calculated as the average value for 50 networks generated for that value of k_{mean}.

Fig. 9a shows the initial characteristics for fully operational networks (number of removed nodes=0). The greatest node degree of scale-free networks exceeds 10 several times, while in the random networks is around 7. Situation in Fig. 9b, where 10 centers were attacked does not differ very much compared to the starting point (the greatest node degree of scale-free networks still exceeds 10).

In contrast, when 20 centers are removed due to successful attacks (Fig. 9c), scale-free networks noticeably migrate to the random ones. This phenomenon achieves its maximum intensity in the next scenario, shown in Fig. 9d, where 30 centers have been eliminated. Both cdf curves are almost the same. This means, that the scale-free networks almost became the random ones.

When the destructive attack is continued, random networks are affected, but probably remain connected (Figs. 9e for 40 nodes removed and 9f for 50 nodes removed, respectively), but scale-free networks suffer to the catastrophic extent. They are certainly disconnected and separated into isolated subnetworks.

In conclusion, we see that if the process of intentional destruction of scale-free networks is performed with the appropriate determination, it leads to the total destruction of the network infrastructure. Unfortunately, this is a relatively fast process and elimination of 5% of centers is sufficient to achieve the destructive result in a short time.

Fig. 10 shows the values of the V_{CDF} parameter used to measure the distance of scale-free network topologies to random ones. The positive values of V_{CDF} denote how much the scale-free topology differs from the random one. The value of $V_{CDF} = 0$ means no difference, i.e. the situation when for a given network, the node degree distribution exactly follows the Poisson law (characteristic to random networks). The obtained results prove that with increasing number of removed important nodes, the scale-free network topological characteristic evolves towards the regular ones. This process is faster for scale-free networks with low rather than high node degrees.

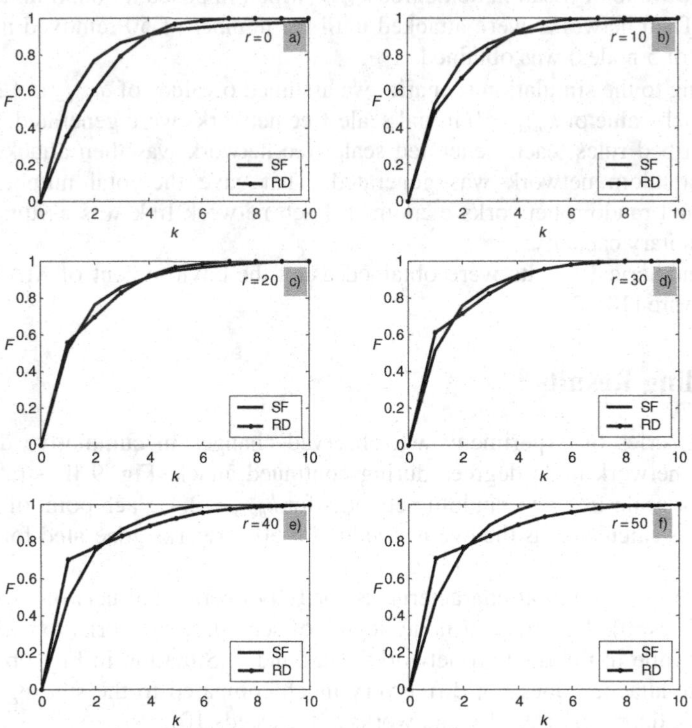

Fig. 9. Cumulative distribution functions for scale-free and random networks for k_{mean}= 2,4 as the function of removed r nodes ($r \in \{0, 10, 20, 30, 40, 50\}$)

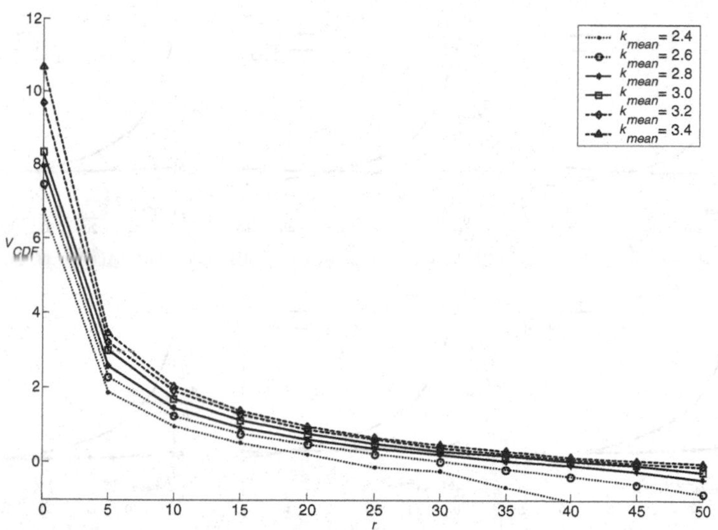

Fig. 10. Values of V_{CDF} for various values of k_{mean} as the function of removed r nodes ($r \in \{0, 10, 20, 30, 40, 50\}$)

In the next series of experiments we compared the dynamic changes of centre of gravity of node degree distribution for scale-free and random networks with $k_{mean} \in \{2.4, 2.6, \ldots, 3.4\}$ as the function of removed (attacked) nodes.

An interesting result is that in all scenarios illustrated in Fig. 11, the average centre of gravity of node degree distribution for random networks was around 5, while for scale-free networks it was systematically decreasing with increasing number of removed centers. This last phenomenon was intuitively expected from the definition (5).

Our original quantitative result is that we give values of the intersection of the two characteristics (for scale-free and random networks, respectively) for various $k_{mean} \in \{2{,}4, 2{,}6, \ldots, 3{,}4\}$.

In Fig. 11a (k_{mean} =2,4), the intersection occurs when about 24 nodes are removed, while in Fig. 11f this happens for about 41 nodes attacked (k_{mean} =3,4). (The exact values are given in Tab. 1).

This observation allows us to state the following conclusions:

1. The process of scale-free networks degradation under intentional attacks is fast, but it is slower in networks with higher node degrees than in networks with smaller node degrees.
2. Random networks are again much more resistant to intentional attacks than the scale-free networks and topology density does not play as important role as in scale-free networks.

In the next series of experiments we compared average maximum flows for scale- free and random networks for $k_{mean} \in \{2{,}4, 2{,}6, \ldots, 3{,}4\}$ as the function of attacked nodes (Fig. 12). Comparing pairs of characteristics for each value of k_{mean} we may identify similar phenomenon, as in Figs. 11. The intersection of average maximum

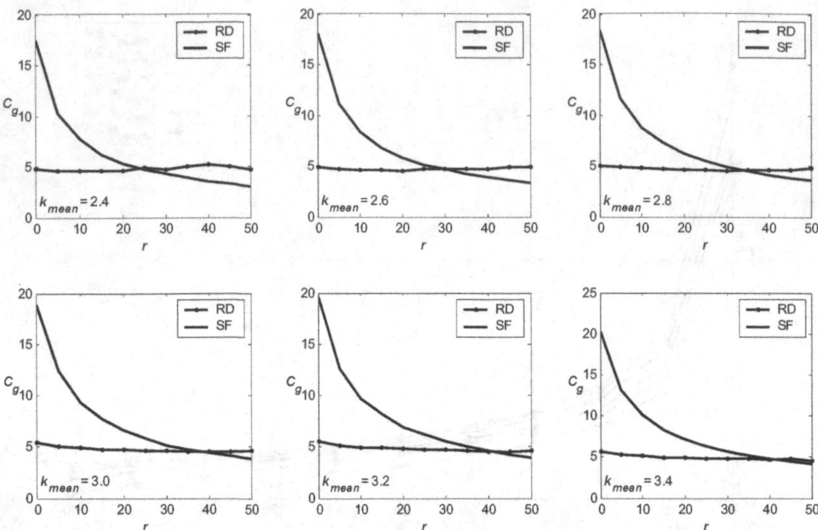

Fig. 11. Centre of gravity of node degree distribution for scale-free and random networks for various values of k_{mean} as the function of removed r nodes (r∈ {0, 10, 20, 30, 40, 50})

Table 1. Numbers of removed r nodes at which the identical values of centre of gravity of node degree distribution for scale-free and random networks were obtained

k_{mean} = 2,4	k_{mean} = 2,6	k_{mean} = 2,8	k_{mean} = 3,0	k_{mean} = 3,2	k_{mean} = 3,4
r = 24	r = 30	r = 34	r = 38	r = 41	r = 41

flows for scale-free and random networks occurs later (i.e. when more nodes are removed) for grater values of k_{mean} . This confirms our earlier observation. There is also good coincidence between the respective values of both kinds of characteristics (compare results in Tab. 1 and Tab. 2, respectively).

Another observation of Figs. 12 is that average maximum flows for fully operational networks are 20-25% better for random networks than for respective scale-free networks. This is due to topological features of networks.

In random networks one can find more alternative routes for source-destination pairs than in scale-free networks. In fact, random network can carry more flows compared to a scale-free network of the same size.

The last series of experiments was performed to measure the spanning cluster size after attacking a scale-free network (Fig. 13). The results prove that the decrease of the size of the spanning cluster with increasing the number of removed important nodes is slower in networks with higher node degrees than in networks with smaller node degrees.

The degradation of scale-free network topology connectivity after an attack seriously affects the performance of higher layer networking protocols (e.g. application layer). In [12] we showed that the attack has the greatest negative effect, if the

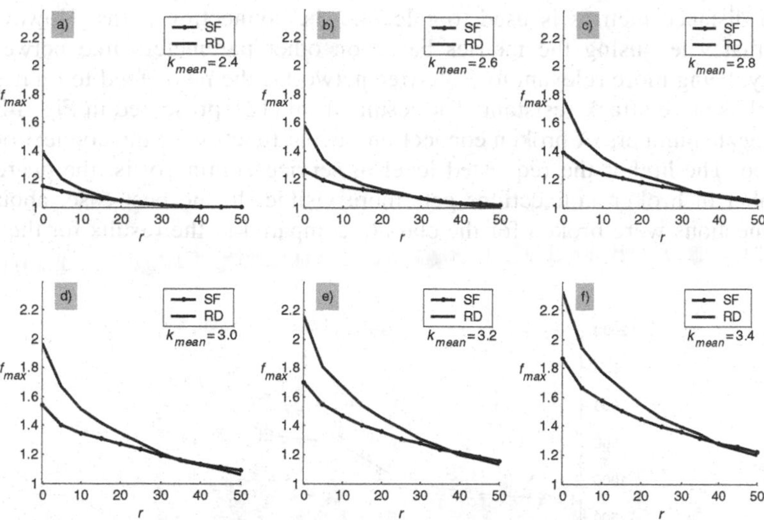

Fig. 12. Average maximum flows for scale-free and random networks for various values of k_{mean} as the function of removed r nodes ($r \in \{0, 10, 20, 30, 40, 50\}$)

Table 2. Numbers of removed r nodes at which the identical values of average maximum flow for scale-free and random networks were obtained

k_{mean} = 2,4	k_{mean} = 2,6	k_{mean} = 2,8	k_{mean} = 3,0	k_{mean} = 3,2	k_{mean} = 3,4
r = 19	r = 27	r = 33	r = 33	r = 38	r = 39

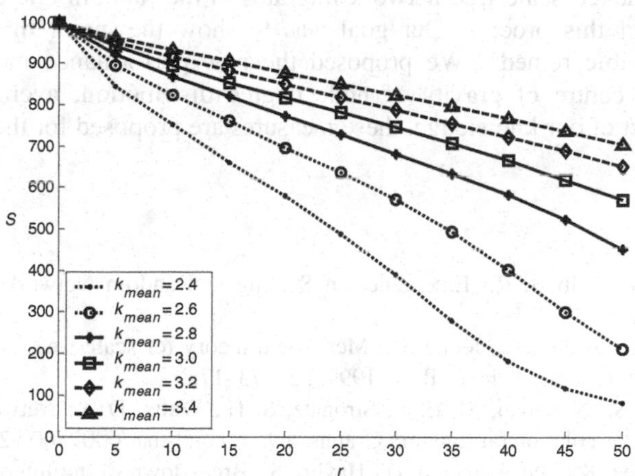

Fig. 13. Spanning cluster size for scale-free and random networks for various values of k_{mean} as the function of removed r nodes ($r \in \{0, 10, 20, 30, 40, 50\}$)

standard distance metrics is used to calculate the connection paths. However, we proved that when using the metrics based on other parameters like betweenness centrality, being more relevant to scale-free networks, the paths tend to omit centers and are thus more attack-resistant. The results from [12], presented in Fig. 14, show the aggregate numbers of broken connections as the function of the connection class of service. The higher the requested level of service continuity is, the decrease in the number of broken connections gets more visible. In the best case, about 67% less connections were broken for the class 0, compared to the results for the lowest class (5).

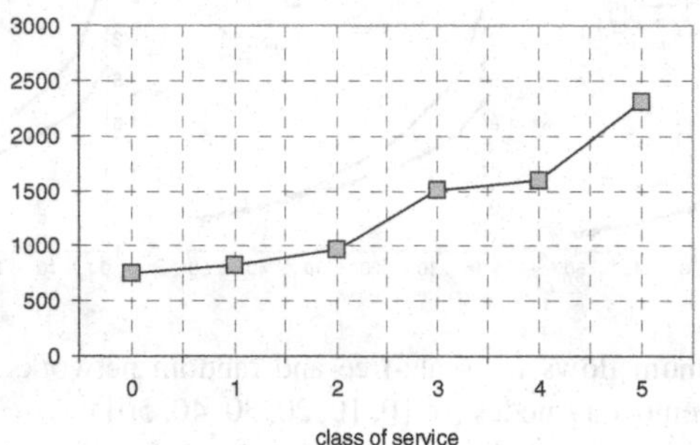

Fig. 14. Aggregate number of broken connections for 6 classes of service

7 Concluding Remarks

We have investigated the dynamics of processes of intentional attacks on scale-free networks. We showed that, if node removing is performed sufficiently long, the topology of an attacked scale-free network migrates to the random one and we evaluated the speed of this process. Our goal was to show the major threats. We also discussed a possible remedy. We proposed the new performance measures: mean maximum flow, centre of gravity of node degree distribution, average maximum flows. To the best of our knowledge, these measures are proposed for the first time.

References

1. Barabási, A.-L., Albert, R.: Emergence of Scaling in Random Networks. Science 286, pp. 509-511, 1999
2. Barabási, A.-L., Albert, R., Jeong, H.: Mean-field theory for scale-free random networks, Physica A 272, Elsevier Science B. V. 1999, pp. 173–178
3. Callaway, D. S., Newman, M. E. J., Strogatz, S. H., Watts, D. J.: Network Robustness and Fragility: Percolation on Random Graphs, arXiv: cond-mat/0007300 v2 19 Oct 2000
4. Cohen, R., Erez, K., ben-Avraham, D., Havlin, S.: Breakdown of the Internet under Intentional Attack, Physical Review Letters, vol. 86, 2001, arXiv:cond-mat/0010251
5. Crucitti, P., Latora, V., Marchiori, M., Rapisarda, A.: Efficiency of Scale-free Networks: Error and Attack Tolerance, arXiv:cond-mat/0205601, 2002

6. Dijkstra, E.: A Note on Two Problems in Connection with Graphs. Numerische Mathematik, 1 (1959), pp. 269-271
7. Ellison, R. J., Fisher, D. A., Linger, R. C., Lipson, H. F., Longstaff, T., Mead, N. R.: Survivable Network Systems: An Emerging Discipline. Carnegie Mellon University, Software Engineering Institute. (1997) (Rev. 1999), Technical Report CMU/SEI-97-TR-013
8. Faloutsos, M., Faloutsos, P., Faloutsos, C.: On Power-law Relationships of the Internet Topology. In SIGCOMM, pp. 251--262, 1999
9. Gierszewski, T., Rak, J.: On Reducing the Value of Aggregate Restoration Time when Assuring Survivability in Scale-free Networks. Proceedings of the 12th GI/ITG Conference on Measuring, Modelling and Evaluation of Computer and Communication Systems (MMB) together with 3rd Polish-German Teletraffic Symposium (PGTS). Dresden, Germany, 12-15 September, 2004, pp. 99-104
10. http://vlado.fmf.uni-lj.si/pub/networks/pajek
11. Mead, N. R., Ellison, R. J., Linger, R. C., Longstaff, T., McHugh, J.: Survivable Network Analysis Method. Carnegie Mellon University, Software Engineering Institute (2000) Technical Report CMU/SEI-2000-TR-013
12. Molisz, W., Rak, J.: End-to-end Service Survivability under Attacks on Networks, Proc. 7th Regional NATO Conference on Military Communications and Information Systems, Zegrze, Poland, 4-5.10.2005, pp. 116-125
13. Molisz, W., Rak, J.: Region Protection/Restoration Scheme in Survivable Networks, 3rd Workshop on Mathematical Methods, Models and Architectures for Computer Network Security (MMM-ACNS 2005) St. Petersburg, Russia, Springer-Verlag, LNCS, Vol. 3685, pp. 442-447
14. Mukherjee, B.: WDM Optical Communication Networks: Progress and Challenges, IEEE Journal on Selected Areas in Communications, Vol. 18, No. 10, Oct. 2000, pp. 1810-1823
15. Siganos, G., Faloutsos, M., Faloutsos, P., Faloutsos, C.: Power-laws and the AS-level Internet topology. IEEE/ACM Transactions on Networking, 11(4): pp. 514--524, August 2003. 41
16. Watts, D. J., Strogatz, S. H.: Collective Dynamics of 'Small-world' Networks, Nature 393, Nature Macmillan Publishers Ltd 1998, pp. 440–442
17. Yook, S.H., Jeong, H., Barabási, A.-L.: Modeling the Internet's large-scale topology, Proc. of the National Academy of Sciences (PNAS) 99 (2002), pp. 13382–13386
18. Zhu, K., Zhang, H., Mukherjee, B.: A Comprehensive Study on Next-generation Optical Grooming Switches, IEEE Journal on Selected Areas in Communications, Vol. 21, No. 7, Sept. 2003, pp. 1173-1186

Verifying a Chipcard-Based Biometric Identification Protocol in VSE

Lassaad Cheikhrouhou, Georg Rock, Werner Stephan,
Matthias Schwan, and Gunter Lassmann

German Research Center for Artificial Intelligence (DFKI GmbH)
Stuhlsatzenhausweg 3, 66123 Saarbrücken, Germany
{Lassaad.Cheikhrouhou, Georg.Rock, Werner.Stephan}@dfki.de
T-Systems Enterprise Services GmbH
Goslarer Ufer 35, 10589 Berlin, Germany
{Matthias.Schwan, Gunter.Lassmann}@t-systems.com

Abstract. In this paper we describe our experiences in specifying and verifying a complex cryptographic protocol actually used in industry that has been developed for the area of chipcard based biometric identification systems. The main emphasis was placed on authenticity, integrity and confidentiality properties. The formal analysis even led to several simplifying modifications of the protocol that facilitate the implementation, yet maintaining the protocol security properties we considered. The formal analysis is based on an inductive approach performed with the help of VSE (Verification Support Environment). The heuristic based proof automation techniques realized in VSE result in an average grade of automation of 80 percent. Thus, VSE provides substantial support for the specification and verification of cryptographic protocols.

1 Introduction

Protocols that (try to) provide certain security properties in open network environments by using cryptographic primitives like encrypting, signing, and hashing, play a crucial role in many emerging application scenarios. Chipcard based biometric identification systems as they are considered in this paper are an example of a technology whose common acceptance heavily depends on how far security properties like confidentiality and authenticity can really be *guaranteed* by their designers. On the other hand the analysis of cryptographic protocols has turned out to be error prone if carried out on an informal basis. Justifiably so, the *formal* specification and analysis of cryptographic protocols has become one of the fastest growing research area with a hardly manageable variety of different approaches.

There is an enormous number of special purpose formalisms and semantic frameworks for the formal analysis of security protocols. Most prominent candidates perhaps are Strand Spaces and the Spi-calculus. Strand Spaces [18] as developed by Thayer, Fábrega, J. C. Herzog, and J. D. Guttman separate a sequence of events into single strands that were associated to one of the protocol participants. Security properties are reduced to properties of graphs. Abadi and Gordon developed the Spi-calculus [19] as an extension of the pi-calculus by cryptographic primitives. Protocols are represented

J. Górski (Ed.): SAFECOMP 2006, LNCS 4166, pp. 42–56, 2006.

as processes and protocol properties are formalized as equivalences on the behavior of processes.

Some of the formal approaches published in the literature have actually been implemented to provide tool support for *debugging* or even complete *verification* of protocols. While debugging means that for fixed settings (scenarios) protocol runs of a given protocol are checked for the violation of certain security properties, verification guarantees appropriately specified security properties for all possible runs in all possible scenarios. In both cases protocol runs include events caused by an attacker whose basic capabilities are given by the so called Dolev-Yao model which (rather implicitly) has been introduced in [1].

As in other areas of formal methods in the formal analysis of protocols we roughly distinguish between approaches that systematically enumerate possible runs of a given protocol including the attacker events and those that perform an inductive proof about protocol traces modeled as sequences of events. Although not being restricted to finite search spaces the former are most often used for detecting situations that indicate security hazards (debugging). Using them for verification requires additional arguments and restrictions. On the other hand successful proofs in the inductive approach, whose feasibility is argued for in this paper, directly provide security guarantees while failed proof attempts in general do not lead to a uniform method for debugging protocols.

Model-checking based approaches have been described in [20, 21, 5, 22, 7, 9, 8, 12, 13, 10, 15]. Basin [16] uses so called *lazy data types* in Haskell for treating infinite state spaces. The protocol as well as the attacker are represented as infinite trees and model-checking techniques for non-finite state spaces are used to explore the state space step by step guided by suitable heuristics. This approach got severely improved by usage of symbolic techniques [17] that allow to get rid of the before mentioned heuristics.

Deductive based approaches can be distinguished primarily by the kind of axiomatization and corresponding inference mechanism that is utilized. For example Weidenbach [11] builds on (first-order) automatic theorem proving as an inference engine to analyze security protocols. The restriction to a special first-order monadic horn logic allows to apply known decidability results. Therefore, a variety of properties can be automatically (dis)proved. For example, the confidentiality of session keys for the Neuman-Stubblebine protocol [14] as well as potential attacks to the protocol can be derived automatically.

The methodology, VSE is based on, is closely related to Paulson's approach [2]. In this method main emphasis is placed on (observable) traces resulting from the execution of protocol rules and attacker events that are axiomatized explicitly. Reasoning about protocol traces and the knowledge gained by (Dolev-Yao) attackers given by sets of messages heavily relies on *inductive* proofs on these very traces.

Briefly, the major features of this approach are: It allows for complete verification, it is extendable (at the level of experienced users) by new types of protocol events and the corresponding capabilities of the attacker (this turned out to be necessary for some examples), it supports the integration of protocol verification into the overall development process, but requires user interaction.

To technically cope with protocol verification problems we make use of the Verification Support Environment (VSE) system. It is a kind of case tool for formal software development that closely combines a front end for specification (including refinement) and the management of structured developments with an interactive theorem prover [23,24,25,26,27,28,29].

The integration of inductive protocol verification in VSE was a major part of the *Valicrypt* project funded by the German Information Security Agency (BSI). These techniques are currently used and extended in the Verisoft [3] project funded by the Federal Ministry of Education and Research (BMBF).

In this paper we focus on the application of VSE to a cryptographic protocol analyzed in the context of the Verisoft project. The techniques that were developed to lower the burden of interactive proof generation to an extent that makes this method applicable within the limited time frames of commercial developments are evaluated using this example. The gained experiences were encouraging. Although the size of proof objects and lemma bases became very large in the real world example that we discuss in this paper we were able to basically keep track with the design team even in the various revisions of the protocol.

The paper is organized as follows: We first present the general scenario with its cryptographic protocol to be analyzed. Then we give a short introduction to the part of VSE that is concerned with the specification and verification of cryptographic protocols. The formalization of the protocol properties is presented in chapter four. The fifth chapter illustrates how the properties were proven. Section six concludes the paper by mentioning the results and experiences gained with VSE and discussing future work planned in this area.

2 CBI-Scenario

The Chipcard based Biometric Identification system (CBI) [4] consists of several components (see Figure 1):

- A chipcard terminal for the communication between the chipcard owner and the host system.
- A chipcard that holds the biometric reference template.
- A computer system (Host) that performs the biometric computations and that contains the biometric feature extracting and matching unit.
- A biometric sensor for capturing the fresh biometric data as, for example, a fingerprint.
- A display that gives the user a feedback on the biometric matching.

The main parts of the CBI-System as shown in Figure 1 are the host and the chipcard. They exchange confidential information that should not be disclosed to an attacker. In order to secure this connection a cryptographic protocol as the one described in section 2.1 is used. A typical behavior of the system can be described as follows:

- The chipcard and the host perform a mutual authentication using pre-shared symmetric keys given in an initial step. After successful authentication a symmetric session key is known to both parties. Otherwise, the session is terminated.

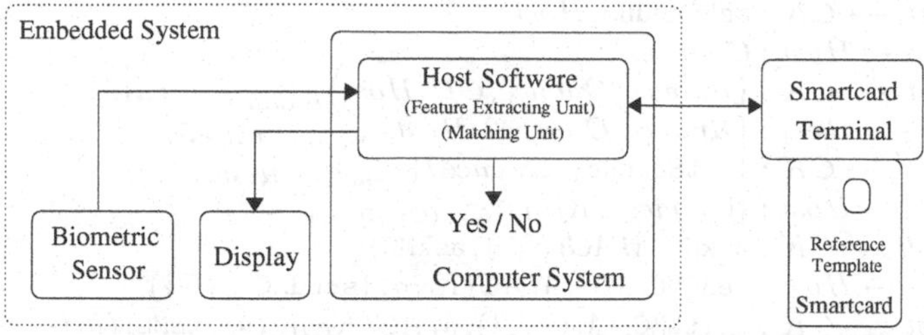

Fig. 1. General structure of the CBI-System

- The host reads the error counter from the chipcard that indicates the number of failed biometric verification attempts. If the error counter is not equal to 0 the host writes the decremented error counter back to the chipcard.
- The host asks for the reference template and receives it together with the electronic signature of the reference template generated by an administrator during the enrollment phase.
- The host asks for the fresh biometric data and receives it from a biometric sensor.
- The host compares the fresh biometric template and the reference template. If the verification is successful the host deletes the fresh biometric data and the reference data, writes the default error counter back on the chipcard and reports the result to the user via a display. In the negative case the host deletes the fresh biometric data and asks for new biometric data. The host repeats this request three times at most.

The output of the CBI-System is "biometrically authenticated" in the positive and "biometric authentication failed" in the negative case. It is clear that such an informal description is usually not enough to come up with a unique formal protocol specification. This is the reason why there are usually several iterations involved in the design of such a protocol. The next section presents a more detailed representation of the protocol and this will be the basis for the formalization described in section 3.

2.1 Specification of the CBI-Protocol

Figure 2 shows the steps of the CBI-protocol used in the identification scenario in the CBI-system described before. The words written in `typewriter` font represent constants whereas the other symbols represent protocol variables, that can be substituted by different instances in different protocol sessions. Encryption of a message m using a key k is written as $\{m\}_k$ and the generation of a message authentication code for a message m using a key k is represented as $MAC(k, m)$ in Figure 2. The keys $K_{auth}(CK, Host)$ and $K_{enc}(CK, Host)$ used in the protocol are assumed to be shared between the host and the chipcard.

Usually the communication between a card and a host is started by a reset and an answer to reset (ATR) command. Since these steps only determine the communication protocol and the communication partners, we omit these steps. In step one of the protocol the host (with identifier) $Host$ sends its identifier to the card CK and asks the card

1. $Host \longrightarrow CK : \texttt{askRandom}, Host$
2. $CK \longrightarrow Host : Cnonce$
3. $Host \longrightarrow CK : \{Rnonce, Cnonce, CK, Host\}_{K_{auth}(CK,Host)}$
4. $CK \longrightarrow Host : \{Rnonce, Cnonce2, Host\}_{K_{auth}(CK,Host)}$
5. $Host \longrightarrow CK : \{\texttt{getSessKey}, Cnonce2\}_{K_{enc}(CK,Host)}$
6. $CK \longrightarrow Host : \{Cnonce2, K_{CH}\}_{K_{enc}(CK,Host)}$
7. $Host \longrightarrow CK : \texttt{askMC}, MAC(K_{CH}, \texttt{askMC})$
8. $CK \longrightarrow Host : \texttt{sendMC}, MC, MAC(K_{CH}, \{\texttt{sendMC}, MC\})$
9. $Host \longrightarrow CK : \texttt{writeMC}, (MC-1), MAC(K_{CH}, \{\texttt{writeMC}, (MC-1)\})$, if $MC \neq 0$
10. $CK \longrightarrow Host : \texttt{sendMC*}, (MC-1), MAC(K_{CH}, \{\texttt{sendMC*}, (MC-1)\})$
11. $Host \longrightarrow CK : \{\texttt{askRefData}\}_{K_{CH}}$
12. $CK \longrightarrow Host : \{Data, \{sha(\{Data, CK\})\}_{sk(Admin)}\}_{K_{CH}}$
13. $Host \longrightarrow Interface : \texttt{askData}$
14. $Interface \longrightarrow Host : Data$
15. $Host \longrightarrow Interface : \texttt{Ok}$

Fig. 2. The CBI-Protocol

to generate a random value. This message allows the chipcard to determine the identifier of the communication partner. In step two the card answers by sending a random *Cnonce* representing a fresh nonce. The message in step three of the protocol contains a challenge (a new nonce) *Rnonce* generated by the host that allows to authenticate the chipcard in step four. The new nonce, *Cnonce*2, inserted in step four is used to prevent replay attacks with the messages from the steps five and six. In step five the card CK is asked by the host to generate a new session key. The card generate the session key K_{CH} and sends it back to the host in step six. This new session key is used for secure messaging in subsequent steps. It ensures confidentiality and integrity of subsequent messages. Steps seven, eight, nine and ten correspond to the read- and write-steps of the error counter MC. This counter is used to restrict the number of trials for biometric identification. In the rest of the protocol the digitally signed[1] reference data and the fresh biometric data are exchanged between the host, the chipcard and the biometric interface. The presented protocol is formally analyzed with the help of the VSE system that is described in the next section.

3 VSE - Cryptographic Protocol Specification and Verification

As part of the projects mentioned above an environment for the formal treatment of cryptographic protocols has been realized in VSE. This environment includes

- a library that provides VSE theories for the basic notions that are needed to formalize protocols,
- an extension of the front end of VSE supporting the user friendly specification of individual protocols and the automatic generation of (individual) lemma bases, and
- a strategy for the interactive generation of inductive proofs about protocols.

[1] This signature is created during the enrollment phase by a trusted third party, called *Admin*.

3.1 Cryptographic Protocol Library

To specify and verify protocols (as the one presented in section 2.1) with Paulson's approach requires the introduction of abstract data types for agents, keys, nonces, messages, events, traces, etc. For these notions the VSE protocol environment provides a structured set of predefined theories.

These theories are generic as they do not contain any definitions that refer to an individual protocol. They include proofs that can be carried out at this generic level.

Some of the theories in this structure are specific for certain classes of protocols. The heuristics used to support the user in proving the desired properties are theory dependent and thus have to be compatible with the configuration chosen for a particular protocol. A suitable configuration management takes care of these dependencies.

The following example specification is taken from the part of the library that defines a protocol *trace* and a protocol *event*.

```
BASIC BProtocolTrace
 USING BProtocolEvent;
       NATURAL
 /* Data type for protocol traces: */
 ProtocolTrace = nullEvent WITH isNullEvent |
                 addEvent(lastEvent : ProtocolEvent,
                          preEvents : ProtocolTrace)
                 WITH isAddEvent
 SIZE FUNCTION ELlength : ProtocolTrace -> NAT
BASICEND

BASIC BProtocolEvent
 USING TMsgList_Thms
 /* Data type for protocol events: */
 ProtocolEvent = Says(sender  : AgentT,
                      address : AgentT,
                      sentMsg : Msg) WITH isSays |
                 Gets(receiver : AgentT,
                      gotMsg  : Msg) WITH isGets |
                 Notes(subject : AgentT,
                       noteMsg : Msg) WITH isNotes
BASICEND
```

In the basic theory `BProtocolTrace`[2] the data type `ProtocolTrace` is defined. Basically, traces are inductively defined by the constructors `nullEvent` (the empty trace) and `addEvent` applied to an event and a trace where events are defined in the basic theory `BProtocolEvent`. The data type `ProtocolEvent` defines the possible events in a protocol trace. A `Says` event represents the sending of a message. It consists of the sender, the address of the intended receiver and the message to be sent. A `Gets` event represents the reception of a message. It consists of the receiver and the received message. A `Notes` event describes the acquisition of some knowledge by some agent. The complete cryptographic protocol library is about 1100 lines

[2] The `With` clauses introduce predicates to check for certain data types.

of specification and contains all definitions to specify cryptographic protocols and their properties.

3.2 Specification of Protocols

In addition to the interactive generation of proofs the VSE system supports the user by an interface that is structured according to the elements of certain development (specification) techniques. Since these frameworks are fixed the actual logical representations including proof obligations are generated by the system. The user has no longer to care about the correct (adequate) axiomatic treatment of certain development methods.

For protocol verification this interface was extended by a language called VSE-CAPSL as an extension of CAPSL [6]. It implements a more user friendly way to specify protocols. These protocols are translated automatically to VSE-SL resulting in protocol specific theories. Such a theory contains the possible protocol steps defined as a predicate (`CBI` in our example) over protocol traces:

```
CBINull : CBI(nullEvent);
CBIAdd : CBI(addEvent(ev,evs)) <->
          (CBI(evs) AND (CBI_Says1(ev,evs) OR
           CBI_Says2(ev,evs) OR CBI_Says3(ev,evs) OR
           .
           .
           CBI_Says15(ev,evs) OR CBI_Oops1(ev,evs) OR
           Gets_event(ev,evs) OR Fake_event(ev,evs)));
```

The events `CBI_Oops1` and `Fake_event` represent the possible actions of an attacker. An example for the specification of a protocol step (step two of our example protocol) is as follows:

```
CBISays2 : CBI_Says2(ev,evs) <->
  EX CK, Hst, Rsc:
   (NOT msgIN(nonce(Rsc), used(evs)) AND
    eventIN(Gets(CK, pair(num(askRandom), agent(Hst))), evs) AND
    ev = Says(CK, Hst, nonce(Rsc)));
```

During the afore mentioned translation process the definition of certain proof-structuring lemmata - like possibility, regularity, forwarding and unicity lemmata, that give rise to the generic proof structure discussed in [2] - are automatically generated by the system.

4 Formal Specification of the CBI-Protocol Properties

The main properties of cryptographic protocols that we are interested in are *confidentiality* and *authenticity*. *Sensitive* data, like session keys or nonces that are often used for the generation of new data items that are not used in the current protocol run, like for example new session keys, have to be protected against a malicious attacker.

Authentication properties are often formulated depending on a particular participant. For the protocol presented in section 2 the authentication property formulated in Theorem 1 is formulated from the chipcard perspective. Authentication proofs are often based on *authenticity* properties of certain messages. The authenticity of such a message is used to identify the sender of that message (see Lemma 1).

In addition to the top-level properties we have to prove so called *structuring lemmata*. These are generated automatically by the system and used by heuristics. Their proof uses the same basic scheme that is used for confidentiality and authentication.

In the rest of this section we list the main properties of the CBI-protocol.

4.1 Mutual Authentication

The CBI-protocol requires mutual authentication of the chipcard and the host (see section 2). This mutual authentication is performed in steps two to four of the CBI-protocol (see Figure 2). There, the chipcard CK authenticates the $Host$ in step three. The message of this step contains the challenge sent before in step two to the host and is encrypted by the shared key $K_{auth}(CK, Host)$. The formalization of this property from the point of view of the chipcard can be found in Theorem 1 where tr represents an arbitrary protocol trace.

Theorem 1 (Authentication of the Host)

$$
\begin{aligned}
&\forall tr, CK, Host, Cnonce, Rnonce:\\
&\quad (tr \in CBI \ \wedge\ \mathtt{says}(CK, Host, Cnonce) \in tr\ \wedge\\
&\quad \mathtt{gets}(CK, \{Rnonce, Cnonce, CK, Host\}_{K_{auth}(CK,Host)}) \in tr\\
&\quad \wedge\, CK \notin bad \ \wedge\ Host \notin bad)\\
&\quad \Rightarrow \mathtt{says}(Host, CK, \{Rnonce, Cnonce, CK, Host\}_{K_{auth}(CK,Host)}) \in tr
\end{aligned}
$$

After having sent a challenge $Cnonce$ to a $Host$ and after having received the corresponding response, a chipcard CK infers that $Host$ is the sender of this response, provided both participants are not compromised. The proof of this theorem uses Lemma 1, that expresses the authenticity of the message in step three of the CBI-protocol.

Lemma 1 (Authenticity of Message in Step 3)

$$
\begin{aligned}
&\forall tr, Rnonce, Cnonce, CK, Host:\\
&\quad (tr \in CBI\ \wedge\\
&\quad \{Rnonce, Cnonce, CK, Host\}_{K_{auth}(CK,Host)} \in parts(spies(tr))\\
&\quad \wedge\, CK \notin bad \ \wedge\ Host \notin bad)\\
&\quad \Rightarrow \mathtt{says}(Host, CK, \{Rnonce, Cnonce, CK, Host\}_{K_{auth}(CK,Host)}) \in tr
\end{aligned}
$$

In the same way, the $Host$ authenticates the chipcard CK with the help of the message in step four of the CBI-protocol. This message contains the challenge $Rnonce$ sent in step three and it is encrypted using the shared key $K_{auth}(CK, Host)$. This property is formulated from the point of view of the host in Theorem 2.

Theorem 2 (Authentication of the Host)

$$
\begin{aligned}
&\forall tr, Host, CK, Rnonce, Cnonce, Cnonce2:\\
&\quad (tr \in CBI\\
&\quad \wedge\, \mathtt{says}(Host, CK, \{Rnonce, Cnonce, CK, Host\}_{K_{auth}(CK,Host)}) \in tr\\
&\quad \wedge\, \mathtt{gets}(Host, \{Rnonce, Cnonce2, Host\}_{K_{auth}(CK,Host)}) \in tr\\
&\quad \wedge\, CK \notin bad \ \wedge\ Host \notin bad)\\
&\quad \Rightarrow \mathtt{says}(CK, Host, \{Rnonce, Cnonce2, Host\}_{K_{auth}(CK,Host)}) \in tr
\end{aligned}
$$

Theorem 2 relies on Lemma 2, that describes the authenticity of the fourth message.

Lemma 2 (Authenticity of the Message in Step 4)
$\forall tr, Rnonce, Cnonce2, Host, CK:$
$(tr \in CBI \wedge$
$\{Rnonce, Cnonce2, Host\}_{K_{auth}(CK,Host)} \in parts(spies(tr))$
$\wedge\, CK \notin bad \wedge\, Host \notin bad)$
$\Rightarrow \mathtt{says}(CK, Host, \{Rnonce, Cnonce2, Host\}_{K_{auth}(CK,Host)}) \in tr$

4.2 Secrecy and Integrity of the Session Key

The session key K_{CH} is generated in step six of the CBI-protocol. It is used to ensure the integrity of the misuse counter MC and the confidentiality of the reference template.

Theorem 3 (Secrecy of the Session Key)
$\forall tr, CK, Host, K_{CH}, Cnonce2:$
$(tr \in CBI \wedge$
$\mathtt{says}(CK, Host, \{Cnonce2, K_{CH}\}_{K_{enc}(CK,Host)}) \in tr$
$\wedge\, CK \notin bad \wedge\, Host \notin bad \wedge \mathtt{notes}(spy, \{Cnonce2, K_{CH}\}) \notin tr)$
$\Rightarrow K_{CH} \notin analz(spies(tr))$

Theorem 3 expresses that the attacker (*spy*) is not able to obtain a session key K_{CH} which is sent by a chipcard CK to a $Host$ within a session of the CBI-protocol, that is represented as (part of) an arbitrary trace tr resulting from the CBI-protocol. The knowledge the attacker can acquire from a trace tr is represented here by the set $analz(spies(tr))$[3]. The theorem requires that the protocol participants CK and $Host$ are not compromised, and that the session key K_{CH} is not revealed accidentally to the attacker[4]. In addition to the confidentiality of the session key, the integrity of the message containing this key has to be analyzed. The integrity is guaranteed by the authenticity of the message in step six, as formulated in Theorem 4. The integrity relies on the assumption that honest participants never generate manipulated messages. Note, that the theorem states that the session key K_{CH} belongs to the session in which the random $Cnonce2$ is created.

Theorem 4 (Authenticity of the Message in Step 6)
$\forall tr, Rnonce, Cnonce2, CK, Host, K_{CH}:$
$(tr \in CBI \wedge$
$\{Rnonce, Cnonce2, Host\}_{K_{auth}(CK,Host)} \in parts(spies(tr)) \wedge$
$\{Cnonce2, K_{CH}\}_{K_{enc}(CK,Host)} \in parts(spies(tr))$
$\wedge\, CK \notin bad \wedge\, Host \notin bad)$
$\Rightarrow \mathtt{says}(CK, Host, \{Cnonce2, K_{CH}\}_{K_{enc}(CK,Host)}) \in tr$

[3] This formula represents all the knowledge an attacker can collect by observing all communications and analyzing the messages by for example decomposing them or decrypting them using the right key.

[4] This is usually represented by an 'oops' event formally written as $\mathtt{notes}(spy, \{Cnonce2, K_{CH}\})$. We consider such an 'oops' event in the protocol model, to investigate whether revealed session keys can be exploited to attack other protocol sessions.

4.3 Integrity of the Misuse Counter MC

The misuse counter MC limits the number of failed biometric identification attempts. As described before the host (i) checks that the current value of MC differs from 0 and (ii) decreases this value by 1 before accessing the reference template. In step eight of the protocol the host accesses the current value of MC on the card. The integrity of the corresponding message guarantees that this value is not manipulated. This again follows from the authenticity of the message in step eight as formulated in Theorem 5.

Theorem 5 (Authenticity of the Message in Step 8)

$$\begin{array}{l} \forall tr, K_{CH}, Cnonce2, CK, Host, MC: \\ \quad (tr \in CBI \wedge \\ \quad \mathtt{says}(CK, Host, \{Cnonce2, K_{CH}\}_{K_{enc}(CK,Host)}) \in tr \\ \quad \wedge\, K_{CH} \notin analz(spies(tr)) \wedge \\ \quad MAC(K_{CH}, \{\mathtt{sendMC}, MC\}) \in parts(spies(tr))) \\ \quad \Rightarrow \mathtt{says}(CK, Host, \{\mathtt{sendMC}, MC, \\ \qquad\qquad\qquad MAC(K_{CH}, \{\mathtt{sendMC}, MC\})\}) \in tr \end{array}$$

By proving this theorem it is guaranteed that the accessed value of MC belongs to the current session and is not replayed from an earlier protocol run.

In step nine of the protocol, the host checks if the current value of MC differs from 0 and asks the chipcard to replace this value with the decremented value $(MC - 1)$. In order to verify that the value of MC is indeed changed accordingly on the card, the host accesses the (changed) value of MC in step ten. Afterwards it compares this value with the one accessed in step eight of the protocol. The integrity of the message in step ten ensures that the changed value on the card is not manipulated. This again is a consequence of the authenticity of the message in step ten formulated in Theorem 6.

Theorem 6 (Authenticity of the Message in Step 10)

$$\begin{array}{l} \forall tr, K_{CH}, Cnonce2, CK, Host, MC: \\ \quad (tr \in CBI \wedge \\ \quad \mathtt{says}(CK, Host, \{Cnonce2, K_{CH}\}_{K_{enc}(CK,Host)}) \in tr \\ \quad \wedge\, K_{CH} \notin analz(spies(tr)) \wedge \\ \quad MAC(K_{CH}, \{\mathtt{sendMC*}, MC\}) \in parts(spies(tr))) \\ \quad \Rightarrow \exists MC': \\ \qquad (MC' = suc(MC) \wedge \\ \qquad \mathtt{says}(CK, Host, \{\mathtt{sendMC}, MC', \\ \qquad\qquad\qquad MAC(K_{CH}, \{\mathtt{sendMC}, MC'\})\}) \in tr \wedge \\ \qquad \mathtt{says}(Host, CK, \{\mathtt{writeMC}, MC, \\ \qquad\qquad\qquad MAC(K_{CH}, \{\mathtt{writeMC}, MC\})\}) \in tr \wedge \\ \qquad \mathtt{says}(CK, Host, \{\mathtt{sendMC*}, MC, \\ \qquad\qquad\qquad MAC(K_{CH}, \{\mathtt{sendMC*}, MC\})\}) \in tr) \end{array}$$

In addition to the authenticity the theorem sates that the current value of MC results from a previous value MC', which was sent by the chipcard CK in step 8 of the protocol.

5 Verification of the CBI-Protocol in VSE

The verification of cryptographic protocols in VSE heavily relies on structural induction on the protocol traces. The basic structure of proof tasks discussed below is common to most induction provers. The heuristics sketched below implement an application specific refinement of this scheme to a certain type of proof goals and a given (but complex) theory structure underneath that includes system generated lemmata.

All inductive proofs of protocol properties are structured into the following (proof-) tasks. For each task there is a collection of heuristics[5] applicable for application.

1. Determine the base case and the induction step for the trace structure.
2. Handle the base case.
3. Handle the step cases:
   (a) Reduce certain formula to *negative* assumptions in the induction hypothesis.
   (b) Add information individual protocol steps.
   (c) Reduce the remaining differences and apply the induction hypothesis.

Currently there are five classes of heuristics used within the different proof tasks.

(1) A heuristic initializes the inductive proof by choosing the induction variable and reducing the proof goals of the base case and the step case to a simplified normal form.
(2) There are heuristics to close the proof goal of the base case by contradiction using pre-stated properties about the empty trace ([]). For instance, the assumption $\texttt{says}(CK, Host, \{Rsc2, K_{CH}\}_{K_{enc}(CK,Host)}) \in []$ occurs in the base case of Theorems 3, 5 and 6. This allows to close the goal using the appropriate axioms about traces.
(3) A class of heuristics performs a difference reduction between the goal assumptions and the corresponding sub-formulas of the induction hypothesis. To give an example we consider the proof attempt of Theorem 3. The (underlined) difference between $\texttt{notes}(spy, \{Rsc2, K_{CH}\}) \notin \underline{(ev\#tr)}$ and $\texttt{notes}(spy, \{Rsc2, K_{CH}\}) \notin tr$, that is part of the induction hypotheses, is eliminated by these heuristics. Thus, the application of the induction hypothesis is prepared.
(4) Other heuristics apply the protocol definition by performing a case split according to the protocol steps, and inserting the conditions of the corresponding protocol step as additional goal assumptions.
(5) There are heuristics that try to derive the missing sub-formulas of the induction hypothesis from corresponding goal assumptions, and this would allow to immediately close the resulting goals.

[5] The developed heuristics extend the proof trees using tactics that apply the basic VSE inference rules.

Heuristics (1) - (5) allow us to close most of the proof goals within a proof attempt. Usually however, some proof goals need further user interaction. These are closed with the help of so-called proof-structuring lemmata, e.g., *regularity lemmata* and *unicity theorems* [2]. For instance, the impossibility for a shared key $K_{enc}(CK, Host)$ to be a member of $analz(spies(tr))$ can be shown with the help of the so-called *elementary regularity lemma*, provided the agents CK and $Host$ are not compromised. This regularity lemma states that such a shared key only belongs to the attacker knowledge if one of the owning agents is compromised. Lemmata of this kind can be defined a-priori in case that the considered shared key is not exchanged during the protocol steps. For the CBI-protocol this condition indeed holds.

For secrecy proofs, the VSE system provides case-specific heuristics that can be invoked by the user to handle complex goal situations. These heuristics are composed of task-specific heuristics, which are also used in (5). They apply task-specific heuristics interleaved with the application of proof-structuring lemmata.

As an example consider the proof of Theorem 3. One of the proof goals that remain open after the application of the heuristics (1) - (5) is concerned with protocol step six. It represents the proof case where the event added to the protocol trace is $\mathtt{says}(CK, Host, \{Rsc2, K_{CH}\}_{K_{enc}(CK,Host)})$[6]. This proof goal is closed by a case-specific heuristic as follows:

1. A task-specific heuristic transforms the assumption $K_{CH} \in analz(spies(\mathtt{says}(CK, Host, \{Rsc2, K_{CH}\}_{K_{enc}(CK,Host)})\#tr))$ by applying the symbolic evaluation of $analz$. This results in two sub-goals depending on the membership of the key $K_{enc}(CK, Host)$ in the set $analz(spies(tr))$. In case that $K_{enc}(CK, Host) \in analz(spies(tr))$ holds the assumption we started with is changed to $K_{CH} \in analz([K_{CH} \| spies(tr)])$, since the attacker is able to decrypt the message. In the other case the assumption is replaced by $K_{CH} \in analz(spies(tr))$.
2. The first subgoal is closed by a regularity lemma for the shared key $K_{enc}(CK, Host)$ together with the assumption that the agents CK and $Host$ are not compromised[7].
3. The second subgoal gets closed by a task-specific heuristic that uses the assumption $K_{CH} \notin used(tr)$ (the freshness condition in protocol step six) contradicting the assumption $K_{CH} \in analz(spies(tr))$.

Case-specific heuristics result in open goal situations when the required proof-structuring lemmata are not available. In this case the user obviously has to analyze the resulting goal situations and to define the suitable lemmata.

6 Summary and Conclusion

The purpose of this paper is to present a case study that was performed during the Verisoft project [3] by DFKI GmbH and T-Systems GmbH. The task was to design, to specify and to verify a real world cryptographic protocol that is indeed used within

[6] Note that this step introduces the session key K_{CH} into the protocol run.

[7] This is expressed by $CK \notin bad$ and $Host \notin bad$.

the context of biometric identification systems. As the basic machinery we used the multi-purpose VSE verification framework.

During the verification process we proved 28 theorems where a typical theorem has about 1600 proof nodes (steps) represented as a VSE proof tree. A proof of this size takes (on Pentium M, 1.7 Ghz, 0.5 Gbyte) in general more than one day. The usage of suitable application oriented heuristics (25 heuristics are currently implemented) reduced the burden of interaction substantially. With their help, the proof effort varies between half an hour (for the less difficult theorems) and three hours. An average grade of automation of more than 80% has been reached. This is encouraging, for it shows that even industrial sized problems have become tractable. It turned out that the VSE approach was not only able to cope with the design team and to deliver the verified versions within the given time frame, but it additionally showed that some simplifying modifications of the protocol won't affect the protocol security properties. For instance, in a previous version of the protocol presented in Figure 2 step six contained a message authentication code (MAC) to protect its integrity. We showed that this MAC can be omitted without losing the integrity of the corresponding message (see Theorem 4). Such simplifications have led to the protocol presented in this paper.

The future work in this area is concerned with the improvement of the user support also in cases where new event types have to be added to the set of possible steps in a protocol specification. In this case, the theory of Paulson [2] and the underlying structuring lemmata have to be adapted accordingly. And of course, some effort is still spent on the realization of new heuristics that lead to a further reduction of user interaction.

References

1. D. Dolev and A. Yao. On the security of public-key protocols. IEEE Transactions on Information Theory, 2(29), 1983
2. L. C. Paulson. The inductive approach to verifying cryptographic protocols. *Journal of Computer Security*, 6:85–128, 1998.
3. The Verisoft Project. http://www.verisoft.de/.
4. G. Lassmann, M. Schwan. Vertrauenswüdige Chipkartenbasierte Biometrische Authentifikation. In Jana Dittmann (Hrsg.), Sicherheit 2006, Sicherheit-Schutz und Zuverlässigkeit, GI-Edition Lectures Notes in Informatics, Gesellschaft fr Informatik, Bonn, 2006.
5. P.Ryan, S. Schneider, M. Goldsmith, G. Lowe, and B. Roscoe. Modeling and Analysis of Security Protocols. Addison Wesley, 2000.
6. G. Denker and J. Millen and H. Rueß. The CAPSL Integrated Protocol Environment. protocol. SRI Technical Report SRI-CSL-2000-02, October 2000.
7. C. Meadows. The NRL Protocol Analyzer: An overview. *Journal of Logic Programming*, 26(2):113–131, 1996.
8. G. Lowe. Casper: A compiler for the analysis of security protocols. *Journal of Computer Security*, 6:53–84, 1998.
9. G. Lowe. Breaking and fixing the Needham-Schroeder public-key protocol using FDR. In *Software—Concepts and Tools*, 17:93–102, 1996.

10. A. Durante, R. Focardi, and R. Gorrieri. Cvs: A compiler for the analysis of cryptographic protocols. In *Proceedings of 12th IEEE Computer Security Foundations Workshop*, pages 203–212, 1999.
11. C. Weidenbach, Towards an automatic analysis of security protocols, Towards an automatic analysis of security protocols. In Proceedings of the 16th International Conference on Automated Deduction, pages 378-382. LNCS 1632, Springer-Verlag, 1999
12. G. Lowe and A. W. Roscoe. Using CSP to detect errors in the TMN protocol. *IEEE Transactions on Software Engineering*, 23(10):659–669, 1997.
13. W. Marrero, E. Clarke, and S. Jha. A model checker for authentication protocols. In *Proceedings of the DIMACS Workshop on Design and Formal Verification of Security Protocols*, 1997.
14. B. C. Neuman and S. G. Stubblebine. A note on the use of timestamps as nonces. *ACM SIGOPS, Operating Systems Review*, **27**(2):10–14, 1993.
15. J. C. Mitchell, M. Mitchell, and U. Stern. Automated analysis of cryptographic protocols using Murϕ. In *IEEE Symposium on Security and Privacy*, 1997.
16. David Basin, Lazy Infinite-State Analysis of Security Protocols, Secure Networking — CQRE [Secure] '99, Springer-Verlag, Lecture Notes in Computer Science, no. 1740, pp. 30–42, Dsseldorf, Germany, November, 1999
17. David Basin, Sebastian Mödersheim, and Luca Viganò. An On-The-Fly Model-Checker for Security Protocol Analysis. *8th European Symposium on Research in Computer Security (ESORICS)*, 2003
18. F. J. Thayer Fábrega, J. C. Herzog, and J. D. Guttman. Strand spaces: Proving security protocols correct. *Journal of Computer Security*, 7(2, 3):191–230, 1999.
19. M. Abadi and A. D. Gordon. A calculus for cryptographic protocols: The spi calculus. In *Proceedings of the Fourth ACM Conference on Computer and Communications Security*, 1997.
20. M. Boreale. Symbolic trace analysis of cryptographic protocols. In *Proceedings ICALP'01*, LNCS 2071, pp. 667 - 681. Springer, 2001
21. R. Donovan, M. Norris, and G. Lowe, *Analyzing a library of security protocols using Casper and FDR*, Proceedings of the FLoC Workshop on Formal Methods and Security Protocols (Trento, Italy), 1999.
22. D. X. Song, S. Berezin, and A. Perrig. Athena: a novel approach to efficient automatic security protocol analysis. *Journal of Computer Security*, 9(1, 2):47–74, 2001.
23. Dieter Hutter, Bruno Langenstein, Claus Sengler, Jörg H. Siekmann, Werner Stephan, and Andreas Wolpers. Deduction in the Verification Support Environment (VSE). In Marie-Claude Gaudel and James Woodcock, editors, *Proceedings Formal Methods Europe 1996: Industrial Benefits and Advances in Formal Methods*. SPRINGER, 1996.
24. Dieter Hutter, Bruno Langenstein, Claus Sengler, Jörg H. Siekmann, Werner Stephan, and Andreas Wolpers. Verification support environment (vse). *High Integrity Systems*, 1(6): 523–530, 1996.
25. Dieter Hutter, Heiko Mantel, Georg Rock, Werner Stephan, Andreas Wolpers, Michael Balser, Wolfgang Reif, Gerhard Schellhorn, and Kurt Stenzel. VSE: Controlling the complexity in formal software developments. In D. Hutter, W. Stephan, P. Traverso, and M. Ullmann, editors, *Proceedings Current Trends in Applied Formal Methods, FM-Trends 98*, Boppard, Germany, 1999. Springer-Verlag, LNCS 1641.
26. Dieter Hutter, Georg Rock, Jörg H. Siekmann, Werner Stephan, and Roland Vogt. Formal Software Development in the Verification Support Environment (VSE). In Bill Manaris Jim Etheredge, editor, *FLAIRS-2000: Proceedings of the Thirteenth International Florida Artificial Intelligence Research Society Conference*, pages 367–376. AAAI-Press, 2000.

27. Georg Rock, Werner Stephan, and Andreas Wolpers. Modular Reasoning about Structured TLA Specifications. In R. Berghammer and Y. Lakhnech, editors, *Tool Support for System Specification, Development and Verification*, Advances in Computing Science, pages 217–229. Springer, WienNewYork, 1999.
28. Georg Rock, Werner Stephan, and Andreas Wolpers. Assumption–Commitment Specifications and Safety-Critical Systems. In Hartmut Knig and Peter Langendrfer, editors, *FBT'98. Formale Beschreibungstechniken für verteilte Systeme*, pages 125–135. Shaker Verlag, Aachen, 1998. 8. GI/ITG-Fachgespräch.
29. Werner Stephan, Bruno Langenstein, Andreas Nonnengart, and Georg Rock. Verification Support Environment. In Dieter Hutter and Werner Stephan, editors, Mechanizing Mathematical Reasoning, Essays in Honor of Jörg H. Siekmann on the Occasion of His 60th Birthday, Lecture Notes in Computer Science, LNAI 2605, pages 476 – 493, Springer Verlag January 2005, ISBN 3540250514

Exploring Resilience Towards Risks in eOperations in the Oil and Gas Industry

Felicjan Rydzak, Lars S. Breistrand, Finn Olav Sveen, Ying Qian, and Jose J. Gonzalez*

Centre for Advanced Manufacturing Technologies, Wroclaw University of Technology, ul. Lukasiewicza 5, 50-371 Wroclaw, Poland
Tel.: +48 71 3204184; Fax: +48 71 3280670
felicjan.rydzak@pwr.wroc.pl
Research Cell "Security and Quality in Organizations", Faculty of Engineering and Science, Agder University College, Grooseveien 36 NO-4876 Grimstad, Norway
Tel.: +47 37253000; Fax: +47 37253001
sqo@hia.no
http://ikt.hia.no/sqo

Abstract. The transition to eOperations in the Norwegian oil and gas industry is expected to yield up to 30% reduction in costs and 10% increase in production. But new information security risks are introduced by substituting traditional offshore operations like drilling, production, delivery, etc, mostly locally operated at the offshore platforms with increasing remote onshore operation via computer networks. In eOperations, security incidents can have serious safety and performance implications. Using a generic risk matrix from case studies and a conceptual system dynamics model we explore policies for resource allocation to production and to security/safety. The simulation model allows studying the resilience of the system depending on management policies and incidents as represented in the risk matrix. We show that there is a region where the system behaviour is very sensitive to changes in resource allocation and to incidents.

1 Introduction

As more and more enterprises conduct a major part of their business from remote centres that are connected with computer networks, the distinction between safety and security becomes blurred. eOperations (also called Integrated Operations), the case of remote operations in the offshore oil & gas industry is particularly interesting. eOperations is a vision of enormous technological and organizational ambition, with huge financial expectations[1] and an extremely complex risk landscape, where information security and HSE aspects are intertwined.[2] Fig. 1 explains the basic operational landscape of eOperations and Fig. 2 depicts its evolutionary perspective.

* JJG is professor and head of the research cell "Security and Quality in Organizations" at Agder University College and adjunct professor at the Department of Informatics and Media Science at Gjøvik University College (both in Norway).

[1] The Net Present Value of the increased value facilitated by eOperations in the Norwegian offshore sector has been estimated as more than 40 billions US dollars. See http://www.olf.no/english/news/?32101.pdf, quoted 24 May 2006.

[2] Health, Safety and Environment. HSE is the acronym used in the oil & gas industry.

J. Górski (Ed.): SAFECOMP 2006, LNCS 4166, pp. 57 – 70, 2006.

For such an inherently HSE risky sector as the offshore oil & gas industry, one powerful driver of the transition eOperations is to diminish the exposure of offshore personnel to potentially dangerous situations. If eOperations succeed, there should be less HSE incidents, and less staff that is affected if incidents happen. But then, it is likely that serious HSE incidents will derive from information security failures.

A recent study by Johnsen et al. [1] has identified the occurrence of generic information incidents with potential of very serious to critical HSE implications in companies operating in the eOperations regime. They are: 1) *Wrong situational awareness* – The ICT system does not give a comprehensive overview of the situation, creating wrong situational awareness among the involved actors; 2) *Denial-of-service attack* on a key communication component, delaying and stopping data communication between onshore and offshore – closing down operations. 3) *Virus/worm* is being spread closing down key components, disturbing the production process. 4) *PCS down*: The process control system is jammed or stopped because of failure in the network.

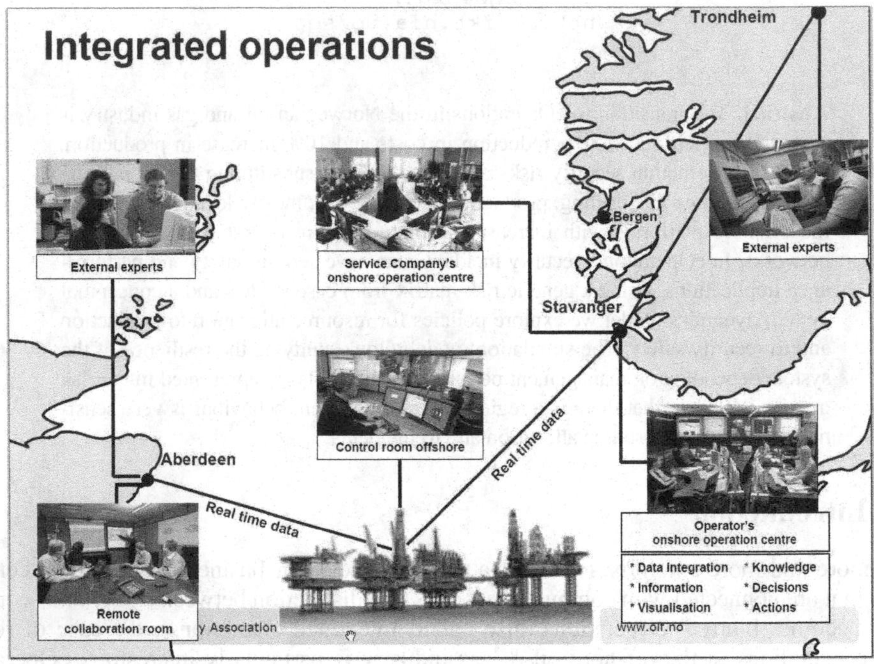

Fig. 1. The operational landscape of eOperations (increasingly called "Integrated Operations"). Source: http://www.olf.no/?26567.pdf , quoted 24 May 2006.

While pilot projects – such as Norsk Hydro's transition from traditional operations to eOperations for the Brage field – seem to prove the technical feasibility and profitability of eOperations, their security (and with it the HSE aspect implied in potential security failures) is less certain. Can such remote operations in computer networks with COTS[3] software be conducted in a secure manner – now, one year from now, in 5-10 years?

[3] Commercial-off-the-shelf.

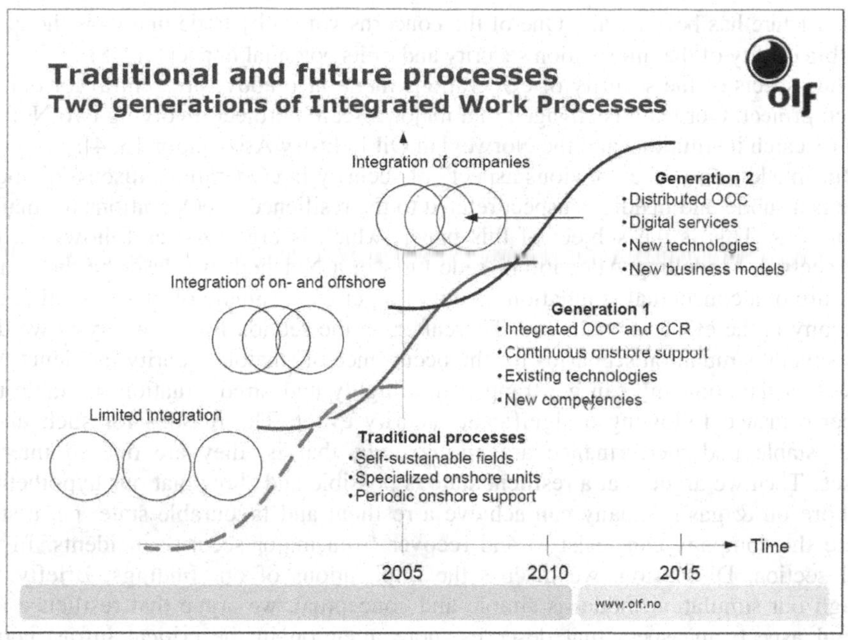

Fig. 2. The transition will go beyond "Generation 1" (eOperations) to "Generation 2" (Integrated Operations). Generation 1 is essentially the transfer of control from offshore to onshore centres. Generation 2 targets the integration of companies, that is, operators, suppliers, vendors, etc, with new digital services, new technologies and new business sectors. The time frames are about 2005-2010 for Generation 1 and 2008-2015 for Generation 2, with some overlap owing to different dynamics in different offshore fields. Source: http://www.olf.no/?26568.pdf , quoted 24 May 2006. (Acronyms: OOC – Onshore Operation Centre; CCR – Central Control Room).

The challenges are enormous, owing to the explosion in attacks and their increasing sophistication,[4] the increasing burden from the exponential growth in internet users, many of them without proper security training, etc. Lipson [2; p. 15] has spelt out the dilemma: «The Internet's original design goals never included the support of today's mission-critical and high-stakes applications in business, energy, transportation, communications, banking and finance, and national defence. These high-stakes Internet applications pose enormously tempting targets of opportunity for criminals, terrorists, and hostile nations, and they overly stress the technology designed for a more innocent time.»

Oil and gas companies need to rely on the information security of the eOperations infrastructure. There is an obvious aspect: Without proper information security a serious incident (or a row of less serious incidents) can lead to costly downtime, with large potential implications for HSE aspects and even for the viability of eOperations. Since much of cost reduction in eOperations will be achieved by a significant reduction of staff, the uneasiness regarding the transition to remote operations based on digital

[4] See the CERT presentation at http://www.cert.org/archive/pdf/k12_netcon_internet.pdf, Slides #9-10.

infrastructure has been strong. One of the concerns voiced by trade unions is the questionable quality of the information security and of its potential impact on HSE.

The aspects of the security of eOperations mentioned above are central for our research project. Our team is engaged in a major research project involving two Norwegian research institutions and the Norwegian Oil Industry Association [3, 4].

But in addition to the "obvious aspect" of security in eOperations discussed above there is a subtle and insidious aspect related to the resilience of eOperations to (major) disruptions. This is the subject of this paper, which is organized as follows: In the next section, Modelling Allocation Trade Offs in a Nutshell, we describe the causal structure of a conceptual simulation model of a generic example of offshore oil & gas company in the eOperations mode. Thereafter, in the section Policy Analysis we discuss several simulation scenarios for the occurrence of (major) security incidents. We show that the company can get trapped in a highly undesired situation of stable underperformance following a significant security event. The reasons for such undesired, stable underperformance are *endogenous*, that is, they are due to internal causes. Then we argue that a resilient state is possible and show that our hypothetical offshore oil & gas company can achieve a resilient and favourable state, i.e. a state where the company can resist to and recover from major security incidents. In the final section, Discussion, we discuss the implications of our findings. Briefly, although our simulation model is simple and conceptual, we argue that resilience is a crucial aspect, an aspect that deserves more attention in the critical infrastructure sector, in particular, for the oil and gas infrastructure.

2 Modelling Allocation Trade Offs in a Nutshell

How can one evaluate such crucial aspects as the resilience of the oil and gas company toward major security incidents? This question is of central importance for eOperations in the oil and gas industry, and for that matter for eOperations and eRemote processes in other branches.

To understand salient issues for how trade offs of resource allocation to production and to security affect resilience we develop a conceptual model of a fictive oil & gas company. We assume that the transition from traditional production processes to eOperations has been completed. Accordingly, our model can be kept simple in that issues such as of deployment of new work processes, development of new know-how and introduction of new technology do not need to be considered.

Consider a generic offshore oil & gas company operating in 2010. By then, the traditional offshore operations – such as drilling, production, delivery, etc are now being mainly operated from remote onshore centres (eOperations). Production has been increased and costs have been reduced through optimization of drilling and production data, and closer collaboration between offshore and land-based personnel. Much of the cost reduction has been achieved by a significant reduction of staff.

Our "nutshell model" represents the generic oil & gas company at a very high aggregation level. The crucial aspects to model the impact of resources on operations are: 1) The oil & gas company generates a stream of revenue in proportion to its uptime. 2) We simplify the operational structure of the company by assuming that managers have to pay attention to two aspects: production and security.[5] 3) Even highly profitable companies in the Norwegian offshore sector have to carefully consider the allocation of resources to production and to security. In the era of globalisation, a highly competitive situation demand that expenses to create and maintain security must be justified by their return on investment. Hence, we assume that there is a strict management policy to keep costs down. One euro spent on resources for production means one euro less spent on resources for security, and vice versa. The trade-offs of this problem resemble features of process improvement.

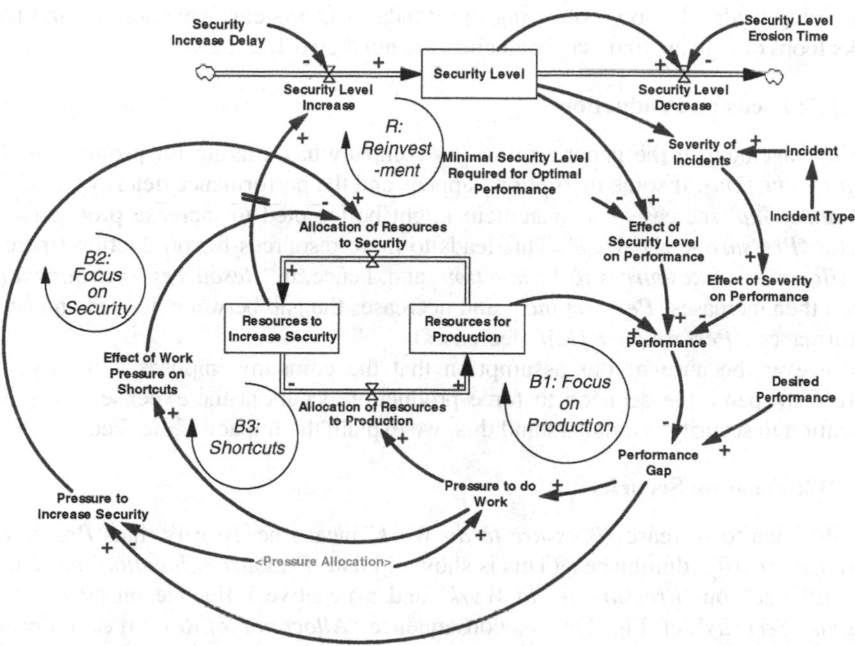

Fig. 3. System dynamics model describing allocation of resources to production and to information security by a fictive offshore oil and gas company. We assume that the offshore processes are mainly run from onshore control centres (eOperations). Hence, information security is of paramount importance for operational aspects and HSE depends critically on information security.

Hence, we adapt and extend an illuminating model that was originally developed by Repenning and Sterman [5] in the context of process improvement. Fig. 1 shows our stock-and-flow model.[6] It consists of three stocks (*Security Level*, *Resources to Production*, *Resources to Security*) and the associated flows (*Security Level Increase*, *Security Level Decrease*, *Allocation of Resources to Production* and *Allocation of Resources to Security*).

---

[5] When speaking of information security we have in mind the integrated aspect of security and safety, and by the impact of security incidents we mean the total aspect of HSE, performance downtime and intangibles, such as reputation.

[6] Developed with Vensim DSS, a system dynamics modelling tool from Ventana Co. (see www.vensim.com). The file with the model equations can be accessed at http://ikt.hia.no/sqo.

The core structure of the model is made up of four feedback loops. A basic understanding of the model dynamic behaviour can be obtained by analyzing the contribution of the four feedback loops determining the performance of the generic oil & gas company: 1) 'B1: FOCUS ON PRODUCTION'; 2) 'B2: FOCUS ON SECURITY'; 3) 'R: REINVESTMENT'; 4) 'B3: SHORTCUTS.' We explain the effect of the feedback loops by "walking through" the feedback loops. The plus and minus signs in the diagram refer to the polarity of the causal influence: A plus sign indicates a causal influence in the same direction; a minus sign indicates an influence in the opposite direction.[7] A balancing loop is indicated by the 'B' preceding the name of the loop. Similarly, a "R" indicates a reinforcing feedback loop. Following the standards of system dynamics [6], the feedbacks loops of a given kind (say balancing) are numbered 1, 2, …

2.1 B1: Focus on Production

The management of the generic oil & gas company has a target for production (*Desired Production*). If some disruption happens and the performance deteriorates ('*Performance Gap*' increases) management might be tempted to increase production by greater '*Pressure to do Work*'. This leads to more resources for production (increase in '*Allocation of Resources to Production*' and, hence, in '*Resources to Production*'), which then increases '*Performance*' and decreases the gap between desired and actual performance ('*Performance Gap*' decreases).

However, because of our assumption that the company imposes a limit on resources to spend, the decision to force production occurs at the expense of resource allocation to security. To understand this, we explain the impact of the feedback loop:

2.2 B2: Focus on Security

The decision to increase '*Pressure to do Work*' means necessarily that '*Pressure to Increase Security*' diminishes. (This is shown in that '*Pressure Allocation*' has a positive influence on '*Pressure to do Work*' and a negative influence on '*Pressure to Increase Security*', cf. Fig. 1). As a consequence, '*Allocation of Resources to Security* diminishes, which then detracts from '*Resources to Increase Security*' and, with a delay (indicated by the double slash //) weakens '*Security Level Increase*' gradually. Since security needs to be continuously maintained and improved in order to keep pace with new threats and increasingly sophisticated attacks, '*Security Level*' starts to decay. Security has a positive impact on production (more security, less disruptions), hence, the decay of '*Security Level*' leads to a decay in *Performance*' (that is production). Alternatively, if management had found a better balance for pressure allocation, both balancing feedback loops B1 and B2 would have acted to close the '*Performance Gap*'. The conditions for this to happen depend on the quantitative impact of the various causal relationships. In other words, we need to simulate the model quantitatively. This we do in the next section, Policy Analysis.

2.3 R: Reinvestment

This reinforcing feedback loop strengthens whichever strategy the management applies. If the management opts for increasing resources to production at the expense of

[7] For a more accurate definition of causal link polarity, see ref. [5] p. 139.

security, too much emphasis on production (increasing '*Pressure to do Work*') diminishes '*Resources to Increase Security*', which via less '*Security Level Increase*', lower '*Security Level*', less '*Effect of Security Level on Performance*' and a negative on '*Performance*' forces management to increase '*Pressure to do Work*' to counteract a drop in performance caused by more security (and HSE) disruptions.

If management had better balanced the allocation of pressure, the effect on security would have been the opposite one: More '*Resources to Increase Security*', which via more '*Security Level Increase*', higher '*Security Level*', higher '*Effect of Security Level on Performance*' and a positive on '*Performance*' (less security and HSE disruptions). As we will show in the next section with quantitative simulations, it is indeed possible to achieve a balance in the allocation of pressure, so that '*Performance*' (i.e. production) and '*Security Level*' attain satisfactory levels.

2.4 B3: Shortcuts

The reason why a good balance between the allocation of resources to production and resources to security is difficult to achieve is the subtle effect of this third balancing feedback loop, i.e. cutting corners or taking shortcuts. All kind of disruptions can occur, e.g. bad weather conditions leading to loss of production. Whether due to security and HSE incidents, bad weather, workforce strikes, ... management react toward an undesired fall in production by "temporarily" increasing resources to production at the expense of resources to security. Indeed, the '*B3: SHORTCUTS*' feedback loop seems like an expedient "solution" to recoup a loss. A shortage in '*Performance*' leads to an increase in '*Performance Gap*', which managements tries to close by what they think is a transient increase in '*Pressure to do Work.*' An increase in '*Pressure to do Work*' means less '*Allocation of Resources to Security*, less '*Resources to Increase Security*', which allows more '*Allocation of Resources to Production*' and increases '*Resources to Production*', thus increasing '*Performance.*'

The reduction of resources to security causes a protracted reduction in '*Security Level*'. Abusing the shortcuts "solution leads ultimately to bad performance. By the insidious effect of the reinforcing loop '*R: REINVESTMENT,*' management is trapped in a vicious circle. The intended temporary shortcut to improve production can lead to so many (or so severe) security and HSE disruptions that performance suffers more or less permanently. The quantitative simulations in the next section will exemplify this.

3 Policy Analysis

We explore policies for resource allocation to production and to security / safety, applied as a response to various types of security incidents. The types of security incidents range from 1 to 6 and they are specified in a generic risk matrix. Incident type 1 occurs very often but its results are insignificant, whereas incident type 6 is very rare and its consequences are catastrophic.[8] It is important to recall that in eOperations, security

[8] The generic risk matrix is expressed in our model through the parameters '*Incident Type*', '*Incident*', '*Severity of Incidents*' and '*Effect of Severity on Performance*' (cf. Fig. 4). The values of these parameters are of the same order of magnitude as a typical risk matrix from our case studies for oil & gas fields in the *eOperations* mode.

incidents can have serious performance and HSE implications. The cost of one day of production downtime in offshore operations is estimated to be 13 million NOK (1.6 million €) for small platforms and up to 200 million NOK (25 million €) for large platforms. However, the short-term consequences of an incident in terms of its HSE implications and its financial impact are not the only results. There are cascading effects, resulting from the interdependences between the production processes, actors and management policies that might eventually lead to a highly undesired system state.

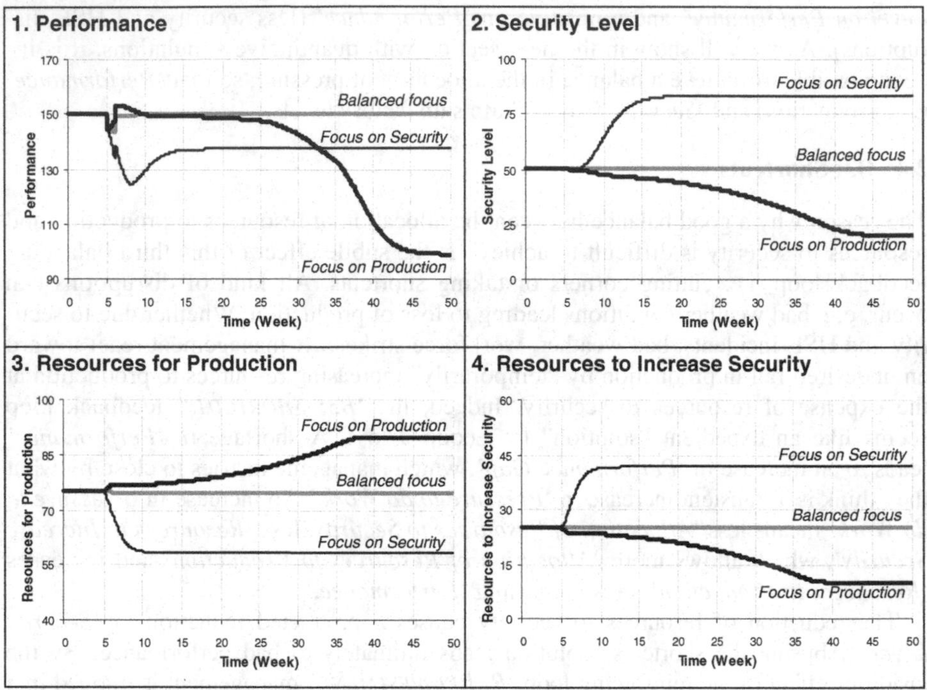

Fig. 4. Graphs illustrating the behaviour of the system resulting from a security incident (*Incident Type* = 3) occurring in week 5, following three production resource allocation policies described by the variable *Pressure Allocation* (***Focus on Production*** **scenario** – *Pressure Allocation* = 0.9; ***Focus on Security*** **scenario** – *Pressure Allocation* = 0.2; ***Balanced focus*** **scenario** – *Pressure Allocation* = 0.6).

Our policy analysis is based on simulation of the system dynamics model described in the previous section. The simulation starts in equilibrium. In week 5 our generic offshore oil and gas company experiences a mild security incident – incident type 3. As an immediate result, the performance is impaired and a gap between actual and desired performance arises. The managerial response to the situation may lead to three generic scenarios, presented together for comparison in Fig. 4.

3.1 Focus on Production

Usually, a backlog in production increases the pressure to work harder. That is, the alarming vision of lost production, and thus of lost revenue, prompts managers to allocate more resources to production. Management expects that such decision will improve the performance and bring back the lost profitability. Fig. 4 shows the system behaviour illustrating this scenario (line marked *Focus on Production*). Indeed, as *Resources for Production* increase (Fig. 4, graph#3) *Performance* quickly recovers and already in week 6 it rises above the desired level (Fig. 4, graph#1). This enables the organization not only to close the performance gap but also to make up for lost production. However, even in profitable offshore oil and gas fields the resources for running operations are limited. Allocation of more resources to production occurs at the expense of *Resources to Increase Security* (Fig. 4, graph#4). Emphasis on production in the aftermath of the incident detracts from a thorough analysis to identify the root causes of the security problem and to implement a proper solution. This leads to a decrease of *Security Level* (Fig. 4, graph#2). In contrast to production, which is precisely measured (e.g. in million barrels per day), security is not a tangible asset. Its status or level can not be easily determined, and thus security is difficult to manage accurately. The situation is even worse, since *Security Level* does not drop right away and the impact of cutting corners / taking shortcuts does not have an immediate effect on performance. High pressure to do work detracts from security maintenance and improvement, and security erodes at the technical and behavioural level (e.g. new patches or intrusion detection systems are not installed / maintained and also people's security consciousness undergoes slow degradation, for instance USB sticks are not tested for viruses). Eventually, about week 45 *Security Level* reaches such a low value (Fig. 4, graph#2) that even though the maximum possible number of resources is dedicated to production, the performance is disrupted, it can not be sustained at an optimal level and it shifts to a highly undesired state (Fig. 4, graph#1). Bringing the performance from that state back to its initial level is a real challenge requiring 'technical' and 'adaptive' changes [7]. Technical changes correspond to know-how, production processes, standards, procedures, and internal regulations whereas adaptive changes relate to people's behaviour, the way they consider the safety issues and perform their tasks.

3.2 Focus on Security

An alternative policy to the previous one (Focus on Production), which can be implemented in face of the incident and the following performance gap, is to prioritize security improvement. The system behaviour illustrating the second scenario is presented in Fig. 4 by line marked *Focus on Security*. Higher pressure to improve security leads to more allocation of *Resources to Increase Security* (Fig. 4, graph#4). Now, 40% of the total available resources are dedicated to security improvement. Managers thoroughly investigate what happened and try to implement a proper solution to the problem, reducing the chance that similar situations might impair the production system again. As illustrated in Fig. 4, graph#2 *Security Level* rises and stabilizes at a high level. However, as in the previous scenario, allocation of resources to one area is at the expense of other operations. *Resources for Production* drops to about 60% (Fig. 4, graph#3). This leads to decrease in *Performance* over week 6 and 7 (Fig. 4, graph#1). Over the next few weeks, though less *Resources for Production* are available, *Performance* recovers. This is due to the increase in *Security Level*, which to some extent leads to improved performance (once the security / safety issues are properly treated, offshore operators are not drawn away from work as very often happens in the case of 'rough and ready', temporary fixes and solutions to security problems). Security itself is a necessary but not sufficient condition to keep production in the oil and gas industry going. *Performance* increases but it levels off below the desired value (Fig. 4, graph#1). From the perspective of the company's effectiveness and profitability, the issue of security is overdone. On the other hand, *Performance* does not reach a highly undesired level, as happened in the previous scenario. The offshore oil and gas company is more resilient to various kinds of incidents and their severity.

3.3 Balanced Focus

The third policy of dealing with the incident is to weigh the pressure allocation and pay sufficient attention to both production and security improvement. The behaviour of the system following this policy is illustrated in Fig. 2 by line marked *Balanced focus*. As a consequence of the incident the pressure caused by performance gap is distributed both to do work and to increase security, so that *Resources for Production* and *Resources to Increase Security* remain at the initial level (Fig. 2, graph#3 and #4). Similarly the *Security Level* remains stable (Fig. 4, graph#2) – there are no changes in resources allocation which could lead to a deterioration of procedures and impair security / safety culture. This policy allows *Performance* to recover right after the incident to the desired level (Fig. 2, graph#1). The oil and gas company suffers a loss due to the unfulfilled production schedule, but still the performance does not shift to the undesired state and the security and safety issues are not overdone, as in the previous scenarios.

Considering all three scenarios illustrated together in Fig. 4, the last policy seems to be optimal. However, this policy is difficult to execute. Managing and weighting the allocation of pressure can be imagined as operating at the razor's edge between the effectiveness of and the security of eOperations. The very fact that assessing the actual level of security / safety in a company is not an easy task further indicates that the identification of an "optimal" policy is a daunting task. Furthermore, we can not assume there is only one incident. During one year of operations several incidents of varying severity can affect the oil and gas company. Hence, we are lead to a different approach, i.e. to investigate the resilience of the oil and gas company towards various types and numbers of incidents. This is the subject of the next two scenarios. One of them will investigate the behaviour of the system to a single, very severe incident. The second scenario will examine the influence of two incidents – type 6 and 3 according to the generic risk matrix.

3.4 Single Incident

The conditions of the model and the values of the model parameters for the purpose of simulation analysis are the same as for the third policy (*Balanced focus* scenario) described above. However, this time, the incident affecting the oil and gas company experiences in week 5, is assumed to be of type 6 – rare and very severe. The response of the system is presented in Fig. 5 by line marked *Single incident*. A more severe incident leads to a larger performance gap. Now, 60% of the pressure to close the performance gap is allocated to production and the rest to improve security. As a result, there is a rise in *Resources for Production* (Fig. 5, graph#3) which is amplified by the shortcuts effect (since pressure to do work still is high, operators try to skip security improvement and spare some more time for production).

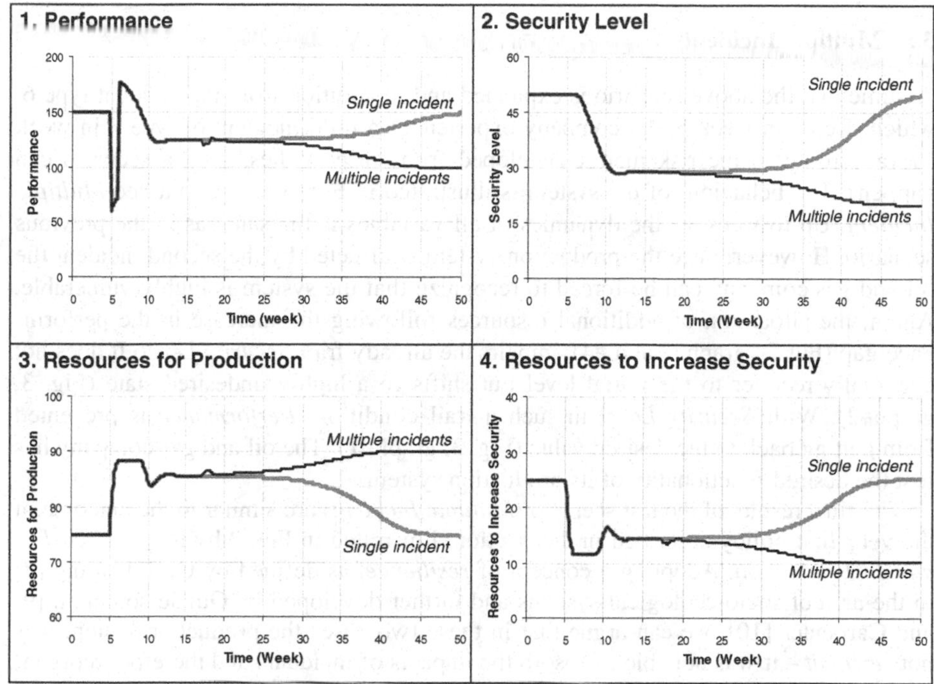

Fig. 5. Graphs illustrating the response of the system to various types and number of incidents: ***Single Incident* scenario** – *Incident Type* = 6 occurring in week 5, *Pressure Allocation* = 0.6; ***Multiple Incident* scenario** – *Incident Type* = 6 occurring in week 5 and *Incident Type* = 3 occurring in week 17, *Pressure Allocation* = 0.6. *Pressure Allocation* describes the extent of allocation to production resources.

At the same time, due to limited availability of resources, *Resources to Increase Security* drops (Fig. 3, graph#4). In such circumstances it is impossible to conduct a thorough analysis of what happened and implement a proper solution. The effect of this is that *Security Level* is reduced (Fig. 3, graph#2). The dynamics of *Resources for Production* and *Security Level* influences *Performance*, the sudden increase of *Resources for Production* over week 5 causes a boost in *Performance* at the start of week 6 (Fig. 3, graph#1). Unfortunately, the decrease of *Security Level* in the following weeks, limits the feasible production. *Performance* is reduced and at about week 15 it levels off below the desired value. Over the next weeks the effect of the incident is mitigated within the production system and *Resources for Production* and *Resources to Increase Security* return back to their initial values (Fig. 3, graph#3 and #4). Simultaneously, *Security*

Level is rebuilt, which enables more effective operations (Fig. 3, graph#2). Eventually at about week 48 *Performance* recovers to the desired level (Fig. 3, graph#1). This result is possible only because security / safety issues were recognised in the given policy and some attention was paid to improve the security level. However, the question is whether this amount of attention is really enough to sustain the desired functionality of eOperations in the oil and gas company.

3.5 Multiple Incidents

Assume that the above scenario is expanded and in addition from the incident type 6, which occurs in week 5, the company experiences a mild incident of type 3 in week 17 (according to the risk matrix developed from case studies, such a scenario can happen). The behaviour of the system is illustrated in Fig. 3 by line marked *Multiple Incident*. Up to week 17 the dynamics of all variables is the same as in the previous scenario. However, once the production system is affected by the second incident the oil and gas company can be forced to recognize that the system is highly vulnerable. Again, the allocation of additional resources following the increase in the performance gap (Fig. 3, graph#3 and #4), impairs the already frail *Security Level*. It does not eventually recover to the initial level but shifts to a highly undesired state (Fig. 3, graph#2). With *Security Level* in such a frail condition, *Performance* is prevented from getting back to the desired value (Fig. 3, graph#1). The oil and gas company has lost the desired functionality of its production system.

The final results of the last scenario (*Multiple Incident*) are similar to the outcome of the very first policy described in this section, illustrated in Fig. 2 by line marked *Focus on Production*. Adopting a concept of *resilience*, as defined by C. S. Holling [8] in the area of socio-ecological systems and further developed by Gunderson et al. [9] and Carpenter [10], we can argue that in these two cases the production system was not *resilient* – it was not able to absorb the impacts of incidents and therefore reorganized its *configuration* (relationships between agents and processes in the system and allocation of strategic resources). The resilience in that context is defined as the capacity of the system to undergo disturbance and still maintain its functions, structures and controls.

Resilience itself is not always a positive property, however. The highly undesired state the oil and gas company reached in the mentioned two cases (*Focus on Production* scenario and *Multiple Incident* scenario) can also be considered as resilient. It requires a lot of effort and expenditure to adjust procedures, standards, processes and, what is even more important, to change peoples' behaviour and attitude in order to rebuild the security level within the company and simultaneously bring back the desired level of performance. Furthermore, this kind of organizational change is not always successful, as examples of reengineering projects show [11].

Hence, we argue that as far as eOperations in the generic oil and gas company are concerned it is crucial to build up the resilience of the desired system configuration in advance (increase the security / safety much above the minimal level required to optimal performance) or, at least, to pay much more attention to security once the production system has experienced a serious incident (as presented by the *Focus on Security* policy described in this section). These approaches would enable the production system to undergo various types and amounts of incidents and still preserve its desired state, as well as to avoid expensive and long-term 'repair' programmes. One may suggest that such policies are less profitable. However, enterprises which strive for long-term effectiveness, profitability and competitive advantage have to consider and secure the desired functionality of their production systems not only in short periods but mainly over long time periods. As Stolz [12] argues '*Resilience is the only sustainable, portable strategic plan. Resilient individuals, teams, and organizations consistently outlast, outmanoeuvre and outperform their less resilient competitors*'.

4 Discussion

How reliable is our analysis? After all the model of the generic oil & gas company is highly aggregated and, thus, "simple." Would a more complex and "realistic" model lead to significantly different results? The question can be rephrased as: Would a more detailed model introduce strong feedback structures that could significantly change the dynamic behaviour? In nonlinear, feedback rich problems the dynamic behaviour is shaped by the feedback loops and the evolution of their strength over time. The dominant feedback loop determines the current dynamic behaviour, the nonlinear relationships lead to shift in dominance, so that a new feedback loop then dominates and determines behaviour [6]. We look forward to adapt and extend our model to more closely describe real oil and gas companies. In the meantime we argue that the four feedback loops 'B1: FOCUS ON PRODUCTION', 'B2: FOCUS ON SECURITY', 'R: REINVESTMENT', and 'B3: SHORTCUTS' are ubiquitous in many enterprises, both in the oil and gas industry and in other sectors. Further, they are strong because emphasis on control and reduction of costs is paradigmatic. Thus, while we do not claim anything like numerical accuracy we do hope that the main qualitative insights about the instability of resource allocation policies and the need to invest in proactive resilience will prove to be "resilient insights" – that is, robust to changes and extensions of the basic analysis in this paper. An encouraging aspect is the structural similarity to findings in other areas, such as in improvement processes [13] and in CSIRT performance [14, 15].

One potential insight, which we believe is worth taking seriously, is the strong impact of the limitation of resources on the resilience of the system. Mostly it makes sense to have a strong budget discipline, but imposing strong resource limits when serious incidents (security / HSE) happen introduces the edge of instability that jeopardizes the system's resilience. In other words, the procedures for business continuity planning in the eOperations mode should have enough resource redundancy.

Acknowledgements

The Research Council of Norway (RCN) has funded the stay of Felicjan Rydzak as visiting researcher at Agder University College.[9] The contribution of the members of

[9] Cultural Agreement Between Norway and Poland, Norwegian Government Scholarship 2005/2006, 'Experimental Exploration of Decision making Focused on Resilience Analysis of Production Systems'.

the research cell "Security and Quality in Organizations" has been funded partly by the AMBASEC project,[10] partly by the ISECBIDAT project.[11] We are greatly indebted to the Research Council of Norway for the support.

References

1. Johnsen, S.O., M.B. Line, and A. Askildsen. Towards more secure virtual organizations by implementing a common scheme for incident response management. In Eight International Conference on Probabilistic Safety Assesment and Management (PSAM8). 2006. New Orleans.
2. Lipson, H.F., Tracking and Tracing Cyber-Attacks: Technical Challenges and Global Policy Issues. 2002, CERT Coordination Center: Pittsburgh, PA. p. 85.
3. Gonzalez, J.J., et al., Helping Prevent Information Security Risks in the Transition to Integrated Operations. Telektronikk, 2005. 101(1): p. 29-37.
4. Rich, E. and J.J. Gonzalez. Maintaining Security and Safety in High-threat E-operations Transitions. In Hawaii International Conference on System Sciences. 2006. Hawaii.
5. Repenning, N.P. and J.D. Sterman, Nobody ever gets credit for fixing problems that never happened. California Management Review, 2001. 43(4): p. 64-88.
6. Sterman, J.D., Business Dynamics: Systems Thinking and Modeling for a Complex World. 2000, Boston: Irwin/McGraw-Hill.
7. Heifetz, R.A. and M. Linsky, Managing Yourself: A Survival Guide for Leaders. Harvard Business Review, 2002. 8(6): p. 65-74.
8. Holling, C.S., Resilience and Stability of Ecological Systems. Annual Review of Ecology and Systematics, 1973. 4: p. 1-23.
9. Gunderson, L.H., C.S. Holling, and S.S. Light, Barriers and bridges to renewal of ecosystems and institutions. 1995, New York: Columbia University Press.
10. Carpenter, S.R., et al., From Metaphor to Measurement: Resilience of What to What? Ecosystems, 2001. 4: p. 765–781.
11. Hammer, M. and J. Champy, Reengineering the Corporation. 1993, New York: Harper Business.
12. Stoltz, P., Building resilience for uncertain times. Leader to Leader, 2004. 31(4): p. 16 -17.

---

[10] AMBASEC, A Model-based Approach to Security Culture, RCN grant number 164384/V30. AMBASEC is funded by the RCN research programme IKTSoS (IKT Sikkerhet og Sårbarhet, i.e. ICT Security and Vulnerability).

[11] ISECBIDAT, Improving Security by Improving Data, RCN grant number 169809/D15. ISECBIDAT is funded by the RCN research programme BILAT.

Computer System Survivability Modelling by Using Stochastic Activity Network

Eimantas Garsva

VGTU, Naugarduko 41, LT-03227 Vilnius, Lietuva
eimaslt@computer.org

Abstract. This article presents the effort to model the computer system security using Stochastic Activity Network (SAN). SAN is a flexible and highly adaptable branch of Stochastic Petri Nets and has a well-developed software tool, Möbius. A known model of incident process and the computer system is adapted and extended. The computer system characterised by the working state and defence mechanism strength is affected by an attack described by using stochastically distributed severity levels. The attempt to bind a stochastic attack severity level to intrusion data parameters collected by Intrusion Detection Systems is presented. The model-based computer system quantitative characteristics are analysed and survivability is chosen to evaluate the modelled computer system security. The article concludes with simulation results and future work guidelines.

1 Introduction

Computer systems are interconnected to achieve more efficiency and better information exchange. The number of potential threats increases because of the computer system integration. Evaluation of the impact on the system is possible when specific features, type and possible influence are known.

A computer system is a heterogeneous, distributed computer network, which faces some attacks. An attack is realisation of the threat, the harmful action aiming to find and exploit the system vulnerability. A successful attack causes intrusion. Vulnerability is some poor characteristic of the system establishing conditions for the threat to arise. The computer system is affected by the active element – a subject (a user or a process) that initiates the query for the object (resource) access and usage. The access is interaction between the subject and the object during which they exchange information. An incident consists of the attack and the response of the computer system to it. An attack can fail to achieve the intended objective for some reasons, but even then there exists possibility that the system becomes more vulnerable.

The quantitative evaluation of the computer system security is usually based on the formal method usage or red team experiment results. Both ways are valuable when determining weaknesses and boundaries of the system. The stochastic-based formal method usage is irreplaceable when modelling and simulating systems which are not implemented yet, or evaluating possible faults and vulnerabilities which are not discovered yet.

J. Górski (Ed.): SAFECOMP 2006, LNCS 4166, pp. 71 – 84, 2006.

Stochastic values are used to describe vulnerability occurrence and discovery, the attacker's behaviour, system response, system state change, intrusion discovery and system function recovery times.

The computer system security as well as information protection modelling and simulation are addressed in a number of researches, articles and theses. Detailed simulation of cyberattack considering possible threat, defender strength, attackers' position to the attack object, and the computer system architecture is performed in [1]. Huge contribution to the computer system security simulation in order to research survivability is presented in [2], later the model was advanced using real intrusion data [3]. Some assumptions based on the ideas from the above-mentioned research will be used in the current article. Dependability and performance evaluation of intrusion tolerant server systems using quantitative cost and benefit values is presented in [4]. Models were constructed using Stochastic Activity Networks.

The primary objective of this article is to model the computer system security using the chosen formal method – Stochastic Activity Network (SAN). The consideration of choosing the formalism and short definition of SAN is presented. The computer system security characteristics were analysed and one was chosen for simulation. The computer system incident numerical evaluation was proposed in order to bind abstract modelling values to the real world taxonomies. The developed computer system security model intended for the evaluation of the characteristics of incident process affecting the computer system security is presented and survivability is simulated, results were analysed and guidelines for future work were formulated.

2 Model Development

The purpose of modelling the computer system and the impact on it is to refine and test the acceptance to the objective security parameters. Incident statistic gathering, analysis and modelling allow constructing incident forecast models, which provides information needed to secure the system. When the system survivability evaluation is performed, the computer system and incident occurrence modelling is needed. It allows revealing a relationship between the computer system survivability and the defence mechanism strength, which depends on their cost. The cost consists of finances, installation, configuration and support time.

2.1 Model of the Computer System

The computer system exists in the space where the threat (planned or incidental) to its security arises, having negative effect on the system itself or on contained information. The intruder performs the action, searching or exploiting the system vulnerability, so called attack. Even if the attack ceases itself it is likely that the system was compromised.

The basic computer system model will be designed, simulated and analysed and later this model will be extended to a more complex system. Let us adopt the basic computer system model using principles described in [2] and [3].

The computer system is a distributed computer network with boundaries defined. The computer system provides service k with some operational grade defined by the system states *{S}:* normal (*s=1*), attacked (*s=2*), compromised (*s=3*), recoverable (*s=4*) and non-functional (*s=5*). The service operational grade in a specific system state and the number of states depend on the system analysed. The initial state of the computer system is normal (*r=1*). The security of the computer system is assured by using security mechanisms, which are defined by their strength *m*. In this case *m* is linearly associated with the cost *C(m)*. The computer system security mechanism cost *C(m)* varies from 0, when no security mechanisms are used, to 100, when all the best possible security mechanisms are used.

It seems likely that a system with correct configuration and resistant design will not be impacted by less severe incidents, although defence mechanisms will not be used. Correct configuration is minimal, designed according to the creator recommendations and updated service collection, needed for the systems mission. Inter incident time is generally longer than a month and recovery time is a lot shorter, so it seems likely that the system before the next serious incident will be in the normal initial state *r=1*. The computer system design resistance is defined by the parameters: π_1, π_3, χ_1 and χ_3. These parameters are the functions depending on the characteristics of an incident (*j*) and the system (*s*).

Incident arrival is a stochastic point process. Incidents arrive at random moments of time t_n and incident type $j \in \{j\}$ is the incident parameter, and incident probability is *P(j)*. Incidents occur at every random rate *a*, which obeys Poisson distribution. The Poisson distribution was chosen because of its simplicity and modelling ability; despite attack motivation relationships with political or technical issues, the occurrence of incidents is approximately Poisson [3]. The incident type describes the severity of incident and probability that there are several incidents at the same time. Incident is most severe when its type *j=1* and least severe when *j=5*.

The computer system state transitions happen with such logic: probability of going to a much worse state is lower than going to a slightly worse state, probability of staying normal is higher if the incident is less severe and the security mechanisms are stronger, and the system must end up in some state.

Statistical data show that the mean time to failure T_{MTTF} is much longer than the system recovery time T_R: ($T_{MTTF} > T_R$), because of that we can consider that the initial state of the system is always normal (*r=1*). Then incident occurs, the next state of the system can be one out of system state space $\{S\}$, but because of the resistive computer system design, the probability that the computer system stays in the normal state P*(1,1)* after the incident is higher. There are two cases:

$$\text{if } s=1, \text{ then } P(1,1) = \pi_2 (1 - e^{-\pi_1 C(m)}), \tag{1}$$

$$\text{if } s>1, \text{ then } P(1,s) = \chi_2 e^{-[\chi_1 C(m)]}. \tag{2}$$

Parameters π_1, for *s=1* and χ_1, for *s>1* determine *P(1,1|m)* and *P(1,s|m)* the probabilities of remaining normal or going to a worse state under attack given a security mechanism *m*. Parameters π_3, for *s=1* and χ_3, for *s>1* determine the levels of transition probabilities *P(1,1)* and *P(1,s)* as the cost changes.

Parameter π_1 depends only on incident severity *j* and parameter χ_1 depends more on the next system state *s* than on the incident severity *j*:

$$\pi_2 = \pi_2(j) = \pi_3 j, \tag{3}$$

$$\chi_2 = \chi_2(j, s) = \chi_3((6 - s) - 0{,}4j). \tag{4}$$

This computer system security model is basic, but highly adaptable in the computer system security simulation.

2.2 Stochastic Activity Networks

Formal methods are widely used for the computer system modelling. Formal methods are mathematical approaches to the system development, which support the rigorous specification, design, verification and modelling of computer systems. There are nearly one hundred of such methods [5], [6]. The modelled computer system is distributed and the aim of modelling is to make the system more secure by improving the security characteristics of the system. For such purpose Petri nets and Performance Evaluation Process Algebra (PEPA) are most useful. Eight popular modelling tools that use high level Petri nets and SAN were tested. Tools were evaluated according to licensing, the operating system, components and documentation. After the analysis was performed, Simulaworks [7], TimeNET [8] and Möbius [9] were selected as most suitable modelling packages. After some modelling performed Möbius was selected as the most powerful and convenient package for the computer system performance modelling. It uses a variety of formal methods: PEPA, SAN, etc. SAN was chosen for the system modelling and construction of the simulation model. SAN is highly adaptable extension of Stochastic Petri nets [9], [10], [11], [12].

Stochastic activity networks (SANs) consist of such primitives: places, activities, input gates, and output gates. Places are as in Petri nets (represented as circles). The number of tokens present in a place is called the marking of that place. Markings of all the places in SAN comprise the marking of the SAN. Activities (similar to transitions in Petri nets) are of two types, timed and instantaneous. Timed activity (represented as thick rectangular or oval) has stochastically distributed latency time. Instantaneous activity (represented as thin rectangular or oval) completes in a negligible amount of time. Instantaneous activities have priority to execute over timed activities. Activity can have one or more cases (represented as small circles on one side of an activity). Input gates have enabling predicates and functions, while output gates have functions. The enabling predicate depends on the places connected to it, and controls the enabling of an attached activity. The function associated with input or output gate describes an action performed upon completion of the activity.

When the activity is activated it stays enabled until completion. Later or when enabled it can be reactivated. Activities are enabled if there is at least one token in each of the places directly connected to the activity and if the predicate of each connected input gate is true. When the activity completes, one token is removed from each of the places directly connected to the input of the activity and one token added to each of the places directly connected to the output of the activity.

The stochastic nature of the SANs is realized by associating an activity time distribution function with each timed activity and a probability distribution with each set of cases. These two choices determine uniquely the next marking of the SAN, which is then obtained by executing the input gates connected to the input of the activity chosen and the output gates connected to the chosen case. Both distributions can depend on the global marking of the network. A reactivation function is also associated with each timed activity.

Performance variables of the modelled computer system are defined using reward models. Reward models consist of three components: a stochastic process, a reward structure, and a performance variable defined in terms of the reward structure and the stochastic process. Rate rewards are assigned to states, and impulse rewards are assigned to state transitions.

The formal definition of Stochastic Activity Networks can be written like this:

$$SAN=(P,A,I,O,\gamma,\tau,\iota,o,\mu_0,C,F,G); \tag{5}$$

where P is some finite set of places, A is a finite set of activities, I is a finite set of input gates, and O is a finite set of output gates. γ specifies the number of cases for each activity and τ specifies the type of each activity. The net structure is specified via the functions ι mapping input gates to activities and o mapping output gates to cases of activities. The next set of parameters represents the stochastic features: μ_0 is the initial marking, C is the case distribution assignment, F is the activity time distribution function assignment and G is the reactivation function assignment.

2.3 Model-Based Computer System Security Characteristics

Researches use different characteristics to describe the computer system and its security features [13], [14], [15]. Most suitable for the computer system security evaluation are these:

Performance shows how well the system intended to perform flawlessly operates and does not estimate the computer failures and recovery. Performance is usually evaluated using throughput (security mechanism ability to process network traffic), different response times (intrusion detection duration, incident response time, etc.) and load of the resource (the number of simultaneous attacks, system load brought by security mechanisms, security mechanism load, etc.).

Reliability is the characteristic assuring that proper service will be provided during the set period of time. It may be evaluated using the probability that the computer system will survive in the normal state.

Availability is the probability that intended service will be provided. The required level of the service, which is needed for proper query processing, depends on the specific computer system, but possible service level change is not estimated.

Safety is the probability that the computer system will not fail causing catastrophic consequences during the set time period. Safety usually depends more on consequences than on causes, and the amount of damage is considered.

Integrity is the characteristic assuring the absence of unexpected changes in the computer system. Integrity can be evaluated using the probability that the computer system state will not change during the set amount of time.

Maintainability is the computer system ability to be repaired and modified and can be evaluated using the system recovery time, cost and the number of operations required.

Performability is the quantitative definition of the system performance in the state of possible failures. Performability combines information of performance and availability characteristics.

Survivability is the computer system ability to resist attacks and to keep functioning at some level after the incident. To achieve that, the system reaction to and evaluation of occurring incidents are needed: to detect incidents, resist to attacks, and keep functionality if compromised. The computer system survivability comprises such areas as reliability, security and interference resistance. A new state of the computer system after the incident s, in common case, is compromised, and the system functions and waits to be restored to full functionality. Survivability can be computed for every computer system service. If service does not change, then the survivability value is equal to 1, if service is sopped, then it equals to 0, other values are distributed between them.

Researchers differently name the computer system ability to function in the presence of attacks. In this article survivability paradigm will be used. Reliability characteristic is the probability that service or the system will survive in the maximal state and can be called maximal survivability S_{max}. Availability is the probability that service will be provided, even in the least operational state that the service has survived and can be called minimal survivability S_{min}. Performability in the modelled computer system does not differ from survivability characteristic $S(s)$.

Stochastic characteristics of the computer system security depend on the system event times, time spent in each system state and the service level in each state. The computer system is brought into production at time $t_{0i}=t_{r(i-1)}$ and is affected by some incident i at time t_{inci}. It is possible that after some impact period T_{imi}, which depends on the computer system response to the attack, system state change will occur at t_{sci}, and that will possibly cause a failure at time t_{fi} and bring the system to non-functional state (s=5). After some recovery period T_{ri}, which depends on fault discovery time and the system repair time, the computer system will be recovered to the fully functional state. These events will occur repeatedly and usage of the system will end at time t_{all}. T_{all} is the time during which simulation is performed in the computer system security model.

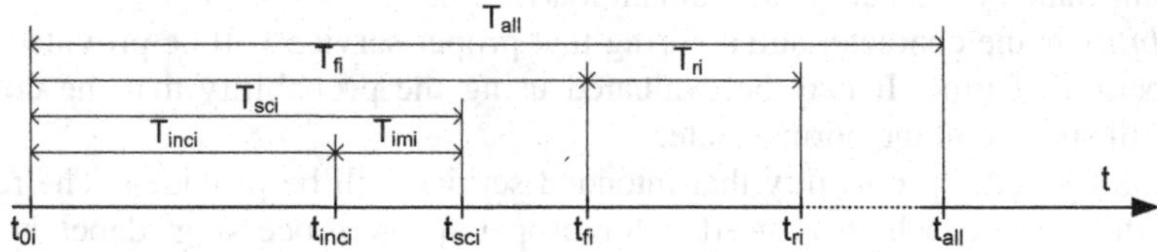

Fig. 1. Computer system events that impact the computer system security characteristics

Performance is described using the computer system mean times to some events and the security mechanism load. Mean time to the incident T_{MTTI} is:

$$T_{MTTI} = \frac{\sum_{i=1}^{N}(t_{inci} - t_{0i})}{N}, \quad (6)$$

where N is the total number of incidents. Mean time to the system state change T_{MTTSC} is:

$$T_{MTTSC} = \frac{\sum_{i=1}^{N}(t_{sci} - t_{0i})}{N}. \qquad (7)$$

Mean time to the system failure is:

$$T_{MTTF} = \frac{\sum_{i=1}^{N}(t_{fi} - t_{0i})}{N}. \qquad (8)$$

The security mechanism load L_m is a ratio of a period of time when the computer system is affected by incidents to all the time when the system is in production:

$$L_m = \frac{T_{all} - \sum_{i=1}^{N} T_{inci}}{T_{all}} = 1 - \frac{\sum_{i=1}^{N} T_{inci}}{T_{all}}. \qquad (9)$$

Maximal survivability S_{max} is a probability that the system will be in the normal state ($s=1$):

$$S_{max} = P_{(s=1)} = \frac{T_{(s=1)}}{T_{all}}, \qquad (10)$$

where $T_{(s=1}$ is the period of time which the computer system is in the normal state.
Minimal survivability S_{min} is the probability that service will be provided, even in the least operational state and it is equal to availability:

$$S_{min} = A = \frac{T_{all} - T_{(s=5)}}{T_{all}} = 1 - \frac{T_{(s=5)}}{T_{all}}, \qquad (11)$$

where $T_{(s=5)} = \sum T_{ri}$ is a time when the computer system is non-functional.
Integrity is a ratio between mean time to the system state change T_{MTTSC} and the time which system spent in the production T_{all}:

$$I = \frac{\sum_{i=1}^{N}(t_{sci} - t_{0i})}{T_{all}}. \qquad (12)$$

Maintainability is evaluated using the average time needed to recover the system:

$$T_{ravg} = \frac{\sum_{i=1}^{N}(t_{ri} - t_{fi})}{N}, \qquad (13)$$

or with the probability that the computer system will be recovered after failure when the incident happens. In the model it is described to be equal to 1.

The general survivability expression [2] is as follows:

$$S(s)=\sum_k w(k)\varphi(s,k)\,,\ 0\le w(k)\le 1;\ \sum w(k)=1\,;\ 0\le \varphi(s,k)\le 1, \tag{14}$$

where $\varphi(s,k)$ is the grade to which service k survived in the system state s, and $w(k)$ is the weight of the service.

The most important is the time that the system spent in the normal state $T_{(s=1)}=\sum T_{sc}$, that is why in this research the maximal survivability characteristic was chosen for the simulation. The composed models permit finding all the defined computer system security characteristics.

2.4 Computer System Attack Severity Numerical Evaluation

Attack severity numerical values are essential for modelling. Using numbers, which represent the attack, it is possible to group, generate and compare attacks as well as their distribution in different computer systems and others. The possible attack severity can be evaluated by the objective of the attack:

1. Super-user privilege gain,
2. User privilege gain,
3. Denial of service,
4. Information integrity violation,
5. Information or system resource confidentiality violation,
6. Malicious code execution,
7. Security policy violation.

The attack severity description must be close to those available in Intrusion Detection Systems (IDS) because IDS are used for the attack statistic data collection. The attack description by the objective is used in SNORT IDS [16] and by CERT [17] organisation, which has most experience in detecting intrusions and evaluating their effect on computer systems. The 5 level attack severity numerical evaluation was organised using the suggested attack classification [18] and above mentioned IDS classifications. The numerical evaluation using 5 severity levels was chosen because the 3 level severity evaluation is not sufficiently accurate for a vast variety of attacks, and the 10 level evaluation would make the model too large and complicated.

First level attacks are most severe, while fifth level attacks are least severe and having least possible effect on the computer system.

A super-user (administrator, root, etc.) has the highest rights in the system and is intended to be used for the system administration. The attacker who gains super-user rights can have the largest influence on the system, these are most severe attacks, $j=1$.

The computer system user has some specified rights and privileges, which depend on security and network access policy. The intruder having ability to connect to the system as a user can affect the system confidentiality, integrity and cause denial of service. User rights make it easier to acquire super-user rights. The total computer system control is usually the final objective of the intruders. The severity level of these attacks $j=2$.

The system availability is the computer system ability to provide proper service during a defined amount of time. When the system fails to provide some service, the computer system does not accomplish its mission and the threat to information confidentiality and integrity arises. The severity level of these attacks $j=3$.

The information integrity violation caused by information corruption, information control between system objects, masquerading as another host and confidentiality violation compromise the system. The severity level of these attacks $j=4$.

The malicious code execution and security policy violation may compromise the system and reveal valuable information to the attacker and encourage striving for larger rights in the system. The severity level of these attacks $j=5$.

3 Computer System Security Simulation Model

3.1 Basic Computer System Security Simulation Model

The SAN based computer system simulation model will be used to evaluate the influence of the parameters of the model on the security of the modelled computer system. The basic computer system model with only two possible types (defined by severity j) of the incidents is presented in Fig. 2.

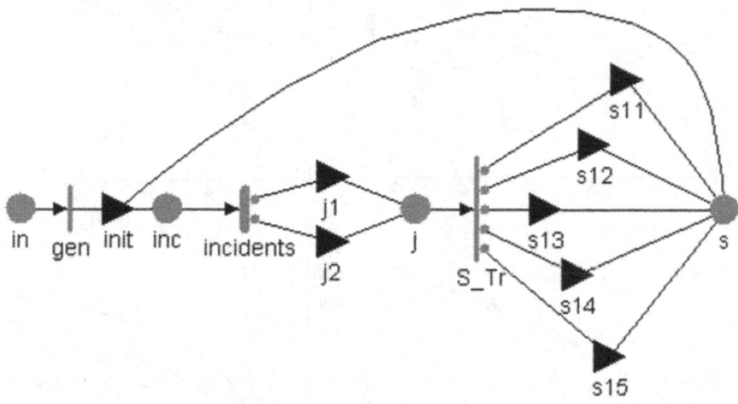

Fig. 2. Basic computer system security simulation model

The number of incidents is defined via place "in" and incidents, one by one through output gate "inc", which assures that the system is in the initial state $r=1$ get into the system. Timed activity "incidents" assure that the incident occurrence is distributed according to Poisson distribution with a parameter a. This timed activity has two cases which determine which type, out of five possible, of the incident will occur, $j=1$ with probability $P(1)$, or $j=2$ with probability $P(2)=1-P(1)$. The probabilities are normalised by the modelling tool. The type of the incident occurred via output gates "j1" or "j2" is transferred to the place "j", which defines the incident type. In this case the system reacts instantaneously to the incident occurred and goes to the state, defined by formulas (1) and (2). Which state the system transition will end up is defined by "S_tr" and output gates "s11", "s12", "s13", "s14", "s15" set the place corresponding to the system state "s" to that numerical value. The influence of the model parameters was found by simulating maximal survivability S_{max} (Fig. 3).

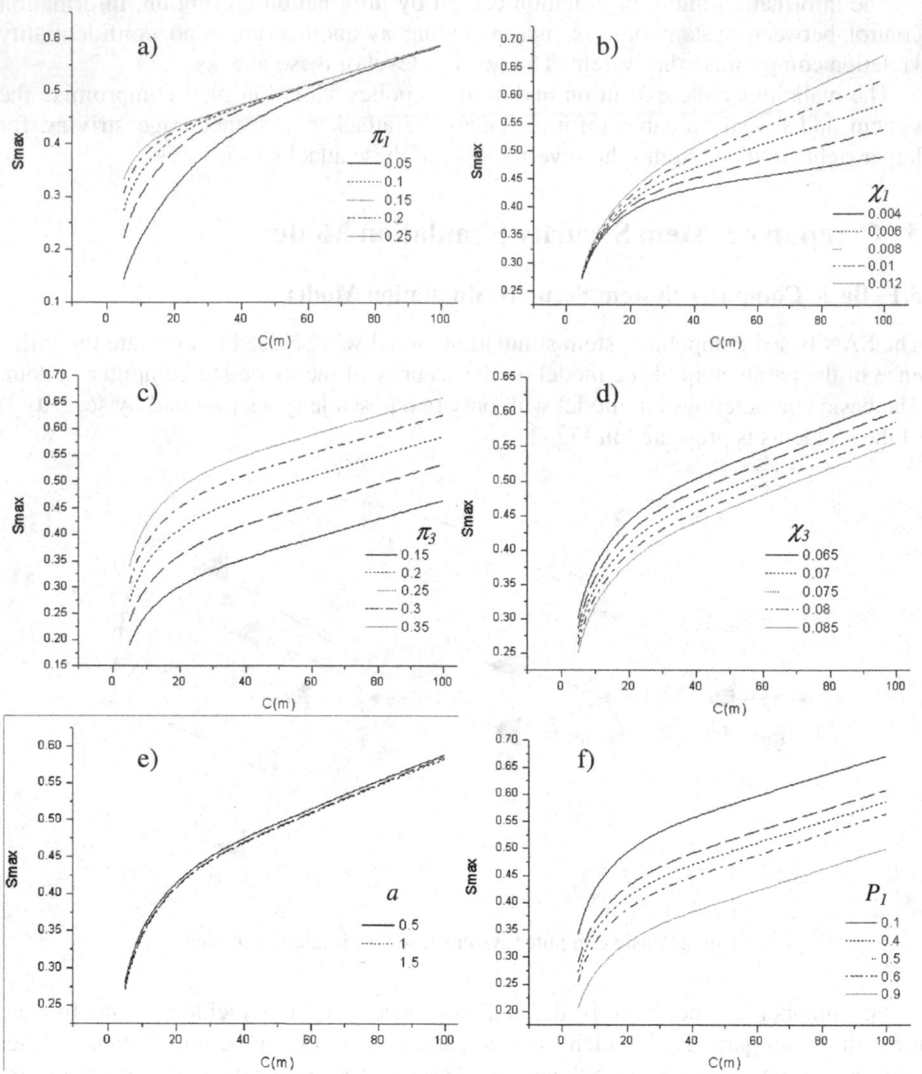

Fig. 3. The influence of the parameters of model and the incident on the modelled computer system is shown via S_{max} dependence on *C(m)*

The parameter π_1 growth (Fig. 3.a) means the growth of the probability to remain in the normal state, it positively influences S_{max}, the influence is higher when security mechanisms are weaker. The parameter χ_1, which determines the probability of going to a worse state *P(1,s)* when higher values are used (Fig. 3.b) S_{max} increases, especially when security mechanisms are stronger.

The higher is parameter π_3 (Fig. 3.c) determining the level of probability *P(1,1)*, the better S_{max} is. The growth of χ_3 negatively influences S_{max} (Fig. 3.d). The influence is lower when security mechanisms are weaker for both parameters.

The higher incident rate *a* makes S_{max} characteristic worse (Fig. 3.e), but not too drastically, because the incidents do happen faster, but the response is similar. If the amount of severe incidents is low, then S_{max} is better (Fig. 3.f). When security mechanisms are weak, resistance to the incidents depends on the system architecture parameter that is why the influence of the incident severity is lower if the security mechanisms are weaker.

Base parameter values were similar to [3] during the simulations: $a=1$, $\pi_1=0.15$, $\pi_3=0.25$, $\chi_1=0.008$, $\chi_3=0.075$ and $P(1)=0.5$. The relative confidence interval, specifying the width of the acceptable interval around the variable estimate, was set to 0.1, the confidence level to 0.95, this means that mean variable will not be satisfied until the confidence interval is within 10% of the mean estimate 95% of the time. Simulation was done for 90 time units, which correspond to 90 days, such period of time is enough for the system features to reveal.

3.2 Computer System Security Simulation Model

Let us extend the earlier analyzed computer system model to the more realistic one and model the computer system, which has two connections to outer systems: Internet (*J1*) and Intranet (*J2*), and provides three services: windows sharing (*k1*), SMTP (*k2*) and HTTP (*k3*) (Fig. 4). These all three services are used by some human resource planning application. Attacks to the services occur with the probabilities and the rate presented in Table 1. These attack severity and service attack probabilities were aggregated from the global sources [19], [20] and adapted to the modelled system.

Table 1. Incident occurrence parameters

	j=1	*j=2*	*j=3*	*j=4*	*j=5*	*a*
J1	0.15	0.15	0.27	0.19	0.24	1
J2	0.25	0.19	0.16	0.16	0.27	2

Modelling logic is the same as used in the basic computer system model. Incidents occur faster from the Intranet (*J1*) than from the Internet (*J2*), because some security measures are implemented by the provider. Generated incidents by "type_2" and "type_1" activities, with appropriate types at the set rate arrive to the system via places "j_1" and "j_2". PS1 and PS2 decide what service is attacked. Activities "S-_ch_1" and "S_ch_2" choose the attacked service at the rate equal to the fastest incident occurrence rate and output gates transfer attack type *j* to the specific service *k1*, *k2* or *k3*. Initialization unit "init" assures that services are recovered to the normal state *s=1* before the incident enters the system. Architecture parameters defining initial service strength (π_1, π_3, χ_1 and χ_3) are the same for all services. Service weights *w(k)* as well as levels at which service *k* is provided in different system states *φ(s,k)* differ. Maximal survivability S_{max} characteristics for all the services (Fig. 4 a), and the

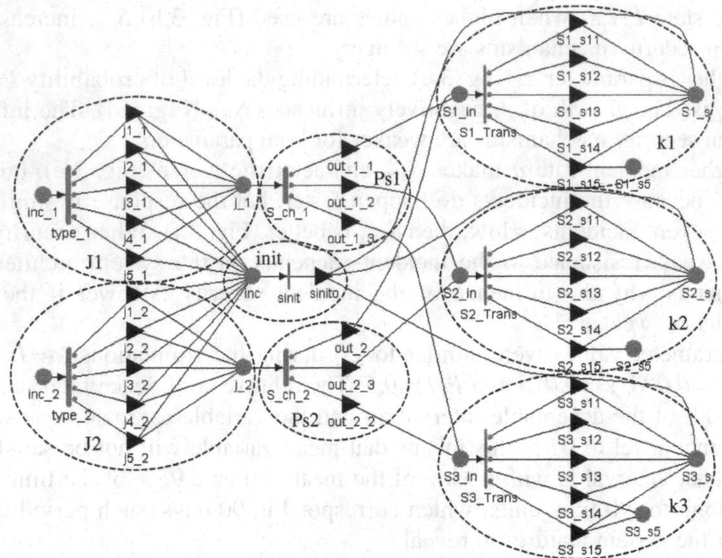

Fig. 4. Computer system security simulation model

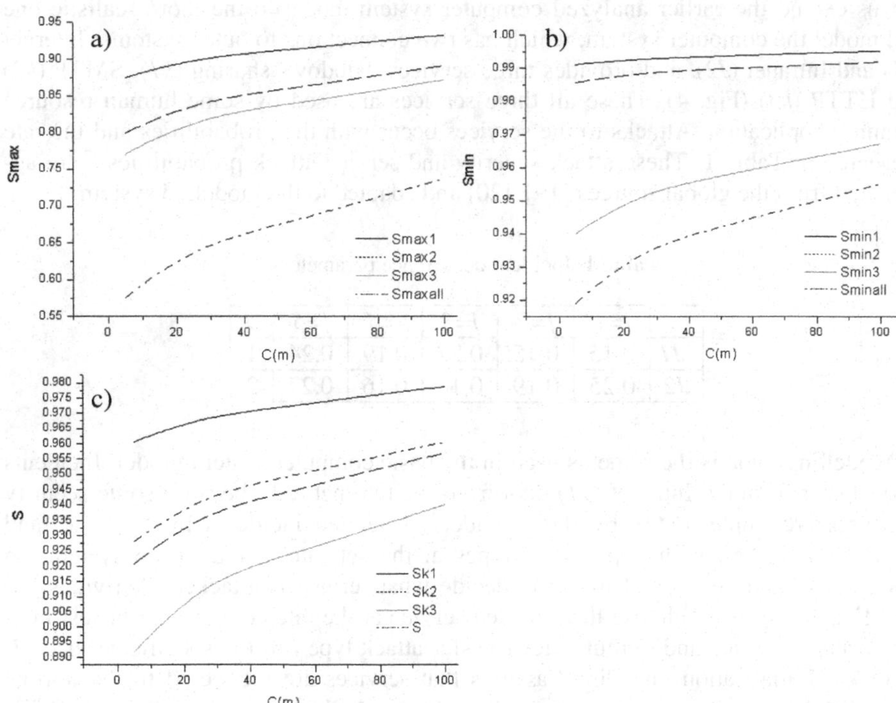

Fig. 5. Survivability characteristics: a) maximal *Smax*, b) minimal S_{min} and c) the system survivability *S(s)*

common maximal survivability S_{maxall}, representing the probability that all the services will be in the normal state $s=1$, were calculated using formula (10). Minimal survivability S_{min} characteristics for all the services (Fig 5. b), and one common, presenting the probability that all the services will be provided at some states, except non-functional, were calculated using formula (11). Then the survivability of all the services, according to the levels that service survives in the specific state were calculated and one value common to the whole system survivability $S(s)$ (Fig 5. c) was found using formula (15). The modelled computer system related parameters used in simulation are shown in Table 2.

Table 2. Service related parameters used in simulation

k	Type	PS1	PS2	$\varphi(1,k)$	$\varphi(2,k)$	$\varphi(3,k)$	$\varphi(4,k)$	$\varphi(5,k)$	$w(k)$	π_1	π_3	χ_1	χ_3
1	Win Shar.	0.1	0.5	1	0.85	0.7	0.55	0	0.4				
2	SMTP	0.4	0.25	1	0.8	0.6	0.4	0	0.3	0.15	0.3	0.01	0.075
3	HTTP	0.5	0.25	1	0.8	0.6	0	0	0.3				

As it is seen from the graphs (Fig. 5) the survivability curves have similar shapes to the basic computer system simulation ones. Because of more distributed incident types they are more flat. Common survivability characteristics S_{maxall} and S_{minall} have lower values, because they represent the worst case in the system. The system survivability $S(s)$ has average values, which depend in the state to which the services have survived and their weight.

4 Future Work

Enhancement of the modelled system architecture parameter impact by finding more adjustable transition probability curve expressions.

Examination of the computer system model behaviour by using extreme parameters and definition of the boundaries of the model.

Research of the differences between the systems in different type organisations (government, commercial, educational, SOHO) by using incident severity levels determined by the collected incident data.

Discovering the best suitable security characteristic for the computer system security simulation by running more different system simulations.

5 Summary

Simulation of the computer system security helps in forecasting and evaluating the computer systems which are in the design phase. The effort to model and simulate the computer system security using SAN is presented in this article. The modelling-related problems, selection of the formalism and tool, defining the computer system security characteristics and quantitative computer system attack evaluation, were solved.

Survivability is a universal and highly adaptable computer system security quantitative characteristic, well suitable for the computer system simulation.

References

1. Cohen, F.: Simulating Cyber Attacks, Defenses, and Consequences. IFIP TC-11. Computers and Security. 1999.: http://all.net/journal/ntb/simulate/simulate.html
2. Moitra S. D., Konda S. L.: A Simulation Model for Managing Survivability of Networked Information Systems. Networked survivable systems. CMU/SEI-2000-TR-020 (2000) 47 p
3. Moitra S. D., Konda S. L.: The Survivability of Network Systems: An Empirical Analysis. CMU/SEI-2000-TR-021 (2000) 41p
4. Gupta, V., Lam, V., Ramasamy, H.V., Sanders, W. H., Singh, S.: Stochastic Modeling of Intrusion-Tolerant Server Architectures for Dependability and Performance Evaluation (2003) 86 p
5. Formal methods Europe.: http://www.fmeurope.org/
6. Virtual library: formal methods.: http://vl.fmnet.info/
7. Simulaworks.: http://mathtools.softlock.net/
8. TimeNET.: http://pdv.cs.tu-berlin.de/~timenet/
9. Sanders, W. H.: Möbius: Model-Based Environment for Validation of System Reliability, Availability, Security, and Performance. User Manual. Version 1.8.0 (2005) 212 p
10. Sanders, W. H.: Construction and Solution of Performability models based on Stochastic Activity Networks. PhD thesis, University of Michigan (1988) 223 p
11. Sanders W. H., Meyer, J. F.: Stochastic Activity Networks: Formal Definitions and Concepts. Lecture Notes in Computer Science, no. 2090, Springer, Berlin (2001) 315-343
12. Williamson, L.: Discrete Event Simulation in the Möbius Modeling Framework. Master's Thesis. University of Illinois (1998) 63 p
13. Avizienis A., Laprie J. C., Randell B.: Basic concepts and taxonomy of dependable and secure computing. Dependable and Secure Computing, Vol. 1. (2004) 11–33
14. Stevens, F., Courtney, T., Singh, S., Agbaria, A., Meyer, J.F., Sanders, W.H., Pal, P.: Model-Based Validation of an Intrusion-Tolerant Information System. Proc. 23rd Symp. Reliable Distributed Systems (2004) 11 p
15. Sanders, W. H., Meyer, J. F.: A unified approach for specifying measures of Performance, dependability, and performability. Dependable Computing for Critical Applications, Vol 4: of Dependable Computing and Fault-Tolerant Systems. Springer-Verlag (1991) 215-237
16. Baker A., Beale J., Caswell, B.: Snort 2.1 Intrusion Detection (Second Edition). Syngress (2004) 751 p
17. Howard, J. D.: An analysis of security incidents on the Internet, 1989-1995. PhD thesis, Carnegie Mellon University, Department of Engineering and Public Policy, (1997).: http://www.cert.org/research/JHThesis/table_of_contents.html
18. N. Paulauskas, E. Garsva. Computer System Attack Classification. Electronics and Electrical Engineering, No. 2(66). Technology, Kaunas (2006) 84–87
19. What Are the Most Dangerous Internet Services?.: www.cisco.com/warp/public/146/news _cisco/ ekits/vulnerability_report.pdf
20. Distributed Intrusion Detection System Reports and Database Summaries.: http://www.dshield.org/reports.php

Software Safety Lifecycles and the Methods of a Programmable Electronic Safety System for a Nuclear Power Plant

Jang-Soo Lee[1], Arndt Lindner[2], Jong-Gyun Choi[1], Horst Miedl[2], and Kee-Choon Kwon[1]

[1] KAERI: Korea Atomic Energy Research Institute, Daejeon, Korea
{jslee, choijg, kckwon}@kaeri.re.kr
[2] Institut fuer Sicherheitstechnologie, Postfach 12 13, 85740 Garching, Germany
{arndt.lindner, horst.miedl}@istec.grs.de

Abstract. This paper describes the relationship between the overall safety lifecycle and the software safety lifecycle during the development of the software based safety systems of Nuclear Power Plants. This includes the design and evaluation activities of the components as well as the system. This paper also compares the safety lifecycle and planning activities defined in IEC 61508 with those in IEC 61513, IEC 60880, IEEE 7-4.3.2, and IEEE 1228. Using the Korean KNICS (Korean Nuclear Instrumentation and Control System) project as an example, the software safety lifecycle is described by comparing it to the software development, testing, and safety analysis processes of international standards. The safety assessment of the software for the KNICS Reactor Protection System and Programmable Logic Controller is a joint Korean/German project. The assessment methods applied in the project and the experiences gained from this project are presented.

1 Introduction

This paper introduces the lifecycle based software safety analysis tasks for the KNICS (Korean Nuclear Instrumentation and Control System) project. The objectives of the safety analysis tasks are mainly to develop the programmable logic controller (PLC) for safety-critical instrumentation and control (I&C) systems, and then to apply the PLC to developing the prototype of the safety-critical software based digital protection system in nuclear power plants.

Safety-critical systems are those in which a failure can have serious and irreversible consequences. For the past two decades, digital technology has been applied rapidly to I&C systems for nuclear power plants, railways, airplanes, vehicles, communication networks, etc. In nuclear power plants more and more digital technology is being applied to I&C systems, too. Programmable logic controller based platforms (e.g., TELEPERM XS, Common Q and Tricon) have been prototyped, evaluated for nuclear safety applications, and installed in several applications. The PLC is a special

J. Górski (Ed.): SAFECOMP 2006, LNCS 4166, pp. 85 – 98, 2006.

purpose digital controller, originally designed to replace the industrial hard-wired control systems. As PLCs are more widely used in digital I&C systems, the safety of the PLC software has become a primary consideration.

Fig. 1 shows the developed PLC prototype of the KNICS project, which mainly consists of power modules, a processor module (embedded with the real-time operating system pCOS), communication modules (HR-SDL, HR-SDN), and I/O modules.

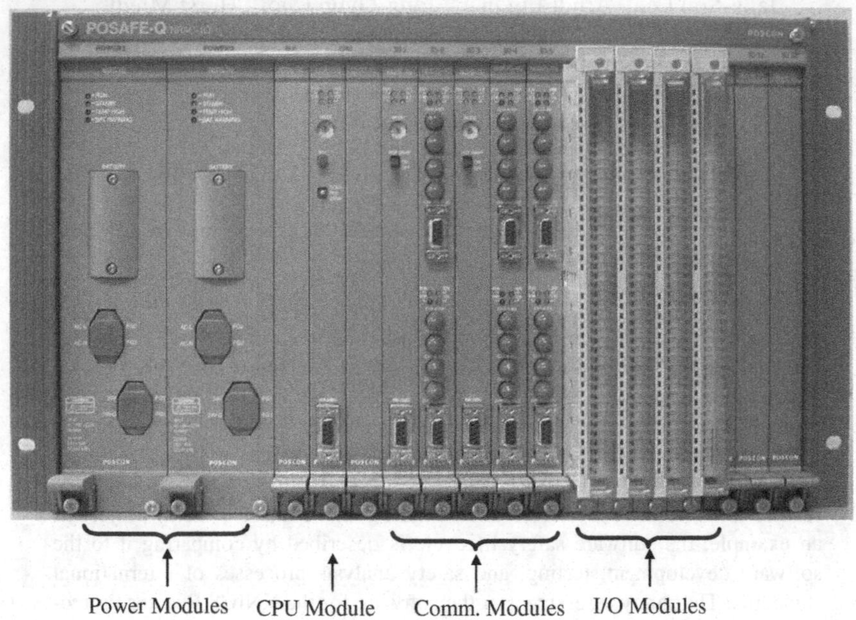

Fig. 1. POSAFE-Q KNICS PLC

pCOS is the software to control the hardware, such as the processors, storage, I/O device, and data communication. It is composed of five components: a scheduler, the inter-tasks communication part, a tick timer, an interrupt handler and application tasks.

As shown in Fig. 2, the plant protection system (PPS) consists of the reactor protection system (RPS) and the engineered safety feature – component control system (ESF-CCS). RPS generates the reactor trip signals and ESF actuation signals automatically whenever the monitored processing variables reach their predefined setpoints. PPS is designed as a PLC-based architecture with four redundant channels/divisions (A, B, C, and D). The software of the prototype of the qualified PLCs (i.e. POSAFE-Q) is implemented by the proprietarily developed engineering tool pSET. The engineering tool pSET is used for developing the functional block diagrams, and for downloading the functional block diagram based programs into POSAFE-Q PLCs via RS-232C interface.

The following chapters deal with the relationship of the overall safety lifecycle to the software safety lifecycle for the development of the components (e.g., KNICS PLC) and the Reactor Protection System (RPS). The software safety lifecycles of the IEC 61508-3, IEC 60880, IEEE 1228-1994, and IEEE standards 7-4.3.2-2003 are com

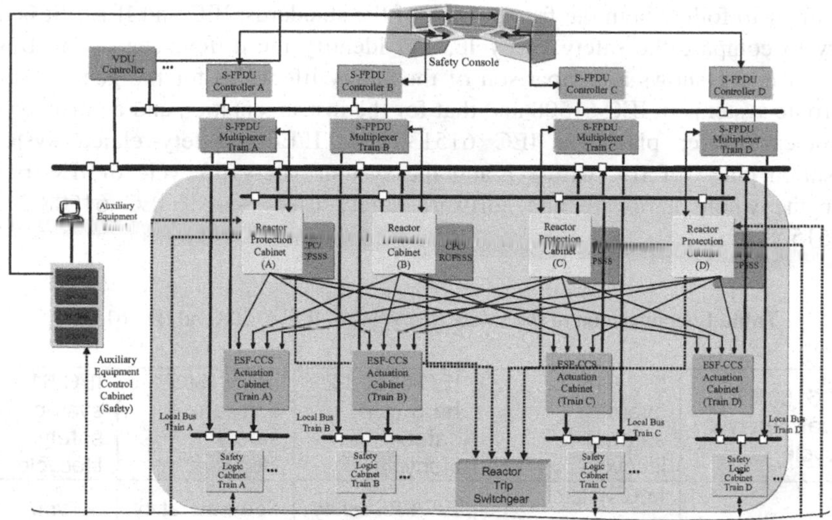

Fig. 2. KNICS Plant Protection System

pared. The software safety lifecycle for the KNICS RPS and PLC systems is introduc ed and the relationship of the safety analysis and testing for a software safety lifecycle is identified. Finally, software safety assessment methods are described for the KNIC S RPS and PLC systems. Experiences of the software safety analysis in the KNICS pr oject are given.

2 Safety Lifecycles in IEC and IEEE Standards

The safety assessment of the software for the KNICS RPS and PLC is an ongoing joint Korean/German project. In the cases where the documents have been evaluated by KAERI, ISTec has checked the results of the evaluation by supplementing spot checks for the development documents according to the following IEC and IEEE standards.

- IEC 61508-1, Functional safety of electrical/electronic/programmable electronic safety-related systems –Part 1:General requirements [6]
- IEC 61508-2, Functional safety of electrical/electronic/programmable electronic safety-related systems –Part 2: Requirements for electrical/electronic/ programmable electronic safety-related systems [7]
- IEC 61508-3, Functional safety of electrical/electronic/programmable electronic safety-related systems –Part 3: Software requirements [8]
- IEC 60880, Nuclear Power Plants – I&C systems important to safety – Software aspects for computer-based systems performing category A functions [9]
- IEC 61513, Nuclear Power Plants – Instrumentation and control for systems important to safety – General requirements for systems [10]
- IEEE Std. 7-4.3.2-2003, IEEE Standard Criteria for Digital Computers in Safety Systems of Nuclear Power Generating Stations [11]
- IEEE Std. 1228-1994, IEEE Standard for Software Safety Plan [12]

In order to follow both the frameworks of the standards, IEC and IEEE, it is necessary to compare the safety lifecycle, and identify the differences of the frameworks. Table 1 shows a comparison of the safety lifecycles for the general safety electronic systems in IEC 61508 and that for the instrumentation and control system of nuclear power plants in IEC 61513. The E/E/PE safety-related systems: realisation phase of IEC 61508-1 and the system safety lifecycle of IEC 61513 cover the whole hardware and software safety lifecycles of IEC 61508-2 and IEC 61508-3.

Table 1. Comparison of the safety lifecycles in IEC 61508 and IEC 61513

IEC 61508-1 overall safety lifecycle	IEC 61513 overall safety lifecycle		IEC 61508-2 hardware safety lifecycle	IEC 61508-3 software safety lifecycle	IEC 61513 system safety lifecycle
Concept	I&C system requirements from the safety design base		E/E/PES safety requirements specification	Software safety requirements specification	System requirements specification
Overall scope definition			E/E/PES safety validation planning	Software safety validation planning	System planning
Hazard and risk analysis			E/E/PES design and development		System specification
Overall safety requirements	Overall requirements specification of the I&C system			Software design and development	System detailed-design and implementation
Safety requirements allocation	Design of the I&C architecture and assignment of the I&C functions		General requirements	Architecture	Design Constraint, System architecture
Overall operation and maintenance planning	Overall operation and maintenance plan		Requirements for hardware safety integrity	Software system design	Design constraint requirements
Overall safety validation planning	Overall integration and commissioning plans and security plan		Requirements for the avoidance of failure	Individual software module design	System safety cycle
Overall installation and commissioning planning	Overall integration and commissioning plans		Requirements for the control of systematic failure	Support tools and programming languages	Defense against propagation of failures

Table 1. (*continued*)

E/E/PE safety-related systems: realisation	System safety lifecycle		Requirements for system behavior on detection of a fault		System architecture, self-monitoring and tolerance to failures
Other technology safety-related systems: realisation			Requirements for E/E/PES implementation	Detailed code implementation	Selection of equipment
External risk reduction facilities: realisation			Requirements for data communication	Software module testing	Internal behavior of the system
Overall installation and commissioning	Overall integration and commissioning			Software Integration testing	
Overall safety validation	Overall commissioning and system qualification		E/E/PES integration	E/E/PES integration (hardware and software)	System integration
Overall operation, maintenance and repair	Overall operation and maintenance		E/E/PES operation, and maintenance procedures	Software operation and modification procedures	System operation plan
Overall modification and retrofit	Implicitly covered		E/E/PES safety validation	Software safety validation	System validation
Decommissioning or disposal			E/E/PES modification	Software modification	System modification
Verification	Overall quality assurance programs		E/E/PES verification	Software verification	System verification plan
Functional safety assessment			E/E/PES functional safety assessment	Software functional safety assessment	

Table 2 shows the differences of the safety lifecycles in IEC 60880, IEC 61513, IEEE 7-4.3.2 and IEEE 1228.

Table 2. Comparison of the Safety Lifecycles between IEC and IEEE standards

IEC 61513 system safety lifecycle	IEC 60880 software safety lifecycle	IEEE 7-4.3.2 computer system safety lifecycle (Annex D)	IEEE 1228 software safety lifecycle
System requirements specification	Software requirements specification	Hazards identification and evaluation plan	Software safety plan
System planning		Safety system hazard identification	Software safety analyses preparation

Table 2. (*continued*)

System specification		Computer system hazards identification	
System detailed design and implementation		Software requirements hazards i dentification	Software safety requirements analysis
System architecture	Software design	Software design hazards identification	Software safety design analysis
Design constraint requirements			
Defense against propagation of failures			
System architecture, self-monitoring and tolerance to failures	Implementation of new software in general purpose language		
Selection of equipment	Implementation of new software in application-oriented language	Software implementation hazards identification	Software safety code analysis
Internal behavior of system	Configuration of pre-developed software and devices	Evaluation of hazards in previously developed systems	
System integration	Software aspects of integration	Computer system integration testing for hazards conditions	Software safety test analysis
System operation plan			
System validation	Software aspects of validation	Computer system validation testing	
System modification		Maintenance and modification hazard analysis	Software safety change analysis
System verification plan			

Most of the IEC and IEEE standards consist of three main phases, planning phase, realization phases according to the plan, and the validation phase. The safety lifecycles for the industry specific standards, for example, IEC 62279 for a railway, IEC 61513 for nuclear power plants, inherit the definition of phases from the generic IEC standard of IEC 61508. However, the detailed phases of the safety lifecycles for the specific industries are different from IEC 61508. Table 2 shows for instance the differences in the safety lifecycles between the IEC and IEEE standards. The safety lifecycles in the IEEE standards require a direct safety analysis at each phase of the lifecycle.

3 Software Safety Planning

In Table 2, there is a safety planning phase in the IEC and IEEE safety lifecycles. However, there are differences in the required activities in the planning between the IEC and IEEE standards. Table 3 shows the differences of the required activities in the planning phases for the IEC and IEEE standards.

Table 3. Planning activities between the IEC and IEEE standards

IEC 61508-3 software safety lifecycle	IEC 61513 I&C system safety lifecycle	IEEE 7-4.3.2 computer system safety lifecycle(Annex D)	IEEE 1228 software safety lifecycle
Software safety validation planning	System planning	Hazards identification and evaluation plan	Software safety plan
schedule	System quality assurance programs	Identify critical functions	1. Purpose, 2. Definitions
qualifier	System verification plan	Identify top-level undesired events	3. Software safety management
operation mode	System configuration management plan	Identify organizational responsibilities	3.1 Organization ~ 3.6 Software safety program record
safety-related software	System security plan	Select the techniques to be used	3.7 Configuration management ~ 3.9 Verification and validation activities
Technical strategy	System integration plan	Identify analysis assumptions	3.10 Tool support 3.11 PDS, COTS
Measures, techniques and procedures	System validation plan	Perform a hazards identification analysis	4. Software safety analysis through lifecycle
Specific references	System installation plan	Evaluate identified hazards for consequences and probability of occurrence	
Required environment	System operation plan	Perform needed corrective actions and re-evaluate the impact of any changes	5. Post development
pass and fail criteria	System maintenance plan		
Policies and procedures for valuating the results			6. Plan approval

4 Software Safety Lifecycle for KNICS

In the KNICS project, the software safety lifecycle was developed based on IEEE 1228, IEEE 7-4.3.2, IEC 61513, and IEC 60880. The software safety lifecycle of IEC 61513[10] is given in Fig 3.

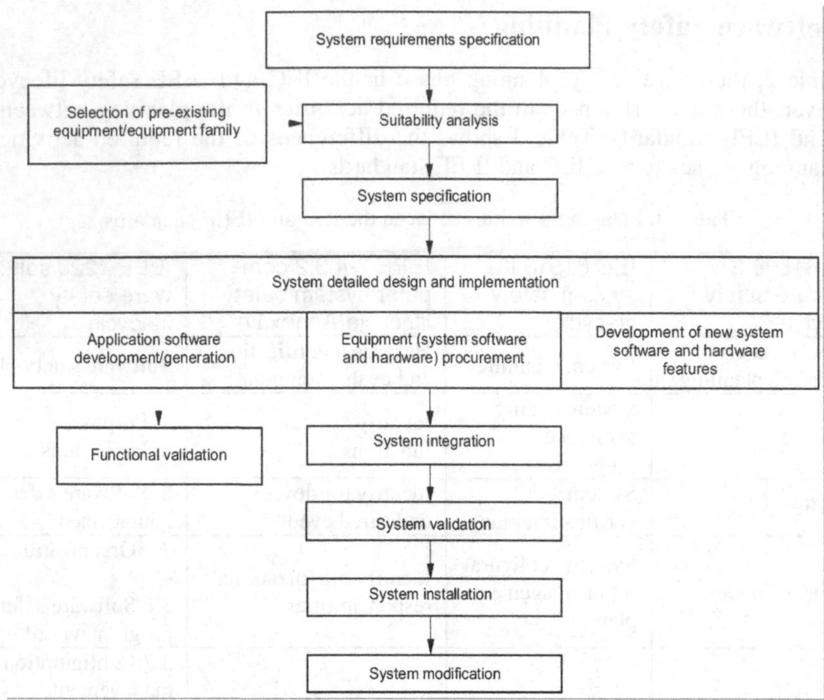

Fig. 3. Software safety lifecycle (IEC 61513)

The software safety lifecycle is tightly coupled with the reliability evaluation process. Software failures cannot be treated as random events and the probabilities for software failures cannot be derived by using historical data [1]. Although attempts have been made to apply a quantitative probability for software [2], this approach is still controversial. For that reason the standards being used to develop and assess the safety critical software for nuclear power plants have established a software safety lifecycle and dedicated requirements to ensure safe and high reliable software.

The software development process is split into consecutive phases. Each phase produces its own set of documents. The change-over from one phase to the next one includes appropriate verification activities. After system integration, a system validation shall demonstrate that the system meets the system requirements specification. The application of standards will provide a solid basis for high quality software.

Nevertheless, software development is a complex process that may result in incorrect final products. Complete tests for all internal state conditions and input scenarios can not be performed due to time constrains. Therefore a software qualification must be complemented by safety and reliability analysis.

Several techniques for a safety analysis have been used by the industries for decades, and some have attracted great attention in the research community. They include Fault Tree Analysis (FTA), Failure Modes, Effects and Criticality Analysis (FMECA), Failure Propagation and Transformation Notation (FPTN), Hazard and Operability (HAZOP), and Preliminary Hazard Analysis (PHA). In Leveson's book,

"Safeware" [5], there is an excellent summary on the techniques for a system's safety and computers.

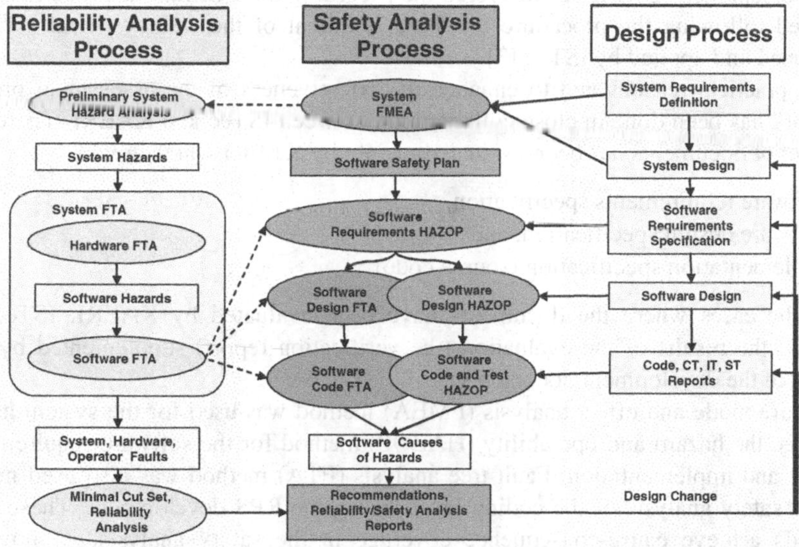

Fig. 4. Software safety lifecycle for the KNICS RPS and PLC systems

Additional failure assumptions are made. The assumed failures must be controlled by the system. Of course support mechanisms to design a fault tolerant system architecture are necessary. Since no single method can prove the case of a correctness of software a set of different measures gives sufficient evidence.

The bundle of different measures and activities to ensure a safety and reliability comprise:

- Application of the safety lifecycle, including verification and validation activities,
- Safety and reliability analysis,
- Fault tolerant system design.

In the KNICS project, a safety lifecycle was developed as shown in Fig. 4 with the quantitative approach for the reliability analysis of the system and hardware levels, but with the qualitative approach for the safety analysis of the software.

We used the software fault tree analysis (FTA) method for the design and coding phases of the lifecycle. After creating the software fault trees by using the procedure, they produced two groups of outcomes from the software FTA. One group is the recommendations to improve the fault tolerance, and the other is the influence on a testing.

5 Software Safety Analysis Methods for KNICS

The safety assessment of the software for the KNICS RPS and PLC is a joint Korean/German project. ISTec is a 3rd party assessor of the software of the real time operating system pCOS and of the safety communication modules HR-SDL and HR-SDN.

The assessment work has been performed in parallel with the development process of the software components pCOS, HR-SDL and HR-SDN. This means that after each development step KAERI has delivered the according documentation which had been assessed following the procedure for the assessment of the safety critical software developed and applied by ISTec [3].

For practical reasons and to enhance the effectiveness of the assessment process the work has been done in close collaboration between ISTec and KAERI. Therefore, a subset of documents has been evaluated mainly by KAERI which are:

- Software requirements specification,
- Software design specification, and
- Implementation specification (source code).

In the cases where the documents have been evaluated by KAERI, ISTec has checked the results of the evaluation (the verification report) supplemented by spot checks of the development documents.

Failure mode and effect analysis (FMEA) method was used for the system hazard analysis, the hazard and operability (HAZOP) method for the software requirements, design, and implementation. Fault tree analysis (FTA) method was also used mainly for the safety analysis of the coding level during the RPS development. These three methods achieve cause-consequence coverage in the safety analysis as shown in Fig 5.

All other documents such as the concept report, test specification, component test report and log, and the integration test report and log have been checked completely with respect to ISTec's assessment procedure for safety critical software. This procedure, the so-called software type test (see Fig. 6), was developed by GRS/ISTec 12 years ago, analogous to the German nuclear safety standard KTA 3503 and in compliance with IEC 60880.

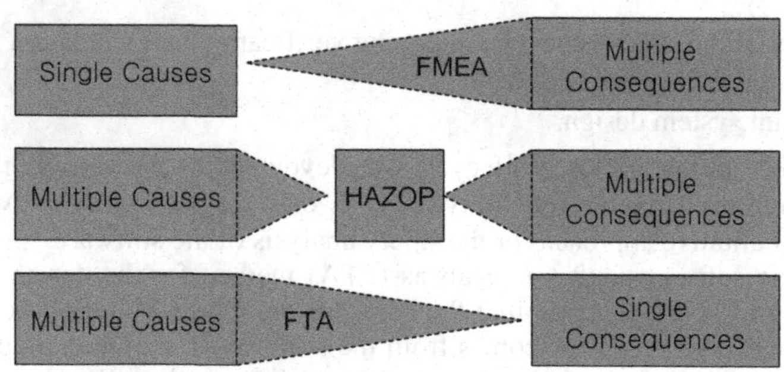

Fig. 5. Cause-consequence coverage of the methods

It has been applied successfully to the qualification of the TELEPERM XS software [3]. This procedure is based on the software lifecycle described in the IEC 60880.

During the assessment all the documents, starting with the concept report to the test reports, are checked for:

- consistency,
- formal correctness, and
- functional traceability.

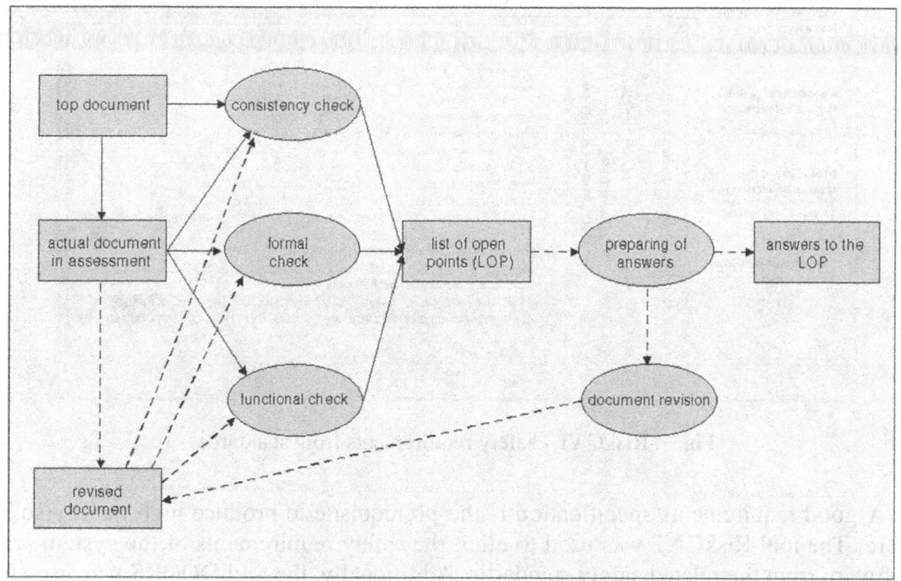

Fig. 6. Software type test procedure

The functional and non-functional requirements are applied as stated in the corresponding IEC and IEEE standards.

Questions and remarks that arise during the checks are collected in "Lists of open points" (LOPs) and they are transmitted to the developers. It is expected that the developers respond to the LOPs and, if necessary, revise the document under assessment. The response is analysed. The procedure is repeated until no open points remain.

The working results are documented in an assessment report. If the assessment succeeds, certificates for the software components are issued.

In the framework of a 3rd party assessment, ISTec evaluated the Concept Report (KNICS-PLC-CR101). The evaluation results were documented in a list of open points. During a workshop meeting the findings of this LOP were discussed in detail and clarified. KAERI documented the answers and sent them to ISTec. Additionally, the Concept Report was subjected to a revision.

Based on the experience as a 3rd party assessor, ISTec could give recommendations which contributed to the KNICS project. In the course of the assessment project several workshop meetings were held which proved to be of great help in clarifying the open points.

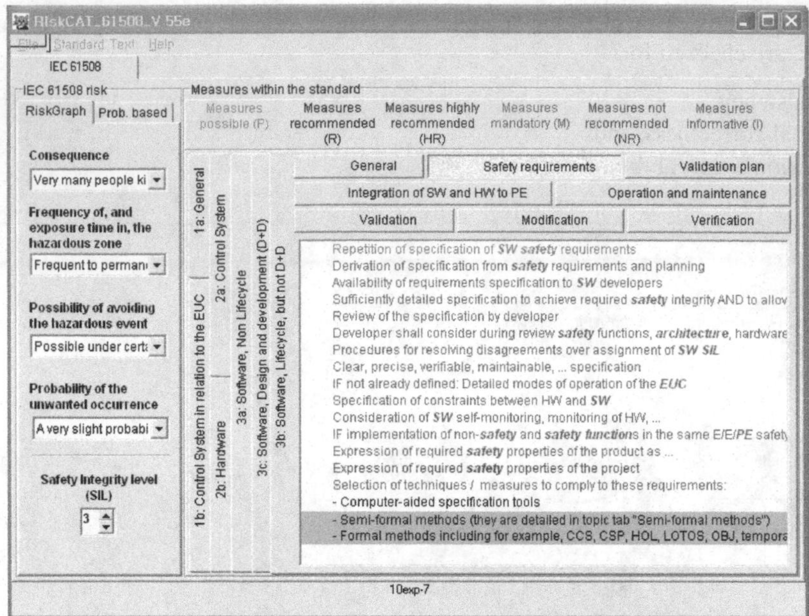

Fig. 7. RiskCAT - safety requirements from standards

A good requirements specification is the prerequisite to produce high quality software. The tool RiskCAT was used to elicit the safety requirements of the system and software from the related safety standards. Additionally, the tool DOORS was used to analyze the traceability of the safety requirements from the standards and customers through the safety lifecycle.

6 Conclusions

This paper discusses the software lifecycle safety analysis tasks for the safety-critical software protection system in nuclear power plants. In order to meet the requirements from both the frameworks of the standards, IEC and IEEE, the safety lifecycles have been compared, and the differences of the frameworks have been identified. The overall safety lifecycle and the software safety lifecycle have been compared for developing a Reactor Protection System and its components by using the KNICS PLC as an example. The differences of the software safety lifecycles of the IEC 61508-3, IEC 60880, IEEE 1228-1994, and IEEE standards 7-4.3.2-2003 have been elucidated. The software safety lifecycle applied for the KNICS RPS and PLC systems was introduced and the relationship of the safety analysis and testing for a software safety lifecycle was identified. Software safety assessment methods were described that have been applied for the KNICS RPS and PLC systems.

When we used the HAZOP method for the hazard analysis of the software requirements in the KNICS project, it was difficult to create the checklists with guide phrases for a real-time operating system pCOS and the communication modules HR-SDL and

HR-SDN. The software FTA method was applied for the RPS software. However, there are general limitations in most software FTA techniques.

- Safety-critical software, whose safety has been analyzed and validated by using the FTA techniques, cannot be re-used in other applications without performing a separate analysis unless its environment is identical.
- Within very large systems, it is often prohibitive to perform a complete FTA as the fault trees become huge and difficult to relate to the plant and its operation.
- Since software FTA is a static technique, it does not lend itself to situations where timing scenarios must be represented and analyzed.

In order to overcome these limitations of a software FTA method, the causal requi rements for a safety analysis (CRSA) method [4] was developed. The KNICS is still an on-going project. New method of a software FTA, CRSA will be applied to the sa fety analysis of the software requirements for RPS system. In addition, the technical experience from the project is expected to be applied to other safety-critical software industries.

Acknowledgment

This work is being carried out for the research entitled "Development of the Licensing Techniques for Digital I&C" as part of the KNICS project, which is under the auspices of the Ministry of Commerce, Industry and Energy (MOCIE), and for the research entitled "Development of Safety Criteria Framework for Railway Software," which is under the auspices of the Ministry of Construction and Transportation (MOCT) in Korea.

References

1. Leveson, N. G. and Stolzy, J. L.: Safety analysis of Ada programs using fault trees. IEEE Transactions on Reliability, Vol R-32, No-5, (1983)
2. Ramamoorthy, C. V. Bastini, F. B.: Software reliability – Status and perspective. IEEE Transactions on Software Engineering. SE-8(1982) 354-371
3. Lindner, A., Wach, D.: Experiences gained from independent assessment in licensing of advanced I&C systems in nuclear power plants. Nuclear Technology Vol. 143 (2003) 197-207
4. Lee J. S., Kwon K. C., and Cha S. D.: Software safety analysis of digital protection system requirements using a qualitative formal method, Nuclear Technology Vol. 147 (2004) 227-239
5. Leveson, N. G.: Safeware: system safety and computers, Addison Wesley, (1995)
6. IEC 61508-1, Functional safety of electrical/electronic/programmable electronic safety-related systems –Part 1:General requirements
7. IEC 61508-2, Functional safety of electrical/electronic/programmable electronic safety-related systems –Part 2: Requirements for electrical/electronic/programmable electronic safety-related systems
8. IEC 61508-3, Functional safety of electrical/electronic/programmable electronic safety-related systems –Part 3: Software requirements

9. IEC 60880, Nuclear Power Plants – I&C systems important to safety – Software aspects for computer-based systems performing category A functions
10. IEC 61513, Nuclear Power Plants – Instrumentation and control for systems important to safety – General requirements for systems
11. IEEE Std. 7-4.3.2-2003, IEEE Standard Criteria for Digital Computers in Safety Systems of Nuclear Power Generating Stations
12. IEEE Std. 1228-1994, IEEE Standard for Software Safety Plan

Regulatory Software Configuration Management System Design

I-Hsin Chou[1, 2] and Chin-Feng Fan[2]

[1] Institute of Nuclear Energy Research, Atomic Energy Council,
P.O. Box 3-11, Lung-Tan, 325, Tao-Yuan, Taiwan, R.O.C
ihsin@iner.gov.tw

[2] Computer Science and Engineering Dept., Yuan-Ze U,
No. 135, Yuan-Tung Road, Chungli, Taoyuan, Taiwan, R.O.C
csfanc@saturn.yzu.edu.tw

Abstract. The gap between nuclear safety-related regulations and the commercial software configuration management causes software quality concerns for Digital Control and Information System (DCIS) of a nuclear power plant. The main reason is that the DCIS of a nuclear plant are usually constructed by multiple vendors and each vendor of the DCIS has its own development environment, such as its development platform, software language and source code. The difficulty often comes from lacking consistence and integrity among the different vendors. Therefore, it is a great challenge to manage all configuration items from multiple vendors and to manage the heterogeneous subsystems within DCIS of a nuclear power plant. The Capability Maturity Model Integrated (CMMI) defines the Configuration Management (CM) as a process area that provides detailed practices of controlling and managing the software work products. This paper proposes an Agent-based Software Configuration Management (ABSCM) System based on the CM process area of CMMI as well as nuclear safety-related regulations to support the operation of nuclear power plant.

1 Introduction

Traditionally, a Configuration Management (CM) program ensures the construction, operation, maintenance, and testing of the physical facilities in accordance with the design requirements as expressed in the design documentation, and to maintain this consistency throughout the operational life-cycle phase, particularly when as changes are being made [2].

Software Configuration Management (SCM) is a process that deals with identifying configuration items, controlling changes to the configuration items, and maintaining integrity and traceability of the configuration items throughout the software development life cycle. The configuration items include software work products delivered to customers and items required to create the software work products such as software design documents, test documents, test data, compilers, etc. Therefore, SCM can be regarded as a subset of general CM [6].

J. Górski (Ed.): SAFECOMP 2006, LNCS 4166, pp. 99 – 112, 2006.

Digital Control and Information System (DCIS) have been used in many industries, including transportation, chemical industry, and conventional power plants [1]. But, the new digital technology has been rarely implemented in nuclear power plants. The most important reason is that the efforts needed to provide adequate evidence that the DCIS can be used in non-safety and safety applications [2]. There are many advantages offered by the DCIS design, but still there are a few disadvantages. One of the main disadvantages is that system designs require interfaces to integrate the individual subsystem into the complex DCIS whose interfaces usually are difficult to be specified, coded, assessed, and tested. Experience has shown that care must be taken during the digital system design in order to handle the interfaces prudently to minimize the possibilities for errors [2]. More specifically, the requirements for design of interfaces shall be specified carefully to ensure successful DCIS system integration, operation, and reliability [1].

The International Atomic Energy Agency (IAEA) Incident Reporting System (IRS) shows that on average 25% of nuclear power plant recorded events were caused by configuration errors or deficiencies [2]. To ensure the consistency of the change with the original software design and to improve the visibility of software changes, it was essential to develop an integrated software configuration management system for DCIS.

For enhancing safety, reliability, plant operability, availability and maintainability of nuclear power plants, U.S. Nuclear Regulatory Commission (USNRC) issued a set of safety system software regulations. Moreover, Software Engineering Institute (SEI) also issued the Capability Maturity Model Integrated (CMMI) to improve deliverable quality of products. The aim of this paper is to propose an Agent-based Software Configuration Management system (ABSCM) based on CM process area of CMMI as well as nuclear regulations to support the operation of nuclear power plants.

We will briefly introduce the system specifications in Section 2. Section 3 describes the results of requirements analysis that consists of functional and non-functional requirements. Then, a Regulatory SCM Process Model (RSCMPM) is presented to identify all activities and to meet system specification in Section 4. The detailed develop processes of ABSCM are presented in Section 5. Finally, some conclusions and our future work are given.

2 Regulatory Software Configuration Management System Specifications

This section firstly describes a requirement acquisition mechanism to meet both nuclear regulations and software quality. Then we will list all detailed items of system requirement resources.

2.1 Requirement Acquisition

The nuclear power industry has developed and implemented a quality assurance program for all aspects of the design, manufacture, construction, documentation, and operation of safety-related systems and components. This is specified in ASME NQA-1-1989. ASME NQA-1-1989 provides the overall quality assurance program requirement. Our regulatory SCM requirements are different and may not directly relate to the overall quality assurance outlined in ASME NQA-1-1989. Therefore, we adopted three software-related resources for our requirement acquisition, namely, Safety-related regulations, CM of CMMI and IEEE standards. This is shown in Fig.1. CM process area of CMMI described generic and specific practices to be referenced. Safety-related regulations indicated these criteria for safety system software. Moreover, IEEE industry standards describe software industry approaches to SCM that are generally accepted in the software engineering community.

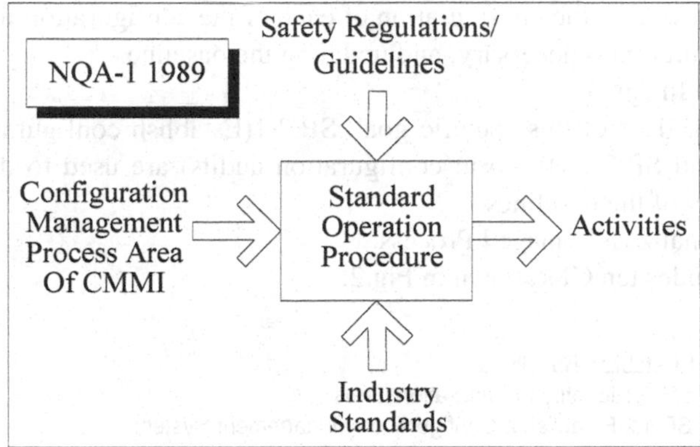

Fig. 1. Activities and requirement acquisition

2.2 Configuration Management (CM) Process Area of Capability Maturity Model Integrated (CMMI)

The Software Engineering Institute (SEI) is a research and development center sponsored by the U.S. Department of Defense and operated by Carnegie Mellon University. The SEI developed the CMMI to help organizations improve development processes and deliverable quality of their products and services through better management and technical practices. There are multiple CMMI models staged or continuous representations are available, as generated from the CMMI Framework. Consequently, you need to be prepared to decide which CMMI model best fits your organization's process-improvement needs. The CMMI staged representation defines five levels of process maturity. Each maturity level builds upon key elements, called Process Areas (PA). The CM is one of PAs at the Level two of the CMMI. The CM includes three Specific Goals (SGs) and one Generic Goal (GG). To achieve specific and generic goal, Specific Practices (SP) and Generic Practices (GP) are included as shown in Fig.2. The related goals are explained below [8]:

- SG 1: Establish Baselines.
To achieve this goal, three practices are covered by this specific goal. SP 1.1 (Identify configuration items) is in charge to identify the configuration items, components, and related work products that will be placed under configuration management. SP 1.2 (Establish a configuration management system) is in charge to establish and maintain a configuration management and change management system for controlling work products. SP 1.3 (Create or release baselines) is used to create or release baselines for internal use and for delivery to the customer.
- SG 2: Track and Control Changes.
The specific practices under this specific goal serve to maintain the baselines. SP 2.1(Track change requests) addresses not only new or changed requirements, but also failures and defects in the work product. SP 2.2 (Control configuration items), this control includes tracking the configuration of each of the configuration items, approving a new configuration if necessary, and updating the baseline.
- SG 3: Establish Integrity.
Both specific practices of this specific goal, SP 3.1(Establish configuration management records) and SP 3.2 (Perform configuration audits) are used to document and audit the integrity of the baselines.
- GG2: Institutionalize a Managed Process.
The process includes ten GPs shown in Fig.2.

SG 1 Establish Baselines
- SP 1.1 Identify Configuration Items
- SP 1.2 Establish a Configuration Management System
- SP 1.3 Create or Release Baselines

SG 2 Track and Control Changes
- SP 2.1 Track Change Requests
- SP 2.2 Control Configuration Items

SG 3 Establish Integrity
- SP 3.1 Establish Configuration Management Records
- SP 3.2 Perform Configuration Audits

GG 2 Institutionalize a Managed Process
- GP 2.1 (CO 1) Establish an Organizational Policy
- GP 2.2 (AB 1) Plan the Process
- GP 2.3 (AB 2) Provide Resources
- GP 2.4 (AB 3) Assign Responsibility
- GP 2.5 (AB 4) Train People
- GP 2.6 (DI 1) Manage Configurations
- GP 2.7 (DI 2) Identify and Involve Relevant Stakeholders
- GP 2.8 (DI 3) Monitor and Control the Process
- GP 2.9 (VE 1) Objectively Evaluate Adherence
- GP 2.10 (VE 2) Review Status with Higher Level Management

Fig. 2. Practice-to-goal relationship table

2.3 Nuclear Safety-Related Regulations and Industry Standards

There are a few safety-related regulations for nuclear digital I&C from the USNRC, such as 10CFR 55, 10CFR 21.51, 10CFR 50 Appendix A and Appendix B. In 10 CFR

Part 50, "Domestic Licensing of Production and Utilization Facilities," paragraph 55a(a)(1) requires, that systems and components are designed, tested, and inspected to meet quality standards commensurate with the safety function to be per-formed. Criterion 1, "Quality Standards and Records," of Appendix A, "General Design Criteria for Nuclear Power Plants," of 10 CFR Part 50 requires, that appropriate records of the design and testing of systems and components important to safety are maintained by or under the control of the nuclear power unit licensee throughout the life of the unit. 10CFR 50 Appendix B, "Quality Assurance Criteria for Nuclear Power Plants and Fuel Reprocessing Plants," to 10 CFR Part 50 describes criteria that must be met by a quality assurance program for systems and components that prevent or mitigate the consequences of postulated accidents. A specific requirement is contained in 10 CFR 50.55a (h), which requires that reactor protection systems satisfy the criteria of IEEE Std 279, "Criteria for Protection Systems for Nuclear Power Generating Stations". Many of the criteria in Appendix B to 10 CFR Part 50 contain requirements closely related to the configuration management activity [4]. However, these regulations do not specify detailed instructions and steps. Therefore, we also have gone through all related Regulatory Guidelines (RG) for digital computer system software used in safety systems in nuclear power plants such as RG 1.169- "Configuration management plans " and RG 1.168 to RG 1.173. We found these regulatory guidelines also endorse industry standards such as IEEE 828-1998 "IEEE Standard for Software Configuration Management Plans" and IEEE 1042- "IEEE Standard for Software Configuration Management". IEEE Standards provide guidance for planning and executing an SCM program. Compliance with standards does not guarantee that regulatory requirements will be met. However, compliance does ensure that practices accepted within various technical communities will be incorporated into the development and quality assurance processes used to design safety systems. Therefore, both safety-related regulations and industry standards are our important requirements resources.

3 Requirements Analysis

After analyzing the system specifications as the above section presented, we mapped each specific item of the specifications to functional or nonfunctional feature as shown in Fig. 3. These features can be modeled as our regulatory SCM process model.

3.1 Functional Requirements

Functional Requirements (FRs) define what is necessary for those specific activities to perform within SCM. That means an activity needs its data inputs or flow in order to be operational. FRs of an activity can be modeled as a data flow that defines input/output relations between activities.

3.1.1 Basic SCM Function

The basic functional requirements of SCM are listed below:

- Identification, trace and control of all design codes, documents generated for the application software and all test procedures including related deficiency reports. It

also includes those specific configuration items in nuclear safety regulations, such as commercial products or components used in a nuclear safety system.
- Provide relationship link from design data document to software application and documentation.
- The change of data and the introduction into the software configuration must be carried out under control of the software maintenance environment. Furthermore, a report is required which identifies all configuration items impacted by the change. Those activities include change request, change analysis, design specification, related document, implementation and system release.
- All changes applied to the configuration need to be recorded automatically in the software maintenance environment.

Source / Feature	Safety Regulation /Regulatory Guide	IEEE Industry Standards	Configuration Management Process Area
Function	•Specific requirement on protection system •Endorse IEEE industry Standards •Reflect to standards review plan	•Specific SCM activities •Change management •Supplier control •Tools, techniques and methodologies •Provide some samples plan	•Specific and generic goal •Specific and generic practice •Refer to other process area
Non-function	•Quality •Reliability •Quality assurance •Manage configuration activities	•Traceability •Consistency •No specific descriptions for safety system	•Integrity •Support other process area •No specific descriptions for safety system

Fig. 3. Functional and non-functional requirements

3.1.2 Workflow Management

Workflow management is used to trace processes by monitoring the review path. SCM workflow should be modeled to follow the standard operation procedures. In the workflow management mechanism, release of Configuration Item (CI) is channeled automatically to the person who has the right to release items. If a CI has interface with any other CI; the workflow mechanism automatically transfers the request to the personnel responsible by E-mail. As a CI action is registered by the system, the authorized persons can see the status and the position of the request.

3.1.3 Web Graphic Interface

It is very convenient to control multiple vendor software by a web enabling graphic interface. Concerning the heterogeneous development environmental used within the system, E-Mail can be used for notification mechanism. Furthermore, the system should select web-based technology such as XML to improve data exchange and communication efficiency.

3.2 Non Functional Requirement

The Non-Functional Requirements (NFRs) of an activity is to specify properties or environmental requirements like the need for traceability, consistence or integrity requirements.

3.2.1 Traceability

The main objective of software configuration management and maintenance is to establish traceability among involved development elements called CI, such as design requirements, firmware/physical configuration, software, documentation, and to maintain the traceability throughout the operational life-cycle phases, particularly as changes are being made. Any changes of made to an element should be reflected in its related elements.

3.2.2 Consistency Maintenance

To ensure the safety of the nuclear power plant, two requirements should be designed in system design: consistency checking and analyzing the impact of change. The consistency checking is to check consistency in one single system or between different systems of the CIs from design specifications to implementation. This may be achieved via analyzing the source file and description of the CI.

For a composite CI, impact analysis may be analyzed according to the architectural description because the change of an element of a composite CI will affect the elements directly connected to the changed element.

3.2.3 Information Integration

Another important requirement is information integration because the ability to automatically update data is needed between related subsystems. This function leads to better decision-making and resolution of problems. Therefore, it is essential to provide comprehensive capability to manage heterogeneous configuration items, which are built from system level including software and hardware.

4 Regulatory SCM Process Model (RSCMPM)

Based on the above results of requirement analysis, we proposed a Regulatory SCM Process Model (RSCMPM) to identify five activities as shown in Fig.4. Each activity is referenced the goals or practices of CM PAs. Moreover, these activities also contain software management mechanisms which refer to nuclear safety-related regulations or IEEE standards, such as defining safety-related configuration items, change control with safety analysis, naming conventions of nuclear power plants, accessing control of critical systems, control sub-vendor document and process audition. We will discuss these activities phase more detailed in the following subsections.

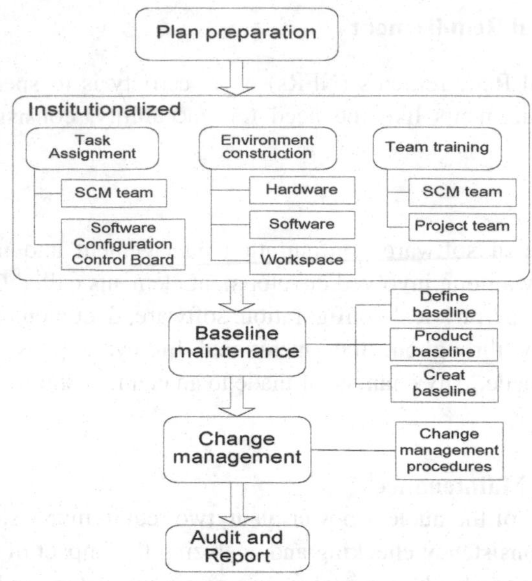

Fig. 4. Regulatory SCM process model

4.1 Plan Preparation

In the plan preparation activity phase, a SCM plan should be produced, which includes the contents as follows:

- Identifies SCM related regulations of nuclear power plants.
- Identifies the responsibilities and authorities for managing and accomplishing the planned SCM activities. [10]
- Identifies all activities to be performed in the project.
- Identifies the required coordination of SCM activities with the other activities in the project.
- Identifies tools and physical and human resources required for execution of the plan.
- Identifies how the plan will be kept current while in effect.

4.2 Institutionalized Activity Phase

Institutionalized activity phase is used for supporting SCM activities, which include task assignment, environment construction and team training tasks needed to perform. In task assignment, both Software Configuration Control Board (SCCB) and SCM team representatives need to be identified firstly from related groups. The SCCB authorizes establishment of software baselines and identification of configuration items. The SCCB also involves in a software change procedure because they represent interests of all groups who are affected by changes to software baselines. Secondly, the project manager should construct a SCM development environment for SCM system developers. Thirdly, all SCM team members are assigned to attend training courses.

4.3 Baseline Maintenance

A SCM repository is constructed in the institutionalized activity phase. In the baseline maintenance activity phase, baselines will be created and defined. The area of baseline repository is divided into two parts: Document Library and Source Library. Before each baseline creation, a baseline report should be published. The SCCB and project team members review the baseline report to ensure the accuracy of the baseline contents and to check if the contents are satisfied the baseline purpose before baseline creation. According to configuration items listed in baseline reports as planned schedule, a baseline will be created. In each baseline creation, a SCM team creates baselines of documents and source code. The baseline of documents is an archive or set of approved documents that satisfy the baseline purpose.

4.4 Change Management

Change management procedure is the most important task in this phase. A SCM team is responsible for managing and controlling the status of a change request in a project. Any updates to change requests and software baselines are performed under authority of the SCCB. Any raised change requests must be documented and sent to the SCM team. The SCM team works with the SCCB for a change request assessment. The SCCB can identify a specialist to assess and to give comments on the request. If any change requests about safety-related, a safety analysis report should be preview before change. The assessment result such as rejection, acceptance, or pending will be recorded as the change request status, and returned to the owner of the change request and to the project team by the SCM team.

4.5 Audit and Report

A baseline is considered as approved for further use after the SCCB considers that the baseline audit report is completed. A SCM team periodically produces SCM reports to inform updated SCM activities to project team members, the SCCB and the affected groups. The reporting period defined in this paper is one month, so the SCM group produces monthly SCM report.

5 Agent-Based Software Configuration Management System (ABSCM)

In this section, we propose an Agent-based Software Configuration Management System called ABSCM to meet the above requirements. More detailed about ABSCM will be presented below respectively.

5.1 System Analysis

Unified Modeling Language (UML) is a widely adopted in object-oriented analysis and design stages. But, sometimes UML is not easy to analyze workflow-based system requirements, moreover, users may not be familiar with UML models, such as use case diagrams, class diagrams and dynamic diagrams. Therefore, Structured

Analysis and Design Techniques (ex: IDEF0, IDEF3 and DFD) were adopted first to analyze all activities within SCM. We propose a combined object oriented analysis and structured analysis technique to analyze data and workflow in system modeling [9]. We then converted the resultant models to UML diagrams for implementation. Our system analysis diagram is shown in Fig. 5.

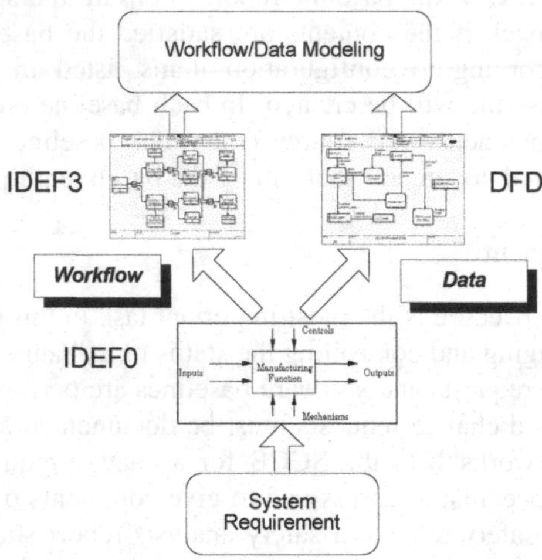

Fig. 5. System flow and data analysis diagram

IDEF0 stands for Integrated DEFinition Language, which is a methodology for describing, managing and improving complex processes and systems. IDEF3 model is a process flow model that graphically describes and documents the process flow, process relationships, and process objects. Data Flow Diagram (DFD) will also be used to describe the process along with input and output data.

5.2 Agent-Based Framework

There are two roles in our ABSCM: I&C SCM system and agent. I&C SCM system will maintain central database and respond to overall system configuration management. Each agent can operate subsystem SCM activities independently (as shown in Fig. 6). We presented three merits of agent-based framework as below:

1. Agent-based philosophy for modeling and managing organizational relationships is appropriate for dealing with the dependencies and interactions that exist in complex systems.
2. Agent-based structure can avoid the complexity of system integration, and each subsystem can operate SCM activities at the same time.
3. Agent-based decomposition is an effective way of partitioning the problem space of a complex system.

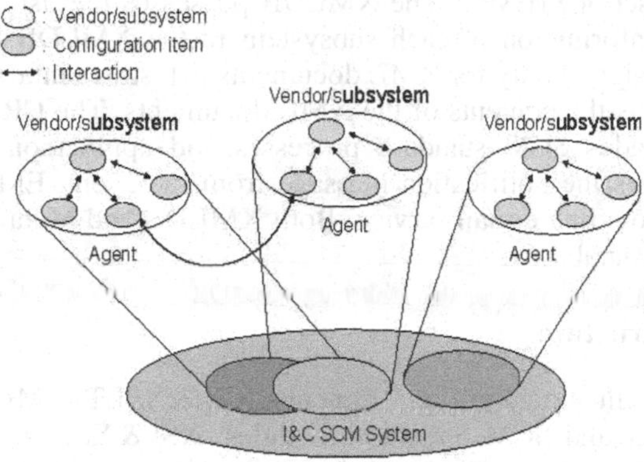

Fig. 6. Agent-based framework

5.3 System Architecture

Figure 7 illustrates the architecture of ABSCM, in which I&C central SCM system controls the configuration information of subsystems equipped with XML-based configuration agents. User can access I&C SCM using browser via any local agent, and all SCM activities will be handled by agents and central SCM system depends on the cross-reference index. The central SCM and agent architecture are described as below.

5.4 Central SCM Database

The central SCM database has five modules: XML database (XMLDB), cross-reference service (CRS), workflow process service (WPS), document service engine

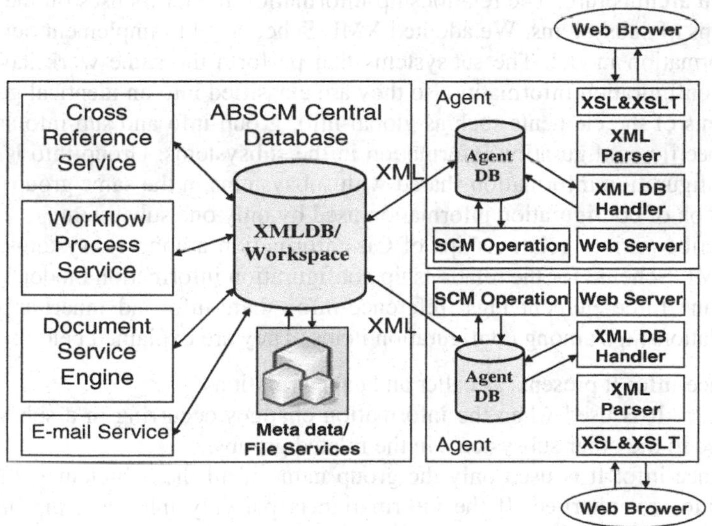

Fig. 7. Architecture of ABSCM

(DSE) and e-mail service (EMS). The XMLDB possesses the list of subsystems and the configuration information of each subsystem in the XMLDB [7]. XMLDB is a special database designed only for XML documents [5], stores intact XML documents and partially controls the contents of the XML documents. The CRS processes information. WPS provides SCM standard processes and application status to various agents. DSE receives the notification message from the agent. EMS connects to the POP3 server for providing e-mail service. Both XMLDB and Meta data are resources of the central SCM database.

5.5 Agent Side Structure

The agent structure illustrated in Fig. 7 contains XSL&XSLT, XML parser, XML DB handler, Web server and SCM operation modules. XSL&XSL transforms the XML form into the HTML form to offer a web-based user interface for browsing users. The XML parser module allows for an agent to parse and access the contents of the XML message. The XMLDB handler module processes information in agent database (agent DB). The SCM operation module has five methods: get, add, delete, modify and create. These methods are used to support SCM activities of agent-based subsystems. Similar to XMLDB of central SCM, agent DB are also special databases designed for storing and controlling XML documents.

5.6 Configuration Information Exchange

XML is particularly useful to integrate and exchange the information in a heterogeneous environment, which can be used to describe the configuration information, exchange messages, relationship information, etc [5]. By using an HTTP interaction operation model, users easily access SCM operations within the agent environment. In order to use automatic reconfiguration of related subsystems, we propose a configuration information model and relationship information model that can apply to DCIS agent-based architecture. The relationship information model focuses on the dynamic relationships of subsystems. We adopted XML Schema [5] to implement our configuration information model. The subsystems that perform the same work have almost the same configuration information, so they are classified into an identical group. The sub-elements of the elements such as global-info, group-info and sub-info are to present the specific configuration information in the subsystems. Group-info is a collection of configuration information shared with subsystems in the same group. Sub-info is a collection of configuration information used by only one subsystem.

To describe various relationships of CIs information among subsystems, we propose an XML Schema for the relationship configuration information model.

We define three-element tags: reference-info, share-info and inheritance-info to express relationships among configuration items. They are explained below:

1. Reference-info: It presents as caller and callee relations.
2. Share-info: It is used when the information changes occurring in a subsystem are delivered to the other subsystems in the related groups.
3. Inheritance-info: It is used only the group name if all the sub-elements under the group-info are inherited. If the information is partially inherited, the inheritance element requires both the group name and the inheritance-info name. It is used

when the child node modifies the inherited information independent of the parent node. We also use "share-info" and "inheritance-info" relations to support analyzers in change impact analysis. At the same time, XML tags also can be used to show change history. The changed fragments may be marked using new/removed/changed tags.

5.7 Implementation

The workflow and data model diagrams were implemented by using AllFusion Process Modeler software. System implement platform and software development tool adopted Microsoft .NET framework and Visual Stduio.Net 2003. For the development of interactive user interface, the technology employed is Microsoft ASP-based IIS.

For validating and simplifing our ABSCM architecture, the first prototype application: Windows Version SCM (WVCM) without web capability has been constructed in our lab. We developed XML-based SCM environment using Microsoft Visual Basic 6.0 and Microsoft Access. User can customize XML tags to markup CIs and select all kind of reference types in WVCM. All basic SCM functions that described in Section 3 are implemented in WVCM. For example, change request form will automatically deliver via e-mail to the designated receivers according to the customized workflow. "Reference-info" and "Inheritance-info" of XML tag are used to support analyzers in change impact analysis and change history.

6 Conclusion

The nuclear industry is one of the most regulated and complex industries in the world. The importance of software configuration management and software maintenance is clearly understood, but there is yet no clear roadmap on planning and implementation. Therefore, we propose an agent-based framework with XML technology to manage and maintain multi-vendor and heterogeneous software environment. We also have presented both configuration and relation information models that can be applied to our agent-based framework using an XML Schema. The pilot windows version is implemented and our results indicated its feasibility.

Taiwan is constructing its fourth nuclear power plant (Lungmen project), which is a full-scope digital I&C developed by General Electric and will ship to Taiwan in 2006. So far, there is no integrated SCM and maintenance environment for I&C of Lungmen project site. Therefore, Institute of Nuclear Energy Research (INER) will cooperate with Taiwan Power Company (TPC) to apply the agent-based SCM concept to manage and maintain digital I&C software of Lungmen project in the near future.

References

1. INTERNATIONAL ATOMIC ENERGY AGENCY: Harmonization of the licensing process for digital instrumentation and control systems in nuclear power plants. IAEA-TECDOC-1327, Vienna (2002)
2. INTERNATIONAL ATOMIC ENERGY AGENCY: Configuration management in nuclear power plants, IAEA-TECDOC-1335, Vienna (2003)

3. U.S. Nuclear Regulatory Commission: Regulatory Guide 1.169, Configuration Management Plans for Digital Computer Software in Safety Systems of Nuclear Power Plants, (1997)
4. INTERNATIONAL ATOMIC ENERGY AGENCY: Modernization of I&C nuclear power plants, IAEA-TECDOC-1016, Vienna (1998)
5. W3C, XML Schema, W3C Recommendation, May (2001).
6. INTERNATIONAL ATOMIC ENERGY AGENCY: Information technology impact on nuclear power plant documentation, IAEA-TECDOC-1284, Vienna (2002).
7. XML: DB, XUpdate, http://www.xmldb.org/xupdate/xupdate-wd.htmSle (2002)
8. Capability Maturity Model® Integration (CMMISM), Version 1.1, Technical Report, CMU/SEI-2002-TR-012, Software Engineering Institute, Pittsburgh, Pa., (2002).
9. I-Hsin Chou, Chin-Feng Fan, Yen-Chang Tzeng: Conceptual nuclear decommissioning knowledge management system design, Proceedings of the Third International Conference on Information Technology and Applications, Sydney, Australia (2005).
10. IEEE 828: IEEE Standard for Software Configuration Management Plans, (1998).

Gaining Confidence in the Software Development Process Using Expert Systems

Mario Brito and John May

Safety Systems Research Centre, Department of Civil Engineering, University of Bristol, Queen's Building , Bristol BS8 1TR - United Kingdom.
{Mario.Brito, J.May}@bristol.ac.uk

Abstract. Software safety standards recommend techniques to use throughout the software development lifecycle. These recommendations are a result of consensus building amongst software safety experts. Thus the reasoning underpinning compliance to these standards tends to be quite subjective. In addition, there are factors such as the size of the project, the effect of a review process on earlier phases of the development lifecycle, the complexity of the design and the quality of the staff, that arguably influence the assessment process but are not formally addressed by software safety standards. In this paper we present an expert system based on Bayesian Belief networks that take into account these and other factors when assessing the integrity at which the software was developed. This system has been reviewed by engineers working with software safety standard IEC61508. In this paper we illustrate some arguments that can be supported using the proposed system.

This paper and the work it describes were partly funded by the Health and Safety Executive. The opinions or conclusions expressed are those of the authors alone and do not necessarily represent the views of the Health and Safety Executive.

Keywords: Software reliability, Safety standards, Integrity claims, Bayesian belief networks.

1 Introduction

Safety critical software is typically developed according to recommendations made by software safety standards. Software safety standards recommend a set of techniques to apply in the various stages of the software development lifecycle. The recommendations made by software safety standards are a result of consensus between software safety engineers. This approach is highly subjective, relying heavily on 'engineering judgment'. Thus when organizations need to follow these standards they face some uncertainty in estimating the rigour at which they managed to comply with the standard. In this paper we address this issue by proposing the use of an expert system based on Bayesian Belief networks (BBNs) to measure the rigour of compliance with software safety standards. Bayesian Belief networks (BBNs) provide a sound framework within which to achieve this.

J. Górski (Ed.): SAFECOMP 2006, LNCS 4166, pp. 113 – 126, 2006.

Expert systems are designed to replicate or replace human reasoning. Since they often focus on a narrow domain it is plausible that under some circumstances they can improve on the performance of humans. For example, these systems can provide powerful reasoning under uncertainty, which humans find difficult especially when confronted with a complex problem containing a large number of factors.

There are two methods for developing expert systems. We can either get the expert system to learn rules from a set of existing data or we can elicit knowledge from a human expert (or group of experts) and develop the expert system to provide the same reasoning as the human expert. The validation of the expert system is done by giving to the expert system unseen scenarios and seeing if predictions made by the expert system matches those of the human expert. Like any other system, expert systems also are developed according to a development lifecycle. Details of the development lifecycle for the type of expert system that we present in this paper are given in [1].

The expert system proposed in this paper is a result of interviews held with experts working with the IEC61508-3 software safety standard [2]. However, it does not restrict its reasoning to that contained within IEC61508; it takes the standard as a guide to process-based integrity assessment, but also includes reasoning paradigms that are not found in IEC61508. The same principles could be applied to other software safety standards such as DO-178 or DEF 00-55.

Bayesian Belief networks were chosen for their ability to capture subjective arguments and because commercial tools already exist to support BBN modeling [3], [4]. One can argue that the process of eliciting expert knowledge is subjective and that it is difficult to build consensus. Whilst this is true, it remains important to reduce subjectivity in safety assessment where possible, and a self-consistent framework for capturing uncertain reasoning is an important step towards that aim. In addition, there are methods that can be applied to reduce the bias in the elicitation process and also to combine opinions of more than one expert, more detail about these techniques can be found in [5],[6]. In order to conduct sensitivity analysis on Bayesian expert systems, Spiegelhalter, Cowell et. al in [7],[8] presented a new approach to measure the expert system's effectiveness. In their publication the authors used logarithmic scoring rules to define monitors for the conditional probability tables. This approach was successfully applied to validate a Bayesian expert system designed to measure the effectiveness of the software inspection process, [9],[10]. We do not apply these sensitivity techniques in this paper, we simply place the experts reasoning within a graphical probabilistic structure.

The use of Bayesian belief networks to predict software integrity based on the software development process has been proposed previously by Hall et. al in the FASGEP project [11]. However the approach presented by these authors is different from ours in the sense that our expert system seeks to assess software integrity based on the principles presented in software safety standards. A number of publications have been published by Fenton and Neil [12],[13],[14] in the development of BBN models for software quality assurance. Models developed by these authors were designed to support software quality assessment, resource management and cost efficiency analysis for software project management. These models do not attempt to measure the rigour of compliance to a software safety standard.

The first application of BBN in the specific context of a software safety standard was presented in [15],[16] by Gran, who studied the standard DO-178. The model presented by Gran comprises two separate blocks, a higher level BBN that represents the quality of product development and a lower level BBN representing the contribution of testing. The higher level BBN is used to provide estimates for the quality of the development process. The BBN representing the testing block uses node Y to estimate the number of failures in N new tests, where N is introduced as hard evidence. The parent nodes of node Y are the number of tests N and the probability of failure P. The latter is estimated based upon the quality of the product development. This BBN can be used to estimate product dependability by linking node P to a node representing the system dependability. Our approach differs from Gran's in the sense that we model the software development lifecycle at a finer level of detail. The BBNs presented in this paper capture the set of activities carried out in each phase of the software development lifecycle, and also interactions between phases. The BBN model presented in this paper combines integrity estimates for all phases of the software development lifecycle in order to compute the overall software integrity. The quality of each single phase is fed forward to affect the quality achieved after subsequent phases. And when errors are found in later phases, that information is fed backward to affect integrity assessments of earlier phases. This phenomenon gives origin to a form of closed loop BBN that has not been proposed before.

In section 2 we provide some background on the type of expert system that we are designing. In section 3 we first address issues concerning compliance to IEC61508-3 and give details of the proposed expert system. In section 4 we provide some examples of how our model can support safety integrity level (SIL) claims within IEC61508-3. Section 5 offers some conclusions and analysis of the results.

2 Background on Bayesian Belief Networks

Expert systems based on Bayesian Belief networks reason about problems that are of a probabilistic nature where there is a causal relationship amongst variables of the domain [17],[18]. The theory supporting Bayesian Belief networks rests on a rich tradition of probability theory, and statistical decision theory and it is supported by excellent axiomatic and behavioural arguments [19]. A Bayesian belief network for a set of variables $\mathbf{X} = \{X_1, X_2, \ldots, X_n\}$ consists of a) a directed network structure that encodes a set of conditional independence assertions about variables in X and b) a set P of 'local' probability distributions associated with each variable, describing the distribution of the variable conditioned on its parent variables. The nodes in the network structure are in one-to-one correspondence with the variables in the probabilistic model.

Typically there are two main tasks in the overall design of BBNs: structure design and parameter elicitation. Structure design involves the task of deciding "what depends on what?" and encoding that using the conditional independence semantics of the network (directed acyclic graph) structure. It can use qualitative information, background knowledge and empirical experience. In some cases, network structure can be learnt, if there is a large body of experimental data. Where this is not the case, the key problem is how to acquire knowledge from domain experts. The task of parameter elicitation, on the other hand, is to fill out the conditional probability tables (CPTs) or node probability tables (NPTs) for every random variable. These can be obtained from either quantitative data or subjective estimation by domain experts. Bayesian belief networks can perform different types of reasoning such as predictions, diagnostics, combined and intercausal. Details about each of these types of reasoning are presented in [19]. Once a Bayesian Belief network is built it can be used to interpret the impact of evidence as it arises, on the distributions of the variables at the nodes.

3 Network Structures

The suggested BBN structures presented in this section represent an attempt to capture the reasoning in software safety standards, but are no means claimed to be fully accurate representations. The structure of the networks, and their conditional probability tables, must be further evolved in a process of expert consensus building. Section 3.1 briefly outlines the process suggested by IEC61508-3.

In order to model the software development process we use two generic BBN structures. One to capture the set of activities that take place in one phase of the development process and a larger BBN to provide interaction between all phases of the development process. Section 3.2 presents the BBN prototype for estimating the integrity of one phase of the software development process and section 3.3 presents the generic model used to capture interaction between several phases of the development process.

3.1 Structure of IEC61508-3 Activities

In IEC61508, system development is structured into three safety lifecycles: the overall, the E/E/PES, and the software. Only the software safety lifecycle is addressed in this paper. The software safety lifecycle phases are ordered according to the well known V diagram for software development.

Table 1. Software safety requirements specification (see part 3 section 7.2 of the standard)

Technique/Measure	SIL 1	SIL 2	SIL 3	SIL 4
1 Computer-aided specification tools	R	R	HR	HR
2a Semi-formal methods	R	R	HR	HR
2b Formal methods including for example, CCS, CSP, HOL, LOTOS, OBJ, temporal logic, VDM and Z	---	R	R	HR
a) The software safety requirements specification will always require a description of the problem in the natural language and any necessary mathematical notation that reflects the application. b) The table reflects additional requirements for specifying the software safety requirements clearly and precisely. c) Appropriate techniques/measures shall be selected according to the safety integrity level. Alternate or equivalent techniques/ measures are indicated by a letter following by a number. Only one of the alternate or equivalent techniques/measures has to be satisfied.				

For each phase, IEC61508 recommends a set of methods to be applied. Table 1 presents all methods recommended by IEC61508-3 for the first phase of the software development lifecycle, software safety requirements specification. More detail about how to apply this standard is given in [20]. Each phase of the software development lifecycle has its own table, and other tables containing recommended methods are presented in appendix A of IEC61508-3. When assessing the integrity of the development process, the safety assessor will try estimate how well an organization complied with the recommendations presented in these tables. Therefore the overall integrity claim for the software development process is a combination of the integrities from individual phases of the development process.

3.2 Single-Phase BBN Prototype

This part of the problem involves prediction of software integrity from the character of the methods used in a single phase of a safety software life-cycle presented in a standard such as IEC61508-3. There is some previous work that is relevant to this problem as summarised briefly in section 1. The network structure in Fig. 1 is proposed.

The main purpose of the BBN is to estimate the significance of the outstanding errors remaining in the system at the end of the phase. This clearly depends on a wide variety of factors, many of which are exposed in the BBN. One important factor that is not present in the BBN is a program's operational profile of inputs during use. A program's reliability depends on this profile. It is assumed (as it is in standards) that such information is implicitly factored in to the assessment i.e. the verification methods used are focused on the proposed usage of the system, so that faults that cause large numbers of failures are found quickly. There is some evidence that if this is true, software reliability (integrity) is predictable provided latent fault numbers can be predicted [21].

In each phase the BBN divides methods into two types: build methods (e.g. in a specification phase, these are the methods used to construct the specification) and verification methods (e.g. methods used within the phase to check that the produced specification is satisfactory).

In the proposed BBN, as a general principle, we model the rigour of application of any method (its effectiveness), in terms of two subsidiary concepts: the inherent power to do the job ('power of build/verification method i' nodes) and the intensity of its application ('intensity at which build/verification method i was applied' nodes). The multiple node notation presented in Fig. 1 is used because every phase of the IEC61508 safety software development lifecycle has one or more build and verification methods, the precise number of nodes depends on:-

1. The number of build and verification methods applied in each phase, and
2. The position of the phase within the whole process (see for example the 'Quality of the verification process…' nodes).

In the generic single phase BBN shown in Fig. 1, phase 'i' is shown with three build methods and three verification methods.

The 'Quality of the development process at phase i' is there to capture the quality of implementation of the build methods. The quality of the development process has a causal effect on the number of faults introduced in the system.

The 'Significance of errors found …' nodes measures the criticality of errors found during the verification process. Errors can have several levels of severity/criticality. This node estimates the criticality of all errors found during the verification process based on estimates for the quality of the 'verification process …', 'quality of the development process…', 'size of the product', 'size of the verification team' and also 'complexity of the verification task'. The node has four possible states {negligible, tolerable, undesirable, intolerable}. Similarly, the 'significance of outstanding errors…' node refers to the effect of the faults that remain undiscovered. The latter node will ultimately feed in to the computation of probable integrity levels (see section 3.3). The computation of the probability distribution for this node from its parents is one of the most contentious aspects of the reasoning in safety standards. In brief, the rationale is that the build processes allow an assessment of integrity prior to verification, and then verification finds errors which results in an improved integrity assessment. It may be that there are other, more comprehensive network structures that can capture the underlying reasoning more accurately. However, it should be possible to capture such reasoning in BBN form, and thus to expose it to expert scrutiny. The central point of each phase is to estimate the significance of the outstanding errors. This is achieved by assessing the confidence levels for the quality of the development process and also for the significance/criticality of errors found during the verification process. This is assumed to have a direct causal link with the SIL that one can claim for phase i. The significance of outstanding errors can take any value of the following set: {negligible, tolerable, undesirable, intolerable}.

The 'complexity of the build task…' nodes capture the inherent difficulty of the tasks being undertaken in a phase. To see why this is an important factor, suppose a phase was modelled in two ways. Firstly, as a single 'meta-phase'. Secondly, as split into two smaller phases. Further, suppose that the same methods were used in all two phases with the same intensity. Without the complexity node, the estimated quality loss in each sub-phase would be equal to the quality loss for the original meta-phase. Depending on how integrity measures from separate phases are composed, the BBN model could be incoherent (self-contradictory).

The 'Quality of the verification process…' nodes take values from a discrete set of values such as {very poor, poor, medium, good, very good}. Estimations of their values are made based on the rigour at which verification methods were applied and their relevance. The 'relevance of the verification method j for phase i' node effectively 'selects' the verification processes that are relevant to previous phases of the software development lifecycle. Finally, the 'Application factor' nodes model the effect that different industrial sectors have different perceptions as to the degree of rigour at which build methods should be applied and their effectiveness. An alternative approach would be to remove this node and use different NPTs for different industry sectors.

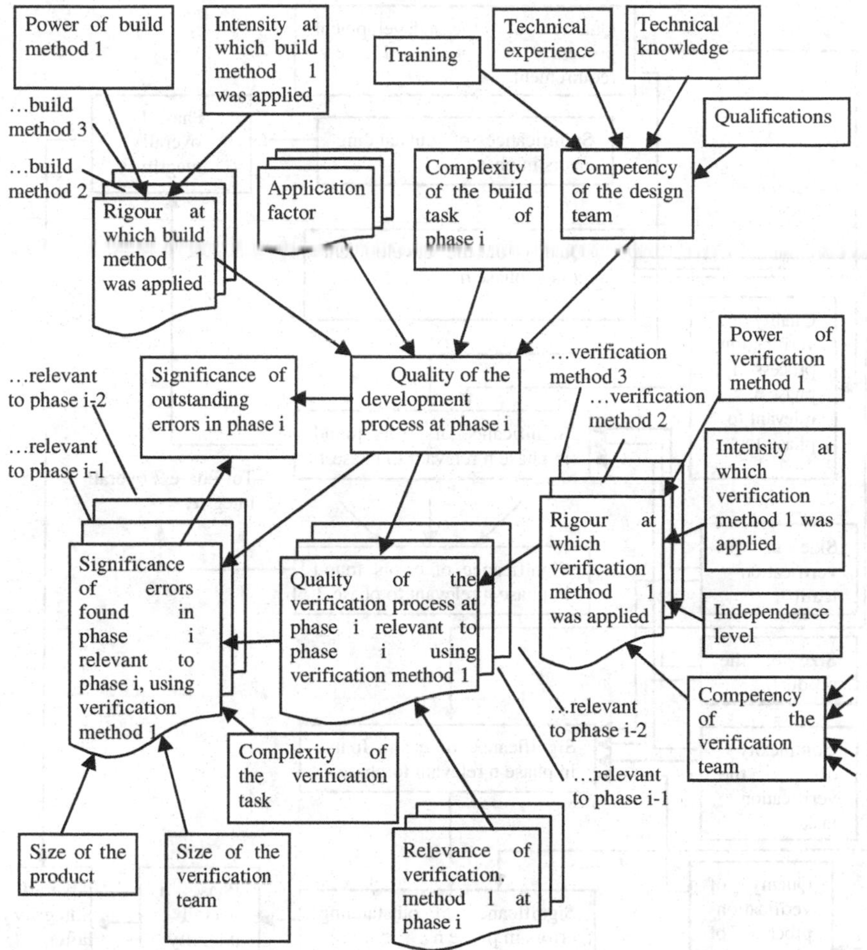

Fig. 1. Generic BBN 'Flat' structure for one phase of the safety software development lifecycle. A rectangular box represents a single discrete variable and a multi-box represents a set of nodes.

3.3 Multi-phase BBN Prototype

In order to model the entire software safety development lifecycle a larger BBN is needed to combine estimations from individual phases. We propose that this larger network should feed forward the quality of the development process of each single phase, since the subsequent development work will depend on that quality. The network also should have a feedback connection so that errors found in later phases have an impact on the contribution to the estimated SIL in a previous phase. This approach allows us to capture intricate influences between 'phases' in a way that goes beyond the reasoning currently used in standards. The generic BBN structure

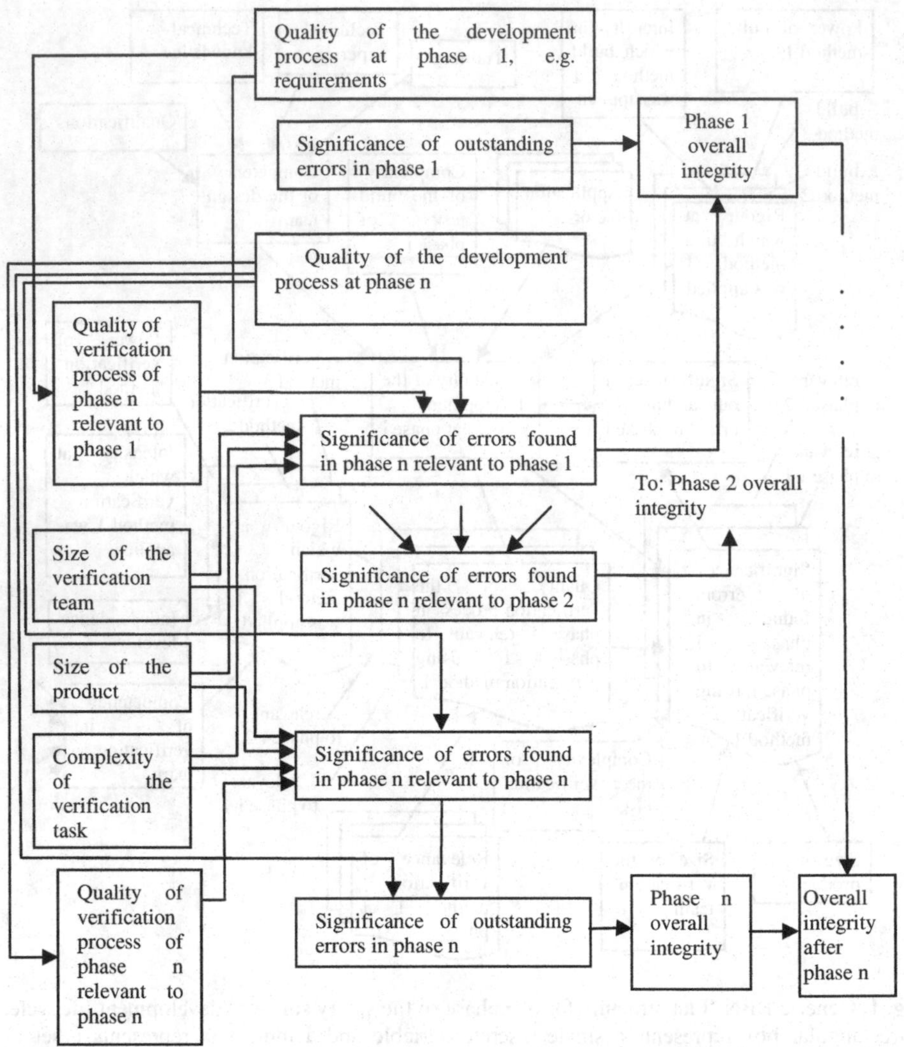

Fig. 2. Generic BBN Multi-Level structure for several phases of the safety software development lifecycle

shown in Fig. 2 presents a sub-net for each phase of the safety software life-cycle and a net for interaction among phases.

The interaction net in Fig. 2 aggregates integrity estimates from multiple phases. In each phase of the safety software development lifecycle, there is a verification exercise that aims to find errors introduced in the development process. This verification exercise, or process, aims to find errors that are relevant to particular phase at which it is being applied. The verification process of a particular phase can clearly also find errors made in previous phases of the safety software lifecycle.

Errors found in later phases are deemed to be corrected resulting in a gain in integrity level achieved at the end of the previous phase. An example is for instance, errors found whilst testing the software. Some of these errors will be relevant to the software implementation phase, however some of these errors may have been introduced in the software functional specification phase.

We implemented a simple rule, that the overall integrity after any phase is the minimum level of integrity achieved for all previous phases including its own. For instance, if one claims SIL 1 for phase 1 and SIL 3 for phase 2, the overall integrity that one can claim after phase 2 is SIL 1. Clearly, this is a candidate for debate, and there is a strong case for additive models (discussed briefly in section 3.2 in the context of the 'complexity…' nodes).

4 Using the BBN

This section gives some examples of the use of BBNs to estimate integrity levels based on the style of reasoning found in safety standards.

4.1 Example 1: Predicting the Criticality of Outstanding Errors in the Software Requirements Specification Phase

This example concerns phase 1 of the safety lifecycle, software safety requirements specification. In the following example, all nodes without parents have been given hard evidence, this means that the variables have been instantiated with a value: a measurement of the quantity being modeled by the variable e.g. the 'Training' node has value 'satisfactory'. This evidence is then propagated through the network updating the belief in the states of the nodes that were not given values. In probability terms, a probability distribution is calculated for each of the latter nodes, conditioned on all of the hard evidence.

The discussion below shows how the integrity level claimed for the safety requirements specification depends on measurements, according to our BBN model.

- Assume that there was overwhelming evidence for the following statements. Formal methods were not applied, the 'Power of the Semi-formal method' used is 'good' and it was applied at a 'low' intensity. In addition, computer aided specification tools were applied at a 'high' intensity. Further more the 'complexity of task' is 'fair'; 'Application factor' is 'medium'. Further, parent nodes of the 'competency of development staff' were set with evidence as follows: 'training' is 'satisfactory', 'technical knowledge' is 'moderate', 'Experience' is 'moderate' and 'qualifications' is 'good'. Then the following distribution would be obtained for the significance of the outstanding errors: {28.28, 35.83, 19.44, 16.44}. This means that there is 28% belief that the criticality of the outstanding errors in phase 1 is negligible, 36% belief that they are tolerable, 19% belief that they are undesirable and 16% belief that they are intolerable. For the same conditions the following distribution is obtained for the 'Overall SIL for Phase 1': {8.23, 14.26, 38.04, 39.47}. This means that there is 39.47% belief that the development process complies with SIL 4, 78% belief that it complies with SIL 3. The states of any node are mutually exclusive, and so by saying that there was 39% confidence that the development process complies with SIL 4 this amount of belief also applies to the statement that the software complies with SIL 3. SIL levels vary from 1 to 4 where level 4 indicates the highest integrity. This scenario is case study 1 in Fig. 3. Note that in Fig. 3, only the confidence estimate that the development process meets SIL 4 is plotted together with the belief that the criticality of the outstanding errors is 'negligible'.

- Consider that all previous evidence remains valid, but semiformal methods were applied at a 'moderate' intensity. Then the following distribution for the 'significance of outstanding errors' would be obtained: {31.02, 37.16, 17.94, 13.89}. Consequently the distribution for the 'Phase 1 overall SIL' would be as follows: {6.81, 12.58, 38.07, 42.55}. Hence one could say with a belief (or 'confidence') of 81% that the development process complies with SIL 3. This scenario is captured in case study 2 in Fig. 3. Whether this improvement of 3% is sufficiently high is a matter for debate, and this shows how these scenarios are a means by which expert consensus can judge the network and subsequently tune the NPTs.
- If in addition to all information previously provided if evidence was collected supporting the fact that a very powerful formal method was applied at a low intensity the following distribution would be obtained for the 'significance of the outstanding errors in phase 1': {54.01, 30.60, 9.53, 5.87}. Consequently the estimated belief that the 'significance of outstanding errors' was negligible increased to 54%. For the same conditions the following distribution would've been obtained for the 'Phase 1 overall SIL': {2.76, 6.59, 29.83, 60.83}. This means that there is now 61% belief that the development process complies with SIL 4. The figures are notional. They are proposed as a basis for future discussion and nothing more. They do however, illustrate the power of the BBN to capture uncertain argumentation of the type needed in standards. This scenario is case study 3 in Fig. 3.
- If formal methods were applied at a high level then the following distribution would be obtained for the 'significance of the outstanding errors in phase 1': {68.87, 23.93, 4.78, 2.42}. For the same conditions the following distribution would be obtained for the 'Phase 1 overall SIL': {1.11, 3.89, 23.45, 71.56}. This means that there is now 72% belief that the development process complies with SIL 4. This scenario is case study 4 illustrated in Fig. 3.

The behaviour of the prototype BBN suggests that the Single-Phase BBN model may usefully be used to capture the reasoning in standards. One idea encapsulated by the BBN in these cases is that using a more powerful method will not necessarily increase integrity unless it is applied diligently.

Fig. 3 presents the belief estimates for the 'significance of outstanding errors in phase 1' and 'Phase 1 overall integrity' nodes.

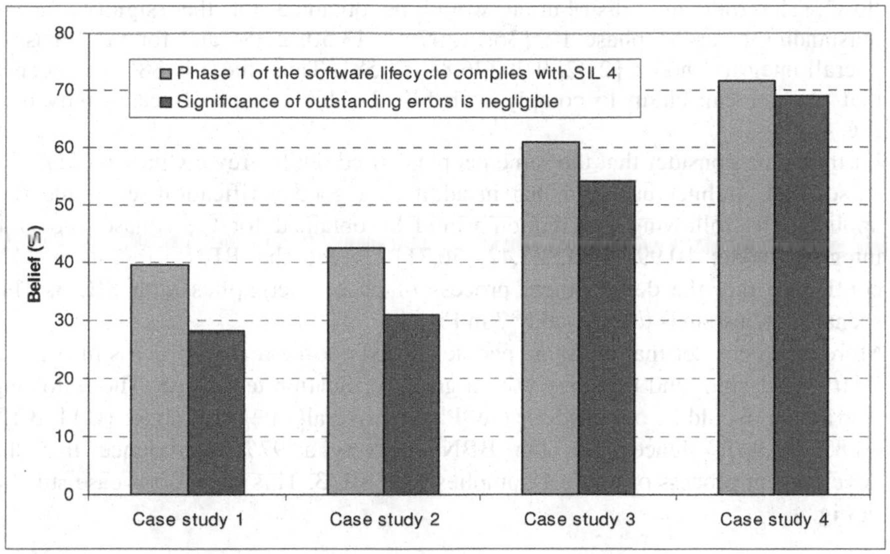

Fig. 3. Estimates of belief that phase 1 complies with SIL 4

4.2 Example 2: Estimating Phase_1 Overall Integrity Taking into Account the Review Process

This example illustrates how evidence gathered regarding the review process of phases 1, 2 and 3 influence the overall integrity claim for phase one. The node capturing the latter measures the integrity level that one can claim for phase 1 and has the following states: {SIL1, SIL2, SIL3, SIL4}. In the following example all nodes concerning the development process of phase 1 were populated with the same evidence as the one considered for case study 1 of the previous example, and then evidence is added concerning review processes.

Fig. 4 presents the belief estimates that 'Phase 1 overall integrity' complies with SIL 3. For this example the following scenarios were considered:

- Consider that there is evidence supporting the following assumptions: the 'power of verification method Y' in phase 1 is 'moderate', the 'intensity at which verification method Y was applied' was 'moderate', the 'relevance of the verification method Y to phase 1' is 'high', the 'independence level' between development team and review team is 'low'. In addition it was also considered that the staff involved in the verification had the same amount of experience, training, technical knowledge and qualifications as the staff used in the development process. Given the above conditions, the following distribution was obtained for the 'significance of outstanding errors in phase 1': {28.53, 36.68, 19.68, 15.41} and for the 'Phase 1 overall integrity' node: {7.78, 14.03, 38.20, 40}. Thus, there is 78% confidence that phase 1 complies with SIL 3. This scenario is case study 5 in Fig. 4.
- In addition to the information provided previously, consider that the independence level between the development team and the verification team is 'high' instead of

'low'. The following distribution would be obtained for the 'significance of outstanding errors in phase 1': {36.71, 47,43, 13.50, 2.35} and for the 'Phase 1 overall integrity' node: {2.32, 9.26, 36.84, 51.58}. Thus, there is 88% confidence that phase 1 can claim to comply with SIL 3. This scenario is case study 6 in Fig. 4.

- Furthermore, consider that the same people carried out the review process *in phase* 2 'software architecture' and that in addition a good verification technique was applied. The following distribution would be obtained for the 'Phase 1 overall integrity' node: {0.99, 4.88, 37.42, 56.71}. Hence the BBN suggests a 94% confidence that the development process of phase 1 complies with SIL 3. This scenario corresponds to case study 7 in Fig. 4.
- Moreover, consider that the same people carried out the review process *in phase 3* 'software design' and that they used a good verification technique. The following distribution would be obtained for the 'Phase 1 overall integrity' node: {0.11, 3.12, 40.83, 55.94}. Hence with the BBN suggests a 97% confidence that the development process of phase 1 complies with SIL 3. This scenario is case study 8 in Fig. 4.

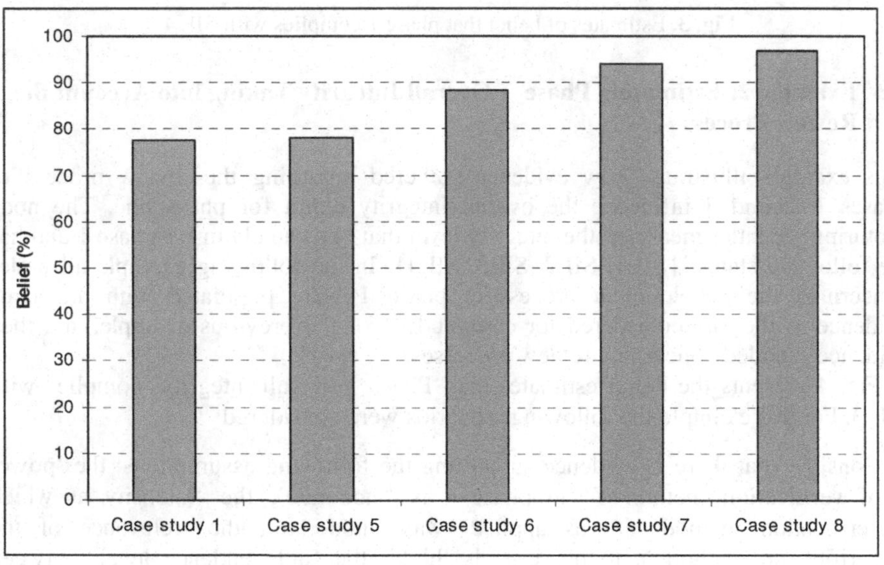

Fig. 4. Estimates of belief that phase 1 complies with SIL 3

The results are a form of 'reliability claim growth' in software development processes; a gain of integrity in an earlier phase due to the effectiveness of the review processes in later phases. This concept is quite different from traditional reliability growth in software testing. Here we are addressing software integrity before code is available, and plausible reliability claims rather than reliability measurement. This modelling goes beyond the reasoning present in standards such as IEC61508.

5 Conclusions

A Bayesian Belief Network model has been proposed to predict software safety integrity based on the type of reasoning present in safety standards such as IEC61508-3. Arguments for this formalisation of the underlying reasoning in such safety standards have been presented. The development and application of a software safety standard such as IEC61508-3 are both highly complex processes. Probabilistic reasoning can provide a sound framework within which to perform them. Although they are currently quite limited, the examples in this paper give an initial indication of the promise of BBNs in this respect. However, it remains possible that some elements of safety standards that cannot be captured in this way.

The proposed prototype BBN structure introduces a novel way to capture the effects that interactions between development phases should have on integrity claims. In doing so, it models the notion of growth in reliability claims.

In the first example studied, we captured the idea that different procedures are not considered to be of equal effectiveness. Effectiveness is not just a matter of the inherent power of procedures. For example, it is tempting to state that the use of formal methods *provides more effective assurance* than, say, the use of traditional code inspection. However, before this statement can be made it is necessary to know how *intensively* the formal method has been applied (e.g. full proof of code, or just a few key system properties?), how many people inspected the code, how long were they given, and their experience/training etc. This rationale was clearly demonstrated in example 1.

With example two we suggested factors that affect software integrity claims that are not addressed by current software safety standards.

One of the benefits of the BBN approach is that tool support that effectively assists in the evaluation of selected methods may result in a more transparent and convincing argument that the software achieves its required SIL. Compliance based on the current static tables of methods may encourage over-prescriptive use of the standard.

The proposed BBN structures and local probability tables represent an attempt to capture the reasoning in safety standards, but are no means claimed to be fully accurate representations. The BBNs will need to be evolved further in a process of consensus building amongst domain experts.

Acknowledgments. We would like to thank our sponsors the Health and Safety Executive (under contract number 6013/R38.039) and Stirling Dynamics Ltd for funding this project.

References

1. Korb, B. K., Nicholson, A.E.: Bayesian Artificial Intelligence. Chapman & Hall/CRC, ISBN:1584883871 (2003)
2. IEC61508 functional safety of electrical/ electronic/ programmable electronic safety-related systems parts 1-7. Published by the International Electrotechnical Commission (IEC), Geneva, Switzerland (1998-2000)

3. Jensen, F.: An Introduction to Bayesian networks. UCL press limited, ISBN: 1857283325 (1996)
4. Hugin A/S: http://www.hugin.com
5. Morgan, M. G., Henrion, M.:Uncertainty.: A Guide to Dealing with Uncertainty in Quantitative Risk and Policy Analysis. Cambridge University Press, ISBN: 0521427444 (1990)
6. Morris, A. P.: Combining Experts Judgments: A Bayesian Approach. Management Science Journal, Vol. 23, No. 7 (1977)
7. Spiegelhalter, D.J., Dawid, A.P., Lauritzen, S.L., Cowell, R.G.: Bayesian Analysis in Expert Systems. Journal of Statistical Science, Vol .8, No. 3 (1993) 219-283
8. Cowell R.G., Dawid A.P., Speigelhalter D.J.: Sequential Model Criticism in Probabilistic Expert Systems. IEEE Transactions on Pattern Analysis and Machine Intelligence, Vol. 15, No. 3 (1993)
9. 9 Cockram, T.: Gaining confidence in software Inspection using a Bayesian Belief Model. Software Quality Journal, Vol. 9, No. 1 (2001) 31-42
10. Cockram, T.: The use of Bayesian Networks to determine software inspection process efficiency. PhD Thesis. England, Open university (2002)
11. Hall, P., May, J., Nichol, D., Csachur, K., Kinch, B.: Integrity Prediction during Software Development. Safety of Computer Control Systems. (SAFECOMP'92), Computer Systems in Safety-Critical Applications, Proceedings of the IFAC Symposium, Zurich, Switzerland, October 28-30 (1992)
12. Fenton, N. E., Neil M., Marsh W., Krause P., Mishra R.: Predicting Software Defects in Varying Development Lifecycles using Bayesian Nets, submitted to ESEC (2005)
13. Fenton, N.E., Krause, P., Neil, M.: Probabilistic Modelling for Software Quality Control. Proceedings of the Sixth European Conference on Symbolic and Quantitative Approaches to Reasoning with Uncertainty, Toulouse, France September 19-21 (2001)
14. Fenton, N. E., Neil, M.:Making Decisions: Using Bayesian Nets and MCDA. Knowledge-Based Systems Vol. 14, (2001) 307-325
15. Gran, B. A.: Assessment of programmable systems using Bayesian Belief nets. Safety Science 40, (2002) 797-812
16. Gran, B. A.: Use of Bayesian Belief Networks when combining disparate sources of information in the safety assessment of software-based systems. International Journal of Systems Science, Vol. 33, No. 6, (2002) 529-542
17. Lauritzen, S.: Graphical Models. Oxford Science Publications, ISBN 0198522193 (1996)
18. Lauritzen, S. L., Spiegelhalter, D., J.: Local Computations with Probabilities on Graphical Structures and their Application to Expert Systems. Royal Statistical Society Journal, Vol. 50, No. 2, (1988) 157-224
19. Pearl J.: Probabilistic reasoning in intelligent systems. Morgan Kaufmann, San Mateo, ISBN: 0934613737 (1988)
20. Smith, D., Simpson. K.: Functional Safety – A straightforward guide to applying IEC61508 and related standards. Elsevier (second edition), ISBN: 0750662697 (2004)
21. Bishop, P.G., Bloomfield, R.E.: A conservative theory for long term reliability growth prediction. Proceedings of the Seventh International Symposium on Software Reliability Engineering (1996) 308-317

Retrenchment, and the Generation of Fault Trees for Static, Dynamic and Cyclic Systems*

Richard Banach[1] and Marco Bozzano[2]

[1] School of Computer Science, University of Manchester, Manchester M13 9PL, UK
banach@cs.man.ac.uk

[2] ITC-IRST, Via Sommarive 18, Povo, 38050 Trento, Italy
bozzano@irst.itc.it

Abstract. For large systems, the manual construction of fault trees is error-prone, encouraging automated techniques. In this paper we show how the retrenchment approach to formal system model evolution can be developed into a versatile structured approach for the mechanical construction of fault trees. The system structure and the structure of retrenchment concessions interact to generate fault trees with appropriately deep nesting. The same interactions fuel a structural approach to hierarchical fault trees, allowing a system and its faults to be viewed at multiple levels of abstraction. We show how this approach can be extended to deal with minimisation, thereby diminishing the post-hoc subsumption workload and potentially rendering some infeasible cases feasible. The techniques we describe readily generalise to encompass timing, allowing glitches and other transient errors to be properly described. Lastly, a mild generalisation to cope with cyclic system descriptions allows the timed theory to encompass systems with feedback.

1 Introduction

Reliability analysis of complex systems traditionally involves a set of activities which help engineers understand the system behaviour in degraded conditions, that is, when some parts of the system are not working properly. These activities have the goal of identifying all possible hazards of the system, together with their respective causes. The identification of hazards is a necessary step for safety-critical applications, to ensure that the system meets the safety requirements that are required for its deployment and use.

Among the safety analysis activities, a very popular one is Fault Tree Analysis (FTA) [30]. It is an example of deductive analysis, which, given the specification of an undesired state –usually a failure state– systematically builds all possible chains of one of more basic faults that contribute to the occurrence of the event. The result of the analysis is a *fault tree*, that is, a graphical representation of the logical interrelationships of the basic events that lead to the undesired state.

The manual construction of fault trees relies on the ability of the safety engineer to understand and to foresee the system behaviour. As a consequence, it is a time-consuming and error-prone activity, and may rapidly become impractical in case of

* Work partly supported by the E.U. ISAAC project, contract no. AST3-CT-2003-501848.

J. Górski (Ed.): SAFECOMP 2006, LNCS 4166, pp. 127–141, 2006.

large system models. Therefore, in recent years there has been a growing interest in formally based techniques to automate the production of fault trees [15, 13].

The starting point is our previous work relating retrenchment [5, 6, 7, 8, 9, 10, 3] and formal system model evolution [4]. Namely, in [4] we showed how retrenchment, as opposed to conventional refinement, can provide a formal account of the relationship between the abstract system model, that is the model of the system in nominal conditions, and the concrete system model, that is the model enriched with a description of the envisaged faults the system is designed to be robust against.

In this paper we show how retrenchment can be developed into a versatile structured approach for the mechanical construction of fault trees. Building on the ideas sketched in [4], where we exemplified the generation of a fault tree on a two-bit adder example, in this paper we show how the simulation relation of retrenchment can be used to systematically derive fault trees built upon the system structure. This is achieved by exploiting the structure of retrenchment concessions, using suitable notions of composition to gather the degraded cases into the concession of a composed retrenchment. We show how these techniques can be readily generalised in order to deal with issues like timing and cycles, thus paving the way for the analysis of dynamic systems and systems with feedback. Finally, we show how the interactions between the system structure and the structure of concessions yield a structural approach to hierarchical fault trees, allowing a system and its faults to be viewed at multiple levels of abstraction.

The techniques we present in this paper improve over the ones discussed in [13], in that they allow the mechanical generation of fault trees built upon the system structure, which are more informative than the flat (two-level) fault trees of [13]. Furthermore, we demonstrate the potential of our approach by exemplifying how these techniques can be fruitfully adapted to address the problem of generating the minimal cut sets of a fault tree. We show that, by annotating the generated subtrees with suitable minimisation directives, it is possible to perform some minimisations locally, thereby diminishing the post-hoc, brute-force subsumption workload of traditional minimisation algorithms.

The rest of the paper is structured as follows. In Section 2 we review retrenchment and relevant notions of composition of retrenchments. In Section 3 we present our retrenchment directed approach to the generation of hierarchical and structured fault trees on a running example. In Section 4 we show how the structured analysis can be modified to reduce the work of finding the minimal cut sets of some fault condition. In Section 5 we extend the method to deal with internal state in the subsystem being treated, which is relatively straightforward as long as the subsystem remains acyclic, and in Section 6 we discuss the issues raised by cyclicity and feedback. Finally, in Section 7 we discuss some related work and we outline some conclusions.

2 Systems, Retrenchments and Compositions

In this paper we describe systems using input/output transformers. So in general, a (sub)system will consist of a collection of I/O relations, each describing the behaviour of a component, and with (sub)system structure expressed by the identification of predecessor component outputs with successor component inputs; obviously some inputs and outputs remain free to allow communication with the environment. We can write such components using a relational notation $Thing(i,o)$, where i and o can be tuples, eg. $i = \langle x,y,z\rangle$ in the case of multi-input/output components.

Retrenchment [5, 6, 7, 8, 9, 10, 3], was introduced to provide a formal vehicle for describing more flexible model evolution steps than the usual technique for formal system development, refinement, conventionally allows. Since refinement was conceived with the desire to ensure that the next model conformed to properties of its predecessor, while moving towards greater implementability, it is no surprise that not all model evolutions that one might conceivably find useful fall under its scope.

In this paper, it is the simulation relation of retrenchment which does the work. This can be expressed as follows. Suppose we have two systems *Abs* and *Conc*, and suppose $Op_A(i,o)$ and $Op_C(j,p)$ are two corresponding operations, aka component behaviours, in *Abs* and *Conc* respectively.[1] A retrenchment simulation between them is given by:

$$W_{Op}(i,j) \wedge Op_C(j,p) \wedge Op_A(i,o) \wedge (O_{Op}(o,p,i,j) \vee C_{Op}(o,p,i,j))$$

Here W_{Op}, O_{Op}, C_{Op} are the *within, output, concedes* relations for the pair of operations Op. The within relation W_{Op} defines the remit of the retrenchment; while the output and concedes relations describe what are to be considered 'normal' and 'deviant' aspects of the relationship between Op_A and Op_C. The aggregate of all the relevant relations for all corresponding operation pairs is collectively called the *retrenchment data* for the particular retrenchment between *Abs* and *Conc* that we have in mind.

To consider large systems, we need mechanisms to express hierarchy and composition. Fortunately these are straightforward. To express hierarchy, it will be sufficient to decompose the concession into a number of cases covering distinct fault possibilities: $C_{Op} \equiv C_{Op,1} \vee C_{Op,2} \vee \ldots \vee C_{Op,n}$. So C_{Op} expresses the high level view while the $C_{Op,k}$ give a more detailed lower level perspective.

For composition, we need sequential and parallel composition mechanisms. Fortunately these are both straightforward, and similar to each other. Given $Op1$ and $Op2$, assuming the outputs of $Op1$ can be identified with the inputs of $Op2$, their sequential composition $Op1;2$ is the relational composition $Op1 ⨟ Op2$. If now both $Op1$ and $Op2$ come in abstract and concrete versions, related by retrenchment data $W_{Op1}, O_{Op1}, C_{Op1}$ and $W_{Op2}, O_{Op2}, C_{Op2}$ respectively, then $Op1;2_A$ and $Op1;2_C$ will be related by retrenchment data:

$$W_{Op1;2} = W_{Op1} \qquad (\textit{provided} \;\; (O_{Op1} \vee C_{Op1}) \Rightarrow W_{Op2})$$
$$O_{Op1;2} = O_{Op1} ⨟ O_{Op2} \qquad C_{Op1;2} = O_{Op1} ⨟ C_{Op2} \vee C_{Op1} ⨟ O_{Op2} \vee C_{Op1} ⨟ C_{Op2}$$

where $\vee$ is relational union. Parallel composition is even easier. Assuming this time that $Op1$ and $Op2$ act on independent sets of variables, and using $|$ to denote parallel composition (which, in terms of logic, is just conjunction), the rules are:

$$W_{Op1|2} = W_{Op1} | W_{Op2}$$
$$O_{Op1|2} = O_{Op1} | O_{Op2} \qquad C_{Op1|2} = O_{Op1} | C_{Op2} \vee C_{Op1} | O_{Op2} \vee C_{Op1} | C_{Op2}$$

We see the strong analogy between the two. Moreover, these interact cleanly both with each other, and with the hierarchy mechanism. Thus if C_{Op1} is a disjunction of n terms,

[1] Correspondence of operations in *Abs* and *Conc* is a meta level concept, which we indicate by using the same name for the operation in the two systems, or by other convenient means.

and C_{Op2} of m terms, the lower level versions of $C_{Op1;2}$ and $C_{Op1|2}$ have $mn+m+n$ terms, corresponding to the substitution of the low level forms into $C_{Op1;2}$ or $C_{Op1|2}$ respectively.

3 Hierarchy and Fault Tree Structure in a Running Example

In Fig. 1 we see a small circuit which will serve as a running example. At a high level it is a black box called *Fred* with two inputs $I1, I2$ and two outputs $O1, O2$. At a low level, it is a circuit in which signals flow from left to right, elements $A1, A2, A3$ are adders, and $F1, F2, F3$ are two-output fanout nodes. We assume that all signals are of a fixed finite number of bits, and that the adders do cutoff addition (which is to say that any value greater than or equal to the maximum representable one is output as the maximum, and there is no overflow). The number of bits is assumed sufficiently large that the cutoff effects do not occur in the examples we treat. The two diagrams in Fig. 1 represent a descent of one level in a hierarchical description of (part of) a large system.

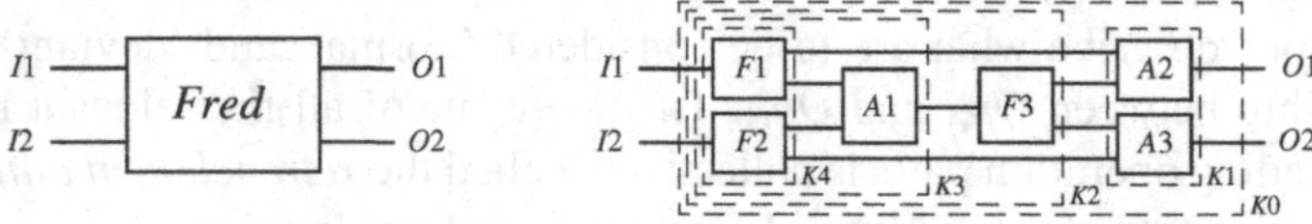

Fig. 1. A subsystem *Fred* and its internal structure

We turn to the internal structure of *Fred*. For the time being, all elements are stateless, and all circuits are acyclic. Such circuits possess a parsing which builds them up via sequential and parallel composition. In general there will be several such parsings. We choose the one in which the elements closest to the inputs are the most deeply nested: it can be derived mechanically from a definition of the circuit in terms of elements and connections, or supplied manually. Such a structure is in sympathy with a top-down fault analysis starting at the outputs. For *Fred* the structuring is illustrated in $K0$-$K4$.

Introducing names for the internal variables implicitly, the ideal $Fred_A$ model is given by fanout component relations: $F1_A(I1, \langle a1, a2\rangle) \equiv a1 = a2 = I1$ (similarly for $F2_A(I2, \langle a3, a4\rangle)$ and $F3_A(a5, \langle a6, a7\rangle)$); and adder component relations, given by: $A1_A(\langle a2, a3\rangle, a5) \equiv a5 = a2+a3$ (similarly for $A2_A(\langle a1, a6\rangle, O1), A3_A(\langle a7, a4\rangle, O2)$).

Fred's potentially faulty behaviour, model $Fred_C$, is given using renamed variables for clarity. Thus the external inputs/outputs are $J1, J2$ and $P1, P2$ respectively, and the internal variables $a1$-$a7$ become $c1$-$c7$. We assume that only the fanouts can have faults, and that these are simply 'stuck_at_0' faults on one or other output, signalled by the truth of additional free boolean variables $F1.c1$ ($F1$ output $c1$ 'stuck_at_0') etc. *We assume (purely for simplicity) that only one fault can be active in any component (at any time).* Thus while the adders $A1_C, A2_C, A3_C$ in $Fred_C$ are given by mere transliterations of the $A1_A, A2_A, A3_A$ relations above to J, P, c variables, the fanouts need full redefinition, eg.:

$$F1_C(J1, \langle c1, c2\rangle) \equiv (F1.c1 \Rightarrow c1 = 0) \wedge (F1.c2 \Rightarrow c2 = 0) \wedge \textsf{ONE} \quad \textsf{ELSE\_IDEAL}$$

In this, $\textsf{ONE} = \neg(F1.c1 \wedge F1.c2)$ and $\textsf{ELSE\_IDEAL}$ represents the transliteration of $F1_A$ to J, P, c variables, when not overridden by the faulty behaviour of the preceding terms.

The ideal and faulty *Fred* models are related by a retrenchment. It will be sufficient to write down the retrenchment data for just the components, since the data for the overall system will emerge as needed from the fault tree analysis below. For the adders, assumed fault-free, we have for $A1$:

$$W_{A1}(\langle a2, a3\rangle, \langle c2, c3\rangle) \equiv \mathsf{true}$$
$$O_{A1}(a5, c5, \langle a2, a3\rangle, \langle c2, c3\rangle) \equiv (c5 = c2 + c3)$$
$$C_{A1}(a5, c5, \langle a2, a3\rangle, \langle c2, c3\rangle) \equiv \mathsf{false}$$

with similar things for $A2, A3$; a consequence of this is that C_A terms can be dropped below. For the fanouts, we need the more complicated ($\oplus$ is 'exclusive or'):

$$W_{F1}(I1, J1) \equiv \mathsf{true}$$
$$O_{F1}(\langle a1, a2\rangle, \langle c1, c2\rangle, I1, J1) \equiv (c1 = c2 = J1)$$
$$C_{F1}(\langle a1, a2\rangle, \langle c1, c2\rangle, I1, J1) \equiv (F1.c1.0 \wedge c1 = 0 \wedge c2 = J1) \oplus (F1.c2.0 \wedge c1 = J1 \wedge c2 = 0)$$

In C_{F1}, following Section 2, we call the two disjuncts $C_{F1,c1}$ and $C_{F1,c2}$ respectively, i.e. $C_{F1} = C_{F1,c1} \vee C_{F1,c2}$. Similar things hold for $F2, F3$. Note that the abstract system is not mentioned in the body of the retrenchment data; it is not needed in this application.

With these ingredients, and a given top level event (TLE), we show how the retrenchment data drive a structured fault analysis. First, if it is of interest to check whether the TLE can arise via fault-free behaviour, it is sufficient to check whether the TLE will unify with O_{Fred}. This is easy to calculate from the assumed parse $K0$-$K4$ and the rules of Section 2, since we will assume that for all components, correct working is given by a total function, and even incorrect working is a total relation.[2] Second, we proceed downward through C_{Fred}, decomposing step by step, eliciting the consequences of composition and of local structure, and deriving a *resolution tree* for all possible ways of satisfying the TLE within the constraints. Values of variables once assigned, remain in force as we descend unless we backtrack past the point of assignment, and once the input values have been reached, any remaining uninstantiated variables can be instantiated within the constraints that hold, case by case, to confirm overall consistency. Now we consider the specific TLE: $J1 = J2 = P1 = 1$ (with $P2$ regarded as irrelevant). It is easy to check that this does not satisfy O_{Fred}. The analysis then proceeds as follows.

TLE: $K0 = K2 \mathbin{⨟} K1$, so $C_{K0} = O_{K2} \mathbin{⨟} C_{K1} \vee C_{K2} \mathbin{⨟} O_{K1} \vee C_{K2} \mathbin{⨟} C_{K1}$. Since $K1$ is nearest the outputs, and we are working backwards through *Fred*, we decompose $K1$ first, i.e. we decompose O_{K1} and C_{K1}. Since $K1 = A2|A3$ and adders don't fail, C_{K1} is false, reducing C_{K0} to $C_{K2} \mathbin{⨟} O_{K1}$, while $O_{K1} = O_{A2}|O_{A3}$. Now O_{A3} merely imposes existential constraints on $P2, c7, c4$ such that $A3(\langle c7, c4\rangle, O2)$ holds; we put these to one side since the TLE does not constrain them further. O_{A2} demands that $c1 + c6 = 1$ (among other things). There are two ways to satisfy this, namely $c1 = 0 \wedge c6 = 1$ or $c1 = 1 \wedge c6 = 0$, giving a top level disjunction into **TLE.L** or **TLE.R** for $C_{K2} \mathbin{⨟} O_{K1}$.

TLE.L: Since $c1$ and $c6$ are outputs of $K2$, we next decompose $C_{K2} = C_{K3;F3} = O_{K3} \mathbin{⨟} C_{F3} \vee C_{K3} \mathbin{⨟} O_{F3} \vee C_{K3} \mathbin{⨟} C_{F3}$. Now $C_{F3} = C_{F3,c6} \vee C_{F3,c7}$, and $C_{F3,c6}$ is inconsistent with $c6 = 1$. Also O_{K3} forces $c5 = 2$, inconsistent with $c6 = 1$ too, so the terms

[2] Similarly, we assume that O_{K4}-O_{K2} can be evaluated immediately from $J1, J2$ when needed. In more general cases, a backwards derivation might be required for some O terms.

containing these are dropped. So $C_{K3;F3} = C_{K3} \fatsemi O_{F3} \vee C_{K3} \fatsemi C_{F3,c7}$. In fact the distinction between these concerns only $c7$, whose precise value is immaterial, so only C_{K3} is of further interest. From $c6 = 1$, we deduce $c5 = 1$. We now decompose $C_{K3} = C_{K4;A1}$ which is just $C_{K4} \fatsemi O_{A1}$ since adders don't fail. Now $c5 = 1$ implies $c2 = 0 \wedge c3 = 1$ or $c2 = 1 \wedge c3 = 0$, giving a disjunction into **TLE.L.L** or **TLE.L.R** for $C_{K4} \fatsemi O_{A1}$.
TLE.L.L: Since $K4 = F1|F2$, we have $C_{K4} = O_{F1}|C_{F2} \vee C_{F1}|O_{F2} \vee C_{F1}|C_{F2}$, with each of C_{F1}, C_{F2} being a disjunction of two faults. However, we earlier derived $c1 = 0$, which is inconsistent with O_{F1} and $J1 = 1$, eliminating a term and forcing $F1.c1$ true. But $c2 = 0$ forces $F1.c2$ true, and we assumed only one fault is ever active in any one component. So we have a contradiction. In such a case we must backtrack to the innermost ancestral nontrivial disjunction, and eliminate the subtree rooted at the relevant disjunct. Thus the subtree at $c2 = 0 \wedge c3 = 1$ is eliminated.
TLE.L.R: As in the previous case we have $F1.c1$ true, but this time $F1.c2$ is false due to $c2 = 1$; so we remain within our constraints. Now $c3 = 0$ forces $F2.c3$ true, and for consistency we must have $F2.c4$ false. This yields a fault configuration for the TLE.
TLE.R: We decompose C_{K2} as in case **TLE.L**, getting $O_{K3} \fatsemi C_{F3} \vee C_{K3} \fatsemi O_{F3} \vee C_{K3} \fatsemi C_{F3}$. The constraint $c1 = 1 \wedge c6 = 0$ and no multiple $F3$ failures, means that this can be made valid by: case **TLE.R.1**, in which $O_{K3} \fatsemi C_{F3,c6}$ holds, with $c5 = 2$; or by case **TLE.R.2**, in which $C_{K3} \fatsemi O_{F3}$ is presumed to hold, with $c5 = 0$; or by case **TLE.R.3**, in which $C_{K3} \fatsemi C_{F3,c6}$ holds, with $c5$ as yet unconstrained; or by case **TLE.R.4**, in which $C_{K3} \fatsemi C_{F3,c7}$ is presumed to hold, with $c5 = 0$.
TLE.R.1: $O_{K3} \fatsemi C_{F3,c6}$ holds, with $c5 = 2$. This is a valid cause of the TLE.
TLE.R.2: We have $C_{K3} \fatsemi O_{F3}$ and $c5 = 0$, so we decompose $C_{K3} = C_{K4;A1} = C_{K4} \fatsemi O_{A1}$ since adders don't fail. Now $c5 = 0$ implies $c2 = c3 = 0$. The latter two imply $F1.c2$ and $F2.c3$ both true, and $c1 = 1$ does not lead to a multiple failure for $F1$. Also $c4 = 1$ is acceptable for $F2$, leading to a valid fault configuration for the TLE.
TLE.R.3: We have $C_{K3} \fatsemi C_{F3,c6}$ as a consequence of which $F3.c6$ holds, and $c5$ is unconstrained. We seek all possible ways of satisfying C_{K3} given the inputs $J1 = 1$ and $J2 = 1$. Now $K3$ is a parallel composition of $F1$ and $F2$, so C_{K3} will contain three terms as usual. Now each of C_{F1} and C_{F2} is a disjunction of two terms, but $c1 = 1$ prevents $F1.c1$ from holding so C_{F1} has just one term that contributes nontrivially. This leads to an overall disjunction of five nontrivial terms.
TLE.R.4: We have $C_{K3} \fatsemi C_{F3,c7}$ and $c5 = 0$. The latter generates only one solution, i.e. $F1.c2$ and $F2.c3$ must both hold.

A tree that depicts the above is shown in Fig. 2. Near the top we show the variable assignments, but suppress them lower down to save space, recording only the fault variables set at various points.[3] Although Fig. 2 is not syntactically a fault tree (FT) according to [30], it is easy to see that it could be straightforwardly transformed into one. We do this in Section 4 after minimisation. At any rate the present tree represents a low level view of the fault analysis.

In terms of the hierarchy of which *Fred* forms a part, a higher level view just represents the fault by a single node: the TLE node itself. Descending the hierarchy thus corresponds to growing the more detailed tree along with uncovering the internal structure

[3] The ellipsis in the root indicates that further facts to be accumulated as the analysis descends are to accumulate *inside* the scope of the quantifier (elsewhere, we suppress the ellipsis).

of *Fred*. Evidently the algorithm described in this section can be easily incorporated into one which deals with large systems in a hierarchical fashion. Whenever a fault tree for a given model has been computed, a pure refinement of a subsystem does not require rebuilding the whole fault tree from scratch. More drastic subsystem evolution, going beyond pure refinements, can imply more widespread changes to fault trees.

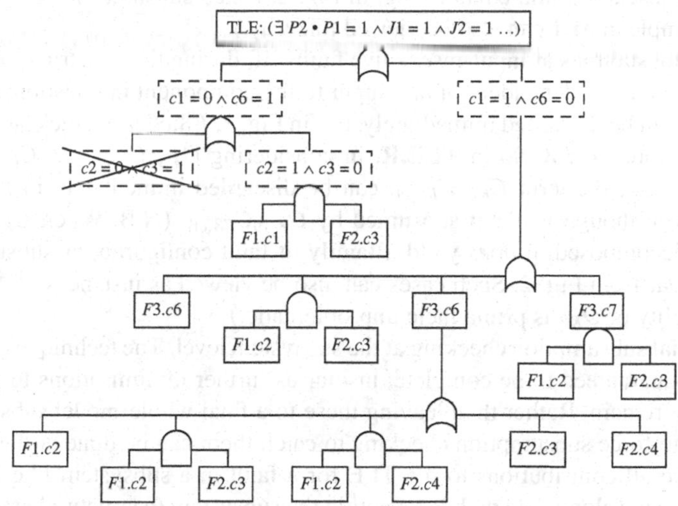

Fig. 2. Part of a Resolution Tree for the TLE of *Fred*

4 Structured Minimisation

In practical fault analysis we are most interested in minimal fault configurations, the so-called *minimal cut sets* (MCSs for short) consisting of the fewest possible basic faults that cause a particular TLE. The traditional technique for discovering MCSs is subsumption. In principle, one needs to generate all possible configurations that cause a fault, and then check them against one another: any that are subsumed by simpler configurations are discarded. These subsumption checks can be quite expensive for a large system model, since the number of leaves in a tree is exponential in its depth, and the number of subsumption checks is quadratic in the number of leaves. Although in practice efficient algorithms [17, 18, 27, 28] based on binary decision diagrams (BDDs) [16] can be used for this purpose, their worst-case complexity is still exponential in the number of variables of the BDD. In this section we explore ways of reducing the subsumption workload by exploiting the structure of the tree construction as guided by the retrenchment data. The various minimisations are illustrated on the running example.

M.1: Discarding non-needed subtrees. If, during the construction, a fault is generated which leads to an assignment to some variable whose value does not affect the validity of the TLE (eg. there is no dataflow from the fault to the TLE), then the fault node (and, implicitly, any subtree rooted at it) can be discarded immediately since the TLE is satisfied without it. In general, we call such faults incidental faults. As in the case of the subtree of Fig. 2 rooted at $F3.c7$, which is an example, such faults can arise by considering the disjunction of the complete range of possible faulty configurations of some otherwise needed component.

M.2: Discarding locally subsumed expressions. If, during the construction, a range of options to explore is generated, some of which are subsumed by others, the subsumed options can be discarded immediately. Eg. in Fig. 2, $F2.c3$ subsumes $F1.c2 \wedge F2.c3$. (N.B. The example in **M.1** can also be viewed this way.)

M.3: Discarding subtrees at input-insensitive faults. If, during the construction, a fault is generated which is independent of any input to the component in question, the subtree beneath it can be discarded immediately. Eg. in Fig. 2, $F3.c6$ is a 'stuck_at_0' fault, insensitive to inputs to $F3$. So in **TLE.R**, in considering $O_{K3\fatsemi}C_{F3,c6} \vee C_{K3\fatsemi}O_{F3} \vee C_{K3\fatsemi}C_{F3,c6} \vee \ldots$, the term $C_{K3\fatsemi}C_{F3,c6}$ can be discarded immediately in favour of $O_{K3\fatsemi}C_{F3,c6}$, even though it is not subsumed by $O_{K3\fatsemi}C_{F3,c6}$. (N.B. When $C_{K3\fatsemi}C_{F3,c6}$ is eventually decomposed, it *does* yield a family of fault configurations subsumed by $F3.c6$, as is clear from Fig. 2. Such cases can also be viewed as instances of **M.2** *provided* satisfiability of O_{K3} is prima facie unproblematic.)

M.4: Doing final subsumption checking at the subsystem level. The techniques outlined above are not guaranteed to be complete, insofar as further minimisations to generate the MCSs may remain. Rather than leaving these to a final whole-model subsumption check, the brute force subsumption checking to catch them can be done at the subsystem level, since all contributions to the TLE for a fault in a subsystem like *Fred* are causally propagated along data pathways within the subsystem (a structural assumption we take for granted.) Thus the inclusion of the rest of the system will result in an overall description which necessarily factorises, regardless of whether or not the factorisation is obscured (whether to a human observer or to some algorithm) by the complexity of the final expression.

The precise way in which the preceding ideas can be implemented in a tool (such as the FSAP/NuSMV-SA platform [13]) remain a matter for implementation tactics. For example, the subsystem parse could be decorated with suitable directives to prompt the FT generation algorithm to apply certain minimisations when the appropriate point is encountered, or the FT generation algorithm may be written so as to check for the whole range of recognised minimisation opportunities every time another stage in the tree is developed. Internal optimisations, such as the sharing of subcomputations not visible at the FT level, can also be deployed. Details lie beyond the scope of this paper.

When we apply the above to the running example whose resolution tree is indicated in Fig. 2, we get a considerably smaller tree. We transform this into a legal FT as per [30], containing just the MCSs, by accumulating the variable assignments along any path between two logical connectives into the label for an intermediate event (IE), and changing the basic fault nodes into round ones.[4] When we do all this, we end up with the minimised fault tree in Fig. 3.

[4] N.B. Where a basic fault occurs in the interior of the resolution tree (eg. the subtrees at $F3.c6$ or $F3.c7$ in Fig. 2, were these trees not discarded), the subtree is manipulated to distribute the interior basic fault into the nearest descendant conjunction(s), and IEs are generated labelled by the relevant logical combinations of the IEs at the roots of the subtrees thus affected.

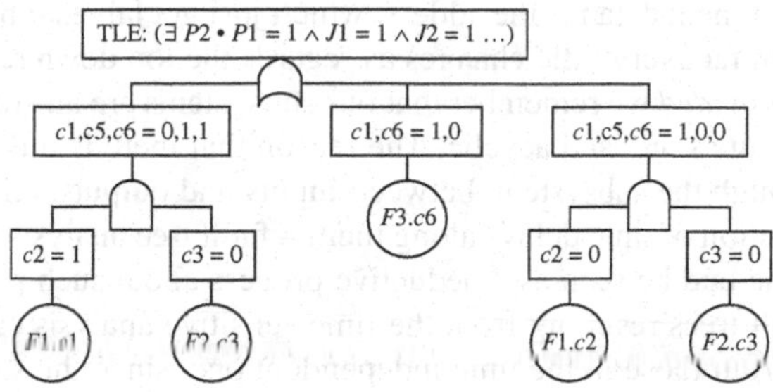

Fig. 3. A Minimised Fault Tree for the TLE of *Fred*

5 Timing and Internal State

Up to now everything has been treated as instantaneous, and the job of fault tree analysis has simply been to trace the possible functional (or more generally, relational) dependencies that connect the inputs and outputs in a given TLE, and thereby, to display the connections between the primitive faults that contribute to valid instances of the TLE. This instantaneous assumption is obviously not adequate for all situations of interest, and so in this section, we introduce a model of time, in order to capture the behaviour of systems in which time delays cannot be neglected. Since many of the digital components that are found in circuits such as our running example are stateful, this generalisation is an important one.

We introduce discrete time, with ticks labelled by integers, and for ease of exposition we just modify slightly our running example. The adders will remain stateless, delivering their result instantaneously, while the fanouts will introduce a unit delay between an input received and the outputs delivered. Thus while the definition of the adders remains unaltered aside from the introduction of a time parameter, eg. $A1_A(\langle a2(t), a3(t)\rangle, a5(t)) \equiv a5(t) = a2(t) + a3(t)$, the definition of the fanouts becomes eg. $F1_A(I1(t), \langle a1(t+1), a2(t+1)\rangle) \equiv a1(t+1) = a2(t+1) = I1(t)$. As well as this, the fault variables become time dependent (to permit the description of eg. glitches), but otherwise, the relational descriptions of components are time independent. So the faulty behaviour of $F1$ becomes:

$$\begin{aligned}&F1_C(J1(t), \langle c1(t+1), c2(t+1)\rangle) \equiv \\ &\quad (F1.c1(t+1) \Rightarrow c1(t+1) = 0) \wedge (F1.c2(t+1) \Rightarrow c2(t+1) = 0) \wedge \\ &\quad \neg(F1.c1(t+1) \wedge (F1.c2(t+1)) \qquad \mathsf{ELSE\_IDEAL}\end{aligned}$$

Let *Fred* with these alterations be renamed *FreT* (we will continue to refer to Fig. 2). With this change, the retrenchment data for *FreT* become:

$$\begin{aligned}&W_{F1}(I1(t), J1(t)) \equiv \mathsf{true} \\ &O_{F1}(\langle a1(t+1), a2(t+1)\rangle, \langle c1(t+1), c2(t+1)\rangle, I1(t), J1(t)) \equiv \\ &\qquad (c1(t+1) = c2(t+1) = J1(t)) \\ &C_{F1}(\langle a1(t+1), a2(t+1)\rangle, \langle c1(t+1), c2(t+1)\rangle, I1(t), J1(t)) \equiv \\ &\qquad (F1.c1.0(t+1) \wedge c1(t+1) = 0 \wedge c2(t+1) = J1(t)) \oplus \\ &\qquad (F1.c2.0(t+1) \wedge c1(t+1) = J1(t) \wedge c2(t+1) = 0)\end{aligned}$$

(We omit the retrenchment data for the adders, which just get labelled by '(t)'.)

With this setup, in fact very little changes as regards the top down resolution driven fault tree analysis, *provided* we remember that our subsystems are all still finite component, finite signal, finite state, and acyclic. The reason that there is little change is that the set of paths through the subsystem, between inputs and outputs, remains unaltered by the mere introduction of time delays along them – fault tree analysis (in the sense of this paper) can in the end be seen as a deductive process about such paths and sets of such paths. The fault trees resulting from the time sensitive analysis can of course be differently shaped from those in the time independent one, since the same component may contribute in different ways at different times.

To illustrate the above, let us do an analysis for the *FreT* subsystem of the same TLE we considered previously, but this time with the output $P1$ instantiated to 1 for some time t (and otherwise unspecified), and with inputs held constant at 1 as before, which we write as $J1 = J2 = P1(t) = 1$. Doing the analysis as described in Section 3, but this time noting the time labels along the way, and then doing the minimisation as described in Section 4, we get the FT in Fig. 4, in which preprimes denote the value at $t - 1$, and the labelling of the IEs is incomplete for space reasons (a full labelling would cite values at t and at $t - 1$ for several variables). Note how the fact that the output is not required to be constant, has spawned a valid instance of the branch of the FT that was cut off in Fig. 2. We are only demanding a glitch, so the two $F1$ faults that could not coexist statically, are permitted to occur at successive instants. Of course if we asked for the glitch to persist for two time ticks, this branch would get cut off once more. This example vividly illustrates the increased expressive power gained by adding timing to essentially the same techniques that we discussed statically.

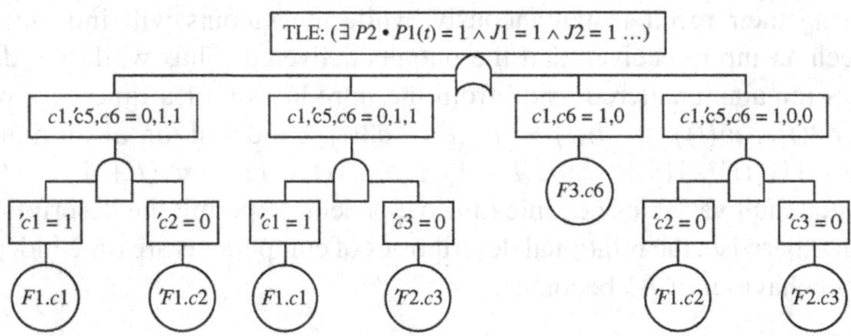

Fig. 4. A Minimised Fault Tree for the TLE of *FreT*

6 Introducing Feedback

The (technically) relatively mild generalisation of the last section becomes more interesting when we include feedback as well as timing delays. We modify our subsystem *FreT* by removing $A3$ and $F2$, and introducing a feedback signal (called k in the concrete system) from $F3$ to $A1$, resulting in subsystem *Jim*. See Fig. 5.

Now we can no longer rely on a static syntactic description of the subsystem as the analysis proceeds, but must unfold a recursive structure. The essentials of this are:

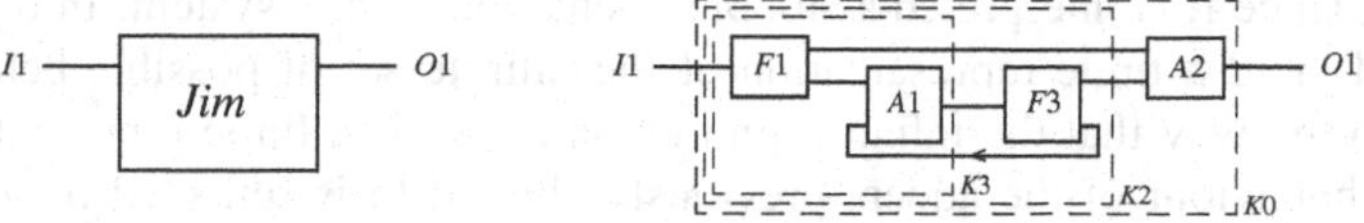

Fig. 5. A subsystem *Jim* with cyclic internal structure

$$O1(t) = (c1(t) + c6(t)) \quad ; \quad c1(t) = c2(t) = I1(t-1)$$
$$c6(t) = c5(t-1) = (c2(t-1) + k(t-1)) = (c2(t-1) + c5(t-2))$$

This is a standard feedback control system, and its I/O behaviour can be computed by standard means. Performing the required back substitutions (details omitted for lack of space), we get:

$$O1(t) = I1(t-1) + I1(t-2) + I1(t-3) + \ldots = \sum_{q=1}^{\infty} I1(t-q)$$

This is a shorthand for describing an infinite set of possible finite behaviours, on the understanding that all values are (bounded) natural numbers, and that an at most finite number of the $I1$ values in the summation are non-zero (and that one cuts off the summation at some point after the earliest non-zero value, to represent initialisation at a point in the finite past). The proliferation in behaviours is due to the fact that $A1$'s output remains stable when its $c2$ input is 0, so that the value held in $F3$ (and hence output at $O1$) remains invariant as long as $I1$ continues to remain at 0. Thus if we stipulate $O1(t) = 2$, then this can arise via $I1(t-1) = 2$, or via $I1(t-2) = 2$, or $I1(t-3) = 2$, etc. (with all other $I1$ values zero). Alternatively we could have $I1(t-1) = 1 \wedge I1(t-2) = 1$, or $I1(t-1) = 1 \wedge I1(t-3) = 1$, or $I1(t-1) = 1 \wedge I1(t-4) = 1$, or ...etc., or $I1(t-2) = 1 \wedge I1(t-3) = 1$, or $I1(t-2) = 1 \wedge I1(t-4) = 1$, etc. etc.

Admittedly we have been considering the fault-free behaviour of *Jim* for the sake of simplicity, but there is no reason at all why similar situations should not arise during the analysis of genuine faults. The back substitutions performed from the TLE '$O1(t) = 2$' are exactly the steps that a retrenchment based fault analysis would dictate.

There are at least three approaches to the question of there being an infinity of possible causes of some situation, just raised. Firstly one could simply regard the TLE as underspecified, since it places no constraints on the input values. Any finite constraint on these that is consistent with the TLE and supplies all the values 'needed' by the TLE[5] would immediately reduce the set of possible causes to a finite one, eliminating the problem. Essentially we would be placing an a priori bound on how far in the past the earliest of the causes of the TLE had occurred, an approach that in general is incomplete.

Secondly, one could examine what a standard model checking approach (such as the FSAP/NuSMV-SA platform [13]) would deliver. Such approaches work by exhaustive search of the state space of the system, keeping an eye out for states already encountered along a given path. Finding a repeated occurrence of the same state, cuts

[5] We are being rather imprecise here about the definition of neededness, since it would depend on the precise nature of the components in the subsystem and their interdependencies.

off the search, since it is interpreted as looping behaviour in the system. In our example this would yield a finite representation of the infinite set of possible behaviours, analogously to the way that the infinite summation above is a finite representation of it. The stable behaviour of the adders previously alluded to is reflected in self-loops on the relevant states generated by the state space search algorithm. Such a representation would require some interpretation as regards the generation of fault trees, since a naive FT generation algorithm would attempt to generate a tree with infinite disjunctions, and not terminate. Adding a finite starting point in the past is an easy way to prevent this, although as above, an a priori finite bound in the past makes the approach incomplete.

A third, and most sophisticated approach to the issue, is to honestly take on board the control nature of the cyclic system, and to combine the model checking strategy with deeper insights about control systems.[6] The benefits of such an approach are that it could yield a complete description, by representing recursive parts of the set of behaviours in a suitably symbolic manner, even extending to situations in which the state space is not finite. However all of this would require deep insight into the relationship between decidabilities in the relevant model checking and control theory domains, since it is well known that combining theories which are decidable on their own, does not automatically lead to decidability of the combination.

7 Conclusions

In this paper we have presented a formal account of fault tree generation based on retrenchment. We have shown how the retrenchment framework is able to capture several aspects of the fault tree generation, namely the mechanical construction of a fault tree based on structural information, fault tree minimization, system model evolution based on a hierarchy of models viewed at multiple levels of abstraction, and fault injection. Finally, the approach can be generalised to deal with dynamic and cyclic systems.

Our work has been inspired by Hip-HOPS (Hierarchically Performed Hazard Origin and Propagation Studies) [24, 25, 26], a framework incorporating a mechanical fault tree synthesis algorithm based on system structure, and taking into account model evolution. The synthesis of the fault tree is based on a preliminary functional failure analysis (FFA) and a tabular technique (IF-FMEA) used to generate a model of the local failure behaviour, activities normally performed manually during system design and safety assessment. Our work addresses the automation of the whole process assuming that a formal specification of both system and fault model is available. Furthermore, we have shown how the synthesis algorithm can be coupled with suitable tactics to perform local minimal cut-set computation, reducing the overall computational effort.

Our techniques can be incorporated into formal tools supporting the safety assessment of complex systems, like the FSAP/NuSMV-SA platform [13, 20]. The algorithms

[6] Certainly the calculation indicated above is standard feedback control theory, and such calculations have been automated (in a suitably symbolic manner) in standard control theory toolkits eg. SIMULINK [1, 21].

described here improve over the ones used there for two reasons. First, they allow the generation of structured fault trees, which are more informative than the flat fault trees produced by the current FSAP platform. Second, they allow the taking of dynamic information into account, eg. they can deal with transient failures (Section 5), and feedback (Section 6). While our focus was on automatic synthesis, the DIFTree (Dynamic Innovative Fault Tree) [22] methodology, implemented in the Galileo tool [29], is mainly concerned with the problem of fault tree evaluation. It uses a modularisation technique [19] to identify (in linear time) independent sub-trees, that can be evaluated using the most appropriate techniques (BDD-based techniques for static fault trees, Markov techniques or Monte Carlo simulation for dynamic ones). In addition, it supports different probability distributions for component failures. A similar modularisation and decomposition technique is advocated in [2]. That technique is orthogonal to our notion of structural generation; in particular, it is concerned with isolating different sub-trees that can be synthesised (or evaluated) separately, whereas our structural information can be used to synthesise (or evaluate) each sub-tree on its own.

Although an experimental evaluation of our algorithm was beyond the scope of this paper, we have provided many hints about the advantages such an algorithm would have with respect to the traditional monolithic algorithms which just flatten the model. First, it makes it possible to synthesise the fault tree by considering each component in isolation, thus avoiding building an internal representation of the whole model (eg. avoiding the generation of a BDD for it). Second, it suggests that the MCS computation can benefit from local minimisation. As future work, we wish to design a practical implementation and evaluate it experimentally against state-of-the-art techniques, eg. the BDD-based routines [17, 18, 27, 28] used in the FSAP platform. Given that integer constraint solving is needed to deal with time, we foresee that there might also be room for using decision procedures for such a theory, eg. MathSAT [11, 23]. Finally, we would like to integrate such algorithms into the FSAP platform [13].

Further issues we would like to address include dynamic aspects (see eg. [22]), that we have only sketched in this paper for lack of space. In particular, we would like to investigate the problem of sequential dependencies and failure duration, and their representation inside the fault tree. Finally, it would be interesting to adapt our algorithms to the truncated computation of prime implicants described in [28].

References

[1] Tewari. A. *Modern Control Design With MATLAB and SIMULINK.* Wiley, 2002.

[2] A. Anand and A.K. Somani. Hierarchical Analysis of Fault Trees with Dependencies, using Decomposition. In *Proc. Annual Reliability and Maintainability Symposium*, pages 69–75, 1998.

[3] R. Banach. Retrenchment and system properties. Submitted.

[4] R. Banach and R. Cross. Safety requirements and fault trees using retrenchment. *Proc. SAFECOMP-04, Springer*, Heisel, Liggesmeyer, Wittmann (eds.), LNCS Volume 3219:210–223, 2004.

[5] R. Banach and C. Jeske. Output retrenchments, defaults, stronger compositions, feature engineering. Submitted.

[6] R. Banach and M. Poppleton. Engineering and theoretical underpinnings of retrenchment. Submitted.

[7] R. Banach and M. Poppleton. Retrenchment: An engineering variation on refinement. *B'98: Recent Advances in the Development and Use of the B Method: Second International B Conference, Montpellier, France, LNCS*, 1393:129–147, 1998.

[8] R. Banach and M. Poppleton. Retrenchment and punctured simulation. *Proc. IFM-99, Springer*, Araki, Gallway, Taguchi (eds.):457–476, 1999.

[9] R. Banach and M. Poppleton. Sharp retrenchment, modulated refinement and punctured simulation. *Form. Asp. Comp.*, 11:498–540, 1999.

[10] R. Banach and M. Poppleton. Retrenching partial requirements into system definitions: A simple feature interaction case study. *Requirements Engineering Journal*, 8:266–288, 2003.

[11] M. Bozzano, R. Bruttomesso, A. Cimatti, T. Junttila, P. van Rossum, S. Schulz, and R. Sebastiani. Mathsat: Tight Integration of SAT and Mathematical Decision Procedures. *Journal of Automated Reasoning, Special Issue on SAT*, 2006. To appear.

[12] M. Bozzano, A. Cavallo, M. Cifaldi, L. Valacca, and A. Villafiorita. Improving safety assessment of complex systems: An industrial case study. *International Symposium of Formal Methods Europe (FME 2003), Pisa, Italy, LNCS*, 2805:208–222, September 2003.

[13] M. Bozzano and A. Villafiorita. Improving system reliability via model checking: The FSAP/NuSMV-SA safety analysis platform. *Computer Safety, Reliability, and Security, LNCS*, 2788:49–62, 2003.

[14] M. Bozzano and A. Villafiorita. Integrating fault tree analysis with event ordering information. *Proc. ESREL 2003*, pages 247–254, 2003.

[15] M. Bozzano, A. Villafiorita, et al. ESACS: An integrated methodology for design and safety analysis of complex systems. *Proc. ESREL 2003*, pages 237–245, 2003.

[16] R.E. Bryant. Symbolic Boolean Manipulation with Ordered Binary Decision Diagrams. *ACM Computing Surveys*, 24(3):293–318, 1992.

[17] O. Coudert and J.C. Madre. Implicit and Incremental Computation of Primes and Essential Primes of Boolean Functions. In *Proc. Design Automation Conference (DAC 1992)*, pages 36–39. IEEE Computer Society Press, 1992.

[18] O. Coudert and J.C. Madre. Fault Tree Analysis: 10^{20} Prime Implicants and Beyond. In *Proc. Annual Reliability and Maintainability Symposium (RAMS 1993)*, 1993.

[19] Y. Dutuit and A. Rauzy. A Linear-time algorithm to find modules in fault trees. *IEEE Transactions on Reliability*, 45(3):422–425, 1996.

[20] The FSAP/NuSMV-SA platform. `http://sra.itc.it/tools/FSAP`.

[21] Nuruzzaman. M. *Modeling And Simulation In SIMULINK For Engineers And Scientists*. Authorhouse, 2005.

[22] R. Manian, J.B. Dugan, D. Coppit, and K.J. Sullivan. Combining Various Solution Techniques for Dynamic Fault Tree Analysis of Computer Systems. In *Proc. High-Assurance Systems Engineering Symposium (HASE 1998)*, pages 21–28. IEEE, 1998.

[23] MathSAT. `http://mathsat.itc.it`.

[24] Y. Papadopoulos. *Safety-directed system monitoring using safety cases*. PhD thesis, Department of Computer Science, University of York, 2000. Tech. Rep. YCST-2000-08.

[25] Y. Papadopoulos and M. Maruhn. Model-Based Synthesis of Fault Trees from Matlab-Simulink Models. In *Proc. Conference on Dependable Systems and Networks (DSN 2001)*, pages 77–82, 2001.

[26] Y. Papadopoulos, J. McDermid, R. Sasse, and G. Heiner. Analysis and Synthesis of the behaviour of complex programmable electronic systems in conditions of failure. *Reliability Engineering and System Safety*, 71(3):229–247, 2001.

[27] A. Rauzy. New Algorithms for Fault Trees Analysis. *Reliability Engineering and System Safety*, 40(3):203–211, 1993.

[28] A. Rauzy and Y. Dutuit. Exact and Truncated Computations of Prime Implicants of Coherent and Non-Coherent Fault Trees within Aralia. *Reliability Engineering and System Safety*, 58(2):127–144, 1997.
[29] K.J. Sullivan, J.B. Dugan, and D. Coppit. The Galileo Fault Tree Analysis Tool. In *Proc. Symposium on Fault-Tolerant Computing (FTCS 1999)*, pages 232–235. IEEE, 1999.
[30] W.E. Vesely, F.F. Goldberg, N.H. Roberts, and D.F. Haasl. Fault tree handbook. Technical Report NUREG-0492, Systems and Reliability Research Office of Nuclear Regulatory Research U.S. Nuclear Regulatory Commission, 1981.

Stepwise Development of Secure Systems

Thomas Santen

Institut für Softwaretechnik und Theoretische Informatik
Technische Universität Berlin, Germany
santen@acm.org

Abstract. System development by stepwise refinement is a well-established method in classical software engineering. We discuss how this method can be adapted to systematically incorporate security issues, in particular, confidentiality into the software construction process. Starting with an abstract system model that precisely captures the relevant confidentiality requirements, subsequent refinements produce models which introduce more detail or relax assumptions on the environment. For each refinement, changing adversary capabilities must be captured and their compatibility with the given confidentiality requirements must be established. In this context, security, and dependability in general, are existential properties: The existence of a secure implementation must be kept invariant during the development process. This considerably adds to the complexity of a development.

1 Introduction

Developing *secure* IT-systems still is a particularly challenging task. Standard systems and software engineering processes focus on the "functional" properties of a system and hardly address "non-functional" properties such as security in a systematic way starting from requirements through design to the final implementation. The reason may be that security concerns – and non-functional properties in general – are less well understood and harder to control during the development process. In particular, confidentiality poses problems because it arguably is the facet of security which is least related to classical functional properties.

The present article discusses a method to develop secure systems in the spirit of *system development by stepwise refinement*. Regarding functional properties, that method has a firm theoretical basis (e.g., Abrial's work [1], but also much work in the context of VDM [12], Z [5], and other specification formalisms), it has been applied in (mostly safety-critical) real-world projects, and it has influenced software engineering at large: Meyer's notion of *design-by-contract* [18] nowadays is accepted best practice in software design. The present work shows how stepwise refinement can be re-interpreted to accommodate security, and confidentiality in particular. The present paper focuses on confidentiality. Therefore, "security" is used as a synonym for confidentiality henceforth. The major issues to address for stepwise secure refinement are the following:

– The *initial model*, which is the starting point of the refinement process, must capture the confidentiality requirements as close as possible, while abstracting from all unnecessary detail.

J. Górski (Ed.): SAFECOMP 2006, LNCS 4166, pp. 142–155, 2006.

- To validate the initial model, the confidentiality requirements should be captured in a descriptive manner. The model should satisfy a *confidentiality property*, which can be validated against the informal requirements independently of the model.
- A refinement step can introduce *new detail* in the model, and consequently offer new ways of the adversary attacking the system. The refinement is to *preserve confidentiality*, i.e., to ensure that the confidentiality property still holds for the refined model, even with respect to the new attacks.
- The influence of the *environment* on security must be systematically addressed during development by "trading" assumptions made on the environment against functionality of the "machine" (cf. Section 2).

The running example illustrating this development process is an anonymization service, a mix [3]. The reader be warned, however, that the results presented here do not provide new insight in the security conditions of mixes. The problems we will touch upon are well-known and it is not the purpose of this paper to suggest any new solutions to these problems.

Section 2 introduces the concept of an adversary model, which comprises a functional model of the system and the possibilities of adversary observations. That section also introduces an abstract model of a mix. Section 3 discusses possibilistic and probabilistic confidentiality properties. In particular, it motivates the existential nature of confidentiality properties. Section 4 introduces confidentiality-preserving refinement. It discusses how new detail in a refined model can extend the observational possibilities of an adversary. The refinement conditions must ensure that the system satisfies the desired confidentiality properties even against this more powerful adversary. Section 5 reduces assumptions on the environment and extends the functionality of the system accordingly. Such trading of functionality is unavoidable if the initial model – for sake of simplicity – captures properties that are crucial for security in the environment process rather than in the system process. Related research is the topic of Section 6. Section 7 summarizes the process discussed in the paper.

2 An Abstract Model to Specify Confidentiality

The first task in a development by stepwise refinement consists in producing a very abstract system model that includes only the necessary detail to express the essential requirements on the system. Subsequent refinement steps add more and more detail[1] until that process reaches a rich model that is equivalent to an implementation.

We use the process calculus of *Probabilistic CSP* (PCSP) [19] to express our models. Previous work [22] introduced the notion of an *adversary model* and possibilistic as well as probabilistic *confidentiality properties* of an adversary model, which we will use to express the specification and its subsequent refinements. In the following, we briefly recap those concepts while introducing the example specification of a mix.

[1] Abrial calls this the "parachute" paradigm: He likens stepwise refinement with a parachute that opens more and more while falling until it is wide open when it reaches the surface (an implementation).

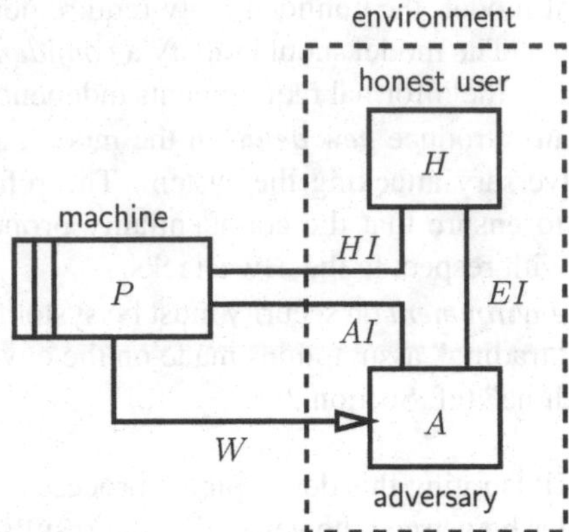

Fig. 1. Adversary Model: Machine, Honest Users, and Adversary

A *mix* [3] is a node in a communication network that mediates the communication between sending and receiving hosts in such a way that an external observer cannot infer who is communicating with whom, i.e., it ensures unobservability of communication relationships although an adversary can observe the sequence of sending events and the sequence receiving events at its interface. It is well-known that this requirement can be established in a strict sense only in an very restricted ("closed") environment but not in an open environment such as the Internet where requirements on the participating hosts cannot be strictly enforced. Knowing this, we formulate the following informal requirement concerning the anonymity provided by our system:

Considering a batch *of* 2*n events at the system interface, n events initiated by sending hosts and n corresponding events forwarding messages to the appropriate receivers, there are at least s different senders and r different receivers involved in the communication. Given the sequences of send events and receive events, the system ensures that all possible communication relationships are approximately equiprobable.*

The sequences of sending or receiving events are called the sender and receiver *anonymity sets*, respectively. Why we use sequences instead of proper sets will become clear shortly.

To capture this requirement, we first set up an abstract adversary model, which models a system with a particular class of adversaries. Following Jackson's [10] terminology, a *system* consists of a *machine* in its *environment* as shown in Figure 1. The machine is to be implemented whereas the environment captures the working conditions of the machine.

In an adversary model, the environment consists of two components: the honest users and the adversary. Formally, an adversary model (P, H, A, AI, EI, W, k) consists of

- a machine process P modeling the machine behavior;
- a process H modeling the admissible behavior of the honest users (or trusted environment);
- a process A modeling the assumed behavior of the adversary;

- a set of communication channels AI, the (functional) adversary interface to the machine;
- a set of channels EI allowing an active adversary to directly influence the honest users;
- a set of channels W, the *adversary window* modeling the adversary's capabilities to observe the system; and
- the maximal length k of system runs that the adversary can observe.

The structure of this model is similar to the one underlying reactive simulatability [20].

The process $Router_1$ models the basic functionality of the mix. It communicates with its environment by the channel ch. An event on that channel either has the form $ch.hs.Send.hr.Rec$ or the form $ch.hr.Rec.hs.Send$ where hs is a sending host and hr is a receiving host. The first message means that hs wishes to send to hr, whereas the second means that hr receives a message that hs initially sent. Note that the model does not mention message content, because the anonymity requirement does not refer[2] to message content.

The router has two modes of behavior: accepting messages from senders, and forwarding previously accepted messages. In a batch, it first (process $Accept(dss, cons)$) accepts n messages from sending hosts and stores them in the sequence dss. In each batch, it accepts each pair of senders and receivers at most once. The set $Connections$ contains all possible sender/receiver pairs. Having accepted n messages, the router forwards those messages to the respective receivers (process $Forward(dss)$). The router nondeterministically chooses the order in which the receivers are addressed ($\bigsqcap_{ds \in dss}$), i.e., it need not respect the order of events in dss.

$$
\begin{aligned}
Accept(dss) \mathrel{\widehat{=}} & \ \textbf{if}\ count(dss) = n\ \textbf{then}\ Forward(dss) \\
& \ \textbf{else}\ ch?hs.Send.hr.Rec \rightarrow \\
& \qquad Accept(dss \frown \langle hr.Rec.hs.Send \rangle) \\
Forward(dss) \mathrel{\widehat{=}} & \ \textbf{if}\ dss = \langle\,\rangle\ \textbf{then}\ Accept(\langle\,\rangle) \\
& \ \textbf{else}\ \bigsqcap_{ds \in dss} ch!ds \rightarrow Forward(dss - \{ds\}) \\
Router_1 \mathrel{\widehat{=}} & \ Forward(\langle\,\rangle)
\end{aligned}
$$

The process $Router_1$ models the basic functionality of the mix but it does not describe the possible observations of a (passive) adversary who gets to see the sender and receiver anonymity sets produced in each batch. The process $Observer$ intercepts the events on channel ch and, for each batch, writes a sender ($sends$) and a receiver ($recs$) anonymity set to the channels ws and wr, which make up the adversary window $W_1 = \{ws, wr\}$.

[2] Nevertheless, whether an implementation actually satisfies that requirement can depend on the way it deals with message content (cf., Section 4).

Summarizing, the process Mix_1, which is the parallel composition of $Router_1$ and *Observer* communicating over *ch*, is an abstract model of a mix system.

$$
\begin{aligned}
Obs(i, sends, recs) \mathrel{\widehat{=}} \; & \textbf{if } i = 2n \textbf{ then} \\
& \quad (ws!sends \rightarrow wr!recs \rightarrow Obs(0, \langle\,\rangle, \langle\,\rangle)) \\
& \textbf{else} \\
& \quad ((ch?hs.Send.hr.Rec \rightarrow Obs(i+1, sends \frown \langle hs \rangle, recs)) \\
& \quad \Box \; (ch?hr.Rec.hs.Send \rightarrow Obs(i+1, sends, recs \frown \langle hr \rangle)))
\end{aligned}
$$

$$Observer \mathrel{\widehat{=}} Obs(0, \langle\,\rangle, \langle\,\rangle)$$

$$Mix_1 \mathrel{\widehat{=}} Router_1 \,|[\{ch\}]|\, Observer$$

The system process Mix_1 alone is not a model of our anonymity requirement, because it does not enforce the lower bounds s and r on distinct senders and receivers in a batch. It also does not exhibit any probabilistic properties that would ensure the required approximate equiprobability of communication relationships in a batch.

For the abstract specification, we shift the responsibility of establishing those requirements to the environment communicating with Mix_1. In particular, the process $Sender_1$ chooses sequences of sender/receiver pairs that satisfy the cardinality requirements. The set

$$
\begin{aligned}
S = \{ & \langle hs_1.Send.hr_1.Rec, \ldots, hs_n.Send.hr_n.Rec \rangle \mid \\
& s \leqslant card(\{hs_1, \ldots, hs_n\}) \wedge r \leqslant card(\{hr_1, \ldots, hr_n\})\}
\end{aligned}
$$

comprises all admissible sequences of sending events. $Sender_1$ probabilistically chooses one of them (according to the distribution $\mathcal{P}$) and successively feeds them to the mix.

$$
\begin{aligned}
Feed(\langle\,\rangle) &= Sender_1 \\
Feed(\langle hs.Send.hr.Rec \rangle \frown t) &= ch!hs.Send.hr.Rec \rightarrow Feed(t) \\
Sender_1 &= \textstyle\bigoplus_{t \in S}^{\mathcal{P}} Feed(t)
\end{aligned}
$$

The process $Receiver_1$ complements $Sender_1$ by receiving any message *ch.hr.Rec....* on *ch*. Finally, the user environment of the mix system is the independent parallel execution Env_1 of those sender and receiver processes. We call $System_1$ the mix communicating with the environment on *ch*.

$$
\begin{aligned}
Env_1 &\mathrel{\widehat{=}} Sender_1 \;|||\; Receiver_1 \\
System_1 &\mathrel{\widehat{=}} Mix_1 \,|[\{ch\}]|\, Env_1
\end{aligned}
$$

We consider a passive adversary only. Therefore, the adversary interface is the empty set, and the process describing the adversary behavior in the adversary model is arbitrary (*Chaos*). The adversary model $AM_1 = (Mix_1, , Env_1, Chaos, \emptyset, \emptyset, \{ws, wr\}, k_0)$ collects all information about the abstract mix model described before and augments it with an upper bound k_0 on the length of system runs that an adversary considers when drawing conclusions from observations: No adversary will be prepared to wait infinitely long for the "next" observation to appear on the adversary window. In our case, a suitable k_0 is a multiple of the batch length $2n$.

3 Confidentiality Properties Are Existential

To validate an adversary model, it is useful to have a descriptive way of stating confidentiality properties that this model is supposed to satisfy. Considering the development process, the abstract specification should model as precisely as possible the *desired* confidentiality properties of the envisaged system. After all, all subsequent refinements will faithfully implement that specification. If the specification is too liberal, then an implementation may not satisfy the confidentiality requirements. If it is too strong, then an implementation may become unnecessarily complex or even impossible to build.

Earlier [22], we have discussed several kinds of confidentiality properties of adversary models. In the following, we state a possibilistic and a probabilistic property of AM_1 that reflect the anonymity requirement on mixes. Furthermore, we discuss the *existential* nature of confidentiality properties of adversary models.

3.1 Possibilistic Confidentiality

The adversary window W of an adversary model induces a partition on the traces of the system into *indistinguishability classes*, also called low-level equivalence sets [25]. Two traces are indistinguishable through W if their projection to the events on the channels in W are identical. For example, the traces

$$\langle ch.h_1.Send.h_2.Rec, ch.h_3.Send.h_4.Rec, ch.h_2.Rec.h_1.Send, ch.h_4.Rec.h_3.Send, ws.\langle h_1,h_3\rangle, wr.\langle h_2,h_4\rangle\rangle$$

and

$$\langle ch.h_1.Send.h_4.Rec, ch.h_3.Send.h_2.Rec, ch.h_2.Rec.h_3.Send, ch.h_4.Rec.h_1.Send, ws.\langle h_1,h_3\rangle, wr.\langle h_2,h_4\rangle\rangle$$

produce the same observation $\langle ws.\langle h_1,h_3\rangle, wr.\langle h_2,h_4\rangle\rangle$. Therefore, an adversary cannot distinguish on the basis of that observation (without further information) whether the system actually performed the first or the second trace. For the mix, this means that the adversary cannot distinguish the communication relations $(h_1 \mapsto h_2, h_3 \mapsto h_4)$ and $(h_1 \mapsto h_4, h_3 \mapsto h_2)$.

A *mask* $\mathcal{M}$ for an adversary model (P,H,A,AI,EI,W,k) is a set of pairwise disjoint subsets of the traces over the alphabet of P such that the members of each set produce the same observation. Thus, a mask represents the requirement that a system shall not allow an adversary to (possibilistically) distinguish between behavior that is in the same member set of the mask. Phrased as a confidentiality property, one can ask whether an adversary model *conceals* a given mask $\mathcal{M}$, i.e., whether each indistinguishability class of the system (communicating with its environment) either contains a member of $\mathcal{M}$ completely or not at all. The system of indistinguishability classes that an adversary model induces is a mask that the adversary model trivially conceals.

Showing that all members of the mask induced by AM_1 satisfy the cardinality requirements on the sets of senders and receivers in each batch, and that each member of a mask actually contains all possible traces satisfying those cardinality requirements, establishes a *possibilistic* validation of the adversary model, i.e., one that abstracts from probabilistic requirements.

3.2 The Refinement Paradox

The process $System_1$ is nondeterministic: *Forward* chooses the order of addressing receivers nondeterministically. Refining $System_1$ allows developers to resolve nondeterminism either by selecting one alternative deterministically or by assigning a probability distribution to the set of alternatives. Therefore, a functionally correct refinement of $System_1$ may implement *Forward* in such a way that it just copies the events in *dss* to the channel *ch in the order of their appearance in dss*. That implementation would *not* conceal the mask induced by $System_1$, i.e., it would violate the possibilistic confidentiality property stated in Section 3.1.

Roscoe [21] showed that possibilistic information flow properties are not preserved under CSP refinement, and he called this observation the *refinement paradox*. Refinement in CSP in particular requires that all traces of the refining process are traces of the refined one (but not necessary vice versa).

To avoid the refinement paradox, Roscoe proposes to consider only deterministic processes to model information flow requirements. Deterministic processes are fully refined, and the refinement paradox does not invalidate propositions about those processes with respect to information flow properties.

From a methodological point of view, however, requiring the initial adversary model to be deterministic seems to be very restrictive. When setting up $System_1$, we do not wish to fix the order in which *Forward* will put the events in *dss* on *ch*. However, we want to be sure that *there is* an implementation of *Forward* (and $System_1$ as a whole) that satisfies the confidentiality requirements.

This observation makes confidentiality properties of adversary models *existential*: An adversary model satisfies a confidentiality property if not necessarily all but at least one functionally correct refinement satisfies that property. This statement in particular applies to probabilistic confidentiality properties.

3.3 Probabilistic Confidentiality

Addressing the requirement that all system behaviors producing the same anonymity sets shall be approximately equiprobable raises two issues: first, what is the probability of a system behavior given an observation on the adversary window *W*; second, what is a general way to capture that kind of probabilistic confidentiality requirement?

Probabilistic CSP [19] extends the (classical) calculus of CSP with a probabilistic choice operator, which we use to model the choice of sender / receiver pairs in the environment process $Sender_1$. Nevertheless, it is impossible to determine the probability of a trace of $System_1$, because Mix_1 does not contain information about the probabilities with which nondeterministic choices are resolved. For this technical reason, it is necessary to consider a *refinement* of the system process that resolves all nondeterminism in a probabilistic way. It is also necessary to require that the environment "drives" the system in such a way that all external choices, where the system accepts input from the environment, are resolved probabilistically. We call such an environment[3] *admissible*.

[3] A *scheduler* [4, 24] for nondeterministic probabilistic processes serves a similar purpose but usually is not specified as a process but as a function on the semantics of processes.

If these conditions hold for a process QE, then the upper bound k on the length of the considered system traces ensures that the *conditional probability* $\mathrm{P}^k_W(t|o)$ of a trace t of QE given an observation o (on W) is well-defined.

The usual probabilistic measure for uncertainty is the entropy of the set of possible (stochastic) events. In our setting, we can define the (conditional) entropy of a class $J^{QE,k}_W(o)$ of indistinguishable system behaviors, which all produce the observation o on W, as follows:

$$H^k_W(QE|o) = \sum_{t \in J^{QE,k}_W(o)} \mathrm{P}^k_W(t|o) \cdot \log \frac{1}{\mathrm{P}^k_W(t|o)}$$

A confidentiality property based on the conditional entropy puts lower bounds on the entropy of each member of a mask $\mathcal{M}$, which the adversary model conceals (for details, see [22]). Let $\mathcal{H} : \mathcal{M} \to \mathbb{R}^+$ map classes of $\mathcal{M}$ to possible values of entropy. The adversary model (P, H, A, AI, EI, W, k) *ensures the entropy* $\mathcal{H}$ *for* $\mathcal{M}$, written $Ent^{\mathcal{H}}_{\mathcal{M}}(P, H, A, AI, EI, W, k)$, if *there exists* a refinement Q of P such that for any admissible environment E, the process QE that is Q driven by E, first, conceals $\mathcal{M}$, and second, produces indistinguishability classes whose entropy respects the bounds given by $\mathcal{H}$. Formally:

$$\forall M : \mathcal{M} \bullet \forall o : \mathrm{Obs}_W(QE) \mid M \subseteq J^{QE,k}_W(o) \bullet \mathcal{H}(M) \leq H^k_W(QE|o)$$

Note that this property only requires a refinement of the machine model P to exist that satisfies the bounds on the entropy. It does not require all possible refinements to satisfy that bound. This is similar to a performance requirement, where one cannot expect all functionally correct implementations to respect performance bounds. Usually, only few of all possible implementations will meet performance requirements.

For the mix specification AM_1, the mask to consider consists of the indistinguishability classes induced by AM_1. The informal requirement calls for approximately equiprobable members of those classes, which corresponds to requiring the entropy of those classes to be nearly maximal. If the distribution $\mathcal{P}$ in $Sender_1$ is uniform, and the nondeterministic choice in Mix_1 is also resolved in that way, then the resulting refinement satisfies the entropy condition. For the purpose of this paper, the exact calculation of the entropy is not important.

However, it is methodologically relevant to note that – as for the possibilistic requirement – we have an adversary model that exactly produces the required bounds.

4 Confidentiality-Preserving Refinement

The adversary model AM_1 captures the essential requirements on a mix, but it does not model a useful system. Refinements must introduce further detail to add useful functionality. This includes extending the model with message content, and reducing nondeterminism. When refining the functionality of the system, the possibilities of an adversary need to be re-evaluated, too. This results in stating an adversary window for the refining model, which in general extends the one of the refined model, because the new model may introduce new means of observation for the adversary. Nevertheless, the refining adversary model must preserve the confidentiality properties of the refined one. Otherwise, the refinement would not be correct with respect to security.

A definition of *confidentiality-preserving refinement* must address two requirements:

1. a confidentiality-preserving refinement must be functionally correct (disregarding the extension of the adversary window);
2. it must establish a sufficient condition to preserve the existence of a deterministic refinement satisfying the required confidentiality property.

The first requirement is easily expressed in terms of the usual refinement of PCSP. For the probabilistic confidentiality of Section 3.3, the second requirement can be captured formally in terms of the mutual information between the behavior of the abstract adversary model and the observations of the concrete model, given an abstract observation, similar to the information flow property of Gray [7]. For the purpose of this paper, it suffices to appeal to the reader's intuition and discuss methodological considerations by way of the running example. A formal definition of confidentiality-preserving refinement [8, 23] has been stated elsewhere.

The adversary model AM_1 abstracts from the message content that senders and receivers exchange because that content is irrelevant for stating the confidentiality *requirements*, i.e., the desired properties of the system. To make the mix practically useful, to transmit message content is an obvious functional requirement. The first refinement AM_2 of AM_1 therefore extends the model by a type of messages that senders and receivers exchange.

For the process definitions, this means to extend each event on the channel *ch* with a new component *m*, the message content. The refined version of the router, $Router_2$ is defined as follows.

$$\begin{aligned}
Accept_m(dsms) \mathrel{\widehat{=}} &\ \textbf{if}\ count(dsms) = n\ \textbf{then} \\
&\quad \textstyle\bigsqcap_{rc:RECODING} Forward_m(dsms, rc) \\
&\ \textbf{else}\ ch?s.d.m \rightarrow \\
&\quad Accept_m(dsms \frown \langle d.s.m \rangle) \\
Forward_m(dsms, rc) \mathrel{\widehat{=}} &\ \textbf{if}\ dss = \langle\,\rangle\ \textbf{then}\ Accept_m(\langle\,\rangle) \\
&\ \textbf{else} \textstyle\bigsqcap_{d.s.m \in dsms} ch!d.s.rc(m) \rightarrow Forward_m(dss - \{ds\}, rc) \\
Router_2 \mathrel{\widehat{=}} &\ Accept_m(\langle\,\rangle)
\end{aligned}$$

The forwarding process now relies on a bijective message recoding function *rc* as an additional parameter. The router chooses that function nondeterministically for each batch of messages. A further refinement would implement *rc* by an asymmetric crypto system where the recoding corresponds to decoding messages with the secret key.

If the adversary's observational power remained the same as in AM_1 then the confidentiality properties of the refined system would not be in question. It is more realistic to assume that the adversary can observe the exchanged messages and the sequence of send and receive events at the interface of the mix as well. The adversary still cannot directly observe the sender / receiver relation. The new observer process produces the corresponding observations at the new adversary window *wm*, which records for each send event the sender *hs* and the message *m*, and for each receive event the receiver *hr* and the associated message *m*.

$$Observer_m \mathrel{\widehat{=}} (ch?hs.Send.hr.Rec.m \rightarrow wm!hs.Send.m \rightarrow Observer_m)$$
$$\Box\, (ch?hr.Rec.hs.Send.m \rightarrow wm!hr.Rec.m \rightarrow Observer_m)$$

The new environment Env_2 behaves similar to Env_1 but, of course, supplies message content as well as sender and receiver information. The processes Mix_2 and $System_2$ are defined as before.

The crucial question now is whether the new adversary model $AM_2 = (Mix_2, Env_2, Chaos, \emptyset, \emptyset, \{ws, wr, wm\}, k)$ is a confidentiality preserving refinement of AM_1. For this to hold, the two refinement conditions mentioned before must be satisfied. First, the new machine process must be a behavioral refinement of the first one. Second, the adversary's possibilities in AM_2 must not allow the adversary to distinguish "more" than the adversary model AM_1 allows him to.

For PCSP, there is a formal notion of refinement $P \sqsubseteq Q$ that basically allows a refining process Q to replace nondeterministic choices of P by probabilistic choices with specific probability distributions (this includes a distribution that assigns a probability of 1.0 to a particular branch and thus makes the refinement deterministic at that choice point). A *renaming* of events allows us to abstract from the newly introduced message data. The relation R_2^1 replaces all events *ch.s.d.m* by events *ch.s.d*.

$$R_2^1 = \{ch.s.d.m \mapsto ch.s.d \mid s,d \in HOST \wedge m \in MESSAGE\}$$

Thus, the renamed process $System_2[\![R_2^1]\!]$ works on the same set of events on channel *ch* as $System_1$. For comparing the functional behavior of the two systems, the extension *wm* of the adversary window in AM_2 is irrelevant. Therefore, this channel is hidden in the following refinement relation:

$$System_1 \sqsubseteq System_2 \setminus \{wm\}[\![R_2^1]\!]$$

This classical correctness condition contributes to integrity and availability because it ensures that $System_2$ actually exhibits the functional behavior that $System_1$ models. It also ensures that the common part of the adversary windows behaves in a compatible way.

Concerning confidentiality, i.e., the anonymity provided by the new model of the mix, we need to compare the observational power described in AM_2 to the one prescribed in AM_1. Obviously, AM_2 allows the adversary to distinguish more detail of a batch of communication: not only the sender and receiver anonymity sets, but also the exact sequence of sending and receiving events, and the message content of those events is visible to the adversary. The crucial question now is whether the newly possible observations break the confidentiality properties of AM_1, i.e., whether they allow the adversary to distinguish members of the same indistinguishability class of AM_1 – possibilistically or probabilistically.

The sequences of events $Observer_m$ contain information about the messages exchanged between senders and receivers. Abstracting from that information (using R_2^1), the remaining sets of indistinguishable traces are covered by the mask that AM_1 induces.

Therefore, it is worthwhile to analyze whether AM_2 preserves the probabilistic confidentiality properties of AM_1. This is the case if there are PCSP refinements of Mix_1 and Mix_2 such that for all refinements of Env_1 there is a refinement of Env_2 such that Mix_1 composed with Env_1 is refined by Mix_2 composed with Env_2, and those processes satisfy the above mentioned condition on mutual information. In the example, this means that there are refinements of Mix_2 such that the choice of a message (which is observable in AM_2) does not provide information about the sender or the receiver of the message. This can be achieved by using recoding functions that do not establish a correlation between messages and their recodings.

5 The Role of the Environment

Technically, the two environment processes H and A are necessary components of an adversary model because they ensure that a probabilistic analysis of a system makes sense (cf., Section 3.3).

However, the environment model also serves a methodological purpose. In an adversary model, the user environment process H models assumptions about the behavior of the legitimate users on which the system may rely. The adversary environment A describes the behavior expected of an active adversary.

Because the user environment process is part of an adversary model, a development can start with an ideal environment, which relieves the initial system model from certain responsibilities. It is then the task of subsequent refinement steps to relax the restrictions on the environment and "trade" them with the responsibilities of the system. Making the environment less restrictive means that the system can rely on weaker assumptions and consequently must incorporate more functionality to achieve the same result as the abstract system interacting with the abstract environment.

In the example, the adversary model AM_1 assumes that the environment process $Sender_1$ triggers the system process Mix_1 such that all sender / receiver pairs (matching given anonymity sets) are equiprobable in each batch. In a second refinement step, the first refinement AM_2 can be developed further to reduce the responsibility of the environment. If the environment $Sender_3$ of the new adversary model AM_3 consists of sender processes which will produce messages at arbitrary rates, then it is the responsibility of the new system process Net_3 of AM_3 to ensure sufficient (and adequately distributed) traffic at the mix node. This means, the system must implement part of the environment functionality of $Sender_2$. It must do this in a distributed manner because the adversary window will still give access to the events on the interface of the proper mix node. The system process therefore consists of a collection of send clients (residing with the senders) and the proper mix node:

$$Net_3 = SendClients \,|[\, \{ch.hs.Send\} \,]|\, Mix_3$$

The refinement condition requires that Net_2 *in the context of the environment* implements the Mix_2 communicating with its environment.

This trading between environment assumptions and machine functionality continues in further refinement steps until the environment process is a realistic model of the true machine environment and (consequently) the machine model incorporates sufficient functionality to satisfy the security requirements in the context of the true environment.

If the trading does not succeed, i.e., there is no realistic way of relaxing the environment assumption to meet the true proposed working environment of the system, then this shows that the security requirements cannot be met without further non-technical (organizational or legal) measures.

6 Related Work

The idea of development by stepwise refinement is perhaps most stringently realized in the *B method* [1], which has been used successfully to support the development of safety-critical systems (e.g., [2]).

Much research has investigated possibilistic [6, 17, 25, 16] and probabilistic [7] information flow properties, but there is little work on a refinement based methodology to develop secure systems. Jürjens [13, 14] introduces notions of secure refinements in the context of UMLsec. Section 8.2 [14] mentions refinement-based development with UML but does not elaborate on methodological issues.

Mantel [15] considers the preservation of information flow properties under refinement. It is well-known that CSP-style refinement does not preserve information flow properties in general [11]. Mantel shows how refinement operators tailored for specific information flow properties can modify an intended refinement such that the resulting refinement preserves the given flow property. He, too, does not elaborate on a refinement-based methodology.

Only recently, Hutter [9] has shown how to preserve possibilistic information flow properties in action refinements, where an atomic abstract action can be refined into a sequence of concrete actions.

A unified model with a refinement relation preserving possibilistic and probabilistic confidentiality properties in the presence of data refinement and action refinement has not been published yet.

7 Conclusion

We have shown the effect of applying the well-known paradigm of stepwise refinement to secure systems development. The following conclusions are of particular importance:

- The first, abstract model should describe the desired security properties as precise as possible. Then, it must be verified whether it satisfies the required security properties.
- That satisfaction relation is existential, not universal: Usually, not all but only few implementations of an abstract model are secure. The refinement process therefore must ensure that each refined model still admits a secure implementation.
- Introducing new detail in a refinement, in particular data-refining the model, usually entails to re-consider the adversary capabilities. Verifying the refinement must

show that those new capabilities do not compromise security. If they do, relaxing the security requirements is a realistic option because one tends to start with overly ambitious idealistic security requirements which may not be achievable in a practical implementation.
- Models of the (friendly) environment and the adversary behavior are integral parts of a system model for security. It is advisable to start the development with a relatively strong environment model and relax the assumptions on the environment in subsequent refinement steps. This eases capturing security requirements in the abstract model, and it allows to gradually increase the complexity of the implementation while reducing the one of the environment. If the achievable environment properties are still stronger than the properties that the true environment guarantees, then non-technical assumptions need to be considered.

Although this paper has discussed a formal notion of system models and refinement, these conclusions can be interpreted in a broader view: It is worthwhile to start with a set of precisely elaborated security requirements and develop a system in a stepwise fashion, introducing new complexity in small, manageable chunks. Frequent evaluation of the resulting security properties can help to early spot states of the development where a trade-off between security and other requirements is necessary – and achieve this trade-off in a systematic and controlled way.

References

[1] J.-R. Abrial. *The B-Book: Assigning programs to meanings*. Cambridge University Press, 1996.

[2] P. Behm, P. Benoit, A. Faivre, and J.-M. Meynadier. Météor: A successful application of B in a large project. In J. Wing, J. Woodcock, and J. Davies, editors, *FM'99 – Formal Methods*, volume I of *LNCS 1708*, pages 369–387. Springer-Verlag, 1999.

[3] D. L. Chaum. Untraceable electronic mail, return addresses, and digital pseudonyms. *Communications of the ACM*, 24(2):84–88, 1981.

[4] F. Ciesinski and M. Größer. On probabilistic computation tree logic. In C. Baier, B. R. Haverkort, H. Hermanns, J.-P. Katoen, and M. Siegle, editors, *Validation of Stochastic Systems: A Guide to Current Research*, LNCS 2925, pages 147 – 188. Springer-Verlag, 2004.

[5] J. Derrick and E. Boiten. *Refinement in Z and Object-Z*. Springer-Verlag, London, 2001.

[6] J.A. Goguen and J. Meseguer. Security policies and security models. In *IEEE Symposium on Security and Privacy*, pages 11–20. IEEE Computer Society Press, 1982.

[7] J. W. Gray, III. Toward a mathematical foundation for information flow security. *Journal of Computer Security*, pages 255–294, 1992.

[8] M. Heisel, A. Pfitzmann, and T. Santen. Confidentiality-preserving refinement. In *14th IEEE Computer Security Foundations Workshop*, pages 295–305. IEEE Computer Society Press, 2001.

[9] D. Hutter. Possibilistic information flow control in MAKS and action refinement. In G. Müller, editor, *Emerging Trends in Information and Communication Security (ETRICS)*, LNCS 3995, pages 268–281. Springer-Verlag, 2006.

[10] M. Jackson. *Problem Frames: Analyzing and Structuring Software Development Problems*. Addison-Wesley, 2000.

[11] J. Jacob. On the derivation of secure components. In *IEEE Symposium on Security and Privacy*, pages 242–247. IEEE Press, 1989.

[12] C. B. Jones. *Systematic Software Development using VDM.* Prentice Hall, 2nd edition, 1990.

[13] J. Jürjens. Secrecy-preserving refinement. In J. N. Oliveira and P. Zave, editors, *FME 2001: Formal Methods for Increasing Software Productivity*, LNCS 2021, pages 135–152. Springer-Verlag, 2001.

[14] J. Jürjens. *Secure Systems Development with UML.* Springer-Verlag, 2005.

[15] H. Mantel. Preserving information flow properties under refinement. In *IEEE Symposium on Security and Privacy*, pages 78–91. IEEE Computer Society Press, 2001.

[16] H. Mantel. *A Uniform Framework for the Formal Specification and Verification of Information Flow Security.* PhD thesis, Universität des Saarlandes, 2003.

[17] J. McLean. A general theory of composition for a class of "possibilistic" properties. *IEEE Transactions on Software Engineering*, 22(1):53–67, 1996.

[18] B. Meyer. Applying "design by contract". *IEEE Computer*, pages 40–51, October 1992.

[19] C. Morgan, A. McIver, K. Seidel, and J. W. Sanders. Refinement-oriented probability for CSP. *Formal Aspects of Computing*, 8(6):617–647, 1996.

[20] B. Pfitzmann and M. Waidner. A model for asynchronous reactive systems and its application to secure message transmission. In *IEEE Symposium on Security and Privacy*, pages 184–201. IEEE Computer Society, 2001.

[21] A. W. Roscoe. CSP and determinism in security modelling. In *Proc. IEEE Symposium on Security and Privacy*, pages 114–127. IEEE Computer Society Press, 1995.

[22] T. Santen. Probabilistic confidentiality properties based on indistinguishability. In H. Federrath, editor, *Proc. Sicherheit 2005 – Schutz und Zuverlässigkeit*, Lecture Notes in Informatics, pages 113–124. Gesellschaft für Informatik, 2005.

[23] T. Santen. A formal framework for confidentiality-preserving refinement. In D. Gollmann and A. Sabelfeld, editors, *Proc. 11th European Symposium On Research In Computer Security (ESORICS)*, LNCS. Springer-Verlag, 2006. to appear.

[24] R. Segala and N. Lynch. Probabilistic simulations for probabilistic processes. In *Proc. 5th Int. Conf. on Concurrency Theory (CONCUR '94)*, LNCS 836, pages 481–496. Springer-Verlag, 1994.

[25] A. Zakinthinos and E. S. Lee. A general theory of security properties. In *Proc. IEEE Symposium on Security and Privacy*, pages 94–102, 1997.

Component-Based Hazard Analysis: Optimal Designs, Product Lines, and Online-Reconfiguration*

Holger Giese and Matthias Tichy

Software Engineering Group, University of Paderborn,
Warburger Str. 100, D-33098 Paderborn, Germany
{hg, mtt}@upb.de

Abstract. Software plays an important role in the safety of today's systems and is increasingly used to create system with variants in form of product families or systems with online-reconfiguration in a cost-efficient manner. Therefore, the required hazard analysis has to consider not only a concrete system and its embedded software but also the different software configurations. We present several extensions to an existing component-based hazard analysis approach. At first, our approach permits to identify the optimal design variant w.r.t. the probabilities of the considered hazard. As the number of variants in a product family is often enormous, our approach secondly supports the hazard analysis of a whole product family at once. The analysis identifies the variant or combination of variants with the worst hazard probability. Finally, we show that also the hazards of systems with online-reconfiguration can be analyzed using the presented approach.

1 Introduction

Advanced mechanical products such as cars or airplanes are today realized as so called mechatronic systems. In these mechatronic systems, beside the classical mechanical, electronic, and control engineering disciplines, software engineering plays an important role, as mechanical solutions are often replaced by pure information processing in order to improve the functionality or reduce costs as in the case of fly-by-wire or drive-by-wire solutions. Therefore, software and the interaction between the different distributed software units of the system has a tremendous impact on the safety of today's systems. One of the most demanding area in this respect is the automotive area. Here software has become an important factor in the development of modern high-end vehicles and grows at an exponential rate while resource and cost constraints make it difficult to apply existing approaches to handle the software from other areas such as avionics. Today, about 70 % of the innovations in these cars are software driven and an increase of the percentage of costs due to the development of software is expected from 20-25 % up to 40 % in the next years (cf. [1]).

Today, not only a single product but a number of basic configurations and a large number of optional features for each new product are typically offered. As the different

* This work was developed in the course of the Special Research Initiative 614 - Self-optimizing Concepts and Structures in Mechanical Engineering - University of Paderborn, and was published on its behalf and funded by the Deutsche Forschungsgemeinschaft.

J. Górski (Ed.): SAFECOMP 2006, LNCS 4166, pp. 156–169, 2006.

variants have to be developed in a cost-efficient manner, the paradigm of software product families [2,3] has therefore been proposed also for mechatronic products (cf. [4]) to enable reuse across several variants of the same product. In the software architecture of these product families the variabilities and dependencies between different features are explicitly modeled and controlled. Therefore, the different variants of the software and the different system configurations can be derived from the same product line model reusing of the same components for a number of system configurations. Often the number of variant combinations which have to be analyzed to cover a product family is too large to apply standard approaches for the safety analysis to each of them. A feasible approach which supports the hazard analysis of a whole product family at once is thus required.

Alternative behavior does not only result from alternative variants which are selected at design time. As reported in [5], we can also expect that that the next-generation of advanced mechatronic systems will adapt their behavior online by means of software that reconfigures itself in response to changes in the observed context (also denoted as self-adaptation or self-optimization [6]). Therefore, also safety analysis techniques which also cover online-reconfiguration are required in the long run.

In this paper we describe a number of extensions to an existing component-based hazard analysis approach (cf. [7]) which exploits the component-oriented character of the software to enable a cost-effective safety analysis by enabling the reuse of component-specific failure propagation information.[1] Assuming a description of the software architecture which covers multiple alternatives, our extensions then permit to identify the optimal design variant w.r.t. the probabilities of all considered hazards. In the case of alternative variants of the system rather than a decision at design time which alternative to chose, the number of variants in a product family is often too large to be able to apply standard safety analysis approaches to each variant. Therefore, our extensions also support to analyze the whole product family at once concerning hazards by identifying the worst case hazard probability for all variants which permit that upper bounds for the whole product family can be established. Also, systems with online-reconfiguration can be analyzed using a slight modification of the proposed extensions.

The remainder of the paper is organized as follows: We at first discuss the current state of the art for the hazard analysis of systems with design alternatives or online-reconfiguration in Section 2. Then, the running example employed to explain our approach is introduced in Section 3 and used to outline the later extended basic component-based hazard analysis approach in Section 4. Thereafter, the extension of the component-based hazard analysis approach towards alternative structures is introduced in Section 5. In Section 6, we then describe how an optimal design alternative w.r.t. the hazard analysis can be identified, how the analysis of product families can be tackled, and how the online case can be addressed. We finish the paper with our final conclusions and an outlook on future work.

[1] It is to be noted that component-based hazard analysis approaches do not address the functional correctness of the components or their correct interconnection. Additional analysis tasks have to ensure that all considered component configurations interact safely (cf. [8]).

2 State of the Art

Component-based hazard analysis is a hot topic in safety-critical systems research [9,10,11,12,13]. The basic idea is to ease the hazard analysis by reusing already available information about failure behavior of the individual components rather than always start from scratch when performing a hazard analysis. The current approaches for component-based hazard analysis have in common that they describe the failure propagation of individual components (cf. failure propagation and transfer nets [3]). Outgoing failures are the result of the combination of internal errors and incoming failures from other components. The failure classification presented in [14,15] is widely employed (as in [10,12]) to distinguish different failures.

Papadopoulos et al. [10] describe an approach for a component-based hazard analysis. The basic idea is a Failure Modes and Effects Analysis (FMEA) for each component based on its interfaces (called IF-FMEA). The outgoing failures are disjunctions of a combination of internal errors and a combination of incoming failures. They employ the notion of block diagrams [16] for their components. The results of IF-FMEA are combined to construct a fault tree for the complete system. A main advantage, besides reusing already available IF-FMEA results, is an improved consistency between the structure of the system design and the fault tree of the system. This approach has been integrated with component concepts of the ROOM [17] methodology in [12]. A major weakness of these approaches (as noted in [9]) is the usage of a fault tree for the combination of the individual IF-FMEA results, since fault trees do not inherently support common mode failures like a hardware crash failure which influences all software components executed on that node. Additionally, the authors impose an unnecessary restriction by the definition that the internal errors are always combined by an logical or with the incoming failures.

Kaiser et al. [11] present a component concept for fault tree analysis. They propose to divide a fault tree into fault tree components. A fault tree component has incoming and outgoing ports. These ports are used to connect the different components and create the complete fault tree. The main advantage of this approach is the possibility to reuse existing fault tree components. Thus, by building a repository of fault tree components for often used system components, the building of fault trees becomes easier. Unfortunately, the proposed fault tree components are not linked in any way to the system components, whose faults they are modelling. In [13] this approach has been integrated with ROOM [17]. The input and output actions are used to derive all failure ports. The failure ports which are used for the connection of the fault tree components are still not typed. In contrast, our approach additionally supports the flexible classification of failures at a greater level of detail. In contrast to all discussed approaches, we explicitly allow cycles in the failure propagation models.

Addouche et al. present an approach for the dependability analysis of systems modeled using structure and behavior UML diagrams [18]. They extend the UML diagrams by probabilistic and timed annotations and use a probabilistic model checker to verify dependability properties. Our approach differs since we pessimistically abstract from behavior and, thus, can provide a more scalable analysis approach.

All above presented approaches do not directly support the hazard analysis of product variants of product lines. Instead, variants must be manually created and analyzed.

Ortmeier et a.l. present in [19] the ForMoSa approach for safety analysis. The approach builds on the foundation of fault tree analysis for hazard analysis. The approach supports the analysis of systems with free parameters, e.g. timing parameters. Model instances with different parameter values can be understand as variants. The approach supports the optimization of the hazard probability by changes to these free parameters. Our approach is different in supporting variants not only for parameter values but also for different *structures*. In addition, our approach can be used to identify the worst variant of a product family with respect to the hazard probabilities.

3 Application Example

A small excerpt from the New Railway Technology project[2] and its safety-critical software is used in the following as our application example. The overall project aims at using a passive track system with intelligent shuttles that operate autonomously and make independent and decentralized operational decisions. Shuttles either transport goods or up to approx. 10 passengers.

The track system, the shuttles are using, is divided into several disjoint sections each of which is controlled by a section control. To enter a section, a shuttle has to be registered at the corresponding section control. The shuttle sends its data, like position and speed, to the section control. The section control in turn sends the data of all other shuttles within the section. Thus, each shuttle knows which other shuttles are nearby. Shuttles can communicate with each other. If two shuttles approach at a switch, they can bargain who has right of way. Depending on the topology, the shuttles speed and its position an optimizer calculates the bid. A more detailed description of this scenario can be found in [20].

In our example, represented in Figure 1, two shuttle components, a switch and a section control interact with each other. A component is depicted as rectangle labelled with at least the component's type (string following the colon) and possibly labelled with the component's name (string preceding the colon). A component represents one instance of a given type. Consider for example the component on the left of Figure 1. This component is an instance of type Shuttle and is named sh1. In our example there is also another shuttle component sh2. This component is of the same type as sh1.

Component ports are shown as small squares at the component's border. These ports are used for interaction with other components. In Figure 1, one port of the shuttle component is connected with the SectionControl. In this case data is sent in both directions which is depicted by arrows at both ends of the connection. Some of the connectors are labelled with nl1..4, this indicates that a network is used for the communication of the corresponding components.

For our example, we consider two variants. The speed and the position of the shuttle can be determined either by employing a SpeedSensor or a GPS sensor. Figure 2 shows the component structure of these two variants.

To describe the connection of hardware and the deployed software components we employ UML deployment diagrams. For presentation reasons, the UML deployment

[2] www.railcab.de/en/

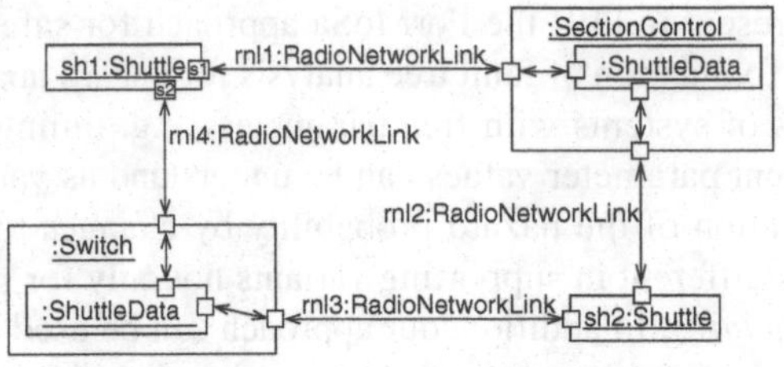

Fig. 1. Component structure with shuttles, switch, and section control

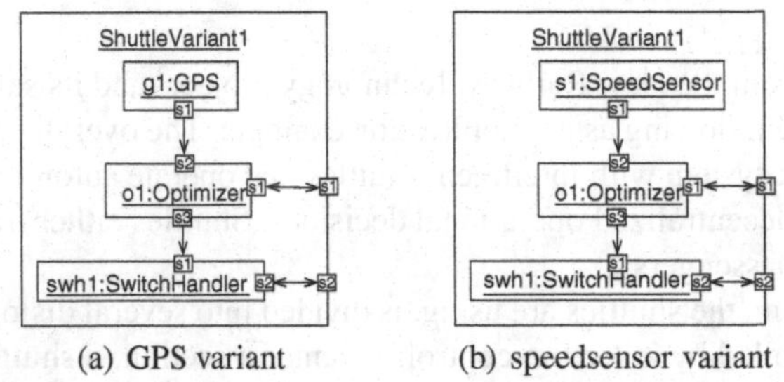

(a) GPS variant (b) speedsensor variant

Fig. 2. Variants of the shuttle component

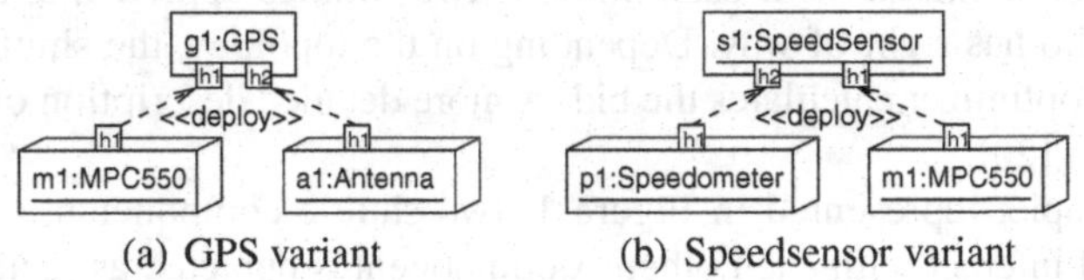

(a) GPS variant (b) Speedsensor variant

Fig. 3. Deployment specification

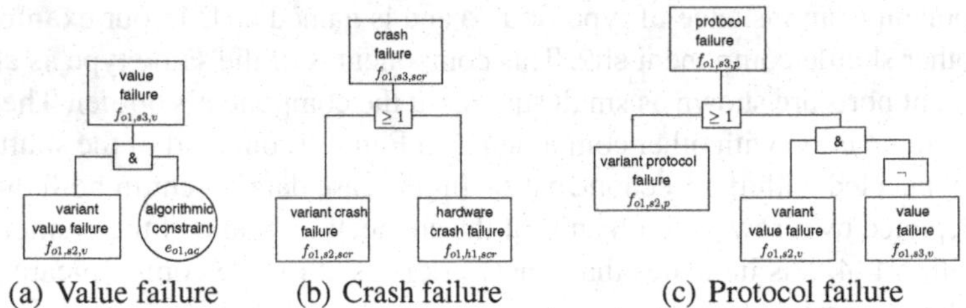

(a) Value failure (b) Crash failure (c) Protocol failure

Fig. 4. Failure propagation of the optimizer component

diagrams are visually slightly extended to include the additional hardware ports. These hardware ports are used to denote the propagation of hardware failures.

Figure 3 shows the deployment specification for the two software variants s1 and g1. Both software components are deployed on the same node m1. Nodes and software components are connected by special deployment connections and, thus, employ the same error and failure propagation concepts. In addition, both sensor software components use special hardware devices for the actual reading of the sensor data (a1 resp. p1). We omit the mapping of the network links nl1..4 of Figure 1 to a wireless network for the sake of clearer presentation.

4 Component-Based Hazard Analysis

The component-based architecture presented in Figure 1 and 2 can be exploited to analyze the systems for hazards in a compositional manner. We will in the following revisit the employed basic component-based hazard analysis technique of [7].

Assuming a set $\mathcal{C}$ of components $c \in \mathcal{C}$ with $\mathcal{C}^h$ the hardware components and $\mathcal{C}^s$ the software components, we use software ports $sn \in \mathcal{P}^s$ and hardware ports $hn \in \mathcal{P}^h$ with $n \in I\!N$ to describe the architecture of a system. A system $\mathcal{S}$ can thus be characterized by a set of components and a connection relation $map \subseteq \mathcal{C} \times \mathcal{P} \times \mathcal{C} \times \mathcal{P}$ between the ports of the components. The component structure of Figures 1 and 3 is formalized using the above defined sets and relations.

For the outlined component-based architecture, we can conclude that *failures* – the external visible derivation from the correct behavior – can only occur at the ports where the components interact with their environment, while *errors* – the manifestation of a *fault* in the state of a component – are restricted to the internal of the component.

The basic idea to formally model the failure propagation of the components and the occurrence of hazards due to failures is to use Boolean logic with quantifiers (cf. [21]) to encode the failure propagation. We use two disjoint Boolean variable sets V_F and V_E for the propagation of failures and probabilistic independent local events (most often errors), respectively.

As outlined in [7], we use an extensible failure classification to ensure that the failure propagation specified for the different components can be combined. In the following, we restrict our considerations on the three general failure types crash failure (scr), protocol failure (p), and value failure (v) which build a complete failure classification $\mathcal{F}$. Failure and event variables are further named according to the following schema: $f_{c,p,t}$ and $e_{c,t}$ for a component $c \in \mathcal{C}$, port $p \in \mathcal{P}$, and failure type $t \in \mathcal{F}$. In the case of the events which do not relate to any specific failure type appropriate event types are simply added. The crash error $e_{m1,scr}$ of hardware component m1 is thus contained in set V_E. A crash failure $f_{o1,h1,scr}$ of the software component o1 incoming from its hardware port h1 is contained in set V_F.

The failure propagation of each component can then be described by Boolean logic expressions over the failure variables ($f_j \in V_F$ where V_F^s are related to software ports and V_F^h are related to hardware ports), event variables ($e_k \in V_E$), and the Boolean constants 1 for true and 0 for false using the basic Boolean operators $\wedge$, $\vee$, $\neg$, $\Rightarrow$, $\Leftrightarrow$ and quantifiers $\forall$ and $\exists$.We use $free(\phi)$ to denote the set of free variables of ϕ.

Definition 1. *For every component* $c \in \mathcal{C}$ *we employ a* failure propagation information $F_c = (O_F^c, I_F^c, V_E^c, \psi_c)$ *which consists of the following four elements: (1) A set of* outgoing failure variables $O_F^c \subseteq V_F$*, (2) a set of* incoming failure variables $I_F^c \subseteq V_F$*, (3) a set of possible internal* event variables $V_E^c \subseteq V_E$*, and (4) a failure dependency* *condition ψ_c which relates the variables for failures and errors to each other by a Boolean logic formula ($free(\psi_c) \subseteq O_F^c \cup I_F^c \cup V_E^c$). We require $O_F^c \cap I_F^c = \emptyset$.*

If an incoming failure represented by the variable f_k directly results in the outgoing failure represented by the variable f_l, the failure dependency ψ_c must include $f_l \Leftrightarrow f_k$. In general, the failure propagation for an outgoing failure $f_j \in O_F^c$ is described by the corresponding formula ϕ_j over the incoming failures and events ($free(\phi_j) \subseteq I_F^c \cup V_E^c$) in the form $f_j \Leftrightarrow \phi_j$.

Figures 4(a) and 4(b) show the failure propagation for value and crash failures of the Optimizer component. As is apparent from the component variant diagrams (Figures 2(a) and 2(b)), the Optimizer uses either the information provided by the GPS or the SpeedSensor to compute the bids for the bargaining. The employed variant is connected to the Optimizer via the $s2$ port. The Optimizer has the ability to detect value failures in the data, provided by the GPS or the SpeedSensor. Due to algorithmic constraints, the failure detection cannot detect small value failures and therefore an internal event (event type ac) is added to model this algorithmic constraint.[3] The second failure propagation model specifies that the optimizer cannot tolerate a crash failure of a sensor variant or the execution hardware. A protocol failure of the sensor variant or detected value failures propagate to an outgoing protocol failure as specified in Figure 4(c). Thus, we get the following failure propagation: $\psi_{o1} = (f_{o1,s3,v} \Leftrightarrow (f_{o1,s2,v} \wedge e_{o1,ac})) \wedge (f_{o1,s3,scr} \Leftrightarrow (f_{o1,s2,scr} \vee f_{o2,h1,scr})) \wedge (f_{o1,s3,p} \Leftrightarrow (f_{o1,s2,p} \vee (f_{o1,s2,v} \wedge (\neg f_{o1,s3,v}))))$.

As depicted in Figure 4, we use standard fault trees which may additionally include negated elements to specify the formulas ψ_k for specific outgoing failures $f_k \in O_F^c$. If an outgoing failure f_j is excluded, we add $f_j \Leftrightarrow$ false to ψ_c. Then, the failure propagation formulas ψ_k for all outgoing failures $f_k \in O_F^c$ are AND-combined to derive ψ_c.

To describe the failure propagation of a composed component structure, we use the AND-composition of the failure information of the involved component instances. Therefore, we employ a failure propagation information per instance and simply renaming the failure and event variables such that the outgoing and ingoing failures are identical ($f_{c,p,t} = f_{c',p',t}$) if and only if their component ports are matched to each other ($(c, p, c', p') \in map$).

A hazard (top event) corresponds to a *hazard condition* γ in form of a Boolean formula without negation which references a subset of the outgoing failure variables of all system components (cf. [7]) and thus an additionally present failure never disables other failures (cf. monotonic increasing formula in [21]). An example hazard is depicted in Figure 5.

In our example, one serious hazard that can occur is a sideway collision of two shuttles on a switch. Here we will mention only two of the possible failures that can lead to this hazard. First, one shuttle component has incorrect own data. Or second, one shuttle has incorrect data of the other shuttle. The incorrect own data can be caused by the SwitchHandler and the incorrect data of the other shuttle is received via the $s1$ port of the shuttle component. As these failures are related to certain components of the system the analysis on this level is stopped.

---

[3] We pessimistically abstract from the deployment of the Optimizer and SwitchHandler components w.r.t. value failures as their crash errors simply result in a fail-safe state of the system.

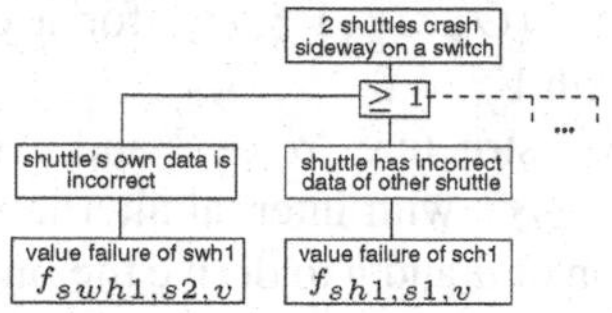

Fig. 5. The hazard condition for the shuttle

The corresponding hazard condition is: $\gamma = f_{sh1,s1,v} \vee f_{swh1,s2,v} \vee \ldots$. To keep the example simple we will in the following focus on the case that the SwitchHandler of sh1 delivers incorrect data. Thus, we only consider the hazard condition $\gamma' = f_{swh1,s2,v}$.

We can then use the satisfiability of the AND-composition of the local failure propagation information of all component occurrences $c_1, \ldots, c_n$ with a hazard condition γ in form of the Boolean formula $\psi_\gamma = \psi_{c_1} \wedge \ldots \wedge \psi_{c_n} \wedge \gamma$ to check whether the hazard is possible at all. Within this check, we can further abstract from the propagated failures $f_1, \ldots, f_m$ using existential quantification and check $\psi_\gamma^\exists = \exists f_1, \ldots, f_m : \psi_{c_1} \wedge \ldots \wedge \psi_{c_n} \wedge \gamma$ instead of ψ_γ.

In our example, we check whether the hazard $\gamma' = f_{swh1,s2,v}$ is possible by combining appropriately renamed version of the failure propagation information for the GPS, Optimizer, and SwitchHandler component. The resulting condition $\psi_{\gamma'}^\exists$ is satisfiable for any assignments for the internal event variables where the GPS unit has a local error which results in a value failure.

Like in our example, very often a hazard cannot be excluded. Therefore, we support to also compute its probability p_γ for a given fixed mission time and given probabilities $p(e_i)$ for the same mission time for all internal events $e_1, \ldots, e_m$ using $\psi_\gamma^\exists$ as follows:

$$p_\gamma = \sum_{v_1,\ldots,v_m \in \{0,1\}} \psi_\gamma^\exists [v_1/e_1, \ldots, v_m/e_m] \; p(v_1, \ldots, v_m) \tag{1}$$

We simply sum up for all possible assignments $v_1, \ldots, v_m$ for the internal event variables $e_1, \ldots, e_m$ the related probability $(p(v_1, \ldots, v_m) := \prod_{i=1}^m (v_i p(e_i) + (1 - v_i)(1 - p(e_i))))$ if the assignment fulfills $\psi_\gamma^\exists$.

For more details and the employed symbolic encoding in form of binary decision diagrams (BDDs) [22] and the efficient computation of p_γ please see Appendix A. In [7], we also outline how to address cyclic dependencies.

5 Introducing Design Alternatives

To further also take alternative system structures into account, we at first extend the failure propagation information. As alternative structures can also result in different required resources and may be subject to additional constraints, we also add an encoding of the resource requirements.

To model the failure propagation of system architectures with alternatives as depicted in Figure 2, we add a set of boolean variables V_A to model alternative substructures. Each failure propagation information without any alternative structures is then extended such that $F_c = (O^c_F, I^c_F, V^c_E, \psi_c)$ for a component $c \in \mathcal{C}$ becomes $F_c = (O^c_F, I^c_F, V^c_E, V^c_A, \psi_c)$ with $V^c_A = \emptyset$.

If in contrast two alternative structures $a \in \mathcal{C}$ and $b \in \mathcal{C}$ should be combined to describe a substructure $c = a \oplus_{\mathcal{C}} b$ with internal alternatives, we combine the related failure propagation information of a and b to derive the one for c as follows:

Definition 2. *Given two component $a, b \in \mathcal{C}$ and two failure propagation information $F_a = (O^a_F, I^a_F, V^a_E, V^a_A, \psi_a)$ and $F_b = (O^b_F, I^b_F, V^b_E, V^b_A, \psi_b)$ with identical interface ($O^a_F = O^b_F$, $I^a_F = I^b_F$, $V^a_E \cap V^b_E = \emptyset$), we can derive the* alternative combination *$F_c = (O^c_F, I^c_F, V^c_E, V^c_A, \psi_c)$ also denoted by $F_a \oplus_F F_b$ for a variable $a \in V_A \backslash (V^a_A \cup V^b_A)$ as follows: (1) $O^c_F = O^a_F = O^b_F$, (2) $I^c_F = I^a_F = I^b_F$, (3) $V^c_E = V^a_E \uplus V^b_E$, and (4) $V^c_A = V^a_A \uplus V^b_A \uplus \{a\}$, and (5) $\psi_c = (a \wedge \psi_a) \vee (\neg a \wedge \psi_b)$.*

If the extended failure propagation information for multiple occurrences of the same component are considered, the renaming of the variables should *not* include the alternative variables in V_A as we study the system under the assumption that the same alternative has been chosen at design time for all occurrences.

The failure propagation for the two shuttle component variants in our example is mostly determined whether the GPS sensor variant or the speed sensor variant is employed. Consequently, this decision is reflected in the failure propagation of the $s2$ port of the Optimizer component. The boolean decision variable a is used to denote whether the GPS sensor variant ($a = true$) or the speed sensor variant is employed ($a = false$) and we get the following failure propagation condition: $f_{o1,s2,v} \Leftrightarrow (a \wedge f_{g1,s1,v}) \vee (\neg a \wedge f_{s1,s1,v})$.

Analogously to the case without alternatives, we can then use the satisfiability of $\psi^\exists_\gamma$ to check whether a hazard is possible. The formula $\psi^\exists_\gamma$ has the internal events $e_1, \ldots, e_m$ as well as the alternative variables $a_1, \ldots, a_n$ as free variables. Thus the question whether any alternative configuration contains the hazard relates to the satisfiability of the formula $\psi^\exists_\gamma$.

A probability function p_γ over the alternative variables $a_1, \ldots, a_n$ can analogously to the basic approach presented in Section 4 (cf. equation 1) be derived from $\psi^\exists_\gamma$ for $p_\gamma(v_1, ..., v_n, w_1, ..., w_n) = \psi^\exists_\gamma[v_1/e_1, ..., v_m/e_m, w_1/a_1, ..., w_n/a_n]\ p(v_1, ..., v_m)$ as follows:

$$p_\gamma(w_1, ..., w_n) = \sum_{v_1,...,v_n \in \{0,1\}} p_\gamma(v_1, ..., v_n, w_1 ... w_n) \tag{2}$$

Equation 2 extends equation 1 only by the free variables $w_1 \ldots w_n$ to encode the alternatives. The advanced analysis techniques presented later in Section 6 use these free variables in different ways.

Referring to the set of boolean variables V_A to model alternative substructures, we further add resource expressions r^{ch}_c with $free(r^{xh}_c) \subseteq V^c_A$ for each hardware port $cp \in P^h_c$ to the failure propagation information $F_c = (O^c_F, I^c_F, V^c_E, V^c_A, \psi_c)$ of a software component $c \in \mathcal{C}^s$. For a given assignment for the alternative variables in V^c_A, the resource expressions r^{ch}_c evaluates to the amount of required resources.[4]

[4] We assume a single resource dimension here, but the outlined concepts can be straight forward extended to n resource dimensions if required.

If two alternative structures $c' \in \mathcal{C}$ and $c'' \in \mathcal{C}$ are combined via the alternative variable $a \in V_A$ to describe a substructure $c = c' \oplus_C c''$ with internal alternatives, we thus also combine the related resource expressions. If the hardware port $ch \in P^h_c$ is connected to both $ch' \in P^h_{c'}$ and $ch'' \in P^h_{c''}$ we then derive r^{ch}_c as $a\ r^{ch}_a + (1-a)\ r^{ch}_b$.

We finally combine these resource expressions for each hardware component $h \in \mathcal{C}^h$ to derive a related constraint ρ_h for an upper resource limit r^u_h as follows:

$$\rho_h := r^\sigma_h \leq r^u_h \qquad \text{with} \quad r^\sigma_h = \sum_{(h,hp,c,ch)\in map} r^{ch}_c$$

r^σ_h is the sum of all required resource for software components c which are connected via hardware ports to the hardware component h. The resulting resource constraint ρ_{m1} for the MPC550 depicted in Figure 3 is thus $a\ r^{h1}_{\mathsf{GPS}} + (1-a)\ r^{h1}_{\mathsf{SpeedSensor}} \leq r^u_{m1}$.

6 Advanced Analysis

Using the beforehand introduced concepts for the failure propagation modeling of architectures with alternatives, we will present in this section that we can determine optimal configurations, can determine solutions which are least sensitive to estimation errors of the internal event probabilities, can analyze whole product families, and can even analyze system architectures with online-reconfiguration.

Optimal Configuration. In a first step, constraints on the likelihood of hazards such as the upper bounds for their probabilities, which are required if a specific SIL level has been assigned to that subsystem or functionality, have to be taken into account. For the hazard γ_i and an upper bound α_i for the likelihood within a given mission time, we have the following constraint: $\zeta_i := p_{\gamma_i} \leq \alpha_i$.

To further define the objective function f which determines which is the optimal solution, a reasonable choice is the *risk*. We thus have $f = \sum_{i\in I} s_i\ p_{\gamma_i}$ for s_i the severity of the hazard γ_i and p_{γ_i} its probability function.

To determine the optimal design we thus have to solve the optimization problem with $f \rightarrow \min$, constraints ζ_i for all $i \in I$, and resource constraints ρ_c for all $c \in \mathcal{C}^h$.

Employing the BDD algorithms of Appendix A, we compute the variant with the minimal hazard probability. The analysis is based on the following component errors and their probabilities (cf. [7]): (1) a value error of the speedometer device $p1$ with probability $p(e_{p1,v}) = 10^{-7}$, (2) a value error of the GPS antenna $a1$ with $p(e_{a1,v}) = 10^{-8}$, (3) a crash error of the executing hardware $m1$ with $p(e_{m1,scr}) = 10^{-6}$, and an error of the algorithmic constraint of the optimizer components $o1$ with $p(e_{o1,ac}) = 10^{-7}$. The following expression f is to be minimized by assigning a boolean value to variable a:

$$f := (a * p(e_{a1,v}) * (1 - p(e_{m1,scr})) + (1-a) * (p(e_{p1,v}) * (1 - p(e_{m1,scr})))) * p(e_{o1,ac})$$

Minimizing this expression results in the selection of $a = 1$ and the solution 10^{-15}. $a = 1$ denotes the GPS sensor variant which, thus, is the optimal one w.r.t. the probability of hazard γ'. It is to be noted that in more complex cases the optimal decision is not simply to chose always the most reliable component variant as resource constraints usually only permit to chose certain combinations and it is not obvious where to invest the resources to achieve an optimal result.

Sensitivity-Based Selection. While taking the risk as an optimization criteria is a straight forward solution, in practice any such optimization has the problem that the estimates for the probabilities of the internal events are often very questionable.

In such cases, we further propose to analyze the considered solutions w.r.t. their sensitivity concerning the estimated internal event probabilities. Therefore, we add to the estimated internal event probabilities $p(e_j)$ a special variable δ and a factor β_j. When building p_{γ_i}, we then use $p'(e_j) = p(e_j) + \beta_j \delta$ instead of $p(e_i)$. The variable δ and the factor β_j basically determine an interval for the error probabilities. The factor β_j determines the individual width of the interval for the error $p(e_j)$. The special variable δ is then used to maximize the interval for all error probabilities.

Depending on the magnitude of the estimates $p(e_j)$ and their known accuracy, appropriate factors β_j should be chosen. Assuming for example that $p(e_j)$ is assumed to be approximately 10^{-6} and the estimation error is about 10^{-7}, we would suggest to use $\beta_j = 10^{-7}$.

To determine the design with minimal sensitivity to estimation errors of the internal event probabilities, we thus have to solve the optimization problem with $\delta \rightarrow \max$, constraints ζ_i for all $i \in I$, resource constraints ρ_c for all $c \in C^h$, and $\delta \geq 0$.

If $\delta_{\max}$ is determined this way, we replace the variable δ by the constant $\delta_{\max}$ and solve $f \rightarrow \min$, constraints ζ_i for all $i \in I$, and resource constraints ρ_c for all $c \in C^h$ in order to derive the design alternative which fulfills all hazard constraints ζ_i while allowing the biggest estimation error of the error probabilities. Thus, this design alternative is the least sensitive to estimation errors (and thus has the maximal safety margin for the error probabilities determined by $\delta_{\max}$).

Product Family Analysis. A product family can also be encoded as a system with alternative designs with free configuration variables $a_i \in V_A$. While in the case of alternative design decisions, the extended failure propagation information for multiple occurrences of the same component are considered, for a product family all combinations of valid product variants have to be considered.

Therefore, the renaming of the variables has to include the alternative variables in V_A as we do not study the system under the assumption that the same alternative has been chosen at design time for all occurrences. Instead, we need that disjoint variables for the alternative substructures ($V_A^a \cap V_A^b = \emptyset$) are employed if these substructures relate to different instances of the same product family.

In the case of product families, the question whether any combination of variants contains the hazard again relates to the satisfiability of the formula $\psi_\gamma^\exists$. We can compute the maximal probability $p_\gamma^{\max}$ of the hazard depending on p_γ from equation 2 with parameters $w_1, \ldots, w_n$ for the alternative variables $a_1, \ldots, a_n$ as follows (in the Appendix A the procedure to efficiently compute this maximum for the employed symbolic encoding in form of BDDs is sketched):

$$p_\gamma^{\max} = \max_{w_1,\ldots,w_m \in \{0,1\}} p_\gamma(w_1, ..., w_m) \tag{3}$$

This maximum for each hazard γ_i and an upper bound α_i for the likelihood within a given mission time can then be used to derive the additional checks $p^{\max}_{\gamma_i} \leq \alpha_i$ which have to be passed to ensure that any combination of product family variants fulfills the safety requirements implied by the assigned SIL levels.

The optimization problem with $f \longrightarrow \max$ for the constraints ζ_i for all $i \in I$ and resource constraints ρ_c for all $c \in \mathcal{C}^h$ can be further employed to optimize the safety of the product family. The optimization result relates to a worst case w.r.t. safety and might relate not to a single product variant but a combination of product variants. Therefore, we propose to study for each of these variants whether recomputing the optimization problem with a special constraint that exclude this specific variant can significantly decrease the likelihood for hazards.

Considering Online Reconfiguration. The outlined encoding for the failure propagation for systems with alternative designs with free configuration variables $a_i \in V_A$ can also be employed to determine the hazard probabilities for systems with online-reconfiguration where the switching between the different configurations is atomic and no cycles in the failure propagation exist. The online reconfiguration can be modeled like alternative designs of a product family. The hazard analysis can be done using the equation 3 for product families.

7 Conclusions and Future Work

Today software in technical systems often has to support multiple variants in order to evaluate different design alternatives, describe product families or system models with online-reconfiguration. Therefore, this paper proposes an extension of a component-based hazard analysis technique which permits to describe alternative structures. It has been described how we can determine optimal configurations, how we can determine the solution which is the least sensitive one w.r.t. estimation errors of the error probabilities, how we can analyze a whole product family at once, and how we can even analyze system architectures with online-reconfiguration using the introduced extension.

Planned future work will include a more tight integration of the approach with modeling techniques for product families and online-reconfiguration.

References

1. Grimm, K.: Software technology in an automotive company: major challenges. In: Proceedings of the 25th International Conference on Software Engineering (ICSE), Washington, DC, USA, IEEE Computer Society (2003) 498–503
2. Knauber, P., Bermejo, J., Böckle, G., do Prado Leite, J.C., van der Linden, F., Northrop, L., Stark, M., Weiss, D.M.: Quantifying product line benefits. In: Proc. of the 4th International Workshop on Product Family Engineering. LNCS 2290, Springer Verlag (2002) 155–163
3. Schmid, K.: A comprehensive product line scoping approach and its validation. In: ICSE '02: Proc. of the 24th International Conference on Software Engineering, New York, NY, USA, ACM Press (2002) 593–603
4. Thiel, S., Hein, A.: Modeling and using product line variability in automotive systems. IEEE Software **19**(4) (2002) 66–72

5. Wirsing, M., ed.: Report on the EU/NSF Strategic Workshop on Engineering Software-Intensive Systems, Edinburgh, GB (2004)
6. Sztipanovits, J., Karsai, G., Bapty, T.: Self-adaptive software for signal processing. Commun. ACM **41**(5) (1998) 66–73
7. Giese, H., Tichy, M., Schilling, D.: Compositional Hazard Analysis of UML Components and Deployment Models. In: Proc. of the 23rd International Conference on Computer Safety, Reliability and Security (SAFECOMP), Potsdam, Germany. Volume 3219 of Lecture Notes in Computer Science., Springer Verlag (2004)
8. Giese, H., Tichy, M., Burmester, S., Schäfer, W., Flake, S.: Towards the Compositional Verification of Real-Time UML Designs. In: Proc. of the 9th European software engineering conference held jointly with 11th ACM SIGSOFT international symposium on Foundations of software engineering (ESEC/FSE-11), ACM Press (2003) 38–47
9. McDermid, J.A.: Trends in Systems Safety: A European View? In Lindsay, P., ed.: Seventh Australian Workshop on Industrial Experience with Safety Critical Systems and Software. Volume 15 of Conferences in Research and Practice in Information Technology., Adelaide, Australia, ACS (2003) 3–8
10. Papadopoulos, Y., McDermid, J., R. Sasse, b., Heiner, G.: Analysis and synthesis of the behaviour of complex programmable electronic systems in conditions of failure. Reliability Engineering & System Safety **71** (2001) 229–247
11. Kaiser, B., Liggesmeyer, P., Maeckel, O.: A New Component Concept for Fault Trees. In: Proceedings of the 8th National Workshop on Safety Critical Systems and Software (SCS 2003), Canberra, Australia. 9-10th October 2003. Volume 33 of Research and Practice in Information Technology. (2003)
12. Grunske, L., Neumann, R.: Quality Improvement by Integrating Non-Functional Properties in Software Architecture Specification. In: Proc. of the Second Workshop on Evaluating and Architecting System dependabilitY (EASY), 6 October 2002, San Jose, California, USA (2002)
13. Grunske, L.: Transformational Patterns for the Improvement of Safety. In: Proc. of the The Second Nordic Conference on Pattern Languages of Programs (VikingPLoP 03), Microsoft Buisness Press (2003)
14. Fenelon, P., McDermid, J.A., Nicolson, M., Pumfrey, D.J.: Towards integrated safety analysis and design. ACM SIGAPP Applied Computing Review **2**(1) (1994) 21–32
15. McDermid, J., Pumfrey, D.: A Development of Hazard Analysis to aid Software Design. In: Proceedings of the Ninth Annual Conference on Computer Assurance (COMPASS94), Gaithersburg, MD, USA (1994) 17–25
16. Ogata, K.: Modern control engineering. Prentice Hall (1990)
17. Selic, B., Gullekson, G., Ward, P.: Real-Time Object-Oriented Modeling. John Wiley and Sons, Inc. (1994)
18. Addouche, N., Antoine, C., Montmain, J.: Combining Extended UML Models and Formal Methods to Analyze Real-Time Systems. In Winther, R., Gran, B.A., Dahll, G., eds.: Computer Safety, Reliability, and Security, 24th International Conference, SAFECOMP 2005, Fredrikstad, Norway, September 28-30, 2005, Proceedings. Volume 3688 of Lecture Notes in Computer Science., Springer (2005) 24–36
19. Ortmeier, F., Thums, A., Schellhorn, G., Reif, W.: Combining Formal Methods and Safety Analysis - The ForMoSa Approach. In Ehrig, H., Damm, W., Desel, J., Grośe-Rhode, M., Reif, W., Schnieder, E., Westkämper, E., eds.: Integration of Software Specification Techniques for Applications in Engineering. Volume 3147 of Lecture Notes in Computer Science. Springer Verlag (2004) 474–493

20. Giese, H., Burmester, S., Klein, F., Schilling, D., Tichy, M.: Multi-Agent System Design for Safety-Critical Self-Optimizing Mechatronic Systems with UML. In Henderson-Sellers, B., Debenham, J., eds.: OOPSLA 2003 - Second International Workshop on Agent-Oriented Methodologies, Anaheim, CA, USA, Center for Object Technology Applications and Research (COTAR), University of Technology, Sydney, Australia (2003) 21–32
21. Rauzy, A.: A new methodology to handle Boolean models with loops. IEEE Transactions on Reliability **52** (2003) 96– 105
22. Bryant, R.E.: Symbolic Boolean manipulation with ordered binary-decision diagrams. ACM Computing Surveys **24**(3) (1992) 293 – 318

A Compute Probability Results for Boolean Formulas

Figure 6(a) presents how we employ Binary Decision Diagrams (BDDs) to calculate the probability of hazards. It shows a BDD containing three nodes for different error events $e_1 \dots e_3$ and special nodes true (0) and false (1). We calculate the probabilities bottom up by starting with node e_1 since both its dependent nodes are already calculated (trivial for the nodes true and false). The probability for a node is computed as follows: $f(node) = p(e_i) * f(node.high()) + (1 - p(e_i)) * f(node.low())$. Thus for node e_1, this results in: $f(e_1) = 0.3 * 1 + (1 - 0.3) * 0 = 0.3$. Propagating this value upward, we get the hazards probability of 0.24.

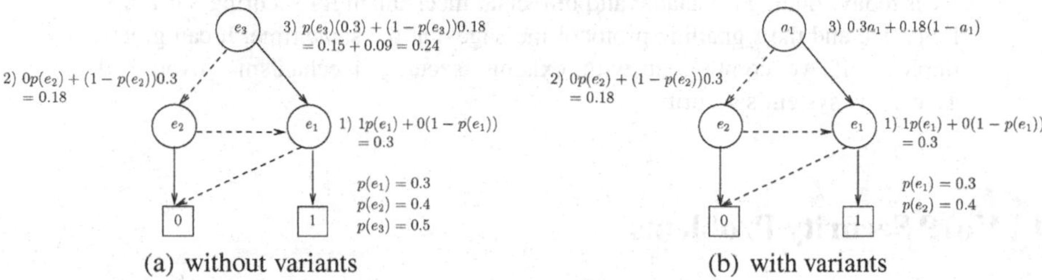

(a) without variants (b) with variants

Fig. 6. Hazard probability calculation using BDDs

A BDD for a hazard analysis with design variants is displayed in Figure 6(b). The difference to the above presented algorithm is the treatment of nodes representing design alternatives, e.g. node a_1 in the example. Here, the following formula is used: $f(node) = a_i * f(node.high()) + (1 - a_i) * f(node.low())$. In our example, this results in the expression: $f(a_1) = 0.3a_1 + 0.18(1 - a_1)$. After the complete expression for the BDD is built, the expression is minimized using a constraint solver. For the given expression, the result is $a_1 = 0$ as this leads to a hazard probability of 0.18 in contrast to 0.3, when $a_1 = 1$.

Using the BDD of Figure 6(b), we can also efficiently compute which variant has the maximum hazard probability also considering the variant nodes a_i: $f(node) = max(f(node.high(), f(node.low()))$ - in our example $f(a_1) = max(0.3, 0.18)$. This means, that the highest hazard probability variant has the probability 0.3.

New VoIP Traffic Security Scheme with Digital Watermarking

Wojciech Mazurczyk[1] and Zbigniew Kotulski[1,2]

[1] Warsaw University of Technology, Faculty of Electronics and Information Technology, Institute of Telecommunications 15/19 Nowowiejska Str. 00-665 Warszawa, Poland
{W.Mazurczyk, Z.Kotulski}@tele.pw.edu.pl
[2] Polish Academy of Sciences, Institute of Fundamental Technological Research
zkotulsk@ippt.gov.pl

Abstract. In this paper we propose a new, lightweight, no bandwidth consuming authentication and integrity scheme for VoIP service based on SIP as a signalling protocol. It is shared password mechanism and this solution exploits digital watermarking. Nowadays, there are many applications of this technique, such as solving copyright protection problems, but we propose to use it to secure the transmitted audio and signalling protocol that IP Telephony is based on simultaneously. This solution can be the potential answer to the problem VoIP faces today: finding a scalable and universal mechanism for securing VoIP traffic (voice and the signalling protocol messages) at the same time. It can greatly improve, if we combine it with existing security mechanisms, overall IP Telephony system's security.

1 VoIP Security Problems

Securing IP Telephony is a complex process. This not only means the ability to make secure conversation between two communicating parties, but also the security of signalling messages used to make this call possible at all. The need to provide certain QoS (Quality of Service) parameters values often results with not enough or no security mechanisms for VoIP service. This is mainly because security mechanisms can be responsible for the increased latency. If latency is too high, it can be the most degenerating constrain for the quality of the VoIP call. So, nowadays we are often facing the necessity of the trade off between providing security and the low latency for real-time service.

That is why our motivation in finding alternative way to handle IP Telephony security (with special emphasize on the authentication and integrity security services) is based on the following facts:

- There is no universal solution for protecting both: audio and signalling messages for IP Telephony systems [8],
- There are drawbacks of SRTP protocol which are discussed in [3]; SRTP is the most popular mechanism to provide authentication and integrity for the data stream,

J. Górski (Ed.): SAFECOMP 2006, LNCS 4166, pp. 170 – 181, 2006.

- The speed of embedding/extracting digital watermark into/from audio is suitable for real-time services,
- Authentication based on digital watermarking scheme is inseparably bound to the data stream content,
– VoIP security is still evolving and still it is time for new solutions and ideas.

That's why, in this paper, we are proposing a novel approach to the IP Telephony security based on digital watermarking. This solution is suitable for the protection of both the audio content and signalling messages simultaneously.

2 Digital Watermarking

Digital watermarking technique is gaining more and more attention these days. It covers a large field of various aspects, from cryptography to signal processing. It is mainly used for marking the digital data (images, video, audio or text). From typical applications for digital watermarks, described in [1] and [2], most important application, which can really improve VoIP security, is the ability of embedding the **authentication and integrity watermark.** Authors can embed data, which is similar to a cryptographic hash, into their digital work. This hash is invisible and inseparable from the data. This way we can achieve the copyright protection by watermarking data with the author's identifier (owner authentication) and we can ensure the authentication and integrity of the data, which allows us to recognize all later data manipulations (a general term in literature is the data authentication [9], [10]).

The watermark that will be used in the authentication and integrity scheme we propose, must possess certain properties like: robustness, security, transparency, complexity, capacity, verification and invertibility. The mentioned properties are described in details in [1] and [2]. The optimization of these properties for real-time audio system is crucial. They are often mutually competitive; that is why there is always a compromise necessary to construct an efficient system. For our purpose the embedded watermark, that we will use, must be characterized by **high robustness** (but only until the semantics of the data is destroyed), **high security** and must be **non-perceptual**. IP Telephony is a demanding, real-time service, so we need the watermarking schemes that deal with the real-time services. The number of such solutions is not high, however, they already exist. Such watermarking algorithms are described, e.g., in [2], [3] and [5].

The general audio watermarking scheme for VoIP traffic consists of two functions: embedding and extractions of the watermark. As soon as the conversation begins, certain information is embedding into the voice samples (as a watermark) and it is sent through the communication channel. After reaching a called party the watermark is extracted, the information is retrieved and verified. If the received watermarked data and extracted parameters are correct, the conversation can be continued.

Most digital watermarking algorithms for the real-time communication are designed to survive typical non-malicious IP Telephony operations like: low bit rate audio compression, codec changes, DA/AD conversion and packet loss. For example, in [2] the watermarking scheme developed at the Fraunhofer IPSI and the Fraunhofer IIS were tested for different compression methods. Those results revealed that the large simultaneous capacity and robustness depend on the scale of the codec compression. When the compression rate is high (1:53), the watermark is robust only when we embed about 1 bit/s. With a lower compression rate we can obtain about 30 bit/s, whereas the highest data rate was 48 bit/s with good robust, transparent and complexity properties. For the monophonic audio signal, which is a default type for IP Telephony, the watermark embedding algorithm appeared around 14 times faster and the watermark detector almost 6 times faster than the real-time.

3 VoIP Security Services

As stated in [16] the security services for system's information security are: authentication (and identification), integrity, authorization (logical access control), confidentiality and non-repudiation/non-denial. But if we take into consideration securing IP telephony systems, the three most crucial security services are: authentication, integrity and confidentiality. The first two can be provided with the use of the watermarking techniques. The third one should be guaranteed in a different manner, e.g., with the use of the security mechanisms (encryption) from the set defined for each VoIP standard.

In particular, the proposed here scheme provides the following security services:

- **Authentication of the data source** (one can be sure of the identity of the caller),
- **Authentication of the signalling messages** (one can prove that the caller is the source of the signalling messages that were exchanged during the signalling phase of the call),
- **Signalling messages integrity** (one knows that the signalling messages were not modified during the transmission through the communication channel)
- **Data authentication** – integrity (one can be sure that the audio comes from the caller and it has not been tampered).

Furthermore, making a call in IP Telephony systems consists of two phases: the initial **signalling phase,** in which certain signalling messages are exchanged between the parties, and the **conversation phase**. Each phase has its disjunctive set of security mechanisms (although, the secure signalling sometimes includes a secure key-setup for the media channels). Nowadays, in SIP and H.323 we can implement different security mechanisms designated for securing the data stream (audio) and other that cover signalling protocols security. Additionally, the security model for the protocols: SIP and H.323 is also different, which means that they use almost disjunctive set of the security mechanisms. What we are proposing in this paper is to move providing the security of the signalling messages from the first phase to the second one (to the conversation phase). We called this method a *post factum* method. This is a first scheme that is using this method. What is characteristic the act of checking the security of the signalling protocol is made after the signalling phase is finished. Such a solution has disadvantages: the most serious one is that a potential attack on the signalling protocol is detected some time after the beginning of the conversation. But on the other hand, this approach has certain advantages:

- It provides one, unified solution for the audio and signalling protocol security,
- It is low-power computing as stated in [2] and no bandwidth consuming mechanism, because we use a channel created in media streams,

- It is signalling protocol independent solution,
- It prevents doubling latency and excessive consuming of the processing time,
- It also reduces complexity (and cost!) of the network equipment on the communication path,
- It is capable of solving the security mechanisms compatibility for various IP Telephony systems that are based on different signalling protocols.

Moreover, it can also help to protect the audio and signalling protocol on the interface between VoIP systems and PSTN (since the watermark is robust, it will survive AD/DA operations).

Unlike the existing security mechanisms for IP Telephony, it provides also real end-to-end security. No network equipment on the communication path will be aware of the embedded watermark, unless it is designed to do so.

Thus, we think that the proposed solution can be an important step in providing authentication and integrity for VoIP traffic.

4 Proposition of Authentication and Integrity Scheme

We assume that proposed mechanism is independent of the watermarking algorithm. It means that it does not depend on watermark embedding and extraction technique. No matter which algorithm for real-time communication is used, the output watermark, if created, has the best properties allowed for the communication environment used. Such an assumption gives this solution flexibility and it will be capable of supporting future ideas of digital watermarking algorithms. Another assumption is that both sides of communication share a secret password (in this paper we do not cover the algorithm used for password exchanging).

4.1 Scenarios for Digital Watermarking in VoIP Security and Related Work

We can point out three possible scenarios, in which we can take advantage of using the digital watermarking to provide authentication and integrity for IP Telephony:

I. We can secure the media stream (audio),
II. We can secure the signalling messages,
III. We can secure both: the audio and signalling protocols at the same time.

Working algorithms for **I** are presented, i.e., in [2], [3] and [5]. We do not fully benefit from the solution **II**, because in this case we still have a disjunction set of the security mechanisms for securing the media stream and a signalling protocol. This is a novel approach and there are no known algorithms that use this approach. As we said at the beginning of Section 3, we want to combine two phases of VoIP call to achieve, mainly, less significant delay. That is why we will focus on the third possible scenario: the simultaneous authentication and integrity protection of audio and signalling messages. All the following considerations, figures and schemes apply to the scenario No. **III**.

4.2 General Digital Watermarking Scheme Modifications

The scheme presented here requires modifications to the general audio watermarking system. First, we are proposing to add a new functional block called Pre-processing Stage (**PPS**). It will be responsible for preparing data before the watermark embedding stage. The modified scheme, with this new block, is shown in the Fig. 1 below:

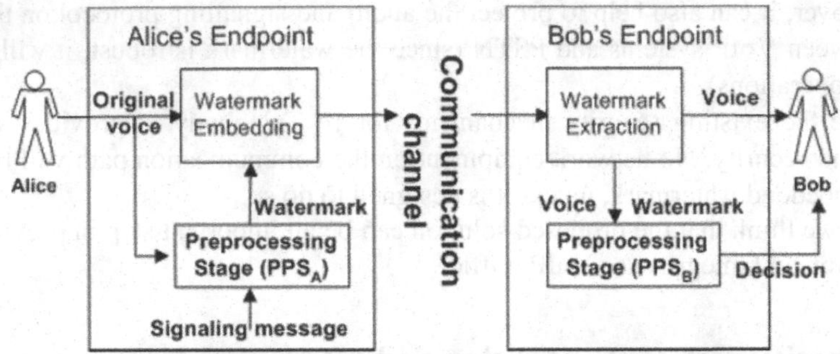

Fig. 1. Modified watermarking scheme with the new Pre-processing Stage (PPS)

As we see in the Fig. 1 we provide a signalling message and a sample of the caller's original voice, as an input to the PPS block in the transmitter. How the PPS block process information will be covered later in the Section 4.4. After the digital watermark is embedded and sent through the communication channel, the information in the receiver is retrieved and verified in an analogous block on the other communication side. If the retrieved information is correct, the connection will continue. We must also consider the problems connected with the call quality degeneration parameters, such as the packet loss and jitter (characteristic for IP networks). The connection cannot break down if the watermark is not retrieved correctly in few samples. The problem will be addressed in the Section 4.5.

The next important thing for this scheme is how much information we are able to embed into the original voice data. This will influence the speed of the authentication and integrity process throughout the conversation. This parameter, in our solution, is expected to be high but it is not crucial. However, the lowest payload watermarks (about 1 bit/s) cannot be accepted in our scheme because, in this case, the conversation would have to last enormously long to work correctly.

4.3 Pre-processing Block (PPS) Description

In this section we will describe how the Pre-processing Stage (PPS) block (presented in Fig.1) is built, in greater details. It consists of functional blocks shown in Fig. 2, which are described below.

The blocks constituting PPS have the following functions:

SB (Signalling Message Buffer): stores the signalling messages from the first phase of the call.

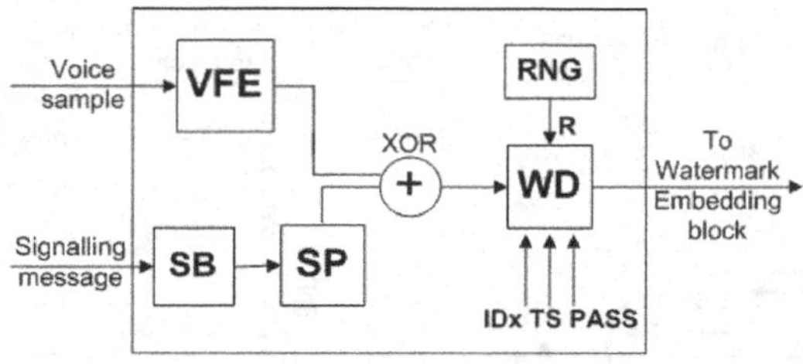

Fig. 2. Architecture of Pre-processing stage block (PPS)

SP (Signalling Messages Processing): in this block a hash function is performed on each signalling message.
RNG (Randomizer): we use it to provide a unique set of data for every embedded watermark, even if the rest of information provided will be the same again (e.g., all the signalling messages were verified, so in this case we use the last one that was sent). It produces a random value R, which is included later in the watermark.
WD (Watermarking Data): in this block the input data is concatenated with the obligatory R parameter (the randomizer value) and other parameters: IDX (unique, global identifier of one side of the connection; X means caller or callee), PASS (the password, which is shared and known to both sides of the conversation) and TS (time stamp). The last parameter can be optional, because it requires tightly synchronized clocks. However, it is useful since it can protect against the replay attacks.
VFE (Voice Feature Extractor): provides characteristic features (VF) of the original voice that we want to protect. Afterwards, a hash is also performed on this value.

As we can see in the Fig. 2, all the sent signalling messages from the first phase of the call are stored in a special buffer (SB). When the voice sample enters the VFE block, the first signalling message is send to the SP block where a hash function is performed. Simultaneously, the same function is performed over the voice sample in VFE. Then, both values are XORed bit by bit and the results enter WD block. The input value is concatenated with the randomizer value (R), the global identifier of caller (IDX), a shared password (PASS) and, eventually, the time stamp (TS). After that, the hash function is performed again. The result, which we will call a **token,** is send to the embedding function and will become a **watermark**. Next, the watermarking process continues for the other signalling messages in the SB buffer. Before the caller's voice reaches the callee, the token from the watermark must be retrieved and verified. This can be done because the callee computes locally the same token, and then the two tokens are being compared.

4.4 The Authentication and Integrity Scheme

The general idea of the proposed scheme is to compare the received token with a locally calculated, appropriate one. Fig. 3 shows how the algorithm works (the inverse communication is analogous).

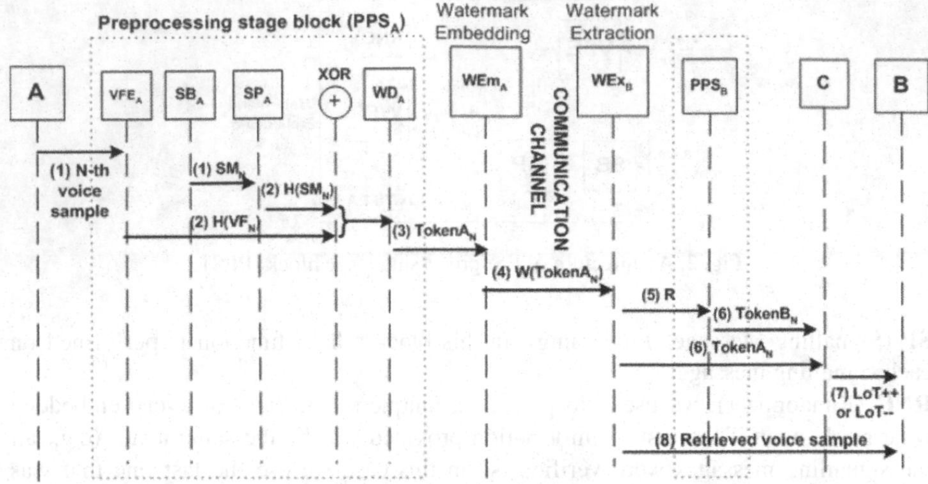

Fig. 3. Architecture of Pre-processing stage block (PPS)

In this situation the values of the tokens A_N and B_N are:

$$\mathbf{TokenA_N = TokenB_N = H}\left(\mathbf{(H(SM_N) \oplus H(VF_N)) \,||} \begin{pmatrix} \mathbf{TS} \\ \mathbf{PASS} \\ \mathbf{ID_A} \end{pmatrix} \mathbf{||\, R} \right) \mathbf{||\, R}$$

PPS_B block is functioning analogously to PPS_A. That is why it is not shown above in details. Additionally, we assume that in the signalling phase some of the signalling messages (SM_N means N-th Signalling Message) were exchanged (and they are stored in SB). Now, in the second phase, they will be verified. **H** stands for the hash function and **W** for the embedding of the digital watermark into audio. The algorithm works as described below:

(1) When the conversation begins, the first voice sample enters VFE_A block and, simultaneously, the first signalling message (SM) is send from the buffer (SB_A) to the SP_A block. In the VFE_A the feature of the voice sample (VF_N) is extracted (for the data integrity) and then the hash function is performed on the result. At the same time, the hash function is performed on the signalling message in SP_A.

(2) The result values from SP_A and VFE_A are, then, XORed (they have the same length). Afterwards, the result is sent to WD_A block, in which **TokenA** is created, together with the other parameters like: the randomizer value (R), the shared password (PASS), the global identifier of A (ID_A) and, optionally, the time stamp (TS).

(3) TokenA is sent to the watermark embedding function and the information, that it contains, is saved there in the caller's voice. Then, the data stream, formed this way, is sent through the communication channel.

(4) Before the voice from A reaches the callee B, the watermark is extracted and send to the comparator (C) on the receiver side.

(5) From the extracted token, the randomizer value (R) is sent to the analogous PPS_B block. In this block some pre-processing had taken place (e.g., the hash function from signalling message was performed). If we have the R-value, then we can compute **TokenB**. It should be equal to TokenA, if the transmission had not been tampered. The result is sent to the comparator (C).

(6) In the comparator (C) both token values are compared.

(7) If TokenA=TokenB, the special parameter LoT (Level of Trust) value (its function will be covered in the Section 4.5) is increased. In any other situation it is decreased. Then, basing on LoT value, the decision is made whether the call should be continued or broken down.

(8) If the call continues, the voice sample finally reaches the callee B.

4.5 Level of Trust (LoT) Parameter

Still we can imagine a situation, in which the retrieved token will be corrupted, due to the packet loss (or some other reason). In this case, we cannot allow the call to be cancelled immediately. That is why both sides will update special parameter named LoT (Level of Trust), during a conversation. As we said, if tokens are equal, the LoT parameter increases. In any other situation its value decreases. If A sends to B a token to compare, the algorithm of handling the LoT parameter (on B side) works as described below in a pseudo-code:

```
/*CL - Critical Level, LoT - Level of Trust, T-timer*/
START
CL = a; LoTA = x; TA = 0; /* Initiating values */
StartTimer(TA);
FOR (i= 0; i++; i< End of Transmission)  /* i - Time
slot */
  {
  IF (TokenA_A = TokenA_B) THEN
    {
    LoTA ++;
    ResetTimer(TA);
    }
  ELSE (LoTA --);
 IF (LoTA <= CL) OR (TA > k) THEN STOP; (1)
 IF (LoTA = a*x) THEN LoT = x; (2)
}
```

As we can see, the breakage of the call will take place if the value of the LoT parameter is equal or below the given threshold (CL value) or if the timer TA expires (1). If the communication continues and every signalling message that was sent is verified, embedding of the digital watermark does not stop. It is a continuous process: to calculate information to be sent, as soon as all the signalling messages are verified, we take the last signalling message. The LoT value changes during the conversation time. If every signalling message is successfully verified the LoT value rises. To prevent its increase from reaching the infinity, we lower it, as soon as it reaches the value of the critical level multiplied by the start value of LoT (2).

This way of decreasing the LoT value has one serious disadvantage: it allows an attacker to wait until LoT= (a*x)-1. However, we must assume that he is able to possess information about its value and then safely spoof ((a*x) - 1 – (CL + 1)) audio packets without LoT's falling below the threshold (CL). To prevent it, one must choose the initiating values (a and x) carefully. Their values should depend on network's parameters e.g. the packet loss and possible delays. So it can be, for example, a function (F) of the following parameters:

LoT = F (Packet_loss_ratio, Delay, Bit_Error_Rate, …)

If the network does not suffer heavily from the packet loss, those values must be low. In the other case, they must be set to a higher level. For example, the network administrator or service provider can circumscribe those parameters for a certain network/user.

5 Implementation of the Scheme for VoIP Based on SIP

SIP is one of the most popular application-layer (TCP/IP model) signaling protocols for IP Telephony that can establish, modify, and terminate multimedia sessions, such as VoIP calls. It is text-based and simple. SIP specification [14] defines only six main methods: REGISTER for registering contact information, INVITE, ACK, and CANCEL for setting up sessions, BYE for terminating sessions and OPTIONS for querying servers about their capabilities. SIP uses network elements called proxy or redirect servers to help route requests to the user's current location, authenticate and authorize users for services, implement provider's call-routing policies, and provide features to users. Our scheme for this signaling protocol is described below. Our mechanism will be integrated with SIP UA and in case of interconnection scenarios also with Media Gateways (MGs). We will show scenario for basic call flow for VoIP based on SIP, which are taken from [15]. In this scenario, Alice completes a call to Bob directly:

Both sides know what signaling messages were exchanged during the signaling phase of the call. The tokens flow for this call is the following:

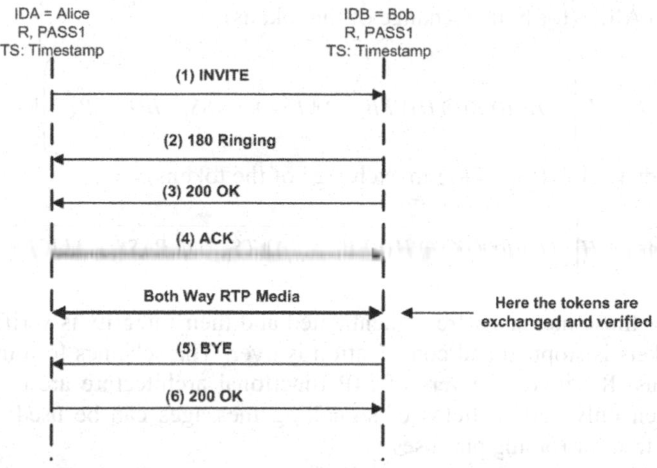

Fig. 4. Connection stages and signalling messages exchanged for SIP

Alice sends to Bob:

(1) $$\mathbf{TokenA_1 = H\left((H(INVITE) \oplus H(VF_{A1})) \parallel TS_1 \parallel PASS_1 \parallel ALICE \parallel R_1\right) \parallel R_1}$$

(4) $$\mathbf{TokenB_2 = H\left((H(180RINGING) \oplus H(VFB_{B1})) \parallel TS_1 \parallel PASS_1 \parallel BOB \parallel R_3\right) \parallel R_3}$$

Bob sends to Alice:

(2) $$\mathbf{TokenA_4 = H\left((H(ACK) \oplus H(VF_{A2})) \parallel TS_2 \parallel PASS_1 \parallel ALICE \parallel R_2\right) \parallel R_2}$$

(3) $$\mathbf{TokenB_3 = H\left((H(200OK) \oplus H(VFB_{B2})) \parallel TS_2 \parallel PASS_1 \parallel BOB \parallel R_4\right) \parallel R_4}$$

If any new message is exchanged during the connection, for example, for negotiation of any parameter of the call, then it does not influence the call until its authentication and integrity is checked. The tokens are analogous as it is shown above.Authentication of BYE (or CANCEL) messages, which is used to terminate a VoIP conversation, has to be treated the same as normal messages that come during the call. Normally, the media channels are terminated, upon receiving this message. In our scheme, it is vital to retain RTP flow until those messages are authenticated. So, the authentication and integrity check of messages BYE and the OK are as follows:

Bob sends to Alice (for N-th exchange of the tokens):

$$\textbf{(5)}\ \ TokenB_5 = H\left((H(BYE) \oplus H(VFB_{BN})) \| TS_N \| PASS_1 \| BOB \| R_N \right) \| R_N$$

Alice sends to Bob (for (N+1)-th exchange of the tokens):

$$\textbf{(6)}\ \ TokenA_6 = H\left((H(200OK) \oplus H(VFB_{A(N+1)})) \| TS_{(N+1)} \| PASS_1 \| ALICE \| R_{N+1} \right) \| R_{N+1}$$

Only after those messages are authenticated and their integrity is verified, the flow of RTP packets is stopped and conversation is over. The schemes for other scenarios are analogous. If network servers of SIP functional architecture are used (proxy or redirect), then only certain fields of signalling messages can be used. Some fields must be left free for routing purposes.

6 Conclusions and Remarks

In this paper the new, lightweight authentication and integrity scheme for VoIP, based on the digital watermarking, has been proposed. It is a new approach that combines securing the signalling protocol's messages and audio, which are exchanged between calling parties at the same. The scheme was described for any VoIP system, in general. The new functional blocks and algorithms were also defined. We showed, how this solution works and how it could be implemented for VoIP based on SIP (Session Initiation Protocol) signalling protocol, for a basic call flow.

The presented solution is a *post factum* method because it works some time after the phase of exchanging the signalling messages took place. So, this mechanism can be used only if the connection was previously established. Nevertheless, we find it useful and flexible because this algorithm does not depend on the signaling protocol, gives new potential possibilities for securing and providing compatibility of IP Telephony. Moreover, it does not consume any additional bandwidth because it uses watermarking technique. As proved in [17], there is a need for using lightweight authentication mechanisms, especially for transmissions that depend on certain values of QoS parameters and VoIP service is the best example of that. Implementing such a solution can greatly reduce number of possible attacks (but it will not eliminate them completely) and improve overall system's security.

References

1. J. Dittmann, A. Mukherjee, M. Steinebach: Media-independent Watermarking Classification and the need for combining digital video and audio watermarking for media authentication, Proceedings of the International Conference on Information Technology: Coding and Computing, IEEE Computer Science Society, Las Vegas, Nevada, USA (2000) 62-67.
2. M. Steinebach, F. Siebenhaar, C. Neubauer, R. Ackermann, U. Roedig, J. Dittmann: Intrusion Detection Systems for IP Telephony Networks, Real time intrusion detection symposium, Estoril, Portugal (2002).

3. S. Yuan, S. Huss: Audio Watermarking Algorithm for Real-time Speech Integrity and Authentication, International Multimedia Conference Proceedings of the 2004 Multimedia and security workshop on Multimedia and security, Magdeburg, Germany (2004) 220 - 226
4. M. Sienebach, A. Lang, J. Dittmann, Ch. Neubauer: Audio Watermarking Quality Evaluation: Robustness to DA/AD Processes, Proceedings of the International Conference on Information Technology: Coding and Computing (ITCC '02), Las Vegas (2002) 100-105.
5. T. Mizrahi, E. Borenstein, G. Leifman, Y. Cassuto, M. Lustig, S. Mizrachi, N. Peleg: Real-Time Implementation for Digital Watermarking in Audio Signals Using Perceptual Masking, 3rd European DSP Education and Research Conference, ESIEE, Noisy Le Grand, Paris (2000).
6. C. Lu, H. Liao, L. Chen: Multipurpose Audio Watermarking, Proceedings of 15th International Conference on Pattern Recognition, Barcelona, Spain, pp. 282-285 (2000).
7. M. Arnold: Attacks on Digital Audio Watermarks and Countermeasures, Third International Conference on WEB Delivering of Music (WEDELMUSIC'03), Leeds, United Kingdom (2003).
8. D.R. Kuhn, T.J. Walsh, S. Fries: Security Considerations for Voice Over IP Systems, Computer Security Division, Information Technology Laboratory, National Institute of Standards and Technology Special Publication 800-58, January 2005.
9. J. Dittmann, P. Wohlmacher, K. Nahrstedt: Using Cryptographic and Watermarking Algorithms. IEEE MultiMedia 8(4): 54-65 (2001).
10. M. Steinebach; J. Dittmann: Watermarking-based digital audio data authentication, EURASIP Journal on Applied Signal Processing, No. 10, September; Hindawi Publishing Corporation, pp 1001 - 1015, ISBN ISSN 1110-8657, 2003.
11. J. Dittmann, F. Nack, A. Steinmetz, R. Steinmetz: Interactive Watermarking Environments, Proceedings of International Conference on Multimedia Computing and Systems, Austin, USA 1998, pp. 286-294.
12. J.D. Gordy, L.T Brutin: Performance evaluation of digital audio watermarking algorithms, in Proc. 43rd IEEE Midwest Symposium on Circuit and Systems (MWSCAS '00), pp. 456-459, Lansing, USA, August 2000.
13. M. Arnold: Audio watermarking: Features, applications and algorithms, in Proc. IEEE International Conference on Multimedia Expo (ICME '00), pp. 1013-1016, New York, USA, July-August 2000.
14. J. Rosenberg, H. Schulzrinne, G. Camarillo, A. Johnston, RFC 3261 - SIP: Session Initiation Protocol, IETF, June 2002.
15. A. Johnston, S. Donovan, R. Sparks, C. Cunningham, K. Summers, RFC 3665 - Session Initiation Protocol (SIP) Basic Call Flow Examples, IETF, December 2003.
16. ISO 7498. International Standards Organisation (ISO). Information processing systems - Open systems interconnection - Basic reference model - Part 2: Security architecture (ISO/IEC 7498-2). 1989.
17. H. Johnson, Toward Adjustable Lightweight Authentication for Network Access Control, PhD thesis, Blekinge Institute of Technology, December 2005.

Towards Filtering and Alerting Rule Rewriting on Single-Component Policies

Joaquín García-Alfaro[1,2], Frédéric Cuppens[1], and Nora Cuppens-Boulahia[1]

[1] GET/ENST-Bretagne, 35576 Cesson Sévigné - France
{frederic.cuppens, nora.cuppens}@enst-bretagne.fr
[2] dEIC/UAB, Edifici Q, Campus de Bellaterra,
08193, Bellaterra, Barcelona - Spain
joaquin.garcia@uab.es

Abstract. The use of *firewalls* and *network intrusion detection systems* (NIDSs) is the dominant method to survey and guarantee the security policy in current corporate networks. On the one hand, firewalls are traditional security components which provide means to filter traffic within corporate networks, as well as to police the incoming and outcoming interaction with the Internet. On the other hand, NIDSs are complementary security components used to enhance the visibility level of the network, pointing to malicious or anomalous traffic. To properly configure both firewalls and NIDSs, it is necessary the use of a set of configuration rules, i.e., a set of filtering or alerting rules. Nevertheless, the existence of anomalies within the set of configuration rules of both firewalls and NIDSs is very likely to degrade the network security policy. The discovering and removal of these anomalies is a serious and complex problem to solve. In this paper, we present a set of mechanisms for such a management.

Keywords: Network Security, Firewalls, NIDSs, Policy Anomalies.

1 Introduction

Many companies and organizations use *firewalls* to police their incoming and outcoming flow of traffic between different zones of the network, as well as *network intrusion detection systems* to monitor and survey such a traffic. A firewall is a network security component, with several interfaces associated with the different zones of the network. The company may partition, for instance, its network into three different zones: a *demilitarized zone* (or DMZ), a private network and a zone for security administration. This way, one may use a single firewall setup, with three interfaces associated with these three zones, to police the protection of each zone[1]. Network intrusion detection systems (NIDSs for short), on the other hand, are complementary network security components which are in charge of detecting malicious or anomalous activity in the network traffic, such as *denial of service* (DoS) attacks or intrusion attempts. NIDSs can employ different families of detection methods, being *anomaly detection* and *misuse detection* two of the most frequently used methods. We refer to [9] for a good survey on the field.

[1] Firewalls also implement other functionalities, such as Proxying and Network Address Transfer (NAT), but it is not the purpose of this paper to cover these functionalities.

J. Górski (Ed.): SAFECOMP 2006, LNCS 4166, pp. 182–194, 2006.

In order to apply a filtering policy, it is necessary to configure the firewall with a set of filtering rules. Similarly, and in order to apply an alerting policy, it is also necessary to configure the NIDS with a set of alerting rules (i.e., *detection signatures* when using misuse detection methods). Both filtering and alerting rules are specific cases of a more general configuration rule, which typically defines a $decision$ (such as $filter$, $alert$, $pass$, etc.) that applies over a set of $condition$ attributes, such as *protocol, source, destination, classification*, etc.

For our work, we define a general configuration rule as follows:

$$R_i : \{condition_i\} \rightarrow decision_i \quad (1)$$

where i is the relative position of the rule within the set of rules, $\{condition_i\}$ is the conjunctive set of condition attributes such that $\{condition_i\}$ equals $C_1 \wedge C_2 \wedge ... \wedge C_p$ – being p the number of condition attributes of the given rule – and $decision$ is a boolean value in $\{true, false\}$.

Let us notice that the decision of a filtering rule will be positive ($true$) whether it applies to a specific value related to *deny* (or *filter*) the traffic it matches, and will be negative ($false$) whether it applies to a specific value related to *accept* (or *pass*) the traffic it matches. Similarly, the decision of an alerting rule will be positive ($true$) whether it applies to a specific value related to *warn* (or *alert*) about the traffic it matches, and will be negative ($false$) whether it applies to a specific value related to *ignore* the traffic it matches.

In the configuration policy of a component, conflicts due to rule overlaps, i.e., the same traffic matching more than one rule, can occur. To solve these conflicts, most components implement a *first matching* strategy through the ordering of rules. This way, each packet processed by the component is mapped to the decision of the rule with highest priority. This strategy introduces, however, new configuration errors, often referred in the literature as *policy anomalies*.

In [5], we presented an audit process to manage firewall policy anomalies, in order to detect and remove anomalies within the set of rules of a given firewall. This audit process is based on the existence of relationships between the condition attributes of the filtering rules, such as coincidence, disjunction, and inclusion, and proposes a transformation process which derives from an initial set of rules – with potential policy anomalies – to an equivalent one which is completely free of such anomalies.

In this paper, we extend our proposal of detecting and removing firewall policy anomalies [5], to a more complete setup where both firewalls and NIDSs are in charge of the network security policy. Hence, assuming that the role of both prevention and detection of network attacks is assigned to these two components, our objective is to completely correct the anomalies within their configuration.

We also extend in this paper the set of anomalies studied in [5] which, in turn, are not reported, as defined in this paper, in none of the studied related work. For such a purpose, we also introduce in this paper the use of a model to specify some properties of the network, e.g., vulnerabilities, as well as to determine whether the network traffic that matches a given configuration rule, may or may not cross the component configured by such a rule.

The advantages of our proposal are threefold. First, when performing our proposed discovery and removal of anomalies, and after rewriting the rules, one can verify that the resulting configuration of each component in the network is free of misconfiguration. Each anomalous rule will be reported to the administration console. This way, the security officer in charge of the network can check the network policy, in order to verify the correctness of the whole process, and perform the proper policy modifications to avoid such anomalies.

Second, the resulting rules are totally disjoint, i.e., the ordering of rules is no longer relevant. Hence, one can perform a second transformation in a positive or negative manner, generating a configuration that only contains positive rules if the component default policy is negative, and negative rules if the default policy is positive.

Third, the set of configuration rules enhanced through our algorithms may significatively help to reduce the number of false positive events warned by NIDSs (i.e., alerts that the NIDS reports when it is not supposed to) since we best fit the number and type of alerting rules to the network properties.

The rest of this paper is organized as follows. Section 2 starts by introducing a network model that is further used in Section 3 when presenting our set of algorithms. Section 4 overviews the performance of our proposed algorithms, and Section 5 introduces an analysis of some related work. Finally Section 6 closes the paper with some conclusions.

2 Network Model

The purpose of our network model is to determine whether the traffic that matches a given configuration rule R_i may or may not cross the component configured by such a rule. It is defined as follows. First, and concerning the traffic flowing from two different zones of the network, we may determine the set of components that are crossed by this flow. Regarding the scenario shown in Figure 1, for example, the set of components crossed by the network traffic flowing from zone $external\ network$ to zone $private_3$ equals [C_1,C_2,C_4], and the set of components crossed by the network traffic flowing from zone $private_3$ to zone $private_2$ equals [C_4,C_2,C_3].

Let C be a set of components and let Z be a set of zones. We assume that each pair of zones in Z are mutually disjoint, i.e., if $z_i \in Z$ and $z_j \in Z$ then $z_i \cap z_j = \emptyset$. We then define the predicate $connected(c_1, c_2)$ as a symmetric and anti-reflexive function which becomes $true$ whether there exists, at least, one interface connecting component c_1 to component c_2. On the other hand, we define the predicate $adjacent(c, z)$ as a relation between components and zones which becomes $true$ whether the zone z is interfaced to

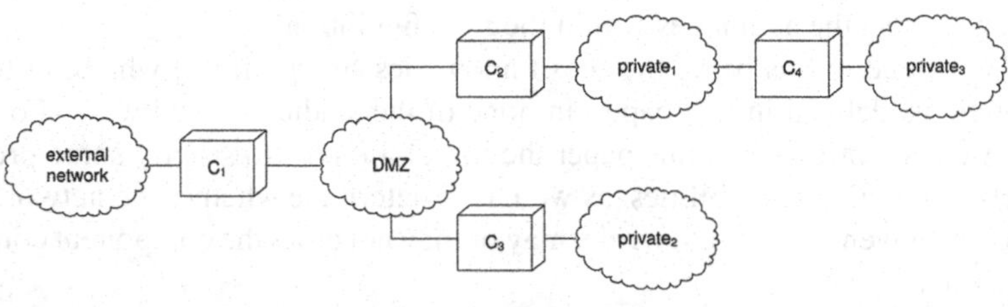

Fig. 1. Simple distributed policy setup

component c. Referring to Figure 1, we can verify that predicates $connected(C_1, C_2)$ and $connected(C_1, C_3)$, as well as $adjacent(C_1, DMZ)$, $adjacent(C_2, private_1)$, $adjacent(C_3, DMZ)$, and so on, become $true$.

We then define the set of paths, P, as follows. If $c \in C$ then $[c] \in P$ is an atomic path. Similarly, if $[p.c_1] \in P$ (be "." a concatenation functor) and $c_2 \in C$, such that $c_2 \notin p$ and $connected(c_1, c_2)$, then $[p.c_1.c_2] \in P$. This way, we can notice that, concerning Figure 1, $[C_1, C_2, C_4] \in P$ and $[C_1, C_3] \in P$.

Let us now define a set of functions related with the order between paths. We first define functions $first$, $last$, and the order functor between paths. We first define function $first$ from P in C such that if p is a path, then $first(p)$ corresponds to the first component in the path. Conversely, we define function $last$ from P in C such that if p is a path, then $last(p)$ corresponds to the last component in the path. We then define the order functor between paths as $p_1 \leq p_2$, such that path p_1 is shorter than p_2, and where all the components within p_1 are also within p_2.

Two additional functions are $route$ and $minimal\_route$. We define first define function $route$ from Z to Z, i.e., $\{route(z_1, z_2) : Z \times Z \ in \ 2^P\}$, such that $p \in route(z_1, z_2)$ iff the path p connects zone z_1 to zone z_2. Formally, we define $p \in route(z_1, z_2)$ iff $adjacent(first(p), z_1)$ and $adjacent(last(p), z_2)$. Similarly, we then define $minimal\_route$ from Z to Z, i.e., $\{minimal\_route (z_1, z_2) : Z \times Z \ in \ 2^P\}$, such that $p \in minimal\_route(z_1, z_2)$ iff the following conditions hold: (1) $p \in route(z_1, z_2)$; (2) There does not exist $p' \in route(z_1, z_2)$ such that $p' < p$. Regarding Figure 1, we can verify that the $minimal\_route$ from zone $private_3$ to zone $private_2$ equals $[C_4, C_2, C_3]$, i.e., $minimal\_route(private_3, private_2) = \{[C_4, C_2, C_3]\}$.

Let us finally conclude by defining the predicate $affects(Z, A_c)$ as a boolean expression which becomes $true$ whether there is, at least, an element $z \in Z$ such that the configuration of z is vulnerable to the attack category $A_c \in V$, where V is a vulnerability set built from a vulnerability database, such as CVE[8] or OSVDB[10].

3 Our Proposal

In this section we present our set of audit algorithms, whose main objective is the complete discovering and removal of policy anomalies that could exist in a single component policy, i.e., to discover and warn the security officer about potential anomalies within the configuration rules of a given component. Let us start by classifying the complete set of anomalies of our proposal.

3.1 Classifying the Anomalies

We classify in this section the complete set of anomalies that can occur within a single component configuration. An example for each anomaly will be illustrated through the sample scenarios shown in Figure 2.

Shadowing. A configuration rule R_i is shadowed in a set of configuration rules R whether such a rule never applies because all the packets that R_i may match, are previously matched by another rule, or combination of rules, with higher priority in order.

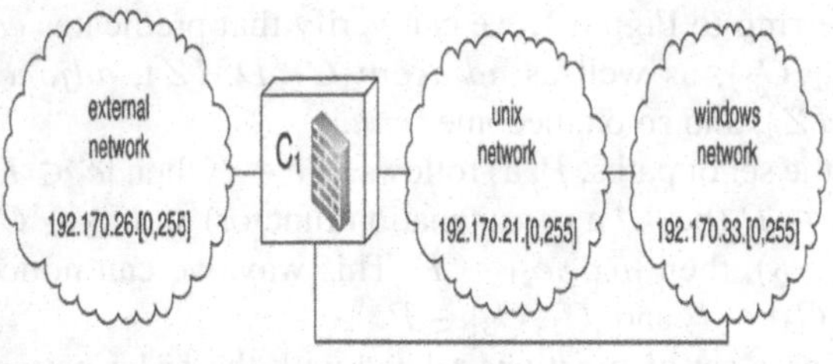

(a) Example scenario with a single filtering policy.

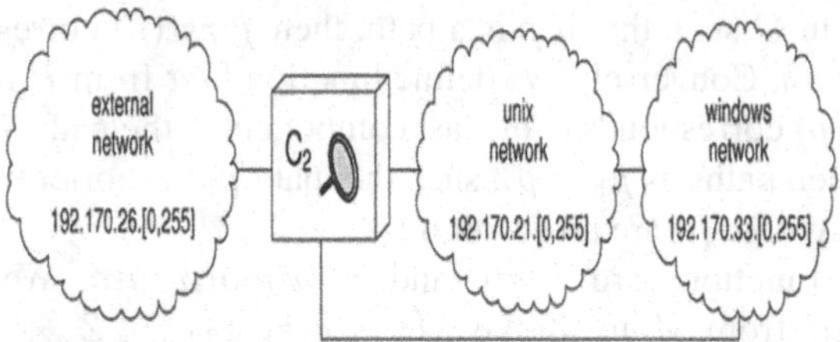

(b) Example scenario with a single alerting policy.

Fig. 2. Example filtering and alerting policies

Regarding Figure 2, rule $C_1\{R_6\}$ is shadowed by the overlapping of rules $C_1\{R_3\}$ and $C_1\{R_5\}$.

Redundancy. A configuration rule R_i is redundant in a set of rules R whether the rule is not shadowed by any other rule or set of rules and, when removing R_i from R, the security policy does not change. For instance, referring to Figure 2, rule $C_1\{R_4\}$ is redundant, since the overlapping between rules $C_1\{R_3\}$ and $C_1\{R_5\}$ is equivalent to the police of rule $C_1\{R_4\}$.

Irrelevance. A configuration rule R_i is irrelevant in a set of configuration rules R if one of the following conditions holds:

(1) Both source and destination address are within the same zone, and its decision is $false$. For instance, rule $C_1\{R_1\}$ is irrelevant since the source of this address, $external\ network$, as well as its destination, is the same.

(2) The component is not within the minimal route that connects the source zone, concerning the irrelevant rule which causes the anomaly, to the destination zone. Hence, the rule is irrelevant since it matches traffic which does not flow through this component. Rule $C_2\{R_3\}$, for example, is irrelevant since component C_2 is not in the path which corresponds to the minimal route between the source zone $windows\ network$ to the destination zone $unix\ network$.

(3) At least one of the condition attributes in R_i is related with a classification of attack A_c which does not affect the destination zone of such a rule, i.e., the predicate affects(z_d, A_c) becomes $false$. Regarding Figure 2, we can see that rule $C_2\{R_2\}$ is irrelevant since the nodes in the destination zone $unix\ network$ are not affected by vulnerabilities classified as $winworm$.

3.2 Proposed Algorithms

Our proposed audit process is a way to alert the security officer in charge of the network about these configuration errors, as well as to remove all the useless rules in the initial component configuration. The data to be used for the detection process is the following. A set of rules R as a list of initial size n, where n equals $count(R)$, and where each element is an associative array with the strings $condition, decision, shadowing$, $redundancy$, and $irrelevance$ as keys to access each necessary value.

For reasons of clarity, we assume one can access a linked-list through the operator R_i, where i is the relative position regarding the initial list size – $count(R)$. We also assume one can add new values to the list as any other normal variable does ($element \leftarrow value$), as well as to remove elements through the addition of an empty set ($element \leftarrow \emptyset$). The internal order of elements from the linked-list R keeps with the relative ordering of rules.

Each element $R_i[condition]$ is a boolean expression over p possible attributes. To simplify, we only consider as attributes the following ones: $szone$ (source zone), $dzone$ (destination zone), $sport$ (source port), $dport$ (destination port), $protocol$, and $attack\_class$ – or A_c for short – which will be empty whether the component is a firewall. In turn, each element $R_i[decision]$ is a boolean variable whose values are in $\{true, false\}$. Finally, elements $R_i[shadowing]$, $R_i[redundancy]$, and $R_i[irrelevance]$ are boolean variables in $\{true, false\}$ – which will be initialized to $false$ by default.

We split the whole process in four different algorithms. The first algorithm (cf. Algorithm 1) is an auxiliary function whose input is two rules, A and B. Once executed, this auxiliary function returns a further rule, C, whose set of condition attributes is the exclusion of the set of conditions from A over B. In order to simplify the representation of this algorithm, we use the notation A_i as an abbreviation of the variable $A[condition][i]$, and the notation B_i as an abbreviation of the variable $B[condition][i]$ – where i in $[1, p]$.

The second algorithm is a boolean function in $\{true, false\}$ which applies the necessary verifications to decide whether a rule r is irrelevant for the configuration of a component c. To properly execute this algorithm, let us define Z as the set of zones, $source(r)$ as a function in Z such that $source(r) = szone$, and $dest(r)$ as a function in Z such that $dest(r) = dzone$.

The third algorithm is a boolean function in $\{true, false\}$ which, in turn, applies the transformation *exclusion* (cf. Algorithm 1) over a set of configuration rules to check whether the rule obtained as a parameter is potentially redundant.

The last algorithm (i.e., Algorithm 4) performs the whole process of detecting and removing the complete set of anomalies. This process is split in three different phases. During the first phase, a set of shadowing rules are detected and removed from a top-bottom scope, by iteratively applying Algorithm 1 – when the decision field of the two rules is different. Let us notice that this stage of detecting and removing shadowed rules is applied before the detection and removal of proper redundant and irrelevant rules.

The resulting set of rules is then used when applying the second phase, also from a top-bottom scope. This stage is performed to detect and remove proper redundant rules, through an iterative call to Algorithm 3 (i.e., *testRedundancy*), as well as to detect

Algorithm 1: exclusion(B,A)

```
C[condition] ← ∅;
C[shadowing] ← false;
C[redundancy] ← false;
C[irrelevance] ← false;
C[decision] ← B[decision];
forall the elements of A[condition] and B[condition] do
    if ((A1 ∩ B1) ≠ ∅ and (A2 ∩ B2) ≠ ∅
    and ... and (Ap ∩ Bp) ≠ ∅) then
        C[condition] ← C[condition] ∪
        {(B1 − A1) ∧ B2 ∧ ... ∧ Bp,
        (A1 ∩ B1) ∧ (B2 − A2) ∧ ... ∧ Bp,
        (A1 ∩ B1) ∧ (A2 ∩ B2) ∧ (B3 − A3) ∧ ... ∧ Bp,
        ...
        (A1 ∩ B1) ∧ ... ∧ (Ap−1 ∩ Bp−1) ∧ (Bp − Ap)};
    else
        C[condition] ← (C[condition] ∪ B[condition]);
return C;
```

Algorithm 2: testIrrelevance(c,r)

```
zs ← source (r);
zd ← dest (r);
if (zs = zd) and (¬r[decision]) then
    warning ("First case of irrelevance");
else if zs ≠ zd then
    p ← minimal_route (zs,zd);
    if c ∉ p and (¬r[decision]) then
        warning ("Second case of irrelevance");
    else if (¬empty (r[Ac])) and (¬affects(zd, r[Ac])) then
        warning ("Third case of irrelevance");
    else return false;
return true;
```

Algorithm 3: testRedundancy(R,r)

```
i ← 1;
temp ← r;
while ¬test and (i ≤ count(R)) do
    temp ← exclusion(temp, Ri);
    if temp[condition] = ∅ then
        return true;
    i ← (i + 1);
return false;
```

Algorithm 4: intra-component-audit(c, R)

```
begin
    n ← count(R);
    /*Phase 1*/
    for i ← 1 to (n − 1) do
        for j ← (i + 1) to n do
            if Ri[decision] ≠ Rj[decision] then
                Rj ← exclusion (Rj,Ri);
                if Rj[condition] = ∅ then
                    warning ("Shadowing");
                    Rj[shadowing] ← true;
    /*Phase 2*/
    for i ← 1 to (n − 1) do
        Ra ← {rk ∈ R | n ≥ k > i and
              rk[decision] = ri[decision]};
        if testRedundancy (Ra,Ri) then
            warning ("Redundancy");
            Ri[condition] ← ∅;
            Ri[redundancy] ← true;
        else
            for j ← (i + 1) to n do
                if Ri[decision]=Rj[decision] then
                    Rj ← exclusion (Rj,Ri);
                    if (¬Rj[redundancy] and
                    Rj[condition] = ∅) then
                        warning ("Shadowing");
                        Rj[shadowing] ← true;
    /*Phase 3*/
    for i ← 1 to n do
        if Ri[condition] ≠ ∅ then
            if testIrrelevance (c,Ri) then
                Rj[irrelevance] ← true;
                r[condition] ← ∅;
end
```

and remove all the further shadowed rules remaining during the latter process. Finally, during a third phase the whole set of non-empty rules is analyzed in order to detect and remove irrelevance, through an iterative call to Algorithm 2 (i.e., *testIrrelevance*).

Let us conclude by giving an outlook to the set of warnings send to the security officer after the execution of Algorithm 4 over the configuration of the two components shown in Figure 2.

First case of irrelevance on $C_1\{R_1\}$ **Redundancy** on $C_1\{R_4\}$ **Shadowing** on $C_1\{R_6\}$	**Third case of irrelevance** on $C_2\{R_2\}$ **Second case of irrelevance** on $C_2\{R_3\}$ **Redundancy** on $C_2\{R_6\}$

3.3 Correctness of the Algorithms

Lemma 1. *Let* R_i : $condition_i \rightarrow decision_i$ *and* R_j : $condition_j \rightarrow decision_j$ *be two configuration rules. Then* $\{R_i, R_j\}$ *is equivalent to* $\{R_i, R'_j\}$ *where* $R'_j \leftarrow exclusion(R_j, R_i)$.

Proof of Lemma 1. Let us assume that $R_i[condition] = A_1 \wedge A_2 \wedge ... \wedge A_p$, and $R_j[condition] = B_1 \wedge B_2 \wedge ... \wedge B_p$. If $(A_1 \cap B_1) = \emptyset$ or $(A_2 \cap B_2) = \emptyset$ or ... or $(A_p \cap B_p) = \emptyset$ then $exclusion(R_j, R_i) \leftarrow R_j$. Hence, to prove the equivalence between $\{R_i, R_j\}$ and $\{R_i, R'_j\}$ is trivial in this case.

Let us now assume that $(A_1 \cap B_1) \neq \emptyset$ and $(A_2 \cap B_2) \neq \emptyset$ and ... and $(A_p \cap B_p) \neq \emptyset$. If we apply rules $\{R_i, R_j\}$ where R_i comes before R_j, then rule R_j applies to a given packet if this packet satisfies $R_j[condition]$ but not $R_i[condition]$ (since R_i applies first). Therefore, notice that $R_j[condition] - R_i[condition]$ is equivalent to $(B_1 - A_1) \wedge B_2 \wedge ... \wedge B_p$ or $(A_1 \cap B_1) \wedge (B_2 - A_2) \wedge ... \wedge B_p$ or $(A_1 \cap B_1) \wedge (A_2 \cap B_2) \wedge (B_3 - A_3) \wedge ... \wedge B_p$ or ... $(A_1 \cap B_1) \wedge ... \wedge (A_{p-1} \cap B_{p-1}) \wedge (B_p - A_p)$, which corresponds to $R'_j = exclusion(R_j, R_i)$. This way, if R_j applies to a given packet in $\{R_i, R_j\}$, then rule R'_j also applies to this packet in $\{R_i, R'_j\}$. Conversely, if R'_j applies to a given packet in $\{R_i, R'_j\}$, then this means this packet satisfies $R_j[condition]$ but not $R_i[condition]$. So, it is clear that rule R_j also applies to this packet in $\{R_i, R_j\}$. Since in Algorithm 1 $R'_j[decision]$ becomes $R_j[decision]$, this enables to conclude that $\{R_i, R_j\}$ is equivalent to $\{R_i, R'_j\}$. □

Theorem 2. *Let R be a set of configuration rules and let $Tr(R)$ be the resulting rules obtained by applying Algorithm 4 to R. Then R and $Tr(R)$ are equivalent.*

Proof of Theorem 2. Let $Tr'_1(R)$ be the set of rules obtained after applying the first phase of Algorithm 4. Since $Tr'_1(R)$ is derived from rule R by applying $exclusion$ (R_j, R_i) to some rules R_j in R, it is straightforward, from Lemma 1, to conclude that $Tr'_1(R)$ is equivalent to R.

Let us now move to the second phase, and let us consider a rule R_i such that $testRedundancy(R_i)$ (cf. Algorithm 3) is $true$. This means that $R_i[condition]$ can be derived by conditions of a set of rules S with the same decision and that come after in order than rule R_i. Since every rule R_j with a decision different from the one of rules in S has already been excluded from rules of S in the first phase of the Algorithm, we can conclude that rule R_i is definitely redundant and can be removed without changing the component configuration. This way, we conclude that Algorithm 4 preserves equivalence in this case. On the other hand, if $testRedundancy(R_i)$ is $false$, then transformation consists in applying function $exclusion(R_j, R_i)$ to some rules R_j which also preserves equivalence.

Similarly, and once in the third phase, let us consider a rule R_i such that $testIrrelevance(c, R_i)$ is $true$. This means that this rule matches traffic that will never cross component c, or that is irrelevant for the component's configuration. So, we can remove R_i from R without changing such a configuration. Thus, in this third case, as in the other two cases, $Tr'(R)$ is equivalent to $Tr'_1(R)$ which, in turn, is equivalent to R. □

Lemma 3. *Let R_i : $condition_i \rightarrow decision_i$ and R_j : $condition_j \rightarrow decision_j$ be two configuration rules. Then rules R_i and R'_j, where $R'_j \leftarrow exclusion(R_j, R_i)$ will never simultaneously apply to any given packet.*

Proof of Lemma 3. Notice that rule R'_j only applies when rule R_i does not apply. Thus, if rule R'_j comes before rule R_i, this will not change the final decision since rule R'_j only applies to packets that do not match rule R_i. □

Theorem 4. *Let R be a set of configuration rules and let $Tr(R)$ be the resulting rules obtained by applying Algorithm 4 to R. Then the following statements hold: (1) Ordering the rules in $Tr(R)$ is no longer relevant; (2) $Tr(R)$ is completely free of anomalies.*

Proof of Theorem 4. For any pair of rules R_i and R_j such that R_i comes before R_j, R_j is replaced by a rule R'_j obtained by recursively replacing R_j by $exclusion(R_j, R_k)$ for any $k < j$.

Then, by recursively applying Lemma 3, it is possible to commute rules R'_i and R'_j in $Tr(R)$ without changing the policy.

Regarding the second statement – $Tr(R)$ is completely free of anomalies – notice that, in $Tr(R)$, each rule is independent of all other rules. Thus, if we consider a rule R_i in $Tr(R)$ such that $R_i[condition] \neq \emptyset$, then this rule will apply to any packet that satisfies $R_i[condition]$, i.e., it is not shadowed.

On the other hand, rule R_i is not redundant because if we remove this rule, since this rule is the only one that applies to packets that satisfy $R_i[condition]$, then configuration of the component will change if we remove rule R_i from $Tr(R)$.

Finally, and after the execution of Algorithm 4 over the initial set of configuration rules, one may verify that for each rule R_i in $Tr(R)$ the following conditions hold: (1) $s = z_1 \cap source(r) \neq \emptyset$ and $d = z_2 \cap dest(r) \neq \emptyset$ such that $z_1 \neq z_2$ and component c is in $minimal\_route(z_1, z_2)$; (2) if $A_c = attack\_category(R_i) \neq \emptyset$, the predicate $affects(A_c, z_2)$ becomes $true$. Thus, each rule R_i in $Tr(R)$ is not irrelevant. □

3.4 Default Policies

Each component implements a positive (i.e., close) or negative (i.e., open) default policy. In the positive policy, the default policy is to *alert* or to *deny* a packet when any configuration rule applies. By contrast, the negative policy will $accepts$ or $pass$ a packet when no rule applies.

After rewriting the rules with our algorithms, we can actually remove every rule whose decision is *pass* or *accept* if the default policy of this component is negative (else this rule is redundant with the default policy) and similarly we can remove every rule whose decision is *deny* or *alert* if the default policy is positive. Thus, we can consider that our proposed algorithms generate a configuration that only contains positive rules if the component default policy is negative, and negative rules if the default policy is positive.

4 Performance Evaluation

In this section, we present an evaluation of the performance of MIRAGE (which stands for MIsconfiguRAtion manaGEr), a software prototype that implements the algorithms presented in sections 3. MIRAGE has been developed using PHP, a scripting language that is especially suited for web services development and can be embedded into HTML for the construction of client-side GUI based applications [3]. MIRAGE can be locally or remotely executed by using a HTTP server (e.g., Apache server over UNIX or Windows setups) and a web browser.

We evaluated our algorithms through a set of experiments over an IPv4 network. The topology for this network consisted of a single firewall based on Netfilter [13], and a single NIDS based on Snort [12] – both of them connected to three different zones with more than 50 hosts. The whole of these experiments were carried out on an Intel-Pentium M 1.4 GHz processor with 512 MB RAM, running Debian GNU/Linux 2.6.8, and using Apache/1.3 with PHP/4.3 configured.

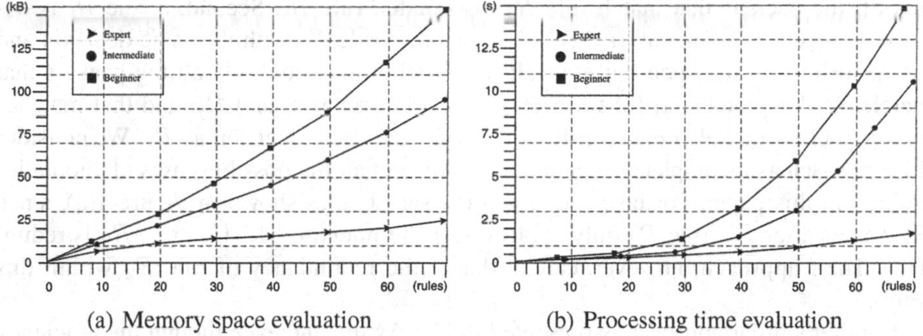

(a) Memory space evaluation (b) Processing time evaluation

Fig. 3. Memory and processing time evaluation

During our experiments, we measured the memory space and the processing time needed to perform Algorithm 4 over several sets of IPv4 filtering and alerting policies for the two IPv4 networks, according to the three following security officer profiles: beginner, intermediate, and expert – where the probability to have overlaps between rules increases from 5% to 90%. The results of these measurements are plotted in Figure 3(a) and Figure 3(b). Although the plots reflect strong memory and process time requirements, we consider they are reasonable for off-line analysis, since it is not part of the critical performance of an alerting or filtering component.

5 Related Work

A first approach to get a configuration free of errors is by applying a formal model to express the network policy. In [4], for example, we presented a model with this purpose. This way, a set of configuration rules, whose syntax is specific to a given component, may be generated using a transformation language.

The proposals in [1,6,7,2], provide means to directly manage the discovery of anomalies from the components' configuration. For instance, the authors in [1] consider that, in a configuration set, two rules are in conflict when the first rule in order matches some packets that match the second rule, and the second rule also matches some of the packets that match the first rule. This approach is very limited since it just detects a particular case of wrongly defined rules in a single configuration, i.e., just ambiguity within the set of rules is detected.

In [6], two new cases of anomalies are considered. First, a rule R_j is defined as backward redundant iff there exists another rule R_i with higher priority in order such

(a) Set of rules A	(b) Set of rules B
$R_1 : s \in [10, 50] \rightarrow deny$	$R_1 : s \in [10, 50] \rightarrow accept$
$R_2 : s \in [40, 70] \rightarrow accept$	$R_2 : s \in [40, 90] \rightarrow accept$
$R_3 : s \in [50, 80] \rightarrow accept$	$R_3 : s \in [30, 80] \rightarrow deny$

Fig. 4. Example of some firewall configurations

that all the packets that match rule R_j also match rule R_i. Second, a rule R_i is defined as forward redundant iff there exists another rule R_j with the same decision and less priority in order such that the following conditions hold: (1) all the packets that match R_i also match R_j; (2) for each rule R_k between R_i and R_j, and that matches all the packets that also match rule R_i, R_k has the same decision as R_i. We consider this approach as incomplete, since it does not detect all the possible cases of anomalies defined in this paper. For instance, given the set of rules shown in Figure 4(a), since R_2 comes after R_1, rule R_2 only applies over the interval $[51, 70]$ – i.e., R_2 is redundant. Their approach, however, cannot detect the redundancy of rule R_2 within this setup.

Another similar approach is presented in [2]. Again, and even though the efficiency of their proposed discovering algorithms and techniques is very promising, we consider this approach not complete since, given a misconfigured component, their detection algorithms could not detect all the possible errors. For example, given the set of rules shown in Figure 4(b) their approach cannot detect that rule R_3 will be never applied due to the union of rules R_1 and R_2.

6 Conclusions

In this paper we presented an audit process to set the configuration of both *firewalls* and *network intrusion detection systems* (NIDSs) free of anomalies. Our audit process is based on the existence of relationships between the condition attributes of the configuration rules of those network security components, such as coincidence, disjunction, and inclusion. Then, our proposal uses a transformation process which derives from an initial set of rules – potentially misconfigured – to an equivalent one which is completely free of anomalies.

We also presented in this paper a network model to determine whether the network traffic that matches a given configuration rule, may or may not cross the component configured by such a rule, as well as other network properties. Thanks to this model, our approach best defines all the set of anomalies studied in the related work, and it reports, moreover, a new anomaly case not reported, as defined in this paper, in none of the other approaches.

Some advantages of our approach are the following. First, our transformation process verifies that the resulting rules are completely independent between them. Otherwise, each rule considered as useless during the process is reported to the security officer, in order to verify the correctness of the whole process. Second, we can perform a second rewriting of rules, generating a configuration that only contains positive rules if the component default policy is negative, and negative rules if the default policy is positive.

Third, the elimination of alerting rules during the audit process helps to reduce future false positive events alerted by a NIDS.

Regarding a possible increase of the initial number of rules, due to the applying of our algorithms, it is only significant whether the associated parsing algorithm of the component depends on the number of rules. In this case, an increase in such a parameter may degrade the performance of the component. Nonetheless, this is not a disadvantage since the use of a parsing algorithm independent of the number of rules becomes the best solution as much for our proposal as for the current deployment of network technologies. The set pruning tree algorithm is a proper example, because it only depends on the number and size of attributes to be parsed, not the number of rules [11].

The implementation of our approach in a software prototype demonstrate the practicability of our work. We shortly discussed this implementation, based on a scripting language [3], and presented an evaluation of its performance. Although these experimental results show that our algorithms have strong requirements, we believe that they are reasonable for off-line analysis, since it is not part of the critical performance of the audited component.

Acknowledgments

This work was supported by funding from the French ministry of research, under the *ACI DESIRS* project, the Spanish Government project *TIC2003-02041*, and the Catalan Government grants *2003FI126* and *2005BE77*.

References

1. Adiseshu, H., Suri, S., and Parulkar, G. (2000). Detecting and Resolving Packet Filter Conflicts. *19th Annual Joint Conference of the IEEE Computer and Communications Societies.*
2. Al-Shaer, E. S., Hamed, H. H., and Masum, H. (2005). Conflict Classification and Analysis of Distributed Firewall Policies In *IEEE Journal on Selected Areas in Communications*, 1(1).
3. Castagnetto, J. et al. (1999). *Professional PHP Programming.*
4. Cuppens, F., Cuppens-Boulahia, N., Sans, T. and Miege, A. (2004). In *Second Workshop on Formal Aspects in Security and Trust.* A formal approach to specify and deploy a network security policy. In *Second Workshop on Formal Aspects in Security and Trust*, 203–218.
5. Cuppens, F., Cuppens-Boulahia, N., and García-Alfaro, J. (2005). Detection and Removal of Firewall Misconfiguration. In *2005 International Conference on Communication, Network and Information Security*. 154–162.
6. Gupta, P. (2000). *Algorithms for Routing Lookups and Packet Classification.* PhD Thesis, Department of Computer Science, Stanford University.
7. Liu, A. X. and Gouda, M. G. (2005). Complete Redundancy Detection in Firewalls. In *Proceedings of 19th Annual IFIP Conference on Data and Applications Security*, 196–209.
8. MITRE Corp. Common Vulnerabilities and Exposures. [Online]. Available from: `http://cve.mitre.org/`
9. Northcutt, S. (2002). *Network Intrusion Detection: An analyst's Hand Book.* New Riders Publishing, third edition edition.
10. Open Security Foundation. Open Source Vulnerability Database. [Online]. Available from: `http://osvdb.org/`

11. Paul, O., Laurent, M., and Gombault, S. (2000). A full bandwidth ATM Firewall. In *Proceedings of the 6th European Symposium on Research in Computer Security (ESORICS 2000).*
12. Roesch, M. (1999), Snort: lightweight intrusion detection for networks. In *13th USENIX Systems Administration Conference*, Seattle, WA.
13. Welte, H., Kadlecsik, J., Josefsson, M., McHardy, P., and et al. The netfilter project: firewalling, nat and packet mangling for linux 2.4x and 2.6.x. [Online]. Available from: `http://www.netfilter.org/`

Using Group Overlapping to Protect Server from Attack in Grid Computing

Byungryong Kim

DongDang Data Technonogy Co., Ltd. No.417, Hanshin IT Tower #235, Kuro-Dong, Kuro-Ku,Seoul, Korea, 152-050
doolyn@gmail.com

Abstract. P2P networks provide a basic form of anonymity, and the participating nodes exchange information without knowing who is the original sender. Packets are relayed through the adjacent nodes and do not contain identity information about the sender. Since these packets are passed through a dynamically-formed path and since the final destination is not known until the last time, it is impossible to know who has sent it in the beginning and who will be the final recipient. The anonymity, however, breaks down at download/upload time because the IP address of the host from which the data is downloaded (or to which it is uploaded) can be known to the outside. We propose a technique to provide anonymity for both the client and the server node. A random node along the path between the client and the server node is selected as an agent node and works as a proxy: the client will see it as the server and the server looks at it as the client, hence protecting the identity of the client and the server from anonymity-breaking attacks.

1 Introduction

Internet has been developed based on information share for recent years. On the other hand, network users are demanding privacy more than share of information. Anonymity is not exclusive to specific system or specific network any more. In fact the most important protocol, TCP/IP protocol puts more emphasis on the improvement of performance such as scalability or efficiency rather than privacy of users. Therefore under open internet environment when sending information, private information which should be secured may be attacked or detected on anonymity-breaking attacks[10,11,12,13].

Under special circumstances, network users may demand different types of anonymity each other. Anonymity can largely be classified into three types: resistant-censorship; anonymity of initiator or responder; mutual anonymity. Mutual anonymity is composed of the following three parts: initiator having anonymity; responder having anonymity; and communication having anonymity between the initiator and the responder. In the most recent studies on mutual anonymity, trusted agent, random agent and random or static proxy techniques are included.

The latest file sharing applications such as Napster[1], FreeNet[2], Gnutella[3], eDonkey[4], KaZaA[5] and distributed Hash Table techniques as in Tapestry[6,7], Can[8], or Chord[9] were designed to make it possible to easily retrieve or share

J. Górski (Ed.): SAFECOMP 2006, LNCS 4166, pp. 195–204, 2006.

information under internet environment. In P2P system peers freely participate in and leave network so they frequently 'join' and 'leave', and each peer performs the roles of provider and consumer at the same time.

P2P systems can largely be classified into centralized system and decentralized system. Centralized system such as Napster can be attacked by denial of service. Decentralized system is strong in terms of high fault-tolerance, high autonomy and flexible scalability. This study puts focus on decentralized and unstructured P2P systems. Nodes participating in P2P systems communicate only with neighbor nodes and finally any node is unable to know the information of node which is more than 2 hops away. Hence Query message requesting for retrieval does not include IP address of node to process the Query[3].

Identity of peer is exposed to all the neighbors and some of malicious peers collect and analyze information with no difficulty by monitoring packet flow. For example type of packet or TTL value, Hops value, retrieval character and so forth can be obtained. Therefore through this method initiator and responder lose the anonymity among their neighbors and at last P2P system as well loses the anonymity.

This study proposes mutual anonymity technique through grouping nodes that can avoid denial of service. Identity is exposed on responder side by initiator receiving QueryHit[3] packet and initiator's identity comes to get exposed to responder by initiator's download request made to responder. Therefore through packet monitoring malicious peer knows who the initiator and responder are. In addition using the information obtained from the information, it can fail initiator and responder with denial of service attack. The proposed technique not only protects identity of initiator and responder through grouping but also enables anonymous communication by performing packet relay for nodes belonging to group in random order. Since cryptography processing implemented in previous papers is not used, it is advantageous in that mutual anonymity can easily be provided using previous protocol as it is without additional overhead.

Other parts of this paper is organized as follows: chapter 2 looks into the unstructured p2p system and Anonymity problem in P2P networks, which are the focus of this paper; chapter 3 looks through mutual anonymity technique, proposed in this paper in detail; chapter 4 tests packet overhead of grouping technique, proposed in this paper; at last chapter 5 draws conclusions.

2 Related Researches

In this Section, we present the unstructured P2P file sharing application and anonymity problem issues in P2P networks. The primary goal for Freenet security is protecting the anonymity of requestors and inserters of files. As Freenet communication is not directed towards specific receivers, receiver anonymity is more accurately viewed as key anonymity, that is, hiding the key which is being requested or inserted. Anonymous point-to-point channels based on Chaum's mix-net scheme[14] have been implemented for email by the Mixmaster remailer[15] and for general TCP/IP traffic by onion routing[16,17] and freedom[18]. Such channels are not in themselves easily suited to one-to-many publication, however, and are best viewed as a complement to Freenet since they do not provide file access and storage. Anonymity for consumers of information in the web context is provided by browser proxy services such as the Anonymizer[19], although they provide no protection for producers of information and do not protect consumers against logs kept by the services themselves. Private information retrieval schemes[20] provide much stronger guarantees for information consumers, but only to the extent of hiding which piece of information was retrieved from a particular server. In many cases, the fact of contacting a particular server in itself can reveal much about the information retrieved, which can only be counteracted by having every server hold all information. Reiter and Rubin's Crowds system[21] uses a similar method of proxing requests for consumers, although Crowds does not itself store information and does not protect information producers. Berthold *et al.* propose Web MIXes[22], a stronger system that uses message padding and reordering and dummy messages to increase security, but again does not protect information producers.

The Rewebber[23] provides a measure of anonymity for producers of web information by means of an encrypted URL service that is essentially the inverse of an anonymizing browser proxy, but has the same difficulty of providing no protection against the operator of the service itself. Publius[24] enhances availability by distributing files as redundant shares among n webservers, only k of which are needed to reconstruct a file; however, since the identity of the servers themselves is not anonymized, an attacker might remove information by forcing the closure of n-k+1 servers. The Eternity proposal[25] seeks to archive information permanently and anonymously, although it lacks specifics on how to efficiently locate stored files, making it more akin to an anonymous backup service. Free Haven[26] is an interesting anonymous publication system that uses a trust network and file trading mechanism to provide greater server accountability while maintaining anonymity.

MUTE[27] forces all intermediate nodes along the path between the client and the server node to work as proxies to protect the identities of the client and the server. Tarzan[28] is a peer-to-peer anonymous IP network overly. so it works with any internet application. Its peer-to-peer design makes it decentralized, scalable, and easy to manage. Mantis[29] is similar to Crowds in that there are helping nodes to propagate the request to the candidate servers anonymously.

3 Providing Anonymity Via Random Agent Nodes

With the technique proposed in this paper neighbor nodes are tied into a group and the group becomes a fixed proxy. Each node belonging to the group processes the request of client in part. Fig. 1 shows the p2p retrieval system of general flooding basis. Whenever client sends Query it has GUID value of its own. Therefore when client receives QueryHit packet, in case that the current guid value and the GUID value of received QueryHit packet are different it is ignored since it is the answer to the former request.

In Fig. 1 client broadcasts Query packet to neighbor node and the node receiving the packet broadcasts it to the neighbor node again. If retrieval matches to among these nodes, it responds as QueryHit packet. In general gnutella system, if receiving Query packet having the same GUID value again, it is aborted. If not, numerous query packets are generated and substantial network traffic may be found. In the proposed technique these rules are ignored according to certain standard. In Fig. 1 Nodes 8 initially received the packet having the same GUID. Then they broadcasts it again to server, the neighbor node. According to general rule, server will respond to one of Queries sent by node 7, or others if it matches to retrieval. However with technique proposed in Fig. 2, if it matches to retrieval, it will respond to all Queries having the same guid value. Nodes X, Y, Z receiving QueryHit packet from server are grouped as one through the exchange of SetGroup packet. Through the exchange of SetGroup packet, it is known that nodes X, Y, Z belong to the same group and finally client communicates with server through the group in the end.

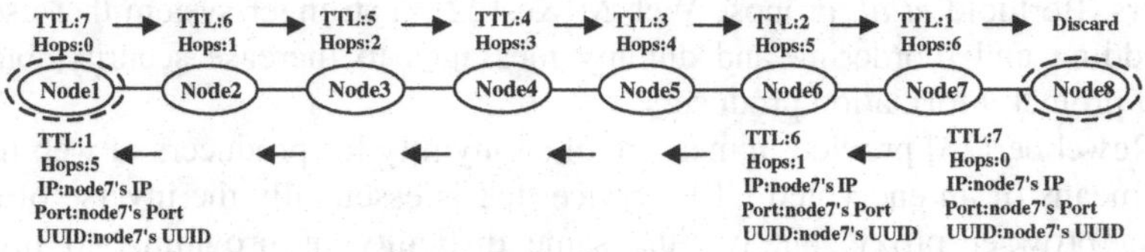

Fig. 1. Flow of Query and Query Hit packets

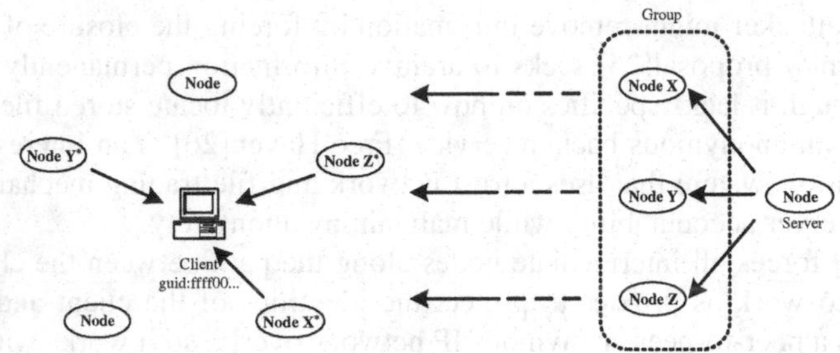

Fig. 2. Intermediate nodes through overlapping receipt of Query message

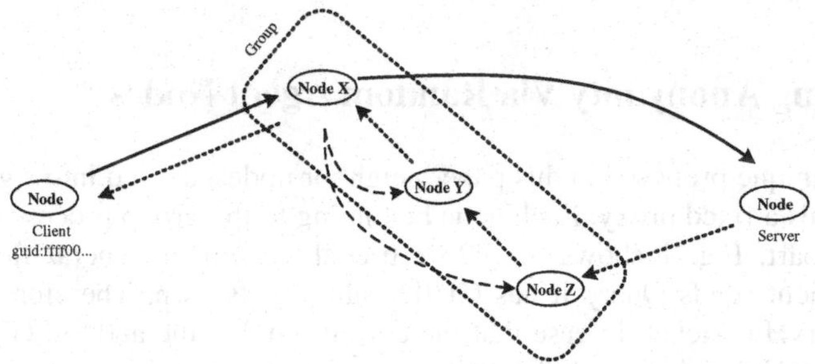

Fig. 3. Anonymous communication flow between server and client

When downloading a file, client can download file from all the nodes, X, Y, Z belonging to group. In Fig. 2, client receives QueryHit packet sent by X,Y,Z server's neighbor nodes from the neighbor nodes, X^*, Z^*, Y^*. In general Gnutella protocol, one retrieval result value is obtained. Where client has same general GUID value and receives QueryHit packet having Servant Session ID value from different node(X^*, Y^*, Z^*), the client is processed as follows:

I-I. If the received packet is QueryHit packet then it is checked that the local GUID value and guid value of packet are identical. If they are not identical, abort it.

I-II. If the received packet is QueryHit packet and the values of local GUID and packet's GUID are the same, then GUID value and Servant Session ID local GUID value are saved to g-table.

I-II-I. If there is the same GUID value and entry which equals to servant session ID value, new entry is added and same Group is set.

I-II-II. In user application, only one group is marked as retrieval result. ii). Users request file download by means of application.

II. If the file download request belongs to g_table a Group, one of them is selected randomly and file request is made. Namely, file download request can be sent to node other than node requested by user.

Fig 3 shows client's downloading flow. In Fig. 2, client tries to download among retrieval list obtained by received QueryHit. If it belongs to a Group at g_table, one of them is randomly selected. In Fig. 3 node X was selected. For node X it conforms to the following process:

I). In node X value obtained from SetGroup packet exchange performed at Fig. 2 process is stored at g_table. So it is known that nodes X and Y belong to the same group.

II). Node X randomly fixes order within the Group. In Fig. 3, number one is X, number two, Y, and number three, Z. Node X sends these order information, SetOrderGroup packet to nodes, X and Z.

III). Node X sends the IP address and Port value of PUSH packet after setting them as IP address and Port of the last node in order, node Z.

IV). Because Server received PUSH packet it tries to connect to node Z and sends filed requested by client.

V). Node Z knows node Y with order number 2 and sends the file sent by Sever to node Y.

VI). Node Y sends it to node X with order number 1 again.

VII). NodeX sends the file to client.

To explain in more detail, random nodes between server and client are tied to one Group and through this group file sharing is performed between server and client. Client sends request for file download randomly selecting one out of this group and node receiving this request settles relay order of each node within group. This request is received to Server after changing it into PUSH packet while sending from Group to Server. Because server received PUSH packet, it requests connection to random node in Group and starts sending file. Finally the file received from server of nodes within Group is sent to client again.

As shown on Fig.3, nodes belonging to the same group, settles the order and performs like proxy between Server and Client. Therefore server and client do not know who the client and the server are. Attacker also has to know all the nodes of the same group when it intends to attack server and client and although if the attacker finds out them, the information of server and client can be known only if it correctly knows the order of packet sending within group.

There is order in nodes in the same group but the order is randomly settled. Pass between client and server in Fig. 3 is for one-time and next time connection path is differently settled and it communicates with other group. Therefore identity of client and Server is protected and anonymous communication between client and server can be kept.

4 Experimentation

We have modified the behavior of Minism[30] to implement our algorithm. Especially a routing table is built to trace the movement of QueryHit packet. Fig. 4 and Fig. 5 shows the inner-working of Minism code. Fig. 4 shows a P2P network generated by Minism. The figure shows each node is assigned a number of neighbor nodes: node 0 has neighbors of node 3 and 4; node 1 has neighbors of node 102, 9789, etc. Fig. 5 shows the propagation of Query packet. The "reached" array shows the nodes the Query packet reached at each stage. In "reached" array, nodes with -1 are ones that are not reached yet; nodes with 1 are those that are visited already; finally a node with (1) is one we are going to visit next. Below "reached" array, we can see the state of the stack that contains the Query packet. To simulate the propagation of a packet, the stack shows at each stage which path each duplicated Query packet should follow (from which node to which node). For example, at stage 1, all nodes are marked with -1 except node 0 since we haven't visited any node yet, and the starting node is node 0. The stack contains the path we should relay the packet: from -1 (no where) to 0 (the starting node). At stage 1, we can see node 0 is already visited (at stage 1); the next node we should visit is node 3 because node 0 has two neighbors - node 3 and 4 - and node 3 is selected as the next one. The stack shows the two path segments we should take (from 0 to 3 and from 0 to 4) for the Query packet. The segment at the top of the stack (from 0 to 3) will be chosen.

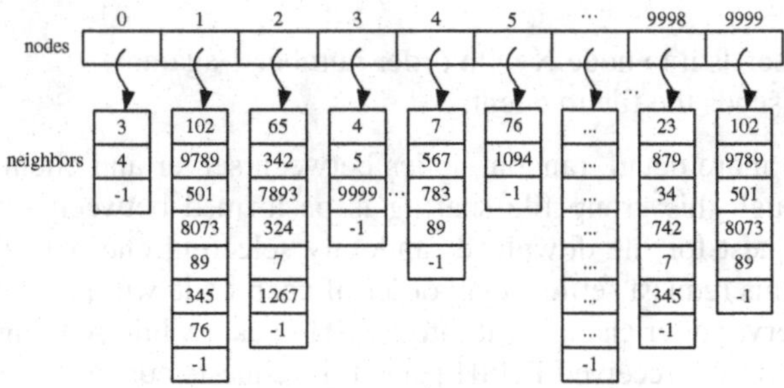

Fig. 4. A P2P network generated by Minism

We have modified the behavior of Minism to implement our algorithm. Especially a routing table is built to trace the movement of QueryHit packet. Fig. 4 and Fig. 5 shows the inner-working of Minism code. Fig. 4 shows a P2P network generated by

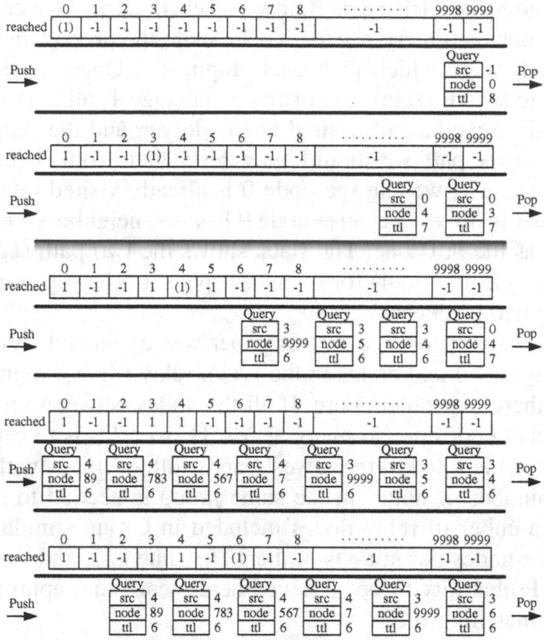

Fig. 5. The propagation of a Query packet

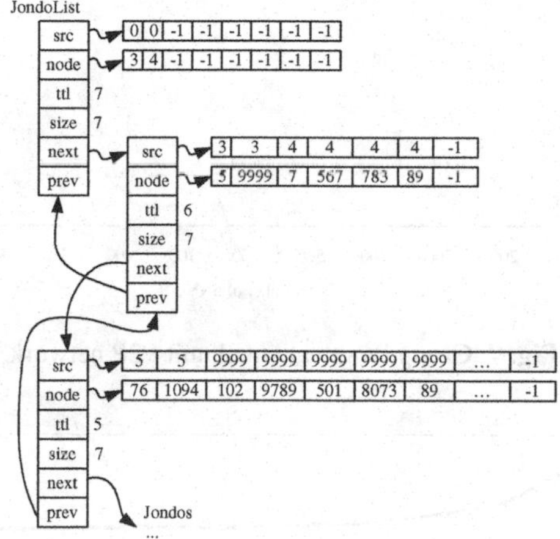

Fig. 6. A routing history table

Minism. The figure shows each node is assigned a number of neighbor nodes: node 0 has neighbors of node 3 and 4; node 1 has neighbors of node 102, 9789, etc. Fig. 5 shows the propagation of Query packet. The "reached" array shows the nodes the Query packet reached at each stage. In "reached" array, nodes with -1 are ones that are not reached yet; nodes with 1 are those that are visited already; finally a node with

(1) is one we are going to visit next. Below "reached" array, we can see the state of the stack that contains the Query packet. To simulate the propagation of a packet, the stack shows at each stage which path each duplicated Query packet should follow (from which node to which node). For example, at stage 1, all nodes are marked with -1 except node 0 since we haven't visited any node yet, and the starting node is node 0. The stack contains the path we should relay the packet: from -1 (no where) to 0 (the starting node). At stage 1, we can see node 0 is already visited (at stage 1); the next node we should visit is node 3 because node 0 has two neighbors - node 3 and 4 - and node 3 is selected as the next one. The stack shows the two path segments we should take (from 0 to 3 and from 0 to 4) for the Query packet. The segment at the top of the stack (from 0 to 3) will be chosen.

In chapter 3 algorithm proposed in this paper was explained. As shown on Fig. 3 several nodes are grouped and nodes in the group relay file between server and client in turn. However there is problem here. If all the nodes between server and client are grouped in one, relay nodes are so many as MUTE so it leads to cause lots of packet and the sending speed is fixed to the lowest bandwidth of nodes within group as well. Accordingly the number of nodes in the same group is needed to be properly fixed. Fig. 4 shows the number of relay nodes included in Group simulated with Minism. Maximum neighbor nodes per node is 5, the TTL value is 7, and the probability to be retrieved is 30%. Probability to be retrieved here means that approximately 30 % of all the nodes have matching file.

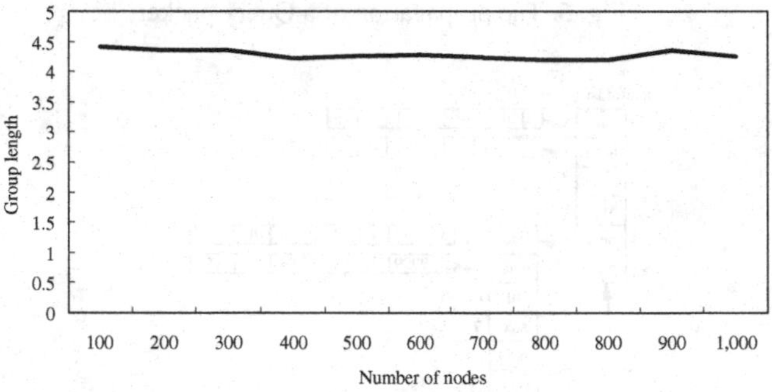

Fig. 7. Group length at small unit P2P network

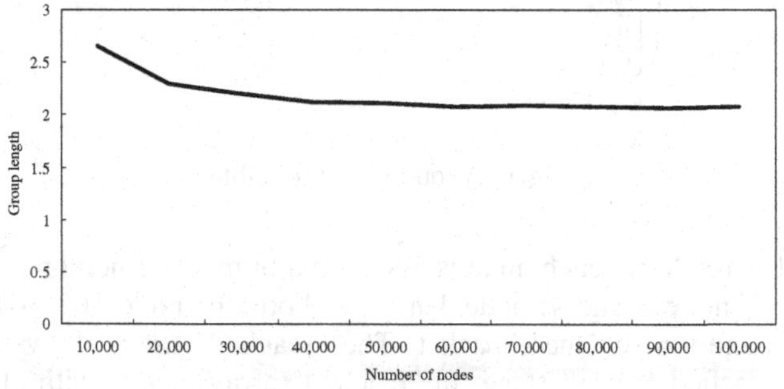

Fig. 8. Group length at large unit P2P network

Fig. 7, 8 shows the number of nodes in a group when the size of P2P network is classified as small, medium, and large unit each. As shown on the figures although the number of nodes participating in network is diminished or increased, the number of node in Group is not so variable. Therefore packet overload is not caused as MUTE.

5 Conclusions

In P2P network without center control each peer is independent and has all the responsibility as well. Accordingly it is relatively weaker in terms of security rather than in centralized P2P network. In this paper we proposed protecting Agent from Attack technique to provide mutual anonymous between server and client when retrieval is made in P2P. Initiator and responder do not exactly know who the initiator and responder are through mutual anonymity technique. Initiator knows that it communicates with specific node of group but does not know node belonging to the group and even if it knows the node the relay order of each node is randomly set that hardly knows the location of responder. It is the same as with responder side that identity of responder and initiator is secured. In proposed technique according to the number of node in one group packet overhead can be made. Test results found that group length is constantly maintained to a certain level regardless of the number of node. Therefore with mutual anonymity technique, since overhead such as cryptography processing is not aroused the mutual anonymity can be provided with relatively little overhead.

References

1. Napster, http://www.napster.com/ 2000
2. I. Clarke, O. Sandberg, B. Wiley, and T. W. Hong, Freenet: A distributed anonymous information storage and retrieval system, In Workshop on Design Issues in Anonymity and Unobservability, pages 46.66, 2000., http://citeseer.nj.nec.com/clarke00freenet.html.
3. The Gnutella Protocol Specification v0.41 Document Revision 1.2., http://rfc-gnutella.sourceforge.net/developer/stable/index.html/
4. eDonkey, http://www.edonkey2000.com/
5. KaZaA, http://www.kazza.com/
6. Kirsten Hildrum, John Kubiatowicz, Satish Rao and Ben Y. Zhao, Distributed Object Location in a Dynamic Network, Theory of Computing Systems (2004)
7. Ben Y. Zhao, Ling Huang, Jeremy Stribling, Sean C. Rhea, Anthony D. Joseph, and John Kubiatowicz, Tapestry: A Resilient Global-scale Overlay for Service Deployment, IEEE Journal on Selected Areas in Communications (2004)
8. Sylvia Ratnasamy, Paul Francis, Mark Handley, Richard Karp, Scott Schenker, A scalable content-addressable network, Proceedings of the 2001 conference on Applications, technologies, architectures, and protocols for computer communications table of contents.
9. Ion Stoica, Robert Morris, David Liben-Nowell, David R. Karger, M. Frans Kaashoek, Frank Dabek, Hari Balakrishnan, Chord: a scalable peer-to-peer lookup protocol for internet applications, IEEE/ACM Transactions on Networking (2003)
10. Neil Daswani, Hector Garcia-Molina, Query-flood DoS attacks in gnutella, Proceedings of the 9th ACM conference on Computer and communications security table of contents (2002)

11. P. Krishna Gummadi, Stefan Saroiu, Steven D. Gribble, A measurement study of Napster and Gnutella as examples of peer-to-peer file sharing systems, ACM SIGCOMM Computer Communication Review (2002)
12. A. Back, U. M¨oller, and A. Stiglic, Traffic analysis attacks and trade-offs in anonymity providing systems, In I. S. Moskowitz, editor, Information Hiding (IH 2001), pages 245.257. Springer-Verlag, LNCS 2137, 2001.
13. J. F. Raymond, Traffic Analysis: Protocols, Attacks, Design Issues, and Open Problems, In Workshop on Design Issues in Anonymity and Unobservability. Springer-Verlag, LNCS 2009, July 2000.
14. D.L. Chaum, Untraceable electronic mail, return addresses, and digital pseudonyms, Communications of the ACM 24(2), 84-88 (1981).
15. L. Cottrell, Frequently asked questions about Mixmaster remailers, http://www.obscura.com/~loki/remailer/mixmaster-faq.html (2000).
16. Roger Dingledine, Nick Mathewson, Paul Syverson, Tor: The Second-Generation Onion Router, Proceedings of the 13th USENIX Security Symposium (2004)
17. D. Goldschlag, M. Reed, and P. Syverson, Onion routing for anonymous and private Internet connections, Communications of the ACM 42(2), 39-41 (1999).
18. Zero-Knowledge Systems, http://www.zks.net/ (2000).
19. Anonymizer, http://www.anonymizer.com/ (2000).
20. B. Chor, O. Goldreich, E. Kushilevitz, and M. Sudan, Private information retrieval, Journal of the ACM 45(6), 965-982 (1998).
21. M.K. Reiter and A.D. Rubin, Anonymous web transactions with Crowds, Communications of the ACM 42(2), 32-38 (1999).
22. O. Berthold, H. Federrath, and S. Kopsell, Web MIXes: a system for anonymous and unobservable Internet access, in Proceedings of the Workshop on Design Issues in Anonymity and Unobservability, Berkeley, CA, USA. Springer: New York (2001).
23. The Rewebber, http://www.rewebber.de/ (2000).
24. M. Waldman, A.D. Rubin, and L.F. Cranor, Publius: a robust, tamper-evident, censorship-resistant, web publishing system, in Proceedings of the Ninth USENIX Security Symposium, Denver, CO, USA (2000).
25. R.J. Anderson, The Eternity service, in Proceedings of the 1st International Conference on the Theory and Applications of Cryptology (PRAGOCRYPT '96), Prague, Czech Republic (1996).
26. R. Dingledine, M.J. Freedman, and D. Molnar, The Free Haven project: distributed anonymous storage service, in Proceedings of the Workshop on Design Issues in Anonymity and Unobservability, Berkeley, CA, USA. Springer: New York (2001).
27. MUTE: Simple, Anonymous File Sharing., http://mute-net.sourceforge.net/
28. Michael J. Freedman, Robert Morris, Tarzan: A Peer-to-Peer Anonymizing Network Layer, in Proceedings of the 1st International Workshop on Peer-to-Peer Systems (IPTPS '02), Cambridge, MA, USA (2002)
29. Stephen C. Bono, Christopher A. Soghoian, Fabian Monrose, Mantis: A Lightweight, Server-Anonymity Preserving, Searchable P2P, Information Security Institute of The Johns Hopkins University, Technical Report TR-2004-01-B-ISI-JHU (2004)
30. Gnutella Developer Forum., http://groups.yahoo.com/group/the_gdf/

The Role of Situation Awareness in Assuring Safety of Autonomous Vehicles

Andrzej Wardziński

PROKOM Software SA
Podolska 21, 81-321 Gdynia, Poland
wardzinskia@prokom.pl

Abstract. Assuring safety of autonomous vehicles operating in an open environment requires reliable situation awareness, action planning and prediction of actions of other vehicles and objects. Factors that also have to be considered are certainty and completeness of available information and trust in information sources and other entities. The paper discusses the problem of autonomous vehicle safety assurance and proposes dynamic situation assessment to cope with the problem of environment dynamics and incomplete and uncertain situation knowledge. The approach is presented for a simple example of a simulated autonomous vehicle. The situation awareness model and autonomous vehicle control system architecture is presented. The problems of justifying system safety are discussed.

1 Introduction

In 1981 the first man was killed by a robot in a manufacturing plant in Japan [1]. The maintenance worker entered the robot's operating zone to fix its component. Instead of opening the robot's safety gate – which was supposed to cut off its power – he jumped over the barrier fence and accidentally switched the robot back on. The robot sensor was activated then the robot decided that he was an industrial component and crushed him. Other similar accidents have been reported [2]. The main cause of this kind of accidents was that a robot was unaware of a human being present in the area it operated. The fatal accidents as described above were caused not by components failures but weak ability to percept and assess the situation.

The objective of the paper is to investigate the problem of safety assurance for autonomous systems where external events and interaction with the environment and other systems have essential influence on safety. The problem and assumptions are introduced in section 2. Section 3 discusses the concept of situation risk assessment, trust in other agents and the problem of uncertain and incomplete knowledge. An example of an autonomous vehicle is introduced in Section 4. Then a situation awareness model is proposed in Section 5. The way how the situation awareness model is applied for the autonomous vehicle control system is presented in section 6. Hazard analysis of presented architecture is discussed in section 7. A vehicle cooperation process that strengthens safety is proposed in section 8. Experiences from autonomous vehicle simulation experiments are discussed in section 9.

J. Górski (Ed.): SAFECOMP 2006, LNCS 4166, pp. 205 – 218, 2006.

2 The Problem of Autonomous Vehicles Safety

Autonomy relates to an individual or collective ability to make decisions and act without outside control or intervention. Autonomy is quite a new concept for safety-critical systems.

Autonomous vehicle (AV) is a vehicle able to perform action planning and control without human interaction in order to accomplish its long-term mission goals. Autonomous vehicles operate in an open (i.e. non-controlled) environment.

Open environment is defined as an environment in which agents operate and can have different, not consistent missions and strategies. Some regulations can be defined for the environment and agents should follow them however it cannot be guarantied that every agent would always act in accordance with the regulations. In an open environment an agent cannot assume that all other agents will cooperate and preserve safety. As an *agent* we understand a vehicle or an object.

An *object* can be able to communicate with other agents but not able to move. Examples of objects are traffic lights (which communicate to vehicles if they should stop or drive on) or a command centre (which communicates missions to vehicles).

The essential feature of an autonomous system is its ability to plan actions and achieve some long-term mission goals. Usually AV objective is to:

- accomplish its mission (a long-term goal),
- comply with the regulations if such rules are defined,
- preserve safety (avoid hazardous events).

An example of a hazardous event is a collision – when a vehicle collides with another vehicle or an object. Intuitionally one can say that a collision will happen when two vehicles have crossing courses. There may be many different causes for this event. It can be a sensor or actuator failure, wrong route planning, unexpected events in the environment or manoeuvres of other vehicles.

Accident models are useful for analysis of accidents causes and possible countermeasures. The sequential accident model is the simplest one. More complex models are also available however the sequential model is a good starting point sufficient for the purpose of the presented analysis. The model starts with the safe state followed by a sequence of states (see Fig. 1).

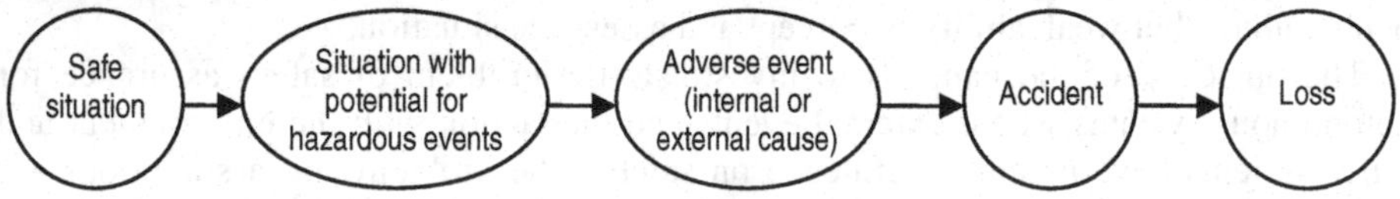

Fig. 1. Sequential accident scenario model

The presented sequential model emphasises that not only adverse events (like components failures) can cause hazards. There are many other factors that have to occur for a hazard to happen. This can be demonstrated on an example of a scenario in which a vehicle starts to overtake another vehicle while being overtaken at the same moment. This hazardous situation is caused by the vehicles interaction and not by a mechanical component failure. Table 1 shows the increasing risk level for the consecutive accident scenario situations.

Table 1. Examples of accidents scenarios

Model state	Industrial robot	Autonomous vehicle	Risk level
Safe situation	Normal robot operation	No other vehicle in close distance	no risk
Situation with potential for adverse events	Preceding robot is off (no part can be passed on to work on)	Another vehicle in front (see Fig. 2.b)	low risk
	A human in operating area	Decision to overtake the vehicle in front	
Adverse event	The robot switched on	Unexpected manoeuvre of the vehicle in front	high risk
	The human activates a robot sensor		
	Robot arm starts the operation	Braking and course change fails	
Accident	Robot arm hits the human	Vehicles collide	unsafe state
Loss	Fatal injury	Vehicles damaged	

A risk level can be attributed to each situation and can be used to denote how far it is from the unsafe state. The longer is the sequence the better are chances that hazard can be avoided. To assure safety the system should continuously assess the situation and act accordingly when some risk factors are detected.

Similar sequential accident model is used by the European Automobile Manufacturers Association (ACEA) [3] for road traffic accidents. The ACEA model distinguishes "danger" state when an accident can be avoided and "crash unavoidable" state. This depicts the problem that to avoid a hazard the countermeasures should be taken before the risk level is too high.

3 Situation Awareness, Risk and Trust

Situation awareness (SAW) is, generally speaking, the knowledge of what is going around. Situation awareness is an area of research in domains of philosophy, logic, psychology, artificial intelligence, computer science (human-computer interface) and robotics. The research goal in psychology is to examine how a human maintains situation awareness, while in robotics the aim is to create machine SAW. Assessment if a situation is safe or dangerous is one of the situation awareness functions.

The general concept of situation awareness is well known however there is no one agreed definition. Endsley introduces three levels of human situation awareness [4]:

1. perception: basic perception of cues based on direct observation.
2. reasoning: the ability to comprehend or to integrate multiple pieces of information and determine the relevance to the goals the human wants to achieve.
3. predicting: ability to forecast future situation events and dynamics based on the perception and comprehension of the present situation.

Situation awareness is necessary for humans to assess the risk, plan actions and avoid dangerous situations. Reason in [5] describes mechanisms how humans perceive situations and the associated risk, how make errors (mistakes and lapses), and how react in case of unexpected events.

Another area of research on situation awareness is focused on remote controlled robots [6]. Its objective is to provide humans (who are regarded as the only entities with the ability of situation awareness) with the right information to ensure situation awareness and safe robot operation.

Situation risk assessment is one of the key human abilities to preserve safety. When someone drives a car at the speed of 50 km/h it is quite normal to pass a person on the pavement. That person is only two meters away from the passing car and no physical barrier exists between them. The driver trusts that the person will not enter the road in front of the car and therefore assesses the risk as low. On the other hand the person on the pavement trusts that the car will not leave the road. But we do not always trust everybody. For example when we see children we usually slow down – the situation is assessed as more risky.

Trust in an entity is related to certainty that the entity will behave in a predicted way and follow the regulations or some rules. Any entity acting in unpredictable way is not trusted. If an entity is trusted and its behaviour is predictable then the vehicle route can be planed with high probability that it will not cause unsafe events.

Rules are used both for assuring safety (the rule says that the person will not enter the road) and prediction of entity actions (the person will stay on the pavement). It is easier to predict future actions when an agent follows the rules.

Another problem is completeness and certainty of available information. The situation knowledge can be incomplete because of perception limitations, unavailable information sources or external factors. The information can come from unreliable sources and turn out to be false. Some attributes cannot be measured and have to be assessed. Such assessments can be uncertain.

Some improvement in completeness and certainty of the situation knowledge can be a result of communication. Examples of the road traffic communication are the use of turn indicator lights (vehicle-vehicle communication) and traffic lights at crossings (agent-vehicle communication). When a person stands on the edge of road he or she communicates the intention to cross the road. Communication helps to ensure more complete and certain situation knowledge and allows for more accurate prediction.

Assessing the risk is a heavy cognitive task requiring perception skills, knowledge and experience. Not always it is possible to correctly assess the risk. Humans make mistakes, especially when in stress conditions and have too little time. What humans do to cope with that problem is to be aware of limitations of their own assessments and take it into account (for example not to drive fast in the fog). Humans recognise situations with a potential for causing adverse events. In these situations they are more attentive and careful. Generally complete and certain knowledge of the situation is practically impossible due to the broad scope of information needed and short time for decision. There is always something that we don't know about the situation. Therefore autonomous machines also need the ability to make assessments based on incomplete knowledge and judge on the credibility of its own assessments.

Summarising the section it can be said that:

- situation awareness is necessary to assess the risk of present and predicted future situations,
- the situation risk assessment depends on trust to other agents that they will act in a predictable way,
- situation assessment can be uncertain due to incompleteness of knowledge and uncertain information sources.

The problem how situation awareness can be used for safety assurance will be discussed for an example of a simple simulated autonomous vehicle presented in the next section.

4 An Example of a Simulated Autonomous Vehicle

Simulation was chosen as the first step of the proposed approach verification. The definition of a simulated autonomous vehicle (SAV) is based on the concept of road traffic on a two-lane road. Vehicles can drive along the road in both directions and each of them has been assigned with its own mission. Some objects are also present in the environment: traffic lights and speed limit signs. Some examples of possible situations are presented in Fig. 2.

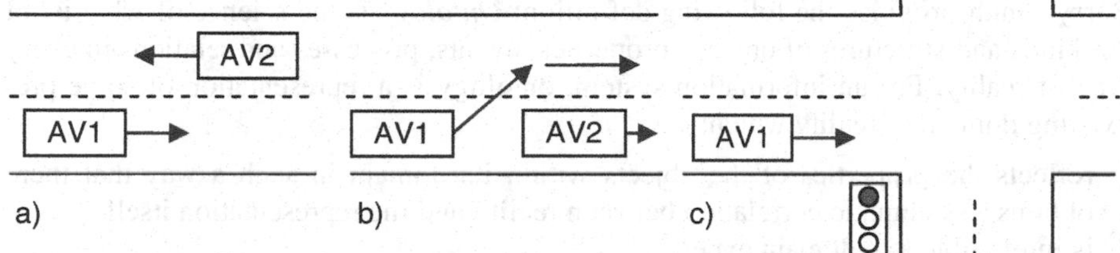

Fig. 2. Examples of simulated autonomous vehicle action scenarios

SAV is equipped with:

- Motors and brakes that enable it to move along the road and change lanes (going off the road is defined as unsafe behaviour and the simulated vehicle is stopped when it leaves the road).
- A set of sensors: speed sensor, clock, position sensor and a set of distance sensors.
- A communication module that allows for communication with other vehicles and objects in a given range.

The objective of SAV is to:

1. accomplish its mission (get to a defined point on the road and then stop),
2. comply with the rules (regulations defined for the environment):
   - drive along the right lane except when overtaking another vehicle,

  - do not overtake on crossings,
  - stop before the crossing when the traffic light is other then green,
  - do not increase the speed when being overtaken,
  - keep the speed in the limit according to the traffic signs,
  - do not go off the road,
3. avoid unsafe event: a collision with other vehicles or objects.

The simulated AV environment is simplified. The main limitations are:

- Properties of agents and the environment are static. Agents do not have to adapt to new conditions, regulations o changed characteristics of other agents.
- The world is limited to the road. The physics of the simulated world is simplified. Discrete time is used in the simulation (a time tick is defined).
- The image recognition problem is excluded from the analysis (SAV does not have to *see* traffic signs or other agents).
- Objects are considered to be reliable. No object failures are simulated.

The problem to be solved is how to assure safety of presented SAV when situations dynamically change depending on behaviour of other vehicles and objects.

5 Situation Awareness Model for SAV

The situation awareness model is proposed in this section. The model uses the concept of ontology.

Ontology is a description of some domain of real world, which is sometimes called a *universe*, which allows for classification and analysis of some properties [7, 8, 9]. Barry Smith provides the following definition: *Ontology* is the science of what is, of the kinds and structures of objects, properties, events, processes and relations in every area of reality. For an information system, ontology is a representation of some pre-existing domain of reality which:

1. reflects the properties of the objects within its domain in such a way that there obtains a systematic correlation between reality and the representation itself,
2. is intelligible to a domain expert,
3. is formalized in a way that allows it to support automatic information processing.

The situation awareness model presented below has been developed for SAV described in the previous section. VDM-like notation [10] is used in the definition of the model. The model has been designed to be as simple as possible to be suitable for SAV. More sophisticated situation awareness models should be built for more complex systems.

Universe. For the analysed system the universe state is a set of information that SAV "knows" about itself and the environment. This can be defined as follows:

UniverseState ::
    InternalState : *AttributeId* → (*Value* × *Certainty*)
    Events : *SensorId* → (*Value* × *Certainty*)
    Environment : <AV knowledge about environment: terrain map (road)>
    Agents : *AgentId* → *AgentInfo*

AgentInfo = *AgentAttributeId* → (*Value* × *Certainty*)

UniverseState describes the AV knowledge about itself and the environment for a given moment of time. *UniverseState* is not a real world. It is a SAV's knowledge of the world. Ontology is well defined if the model complies with three conditions defined at the beginning of this section.

InternalState incorporates attributes such as the time, position, speed, mission goal, command for actuators. Examples of agents attributes are agent type, position and speed. Information about environment is static and limited to the road coordinates (that's one of the SAV limitations).

Certainty. Knowledge about the situation can be uncertain and therefore *Certainty* type was introduced to the model. Certainty here does not mean objective probability but a result of SAV assessment on how certain is particular value of an attribute. This was achieved by introducing *BasicProbability* type. The Basic probability is a concept from Dempster-Shafer theory [11, 12]:

$$
\begin{aligned}
&BasicProbability ::\\
&\quad belief \quad : \mathbf{R}\\
&\quad disbelief \quad : \mathbf{R}\\
&\quad \text{invariant}(\,belief, disbelief\,) \equiv\\
&\qquad\qquad belief \geq 0 \wedge disbelief \geq 0 \wedge belief + disbelief \leq 1\\
&Certainty = BasicProbability
\end{aligned}
$$

BasicProbability is a tuple of two values: *belief* and *disbelief. Belief* is an assessed probability that the value is *true*, while *disbelief* indicates assessed probability of *false*. Basic probability can be used to represent certainty that a situation is safe. Value (1, 0) means that there is 100% assessed probability that the situation is safe. Value (0.5, 0.5) relates to fifty-fifty assessment that the situation is safe or not safe.

When the situation assessment is uncertain, the sum of *belief* and *disbelief* is less then 1. Value (0.2, 0.3) means that there is 20% probability that the situation is safe, 30% that it is not safe however the remaining 50% is uncertain – it's not known if it is safe or not. In other words it can be said that because of incomplete knowledge and uncertain assessment the probability of the safe situation is believed to be somewhere from 20% to 70%. Uncertainty is calculated by function:

$$
\begin{aligned}
&\text{uncertainty}: BasicProbability \rightarrow \mathbf{R}\\
&\text{uncertainty}(\,bp\,) \equiv 1 - bp.belief - bp.disbelief
\end{aligned}
$$

Situation assessment. Basic probability is used to represent assessments if the situation is safe, the rules (regulations) are followed and whether there is a progress in achieving mission goals:

$$
\begin{aligned}
SituationAssessment \quad :: \quad & missionProgress : BasicProbability\\
& rulesAccordance : BasicProbability\\
& safetyLevel : BasicProbability
\end{aligned}
$$

Trust. Trust to other agents and sensors is also represented by basic probability:

TrustAssessment = (*AgentId* ∪ *SensorId*) → *BasicProbability*

Situation awareness. *UniverseState* represents knowledge about a situation at a given moment of time. The Situation awareness is not only the knowledge of the current universe state, but also the past and future states.

SituationAwareness ::	*now*	: *Time*
	observedSituations	: *Time* → *UniverseState*
	predictedSituations	: *Time* → *UniverseState*
	assessment	: *SituationAssessment*
	trust	: *TrustAssessment*

invariant(mk-*SituationAwareness*(*now, observed, predicted, sa, ta*)) ≡
$\forall\, t \in$ dom(*observed*) $\cdot\; t \leq now$

There is a question if the perception, prediction and assessment methods should be included as part of the situation awareness model. This has not been done for the presented example. Intuitively the situation awareness model should comprise this kind of knowledge. This knowledge may also evolve in order to adapt to changing environmental conditions, new agent types or new possible accident scenarios. The problem of adapting and learning from experience is out of the scope of this paper.

6 SAV Control System

SAV control system has been designed using the layered architecture [13, 14]. The system is decomposed into policy layer, mission layer, tactical layer and control layer. Situation assessment and action planning is located in the tactical layer and this layer is described in this section. The SAV tactical layer is decomposed into two main processes: Situation analysis (SA) and Task planning (TP) presented in Fig. 3.

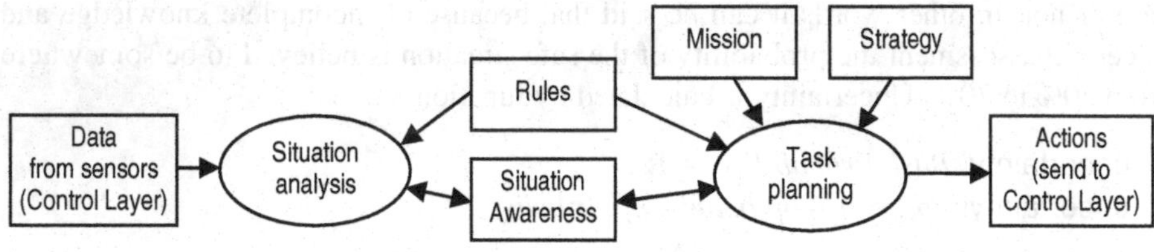

Fig. 3. SAV control system Situation analysis and Task planning processes

The goal of Situation analysis (SA) process is to collect information from available sources to provide situation awareness knowledge. The process is decomposed into following subprocesses:

SA.1. Read sensor values and update *observedSituations*(*now*).*Events* (use sensors *trust* as initial value for data *certainty*)

SA.2. Calculate *observedSituations(now).Agents* and *InternalState* attributes and check for data consistency (rise or lower trust in appropriate data sources)
SA.3. Update *trust* in other agents depending on their observed behaviour

Task planning process (TP) objective is to predict possible situations and then choose the optimal sequence of actions. The process is decomposed into the following steps:

TP.1. Generate a set of possible scenarios of actions.
TP.2. Assess each scenario for:
 TP.2A. progress towards mission goals,
 TP.2B. compliance with formal rules (regulations),
 TP.2C. situation risk level.
TP.3. Choose the optimal scenario (according to SAV strategy). Update *predicted-Situations* and *assessment*
TP.4. Chosen scenario tasks are communicated to the Control layer.

TP.1 process generates a set of possible action scenarios determined by possible AV actions and predicted behaviour of other agents. Generally the range of possible actions of other agents is very broad. This depends mostly on an agent decision to obey the rules or not. For example for a situation presented in Fig. 2.a an agent AV1 must predict possible set of AV2 actions. If AV2 does not intend to follow the rules then it will be possible that AV2 will suddenly change lane in front of AV1. This could lead to a collision. This would not happen if AV2 followed the regulations. What is needed here is trust. Both agents need to trust each other that they will conform to the regulations (precisely: obey the rule to drive along the right lane).

When the trust in other vehicle is equal to (0.9, 0) it is interpreted as 10% uncertainty that the vehicle will follow regulations. In such case more scenarios of its behaviour would be analysed.

The effectiveness of the situation risk assessment generally depends on two factors. The first is the span, certainty and completeness of the prediction (TP.1). The second factor is the ability of TP.2C function to assess the risk depended on the current situation knowledge. The value of joining risk assessment with prediction algorithm comes from the possibility of examining possible actions for hazard avoidance when unexpected events occur. Even for high risk situations the prediction function will provide for possible scenarios to reach safe state (propose actions that lead to situations with lower risk level).

Two safety assessment functions TP.2B and TP2C have been defined. The first one uses static rules (regulations). The second assessment function examines current and expected future situations to judge the possibility of a hazard. These two assessment functions are both necessary for safe operation of the vehicle. The comparison of these two functions is presented in Table 2.

Three different assessment functions are used in the TP.2 process and a question arises what strategy should be used to choose the so-called optimal scenario (TP.3 process). Many different strategies are possible. Three of them are:

1. *Care for yourself* strategy – if there are some risk factors (*safetyLevel.disbelief* > 0) then choose the safest scenario or otherwise select the scenario with the best combination of assessment values. In case of any risk factor the vehicle will ignore all rules and will perform any action to achieve no-risk state.

2. *Stick to the rules* strategy – always choose the scenario with the highest TP.2B assessment, then the second priority is the safety level and mission progress.
3. *Mission first* strategy – always choose scenario with the best mission progress assessment (this strategy can be used to implement hostile vehicles).

Table 2. Rule-based and risk-based assessment function comparison

Rules Compliance (TP.2B)	Situation Risk Assessment (TP.2C)
Based on static rules	Based on dynamic risk assessment
Easier for design and verification	More difficult for design and verification
Supports external judgment if a vehicle obeys the rules	Supports decision making when planning individual and group actions
Can be used to assure safety in normal situations. May not assure safety if rules are violated in the environment	Can be used to assure hazard avoidance in any situations
Will not assure safety if rules are incomplete for a context of a given environment	Will not assure safety if the knowledge is incomplete or uncertain in context of a given environment
When function fails: breaking the rule will sometimes (but not always) cause a hazard depending on the situation	When function fails: choosing unsafe scenario of actions will lead to hazard if no other countermeasures are taken
Is required in order to assure compliance with the regulations	Is required in order to assure hazard avoidance in open environment

A question comes to mind what strategy is the right one. Even when more sophisticated strategies are defined, the question remains when an autonomous agent can violate regulations in order to avoid hazard. Never? Whenever it perceives any risk factor? Only when the risk is high? How high? All rules can be violated or only some of them? And what if the agent risk assessment is wrong? These are hard questions to answer.

7 The Problem of Autonomous System Hazard Analysis

The autonomous vehicle is considered to be a safety-critical system therefore demonstrating that the solution assures safety is essential. This can be done by developing a safety case for the system. The system architecture is more complex then for most embedded systems and to develop such a safety case can be a nontrivial task.

The first problem encountered when constructing the safety case was the decision how the hazards should be defined. The first attempt was to define accepted probability of hazard occurrence. This led to probabilistic claims and assumptions on external events (like behaviour of other vehicles). Quantitative arguments were left off for the moment and the analysis focus was on what situations and combinations of events can lead to hazard (qualitative arguments).

The argument for the claim that the hazard will be avoided (e.g. SAV will not collide) intuitively leads to safety requirements like: the Task Planning process will not give unsafe action plan as an output. A fault tree-like analysis can be used to track down the causes for such event and then define requirements for processes and their input data. Such analysis on the components level has been carried out. The result of this analysis was a set of safety requirements. Some of them relate to situation awareness model and assessment functions.

Justification for claims like completeness of situation awareness model, correctness of prediction process TP.1 or correctness of risk assessment function TP.2C requires providing evidence based on the environment and AV mechanical engineering models and accident models. This is an area of future research.

8 Extending SAV with a Collaboration Process

The vehicle presented in Section 4 is fully autonomous. It does not cooperate with other agents and does not exchange any information with them. Cooperation can offer possibility for:

- verification of situation awareness knowledge by comparison to information from other agents,
- more reliable prediction of other agents behaviour,
- using recommendation mechanism for more accurate assessments of trust in other agents.

These properties strengthen justification for some safety requirements identified in the safety case.

Extending AV with a communication process is a big change of autonomous vehicle characteristics. A set of non-communicating autonomous vehicles is now transformed into a set of vehicles which cooperate to assure safety although each of them has its own mission.

The proposed solution is to extend Situation analysis process (described in section 6) with additional process decomposed into four steps:

1. Communicate with other agents to exchange a subset of situation awareness information. The scope of the information exchange depends on the AV strategy. For the simulated AV the data exchange scope is the vehicle identification data, position, speed, planned actions and also trust levels to other vehicles.
2. Analyse consistency of the recommendations and own trust assessments and accordingly update trust in a recommended agent, the recommender and own trust assessment function data sources.
3. Consistency check – for each situation awareness attribute find related data received from other agents, if found then check consistency and adjust the data, its certainty and the data sources trust levels according to the detected data consistency or discrepancy.
4. Situation awareness extention – add information on other agents planned actions.

The proposed cooperation process makes stronger arguments for justification of claims like completeness of situation awareness model, correctness of prediction process TP.1 or correctness of risk assessment function TP.2C.

9 Experiments Results

A simulation tool has been designed and developed using Java development environment. Some number of simulation experiments has been carried out to verify the approach. The main limitation of the simulation tool is that AV processes are run as sequential tasks for each simulated time tick. No concurrency has been implemented and no time requirements have been analysed.

Analysis of simulation results is difficult except for simple situations. For a given scenario the risk and trust evolve in time but have no directly measurable values in the real world. The problem is that humans also have different perception of how risky are some situations. Therefore justification for a particular risk value for a given situation is usually questionable. Risk assessment function results depend on many parameters. Changing slightly some parameters can sometimes cause big change in the risk assessment value. Designing the risk assessment algorithms is a non-trivial task even for the simple simulated AV. The conclusion of the experiments is that the critical issue is to start with explicit definition of safe and unsafe situations, which are denoted as the extreme *BasicProbability* values (1,0) and (0,1).

The safe level assessment value (1,0) was defined as lack of any risk factors and full certainty of the situation knowledge. The risk factors are derived from the accident model analysis. The safety level value (0,1) has been defined as accident (vehicles collide). It is not required to justify the exact risk assessment values however risk assessment consistency should be justified (the same risk value should be assigned to the situations of the same risk level).

The SAV accident scenario analysis was made manually and tool support for this task is needed. The plan is to use accident scenario risk profiles. A risk profile is a chart showing change of safety level in time together with labels for relevant events. The objective of using risk profiles is to ensure that the assessment is consistent with the concept of the increasing risk level for accident scenarios (compare to Table 1) and to stretch the period of time when the risk is perceived.

Another issue analysed in the experiments was what initial trust level should be assigned to other vehicles. Three approaches were tested: full trust, uncertain or no trust. Also the ways how humans assess trust have been analysed. This led to the first impression mechanism. Humans usually judge any person within the first three seconds when they meet. This strategy was chosen as the best one. Initial trust level for any new vehicle should be uncertain, denoted as value (0,0). For some short period of time the trust assessment function should be more sensitive to make wide range of trust adjustment possible. When the trust level is stabilized, the function should become less sensitive. That leads to the problem which factors should be considered as relevant for initial trust or distrust. Some strategies for building trust (e.g. regulations conformance, identifying itself to other vehicles, cooperation) have been analysed. The mechanism of the first impression needs further research.

Some number of scenarios have been simulated and analysed.

Scenario 1 (see Fig 2.a in section 4) relates to a situation when two vehicles pass each other on separate lanes. The situation risk level depends on the distance, speed and direction of the vehicles and available space (limited to the road by the rule). When AV does not fully trust other vehicle then it tries to keep safe distance. That may lead to speed decrease and turning to the road side. The safe passing scenario (Fig. 2.a) is possible when vehicles follow the rules and trust each other.

Scenario 2 (see Fig. 2.b) relates to a situation when one vehicle is followed by another one and finally can be overtaken. The first issue is the safe distance between the two vehicles. When vehicles cooperate and trust each other the distance can be smaller. When there is no trust relation then the safe distance is longer. The second issue is the decision when to overtake safely. Some problems were caused by limitations of the prediction function as the predicted scenario was shorter then the overtake manuevre. Longer scenario would ease the risk assessment. Some work was needed to elaborate a risk assessment function that would preserve safety when for example another vehicle is approaching on the left lane or there is a crossing not far away. Effect of safe overtaking was achieved after some experimental trials however the systematic process for accident model analysis is needed.

Scenario 3 (see Fig. 2.c) was introduced to investigate how cooperating vehicles behave in dynamically changing environment. The first problem encountered was the influence of action plan changes on trust. In the tested scenario two vehicles were driving one following another. The first vehicle stopped when the traffic lights changed from green to yellow. When the second vehicle noticed the change in planned actions it lowered the trust level in AV1. This approach is too simplified. The justification for other vehicle plan change should be assessed before the trust level is altered. Analysis how this can be achieved is a possible future work.

Another problem encountered in the experiments was that the risk level definition does not take in account the hazard consequences. The conclusion was to extend the situation risk definition from *BasicProbability* to a set of tuples containing accident consequences (the loss) and probability assessment. Quite interesting is that such model could be used for risk assessment compliant with Three Laws of Robotics defined by Asimov [15]. An example of such situation risk assessment can be a set { (*human-harm*, (0, 0.9)), (*robot-damage*, (1,0)) }. Other possibilities for the situation awareness model extensions are also analysed.

10 Summary

The main conclusion of the paper is that the situation awareness is the key factor in autonomous vehicles safety assurance. Autonomous vehicles need to be able to perceive current situation, assess it and predict future situations. Situation awareness model should be built on a sound ontology which describes the vehicle and its environment. The model should provide means to cope with the problems of trust in other agents and uncertain and incomplete knowledge. The proposed solution is based on simple patterns of human situation awareness.

Three situation assessment functions were distinguished: situation risk level assessment, regulations compliance assessment and mission progress assessment. Hazard avoidance is dependent on the perception and assessment of the situation risk.

Communication and cooperation has been proposed to strengthen safety in a situation of dynamic agent interactions.

The proposed approach was demonstrated on a small simulated example of an autonomous vehicle. For most scenarios the simulated vehicle could perceive unsafe situations and avoid them. Limitations of the method and experiences from the experiments have been discussed in Section 8.

Systematic process for accident model analysis and building safety argument is an area of planned research. Plans for future work include also application of presented approach to a laboratory autonomous vehicle and extending the situation awareness model. A challenge that is foreseen is to enable AV to adapt to changing environment characteristics. Autonomy is a novel concept for safety-critical systems and will require a lot of research work to provide sound arguments for safety justification.

References

1. Dennet, D. C.: Did HAL Commit Murder?, Cogprints Cognitive Science E-print Archive, http://cogprints.org/430/00/didhal.htm (1998)
2. Fatal Accident Summary Report: Die Cast Operator Pinned by Robot, FACE Report 8420, National Institute for Occupational Safety and Health, http://www.cdc.gov/niosh/face/In-house/full8420.html (2005)
3. Huang Y., Ljung M., Sandin J., Hollnagel E.: Accident models for modern road traffic: changing times creates new demands, IEEE International Conference on Systems, Man and Cybernetics (2004)
4. Endsley, M. R.: Direct Measurement of Situation Awareness: Validity and Use of SAGAT in (Eds.) Mica R. Endsley and Daniel J. Garland, Situation Awarenss Analysis and Measurement (2000)
5. Reason J.: Human Error, Cambridge University Press, (2000)
6. French H. T., Hutchinson A.: Measurement of Situation Awareness in a C4ISR Experiment, In: The 7th International Command and Control Research and Technology Symposium, Quebec City (2002)
7. Goczyła K., Zawadzki M.: Processing and inferring from knowledge of different trust level, In: Kozielski S., Małysiak S., Kasprowski P., Mrozek P. (eds.): Data Bases – Models, Technologies, Tools, WKŁ (2005) 207-213 (in Polish)
8. Matheus C. J., Kokar M. M., Baclawski K.: A Core Ontology for Situation Awareness, International Conference of Information Fusion, IEEE, Cairns, Australia (2003) 545-552
9. Smith B.: Ontology, in Floridi (ed.) Blackwell Guide to the Philosophy of Computing and Information, Oxford: Blackwell (2003) 155–166
10. Jones, C.: Systematic Software Development using VDM, Prentice Hall International (1990)
11. Shafer, G.: Mathematical theory of evidence, Princetown University Press (1976)
12. Górski J., Zagórski M.: Using Dempster-Shafer approach to support reasoning about trust in IT infrastructures, In: Warsaw International Seminar on Intelligent Systems (WISIS 2004), Warsaw (2004) 39-57
13. Kelly, A. J.: Predictive Control Approach to the High-Speed Cross-Country Autonomous Navigation Problem, Ph.D. thesis, Carnegie Mellon University, Pittsburg (1995)
14. Broten G., Monckton S.: Unmanned Ground Vehicle Electronic Hardware Architecture – A Flexible and Scalable Architecture for Developing Unmanned Ground Vehicles, Defence R&D Canada – Suffield TM 2004-122 (2004)
15. Asimov I., I, Robot (1950)

Demonstration of Safety in Healthcare Organisations

Mark A. Sujan[1], Michael D. Harrison[2],
Alison Steven[3], Pauline H. Pearson[3], and Susan J. Vernon[4]

[1] Department of Computer Science
University of York, York, YO10 5DD, UK
sujan@cs.york.ac.uk
[2] Informatics Research Institute,
University of Newcastle, Newcastle NE1 7RU, UK
michael.harrison@ncl.ac.uk
[3] School of Medical Education DevelopmentUniversity of Newcastle,
Newcastle NE1 7RU, UK
{alison.steven, p.h.pearson}@ncl.ac.uk
[4] School of Clinical Medical Sciences, University of Newcastle,
Newcastle NE1 7RU, UK
s.j.vernon@ncl.ac.uk

Abstract. The paper describes the current regulatory situation in England with respect to medical devices and healthcare providers. Trusts already produce evidence to the Healthcare Commission that they operate in accordance with standards set out by the Department of Health and the NHS. The paper illustrates how the adoption of an explicit goal-based argument could facilitate the identification and assessment of secondary implications of proposed changes. The NHS is undergoing major changes in accordance with its 10-year modernisation plan. These changes cannot be confined to the Trust level, but will have NHS-wide implications. The paper explores the possibility of an organisational safety case, which could be a useful tool in the management of such fundamental changes.

1 Introduction

Healthcare organisations are undergoing major changes everywhere, both technical and organisational. The NHS in England is currently implementing a 10-year modernisation plan [1] that will have implications for all areas of healthcare provision. Managing change in a safe and effective way poses major challenges. Similar restructurings of this scale have had serious implications; compare for example the privatisation and reorganisation of the UK railways. To deal with these implications in aviation, Eurocontrol explored the possibility of producing a whole-airspace safety case [2]. Railways, air traffic control and even more so healthcare are instances of complex socio-technical systems. Different authors characterise complex systems [3], [4] in different ways, but in general there is agreement that complex systems possess a large number of individual components or agents, whose rich interactions are difficult and sometimes impossible to predict. These interactions and the interactions with the environment often are non-linear and they are sensitive to the system's history and initial conditions. Complex systems exhibit emergent properties, i.e. properties that cannot be anticipated from a functional decomposition, and that are the result of

J. Górski (Ed.): SAFECOMP 2006, LNCS 4166, pp. 219 – 232, 2006.

unexpected non-linear interactions that occur between the components and the environment (e.g. [5], [6], [7], [8], see also [9] for a discussion about emergent properties). In [10] it is argued that changes in such complex systems produce "a set of organizational reverberations that are difficult to anticipate or predict and may go far beyond the expectations of designers".

This paper explores such safety challenges within the health sector and how these might be addressed by supporting risk and change management through the construction and use of system-wide safety cases. The present exploration may be set within our broader work agenda. In particular there are a number of concerns:

- *Institutional and organisational issues (the scope of this paper):*
  As a necessary first step, this paper discusses the institutional and regulatory background in order to identify, for example, relevant requirements, standards, stakeholders, organisational structure, and the type of evidence currently available. This forms the basis for all subsequent work, and is used in the discussion about formal characteristics of a system-wide argument including appropriate level, ownership and structure.
- *Technical issues (future work):*
  The discussion of the paper raises questions about how a safety case could be realised in practice. The last 10 years have seen substantial progress in safety case development. There has been a shift from prescriptive to goal-based regulation [11], and a graphical notation (GSN) has been developed [12], which facilitates the construction and communication of safety cases of large-scale systems. A study needs to investigate how this and subsequent work on maintenance [13] and on modularisation of safety cases [14] may render the construction of safety cases for large, complex systems, such as healthcare organisations, technically feasible.
- *Application of the safety case (addressed in this paper and future work):*
  The activity of producing a safety case requires explicit consideration of safety-related issues, and provides assurance to both the organisation and to regulators that the system is adequately safe. The safety case has also the potential to be a useful tool in assessing the implications of change, both technical and organisational. A methodology for systematically utilising a system-wide safety case to support the management of change will be explored.
- *Safety cases for systems exhibiting strong emergence (future work):*
  This is the most challenging aspect and more about this issue will be said in the discussion. Strong emergence [15], [9] refers to properties or patterns that cannot be derived from models of interaction of components at lower hierarchical levels. This has far-reaching consequences for the way risk analysis is conducted (see e.g. [16]) and for the way safety cases are to be understood in the future and the type of evidence that needs to be provided.

The next section describes the regulatory context in England, and briefly outlines the large-scale organisational changes that are still ongoing in this domain. In this context two simplified yet realistic examples are considered at different levels of representation. Firstly a technical change within a hospital environment is used to discuss how a goal-based argument could facilitate the identification and assessment of implications of that change. This addresses interactions that may be difficult to spot, but that may be handled given appropriate representational tools (such as a safety case). Secondly, an organisational change is considered in the context of the modernisation plan of the NHS in order to discuss the possibility that a safety case could be used to support the management of this change. This also touches upon the issue of interactions that may be impossible to predict, and thus raises questions about the suitability of current safety cases to deal with such complex systems. The concluding section follows this up by discussing ongoing work and by reflecting on possible limitations.

2 The Regulatory Context in England

In England, as in other comparable European healthcare systems, there is a differentiation between manufacturers of medical devices on the one hand and healthcare providers as users or consumers of such devices on the other hand. Both are regulated by and are accountable to the Department of Health, albeit through different agencies and institutions. In general, manufacturers have to provide evidence that their devices are tolerably safe for a particular use in a specific environment. Healthcare providers, on the other hand, are audited to ensure that the care they provide meets national standards. A part of this is the requirement to utilise only previously certified medical devices.

2.1 The Certification of Medical Devices Within the UK Environment

The UK Medical Devices Regulations 2002 (MDR 2002) implement a number of European directives relevant to the certification of medical devices (MDD 93/43/EEC; IV-Diagnostic MDD 98/79/EC; Active Implantable MDD 90/385/EEC). The definition of what constitutes a medical device is broad and comprises devices as diverse as radiation therapy machines, syringes and wheelchairs. The Medicines and Healthcare Products Regulatory Agency (MHRA) acts as the *Competent Authority* overseeing the certification of medical devices. *Notified Bodies* of experts provide evaluation of high and medium risk medical devices undergoing certification to the Competent Authority.

The medical devices directive consists of three parts:

1. Essential Requirements that have to be met by any medical device to be marketed in the EU. Six requirements are regarded as essential including: defining acceptable levels of risk; applying safety principles during design and construction; establishing and meeting performance criteria, ensuring that undesirable side effects constitute an acceptable level of risk.
2. Classification Rules that specify four classes for medical devices. Class I devices pose little risk and are non-invasive. Classes IIa and IIb devices pose medium risk (medium to low risk, and medium to high risk, respectively), while Class III devices pose high risk.

3. Conformity Routes specifying different ways of manufacturer compliance with the Essential Requirements. In the case of Class I devices the manufacturer has to declare through a self-documentation process (no Notified Body is involved) that the Essential Requirements are met, and compile adequate technical documentation. For devices of the other classes a number of methods for demonstrating conformity are available. This is frequently done through a Full Quality Assurance System assessment (ISO13485:2003). In the case of Classes IIa and IIb it is also possible to provide evidence, including the results of risk analysis, test and inspection reports, design documentation, instructions for use and so on. The manufacturer is expected to have a systematic risk management process in place (e.g. ISO14971).

All of these standards are addressed to the manufacturer of medical devices. When healthcare providers assemble different devices to create a system, the safety of the resulting system generally will not have been assured. As indicated in [17], the role of a systems integrator, with the responsibility of installing medical devices according to the manufacturers' instructions for use, of demonstrating the safety of the resulting system, and of providing documentation, training and support to the actual end users would be an important contribution to ensuring patient safety.

Apart from issuing instructions for use, the manufacturer has little influence on the way the devices are actually used in practice. More importantly, the manufacturer does not have detailed information about the specific environment and the processes within which the device will be operated within a particular healthcare provider's setting. In complex systems this is a serious cause for concern, as in this way the possible interactions between system components and interactions with the environment as well as the system's particular history will not have been accounted for. It is reasonable, therefore, to expect healthcare providers to demonstrate that the services they are providing are acceptably safe. Such a demonstration should make use of data supplied by the manufacturers.

2.2 Auditing of Healthcare Providers

Healthcare in England involves a diversity of actors. The Department of Health is responsible for setting the overall strategic direction of the NHS, for setting national standards for improving the quality of health services, and for securing adequate funding for the NHS. At the time of writing there were 28 Strategic Health Authorities (SHA) responsible for setting and managing the local strategic direction of the NHS. However, this situation is still undergoing change. The SHA develops plans to improve local services, and monitors the performance of healthcare providers within their region. The monitoring function is increasingly being taken over by the Healthcare Commission (HC), which assesses all healthcare providers against national standards. Primary Care Trusts (PCT) are local healthcare organisations responsible for assessing the healthcare needs of the local communities, and for commissioning services from GPs, hospitals and so on. NHS Hospital Trusts manage hospitals ensuring healthcare provision is of sufficient quality, and that finances are managed effectively. PCTs purchase these services on behalf of their patients. On top of all this there are a large number of additional actors such as pharmacies, dentists, walk-in centres, NHS direct telephone services and so on. For the purpose of this paper it is sufficient to give a simplified version of the organisational structure including regulatory bodies and agencies, see fig. 1. These organisational arrangements are still fairly recent and are undergoing continuous change.

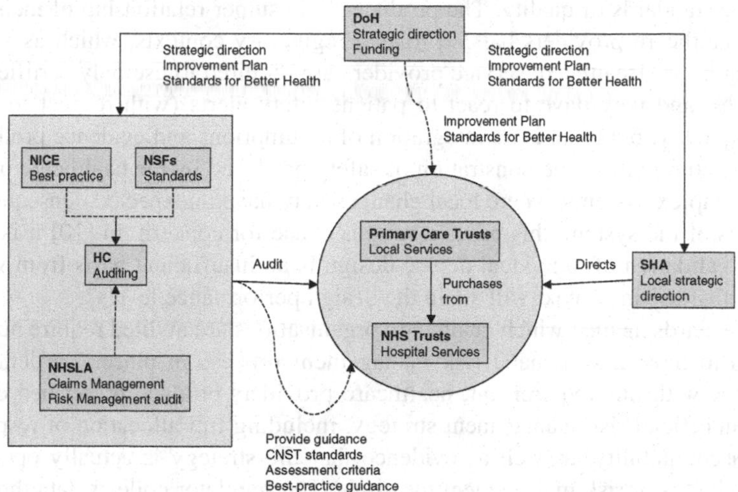

Fig. 1. Simplified structure of regulatory context of healthcare provision in England

In 2004 the Department of Health published the 'Standards For Better Health' [18] to set out quality expectations for all organisations providing NHS care in England. The standards focus on a broad spectrum of seven domains designed to cover the full spectrum of healthcare: safety; clinical and cost effectiveness; governance; patient focus; accessible and responsive care; care environment and amenities; public health. Each domain incorporates two types of standards: *core standards* and *developmental standards*. The 24 core standards are based on a number of standards or requirements that already exist. Developmental standards, on the other hand, outline requirements towards which continuous progress is expected.

Safety and risk management aspects are covered in particular in domains 1 (Safety) and 3 (Governance). The corresponding core standards for safety focus on learning from incidents, fast response to incidents, adherence to NICE (National Institute for Clinical Excellence) guidance, decontamination of medical devices, minimisation of risks associated with the acquisition and use of medical devices etc. The developmental standard requires healthcare providers to continuously review and improve all aspects of their activities that directly affect patient safety, and to apply best practice in assessing and managing risks to patients, staff and others.

The Healthcare Commission (HC) undertakes annual reviews of the provision of healthcare by each NHS organisation in England including PCTs, ambulance trusts, mental health trusts, and acute trusts. These reviews aim to verify compliance with the core standards, as well as the achievement against the developmental standards.

2.3 The Need for Integration

In conclusion therefore, within the regulatory context both manufacturers of medical devices and healthcare service providers are regulated and are required to provide evidence that their devices and the services they provide are tolerably safe and meet acceptable standards of quality. The producer - consumer relationship of manufacturers and healthcare providers has led to two regulatory contexts, which as yet show little integration. Healthcare service providers are required to use only certified medical devices, and they have to react to patient safety alerts (with respect to medical devices) quickly, but there is no integration of assumptions and evidence produced by the manufacturers into a demonstration of safety produced by the healthcare organisation. In complex systems, where local changes may have unexpected consequences in other parts of the system, this poses a serious cause for concern. In [10] it is pointed out that "validation of individual device design is an insufficient basis from which to conclude that use in context will attain the design performance levels".

The standards against which healthcare organisations are audited require healthcare providers to have a systematic risk management process in place. To demonstrate compliance with this requirement, healthcare providers produce prescribed evidence such as an official risk management strategy, including full allocation of responsibility and accountability, as well as evidence that the strategy is actually operational, such as minutes of risk management meetings. The regulator collects data throughout the year from a number of different sources. However, no formal argument (as required in aviation, for example) on the part of the healthcare organisation is required. This implies that assumptions and dependencies may not be documented properly, that interactions and unintended consequences of changes may go unnoticed, and that there are no formal notions of issues such as confidence in the evidence or diverse evidence to mitigate possible uncertainty.

Having identified and described the current regulatory context, we will briefly explore in the remaining sections the role that safety cases could play in managing technical and organisational changes.

3 Assessment of Technical Changes

This section describes a possible technical change in a hospital context. The demonstration of adequate levels of safety for complex systems cannot be achieved at the level of the individual device. The actual changes taking place within the setting depend on the particular history of that setting, and are a result of the numerous interactions of a variety of actors and other sub-systems.

It is argued that a goal-based safety argument at the hospital level could facilitate the assessment of potentially adverse implications of the change and would enable an analysis of dependencies that might otherwise go unnoticed. The safety case becomes a tool for documenting assumptions and dependencies, and for the systematic identification of predictable, yet otherwise difficult to spot, interactions, both locally, where the change is introduced, as well as in other areas of the hospital.

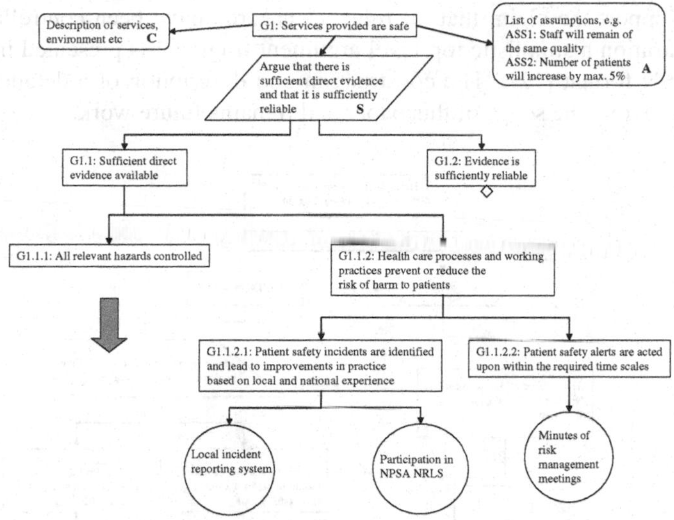

Fig. 2. Simple top-level argument fragment

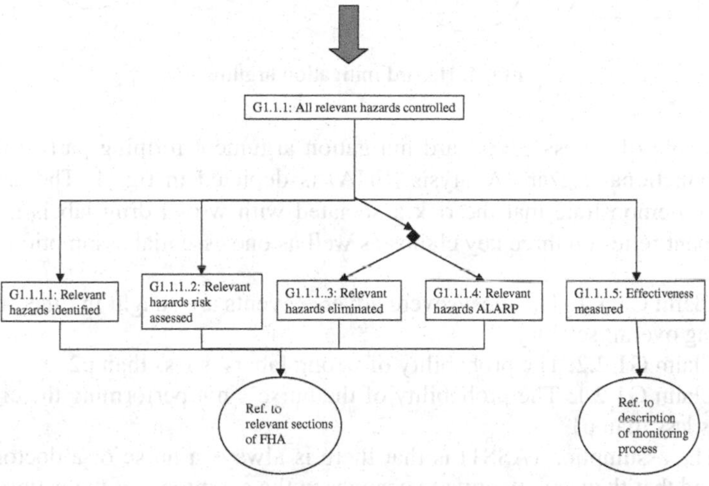

Fig. 3. Simple top-level argument fragment (ctd.)

Medication administration on a typical ward within a hospital relies on the nurse's matching of patients to the identity and quantity of drugs to be administered [19]. Usually such practices are not risk-assessed. However, clinical risk management will aim to ensure that all incidents concerning patient mismatching are reported, and best-practice guidance issued by agencies such as the NPSA is implemented.

Structurally a safety case would include as evidence a risk assessment of the above activities that would support the claims that all hazards have been identified, risk-assessed, and eliminated or reduced to be as low as reasonably practicable. This in turn could support the claim that all relevant hazards have been controlled. For the sake of illustration a simplistic top-level argument fragment is presented in fig. 2 and fig. 3 (in GSN format [12]). The construction and description of a detailed top-level argument is beyond the scope of this paper and remains future work.

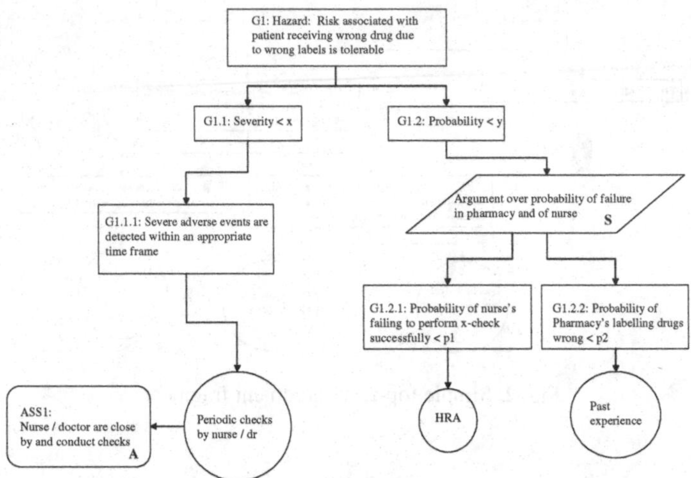

Fig. 4. Hazard mitigation argument

An example of a possible hazard mitigation argument forming part of the (hypothetical) Functional Hazard Analysis (FHA) is depicted in fig. 4. The argument is intended to demonstrate that the risk associated with wrong drug labels is tolerable. The argument relies on three key claims as well as one essential assumption:

- Claim G1.1.1: The most severe adverse events are caught in time, thus reducing overall severity
- Claim G1.2.2: The probability of wrong labels is less than p2
- Claim G1.2.1: The probability of the nurse's not performing the cross-check is less than p1
- The assumption (ASS1) is that there is always a nurse or a doctor close by and that they are attentive to changes in the symptoms of the patient.

Consider now a situation where the claims pertaining to the nurse (G1.2.1) and to the pharmacy (G1.2.2) are considered to be untenable, and a technological solution, namely bar-coding, is proposed as a means of conforming to the required targets. The bar-coding hardware and software will be identified as a medical device, and the manufacturer will have conducted and documented a risk assessment of the device. The hospital as a consumer would purchase the device possibly with initial support for installation and operation. In purchasing the equipment the hospital would be required to conduct its own risk assessment.

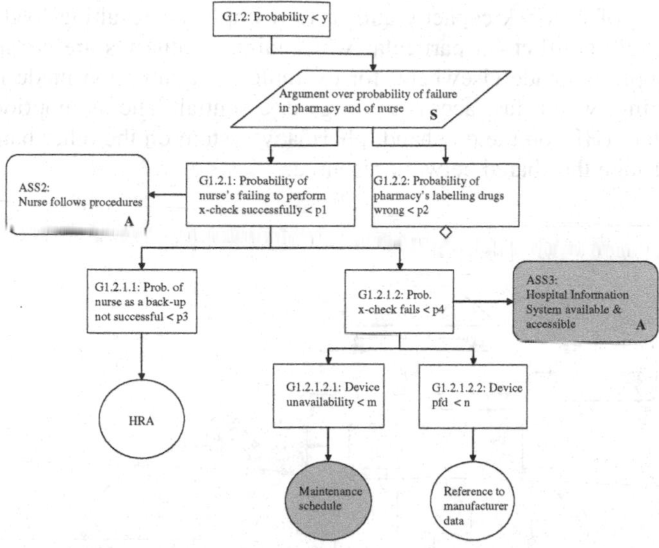

Fig. 5. Modified hazard mitigation argument (probability branch)

The paper focuses on the (possible) modifications to the (hypothetical) hazard mitigation argument pertaining to the support of claim G1.2.1 (probability of nurse's failing to perform cross-check successfully) as illustrated in fig. 5. An assumption (ASS2) would now be required that the nurse follows the new procedures (i.e., uses the bar-coding device to identify patients, and then administers drugs to the previously identified patient). The support comes from a pair of claims relating to the probability of failure of the bar-code x-check (G1.2.1.2), and to the fact that the nurse will act as a back-up in case there is a problem with the bar-code x-check (G1.2.1.1).

There is an assumption that the Hospital Information System (required for a successful x-check) is available and accessible through the network (ASS 3). The bar-code x-check claim (G1.2.1.2) is supported essentially by reference to the probability of failure on demand as supplied by the manufacturer's documentation (G1.2.1.2.2). In addition, the implicit assumption that the bar-coding hardware is available to the nurse and operational is made explicit (G1.2.1.2.1).

To ensure that the availability claim is supported by valid evidence, sufficient technical staff time has to be allocated, training will have to be provided, facilities may have to be changed and so on. Establishing that this evidence is required may have the effect of altering the activities of the technicians (they may have to do work on wards when they previously did not), it requires their time, and it may conflict with similar statements made elsewhere for other hardware. In fig. 6 this is illustrated by the link to an argument fragment claiming the availability of pharmacy label printers (i.e. a completely different context). Potential conflicts are of particular concern in the sense that they represent a class of assumptions about dependencies that often remain undetected.

Fig. 6 illustrates also a second instance of possible conflict due to shared resources. The assumption that the Hospital Information System (HIS) is accessible presupposes the availability of network capacity and in turn implies a resulting load on the network. This could conflict (in particular when failure scenarios are considered) with similar assumptions made elsewhere, for example an assumption made in the intensive care setting, where fast access to drugs is essential. The assumption is about a different system (HIS on the one hand, pharmacy system on the other hand), but they are linked through the shared network resource.

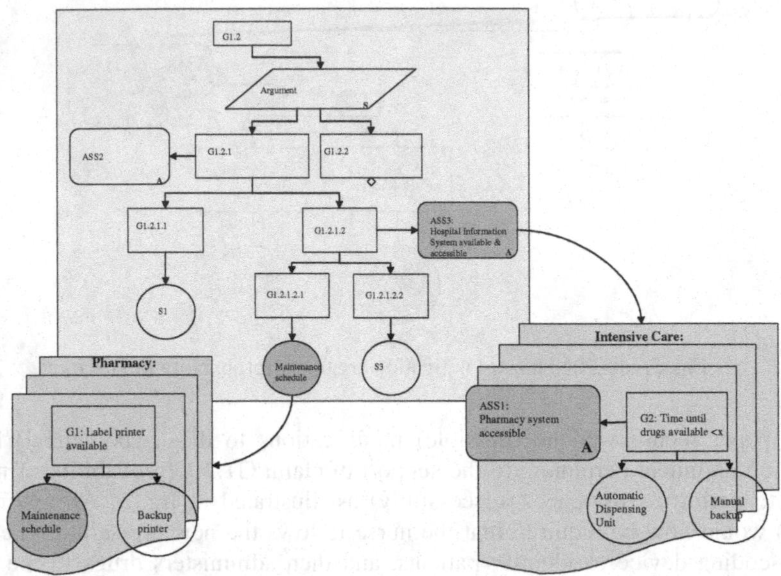

Fig. 6. Example of possible interactions

Two problematic issues have been outlined through this scenario: The first problem arises from the fact that medical devices and healthcare providers are certified and audited separately. Assumptions and information "hidden" within the documentation of the medical device may not be acknowledged or used properly within the auditing process of the healthcare provider. Likewise, device manufacturers possess only limited information about the specifics of the settings within which their devices will be employed, and of the systems which the devices will become part of.

The complexity of the setting with the resulting tight integration of the various activities within the healthcare organisation implies that changes cannot be assessed properly within their local context in relation to the activities that are immediately affected. Secondary effects may propagate throughout the organisation. These effects may have unintended or adverse consequences if not properly taken into account.

A (more) formal demonstration of safety in the form of an explicit argument could be a valuable tool. Such a demonstration would need to integrate information and assumptions of arguments produced by manufacturers into the larger perspective of an organisation-wide safety argument. The process of producing a formal argument could in itself prove to be valuable, as it would prompt risk managers and other stakeholders to reason about such issues. In addition, once such an organisation-wide argument exists that makes all assumptions explicit, it will facilitate the assessment of both direct and secondary effects of changes, as well as previously hidden or undocumented dependencies.

The process for identifying dependencies and interactions followed in this paper consisted of the identification of newly added solutions, assumptions, and changes to the context elements, and the subsequent search for occurrences elsewhere. In the example above, the common elements were shared resources (maintenance personnel, network). This is similar to the process outlined in [14] for safety case maintenance. A more formal approach is conceivable as well. [20] describes an approach that augments each claim with a UML context representation. In cases, where all claims are specified using a formal language, shared occurrences could be detected automatically.

The dependencies and interactions that can be identified with such an approach are "predictable", i.e. a person with a thorough understanding of the overall system is expected to spot them. In this respect, the approach can be regarded as a tool contributing to a thorough understanding of the system. However, complex systems also exhibit emergent forms of behaviour that cannot be predicted in such a way. While the next section outlines that the safety case approach may still be a valuable tool at higher hierarchical levels, it becomes also clear, that novel approaches to risk assessment and to safety case construction are required to take account of the complexity of healthcare organisations.

4 Assessment of Organisational Changes

A major concern in the NHS has been the problem of patient waiting times. Treatment waiting times of up to 18 months are to be reduced to a target of 18 weeks for the entire "patient journey". One of the changes directed at achieving the aims of higher quality, personalised care, and reduced waiting times is the introduction of specialist nurses as mediators between primary and secondary care. A simplified scenario is described below in order to explore the implications of such change (see [21] for a detailed description).

Urinary tract infections (UTI) in children may lead to renal scarring and other adverse consequences when not diagnosed and treated quickly and adequately. The previous referral pathway for the investigation of childhood UTI required often a minimum of three interactions between practitioners and the children and their parents, taking up to a year.

The aims of the introduction of a UTI specialist nurse included improved awareness among primary care teams, increased detection rates, reduction in time required of patients and parents, streamlined working with other agencies involved in the investigation process, reduction in overall duration of the process, and improved relationship with patients and parents.

The new solution is a nurse-led service for childhood UTI, combined with an education package for primary care teams, and available telephone support. The specialist nurse is autonomous, not supervised directly by a consultant. The nurse acts across the interface between primary care and secondary care. A consultant gets involved only when the nurse determines that a particular case requires such attention based on clinical judgment. The nurse will make decisions based on the test results, and she will inform both the GP and the patient and parents promptly.

Proactive assessment of such change is not straightforward as comprehensive representations of how the various actors and systems interact for the whole system are more or less completely absent even though limited safety cases of sub-systems sometimes do exist for the local environment.

The interface between primary and secondary care leads to a large number of interactions. The GP decision-making process is now different, from a diagnosis to a fast referral for in-depth consideration by the specialist nurse. This will release GP resource and will modify the GP's communication and relationship with hospital consultants. Testing services will interact only with the specialist nurse. The Consultant will deal with a smaller proportion of cases. There will be a redistribution of resources to finance the new role on part of the Hospital Trust. The far-reaching consequences of this change (consequences that have only been hinted at) can only be assessed with proper models of the organisation, and in particular with models of how the organisation achieves safe operations. This becomes even more relevant when this change is seen in the broader view of all the other changes taking place concurrently. In addition to the UTI specialist nurse, other similar specialist roles are being introduced (e.g. diabetes, palliative care etc.), all changing the activities of GPs, consultants, test facilities, patients and so on, and all possibly interacting with one another.

A formal safety argument could be used to make explicit how the overall organisation is achieving safe operations by making explicit the assumptions, dependencies and interactions that could be used to identify and to resolve interactions between changes. To make the use of such a safety argument possible a number of problems would need to be addressed. Currently, manufacturers of devices are certified by the Competent Authority. Healthcare providers (PCT, NHS Trust etc.), on the other hand, are audited independently by the HC. As already discussed changes often cut across sub-systems and responsibilities and may involve transfer of responsibility, transfer of resources and introduction of new technologies all at the same time. Any overarching safety argument would need to integrate information from all of these actors and, for this to happen, one actor would need to take overall responsibility. The SHA seems a possible candidate for this as it is involved in the process of performance monitoring of the healthcare providers, whereas auditing is increasingly being taken over by the HC. The SHA could thus assume the responsibility of compiling a safety argument for its area of responsibility. This safety argument would function as a tool within the management of change process rather than being part of the auditing process (as the HC does not audit the SHA) and would contribute to the achievement of the SHA's aim of providing higher-quality care within its region.

Achieving management of change through such arguments presents problems for the developers of safety arguments. They would need to integrate a substantial number of autonomous actors and would need to develop an underlying model upon which the argument could be constructed. Traditional analytical models often fall short of providing adequate representations of organisations. A decomposition of the organisation into its elements for analytical reasons would not be an appropriate way of dealing with the emergent properties resulting from the manifold and complex interactions of all the elements of an organisation. Alternative models and representations are required that can interpret the organisation's defences or barriers in terms of human activity, and make this explicit to prevent unwanted and unsafe interactions.

5 Conclusion

This paper discusses the role that a safety argument might play in managing the safety implications of organisational change. Specifically, healthcare organisations are complex systems characterised by a large number of interactions and interrelationships. Safety of such complex systems is an emergent property of these interactions. The complexity of healthcare organisations, the large number of autonomous actors, and the disjoint regulation of healthcare providers and medical device manufacturers renders the assessment of the implications of change very difficult. The paper demonstrates that the construction of a safety case at the appropriate level can be a useful tool for identifying possible predictable interactions and dependencies.

However, the complexity of whole-system safety arguments makes the possibility of their construction and management a matter of concern. The example of organisational change used for illustration was relatively simple involving few agents and yet many issues emerged through the discussion. For example no one actor in the organisation has responsibility for maintaining the whole safety of the system and therefore the overall safety argument. It is not clear how well existing argumentation techniques would manage the unforeseen emergent properties of these complex systems. As yet no systematic techniques exist for managing effectively change through these arguments – an issue that we wish to explore in our future research agenda.

As indicated in the introduction, we are particularly interested in exploring ways of assessing risks and of demonstrating safety that take into account the fact that certain patterns of behaviour exhibited by the system are emergent and cannot be predicted using traditional decomposition. This undertaking is somewhat aporetic, and may consequently require a debate about the perception and acceptability of risks, and the reformulation of the purpose of safety arguments. Maybe the emphasis will need to shift towards more reliable monitoring of system performance and faster and more flexible reaction to abnormalities, while at the same time accepting that some accidents are inevitable [5].

References

1. Department of Health: The NHS Plan: a plan for investment, a plan for reform (2000)
2. Kinnersly, S.: Whole Airspace ATM System Safety Case – Preliminary Study, Eurocontrol (2001)
3. Cilliers, P.: *Complexity and Postmodernism*, Routledge, London (1998)
4. Gleick, J.: *Chaos*, Minerva, London (1997)
5. Perrow, C. *Normal Accidents*, Basic Books (1984)
6. Pavard, B. and Dugdale, J.: The contribution of complexity theory to the study of socio-technical cooperative systems, In *InterJournal of Complex Systems*, 335 (2000)
7. Sweeny, K. and Griffiths, F.: *Complexity and Healthcare*, Radcliffe MP (2002)

8. Plsek, P.E. and Greenhalgh, T: The challenge of complexity in healthcare, BMJ, 323 (2001) pp. 625-628
9. Johnson, C.W.: What are emergent properties and how do they affect the engineering of complex systems?, Reliability Engineering & System Safety (in press)
10. Wears, R.L. and Cook, R.I.: Automation, Interaction, Complexity, and Failure: A case study, Reliability Engineering & System Safety (in press)
11. Penny, J., Eaton, A., Bishop, P.G., Bloomfield, R.E.: The Practicalities of Goal-Based Safety Regulation, In Redmill, F. and Anderson, T. (eds): Proc. 9th Safety-Critical Systems Symposium, Springer Verlag (2001), pp. 35-48
12. Kelly, T.P.: Arguing Safety – A Systematic Approach to Safety Case Management, DPhil Thesis, Department of Computer Science, York (1998)
13. Kelly, T.P. and McDermid, J.A.: A Systematic Approach to Safety Case Maintenance, Reliability Engineering and System Safety 71, Elsevier (2001), pp. 271 – 284
14. Bate, I. and Kelly, T.: Architectural considerations in the certification of modular systems, Reliability Engineering and System Safety, 81, Elsevier (2003), pp. 303 – 324
15. Bedau, M.: Weak Emergence, In Tomberlin, J. (ed), *Philosophical Perspectives, 11: Mind, Causation, and World* (1997), pp. 375-399
16. Hollnagel, E.: Barriers and Accident Prevention, Ashgate (2004)
17. Jordan, P.A.: Medical Device Manufacturers, Standards and the Law, paper presented at DIRC Workshop on Software Quality and the Legal System (2004)
18. Department of Health: Standards for Better Health (2004)
19. Sujan, M.A., Henderson, J., Embrey, D.: Mismatching between planned and actual treatments in medicine – manual checking approaches to prevention, Human Reliability Associates (2004)
20. Gorski, J. et al.: Trust Case: justifying trust in an IT solution, Reliability Engineering & System Safety, 89 (2005), pp. 33-47
21. Coulthard, M.G., Vernon, S.J., Lambert, H.J., Matthews, J.N.S.: A nurse led education and direct access service for the management of urinary tract infections in children: prospective controlled trial, British Medical Journal (2003)

Healthcare System Architecture, Economic Value, and Policy Models in Large-Scale Wireless Sensor Networks

Won Jay Song[1], Moon Kyo Cho[2], Im Sook Ha[2], and Mun Kee Choi[2]

[1] Department of Computer Science, University of Virginia, VA 22904-4740, USA
[2] School of IT Business, Information and Communications University, 305-732, Korea
wjsong@cs.virginia.edu

Abstract. In this paper, we have designed and modeled the ubiquitous RFID healthcare system architecture and framework workflow, which are described by six classified core players or subsystems, and have also analyzed by an economic value-chain model. They consist of the patient and wearable ECG sensor, network service, healthcare service, emergency service, and PKI service providers. To enhance the security level control for the patient's medical privacy, individual private and public keys should be stored on smart cards. All the patient and service providers in the proposed security control architecture should have suitable secure private and public keys to access medical data and diagnosis results with RFID/GPS tracking information for emergency service. By enforcing the requirements of necessary keys among the patient and service providers, the patient's ECG data can be protected and effectively controlled over the open medical directory service. Consequently, the proposed architecture for ubiquitous RFID healthcare system using the smart card terminal is appropriate to build up medical privacy policies in future ubiquitous sensor networking and home networking environments. In addition, we have analyzed an economic value-chain model based on the proposed architecture consisting of RFID, GPS, PDA, ECG sensor, and smart card systems in large-scale wireless sensor networks and have also analyzed two market derivers – customer demands and technology – in the proposed service architecture using the value-chain model. Finally, policy modeling for privacy and security protection for customers, service providers, and regulatory agency is considered to promote beneficial utilization of the collected healthcare data and derived new business of healthcare applications.

1 Introduction

Recently, electronic healthcare systems have extended to ubiquitous healthcare systems such as personal home networking healthcare. They enable medical professionals to remotely make real-time monitoring, early diagnosis, and treatment for potential risky disease, and to provide the medical diagnosis and consulting results to the patient via wired/wireless communication channels. In addition to new ubiquitous medical equipments for patients (e.g., wearable healthcare sensor systems), smart home/sensor networks, radio frequency identification (RFID), public-key infrastructure (PKI), and Grid computing technology for large-scale physiologic and electrocardiogram (ECG) signal analysis have been studied and developed [1]-[8].

J. Górski (Ed.): SAFECOMP 2006, LNCS 4166, pp. 233–246, 2006.

In spite of all the research and development in ubiquitous healthcare systems for a variety of applications, the system should still have to address both access control and privacy protection issues for the patient's individual medical data. These problems are serious when unauthorized persons or groups trying to monitor and access to the systems, remotely and stealthily. The problem can be complicated since it is possible to collect the patient's medical data from a wide variety of ubiquitous sensor nodes and to track an individual patient's location in ubiquitous networking world. To address those issues systematically, advanced study of privacy and security control architecture is critical. We have designed and modeled an architecture based on RFID and smart card technologies for ubiquitous healthcare in wireless sensor networks. Our novel architecture can effectively protect personal medical data and diagnosis results [4],[9]-[11].

Additionally, a need for an efficient method of storing personalized medical data, while providing security, reliability and portability, has arisen for ubiquitous RFID healthcare system in large-scale wireless sensor networks. The current PC-based smart card terminal should not only be designed to interface with smart cards and to control the retrieval or storage of data on the card but should also consist of several hardware components [12]. The microprocessor, memory, and the other hardware components needed for data encryption are embedded in the IC chip of the smart card. Therefore, smart cards are usually used in the area of wireless sensor networks. There is a need for smart card terminal-based systems with technical specifications for specific IC card operations [13],[14].

Finally, most research for new system architectures has only focused on technical aspects. In this paper, however, we have described not only the technical approach but also performed economic evaluation of the architecture using a value chain model and proposed policy modeling process of privacy and security protection. The value chain is a systematic approach to examining the development of competitive advantage and it was introduced by M.E.Porter [16]. The chain consists of a series of activities that create and build value. Moreover, it serves a useful analytical tool of emerging new system or service, particularly under rapidly changing telecommunications environments [17]. Thus, this paper describes that a value chain of the healthcare system and core players of each stage exist for value creation of RFID wearable sensor healthcare systems. For the business value to make new healthcare industry, the system must operate based on confirmed policies of privacy and security protection. For the policy modeling, this paper proposes a scheme of confidentiality and patient-identifiability to utilize collected healthcare data for public benefit. Service providers are required to allocate privacy and security rules to procedures and technologies to implement the levels of protection.

2 Architectural Design Process

2.1 Ubiquitous RFID Healthcare System

In the proposed security control architecture for ubiquitous healthcare system, we use radio frequency identification (RFID) tag, wearable electrocardiogram (ECG) sensor, smart card, Grid computing, PhysioNet, wired/wireless networks, and public-key infrastructure (PKI) technologies. The system architecture and framework are described by six classified core players or subsystems as shown in Figure 1.

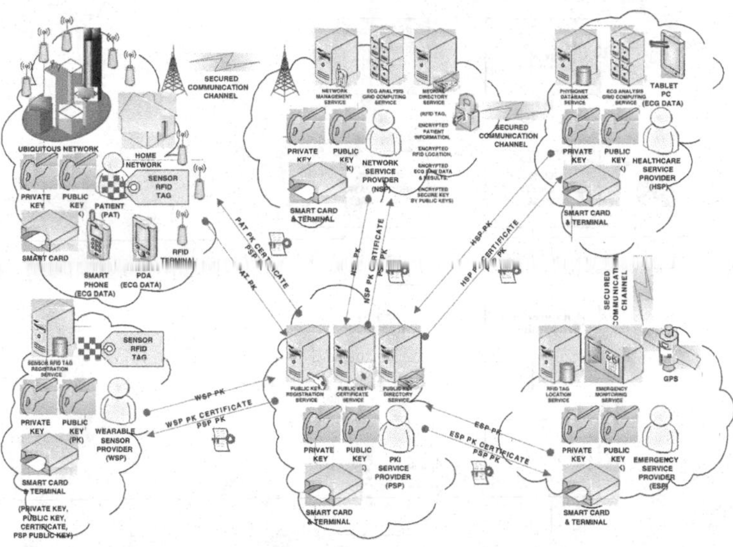

Fig. 1. The schematic diagram consisting of six core player or subsystems with their individual components and functions at privacy and security control architecture for ubiquitous RFID healthcare system

They consist of the patient (PAT) and wearable ECG sensor provider (WSP), network service provider (NSP) with encrypted medical database and Grid computing, healthcare service provider (HSP) with PhysioNet database, emergency service provider (ESP), and PKI service provider (PSP) with certificate and directory databases. The individual private and public keys should be stored on the smart card and be used to enhance security level control for the patient's medical privacy.

The WSP supplies its wearable ECG sensor system with RFID tag to the PAT, whose tag has unique identification information for the wearable sensor node. In order to protect the patient's privacy, all of the providers only recognize and use the tag information, instead of directly accessing to the patient's personal data. In addition, unique RFID tag information can be also used to track a patient in wearable RFID sensor system for emergency service by the ESP under ubiquitous RFID terminal network environments.

All individual public keys with correspondence to each private key should be stored on the PKI key server at the PSP. To verify the unique identification of each player or subsystem, the certificate of each public key should be issued by using the private key of the PSP and be stored on the PKI directory server. Then, both the certificates and the public key with correspondence to the private key of the PSP should be in service to all of the patient and providers via wired/wireless secure communication channels.

2.2 Security Features of Healthcare Smart Card

Digital Signature. A smart card can carry all the data needed to generate the holder's digital signature in sensor networks. The main components are encryption and

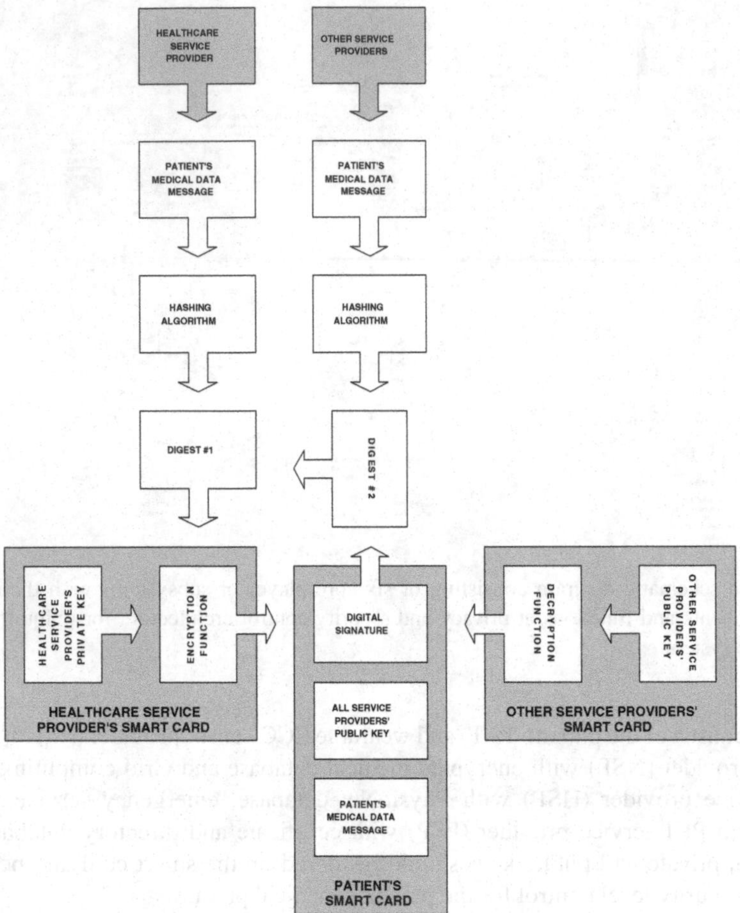

Fig. 2. The first processing sequence required to generate a digital signature for authentication purposes in ubiquitous RFID healthcare systems

decryption keys (private/public key pair) and a signed digital certificate. Digital signatures use a method of encryption and decryption known as 'asymmetric.' This method uses two keys, one to encrypt and the other to decrypt. If a message is encrypted using one key, it can only be decrypted using the other. These key pairs need not both be secret.

In 'public-key encryption' systems, one key is private, the users, and the other is the public domain. Note that in these cases, key distribution is trivial since the private key is never conveyed to anyone and the public key is available to everyone. An electronic signature cannot be forged. It is a computed digest of some text that is encrypted and sent with the text message. A digital signature ensures that the document originated with the person signing it and that it was not tampered with after the signature was applied.

Smart Card Authentication. As shown in Figure 2, you have to have access to that public key. Not only do you need that access, but you also need to be sure that the public key you obtain really is the public key for the person in question. One way to verify the validity of a public key is to sign it with yet another key, whose public key you know to be valid. Thus, it belongs to a trusted third party and a patient's smart card. This is the 'signed' digital certificate [15].

Public-Key Infrastructure. A Public-Key Infrastructure (PKI) is a collection of services that enables the use of public-key encryption techniques. The functions of a PKI include creating digital certificates, storing public keys, and tracking expiration dates of certificates. A public key obtained through a PKI is trustworthy. By managing these keys and certificates, an organization, such as the National Health Service (NHS), establishes and maintains a trustworthy networking environment. The existence of a PKI is therefore a critical factor in the use of the HPC in the NHS.

As commonly used, a digital certificate contains: (1) an expiration date, (2) the name of the certifying authority that issued the certificate, (3) a serial number, (4) the digital signature of the certificate issuer and the Certification Authority (CA), (5) the identity of the registered holder, and (6) the holder's public key. Using smart cards in conjunction with a PKI implies that the CA issues the card with certificates and key pairs already written on it. This would apply both to the healthcare professional card and the patient's data card. Signed public keys are stored in a public directory. In the NHS, this would be the managed directory service [15].

2.3 Functions of Healthcare Smart Card

Login Process. The Healthcare Professional Card (HPC) is the core of the login process, which involves verification of the user and authentication of the HPC. Authentication is the process that identifies and validates either the principal(s) involved in a transaction, or the origin of a message. We assume for the sake of illustration that the HPC holder wishes to use a healthcare application. We also assume that the application is a client/server system with a wireless PDA acting as the user terminal and that it is fitted with a smart card terminal.

The first part of the login process will comprise the user inserting the HPC into the terminal. The application will request the HPC to generate the holder's digital signature. At the same time, the application will request the user to enter identification details. This will enable the application to verify that the user is the authorized holder of the HPC and that the card is genuine, and then start the session. The user identification might include the use of a Personal Identification Number (PIN) or password. This method has often been dismissed as 'weak' security and easily compromised. However, this is not necessarily the case, and the weaknesses often lie in sending clear text to the authentication server [15].

Request and Response Procedures. The authentication process performed by the application is achieved using a request and response procedure employing the cryptographic algorithm recorded on the HPC. To authenticate the HPC, the system requests the card by sending a random number. Figure 2 shows the first part of the request pro-

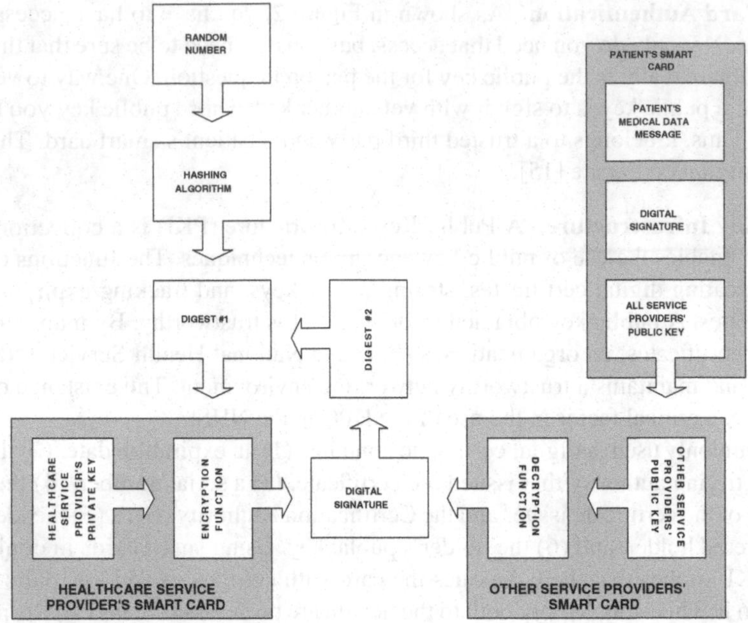

Fig. 3. The second processing sequence required to generate a digital signature for authentication purposes in ubiquitous RFID healthcare systems

cess. i.e., the 'message' sent to the card being the random number. The card uses this number and its own secret (private) key as input to its cryptographic algorithm [15].

The output of the calculation is then transmitted to the application as a digital signature. The application decrypts the signature using the public key obtained through the Public-Key Infrastructure (PKI). It compares the result with the original. If the two match, the card is considered to be genuine. Figure 3 shows the authentication process, the second part of the request-response. The application obtains the public key for the user from the PKI, using the identification details supplied.

Authentication and Access Control. For security purposes it is necessary for the healthcare application to check that the card is genuine. This means that the card must be issued by the National Health Service (NHS) Certification Authority (CA) for the holder's GP and initialized with signed security data. For the Healthcare Professional Card (HPC) and Patient's Data Card (PDC) interaction, two services are required as the PDC has to prove its authenticity and the healthcare professional has to prove access rights [15]. When proving access rights, an authentication procedure has to be performed. If after successful authentication a read or update command is performed on a smart card file, the application has to verify that the respective security condition described in the security attributes of this PDC file is fulfilled. Access rights can be expressed in terms of either individual professionals or identifiable groups, or both. The problems with the application can therefore be complicated by the need to recognize the HPC holder as a member of an access group [15].

The PDC authentication procedure assumes that the professional has already logged into the healthcare application using an HPC. The patient holds a healthcare smart card, which is plugged into the auxiliary card terminal. The PDC is authenticated by the challenge-response method. This entails the professional entering the patient's NHS number at the user terminal.

Authentication proves that the PDC belongs to the NHS number supplied and was created by an authorized professional. When the application reads data from the card, it checks that the professional currently in session has the right to access that data. If not, the application will inform the professional that access has been denied, but provide an override facility for emergency purposes. If the professional makes a decision that affects the card's data, the application will check that the professional has the right to amend the data. If the professional is not authorized, an emergency override facility will be offered [15]. Any data written will have the professional's digital signature attached. Referring to Figure 2, the 'message' represents the data to be written to the card. The digital signature is a function of the data written. Therefore any later unauthorized attempt to alter the data written will result in the digital signature not matching the data.

3 Architectural Integration Process

In the proposed architecture combined with wearable and wireless sensor network environments, the patient's ECG signals should be automatically measured and periodically stored on the internal flash memory of the wearable ECG sensor system. The stored medical raw data will be transferred to the patient's or medical professional's wireless PDA with a 2-way double-type smart card terminal or GPS smart phone. For the data transfer, near-field wireless communications such as the Bluetooth wireless technology is used. The transferred data should be encrypted by using the patient's one-time secure key at the handheld devices.

As illustrated in Figure 4, all the data in wearable ECG sensors as well as analyzed data in Grid computing with PhysioNet should be encrypted by using an individually generated one-time secure key with expire-time by the PAT's and HSP's private keys, respectively. Additionally, the issued one-time secure keys are also encrypted by using public keys of the patient and pre-approved service providers. These encrypted medical data and encrypted secure keys will be also transferred to the network service provider via secured communication channels in wired/wireless networks. The encrypted data and keys with unique RFID tag information should be stored on the secured database directory of network service provider. The database meta-schema has decrypted and encrypted fields, that are used to make access control among the patient and providers.

4 Economic Value Modeling Process

Value chain is the linkage and integration of a series of activities in which enterprises deliver the created and valued products or services to customers. The value chain of enterprises is essentially encompassed in a broader value system. This consists of activities

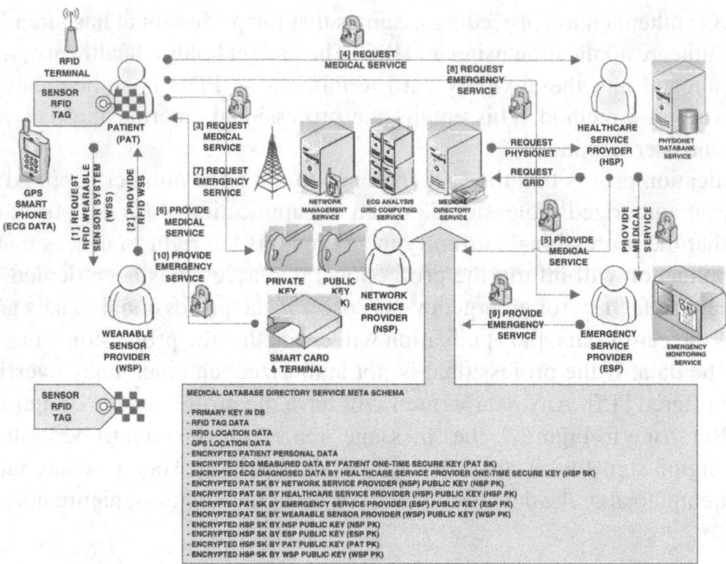

Fig. 4. The schematic diagram consisting of five core player or subsystems without public-key service provider

such as design, production, marketing, distribution, and support to the final consumer [16]. In the value chain of ubiquitous system, however, subsystems of the existing value chains are regrouped in response to major function of system's players. The proposed six classified core players in large-scale wireless sensor networks should match with five activities in value chain corresponding to common function. The Figure 5 shows the players of each activity. Therefore, the reconfiguration value chain of the system consists of four parts; sensing, networking, diagnosis, and acting stages. Figure 6 shows the reconfigured value chain. Each stage has its own customer demands and technology derivers that define the speed and direction of evolution path for RFID wearable healthcare systems. Customer evaluates and responses the service level of health care system. Their responses are not only critical of success and failure of the system but affecting the scale of service market. Additionally, evolution of each technology accelerates new system. Two major market drivers – customer demands and technology – can be defined by stages.

Sensing Stage. In the sensing stage, it is essential to have a precise awareness and convenient sensing technology. Through the ubiquitous RFID/GPS technology, the patients can be diagnosed in any place at any time so that the importance characteristic of this stage is sensor and sensing technology such as wearable ECG sensor. Additionally patients can feel comfortable to attach senor without any trouble. The technology for sensing is RFID technology in terms of weight and easy of use (e.g., tag, reader, and server).

Networking Stage. The following stage is networking. Privacy and security are critical for the customer, especially in this stage. Network service provider provides

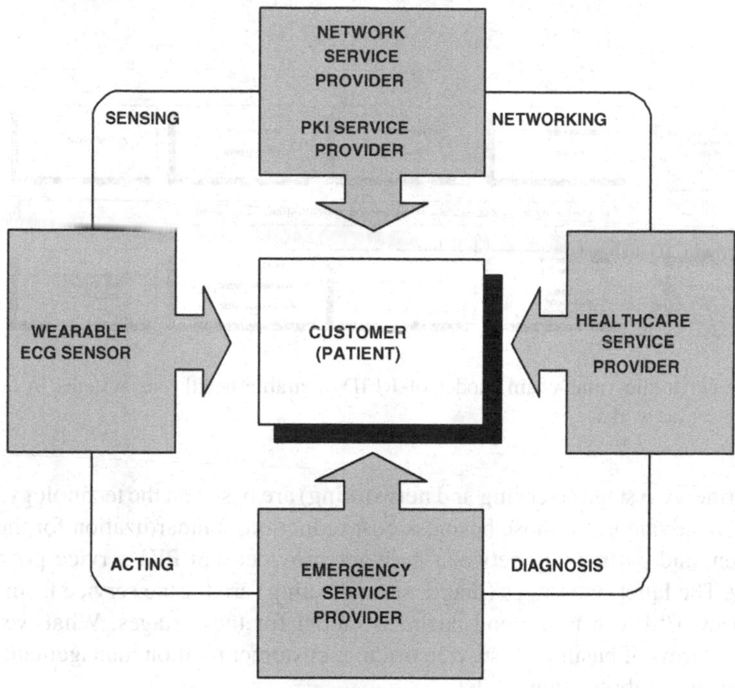

Fig. 5. The players and activities of RFID wearable healthcare system in large-scale wireless sensor networks

wireless sensor networks, and PKI service provider supports high-level encryption and decryption algorithm for the protection of patients' medical data. Thus, the two players carry out important technical issues. Moreover, high-bandwidth infrastructure for huge data handling is also essential.

Diagnosis Stage. The third stage is a diagnosis stage. The correct and high-quality diagnosis service of a medical specialist is major customer needs based on the collected patients' medical data. The major technical issue of this stage is grid computing technology. It also provides the ability to perform computations on large medical data sets and to accomplish more computations at once with accuracy. From the accumulating patient's medical data, healthcare service provider analyzes the symptom and prescribes the medicine or treatment.

Acting Stage. Finally, last stage is an acting stage which is the reaction and control of hospital or pharmacy for the diagnosed patients. Emergency service provider (ESP) can be a core player of this stage. When any alerts from the diagnosis is announced, the ESP can track him through location-based system and then it gives expediency and bring the patients to the proper hospital or organization within a short time. The technology issue of this stage is location-based sensor and sensing, for example, RFID and GPS.

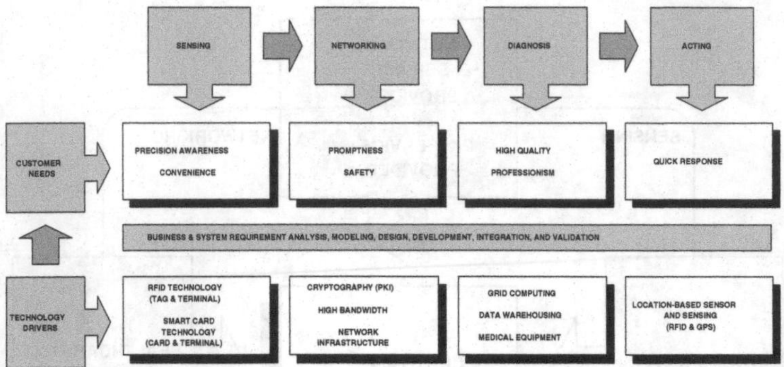

Fig. 6. The economic value-chain model of RFID wearable healthcare systems in large-scale wireless sensor networks

The former two stages (sensing and networking) are based on the technology. To have comparative advantage in those business cost reduction, standardization for the market domination, and partnership between network provider and PKI service provider are necessary. The latter two stages (diagnosis and acting) are for the service from hospital or pharmacy. ESP can be a good business model for these stages. What we have to consider in terms of business is service pricing, customer relation management (CRM), advertising, and subscription model.

5 Policy Modeling Process

For the business about healthcare information, customer's privacy concern is not confined within unauthorized access but extended to the scope of its utilization for business. Although RFID and smartcard can offer access control and privacy protection for a specific service, the customer always worries about the abuse of private information, and the provider always wants to create economic value from the information to make new business. Therefore, we need a set of rules to make a compromise between the protection and the utilization of private information. We describe policy modeling process that can be deployed to the healthcare system on the sensor networks.

Generally disclosure of private information has negative effects on the attitude to the related service. In other words, the customer undertakes some cost based on the quality and quantity of their private information. The cost depends on some factors, such as importance of the information for the service proposition, legitimacy of collecting the information, and perceived difficulty of response [19]. At the case of the proposed sensor networks, they may relive the difficulty of response, but the customer does not easily control the flow of critical information. One approach to empower the customer to control private information is the standard of Platform for Privacy Preferences Project (P3P). On the platform, a user's Internet browser and a web site contract the degree of privacy disclosure based on the user's privacy preference and the site's P3P profile [20]. Such a contract-based approach is more useful when many applications are provided on the sensor networks because it relieves the user's burden

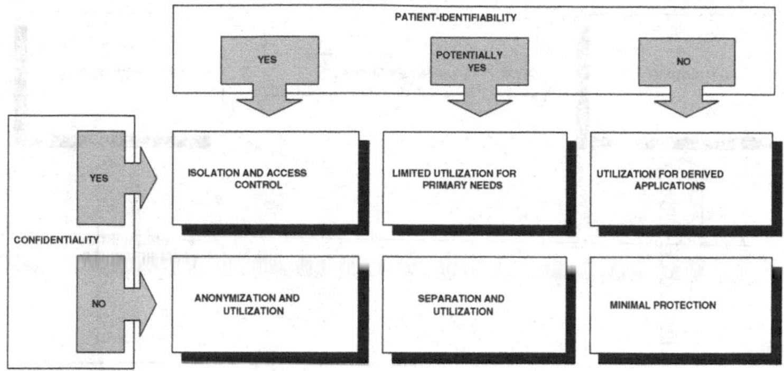

Fig. 7. The categories and required privacy protection levels of healthcare information in large-scale wireless sensor networks

of manual confirmation and promotes development of various derived services. Based on the contract, service providers can develop new business and research for public benefit.

To classify the sensitivity of healthcare information, we use a scheme of confidentiality and patient-identifiability of the information [21]. However, the proposed application also collects GPS data, which may be potentially used to identify the patient combined with other trivial information. Therefore, we add one more category on patient-identifiability, and consider privacy protection levels respectively as shown in Figure 7. For the information with confidentiality, its scope of utilization is broadened as the information lacks patient-specific data. If the information is not secret, patient-identifiable information must be anonymized to be used outside. At the case of potential risk of patient-identification, separating location data from other information is a possible solution to protect privacy. Regulatory agency may play a role in making the policy and persuading customers because it costs too much for each service provider to develop the policy case by case.

For service providers, the levels of privacy protection are implemented through a set of security and privacy rules. Since the system can not operate without manual procedures, the rules are enforced via procedures and via technologies [22]. For example, transferring critical data to removable electronic media or hardcopy involves security rules allocated to procedures. However, most of a healthcare system is protected by secure technology about user management, data management, logging and accounting, digital signature, and so on. Recently Health Insurance Portability and Accountability Act (HIPAA) in the USA explicitly mentioned the security and privacy regulations [23].

Consequently, as shown in Figure 8, healthcare systems on sensor networks face new challenges in policy-based privacy protection. As the customer must control the privacy information, the service provider must be able to make new business. The regulatory agency coordinates them and pursues public benefit. Policy models of privacy protection levels and security rules are indispensable to the goals of all players in healthcare industry.

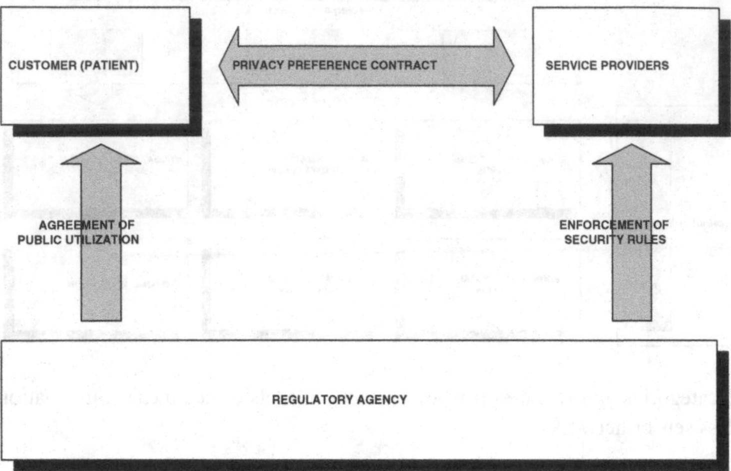

Fig. 8. The cooperation of privacy and security policies among customer, service providers, and regulatory agency in healthcare industry

6 Conclusion

In the proposed privacy and security control architecture for ubiquitous RFID healthcare systems in large-scale wireless sensor networks, all of the patient and providers need suitable secure private and public keys in order to access to ECG medical raw data and diagnosis results with RFID and GPS tracking information for emergency service. By enforcing the requirements of necessary keys among the patient and providers, the patient's ECG data can be protected and effectively controlled over the open medical directory service of network service providers. Consequently, the proposed architecture for ubiquitous RFID healthcare system is appropriate to build up medical privacy policies. The architecture can provide a new business model to wired/wireless network service providers. In the future, the system architecture workflow and protocols will be modeled and verified using Petri nets.

The new emerging system and service have only been considered customer requirements analysis, systems design, integration, implementation, and verification passing over economic aspects. However, this paper analyzes not only the verification of proposed system architecture in technical aspect but also evaluating economic value creation through developing an economic value-chain model. The value chain model developed in this paper is also reconfigured in response to common function of classified six players. The reconfiguration value chain of the system describes five activities: (1)customer, (2)sensing, (3)networking, (4)diagnosis, and (5)acting stages. The results show that the customer is the patients, the sensing stage contains wearable ECG sensor, the networking stage has network service provider and PKI service provider, the diagnosis stage has healthcare service provider, and the acting stage contains emergency service provider. In addition, it should be analyzed customer demand and technology derivers for four service providers. Therefore, this new value-chain should be contributed to a better understanding of RFID wearable healthcare system in large-scale wireless sensor networks. It will be expanded by examining six players considering the evolution of networks.

For the business the system must establish policies of privacy and security protection also. For the policy modeling, this paper proposes a scheme of confidentiality and patient-identifiability to utilize collected healthcare data considering the characteristics of ubiquitous service. Recent legislation specifies the obligation of service providers to allocate privacy and security rules for privacy protection. The regulatory agency's coordination and enforcement are critical to the industry.

Acknowledgement. This research work has been supported in part by the Korea Research Foundation Grant (KRF-2005-M01-2005-000-10434-0) and the Information Technology Research Center program supervised by the Institute of Information Technology Assessment in Republic of Korea.

References

1. W.J.Song, S.H.Son, M.K.Choi, and M.H.Kang, "Privacy and Security Control Architecture for Ubiquitous RFID Healthcare System in Wireless Sensor Networks," *Proceedings in the IEEE ICCE 2006*, January 2006.
2. S.S.Choi, W.J.Song, M.K.Choi, and S.H.Son, "Ubiquitous RFID Healthcare Systems Analysis on PhysioNet Grid Portal Services Using Petri Nets," *Proceedings in the IEEE ICICS 2005*, December 2005.
3. G.B.Moody, R.G.Mark, and A.L.Goldberger, "PhysioNet: A Web-Based Resource for the Study of Physiologic Signals," *IEEE Engineering in Medicine and Biology*, vol.20, no.3, pp.70-75, May/June 2001.
4. K.Finkenzeller, *RFID Handbook*, 2nd Edition, Wiley & Sons, April 2003.
5. D.S.Nam, C.H.Youn, B.H.Lee, G.Clifford, and J.Healey, "QoS-Constrained Resource Allocation for a Grid-Based Multiple Source Electrocardiogram Application," *Lecture Notes in Computer Science*, vol.3043, pp.352-359, 2004.
6. G.Eysenbach, "What is e-healthcare?" *Journal of Medical Internet Research*, vol.3, no.2, 2001.
7. J.Marconi, "E-Health: Navigating the Internet for Health Information Healthcare," *Advocacy White Paper*, Healthcare Information and Management Systems Society, May 2002.
8. J.Joseph and C.Fellenstein, *Grid Computing*, Prentice Hall, 2004.
9. H.Chan and A.Perrig, "Security and Privacy in Sensor Networks," *IEEE Computer*, vo.36, no.10, pp103-105, October 2003.
10. C.H.Fancher, "In Your Pocket: Smartcards," *IEEE Spectrum*, vol.34, no.2, pp.47-53, February 1997.
11. R.W.Baldwin and C.V.Chang, "Locking the e-safe," *IEEE Spectrum*, vol.34, no.2, pp.40-46, February 1997.
12. W.Rankl and W.Effing, *Smart Card Handbook*, 2nd Edition, New York, John Wiley & Sons, 2000.
13. ISO/IEC 7816-1:1998, *Identification Cards – Integrated Circuit(s) Cards with Contacts - Part 1: Physical Characteristics*, International Organization for Standardization, 1998.
14. W.J.Song, W.H.Kim, B.G.Kim, B.H.Ahn, M.K.Choi, and M.H.Kang, "Smart Card Terminal Systems Using ISO/IEC 7816-3 Interface and 8051 Microprocessor Based on the System-on Chip," *Lecture Notes in Computer Science*, vol.2860, pp.364-371, November 2003.

15. NHS, *NHS IT Standards Handbook*, National Health Service (NHS) Information Authority, June 2001.
16. M.E.Porter, *Competitive Strategy: Techniques for Analyzing Industries and Competitors*, New York: Free Press, 1980.
17. P.Olla and N.V.Patel, "A Value Chain Model for Mobile Data Service Providers," *Telecommunications Policy*, vol.26, no.9-10, pp.551-571, 2002.
18. Y.H.Lee, H.W.Kim, Y.J.Kim, and H.Sohn, "A New Conceptual Framework for Designing Ubiquitous Business Model," *IE Interfaces*, vol.19, no.1, pp.9-18, March 2006.
19. S.Spiekermann, J.Grossklags, and B.Berendt, "E-privacy in 2nd Generation E-Commerce: Privacy Preferences versus Actual Behavior," *Proceedings of the 2001 ACM Conference on Electronic Commerce*, Association for Computing Machinery, pp.38-47, October 2001.
20. *The Platform for Privacy Preferences 1.0 (P3P1.0) Specification*, W3C Recommendation, http://www.w3.org/P3P/, April 2002.
21. L.Janczewski and F.X.Shi, "Development of Information Security Baselines for Healthcare Information Systems in New Zealand," *Computers & Security*, vol.21, no.2, pp.172-192, March 2002.
22. D.E.Gobuty and Joint NEMA/COCIR/JIRA Security & Privacy Committee (SPC), "Organizing Security and Privacy Enforcement in Medical Imaging Technology," *International Congress Series*, vol.1256, pp.319-329, June 2003.
23. *Health Insurance Portability and Accountability Act of 1996*, Public Law 104-191, 104th United States Congress, http://www.aspe.hhs.gov/admnsimp/pl104191.htm, 1996.

Assessment of Hazard Identification Methods for the Automotive Domain

Fredrik Törner [1], Per Johannessen [1], and Peter Öhman [2]

[1] Volvo Car Corporation, Department 94120, 405 31, Gothenburg, Sweden
ftorner@volvocars.com, pjohan1@volvocars.com
[2] Chalmers University of Technology, Gothenburg, Sweden
peter.ohman@chalmers.se

Abstract. Many automotive electronic systems are safety related and therefore need to be developed using a safety process. A preliminary hazard analysis, PHA, is one of the first and vital steps in such a process. In this paper, two methods with different approaches are experimentally evaluated using an electrical steering column lock system. The two methods are an adapted FFA, functional failure analysis, method based on induction with generic failure modes and a method from ESA based on induction with generic low level hazards. In the evaluation, interviews and questionnaires are used to triangulate the results. Both methods are found to be applicable for hazard identification in the automotive system context. The experiments conducted also show, with statistical significance, that the adapted FFA method is less time consuming and easier to use than the ESA method. Hence, the FFA method is found to be more suitable for hazard identification in early phases of development in this context.

1 Introduction

Active safety systems can, together with passive safety systems, increase road safety. Normally, active safety systems require complex implementations in both software and hardware. As these systems are inherently safety related they must be developed according to a rigid system safety process.

One of the first steps in the safety process is to do a Preliminary Hazard Analysis, PHA [1]. The PHA includes identification of the system's hazards and a consequence evaluation, a severity grading and exposure estimations of the identified hazards. A hazard is defined by Storey in [2] as "*a situation in which there is actual or potential danger to people or to the environment.*" The PHA serves several purposes in the system's development, including early assessment of required safety level, elicitation of safety requirements, identification of safe states, and support to the organization in gaining an understanding of the system and its functionality.

Automotive related standards, such as IEC-61508 [1], MISRA [3], and the working draft version of ISO-26262 [4], dictate the usage of early hazard analysis. These standards have slightly different guidance for determining the required safety level of the system given the list of hazards. The IEC-61508 defines Safety Integrity Levels while ISO/WD 26262 [4] defines a concept of Automotive Safety Integrity Levels.

J. Górski (Ed.): SAFECOMP 2006, LNCS 4166, pp. 247 – 260, 2006.

The standards all target the development of safety related systems to ensure safe products and are currently used in the automotive industry. This is achieved by defining process requirements and detailed technical requirements. However, methods for performing the hazard identification are not specified in these standards, in order to allow adaptation to advancements and company specific practices.

As the PHA is a critical step in the development process, an unsuitable identification method will drastically reduce the trustworthiness of the safety argumentation for the system implementation, complicate development, and increase cost. Hence it is important to use a method that is both simple and identifies all relevant hazards. This paper evaluates two principally different methods for conducting hazard identification, both of which provide the basis for the safety level classification.

Figure 1 shows two different approaches to identifying hazards, from system failure modes and from low-level hazards.

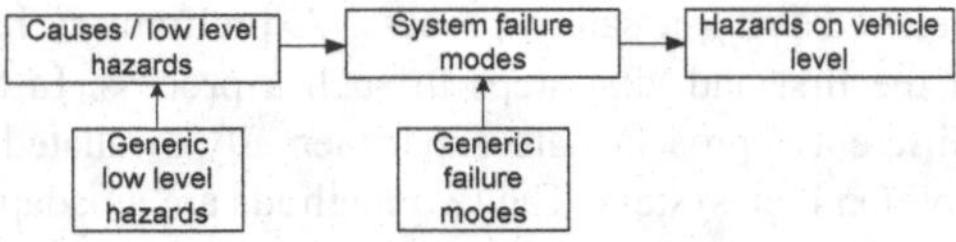

Fig. 1. Approaches to hazard identification

Three different approaches for identifying system hazards have been identified:

- *Ad hoc* or unstructured methods such as brainstorming.
- Induction with generic failure modes, in which failure modes are applied to actuators, functions or system states to identify the system hazards. FFA [5] and HAZOP [6] are typical examples of this type of method.
- Induction with generic low-level hazards, in which a generic set of hazards is applied to the system components to derive the system failure mode. ESA [7] and FMEA [2] are examples of this type of approach.

An *ad hoc* approach is highly dependant on the expertise of the engineers who are using it, since it does not provide structure or guidance. Therefore, it is not suitable for hazard identification for safety relevant systems.

In this study, one method representing each of the approaches was selected for evaluation. The first method chosen was the ESA hazard analysis method [7] and the second method was an adapted FFA presented in [8]. The main criterion in choosing these two methods is that they are currently used in the automotive industry.

2 Related Work

The concept of PHA has been used in several standards in the area of system safety development and hazard analysis. The value of early hazard analysis has been thoroughly discussed by Leveson [9] and Storey [2].

The automotive industry is dependant on several standards. One standard is IEC-61508 [1], which is a meta standard for developing functional safe systems and is currently in use in the automotive industry. The initiative for ISO-26262 [4] is working on an instantiation of the IEC-61508. A third standard is the MISRA guideline [3] that provides a supplement in severity rating. All these standards include requirements on classification of the system based on hazard analysis.

Hazard analysis is addressed in several methods such as FFA [5], HAZOP [6], HipHops [10], and an extended FFA proposed by Johannessen et al. [8].

Also included in hazard analysis is a root cause analysis. This provides a necessary basis for deriving detailed safety requirements. The state of the art for this purpose is the fault tree analysis, FTA [2]. This method, however, like FMEA, is better suited for later stages where more information about the system solution is available.

3 Methodology

The base of this study is an experiment, which is followed by a questionnaire and an interview to make it possible to triangulate the results. Hence, the study has an experimental set up with both qualitative and quantitative measurements. Figure 2 shows an overview of the study.

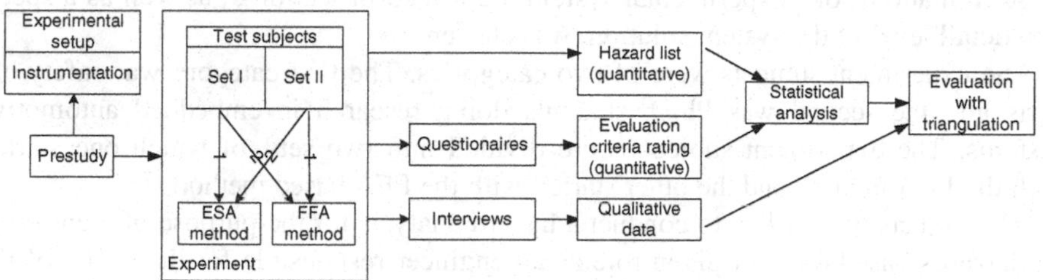

Fig. 2. Research process overview

In order to evaluate the methods, seven evaluation criteria were defined. Each evaluation criterion is presented in Table 1 with the corresponding metric and definition.

Table 1. Evaluation criteria, corresponding measurement method and definition

Evaluation criteria	Measurement method	Definition
Ease of use	Questionnaire, interviews	Subject's rating of the ease of use of the method.
Efficiency	Experimental results, interviews	Time required to carry out the method.
Applicability	Experimental results, interviews	Answers the question of whether the method serves the purpose of identifying the hazards.
Understandability	Questionnaire, interviews	Subject's rating of the method's learning curse
Confidence	Questionnaire, interviews	Subject's rating of perceived confidence in the method.
Level of engineering judgment	Experimental results, interviews	The method's inherent need for engineering judgment.
Scalability	Experimental results, interviews	The growth of the information generated based on the system's size.

In order to determine which properties each of the methods provides, a statistical analysis was made of the empirical data from the questionnaire. This analysis was based on the following hypothesis:

H_X: There is no difference between the methods in regard to criteria X.

To conduct the study, an experimental system was needed. Requirements were identified and four systems of different size and complexity were developed during the pre-study, in different detail levels.

The descriptions of both methods and step by step instructions were developed based on the ESA standard [7] and the papers by Johannessen et al. [8] [12].

In the pre-study, a questionnaire whose purpose was to measure some of the above stated criteria was also developed. Further, the methods were applied to the experimental systems in order to gain experience. The results were concluded to be the basis for a "Golden Run" and the experiences were noted and used as discussion material in the interviews.

Given the limitations of the subjects' availability, it was decided that each subject should be able to complete the experiment and interview within four hours. Given these limitations, one experimental system, described in section 5, as well as a specified detail level of the system solution, was chosen.

The experiment subjects were of two categories. The first category was safety experts and the second was Ph.D. students doing research in embedded automotive systems. The experiment subjects were divided into two sets, of which one started with the ESA method and the other started with the FFA based method.

All subjects were asked to conduct a hazard analysis for the purpose of identifying the hazards based on their given role as an engineer responsible for the safety of the system. The researcher's interference during the experiment was limited to clarifying questions regarding the system specification and the two method instructions.

The results of the experiment and the time spent on each method were logged in a spreadsheet.

The interviews were conducted to further investigate opinions and thoughts about the methods and hazard identification in general as well as to explore the potential bias of the subjects. Hence, an interview was held with each subject.

The qualitative data from the experiment and the questionnaire were analyzed for descriptive statistics. The statistical test (the Wilcoxon matched-pairs signed ranks test [11] with $p=0.05$) was used for testing the hypothesis on the basis of the results of the questionnaire and the measured times.

After completion of the experiment with all subjects, the "Golden Run" was updated. Further, the questionnaire and interview data were compiled in a spreadsheet.

The three data sources were used to verify the results, with the emphasis being on the interviews with the expert safety group. Further, the results of the analysis were discussed to evaluate the suitability of the methods for the given context.

3.1 Validity Evaluation

There are two basic threats to validity in this study. The first is that the sizes of the subject categories are small, and the subjects have similar backgrounds. The second is the limited size of the experiment system. However, threats to validity can be discussed in terms of Conclusion, External, Internal and Construct validity according to [11].

Conclusion validity. The subjects received the same introductory lecture and were given the same material. It is thus unlikely that the subjects perceive the system and the methods differently, influencing the results excessively. However, the answers of human subjects are used and the measures gathered are therefore not fully repeatable.

Another threat is that the chosen statistical test has too low a power, which results in a false hypothesis not being rejected. However, the Wilcoxon matched-pairs signed ranks test used in the analysis is a well known instrument and is a non-parametric alternative to the paired t-test. Measuring dependent variables is a threat to conclusion validity when treated as independent variables in the statistical analysis. However, in this study the criteria are fairly orthogonal and the interviews have been used for verification.

Internal validity. Instrumentation, such as the questionnaire and interview technique, may be flawed. However, this is mitigated with triangulation with both qualitative and quantitative data. Further, the subjects are neutral to the research question and are therefore not constrained in their answers. Further, they all have a background in research oriented work and thus have limited their potential bias.

The subjects' maturity in conducting the second method may also be a threat since the same experiment system is used for both methods and a subject can learn from the first method. This is mitigated by dividing the subjects into two sets, one starting with the ESA method and the other starting with the FFA method, which should balance this effect.

Construct validity. Interviews and questionnaires developed during the pre-study are dependent on subjective measurements, which are difficult to define using a scale.

However, the questionnaire is designed to be as non-leading as possible and to reflect only the opinion of the subject himself.

Mono-method bias is avoided by utilizing several methods for measuring. However, since a single system is used in this experiment, there is a risk that the choice of the system influences the results more than the methods under evaluation. However, since the system was simple, the subjects could focus on the methods instead of the system. The experiment was conducted with one subject at a time and the researcher was present during the experiment to observe. Further, the subjects may be biased towards one of the methods and thereby intentionally favor it, although no indication of this was observed during the interviews.

The researcher has contributed to the development of the adapted FFA, but acknowledged this from the beginning. Further, the researcher did not answer questions during the experiment, except to clarify the methods and the system solution. The subjects had limited or no earlier experience from the methods.

External validity. The important generalization in this study is to determine the applicability and efficiency of the methods in the automotive domain.

The subjects shall represent the total population of all engineers that may receive the task of carrying out the method. In this study, the subjects are chosen from two categories. The first category, safety experts from the automotive industry, is chosen for their competence and experience. Further, the three safety experts are employed by three different companies, all working in the Swedish national ISO standardization group for ISO-26262. The second category of subjects is Ph.D. students, who are active in automotive embedded system research, and represent engineers who could be assigned to conducting a hazard analysis in the industry. By making this selection, the two major industrial user groups are represented. However, the group is small and may therefore not be completely representative of the total population. Further, the system that is used in this experiment is representative for the automotive domain, although simplified.

4 Description of the Methods

Two following sections will give background and approach descriptions.

4.1 The ESA Method

The ESA method is based on the assumption that all hazards of the system originate from the environment. The method is fully described in European Space Agency standard PSS-01-403 [7] and is aimed at space applications. However, other industries have found it to be useful, including the automotive industry, where it is currently used.

The approach is to provide a set of generic hazards that should be applied to the system's components and characteristics in order to derive the induced possible failure behavior, hence hazards. The generic hazard list is the key to the method. It consists of environmentally based hazard inducers such as "AB2-high temperature". Since the origin of the method is the space industry, the generic hazards have been influenced by this. As a consequence, generic hazards such as "Zero gravity" should be disregarded when it is applied to an automotive system. The ESA method is also extensive and covers hazard analysis for all stages of product development. However, given the scope of this paper, the method is applied as described to a conceptual design.

In addition to hazard identification, the ESA method's hazard analysis also specifies how to determine exposure, severity etc. These parts have been removed within the scope of this study. A few generic hazards have also been added that concern malfunctioning of processors and electrical networks [13].

4.2 The Adapted FFA Method

The adapted FFA method is derived from FFA, Functional Failure Analysis, described in aerospace standard ARP-4761 [5]. However, the method was adapted by Papadopoulos et al. [6] and further enhanced for the automotive domain by Johannessen et al. [8] [12]. It is based on the assumption that the only part of a system capable of affecting the environment is the actuator. Hence, by applying failure modes to the actuators, the system's hazards and their effects can be determined. By extending the analysis to also include the functionality itself, multiple failure induced hazards can be covered.

The generic failure modes are driven by the guide words Omission, Commission, Late, Early, Less, More, and Stuck. These guide words refer to the behavior of an actuator in comparison to the intended behavior. In this study, the set of guide words has been simplified to include only Omission and Commission in order to limit the time needed for the analysis. This is further discussed in section 7.2.2.

This method has, as well as the ESA method, a part that determines a severity rating, and hence this part has been removed to serve the context of this study [13].

5 Experimental Set Up

To be able to evaluate the two methods, one experiment system was needed. The following requirements for the system were identified:

- Relevant – The system should be in the automotive context.
- Simple – In order to limit the number of potential hazards.
- Easy to understand – To be able to complete the study in a reasonable time.
- Granularity – The system should be available on several detail levels.

Some limitations of the system were also made in order to match the early design phase automotive context. The power supply was removed since both methods cover this as a failure mode or a generic hazard. Further, the diagnostic system was removed since this may not yet be decided in the early stages of development.

Of three candidate systems, the Electrical Steering Column Lock was found to be the most suitable.

5.1 Electrical Steering Column Lock System

The electrical steering column lock system has the purpose of prohibiting theft of the vehicle by locking the steering wheel when no valid key is present. It is a mechatronic system but has the same basic functionality as a traditional mechanical column lock. The system includes a sensor for reading the presence of a valid key, an ECU for computations, and an actuator controlling the column lock.

The system was developed in four levels of detail spanning from a solution with two interacting ECUs and signal sequence diagrams to a rudimentary solution with only one ECU, an actuator, and a sensor. In order not to favor one of the methods a detail level including one ECU, basic signals, and a CAN network was chosen, as shown in Figure 3.

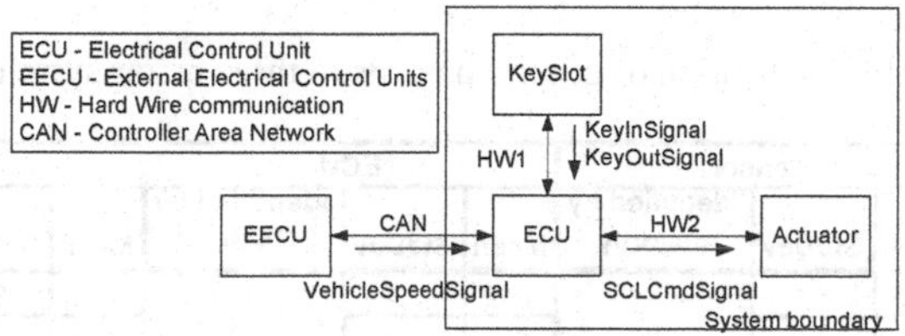

Fig. 3. The Electrical Steering Column system overview

In addition to the conceptual design, the functionality was described in UML use cases. The use cases of the system are two scenarios or functionality modes, Lock and Unlock.

6 Empirical Data

This section gives the empirical data collected in the experiment and data from the questionnaire and interviews. The analysis and discussion are found in Sections 7 and Section 8. The study includes in total seven subjects, four Ph.D. students and three safety experts.

Table 2 presents the vehicle phases that the subjects identified. The vehicle phase is a key element in both methods and it is therefore important that it is identified correctly.

Table 2. Vehicle phases identified in the experiment

Vehicle phase	PhD students	Safety Experts	All
"Vehicle moving"	4	3	7
"Vehicle standing still"	4	3	7
"Vehicle moving with valid key"	1	1	2
"Vehicle standing still with valid key"	1	1	2

Table 3 shows the results of the hazard identification experiment for the two methods. The data are presented in number of subjects who identified the hazards, both in each group and as a total.

Table 3. Hazards identified in the experiment

	PhD students		Safety Experts		All	
Hazard	ESA	FFA	ESA	FFA	ESA	FFA
"System locks the steering when vehicle is moving."	4	4	3	3	7	7
"System does not unlock when vehicle starts to move"	3	3	2	2	5	5

Table 4 shows the mean and standard deviation of the number of generic hazards that were identified as applicable, compared to the number of hazards identified by the majority, i.e. by at least four of the subjects.

Table 4. Data for application of generic hazards to three major system components

	Sensor			ECU			Actuator		
Group	**Mean**	**StdDev**	**Identified by majority**	**Mean**	**StdDev**	**Identified by Majority**	**Mean**	**StdDev**	**Identified by majority**
PhD students	14,5	6,1	8	14,8	3,1	11	13,3	3,6	10
Safety Experts	9,7	0,9		8,3	2,1		9,0	1,6	
All	12,4	5,2		12,0	4,2		11,4	3,6	

The questionnaire results are presented in Table 5 and Table 6 for the ESA and the FFA method with descriptive statistics.

In Table 5 adjustment was made of one subject's time for the ESA method since the task was abandoned before completion. The task was judged to be 50% complete; hence the time was multiplied by two, indicated by a '*' in the table.

Table 5. Empirical data for the ESA method collected in the questionnaire

ESA method	PhD Students		Safety Experts		All		Scale
Property	Mean	Std dev	Mean	Std dev	Mean	Std dev	
Ease of use	4,3	1,3	2,7	0,5	3,6	1,3	1=Easy..5=Hard
Understandability	3,0	0,7	2,7	0,5	2,9	0,6	1=Easy..5=Hard
Percieved confidence	3,0	1,0	2,0	0,8	2,6	1,0	1=Weak..5=Strong
Spent time	148,3	4,9	103,3 *	17,0	129,0	25,1	Minutes
Number of subjects	4		3		7		Persons

Table 6. Empirical data for the FFA method collected in the questionnaire

FFA method	PhD Students		Safety Experts		All		Scale
Property	Mean	Std dev	Mean	Std dev	Mean	Std dev	
Ease of use	2,0	0,0	1,3	0,5	1,7	0,5	1=Easy..5=Hard
Understandability	2,5	0,9	1,3	0,5	2,0	0,9	1=Easy..5=Hard
Percieved confidence	2,8	0,4	4,3	0,5	3,4	0,9	1=Weak..5=Strong
Spent time	57,5	17,5	45,0	4,1	52,1	14,8	Minutes
Number of subjects	4		3		7		Persons

Hypothesis H_X was tested for the applicable criteria presented in the Table 1. For the total population, the hypotheses $H_{\text{Ease of use}}$ and $H_{\text{Spent time}}$ can be rejected according to the Wilcoxon matched-pairs signed ranks test with p=0.05. Hence, there is a difference in the means with regard to ease of use and time spent in the two methods.

Table 7 shows how many lines in the spreadsheet were needed by each method to evaluate the system. A line in the spreadsheet corresponds to a potential hazard that must be considered in the analysis.

Table 7. Lines in spreadsheet to be evaluated for identification of a hazard

System Characteristic	ESA	FFA
ECU	48	-
Actuator	46	8
Sensor	48	-
Functionality	-	8

7 Analysis

The first part of this analysis discusses the empirical results and the second part discusses the characteristics of each method.

7.1 Analysis of the Empirical Results

Table 2 presents the phases identified by the subjects to be relevant for the test system: "Vehicle moving", "Vehicle standing still" or the equivalent of these.

Further, two subjects identified the presence of a valid key as giving another dimension to the vehicle phase and hence concluded that four vehicle phases were relevant. It is important for the subsequent analysis to have correctly identified the right vehicle phases. The phases should describe the vehicle states that are relevant for the functionality under analysis.

The results of the hazard identification experiment are given in Table 3 and the following functional hazards were identified with both the ESA and FFA methods by all subjects: *"The system locks the steering when the vehicle is moving."* or derivates thereof. Further, five of seven subjects identified the hazard *"System does not unlock when a driver inserts the key and starts the vehicle"* or derivates thereof using the ESA method. One of the subjects, who did not identify the last hazard, completed only half of the task due to time constraints. The second hazard was also identified by five of seven subjects using the FFA method. However, for both subjects that did not identify the second hazard, the first hazard was formulated such that it implicitly covered the second hazard. The hazards identified were compared to the Golden Run and it was concluded that all functional hazards were found.

Some of the subjects also identified hazards not related to the system's functions utilizing the ESA method. One example is *"Driver may get an electric shock from the key slot"*. Since these hazards are not functional hazards and are outside the electrical system's boundary, they are not focused on in this paper.

The ESA method relies on the generic hazards and their application to the system's characteristics. Table 4 shows that there is a major difference in how many generic hazards are identified. On average, 12.4 generic hazards were identified to be applicable to the sensor component of the experiment system. However, only 64% of them were identified by more than four persons.

Hypothesis $H_{\text{Ease of use}}$ was rejected and given the averages shown in Table 5 and Table 6. It is concluded that the FFA method is statistically significantly easier to use than the ESA method, according to the subjects.

It was difficult for the subjects to fully complete the ESA method within a reasonable time. A limitation had to be included stating that only three hazards for each System Characteristic should be evaluated. The test subjects decided which three of the possible hazards were to be evaluated. This decreased the actual time needed to complete the ESA method. Hypothesis $H_{\text{Time spent}}$ was still rejected and, when the information in Table 5 and Table 6 is combine, it can therefore be concluded that the FFA method was less time consuming, with a mean completion time of 52.1 minutes.

However, with respect to the criterion of Understandability and Confidence, the hypothesis could not be rejected. Hence, the study can not conclude that any method is better in these regards.

As a system's size and complexity increases, the demands on scalability of the methods will be higher. Table 7 shows the number of lines in a spreadsheet that must be evaluated in order to identify the relevant hazards. The ESA method requires more than eight times as many lines as the FFA method.

7.2 Experiences from the Methods

This section will discuss the characteristics of the two methods. The material is based on the interviews and the pre-study results.

ESA method experiences. When the generic hazards are applied to the system characteristics, there is always a question of whether the hazards are applicable.

As presented in Table 4, there are considerable differences among the test subjects' engineering judgment of which generic hazards should be applied to each system characteristic type. Hence, an uncertainty exists which creates a possible threat of inconsistency. One subject identified the problem as "The relevance and effect of certain generic hazards are difficult to determine".

However, it is apparent that a skilled engineer needs to utilize his judgment to identify the relevant hazards among all those generated. There is no guidance as to what level these generic hazards should be applied. Further, some generic hazards, such as "zero gravity", are not suitable for the automotive domain. This could however be remedied by further adapting the list to the automotive domain. The generic hazards also exist on different levels. It should be possible to remove some of the generic hazards since they only cause other generic hazards. One example is the generic hazard of "wetness", which can lead to the generic hazards "short circuit" and "high current". The list of generic hazards is said to be non exhaustive and should build on experience from earlier projects as well as actual failure data.

On the other hand, the generic hazards can easily be reused. Most systems today include at least one ECU, a network, a sensor, and an actuator. All these component types could have specified hazard profiles, eliminating a part of the engineering task.

Further, the ESA method does not consider the functionality in itself. This is not apparent in this experiment since there is an input signal that triggers the functionality; hence this signal's hazards will coincide with the functionality's hazard.

FFA method experiences. The engineering judgment in this method is related to the application of the generic failure modes and the interpretations of these guide words.

In this experiment, only two guide words were used since "Omission" and "Commission" can be considered to cover the other proposed guide words. This is possible since "Late" and "Early" add a time aspect to the actuator's behavior, which can be considered to be omission or commission. "Less", "More", and "Stuck" can be interpreted in a similar manner depending on the situation. Further, this reasoning is strengthened by the available information regarding the actuators behavior perhaps not being sufficiently detailed in this early design phase. However, if the time aspect is introduced, e.g. by adding "Late" and "Earlier", the spreadsheet lines in Table 7 would increase by 100%, but the identification rate of the second hazard, presented in Table 3, would probably increase. This would also increase the time required to conduct the FFA method but would most likely not reach the level of time required by the ESA method.

8 Evaluation

The importance of identifying the major hazards as early as possible implies that a good hazard identification method should be well structured and repeatable. This study shows that both methods are capable of solving the hazard identification task and do so with a well defined structure for guiding the engineer. Thus both methods are considered to be applicable in the automotive context.

While the study has provided a basis for an informed selection, in this section we also present our evaluation of which method is most suitable in the context of the early design phase in the automotive industry.

As a basis for this evaluation, the three data sources have been triangulated where applicable. As can be seen in Table 8, the FFA method is preferred for most of the evaluation criteria. Further, a qualitative evaluation is given below to place the results in an overall perspective.

Table 8. Triangulation of criteria evaluation

Evaluation criteria	Experiment	Questionnaire	Interview
Ease of use	FFA	FFA	FFA
Efficiency	FFA	N/A	FFA
Understandability	N/A	Undecided	Undecided
Confidence	N/A	Undecided	Undecided
Level of engineering judgment	FFA	N/A	FFA
Scalability	FFA	N/A	Undecided

Given that the method is applicable it must also be easy to use to be of value in an industrial setting. As shown in this study, the FFA method is clearly considered to be easier to use than the ESA method.

Understandability is primarily important for estimating the level of training needed when the method is introduced in an organization. However, this study cannot show any difference between the two methods. Nevertheless, both methods can be argued to be easy to learn, since the subjects in this study learned how to use the methods, conducted the analysis, and were interviewed within four hours.

The two methods rely on engineering judgment to different extents. It is important to minimize the necessary experience since engineers at different levels of experience may be assigned the task of hazard identification. As the study shows, the application of generic hazards, which the ESA method uses, is highly dependent on experience. However, this may be compensated for by a standard library of generic hazards that should be applied to certain system characteristics or components.

As the study also shows, the ESA approach results in many potential hazards, and it is up to the engineer to decide which of them are valid. The approach of the FFA method is also inductive but, by applying common failure modes to the relevant parts of the system, fewer potential hazards are derived. Since both methods identify the relevant hazards, it can be concluded that the FFA method is more efficient. Another aspect is that the FFA method scales better when the method is applied to larger systems. While the FFA method can be handled within a spreadsheet for large systems, the ESA method would need specialized software to support ease of use.

Both methods are affected by engineering judgment regarding identifying the necessary vehicle phases. This is unavoidable but can be mitigated with a catalogue of standard vehicle phases, which can be provided by standards.

As the empirical data clearly shows, the ESA method takes considerably more time to complete than the FFA method in this experiment. Hence the FFA method is concluded to be the most suitable, among the two evaluated methods, for conducting hazard identification in a PHA in the automotive context.

However, the interviews indicate the ESA method to be a better basis for deriving safety requirements. Reasons for this could be that the method gives a deeper understanding of the system design and that it works at a more detailed level.

9 Conclusions

The two methods, ESA and FFA, for hazard identification in a PHA are found to be applicable to the automotive system context. Further, the results of the experiment conducted show with statistical significance that the FFA method is less time consuming and easier to use than the ESA method for detection of the same hazards. Hence, the FFA method is found to be the most efficient method for hazard identification in early phases of development.

Acknowledgments

This research has been partially funded by the Swedish Automotive Research Program. The authors would also like to thank the safety experts and the Ph.D. students for their participation and ideas.

References

1. International Electro-technical Commission: IEC-61508: Functional safety of electrical / electronic / programmable electronic safety-related Systems. IEC, (1998)
2. Storey, N.: Safety-Critical Computer Systems. Addison Wesley Longman, Essex, (1996)
3. The Motor Industry Software Reliability Association: Development Guidelines for Vehicle Based Software. MISRA, (1994)
4. International Organization for Standardization: ISO WD 26262, ISO, (2006)
5. Society of Automotive Engineers: ARP-4761: Aerospace Recommended Practice: Guidelines and Methods for Conducting the Safety Assessment Process on Civil Airborne Systems and Equipment. SAE, (1996)
6. UK Ministry of Defence: HAZOP Studies on Systems Containing Programmable Electronics, UK Ministry of Defence, Glasgow, (2000)
7. European Space Agency: PSS-01-403: Hazard Analysis and Safety Risk Assessment, ESA, (1989)
8. Johannessen, P., Grante, C., Alminger, A., Eklund, U.: Hazard Analysis in Object Oriented Design of Dependable Systems. Proceedings of the 2001 International Conference on Dependable Systems and Networks, IEEE CS Press, (2001)
9. Levesons, N.: *Safeware: System Safety and Computers*, Addison-Wesley Publishing Company, Reading, MA, (1995)
10. Papadopoulos, Y., McDermid, J.A., Hierarchically Performed Hazard Origin and Propagation Studies. Proceedings of SAFECOMP'99, 18Th International Conference on Computer Safety, Reliability and Security, Toulouse, (1999)

11. Wohlin, C., Runeson, P., Höst, M., Ohlsson, M.C., Regnell, B., Wesslén, A.: Experimentation in Software Engineering. Kluwer Academic Publishers, Norwell, (2000)
12. Johannessen, P., Törner, F., Torin, J.: Actuator Based Hazard Analysis for Safety Critical Systems. Proceedings of SAFECOMP´04, 23rd International Conference on Computer Safety, Reliability and Security, Potsdam, (2004)
13. F. Törner: Hazard Identification Methods. Technical Report no: 2006:11 Chalmers University of Technology, Gothenburg, (2006)

A Tool for Databus Safety Analysis Using Fault Injection

Dawid Trawczynski[1], Janusz Sosnowski[1], and Janusz Zalewski[2]

[1] Institute of Computer Science, Warsaw University of Technology,
Nowowiejska 15/19, 00-665 Warsaw, Poland
{d.trawczynski, jss}@ii.pw.edu.pl
[2] Computer Science Department, Florida Gulf Coast University,
Fort Mayers, FL 33965-6565, USA
zalewski@fgcu.edu

Abstract. In real-time safety-critical systems, it is important to predict the consequences of specific faults in databus logic and driver software on the safe operation of a databus. For this purpose we have developed a test-bench based on the TrueTime simulator extended by adding a fault injection capability, with new network models and fault modeling strategy. Faults are simulated by disturbing specified parameters of the databus model. In this paper, we present the modeling approach, the fault injection scenarios, and illustrate it with examples of the impact of the simulated faults on data throughput, message latency and bus scheduling for CAN and TTCAN networks.

1 Introduction

The communication standards in real-time safety, critical systems should assure high dependability; hence there arises the problem of the definition and verification of safety requirements. This paper presents a new approach to evaluate safety-critical network interfaces in the context of their performance capabilities, based on the TrueTime simulator developed at Lund Institute of Technology [3,7] and extended in our Institute. Previous research [2,8] has shown that performance alone cannot guarantee safety, but system's performance evaluation can provide meaningful insights into dependability and safety aspects only when evaluated in an appropriate context. Various fault injection scenarios presented in [5] and in this paper facilitate dependability and safety assessment.

The TrueTime simulator allows us to model the system under test and its interaction with the external environment. In our case we simulate communication interface of a distributed network and its environment, which is a set of real-time operating system kernels (in the network nodes) that process data transferred via the network interfaces. The simulation process can be supplemented with the specified application algorithms that communicate with the kernel models. This is assured by S-function programming (due to Simulink and Matlab used in TrueTime). It facilitates creation of specific interfaces that can be used to transfer application data to and from the operating system kernel data structures. We have extended the network interface model with fault injection capabilities for dependability assessment purposes.

J. Górski (Ed.): SAFECOMP 2006, LNCS 4166, pp. 261 – 274, 2006.

In our approach we generate abstract state-space models of the studied network protocols and analyze their behavior in the presence of injected faults, simulated by disturbing model variables. The results of fault injection scenarios are compared with fault-free cases. This approach is useful in the analysis of fault effect propagation and identification of critical paths within the state space models of the network protocols.

In the next three sections, we present the simulation network model, our new fault injection model and experimental results that show the impact of the faults on the performance of network interfaces. The last section presents the conclusion and suggestions for the future research.

2 Modeling and Simulation Approach

All simulations within the TrueTime simulator are performed according to the following steps. First, all necessary distributed environment entities are instantiated by the user. The user determines the number of nodes, the type of the communication network and then instantiates the appropriate kernel, network interface and fault model entities. Next, the user enables the simulation and all control algorithms described by necessary application tasks. Those tasks are executed with the help of the associated kernel entities.

The most important model for our simulations is the network interface model. When initializing a specific network model a user specifies an instance of the model. This instance of a network model forms an entity that follows a specific network interface behavioral model. The TrueTime network interface entities function as units under test. Each behavioral model is configured during simulation initialization phase in which the user specifies configuration parameters for each network entity. These parameters include network interface type, data throughput rate, communication schedule, total number of nodes that utilize the given network model, bit error probability in the communication channel, etc. After the initialization, messages can be exchanged among nodes that belong to a specific network model instance.

In addition to the network entities our simulations also instantiate necessary kernel entities. Each kernel entity in a simulation models the functionality of a physical real-time operating system. The kernel model is quite complex. The most important mechanism of the kernel model is the task scheduling mechanism which defines task triggering, suspension and execution points in time. Tasks triggered by kernel entities are of the following types: network interface, operating system, or application. Network related interface tasks are those responsible for transmission and reception of data and servicing of some network interrupts. Operating systems tasks are tasks directly responsible for the management of computational resources. Application tasks are tasks that execute the application or high-level, user control algorithms.

The developed fault injection functionality is modeled as fault entities (they disturb network performance parameters) embedded within the network interface entities. Figure 1 presents an example of a distributed simulation environment with a network interface, kernel and fault entities instantiated. In this diagram a tree like architecture can be observed for each entity; namely its associated tasks, task segments and data variables. The original TrueTime provides only selected and simplified models of the kernel and network interfaces (K_i and I_i on the diagram). The application model A_i has to be defined by the user. We have also defined the fault injection model (its instance F_i is shown in fig. 1). Details of the fault model are presented in section 3. In section 2.1, we describe in more detail how the actual modeling and simulation are performed in TrueTime with explicit emphasis on the network interface. In section 2.2 we present the bus access technique for CAN interface.

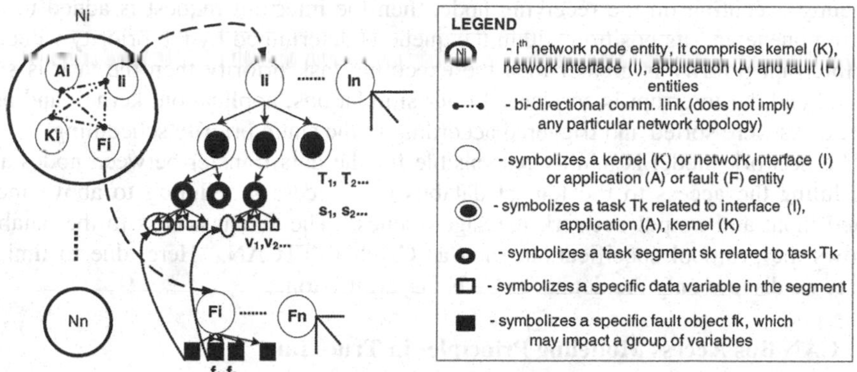

Fig. 1. Model of a distributed network and associated entities with their structures

The authors of the TrueTime simulator concentrated on applications for discrete automatic control [5]. Some details regarding the models used in the simulator are described in [3] and are mainly related to the task structural, scheduling and timing models of TrueTime. Network interface modeling is described rather vaguely, so here we present a more elaborated network model, in the context of dependability issues.

2.1 Network Interface Model in TrueTime

In the TrueTime simulator the kernel model reflects a physical real-time operating system whose function is to handle internal and external interrupts and trigger tasks according to the appropriate scheduling policy. Interrupts and task triggering instances are all modeled as events and therefore the kernel model is an event model. All events that need to be serviced by the kernel are temporally ordered according to the global simulator time t_{sim}; this is the simulated real-time variable, which synchronizes all events in the kernel.

The kernel is a process, which executes periodic and aperiodic tasks according to a specific schedule. In the TrueTime each task T_k executed on kernel K_i is divide into segments. Segments are task intervals with specified worst-case execution times. After triggering a task by the simulator the kernel executes its segments sequentially. The calls to the network interfaces take place in task segments. An example of such interface is the call to the `ttSendMsg()` function. A call to this function schedules a network interrupt and transmits data via a logical channel. This channel is formed by a pair of queues (input and output) - at least one queue pair exists.

The input queue is responsible for receiving local node messages generated by kernel tasks, whereas the output queue receives messages from all nodes in the network.

During the transmission, a message is first stored in the input queue and when a task gains access to the channel, this message is removed from the input queue and appended to the output queue of the corresponding reception node. When a node receives a message, it also receives an interrupt from the network entity. This interrupt is then serviced by an appropriate interrupt handling function. A priority value may be assigned to the handling function. If this value is lower then the priority of a task currently executing on the receiving node, then the interrupt request is added to the waiting queue and its position within the queue is determined by the priority value. If the interrupt priority is greater then the executing task priority then the task is suspended and the interrupt is serviced. In our simulations, application, kernel, and network tasks were sorted and triggered according to the static priority scheduling.

The network model is mainly responsible for the data transfer between nodes and scheduling the access to the logical databus (i.e. access scheduling to above mentioned input and output network message queues). The actual access to the databus follows the protocol specification, such as CAN or TTCAN. Here, due to limited space, we discuss only the details of CAN bus arbitration.

2.2 CAN Bus Access Modeling Principles in TrueTime

In the CAN databus, bus access occurs on the first-come first-served basis. If during a simulation, two task messages try to access the databus at the same time interval, the access problem is resolved through message contention. The task with higher priority message wins the contention, the losing task backs off for a certain amount of time and later tries again to gain the access to the databus. This bus access strategy is then followed by the data transmission. Next we explain essential steps performed by the CAN state machine before every transmission.

The protocol first determines if anyone has been transmitting on the bus in the previous event instance. If a node has been transmitting on the bus during the currently handled event, the protocol attempts to continue this transmission. Let us assume that during the execution of task T_i a new event occurs related to transmission of task T_j. If the priority of task T_j is greater than T_i then the task T_i is suspended till the execution of the higher priority task transmission. In the opposite case task T_i is continued (including its transmissions) and then lower priority transmission of the second task will be executed.

When the transmission is finished the receiving node protocol must make a decision where to put the data. If the transmitter designates a message as a unicast message then this message is appended to the output queue of only one receiver. In the other case (broadcast), the message is appended to all output queues of all nodes in the network. After this the transmitter node sets necessary state variables to indicate that the transmission is finished and the transmitting node is now idle.

Note that events in the event queue of the simulator are either generated by network, kernel or application entities. Some events are detected by an event sampling operation which detects changing signals at the input ports of entities (i.e., network interface inputs) and others may be specified explicitly by setting the *Next Hit* event variable. A detection of an event with the *Next Hit* variable is possible through a special MATLAB function `detect_zero_crossing()`. This function detects a zero difference between t_{sim} and t_{event} = *Next Hit*. Therefore detection of events can occur in two ways – either through constant entity input sampling or value adjustment of the *Next Hit*. After a detection of an event, a Simulink engine invokes a MATLAB function `mdlOuputs`. This function updates all outputs associated with the detected event. The event detection, evaluation and update processes continue within a loop until the simulation terminating time is reached.

In cases when the databus is not occupied, i.e., no one has been transmitting on the bus during the last event time, appropriate state variables are checked to see if any node has messages waiting in their input queues. If so, the protocol prepares for a new transmission on the bus. This means that the protocol once again checks the bus to see if the bus is still idle and if this is true then it designates the node wishing to transmit as the transmitting node. The *Next Hit* is then updated (taking into account the predicted transmission time), so that when the protocol executes at the next event interval it will know that a node has been transmitting on the bus in the past. If during bus

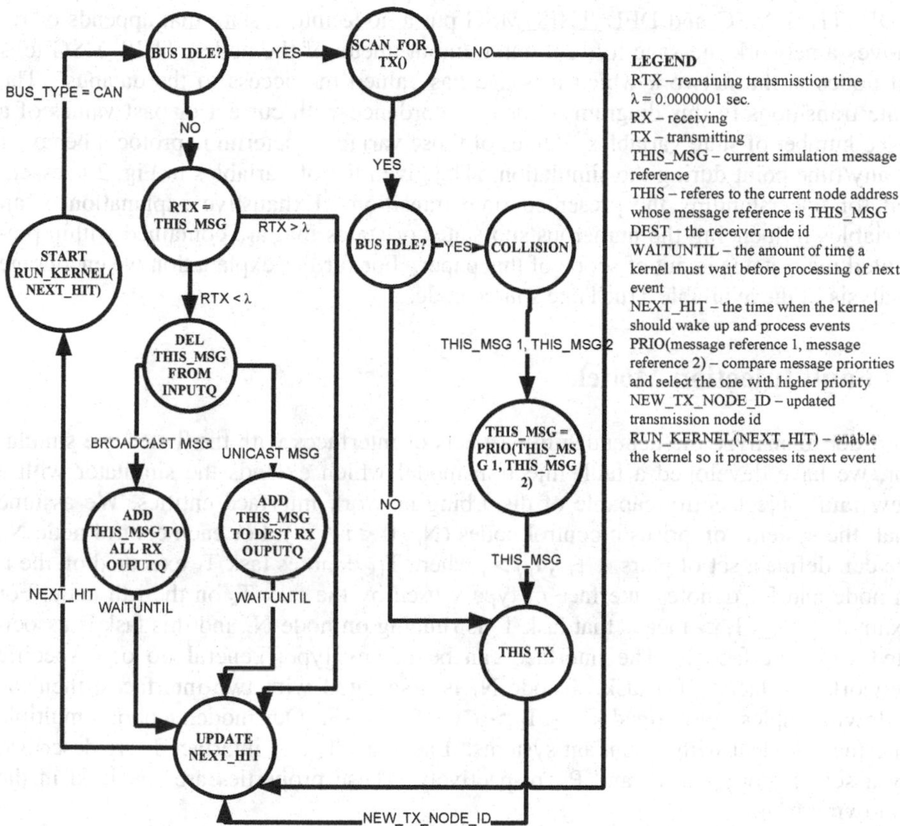

Fig. 2. CAN state diagram

occupation analysis, the protocol determines that someone else is trying to access the databus, then it compares both message priorities and goes into a contention process.

The winning node transmits the message, the loser stops requesting transmission and awaits some time before it attempts again to transmit. This gives an overview of the simulated CAN model. Figure 2 presents a simplified CAN state machine description. This state machine description contains only 12 most relevant states for the purpose of understanding CAN's control flow. Such machines are created for all nodes. They communicate via appropriate variables.

The START state initializes all protocol variables. The BUS IDLE state determines if the bus is currently idle. The SCAN_FOR_TX state allows each node in the network to check if any other node is currently accessing the databus. The COLLISION state puts the protocol in a contention mode if two or more nodes (in fig.2 collision is shown for two nodes – branch with THIS_MSG1 THIS_MSG2) attempt to access the databus at the same time interval. When a node is in the THIS_TX state then all other nodes in the network will see that node as the one that has gained access to the databus. When a node is in the UPDATE_NEXT_HIT state this means that it has finished processing of a job and needs to update future event processing time. ADD_THIS_MSG and DEL_THIS_MSG put a node into a state that appends or removes a network message to/from output/input queue of the node. THIS_MSG tells all nodes in the network which message has gained the access to the databus. The state transitions in this diagram occur in accordance with current or past values of a large number of state variables. Values of those variables determine protocol behavior at any time point during the simulation. The given list of variables in Fig. 2 is essential for understanding the presented state transitions. Exhaustive explanation of all variables influencing the numerous sub-states or states that are contained within presented main states is out of scope of this paper. For further explanation we encourage analysis of the available TrueTime source code.

3 Fault Injection Model

In order to analyze the dependability aspects of interfaces with the TrueTime simulator, we have developed a fault injection model which extends the simulator with a new fault object entity capable of disturbing network interface entities. We assume that the system comprises n control nodes (N_i , $0 < i \leq n$). For each control node N_i, we can define a set of pairs $< T_{i,k}, I_{i,y} >$, where $T_{i,k}$ denotes task T_k executed on the i-th node and $I_{i,y}$ denotes interface of type y used by the task T_k on the i-th node. For example, $<T_{1,2}, I_{1,1}>$ means that task T_2 is running on node N_1 and this task is associated with interface I_1. The interface can be of any type: general i/o or a specific network interface. If a task of node N_1 is associated with two interfaces, then the following tuples are defined $<T_{1,2}, I_{1,1}> \cap <T_{1,2}, I_{1,2}>$. Our model supports multiple interfaces to deal with redundant systems. Each task T_k and interface I_y are described by a set of properties P_k and P_y, respectively. These properties are specified in the following form:

$$P_k : <t_d, t_{wcet}, p, r, S, \mathbf{F}_k >, P_y : <t_d, t_{wcet}, p, r, S, \mathbf{F}_y>$$

where t_d is the task's relative deadline, t_{wcet} is task's worst-case execution time (it is calculated as the sum of the worst-case execution time of all segments belonging to the considered task), p is the task period, r is the task priority, $\mathbf{F}_k$ and $\mathbf{F}_y$ are sets of the simulated fault vectors for the considered task and interface. The fault vectors are defined as 5-tuple: <f_{typ}, f_d, f_p, f_{occ}, f_{rand}>. Each element of the vector specifies value of the corresponding variable describing fault properties. They are explained in the next section. If a particular variable (parameter) is not applicable, then its value is set to 0.

3.1 Description of Fault Parameters

In the previous section we have introduced the fault vector composed of a set of 5 parameters (variables). These parameters are defined as follows:

- f_{typ} ≡ `flt_type` designates which fault from the fault type set **G** = {$type_1$,$type_2$,$type_3$,…} is to be utilized by the model, where the parameter value is the fault enumeration value or $type_1 \equiv 1$.
- f_d ≡ `flt_dur` is the fault duration; specified by time moments corresponding to variable disturbance (simulating fault) and its recovery to the previous state;
- f_p ≡ `flt_per` is the fault period and specifies the time between consecutive fault activations of the same fault type;
- f_{occ} ≡ `flt_nbr_occ` specifies the maximal number of fault activations;
- f_{rand} ≡ `flt_rand` specifies the random properties of fault activation; if `flt_rand` is set to 0, it means that the fault element is deterministic; if this value is set to 1, then the fault's activation pattern follows uniform distribution; if `flt_rand` is set to 2, then the fault element activation pattern follows Gaussian distribution; therefore, if `flt_rand` > 0 our model effectively sets `flt_per` and `flt_dur` according to a probabilistic distribution desired by the user - currently only time is supported by probabilistic activation; values of `flt_nbr_occ` and `flt_type` cannot be set explicitly as probabilistic but future improvements of our model will include this possibility.

In a general case where our fault model ($f_{rand} > 0$) probabilistically adjusts all parameters of fault vector F, we define a fault transformation operator *RFT{.,}*, which generates appropriate values of these parameters. In the performed simulations our objective was to trace the effect of selected (*a priori*) fault element F in relevance to the network safety and performance. In order to accomplish this, the elements in the set of considered fault vectors **F** were transformed only partially. This means that only activation times of F may be random, but `fault_type` parameter in F is deterministic, i.e., we know what faults types will occur but possibly not their activation and duration time. Transforming all fault parameters render the actual nature and timing of faults unpredictable.

In the paper we describe fault models which disturb only network interface entities. This means that faults affect interface functions, which allow application and kernel tasks to interact with the network model. When an application task calls one of the network interface functions, it effectively passes control to the appropriate safety-critical communication protocol. Once this redirection of the control is performed, the respective protocol state machine model is responsible for scheduling a databus access and message transmission. Our faults are injected at the state machine level. In the sequel, we explain the logic of fault injection at this lower level of abstraction for some of the faults implemented in our model.

At the lower level of abstraction our fault types disturb protocol state machines, namely, their respective state variables. An interesting problem is mapping physical faults into logical ones. We deal with this problem in the on-going research.

3.2 State Variable Level

Below we present a more detailed explanation of some state variables, which we disturb in experiments. This approach addresses specific logical faults at the lower level of abstraction – the state variable abstraction.

The first state variable that we decided to disturb is the *Broadcast* conditional variable. Setting the value of this variable to 1 means that the protocol is dealing with a broadcast message. Any other value for this variable ≥ 0 designates the node id of the receiving node. Changing the value of this variable will convert a broadcast message to a unicast message or vise versa (wrong id in the unicast transmission is also possible). In cases where unicast messages are converted by a fault to broadcast messages, we expect to increase network interrupt processing delays (the nodes will have to process extra messages regardless of their actual significance). A significant message is a message that contributes to either protocol state machine transition or application state transition. Other messages simply occupy network bandwidth with redundant information.

Another important state variable that we decided to disturb is the *Remaining Number of Bytes for Transmission* conditional variable. Setting this variable to any value tells the state machine how many bytes still need to be transmitted for the message under consideration. Decreasing the value of the considered variable will allow the state machine to cease the data bus access prematurely, increasing the value of this variable extends transmission time. This may cause incomplete message transmission (partial data transmission) or inefficient message transmission (allocated frame size is larger than required for efficient transmission).

The next disturbed state variable in our experiments is the *Remaining Tx Time* conditional variable. This variable specifies how much time is needed for the transmission of a message. Each protocol finite state machine (PFSM) found in each node computes this value separately. A *Remaining Tx Time* ≈ 0 enables the PFSM transition into the next state that appends the transmitted message into the appropriate queue of the receiver. Disturbing this variable we may simulate value and slightly off-specifications faults (compare [1]). For example, if the protocol state machine determined that at 1 Mbps (transmission speed) it will take 0.512 ms to transmit a 64 byte message, then under ideal conditions a complete message transmission occurs at t = 0.512 (assuming that transmission starts at t=0). Inserting a fault into *Remaining Tx Time* by changing this value to 0.500 ms decreases the amount of information transmitted in a message to 500 bits. If the last eight least significant bits of information are shortened from 10110010 to 1011(0000) then the application may interpret an incorrect sensor reading resulting in a slightly off specification error. Faults injected into this state variable are also expected to generate timing errors because in some instances data may not meet its assigned delivery deadline.

Another important variable in our fault injection model is the *Next Hit* conditional variable. Detailed explanation of this variable is given in section 2.2. Increasing the *Next Hit* value (due to a fault) will result in processing the associated event later than expected. Such fault will lead to increased delays experienced by network messages. Under some circumstances excessively delayed messages can be considered invalid by an application. Rejection of late messages often degrades control performance of an application algorithm. This discussion only described a sample of fault types implemented in our model. In addition to the faults mentioned above, we have disturbed state variables that tell the PFSM if the node is currently sending, receiving or in the idle mode of operation. Moreover, we disturbed the message content of a node, and the state variable that tells the PFSM the size of the transmitted message. In addition to those experiments, we also injected a fault into the PFSM variable responsible for network event suspension and activation. In the next section we present a specific simulation scenario and sample results obtained with our fault injection model.

4 Examples of Simulation Results

To illustrate the capability of the implemented model we give some examples of results obtained for CAN and TTCAN networks. Namely, we present the effects of *Next Hit* faults on the global network throughput and node message delay. Finally, we present the effects of *Remaining Tx Time* faults on CAN bus access scheduling.

In our experiments the simulation environment consisted of a distributed network with 8 nodes communicating on a CAN or TTCAN logical data bus. This setup is a good representation of a physical network, and may model a distributed control network in a vehicle active suspension system. As shown in Fig. 1 each node N_i in the simulation environment encapsulated a network interface I_i, an application A_i, a kernel K_i and a fault F_i entity. In order to enable proper simulation of all entities, specific parameters for each entity were configured. When evaluating a simulation experiment the reader must refer to these parameters for correct interpretation of results. Detailed explanation of these parameters can be found in [3].

Data transmission is realized through network interface functions of the simulator. When the application task is ready to send data it calls the `ttSendMsg()` network interface function. If an application is expecting to receive a message from the network interface it calls the `ttGetMsg()` function. When new data arrives at its destination, an interrupt is triggered in the receiving node and the real-time kernel invokes an interrupt handler. The handling task then determines how the received data is processed. In our simulation model, the node forwards the incoming network data to the next node in the network. For example, when node N_i receives a message M from node N_{i-1}, this message generates an interrupt in the node N_i. An interrupt handler function in N_i is invoked and the message is received by the handling function. This handling function then sends the message M again to the next node in the network, namely node N_{i+1}. This type of data flow proceeds in a circular way but still respects the databus scheduling policy of its protocol. This type of traffic flow can model sensor traffic for a shock absorber in an automotive suspension control system. All controller nodes that control the mechanical actuators process this sensor reading and compute appropriate control.

The circular data flow generates a traffic that monotonically increases network congestion. Network congestion in this case refers to the total number of messages W_M waiting in input and output queues of all nodes in the network. Increasing W_M at a rate ΔW_M leads to increased message delays and effectively models traffic flow in physical networks. In our simulations we generated network messages at an exponential rate (in node 1) and measured the associated global network throughput and message delay. The delay has been measured as the difference between the message send and receive time points. This approach effectively measures the application message end-to-end delay. The global network throughput (GNT) and message delay (MD) are calculated according to the following formulas:

$$GNT=\left|\frac{\sum_{i=0}^{Nn} NTXi(Tk)\times MSi-\sum_{i=0}^{Nn} NTXi(T\times(k-1))\times MSi}{T}\right|. \quad (1)$$

$$MD=\left|MSGTXTIME(M)-MSGRXTIME(M)\right|. \quad (2)$$

where NTXi is the total number of databus transmissions performed by the i-th network node at time kT, and k is the integer multiple of period T. This period defines the length of a time interval or its granule for which GNT is computed. In our simulations T has been selected to be small enough so that throughput measurements would be accurate and still efficient. By efficiency we mean that the measurements themselves did not introduce considerable delays due to increased fine grained computational demands by the MATLAB simulator engine. MSi is the size of the message sent by the i-th node. In equation (2) MD represents a delay a single message experiences in a CAN or TTCAN network. MSGTXTIME is the timestamp for the message M, it specifies the time at which an application task invoked the `ttSendMsg()` network interface function. The MSGRXTIME defines the time at which the receiver's application task invoked the `ttGetMsg()` function and obtained the associated message M from the node's associated output queue.

In our experimental network all nodes access a network data bus through the above mentioned interface functions. Each node in our network executes three tasks namely task A_1, A_2, and I_1. Therefore the total number of tasks executing on 8 nodes is 24. A_1 task is a periodic task that generates some data and sends this data to other network nodes. Task A_2 is an interference task whose priority $r_{A2} > r_{A1}$. Each interference task sends messages via respective network interface once every 10ms with varying time offsets. Task I_1 is the network interface task and in our simulations its priority r_{I1} fulfills relation $r_{A2} > r_{I1} > r_{A1}$. Therefore in all experiments presented in this section every node executes three tasks that model a simple case of a physical situation. In more complex simulation scenarios, greater number of tasks may be executing on each node.

Our fault injection model disturbs the network interface model. In the next subsections we explain the effect of injected faults on the network throughput, message delay and bus scheduling. Those three parameters are compared against the total network traffic or total number of transmissions completed by all nodes at any given simulation time t. The simulation results present the effects of two fault types; namely the *Next Hit* and *Remaining Tx Time* fault effects.

4.1 Network Throughput vs. Number of Transmissions

This section presents results of experiments with respect to network throughput. The experiments were performed under one set of tasks. In each simulation run only one fault of the same type had been injected into all nodes in the network. By injection of only one fault at a time we avoided fault effect correlation and were able to directly observe the effects of the injection. All faults were active for 1 second. This time was sufficient to analyze the network properties, which means that we were able to obtain enough state transitions within the PFSM to evaluate the behavior of the protocol.

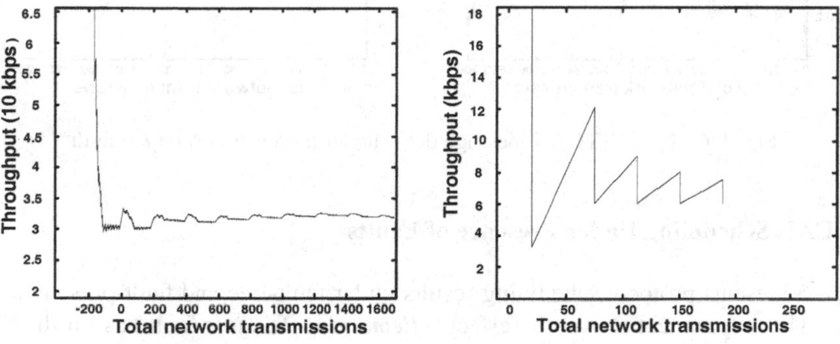

Fig. 3. CAN and TTCAN throughput under presence of *Next Hit* fault

The experiment measured how the global network throughput (GNT) can be affected by a fault in the *Next Hit* variable. Figure 3 presents the results for CAN and TTCAN in a situation where this state variable is increased by 1 second. Adjustment of this variable changes the time a kernel waits before it processes its next internal or external event. Therefore, as this time was increased, the throughput decreased considerably from an ideal 1 Mbps to less then 35 kbps in case of CAN and 12 kbps in case of TTCAN. The higher decrease in throughput of TTCAN network can be attributed to its scheduling policy. Once a message in TTCAN misses its transmission slot it must wait until the next cycle. Variation of *Next Hit* further increases this waiting time which leads to further degradation of throughput. The performance of both protocols with respect to throughput is highly sensitive to this type of fault. By sensitivity we mean that small variation in *Next Hit* can have a significant effect on the network ability to handle traffic.

4.2 Message Delay vs. Number of Transmissions

Figure 4 presents simulation results for message delay (MD) under the presence of *Next Hit* fault (delay between node 1 and 2). Here, too, *Next Hit* was incremented in value by 1 second and no other faults were injected into the PFSM of each node besides the *Next Hit* fault. The generated discrete levels correspond to task triggering times, which increase message delays. For the same simulation time in TTCAN, only 200 message transmissions were completed with a delay of 0.7ms. This is due to the scheduling mechanism of the protocol which prevented other transmissions to take place under the conditions of *Next Hit* fault.

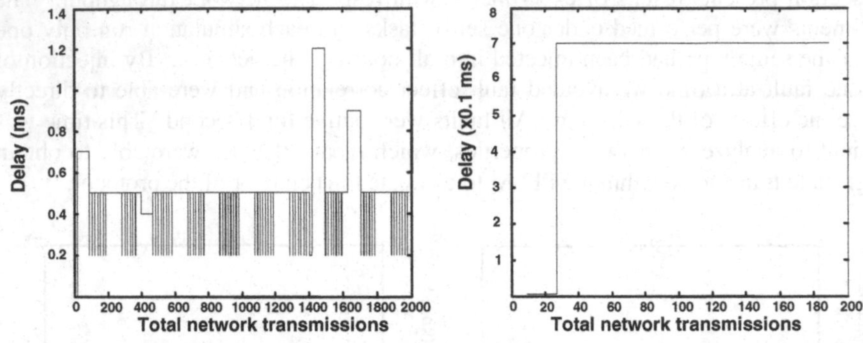

Fig. 4. CAN and TTCAN message delay under presence of *Next Hit* fault

4.3 CAN Scheduling Under Presence of Faults

Figure 5 presents protocol scheduling results under fault-free and fault-present conditions. This experiment shows the effect a *Remaining Tx Time* fault has on the CAN databus utilization. This fault increased the *Remaining Tx Time* variable by one second. In this diagram a high signal (1) represents time interval during which the i-th node N_i is accessing a databus. A low signal indicates that the databus is idle. Databus access performance is often measured according to the utilization parameter $U = t_{acc} / T$ where t_{acc} is the total access time for all nodes in the network and T is the simulation time interval. In CAN we notice much lower bus utilization in a simulation window of 50 ms.

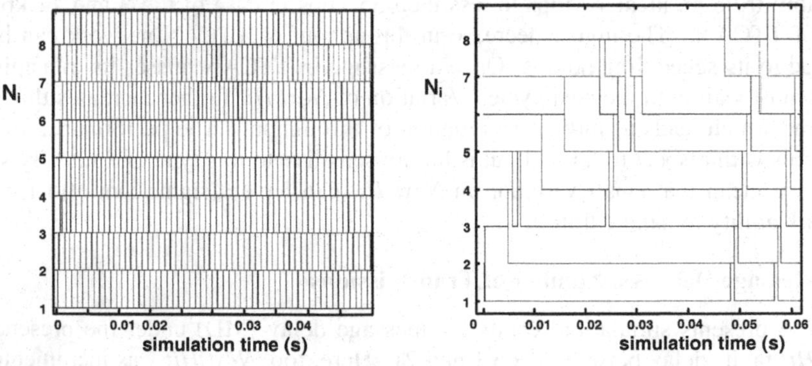

Fig. 5. CAN Schedule (a) fault free and (b) under influence of *Remaining TX Time* fault

This low bus utilization occurred in a situation when *Remaining Tx Time* faults were present in all eight nodes in the network. The utilization was measured to be less then 10%, when a fault-free CAN protocol achieved a utilization of over 75%. This experiment shows that, in situations when such fault types occur, utilization can drastically affect the performance of a protocol. Reduction of utilization under heavy loads is problematic and negatively affects dependability of a network interface.

5 Conclusion

The main benefit of extending the TrueTime simulator with our fault injection modeling, compared to other dependability evaluation methods, is that we are able to simulate faults at the logical level of the network protocol state machine and, at the same time, simulate a real-time operating system kernel. Co-simulation of the network interface and real-time kernel allows us to create more realistic traffic flows where control, interrupt, protocol and interference tasks all compete for bus access. Additionally, with our model we could inject faults into specific areas of the state machines, while in other models errors are often injected randomly. Such approach allows tracing the injection effects and mapping them onto performance issues. This can be combined with fault effect analysis at other abstraction levels (compare [4]).

In the sample simulations performed we found that both data buses used, CAN and TTCAN, can be realistically modeled and evaluated with respect to safety, when certain parameters are disturbed. TTCAN performed more predictably in cases where additional time delays were introduced by fault injection. In those instances the scheduling mechanism of this protocol ensured that "useless" time delays were limited by the specified slot size. CAN, however, performed better in instances where the time when the kernel should wake up and process its input/outputs, was disturbed with a faulty value. By better performance we mean that more information had been transferred by CAN than TTCAN due to the event driven nature of the protocol. TTCAN transferred less information because of its strict scheduling policy. According to this policy, if a message misses its slot it must wait at minimum one cycle before it can be transmitted over the network. For example, incrementing a value of the *Next Hit* variable delays this message and causes more slot misses. Effectively, this causes decreased global network throughput in TTCAN.

Future extensions of the models will cover fault tolerant mechanisms that will prevent state machine faults that manifest themselves as errors and degradations of network performance. Finally, future research will also include implementations of other safety-critical data buses, such as TTP or FlexRay, and their comparisons with the two discussed in this paper in the context of their impact on safety.

References

1. Adermaj A.: Slightly-of-specification failures in the time triggered architecture. Proc. of 7th IEEE Int. Workshop on High Level Design and Validation and Test (2002) 7-12
2. Albert, A., Gerth, W.: Evaluation and Comparison of the Real-Time Performance of CAN and TTCAN. Proc. of 9th CAN Conference, Munich (2003)

3. Anderrson, M., Henriksson, D., Cervin A.: TrueTime 1.3 Manual. Lund Institute of Technology, Sweden (2005)
4. Anghel L., Leveugle R., Vanhauwaert P.: Evaluation of SET and SEU effects at multiple abstraction levels. Proc. of the 11-th IEEE International On-line Test Symposium, (2005), 309-314
5. Arlat, J., Crouzet, Y., Karlsson, J., Folkesson, P., Fuchs, E., Leber, G.H.: Comparison of physical and software implemented fault injection techniques. IEEE Transactions on Computers, vol. 52, no.9 (2003) 1115-1133
6. Henriksson, D., Cervin, A., Arzen, K.: TrueTime: Real-Time Control System Simulation with MATLAB/Simulink. Proceedings of the Nordic MATLAB Conference, Copenhagen, Denmark (2003)
7. TrueTime 1.3 Simulink Simulator. Lund Institute of Technology, Sweden. http://www.control.lth.se/~dan/truetime/
8. Zalewski, J., Trawczynski, D., Sosnowski, J., Kornecki, A., Sniezek, M.: Safety Issues in Avionics and Automotive Databuses. IFAC World Congress, Prague Czech Republic (2005)

Towards a Unified Model-Based Safety Assessment*

Thomas Peikenkamp[1], Antonella Cavallo[2], Laura Valacca[3], Eckard Böde[1], Matthias Pretzer[1], and E. Moritz Hahn[1]

[1] Kuratorium OFFIS e.V., Escherweg 2, 26121 Oldenburg, Germany
{peikenkamp, boede, pretzer, ernst.hahn}@offis.de

[2] Alenia Aeronautica S.p.A., Strada Malanghero 17, IT-10072 Caselle, Turin, Italy
acavallo@aeronautica.alenia.it

[3] Societa' Italiana Avionica S.p.A, Strada Antica di Collegno 253, IT-10146 Turin, Italy
valacca@sia-av.it

Abstract. The increase of complexity in aircraft systems demands for enhanced analysis techniques. Methods are required that leverage the burden of their application by reusing existing design and process information and by enforcing the reusability of analyses results allowing early identification of design's weak points and check of design alternatives. This report elaborates on a method that assumes a system specification in an industrial standard notation and allows to perform several formal safety analyses. Based on a collection of failure models and means of specifying safety requirements, the techniques produce results along the lines of traditional methods.

We show how to combine traditional techniques, required by the Aerospace Recommended Practice (SAE-ARP) standards, like Fault Tree Analysis, Failure Mode and Effect Analysis and Common Cause Analysis and also how to automate most of the analysis activities.

The methods described in this paper can be used as means to support the Certification process.

1 Introduction

As avionic systems are getting more complex, it becomes increasingly difficult to perform safety assessment activities required by Aerospace Recommended Practice standards. In particular, the need of having considered all safety-related aspects on a high level of confidence demands for a more systematic and automatic way for performing safety analyses. To address these problems, we present an integrated model-based safety assessment framework, which automates ARP 4761 safety assessment techniques such as Fault Tree Analysis (FTA), Failure Modes and Effects Analysis (FMEA) and Common Cause Analysis (CCA). The

* This work was supported by the European Commission within the projects ESACS (Enhanced Safety Assessment for Complex Systems, FP5), http://www.esacs.org/, and ISAAC (Improvement of Safety Activities on Aeronautical Complex systems, FP6), http://www.isaac-fp6.org/

J. Górski (Ed.): SAFECOMP 2006, LNCS 4166, pp. 275–288, 2006.

framework uses a sound formal approach by employing formal methods to assess the safety of system models implemented in industrial modelling tools such as Statemate [1] or Simulink [2]. We will show the approach to be more comprehensive in respect to the traditional approach since it allows to consider the full temporal properties of the system, for example allowing safety-critical events to be specified by temporal patterns stating that events need to occur in a particular order to be safety-relevant. The underlying analysis techniques elaborate on these specifications and allow, for instance, to identify and relate failure causes and consequences even if they happen at different time instances with several system interactions between them. The possibility to automatically generate results which are easily update-able when the system model changes allows to quickly verify possible design alternatives. This approach can be applied since the first system development phases, therefore identifying potential weak design points with timeliness avoiding later and costly design changes. By applying some of the developed techniques to a given case study we will moreover show that we achieve results beyond those that can be achieved by classical verification techniques [3,4] like model-checking, yet having the same degree of accuracy. The two main enablers for these are, first, a failure injection (c.f. section 3.2) that essentially allows to maintain nominal and dysfunctional system behaviour within one model and, second, the corresponding analysis algorithms (c.f. sections 3.3–3.6). The latter allow to reduce the number of verification runs by a factor that (e.g. in the case of FTA) is exponential in the number of failures.

Typical questions that will be answered by the techniques presented are "Is it possible to violate a certain safety requirement?", "Which failures and failure combinations need to occur to violate the safety requirement and which additional timing constraints are necessary?", "Is it possible for a fault to occur undetected?", "Will a list of impacted items violate independence assumptions underlying a system design?", "Is it possible to continue a flight in a failed configuration?", "Will an erroneous flight procedure lead to a safety requirement violation?". In the following it is shown how such questions can be answered by performing several analyses on the braking system of an aircraft. All analyses were carried out with STSA, a Statemate [1] Plug-in for supporting safety assessment actions. The paper is structured as follows: Section 2 explains the model of a braking system to be used as an example throughout the following sections. Section 3 shows how to apply several traditional and new safety analysis methods on the braking system model. Section 4 discusses related work and section 5 concludes with the indication of future work.

2 Braking System Example

We illustrate our approach by applying it to the model of the wheel brake system as described in appendix L of ARP 4761 [5]. The example was chosen due to the fact that the systems description is relatively concise while retaining a lot of interesting features w.r.t. to safety analysis. Since it is featured in the ARP, it should be well known to safety engineers. Incidentally, [4] uses the same example (albeit modelled in Simulink rather than Statemate), which gives us the opportunity to directly compare their results with ours. A detailed description of the Statemate model can be found in [6].

The braking system, whose architecture is depicted in figure 1, controls the amount of hydraulic power applied to the brake pistons installed at the main landing gears. Hydraulic power is supplied via two independent hydraulic lines, the normal and the alternate line. The normal line is powered by the green hydraulic pump, the alternate line by the blue one. Additionally, the blue pump is backed up by an accumulator. Thus, the system distinguishes three operational modes, normal (powered by the green pump), alternate (blue) and emergency (accumulator). In normal mode, the valves regulating the flow of the hydraulic pressure are completely controlled by the BSCU (Braking System Control Unit), a computer which computes braking and anti-skid commands. In alternate mode, the BSCU provides anti-skid commands, as long as it is working. The normal braking commands are directly taken from the mechanical position of the brake pedals. In emergency mode, anti-skid is disabled completely.

The BSCU itself consists of two redundant command units and two monitoring units which supervise their respective command units. A switch is used to select the active command unit based on the output of the first monitor. When the monitor signals a failure in the first command unit, the switch selects the second one.[1] When both monitors signal failure of their respective command units, the shutoff signal is issued.

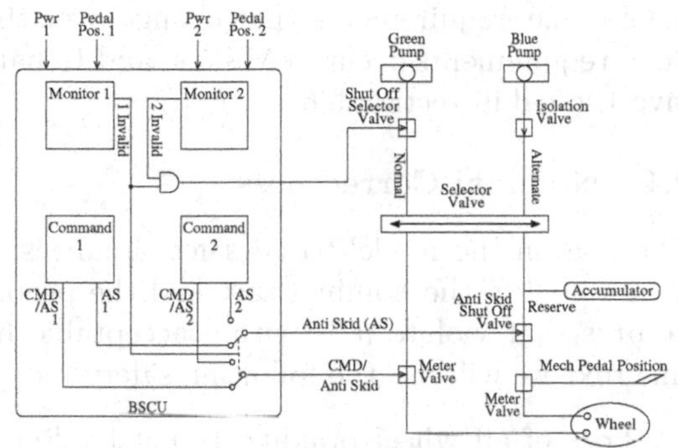

Fig. 1. Architecture of the wheel braking system

The shutoff signal closes the "Shut Off Selector Valve", which inhibits the green pressure from reaching the "Selector Valve". The Selector Valve engages the alternate mode as soon as the green pressure is not available (which can be caused by the described BSCU shutoff or the failure of the green pump). Also, switching between modes can be commanded manually by the pilot.

The presented Statemate model of the braking system is largely a direct formalisation of the model described in the ARP [5]. The main differences are the missing autobrake mode in our model and the restriction to one braking pedal. However, these differences are irrelevant w.r.t. the analyses carried out in the later sections.

[1] Note that our model uses an invalid signal, while the original ARP model uses a valid signal. However, this is equivalent on the model level.

3 A Stepwise Approach to Safety Analysis

Before we start looking at possible failures, causes, and impacts, we assume that the model is free of design errors. The validation of this assumption will be done with available verification tools [3]. For the braking system this is outlined in section 3.1. Having passed this check we extend the nominal behaviour by failure behaviour as shown in section 3.2. After this we pass to more traditional methods used in safety assessment. All of them are applied on the extended model ensuring consistent results. In section 3.3 we are looking for a complete set of causes for a given failure by performing a fault tree analysis (FTA) and a refinement of this analysis allowing the simulation of identified cut-sets. Looking in the other direction, i.e. by investigating failure impacts, we will perform a Failure Mode and Effect Analysis (FMEA) in section 3.4. After this we "jump" over system boundaries and look at causes that arise external to the system. In particular, we will investigate, how to identify *common causes* that lead to a violation of failure independencies. In section 3.5 we show how to perform the necessary Common Cause Analysis (CCA) and how to incorporate the results in the FTA of section 3.3. The final aspects we will consider are "dynamic safety requirements", i.e. requirements that change over the time of the system's operation. Such requirements occur in Mission and Reliability Analyses (MRA) and will be investigated in section 3.6.

3.1 Nominal Correctness

The goal in the model-based safety-analysis is to show that all safety requirements hold in the nominal case and the probability for all scenarios containing failures that violate it is within acceptable limits. As an example throughout this text we will use the following safety requirement from ARP 4761:

> Loss of all wheel braking during landing or Rejected Take Off (RTO) shall be less than $5 \cdot 10^{-7}$ per flight.

Since we are performing a qualitative rather than a quantitative analysis we do not compute the probability itself. Rather we determine the failure combinations qualitatively that contribute to this probability. So we rephrase the requirement and ask for:

> Loss of all wheel braking shall not occur.

Having a formalisation of the model (from section 2), we need to formalise the safety requirement as well. In simple setting such formalisation may be done by characterising a safety-critical state (e.g. by specifying that the pressure of the blue line is above a given limit). If timing is important for the specification of the safety requirement, temporal logic may be used [7]. Although being quite expressive, temporal formulas are sometimes not easy to understand. A reasonable approach is to use *patterns* for typical temporal relationships occurring in safety requirements. For establishing the nominal correctness of the design we use the *ModelCertifier* from OSC [8] that comes with a library of patterns for typical safety requirements. The most obvious way to formalise the above safety requirement is to state that whenever the pilot pushes the braking pedals, either the green or the blue line have to supply pressure to the wheels subsequently. Due to the stepwise propagation of the braking commands we cannot simply use a safety requirement of the form

(Pedal pressed) implies ((Green pressure high) or (Blue pressure high)).

Instead, we use the following pattern supplied by the OSC pattern library:

P_stable_X_steps_implies_finally_Q_B.

This pattern states that whenever P (the pressed pedal in our case) is true for X steps then Q has to hold after at most B steps. In our case, Q is instantiated with the disjunction from above, while we set X and B to 10 milliseconds, each. We require the pedals to be pressed for at least 10 milliseconds in order to avoid situations where the pedal is pressed and released over and over again. Otherwise, we run into situations, where one of the different valves along each line is always closed thus blocking the pressure from reaching the wheels. Another solution to overcome this problem is to change the system to open all the valves for a certain amount of time, whenever the pedals are pressed (or to check whether physical laws ensure this). Using this pattern, we can prove the nominal correctness of the system model with the ModelCertifier. Further verification tasks solvable with the ModelCertifier include checks for non-determinism, races, range violations and others.

3.2 Failure Injection

After the nominal correctness has been established, the next steps will evaluate the system behaviour in case of failures. Thus, the model has to be extended to reflect the possible behaviour of the system in the presence of failures. This is accomplished by injecting a number of (candidate) failures, i.e. failures that *might* occur. As a consequence, the resulting model may behave as in the nominal case or it may behave as if some combination of the injected failures have occurred. In the latter case it is free to apply the failures in any order with any kind of time passing between their occurrences. Figure 2 indicates three possible runs of a system with three failures (F_1, F_2, F_3) injected. It is this kind of generality that allows to do an exhaustive investigation of possible failure scenarios (as outlined, for instance, in section 3.3).

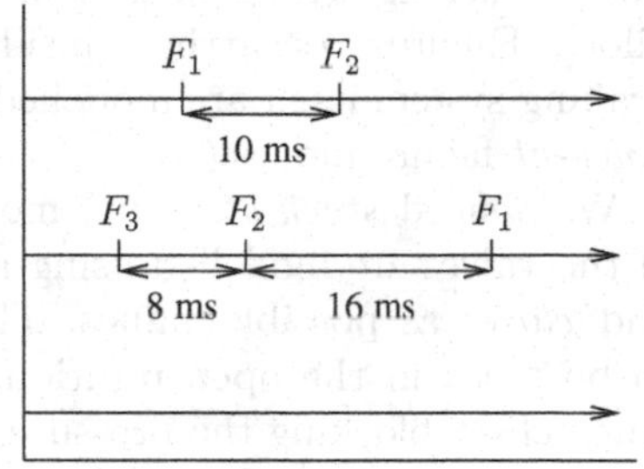

Fig. 2. Different system runs with three injected failures

For the sake of the analyses presented in the following sections we require the failures to be observable, so in addition to the actual failure behaviour an *observer* is introduced for each injected failure that is able to detect whether (and when) the failure occurs. By this means we guarantee that nominal and failure behaviour are strictly separated. In particular it allows to check whether failures or failure combinations are *causal* for some safety-critical event. This fact will be exploited in section 3.3 to guarantee *minimality* of cut-sets.

The internal complexity of the failure injection is hidden to the user of STSA, who is only required to identify the affected system variable, selecting a failure-mode that should be applied to the variable, and, if necessary, supply failure-mode parameters (see figure 3). Again, a pattern-based approach is used to provide a list of failure-mode templates including *stuck-at*, *delay*, *noise*, and *random* failures. When the provided failure-mode patterns are insufficient, e.g. if the failure affects several model variables in a complex fashion, or the failure makes use of some internal system mode (degraded system mode), it is possible to apply *user-defined* failures, i.e. failures that are defined within Statemate. In this case the system ensures that nominal and failure behaviour is separated by requiring the user to specify an input that triggers the failure behaviour. After all failure candidates are specified, STSA injects them without any additional interaction in the aforementioned way.

The failure injection was applied to the braking system in the following way: Failures of the electrical and hydraulic power supplies are represented by *user-defined* failure-modes, since the supplies are modelled as inputs to the model. A *user-defined* failure-mode may also be applied to the manual mode selection thus modelling wrong behaviour of the pilot. Failures occurring inside the braking system itself are modelled using *stuck-at* failure modes.

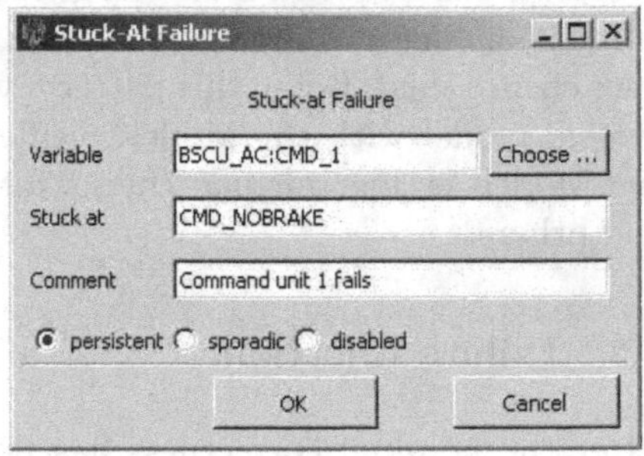

Fig. 3. Specifying a stuck-at failure

We defined *stuck-at* failure-modes for a variety of variables. Failures of each of the valves are modelled using a *stuck-at* failure-mode with both states (*open* and *close*) as possible values. This way, the failure-mode can force the valve to be stuck in the open position, passing the incoming hydraulic pressure, or stuck close, blocking the pressure. Similarly, the validity signals from the BSCU monitors can either be made stuck *true* or *false*. Further failure-modes were created for the braking commands computed by the two redundant BSCU units and the reference commands the monitoring units compute. Another failure-mode was created to model the failure of the switch unit inside the BSCU.

3.3 Fault-Tree Analysis

After the nominal correctness has been analysed and the system model has been extended with failure-modes it is now possible to perform a fault-tree analysis (FTA). In order to do this the next step is the definition of a *Top-Level Event* (TLE). A top-level event describes a system state that should not be reachable in the nominal behaviour. In most case there is a direct relation between a top-level event and a safety requirement in the sense that $TLE = \neg SafetyRequirement$ so that is is possible to reuse the definition of safety requirements as they are described in section 3.1.

After all the basic parts of the analysis definition are in place we can start with the analysis. The algorithms we are using to perform an FTA are build on BDD techniques and are related to BDD model-checking. Although our approach shares the fundamental attributes of these techniques it has been extensively enhanced. The main enhancement is in the results that are obtained from the analysis, traditionally model-checking algorithms only analyse whether a certain property can be proven correct or try to find a counter example if the property has been found to be be invalid. In our analysis we are not only interested in a single counter example but in finding all the causes for a TLE. During our FTA analysis a set of all failure-combinations that are necessary to reach the TLE are computed. As these combinations are minimal by construction, they are similar to the well known *minimal cut-sets* that are often used in traditional safety-analysis [9].

Minimal cut-sets are an abstraction notion of a failure-situation. Even for a designer who has an in-depth knowledge of the system it is often not easy to understand the interaction of failure-modes and how they lead to the TLE. In order to ease this task it is possible to use STSA to generate a concrete counter example that shows not only the development of the failure-modes but also that of the the system variables. While the fault-tree generation employs a *free-ordering semantics*, i.e. the order of failures is not restricted in any way, the generation of a counter example produces one concrete ordering. The usefulness of this approach is that the generated fault-tree is complete since it considers *all* possible orderings of failures, while the generated counter examples show a concrete ordering enabling the designer to easily find the deficiencies in the system. One should also note that this kind of analysis is hardly to be achieved by a simulation-based approach, since then one is required to actually specify the order and duration of failures during simulation. Thus to achieve the same quality of result one had to do a lot of iterations.

We applied the fault-tree generation to the braking system using the safety requirement described in section 3.1 (loss of wheel braking) and a subset of the failure-modes described in section 3.2. The INVALID signals of the BSCU monitors and the complete shutoff of the BSCU were used as intermediate events. This results in the fault-tree shown in figure 4. We will have a closer look at the two highlighted subtrees.

Subtree b) is directly related to the one depicted in the ARP [5, page 200], except that we did not include failure-modes for the electrical power or the failure of the hydraulic system (except for the pumps). The subtree shows that the safety requirement is violated, when all three modes fail to operate. The reason for the failure of the normal mode is further broken down to be caused by the failure of the green hydraulic pump or failure of the BSCU units to command braking. Note that this also occurs, when the BSCU monitors fail to

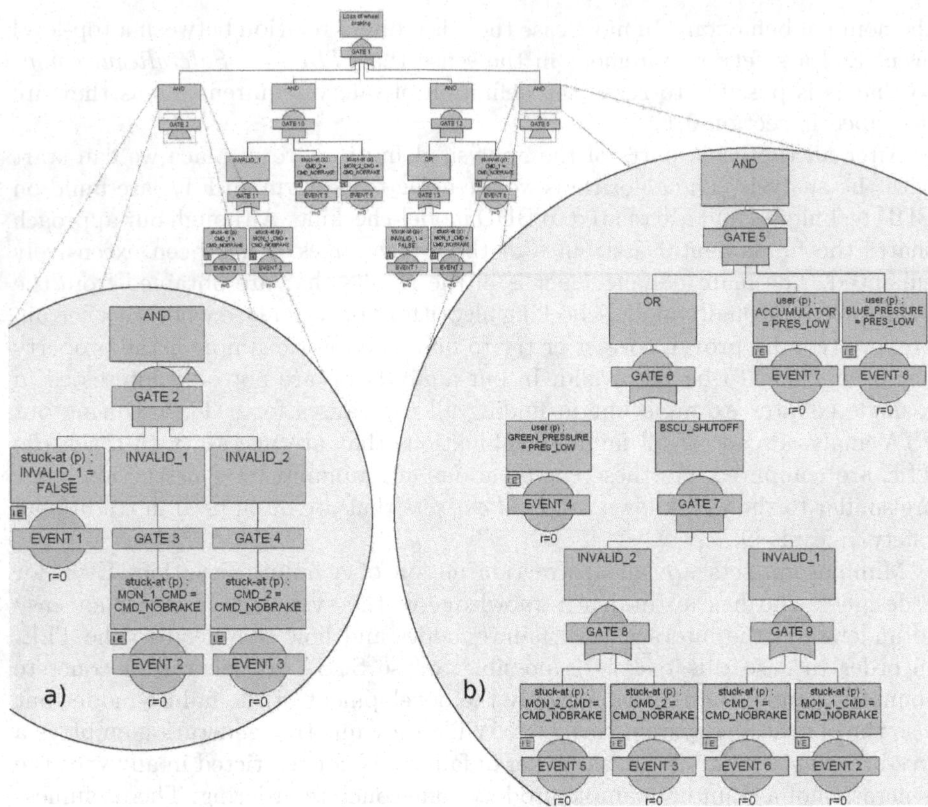

Fig. 4. Auto generated fault-tree

correctly compute the reference signal, which is covered by the events 5 and 2 in the fault-tree.

The consideration of monitoring failures is also the reason for the generated fault-tree to be more comprehensive than the one depicted in the ARP, where the occurrence of monitoring failures seems not to be considered. Subtree a) of figure 4 is one of the additional subtrees stemming from this fact. The first remarkable observation of this subtree is the circumstance that it only features failures occurring inside the BSCU, i.e. the TLE is reachable without any failure of the alternate and emergency mode. This is due to the fact that the failure of the monitoring unit inside the BSCU can inhibit its shutoff, thus preventing the system from changing to alternate mode. Nevertheless, a closer look at the minimal cut-set of subtree a) in figure 4 reveals a situation which is confusing at first. The failure of the first monitor (Event 2) activates the first invalid signal, yet the subtree also contains a failure which makes the same signal stay inactive. We can find an explanation for this by letting STSA compute a counter example, which shows the temporal ordering of the involved failures.

Such a trace is depicted in figure 5 which easily explains the odd situation in the fault-tree. One can see, that the first failure occurring is the failure of the first monitor. Due to this, the BSCU switches to the second command unit, which subsequently fails. At last, the invalid signal fails, inhibiting the shutoff of BSCU.

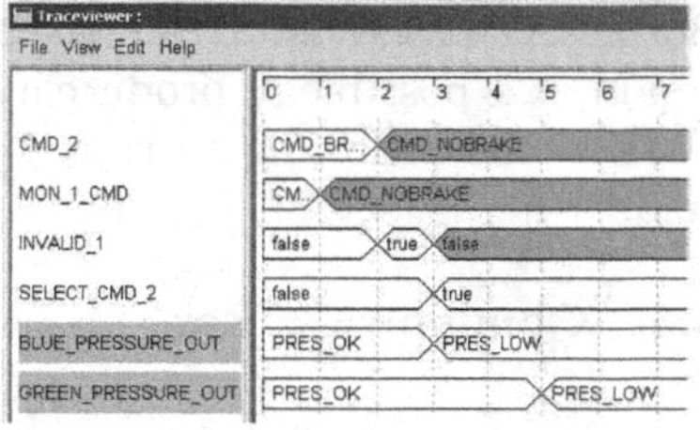

Fig. 5. Traceviewer showing the temporal ordering of failures

We conclude by referring to [10], where the technique has been applied to the high-lift system of an aircraft.

3.4 FMEA

Each of the cut-sets that has been computed may give rise to other questions, for instance, whether there are other impacts. Since all kind of analyses are performed on unique system and failure models we may proceed to investigate cut-sets for further possible impacts. The traditional way for answering this question is to perform a Failure Mode and Effect Analysis (FMEA), also embedded in STSA. An important difference to the traditional (application of the) FMEA method is that it is possible not only to investigate single failures for their effects, but also failure combinations. In particular the minimal cut-sets that have been identified during fault tree analysis may be imported and further investigated. This idea of having formal tools *guiding* the safety assessment process will be further followed in the following section about the identification of common causes. It is in contrast to [4] where the idea is "to try to pose the right verification questions to formal tools". Although we agree that standard verification tools can be used *in principle* to perform safety assessment activities (and in fact we use several classical verification engines), they need to be adopted for safety assessment purposes (e.g. the setting in [4] does not even allow to detect causality of failures).

icrosoft Excel - fmea.xml

Datei Bearbeiten Ansicht Einfügen Format Extras Daten Fenster ? Adobe PDF

A7

Failure Mode Variable	Failure Mode Description	Effects on TLEs
stuck-at (p) : CMD_2 = CMD_NOBRAKE & stuck-at (p) : MON_1_CMD = CMD_NOBRAKE & stuck-at (p) : INVALID_1 = FALSE	Cmd 2 Stuck & Monitor 1 fails & Invalid 1 fails	Loss of wheel braking
stuck-at (p) : CMD_2 = CMD_NOBRAKE & stuck-at (p) : MON_1_CMD = CMD_NOBRAKE	Cmd 2 Stuck & Monitor 1 fails	BSCU_SHUTOFF (length:1)
stuck-at (p) : MON_1_CMD = CMD_NOBRAKE	Monitor 1 fails	INVALID_1 (length:1)
stuck-at (p) : CMD_2 = CMD_NOBRAKE	Cmd 2 Stuck	INVALID_2 (length:1)

Fig. 6. Auto generated FMEA table

Usually FMEA result are given in the form of tables, as shown in figure 6. Each row shows the effect of (a subset) of the failure-modes under consideration, if any. In this case, the first row corresponds to the cut-set depicted in subtree a) of figure 4, which was used as an input to the analysis. The other rows depict the effects that different subsets of the failure-modes have on the system. Subsets without any effect on the TLEs are not shown (e.g. the sole failure of the INVALID_1 signal in our example).

Depending on the size of the state space of the model and the length of propagation paths several kinds of analysis techniques are used in the implementation.

Both, SAT-based and BDD-based [11,12] techniques are used in several variants. Again, it is possible to produce a simulation trace for each effect detected during FMEA, thus allowing to trace problems down to concrete runs of the system (model).

3.5 Common Causes

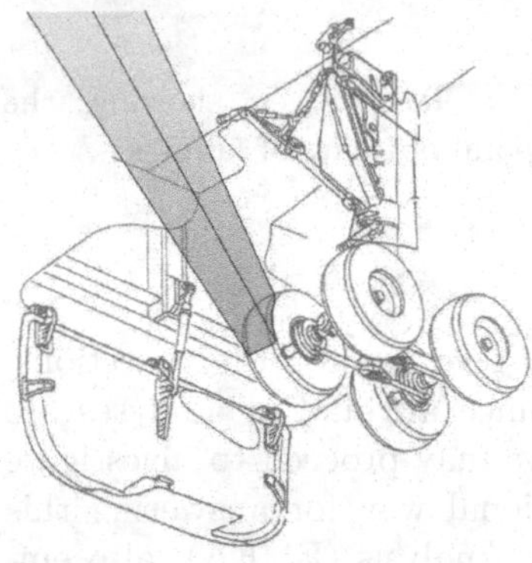

Fig. 7. Tyre burst trajectories

The idea behind failure-modes that have been described in section 3.2 is that all failure-modes are independent. The goal in the common cause analysis is to evaluate the consequences of violations to these independence assumptions. For instance, the violation of independence hypothesis for AND-ed failure events implies the invalidation of basic redundancies foreseen by the aircraft system's architecture and then different qualitative and quantitative assessment about the violation of safety requirements. As recommended by the ARP, it is therefore necessary to ensure that such independence exists, or that the risk associated with dependence is deemed acceptable in respect to the applicable certification standard requirements.

Typically the violation of independence assumption is caused by an external event establishing dependencies that are not represented in the system model. An example for such an external event could be a tyre burst where the ejected particles hit several components that are independent in the functional design model but closely located within the physical structure (see figure 7). Taking such dependencies into account requires the integration of the functional models with the the geometrical representation of the system installation. This integration is performed in the context of a stepwise process that starts from the geometry and moves towards the functional tools. The results of safety analyses are then translated back into the geometrical domain to highlight the potential weak points of design installation in terms of violation of safety requirements.

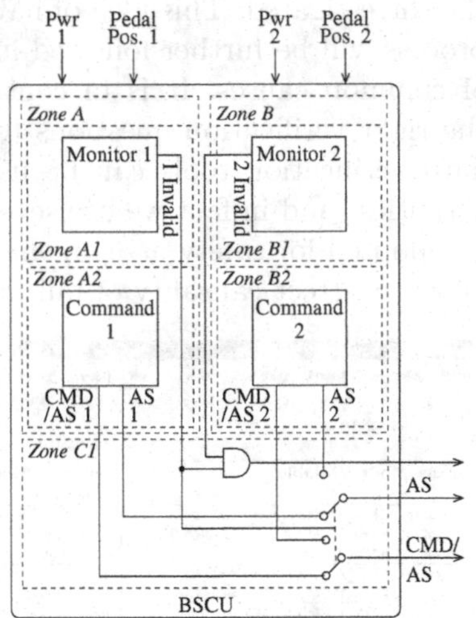

Fig. 8. Zones for the BSCU

The main steps of the process are detailed in the following. Geometrical models of fragments and relevant trajectories — picked up from a library and built in agreement with the reference standards — are located on geometrical item/s potentially interested by a particular risk event (for instance a rotor stage of an engine or a tyre). In this extended geometrical environment (including aircraft systems and fragments trajectories), the consequences of a particular risk event are evaluated by means of interference analysis facilities. The output of this first phase of the process is a list of impacted geometrical components for each possible trajectory of the ejected debris. In the second step of the process the list of impacted items for each trajectory is translated into the list of functional failure-modes through a dictionary. The output of this step is a list of groups of failures that are triggered by the same cause. We call each group of failure-modes a *failure-set*. Each failure-set is identified by the angular coordinates of one or more possible trajectories of the considered fragment. The BSCU from the braking system is divided into several zones (see figure 8). In the example analysis we are presenting there is one trajectory that hits the zones A1 and A2 thereby failing both *Command1* and *Monitor1*. This information is then imported into the analysis tool as a new failure-set that references the failure-modes that have been defined for the affected components.

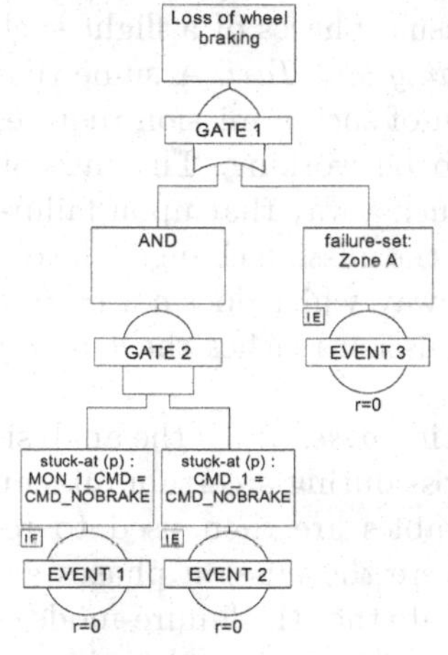

Fig. 9. Fault-tree with Common Causes

The last step of forward flow of the process consists in performing the same safety analyses described in previous sections 3.3 (FTA) and 3.4 (FMEA), this time taking into account common causes. To do that, the failure-sets imported into STSA are treated as additional failure-modes in the elaboration of safety results. As we can see from figure 9 the fault-tree now contains a single failure-mode cut-set that is relevant to tyre burst fragment trajectories. This has an obvious impact from the quantitative point of view. The critical trajectories identified in the analysis (i.e. those trajectories that invalidate safety requirements) can be highlighted in the 3D tools afterwards. If the quantitative requirements are not satisfied, our integrated approach eases the verification of possible design alternatives.

As final note, we highlight an alternative use of the failure-set facility. The user has the possibility to bypass the interference analysis by manually creating groups of dependent failures. This could be helpful in order to perform user-guided grouping of failures sharing one or more geometrical attribute. A possible useful application of this manual definition of failure-sets could be in performing the Zonal Hazard Analysis [5]: in this case the failure-sets will be relevant to failures of components located in the same Aircraft zone (see figure 8).

3.6 Mission and Reliability Analysis

So far, our example safety requirement (c.f. section 3.1) did not take different flight phases into account. This section shows, how this can be done by specifying the successful completion of the aircraft's mission as the safety requirement. The goal of the mission analysis therefore is to determine to what extent the success of a mission depends on the availability of certain functions (in certain phases of the mission).

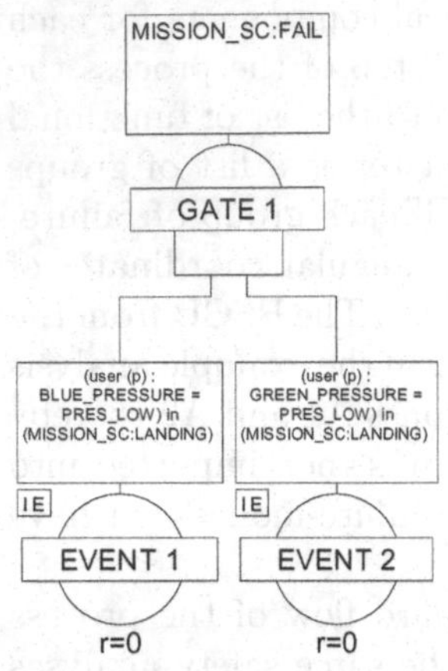

Fig. 10. Fault-tree with mission phases

In order to reason about the aircraft's mission, a formal model of it is needed. We refer to such a model as the *mission manager*. Usually, it consists of a statechart describing the succession of the different mission phases. Transitions between the phases are annotated with the requirements for the successful completion of the phases. Failure to meet these requirements can either result in the transition to an alternative successor phase or the failure of the mission.[2]

For the braking system example, we created a mission whose objective is to land on an icy runway. The mission consists of the usual phases of a flight such as *Cruise*, *Descent*, *Landing* and *Taxi*. Assume that the successful completion of such a mission requires the anti-skid function to be working. The mission manager is designed in such a way that upon failure of the anti-skid function, the mission changes the objective to use another runway, which does not require anti-skid. However, this is only possible before the mission reaches the *Landing* phase.

By defining the phases of the mission to be interesting *observables* the analysis can be used to determine the impact of a function loss during a certain mission phase (on the success of the mission). The observables are then used to reorganise the tree that results from the analysis, where the mission phases are reported in the description of the basic events to indicate that the failure-mode of the system items has to occur in a specific phase to have an effect on the missions failure. Figure 10 shows a fault-tree where the occurrence of the failures is only relevant during the *Landing* phase – earlier occurrences do not lead to the failure of the mission (because an alternate runway can be used).

4 Related Work

Model-based verification of fault-trees is shown, for instance in [13,14]. They allow for a very detailed specification of (intermediate) events. The fault-tree itself has to be created manually. However, some work exists how to complete an incomplete fault-tree [15]. The Hip-HOPS [16,17] method is based on the construction of a failure propagation model that is afterwards analysed. The result of the first step is usually a model that is simple in structure when compared with a typical functional model that is created by tools like Statemate [1]

[2] Where the mission's failure is considered to be catastrophic.

or Simulink [2]. Another model-based safety analysis approach, derived from methods we jointly developed in [18] within the ESACS consortium, is presented in [4]. The method applies standard verification tools to produce single failure scenarios and is based on a taxonomy of failure models and failure semantics that were developed in [18]. From the safety point of view, however, it suffers from an important drawback: Because standard verification algorithms are used, the method is bound to investigate only single failure scenarios, i.e. each failure combination has to be specified and investigated independently implying that for n failure candidates in the worst case 2^n analysis runs have to be performed to completely traverse the search space induced by the failure combinations. Even this number increases if system modes or mission phases are taken into account. Another weakness of the approach is that it does not take *causality* of failures into account leaving the safety engineer alone with the question of whether a given cut set is *minimal.* In contrast to the pattern-based failure injection presented here, they have chosen a manual injection method that, beside being time-consuming, leaves the system engineer alone with the question of what is the system and what are the failures. It seems questionable whether such manual injection can be carried out practically on larger designs.

5 Conclusion, Further Work

We have presented a tool-supported method for performing a model-based safety assessment. A unique model of the system extended with failure modes — obtained by instantiating pattern from a failure mode library — was used to perform several traditional safety analysis techniques, namely FTA, FMEA, CCA, and MRA. By identifying *causal failure combination* in the ARP 6741 braking system model it was demonstrated that the results are beyond those that are achievable by standard model checking techniques. Other improvements were achieved by exploiting synergies from a combination of analysis results, so that common causes could be incorporated in a fault tree and the role of mission phases could be identified when investigating requirement violation in a MRA. The failure injection and the analysis methods were implemented as a plug-in for Statemate, allowing easy definition and execution of safety analysis tasks. The techniques allows to analyse system models up to 10^{100} states without modifications. Further work includes the adoption of abstraction techniques to address more complex models.

There are no general obstacles in extending the presented analyses to the quantitative, i.e. probabilistic case. The necessary models are at hand (c.f. [19]) and also existing stochastic analysis techniques (e.g. [20]) are waiting to be extended much like we have extended traditional verification techniques to cope with qualitative questions of safety. The challenge will be to apply these to models of realistic size. The necessary state aggregation techniques have already been set up in [21]. Thus, most of the presented techniques are likely to be lifted to the quantitative case in the near future.

References

1. Harel, D., Politi, M.: Modelling Reactive Systems with Statecharts: The STATEMATE Approach. McGraw-Hill (1998)
2. The MathWorks: Simulink — Model-Based and System-Based Design. (2004)
3. Bienmüller, T., Damm, W., Wittke, H.: The STATEMATE Verification Environment - Making It Real. In: Proc. of CAV. Volume 1855 of LNCS. (2000) 561–567
4. Joshi, A., Heimdahl, M.P.: Model-Based Safety Analysis of Simulink Models Using SCADE Design Verifier. In: SAFECOMP. Volume 3688 of LNCS., Springer-Verlag (2005) 122–135
5. ARP4761: Guidelines and Methods for Conducting the Safety Assessment Process on Civil Airborne Systems and Equipment. Aerospace Recommended Practice, Society of Automotive Engineers, Detroit, USA (1996)
6. Peikenkamp, T., Cavallo, A., Valacca, L., Böde, E., Pretzer, M., Hahn, E.M.: http://seshome.informatik.uni-oldenburg.de/~sesdocs/safecomp2006 (2006)
7. Clarke, E., Grumberg, O., Peled, D.: Model Checking. MIT Press (1999)
8. I-Logix: ModelCertifier User Manual. I-Logix, Andover, MA (2002/2003)
9. Vesely, W.E., Goldberg, F., Roberts, N.H., Haasl, D.F.: Fault Tree Handbook. NUREG-0492. U.S. Nuclear Regulatory Commission, Washington DC (1981)
10. Peikenkamp, T., Böde, E., Brückner, I., Spenke, H., Bretschneider, M., Holberg, H.: Model-based Safety Analysis of a Flap Control System. In: Proc. of INCOSE, Toulouse (2004)
11. Drechsler, R., Becker, B.: Binary Decision Diagrams – Theory and Implementation. Kluwer Academic Publishers (1998)
12. Somenzi, F.: CUDD: CU Decision Diagram Package Release 2.4.1. University of Colorado at Boulder (2005)
13. Schellhorn, G., Thums, A., Reif, W.: Formal fault tree semantics. In: IDPT2002: Interated Design and Process Technology. (2002)
14. Hansen, K.M.: Linking Safety Analysis to Safety Requirements. PhD thesis, Institut for Informationsteknologi, DTU Lyngby (1996)
15. Schäfer, A.: Combining real-time model-checking and fault tree analysis. In Mandrioli, D., Araki, K., Gnesi, S., eds.: FM 2003: the 12th International FME Symposium. LNCS (2003)
16. Papadopoulos, Y., Maruhn, M.: Model-based synthesis of fault trees from Matlab-Simulink models. In: The International Conference on Dependable Systems and Networks (DSN'01). (2001)
17. Papadopoulos, Y., McDermid, J.A.: Hierarchically performed hazard origin and propagation studies, Springer-Verlag (1999)
18. Bozzano, M., et al.: ESACS: An integrated methodology for design and safety analysis of complex systems. ESREL (2003)
19. Hermanns, H.: Interactive Markov Chains: The Quest for Quantified Quality. Volume 2428 of LNCS. (2002)
20. Baier, C., et al.: Efficient computation of time-bounded reachability probabilities in uniform continuous-time markov decision processes. Theor. Comput. Sci. **345**(1) (2005) 2–26
21. Herbstritt, M., Wimmer, R., Peikenkamp, T., Böde, E., Hermanns, H., Adelaide, M., Becker, B.: Analysis of Large Safety-Critical Systems: A quantitative approach. Reports of SFB/TR 14 AVACS 8 (2006) ISSN: 1860-9821, `http://www.avacs.org`.

Reliability Analysis of Resilient Packet Rings

Piotr Chołda*, Jerzy Domżał, Andrzej Jajszczyk, and Krzysztof Wajda

Department of Telecommunications, AGH University of Science and Technology
Al. Mickiewicza 30, 30-059 Kraków, Poland
Tel.: (+48 12) 617–35–38, Fax: (+48 12) 634–23–72
{cholda, jdomzal, jajszczyk, wajda}@kt.agh.edu.pl
http://kt.agh.edu.pl

Abstract. Resilient Packet Ring is a novel metro access standard. Here, we analyze it from the reliability viewpoint. The *reliability function*, *availability* as well as *Mean Time to Failure* metrics are analyzed. Simulation experiments are performed to confirm that the formulas obtained on the theoretical basis are correct.

1 Introduction

RPR (*Resilient Packet Ring*) is a standard finished and approved in June 2004 and marked as IEEE 802.17 [1]. It is based on DPT (*Dynamic Packet Transport*), the solution for MAN and WAN networks proposed by Cisco in 2000 [2]. The main goals of DPT (and also RPR) are: fast and manageable transmission, spatial reuse, fairness and fast reaction to any failure. There are many papers published on conferences or in magazines where RPR features are described and propositions how to develop the 802.17 standard are presented. The problem of RPR reliability estimation is not widely studied. This is rather strange, as RPR is substantially a resilience assurance technique and the reliability assessment of it could be very useful in designing networks based on that paradigm as well as to compare with alternative solutions. In this paper, we analyze this problem and present a simple mathematical model. Nevertheless, results obtained by simulation experiments suggest that even such a simple analysis is very useful.

The structure of the paper is as follows. In Section 2 the architecture of RPR together with the main features of RPR are shown. In Section 3 the reliability analysis is introduced, including the methodology, reliability function, availability and Mean Time to Failure parameter of the network based on RPR. In Section 4 numerical example and simulation results are presented. They show that the derived formulas can be used as a good estimate of reliability factors for RPR and that the presented conclusions are correct.

2 Resilient Packet Rings: Short Overview

The RPR standard is proposed to be use in MAN and WAN networks. The architecture is based on a ring topology with two counter-rotated rings. The

* The author was supported by The Foundation for Polish Science.

J. Górski (Ed.): SAFECOMP 2006, LNCS 4166, pp. 289–301, 2006.

packets of traffic flows may be sent in both rings at the same time, but while packets of the flow are sent in one ring, the control packets of this flow are sent in the opposite direction in other ring. The architecture of an RPR ring with four nodes is presented in Fig. 1.

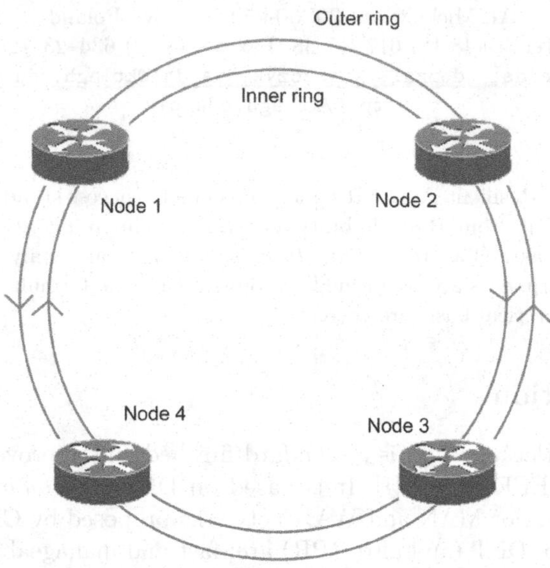

Fig. 1. Simple RPR network with four nodes

There are three traffic classes described in the RPR standard. The highest priority is given to *class A* packets. Within this class two subclasses are described and named *A0* and *A1*. The *class A* packets are usually used for real time transmissions, where no delays are acceptable. Medium priority packets (*class B*) are used for real time transmissions where low packet delays are acceptable. Within this class two subclasses are defined: *B-CIR* (provides bounded delay transfer of traffic at or below the committed information rate) and *B-EIR* (the traffic with rate beyond the committed rate is treated as best effort traffic). The lowest priority packets (*class C*) are used for best effort transmissions [3].

The transmission of best effort traffic is additionally controlled by a fairness algorithm. The available bandwidth is fairly divided and assigned to each flow. The concept of such a mechanism allows for using the *Spatial Reuse* concept. It assumes that more bandwidth than computed by the fairness algorithm may be assigned to a traffic flow in a selected part of the ring. Such method allows for increased bandwidth utilization and decreasing packet latency. The concept of the fairness algorithm and spatial reuse mechanism is presented in Fig. 2.

The dual-ring architecture is the most important advantage from the resilience point of view. The alternative path between a source and a destination is available after a single node or span failure. There are two approaches to react to a

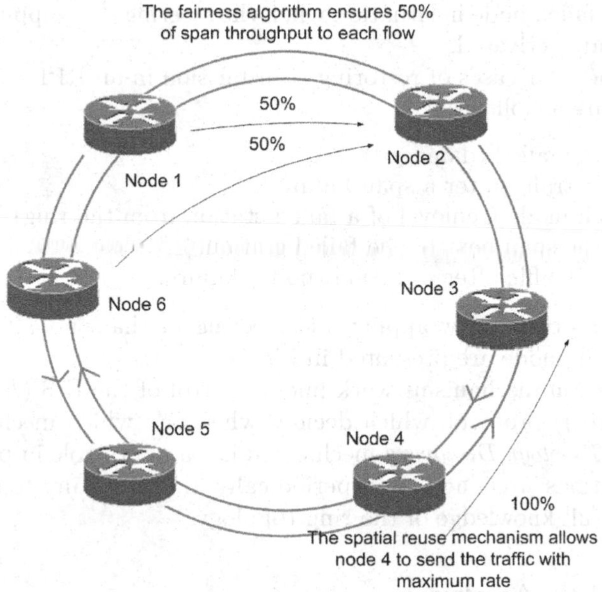
The fairness algorithm ensures 50%
of span throughput to each flow
50%
50%
Node 1
Node 2
Node 3
Node 4
Node 5
Node 6
100%
The spatial reuse mechanism allows
node 4 to send the traffic with
maximum rate

Fig. 2. Fairness algorithm and spatial reuse mechanism

failure: *protection* and *passthrough*. Two *protection* mechanisms are described in the RPR standard:

- *steering*: an obligatory mechanism for each node in the RPR ring; when a link or node along a packet route fails, the packets are redirected in the source node to the opposite ring;
- *wrapping*: an optional mechanism for nodes in the RPR ring; if implemented in a node placed next to a failure point, packets are redirected in this node; it allows for lossless transmission but with higher delays.

Obviously, if only steering mechanism is used, packets sent towards the failure point are lost. Thus, the most popular and suitable proposition to use is the *wrapping-then-steering* mechanism. In such a case, packets sent towards a failure point are redirected to the opposite ring in node placed next to the failure point. Then, other packets (from time instant when the source node is aware of the failure point) are redirected in the source node. It decreases the probability of packet loss. The main objective of using protection mechanisms is limitation of service interruption to 50 ms.

The *passthrough* mode is also described in the RPR standard. When the node failure occurs, the node may be just removed from the ring. It allows for continuation of transmission in both rings [4]. The passthrough mode is optional. It may be activated by a failed node (the way of activating the mode depends on implementation). What is very important, the failure cannot be physical (the network cards must be in the working order). The passthrough mode is usually activated by a failed node in situation when the steering or wrapping mechanism has been already activated.

The most popular cases of restoring transmission in an RPR network after a single failure are as follows:

- wrapping the failed (damaged) span,
- steering the traffic after a span failure,
- passthrough mode (removal of a failed station from the ring),
- wrapping the span next to the failed station,
- steering the traffic after a station (node) failure.

The examples of using wrapping and steering mechanisms after link failure and passthrough mode are presented in Fig. 3.

Both protection mechanisms work under control of the IPS (*Intelligent Protection Switching*) protocol, which decides when and which mechanism should be used. The *Topology Discovery* mechanism has a major role in protection and restoration actions. It is activated periodically and after any topology change and gives the full knowledge of the ring topology.

3 Reliability Analysis

3.1 Applied Methodology

We apply the following commonly used metrics for network resilience assessment:

- *Reliability function* $R(t)$ which can be defined as the probability that the system operates successfully for a given period of time $(0, t)$ if we assume that in time 0 the system is operational [5];
- *Steady-state availability* A defined as the limit (if exists), when time t tends to infinity, of the probability that a system is in the operational state at time t [6]. Unlike the reliability, it is a number, not a function;
- *Mean Time to Failure* $MTTF$, i.e., the average amount of time before the system fails.

For each structure we derive two types of reliability (and analogously, availability as well as $MTTF$):

- the *all-terminal* reliability: if a network consists of N nodes, it is defined as the probability that all N nodes are connected for a given period of time $(0, t)$;
- the *two-terminal* reliability: if a network consists of N nodes, it is calculated for selected source node s and termination node t, and equals the probability that these nodes are connected (it is also called $s - t$ reliability)

While the all-terminal metrics can be used as an overall assessment of the network resilience, two-terminal metrics can be treated as some Quality of Service parameter related to a given connection.

Closed-form formulas usable to draw practical conclusions are desired. Therefore, to simplify the derivation, we take some common simplifying assumptions:

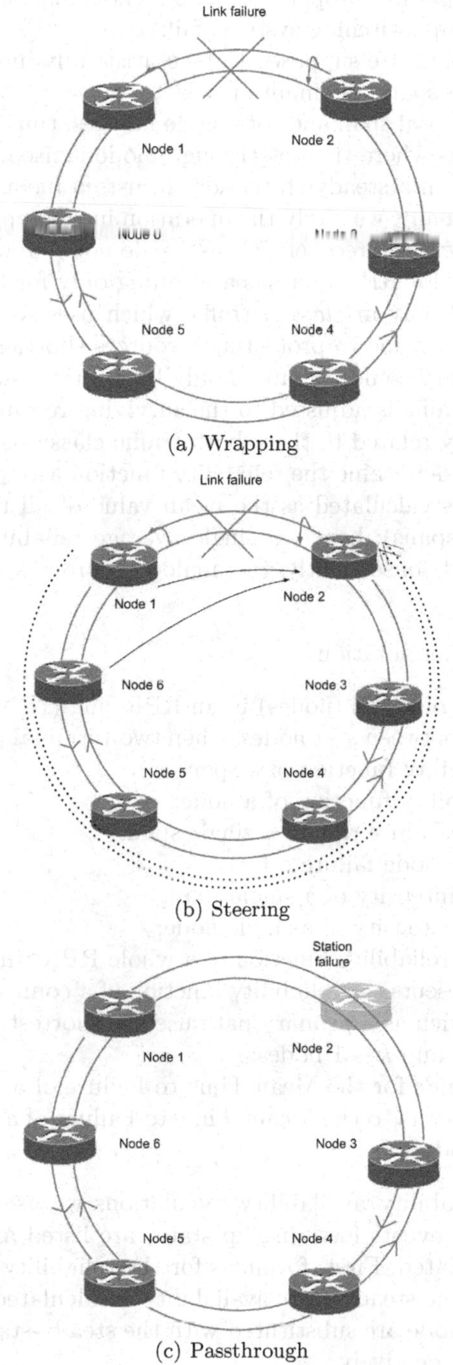

(a) Wrapping

(b) Steering

(c) Passthrough

Fig. 3. Examples of steering and wrapping mechanisms and passthrough mode

- the self-healing operates properly, i.e., we do not take into account the probability that backup switching systems fail;
- failures of two spans are supposed to be statistically independent;
- both ringlets in a span fail simultaneously;
- we consider only total span and total node failures, thus, we do not take into account situations where the possthrough mode is used;
- we are interested in a steady-state, not an instantaneous behavior of a network and additionally, we study the operation in the sense of physical recovery (not the packet level recovery); thus, we do not deal with wrapping which is not mandatory for RPR and has a meaning only for the fast recovery;
- we are interested only in *class A* traffic which uses so little resources that a failure of recovery due to protecting resources shortage is impossible, i.e., a failure of recovery could be caused only by multiple simultaneous failures; *class B* and *C* traffic is adjusted to the surviving resources so a notion of a failure of recovery related to these both traffic classes is not relevant;
- for each span we determine the reliability function as: $\forall_i r_{span_i}(t) \equiv r_s(t)$ (in Section 4, $r_s(t)$ is calculated as the mean value of all reliabilities resulting from lengths of spans); hence, a single average reliability function is used for all spans (and consequently, the analogous process is performed for the availability).

We use the following notation:

- N is the number of spans (nodes) in an RPR ring ($N \geq 3$);
- k is the distance between $s-t$ nodes, when two-terminal metrics are assessed;
- $r_s(t)$ is the reliability function of a span;
- $r_n(t)$ is the reliability function of a node;
- λ_s represents the failure rate of a single span;
- λ_n represents the node failure rate;
- μ_s, is the repair intensity of a single span;
- μ_n, is the repair intensity of a single node;
- $R_{\mathrm{RPR}_{\mathrm{all}}}(t)$ is the reliability function of a whole RPR ring;
- $R_{\mathrm{RPR}_2}(k,t)$ represents the reliability function of a connection between a pair of $s-t$ nodes which as a primary path use the shortest path composed of k contiguous spans and $k-1$ nodes;
- $MTTF_{\mathrm{RPR}_{\mathrm{all}}}$ stands for the Mean Time to Failure of a whole RPR ring;
- $MTTR_{\mathrm{RPR}_2}(k)$ refers to the Meant Time to Failure of a connection between a pair of $s-t$ nodes.

In the case of reliability/availability calculations we use the state enumeration method, i.e., all events fostering up states are listed and the sum of their probabilities is calculated. First, formulas for the reliability function are found. Then, on this basis, the steady-state availability is calculated, i.e., the reliability functions of a span/node are substituted with the steady-state availability value of a span or node, respectively.

In the case of $MTTF$ calculation, we model the behaviour of a system as a continuous time Markov chain [7], where states are related to different failure situations. We assume that failure as well as repair processes are memoryless and we take into consideration failure/repair intensities in appropriate transitions. Thus, we use the homogeneous Markov chains. To obtain $MTTF$ easily, the Laplace transform is used. Then, the sum of probabilities in limit where the imaginary variable tends to 0 gives $MTTF$ values.

The similar methodology of the reliability function in the communication connections context was used for instance in [8]. The methodology of network-related $MTTF$ assessment is similar to the one presented in [9].

3.2 Reliability Function and Availability

All-terminal Reliability/Availability. There are only two classes of probability events resulting in the situation in which all RPR nodes are connected:

(a) all nodes as well as all spans are operational;
(b) all nodes are operational and only one among the spans is faulty, all remaining spans are operational.

On the basis of such analysis the following formula for the all-terminal reliability of an RPR ring can be derived:

$$R_{\mathrm{RPR_{all}}}(t) = \underbrace{r_n^N(t) \times r_s^N(t)}_{\text{(a)}} + \underbrace{N \times r_n^N(t) \times r_s^{N-1}(t) \times \left[1 - r_s(t)\right]}_{\text{(b)}} \tag{1}$$

From the all-terminal reliability viewpoint, the behavior of an RPR is the same as a BLSR (Bidirectional Line-switching Ring) or a p-cycle.

Two-terminal Reliability/Availability. The two-terminal reliability for a pair of nodes can be calculated when a 'span distance' between them equal to k ($1 \le k \le \lfloor N/2 \rfloor$) is assumed. The reliability is related to the parallel structure built by two elements:

(a) shortest path;
(b) recovery path.

While also two end nodes of the connection (s and t) must be up to ensure the connectivity reliability block diagrams representing these nodes are treated as an element connected serially in the reliability sense **(c)**.

Thus, the two-terminal reliability of a connection in an RPR ring is equal to:

$$R_{\mathrm{RPR_{all}}}(t) = \left\{1 - \left[1 - \underbrace{r_n^{k+1}(t) \times r_s^k(t)}_{\text{(a)}}\right] \times \left[1 - \underbrace{r_n^{N-k+1}(t) \times r_s^{N-k}(t)}_{\text{(b)}}\right]\right\} \times \underbrace{r_n^2(t)}_{\text{(c)}} \tag{2}$$

3.3 Mean Time to Failure

All-terminal Case. As it was said before, to calculate $MTTF$ we will need state space models instead of combinatorial ones used previously. In this section

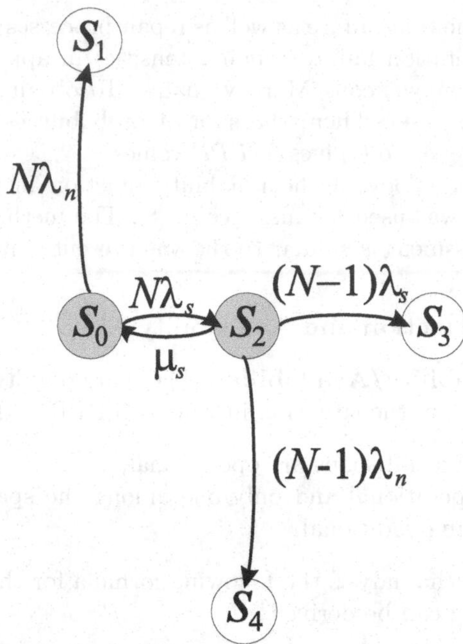

Fig. 4. Markov reliability model related to the all-terminal reliability of an RPR ring

we present the methodology of calculations and not the final formulas as they are, generally, very long and hard to understand. The values are calculated with the SHARPE modeling tool [10]. The modeling will be shown by using an example of the simplest model, i.e., $MTTF$ of a system which is here an all-terminal RPR ring. To obtain the formula describing the *Mean Time to Failure* when repairs are taken into account, a Markov model of failure states, presented in Fig. 4, will be used. In the Markov model we assume that it is impossible to have more than a double failure in a network. This allows us to have a relatively small state space. In fact, it is not so small, especially in the two-terminal cases. The influence of triple, quadruple, etc. failures is negligible. Therefore, we do not consider any transitions related to triple and higher order failures. Let us denote the states in the model presented in Fig. 4:

- s_0 the state where all spans and nodes are operational; it is an initial state, i.e., the state in which the system starts to work;
- s_1 the state where one node is faulty; this state is treated here as the absorbing one;
- s_2 the state where one span is faulty (and steering is activated)
- s_3 the state where one span and one node are faulty (absorbing state);
- s_4 the state where two spans are faulty (absorbing state).

The intensity of the transition from s_0 to s_2 equals $N\lambda_s$ as there are N spans that can fail. The intensity of the transition from s_2 to s_0 is equal to μ_s as

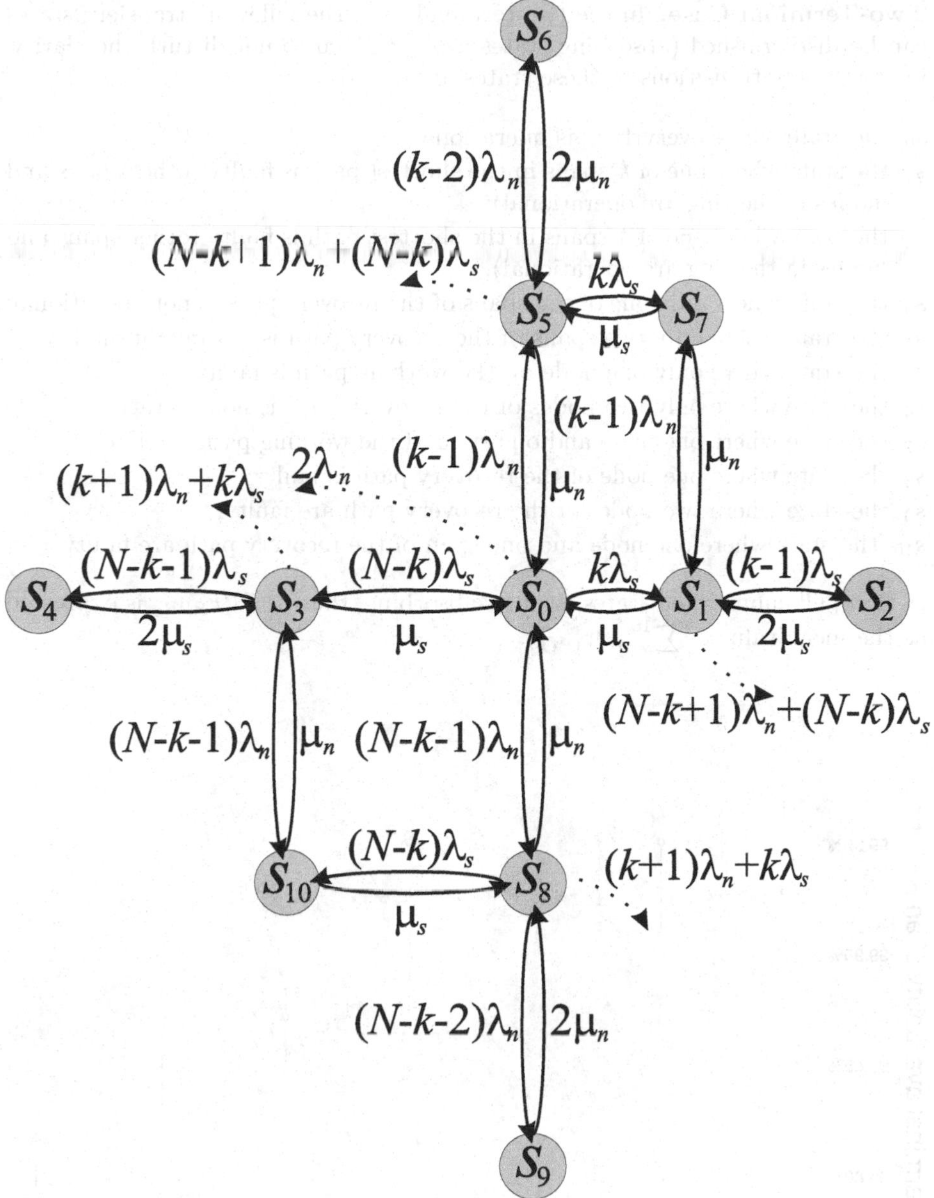

Fig. 5. Markov reliability model related to the two-terminal reliability case in an RPR ring

in this case only one span can be recovered. Other transition intensity values are determined in the analogous way. $MTTF_{\mathrm{RPR_{all}}}$ is here expressed as the mean value of the sum of the probabilities of non-absorbing states [11] (here: $\Pr\{s_0\} + \Pr\{s_2\}$).

Two-Terminal Case. In the two-terminal case, the following transient states can be distinguished (absorbing states are not given to not disturb the clarity, in Fig. 5 only transitions to these states are given):

s_0 the state where everything is operational;
s_1 the state where one of k spans in the shortest path is faulty (other spans and nodes in the ring are operational);
s_2 the state where one of k spans in the shortest path is faulty (other spans and nodes in the ring are operational);
s_3 the state where only one of the spans of the recovery path is not operational;
s_4 the state where only two spans of the recovery path is not operational;
s_5 the state where only one node on the working path is faulty
s_6 the state where only two nodes of the recovery path is not operational;
s_7 the state where one node and one span of the working path are faulty;
s_8 the state where one node of the recovery path is faulty;
s_9 the state where two nodes of the recovery path are faulty;
s_{10} the state where one node and one span of the recovery path are faulty;

Here, all enumerated states are non-absorbing, thus $MTTF_{\mathrm{RPR}_2}$ is expressed as the mean value of $\sum_{i=0}^{10} \Pr\{s_i\}$).

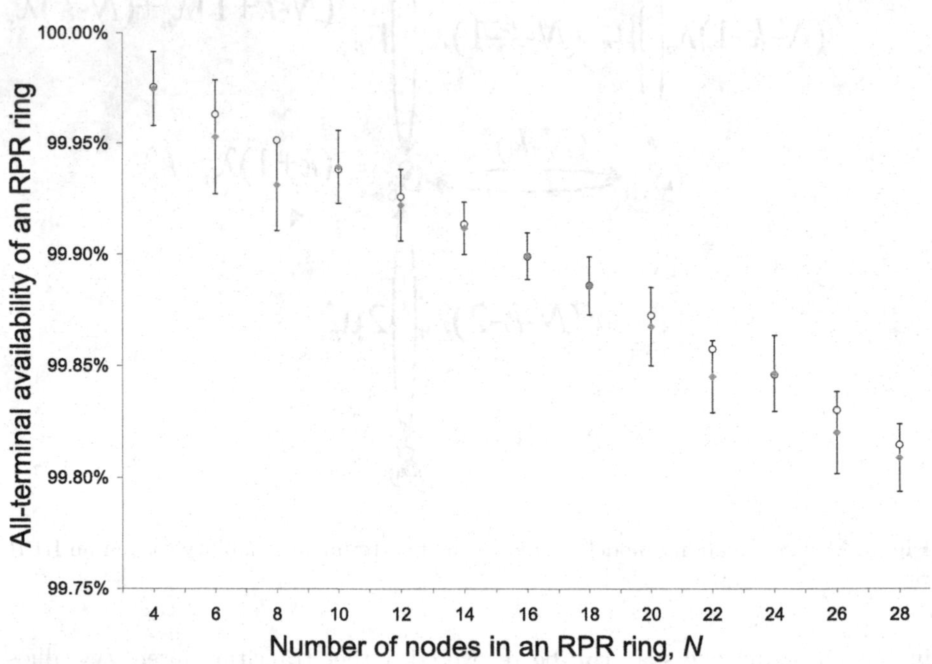

Fig. 6. Comparison of theoretical (circle) and simulation results (squares) in example RPR rings: all-terminal availability. 95% confidence intervals are marked.

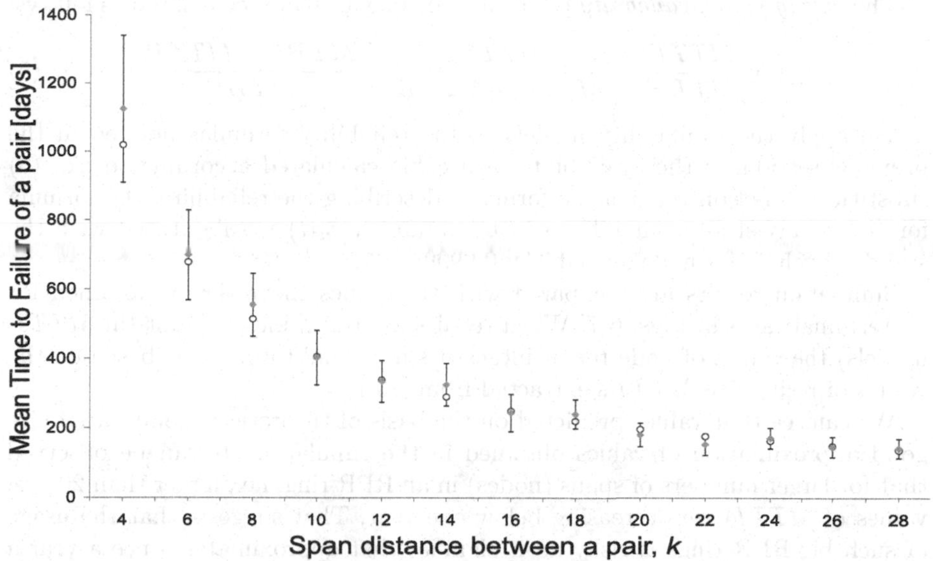

Fig. 7. Comparison of theoretical (circle) and simulation results (squares) in example RPR rings: *Mean Time to Failure*: all-terminal availability. 95% confidence intervals are marked.

4 Numerical Example

To verify the results of our analysis we performed some simulation experiments as we lack empirical data from carriers' statistics. To show that the derived formulas were calculated properly and can be used as resilience performance estimates, we simulated failures in an RPR ring with different number of nodes. Span lengths were chosen randomly on the basis of the normal distribution $N(200, 100)$ (distance is given in km).

In the steady state, we have the well known relation:

$$MTBF = MTTF + MTTR \tag{3}$$

where: $MTTR$ is the *Mean Time to Repair* ($MTTR = 1/\mu$) and $MTBF$ represents *Mean Time Between Failures* ($MTBF = 1/\lambda$). It can be useful as an input in some studies, because its value is based of statistical studies derived from the data collected by operators, i.e., the frequency of cable cuts. Let CC (cable cuts parameter, measured in km) represents the average length of a fiber which is cut once a year. Provided it is known, the value of $MTBF$ (in hours) of a fiber, which is l miles long, can be calculated according to the following relation [12]:

$$MTBF = (CC \times 365 \times 24)/l \tag{4}$$

In our simulations $CC = 530$ km.

The *steady-state availability* for a cable forming a span is calculated as follows:

$$A = \frac{MTTF}{MTBF} = \frac{MTTF}{MTTF + MTTR} = \frac{MTBF - MTTR}{MTBF} \quad (5)$$

We apply the availability models to the reliability formulas derived in the previous section. If the availability of a cable calculated according to Eq. (5) substitutes function $r_s(t)$ in the formulas describing the reliability, the formula for the steady-state availability will be obtained. $r_n(t)$ is substituted with the standard value of a node availability 0.99994 [13].

Simulation results are compared with the values theoretically obtained for all-terminal cases in Figs. 6-7. When repairs are taken into account (in $MTTF$ models) the values of node repair intensities are equal to: $\mu_n = 4$ (based on the values of respective $MTTR$s extracted from [13]).

We can see that values predicted on the basis of theoretical models are quite good approximation of values obtained in the simulation. It can be observed that for larger numbers of spans (nodes) in an RPR ring, i.e., larger than 20, the values of $MTTF$ are decreasing below one year. That suggests that the usage of such big RPR rings is risky ad it signifies that approximately once a year a carrier will have problems with transporting some quantity of traffic according to not restored faults.

5 Conclusion

In the paper, different reliability models related to an RPR rings were applied. This is the first approach to the RPR reliability analysis. The reliability function as well as Mean Time to Failure are covered. All- and two- terminal cases are taken into account. The simulation results confirm that they can be successfully used to assess the resiliency features of this technique. Further works will focus on more systematic analysis of reliability aspects when the RPR protocol is embedded in a wider system (e.g., MPLS-over-RPR).

References

1. IEEE 802.17: IEEE Standard for Information Technology–Telecommunications and Information Exchange between Systems–Local and Metropolitan Area Networks–Specific Requirements-Part 17: Resilient Packet Ring (RPR) Access Method & Physical Layer Specifications (2004)
2. Spadaro, S., Solé-Pareta, J., Careglio, D., Wajda, K., Szymański, A.: Assessment of Resilience Features for the DPT Rings. In: Proc. Eurescom Summit 2002, Heidelberg, Germany (2002)
3. Spadaro, S., Solé-Pareta, J., Careglio, D., Wajda, K., Szymański, A.: Positioning of the RPR Standard in Contemporary Operator Environments. IEEE Network **18**(2) (2004) 35–40
4. Domżał, J., Wajda, K.: Recovery, Fairness and Congestion Control Mechanisms in RPR Networks. In: Proc. 12th Polish Teletraffic Symposium PSRT'2005, Poznań, Poland (2005)

5. Shooman, M.L.: Reliability of Computer Systems and Networks: Fault Tolerance, Analysis, and Design. John Wiley & Sons, Inc., New York, NY (2002)
6. ITU-T Rec. E.800: Terms and Definitions Related to Quality of Service and Network Performance Including Dependability (1994)
7. Bolch, G., Greiner, S., de Meer, H., Trivedi, K.S.: Queueing Networks and Markov Chains: Modeling and Performance Evaluation with Computer Science Applications. John Wiley & Sons, Inc., New York, NY (1998)
8. Logothetis, D., Trivedi, K.S.: Reliability Analysis of the Double Counter-Rotating Ring with Concentrator Attachments. IEEE/ACM Trans. Networking 2(5) (1994) 520–532
9. Chołda, P., Jajszczyk, A.: Reliability Assessment of p-Cycles. In: Proc. 2005 IEEE Global Telecommunications Conference GLOBECOM'05, St. Louis, MO (2005)
10. Sahner, R.A., Trivedi, K.S., Puliafito, A.: Performance and Reliability Analysis of Computer Systems: An Example-Based Approach Using the SHARPE Software Package. Kluwer Academic Publishers, Dordrecht, Holland (1996)
11. Trivedi, K.S.: Probability and Statistics with Reliability, Queuing, and Computer Science Applications. John Wiley & Sons, Inc., New York, NY (2001)
12. Vasseur, J.P., Pickavet, M., Demeester, P.: Network Recovery. Protection and Restoration of Optical, SONET-SDH, IP, and MPLS. Morgan Kaufmann Publishers, San Francisco, CA (2004)
13. Verbrugge, S., Colle, D., Demeester, P., Huelsermann, R., Jaeger, M.: General Availability Model for Multilayer Transport Networks. In: Proc. 5th International Workshop on the Design of Reliable Communication Networks DRCN 2005, Lacco Ameno, Island of Ischia, Italy (2005)

Experiences with the Design of a Run-Time Check

Meine J.P. van der Meulen[1] and Miguel A. Revilla[2]

[1] City University, Centre for Software Reliability, London, UK
http://www.csr.city.ac.uk
[2] University of Valladolid, Valladolid, Spain
http://www.mac.cie.uva.es/~revilla

Abstract. Run-time checks are often assumed to be a cost-effective way of improving the dependability of software components, by checking required properties of their outputs and flagging an output as incorrect if it fails the check. Run-time checks' main point of attractiveness is that they are supposed to be easy to implement. Also, they are implicitly assumed to be effective in detecting incorrect outputs. This paper reports the results of an experiment designed to challenge these assumptions about run-time checks.

The experiment uses a subset of 196 of 867 programs (primaries) solving a problem called "Make Palindrome". This is an existing problem on the "On-Line Judge" website of the university of Valladolid. We formulated eight run-time checks, and posted this problem on the same website. This resulted in 335 programs (checkers) implementing the run-time checks, 115 of which are used for the experiment.

In this experiment: (1) the effectiveness of the population of possibly faulty checkers is very close to the effectiveness of a correct checker; (2) the reliability improvement provided by the run-time checks is relatively small, between a factor of one and three; (3) The reliability improvement gained by using multiple-version redundancy is much higher. Given the fact that this experiment only considers one primary/Run-Time Check combination, it is not yet possible to generalise the results.

1 Introduction

Redundancy is a means to improve the reliability of software components. Much research has been invested in multiple-version redundancy, e.g. 1-out-of-2 systems. Much less research has been invested in asymmetrical redundancy, e.g. the use of run-time checks, RTCs, see Figure 1. In these cases a primary program is checked by an, ideally relatively simple, RTC.

RTCs are often proposed as a means to improve the dependability of software components. They are seen as cheap compared to other means of increasing reliability by run-time redundancy, e.g. N-version programming. We are interested in answering questions like whether RTCs are effective and how their performance compares to that of symmetrical redundancy. We also want to confirm or reject common conjectures, such as that RTCs are so simple that we may assume that they are correctly programmed.

J. Górski (Ed.): SAFECOMP 2006, LNCS 4166, pp. 302–315, 2006.

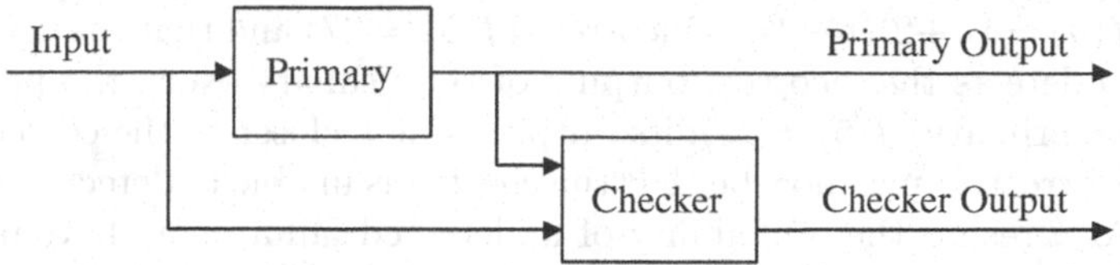

Fig. 1. Primary/Checker model

Table 1. Sample inputs and sample outputs for the primary

Sample Input	Sample Output
`abcd`	`3 abcdcba`
`aaaa`	`0 aaaa`
`abc`	`2 abcba`
`aab`	`1 baab`
`abababaababababa`	`0 abababaababababa`
`pqrsabcdpqrs`	`9 pqrsabcdpqrqpdcbasrqp`

RTCs (also called *executable assertions* and other names) can be based on various principles (see e.g. Lee and Anderson [3] for a summary), and have wide application. For instance, the concept of design by contract [5] enables a check on properties of program behaviour.

Some RTCs can detect all failures, for example checks that perform an inverse operation on the result of a software component [1,2]. If the program computes $y = f(x)$, an error is detected if $x \neq f^{-1}(y)$. This is especially attractive when computing $f(x)$ is complex, and the computation of the inverse f^{-1} relatively simple. The argument is then that because computing f^{-1} is simple, the likelihood of failure of this RTC is low. Also, it seems unlikely that both the primary computation and the RTC would fail on the same invocation and in a consistent fashion. Together, these factors lead to a high degree of confidence that program outputs that pass the check will be correct. However—as these authors readily admit—such theoretically perfect checks do not exist in many cases, maybe even not in the majority of cases. RTCs can then still be applied, but they will in general not be capable of finding all failures. Examples of these partial RTCs are given by e.g. [11].

Previous empirical evaluation of RTCs have generally used small samples of programs, or single programs [4,7,10]. Importantly, our experiment involves a *population* of programs, both of the primary and of the checker, because we think that in order to learn something general about RTCs, we need a statistical approach. We can now study the complex interplay between (possible faulty) primaries combined with (partial, possibly faulty) checkers.

The interaction between the primary and the checker is complex because the performance of the checker is dependent on that of the primary. An example of this interaction is that it may be that improving the primary may lead to a rise in the probability of undetected failure. Suppose that a primary (e.g., to compute $f(n) = (n+2)(n-2)$) is incorrect ($f(5) = 27$) and that the checker (e.g., $f(n) \leq n^2$) detects the incorrect outputs of the primary. Now, the programmer changes the primary ($f(5) = 23$); its output is now closer to the correct answer, but still incorrect. It may now be that the checker is unable to detect the incorrect outputs. As a result, the probability of undetected failure may have increased.

2 The Experiment

2.1 The UVa Online Judge

The "UVa Online Judge"-Website (`http://acm.uva.es`, [8]) is an initiative of one of the authors (Revilla). It contains program specifications for which anyone may submit programs in C, C++, Java or Pascal intended to implement them. The correctness of a program is automatically judged by the "Online Judge". Most authors submit programs repeatedly until one is judged correct. Many thousands of authors contribute and together they have produced more than 3,000,000 programs for the approximately 1,500 specifications on the website.

2.2 Specification of the Primary

For the primary, we took a specification from the Online Judge formulated by Md. Kamruzzaman: a program to generate palindromes. It takes an input string of 1000 or less lower case characters and makes it into a palindrome by inserting lower case characters into the input string at any position. The number of characters inserted shall be as low as possible. The output is the number of characters inserted, followed by the resulting palindrome. See for a complete specification the Online Judge website, `http://acm.uva.es/p/v104/10453.html`, and Table 1 for some examples of correct input and output combinations.

2.3 Specification of the Checker

Based on the specification of the primary, we formulated a specification for its checker. The checker (`http://acm.uva.es/p/v104/10848.html`) takes as its input a string of 5000 or less ASCII characters (5000 to allow for faults in the primary, leading to the output of many characters). It tests this string for the following properties:

- P1. It consists of a first string of lower case characters (length ≤ 1000), a single space, an integer (≥ 0, ≤ 1000), a single space, and a second string of lower case letters (length ≤ 2000).
- P2. P1 & the second string is a palindrome.
- P3. P1 & all letters of the first string appear in the second string.
- P4. P1 & the frequency of every letter in the second string is at least the frequency of this letter in the first string.
- P5. P1 & the first string can be made out of the second string by removing 0 or more letters (and leaving the order of the letters intact).

Table 2. Sample inputs and sample outputs for the checker

Sample Input	Sample Output
`abcd 3 abcdcba`	`TTTTTTT The solution is accepted`
`aaaa 3 abcdcba`	`TTTFFTT The solution is not accepted`
`abc 2 abdcba`	`TFTTTFT The solution is not accepted`
`aab b baab`	`FFFFFFF The solution is not accepted`
`abababaababababa 0 abababaababababa`	`TTTTTTT The solution is accepted`
`pqrsabcdpqrs 9 pqrsabcdpqrqpdcbasrqp`	`TTTTTTT The solution is accepted`

P6. P1 & the length of the second string is equal to the length of the first string plus the value of the integer.
P7. P1 & the value of the integer is smaller than the length of the first string.

Obviously, when all properties are true, the output of the primary may still be faulty.

The output consists of the value "T" or "F" (for True and False) for every property in the list above, and a statement "The solution is accepted" if all properties are true, and "The solution is not accepted" otherwise. We will call this property P8. See Table 2 for some examples of correct input and output combinations.

Although the checkers implement all eight different properties, we will analyse these separately, as if the checker programs only implement one of these. When we address any of the run-time checks, we will use the abbreviation RTC. When we address the implementations of one of the properties P1-8, we will use the abbreviations RTC1-8.

2.4 System Behaviour

Table 3 shows how we classify the effects on the system based on the outputs of the primary and the run-time checks. The effects from the system viewpoint are rather obvious, except for the consequences of “No output” from the RTC (this includes invalid output). We have chosen to accept the output of the primary in these cases; the other option would also have been possible, it would have increased the number of false alarms. Our choice is based on the assumption that false alarms of RTCs are in general very undesirable.

RTC1 differs from RTC2-8, because it is purely a syntactical check of the input. It is a necessary precondition to be able to do any of the other checks. It is interesting to separate this check from RTC2-8, because it gives us an idea how much the more application specific RTC2-8 add to this basic syntactic check.

2.5 Equivalence Classes

We subjected the primary to 10,000 demands: strings of lower case characters. Each string has a random length between 1 and 30 characters with random characters from the set “a”..“e”. The reason for the limited character set is that

Table 3. Classification of execution results with RTCs

Output of primary	run-time check	Effect from system viewpoint
Correct	Accept	Correct
Correct	Reject	False alarm
Correct	No output	Correct
Incorrect	Accept	Undetected failure
Incorrect	Reject	Detected failure
Incorrect	No output	Undetected failure

cases with character repetition will more frequently occur. The reason for the maximum length of the string is to limit the execution time of the primary.

We sorted the primaries in "equivalence classes", i.e. sets of programs producing exactly the same output. There is more than 1 correct equivalence class, because for almost all inputs there is more than one correct solution, e.g. the correct output to the input "`ab`" may be "`1 aba`" or "`1 bab`".

The primaries gave mostly equal, but also many different outputs to the 10,000 demands; in total there were 529,433 different outputs to the 10,000 inputs. to reduce computing time, we randomly selected 17,241 of these (approximately 1/30). We generated an input file to the checkers by combining each output with the corresponding input. This input file is used to determine the equivalence classes of the checkers and was only used for this purpose; for the rest of the experiment we used the 10,000 demands as used for determining the primary equivalence classes. We assumed that these 17,241 demands are sufficient to discern the different checker equivalent classes.

For every primary equivalence class we made an input file for the checkers by combining the 10,000 demands (the same for every primary) and their outputs. We executed every combination of primary and checker equivalence classes with the appropriate input files. This was computationally quite intensive; the computation took approximately three days.

2.6 Score Functions

Assume a specification for the primary, S_π:

$$S_\pi(x,y) \equiv \text{“}y \text{ is valid primary output for input } x\text{”} \tag{1}$$

Then, we define the score function ω_π for a random primary π as:

$$\omega_\pi(\pi, x) \equiv \neg S(x, \pi(x)) \tag{2}$$

I.e., the score function is true when the primary π fails to compute a valid output y for a given input x.

The behaviour of an RTC σ can be described as:

$$\sigma(x,y) \equiv \text{“}y \text{ is accepted as valid primary output for input } x\text{”} \tag{3}$$

Note the similarity to the specification of the primary, S_π. Whereas the specification is supposed to be correct, we assume that the checker may be faulty: it may erroneously accept an incorrect pair (x, y). The checker fails if there is a discrepancy with the specification. The score function ω_σ for an RTC is:

$$\omega_\sigma(\sigma, x, y) \equiv S_\pi(x, y) \oplus \sigma(x, y) \tag{4}$$

I.e., the score function is true when the checker fails to recognize whether y is valid primary output for input x or not.

For our system as depicted in Figure 1 and the variables (x, π, σ) for the input, the primary and the checker, there are four possibilities:

1. $\neg\omega_\pi(\pi, x) \wedge \neg\omega_\sigma(\sigma, x, \pi(x))$: Correct operation.
2. $\neg\omega_\pi(\pi, x) \wedge \omega_\sigma(\sigma, x, \pi(x))$: False alarm.
3. $\omega_\pi(\pi, x) \wedge \neg\omega_\sigma(\sigma, x, \pi(x))$: Detected failure.
4. $\omega_\pi(\pi, x) \wedge \omega_\sigma(\sigma, x, \pi(x))$: Undetected failure.

We have calculated the score functions $\omega_\pi(\pi, x)$ and $\omega_\sigma(\sigma, x, y)$ for the primary and the checker equivalence classes.

2.7 Subsets for the Experiment

There are 867 submissions for the primary specification. We included the primaries that are written in C, C++ or Pascal, compile and provide output within one second. This left 566 primaries. Then we excluded primaries that fail for all inputs, that left 484 primaries. From these we used the first submission of each author: 196 primaries. There are various reasons for selecting the first submissions:

1. We do not want to include more than one submission of a single author, because subsequent submissions are shown to be highly similar, and that would corrupt our statistical analyses.
2. The variability between first versions is higher, e.g. because later submissions are more likely to be correct. This gives more room for statistical analyses.
3. A first submission is most comparable to a first submission in a "normal" development process, because feedback to the authors differs from normal feedback in various ways, e.g. the Online Judge will not communicate for which input the program failed.

There are 395 submissions for the checker specification. We included the checkers that are written in C, C++ or Pascal, compile and provide output within one second. This left 335 checkers.

For these checkers we compute the average FAR (false alarm rate, the fraction of false alarms) for a specific primary π for RTC8 (for the calculations: $TRUE = 1, FALSE = 0$):

$$FAR(\pi) = \sum_{x \in D} \sum_{\sigma \in R_\sigma} (1 - \omega_\pi(\pi, x)) \cdot \omega_\sigma(\sigma, x, \sigma(x)) \cdot Q(x) \tag{5}$$

R_σ is the set of checkers, $Q(X)$ is the demand profile over the demand space D. D is the test set of 10,000 demands; we assume that each of the 10,000 demands is equiprobable, and therefore: $Q(x) = 1/10,000$.

We excluded checkers that have a FAR of more than 0.1 for any primary or do not provide sensible output at all (manual check), that left 306 checkers. From these we used the first submission of each author: 118 checkers.

The rationale for excluding checkers with a high FAR is that these will normally be quickly detected during development. This is our modelling of the debugging process of the checkers. There is only one checker left with a FAR larger than zero. This checker fails for RTC1 (and subsequently often for RTC2-8) in a rather erratic way.

3 Observations

3.1 General

The first observation was already done during selection of a suitable primary for this research. It appeared that it is only possible for a small subset of the problems of the Online Judge to formulate meaningful RTCs. In many cases, the output of a program is a (set of) number(s) for which it is not possible to formulate an inverse function to the input, or even an interesting weaker relationship.

We chose this primary because it is possible to define RTCs, and a sufficient number of submissions for the primary is available.

3.2 The Specification of the Checker

The checker specification appeared to be incomplete: we forgot to specify a lower bound on the length of the strings. This leaves it to the programmers to decide whether an empty string is correct input or not. As it appears, some of the authors allow empty strings. This ambiguity has consequences for property 2: is an empty string a palindrome or not? As it happens some authors who accept empty strings consider an empty string to be a palindrome, others don't.

A peculiar problem occurs for property 4: P1 & the frequency of every letter in the second string is at least the frequency of this letter in the first string. We intended to write: P1 & the frequency of every letter in the first string is smaller than or equal to the frequency of this letter in the second string. Peculiarly, most authors interpreted it this way. They thus wrote a stronger test than was specified.

We argue that problems with specifications are common, and that this observation does therefore not invalidate the conclusions of the paper. Maybe even to the contrary: they might even be supporting it, since specifying is part of the development process, and a possible source of errors.

There is one equivalence class containing a correct checker, i.e. a program that does not accept empty strings and interprets P4 as written in the specification. Nobody submitted a correct program as their first submission. This implies there

Table 4. Most frequent equivalence classes in the first submissions for the primary

Fault	Freq.	PFD	Detection
Correct	129	0.00	No detection.
Adds too many characters to input string.	5	0.54	No detection.
Forgets last character in input string.	2	0.69	P3 (28%), P4 (55%), P5 (100%), P8 (100%)
Adds too many characters to input string.	2	0.55	No detection.
Output string is not always a palindrome.	2	0.12	P2 (100%), P8 (100%)
...			
Often fails to output second string.	1	0.94	P1-8 (100%)
Often outputs very large integers.	1	0.99	P126 (93%), P345 (96%), P8 (100%)
...			
No integer in output.	0	1.00	P1-8 (100%)
Often outputs control character at end of second string.	0	0.94	P1-8 (100%)

is no correct submission in the set of programs we do our analyses on in this paper, c.f. 2.7.

3.3 Faults in the Primary

To give an idea of the kinds of faults made, Table 4 presents some of the equivalence classes of the primaries. There are 17 correct equivalence classes, with in total 129 submissions. There are 67 incorrect submissions in 59 equivalence classes. Only five equivalence classes contain more than one submission, these are listed in the table. The fact that equivalence classes tend to only contain one program indicates that authors tend to choose different approaches and tend to make different mistakes. Furthermore, the presence of many different equivalence classes for correct solutions indicates that authors do not tend to copy solutions from each other, one of the worries for the usefulness of the data.

The table also shows whether the faults are detected by a correct checker, and how effective these checks are.

3.4 Faults in the Checker

Table 5 presents some of the equivalence classes of the checkers. There are 54 correct submissions in one equivalence class (there is only one way to solve this problem). There are 64 incorrect submissions in 51 equivalence classes, only seven of these contain more than one submission. This again indicates that the authors do not tend to make exactly the same mistake.

Seven submissions give no output when the second string is empty.

The most frequent mistake is that a checker fails when there are special ASCII characters in the input string, e.g. the NULL character. This is problematic, because some primaries fail in a way that produces exactly these characters. This is caused by the fact that the solution to the "Make Palindrome"-problem typically

Table 5. Most frequent equivalence classes in the first submissions for the checker

Fault	Freq.
Correct, except that P4 is interpreted more extensively.	54
Fails when input contains control characters.	5
Fails when integer in input string is very large.	4
Always outputs "TTTTTT The solutions is accepted".	3
Fails when second string is absent.	2
Fails when there is a control character in the second string.	2
Fails when integer in input string is very large.	2
Fails when there is a control character in the integer or in the second string.	2
...	
Fails for P4, behaves partly as specified.	1
Fails for P4, behaves as specified, but strange other fault.	1
Accepts empty second string, assumes empty string is palindrome.	1
...	
Correct.	0
...	

includes array manipulation. This, combined with a bug leading to a pointer being out of array bounds, leads to possibly outputting these characters. Important is here that this observation may undermine the conjecture of independence between primaries and checkers.

4 Statistical Calculations

4.1 Reliability Improvement

To know the reliability improvement the checkers give, we first have to compute the probability of failure on demand of the primaries:

$$PFD(\pi) = \sum_{x \in D} \omega_\pi(\pi, x) \cdot Q(x) \tag{6}$$

Figure 2(a) presents the distribution of the PFDs of the primaries in a histogram.

The probability of undetected failure of a primary, averaged over the checkers is:

$$PUFD(\pi) = \sum_{x \in D} \sum_{\sigma \in R_\sigma} \omega_\pi(\pi, x) \cdot \omega_\sigma(\sigma, x, \sigma(x)) \cdot Q(x) \tag{7}$$

Figure 2(b) shows the distribution of the probability of undetected failure after applying RTC8. As can be expected, there is a significant shift to the left.

We now calculate the improvement of the primary PFD for various checkers for subsets of the primary programs:

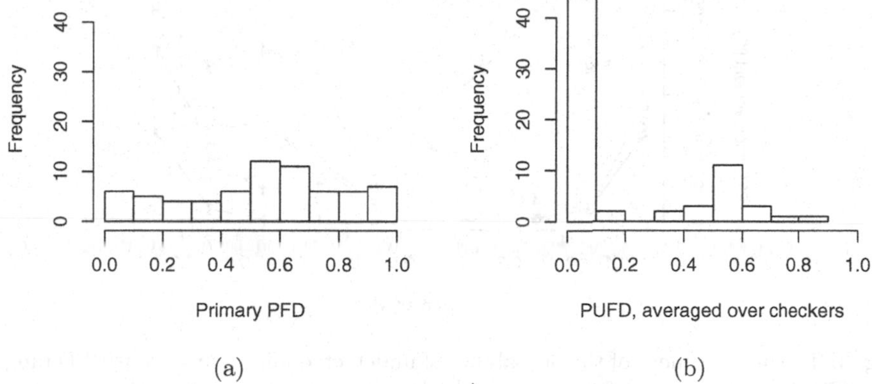

(a) (b)

Fig. 2. (a) Histogram of the PFDs of the primaries; (b) Histogram of the average probability of undetected failure for the same primaries, with RTC8. Both graphs exclude the 129 correct primaries.

$$I(PFD_{min}, PFD_{max}) = \frac{\sum_{\pi \in \hat{R}_\pi} PFD(\pi)}{\sum_{\pi \in \hat{R}_\pi} PUFD(\pi)} \tag{8}$$

with $\hat{R}_\pi = \{\pi | PFD_{min} < PFD(\pi) \leq PFD_{max}\}$.

We choose 10 subsets $\hat{R}_\pi$ of the primary programs such that: $0 < PFD(\pi) \leq 0.1$, $0.1 < PFD(\pi) \leq 0.2$, and so on. Figure 3 shows the improvement of the probability of undetected failure in the various PFD ranges for RTCs 1, 2, 4, 6 and 8 for a correct checker (we do not show all, because this makes the figure unreadable; the other RTCs show similar erratic behaviour). There appears to be no obvious relation between the PFD of the primaries and the effectiveness of RTCs. Who would have expected that RTC6 would be very effective for reliable primaries?

Some RTCs are very effective, others are not. Some are effective for low primary PFDs, others for high. It is however not predictable which RTCs will be effective, since this depends on factors as the demand space and the programming faults made in the primary.

The graph gives rise to one possible conclusion: RTCs may still be effective for reliable primaries.

4.2 Effectiveness of the RTCs for Decreasing Average PUFD

We now investigate the effectiveness of RTCs as a function of the average PFD of primaries. To vary the PFD, we take the pool of 196 primaries and we one after another remove primaries with the highest PFD. The result is shown in Figure 4.

As observed in our earlier paper [9], the effectiveness of RTCs shows a rather unpredictable pattern. The PFD-improvement of RTC1-7 remains well below a factor three in almost the entire graph. RTC6 and 8 become infinity for low PUFDs, but that is mainly caused by the fact that the number of primaries in this region becomes very small and the checkers manage to capture the faults in

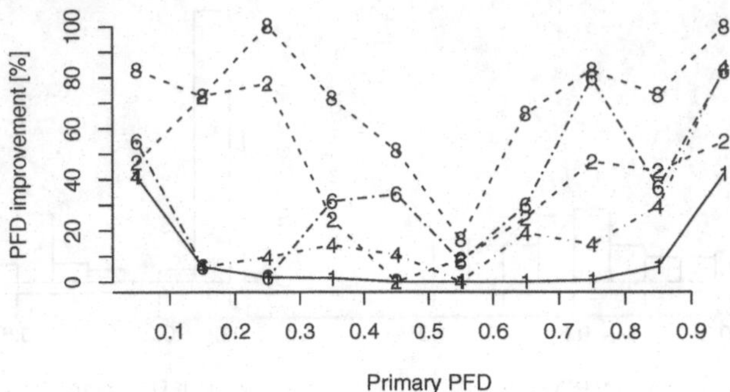

Fig. 3. The improvement of the probability of undetected failure in various PFD ranges for RTCs 1, 2, 4, 6 and 8 for a correct checker. The improvement in the range 0-0.1 excludes correct primaries.

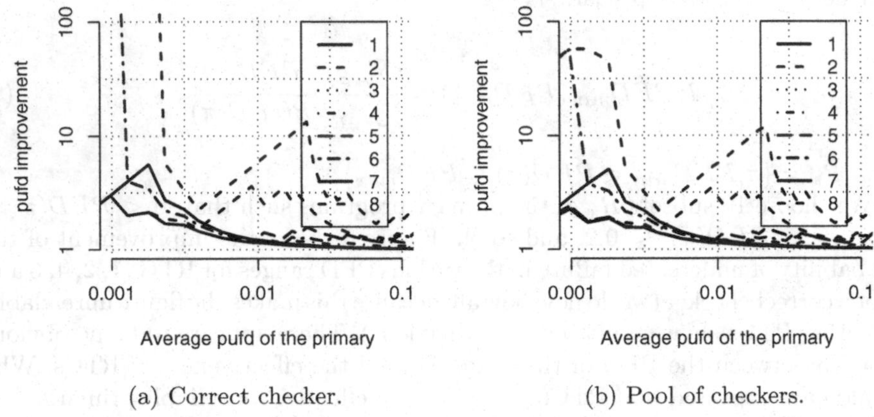

Fig. 4. The effectiveness of the eight RTCs as with decreasing average PFD of the pool of primaries. The PFD is lowered by subsequently removing the most unreliable programs. (a) For a correct checker; (b) averaged over the pool of checkers.

these few programs. The numbers computed in this region of the graph should be considered with care. RTC8 is the conjunction of RTC1-7, and reaches an average PFD improvement of about a factor three.

When we compare the PUFD of the correct checker with the average of the checkers, we can observe that there is little difference, except for highly reliable primaries. Here, the performance of the checkers is reduced, because of faults in some checkers.

There may be a turning point at which a checker's effectiveness becomes questionable: when the ratio between false alarms and detection of primary failure becomes worse. Here we see a complex interplay between improving the quality of the primary and the checker. Improving the quality of the checker may have low priority, thus possibly resulting in poor specificity of the average checker.

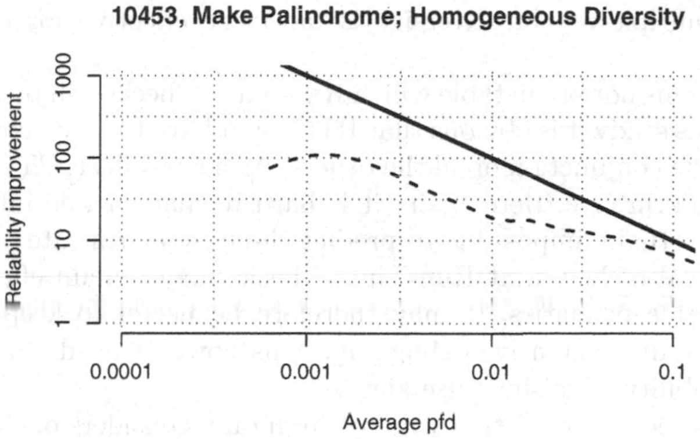

Fig. 5. Improvement of the PUFD of a pair of randomly chosen primaries, relative to a single version. The horizontal axis shows the average PUFD of the pool from which both primaries are selected. The vertical axis shows the PUFD improvement ($PUFD_A/PUFD_{AB}$). The diagonal represents the theoretical reliability improvement if the programs fail independently, i.e. $PUFD_{AB} = PUFD_A \cdot PUFD_B$.

5 RTCs vs. Multiple-Version Diversity

We now compare the effectiveness of RTCs with 1-out-of-2 diversity. We make a graph in the same way as Figure 4, except that we take two primaries from the pool instead of one.

We observe (see Figure 5) that 1-out-of-2 diversity becomes more effective with decreasing PFD of the pool of primaries from which the pair is selected. The reliability improvement ranges from a factor 25 to 100 for primary PFDs between 0.01 and 0.001. The effectiveness seems to reach a peak at a PFD of 0.001. (note that the opposite trend—effectiveness decreasing with decreasing mean PFD—is also possible, as proved by models and empirical results [6]). The improvement factor of most run-time checks remains fairly constant between 1 and 3 over this range, depending on the RTC. Only RTC8 reaches a factor of 10, when the PFD of the primaries is around 0.02. The improvement factor of using diversity is significantly higher than that of applying RTCs.

These results also confirm those in our earlier publication on the effectiveness of RTCs [9].

6 Conclusions

In this paper, we examined the effectiveness of Run-Time Checks without the assumption that these are fault-free. The effectiveness of the average checker appears to not deviate much from that of a perfect checker.

The effectiveness of the Run-Time Checks is comparable to that in our earlier study [9], a factor between one and three. We also confirmed the earlier result that multiple-version diversity is far more effective for decreasing the PUFD.

As yet, it seems not predictable which Run-Time Checks will be most effective, although in this study it is obvious that RTC8 will have the best coverage, simply because it is the conjunction of all the others. As a side effect, RTC8 also has the highest false alarm rate. Here again, it is hard to make a well-informed choice, because it is virtually impossible to predict the false alarm rate.

The results also show that Run-Time Checks may remain effective, also for the more reliable primaries. It may therefore be useful to keep the RTCs in primaries, also after extensive debugging. This however needs to be a trade-off with the possibility of raising false alarms.

We have to keep in mind that this research only considers one primary/Run-Time Checker combination, and that we can as yet not generalise, except perhaps for those observations that confirm those in our earlier publication on Run-Time Checks.

Acknowledgement

This work was supported in part by the U.K. Engineering and Physical Sciences Research Council via the Interdisciplinary Research Collaboration on the Dependability of Computer Based Systems (DIRC), and via the Diversity with Off-The-Shelf Components (DOTS) project, GR/N23912.

References

1. M. Blum and H. Wasserman. Software reliability via run-time result-checking. Technical Report TR-94-053, International Computer Science Institute, October 1994.
2. A. Jhumka, F.C. Gärtner, C. Fetzer, and N. Suri. On systematic design of fast and perfect detectors. Technical Report 200263, École Polytechnique Fédérale de Lausanne (EPFDL), School of Computer and Communication Sciences, September 2002.
3. P.A. Lee and T. Anderson. *Fault Tolerance; Principles and Practice*, volume 3 of *Dependable Computing and Fault-Tolerant Systems*. Springer, 2nd edition, 1981.
4. N.G. Leveson, S.S. Cha, J.C. Knight, and T.J. Shimeall. The use of self checks and voting in software error detection: An empirical study. In *IEEE Transactions on Software Engineering*, volume 16(4), pages 432–43, 1990.
5. B. Meyer. Design by contract. *Computer (IEEE)*, 25(10):40–51, October 1992.
6. P. Popov and L. Strigini. The reliability of diverse systems: A contribution using modelling of the fault creation process. *DSN 2001, International Conference on Dependable Systems and Networks, Göteborg, Sweden*, July 2001.
7. M. Rela, H. Madeira, and J.G. Silva. Experimental evaluation of the fail-silent behavior of programs with consistency checks. In *FTCS-26, Sendai, Japan*, pages 394–403, 1996.
8. S. Skiena and M. Revilla. *Programming Challenges*. Springer Verlag, March 2003.

9. M.J.P. van der Meulen, L. Strigini, and M. Revilla. On the effectiveness of run-time checks. In B.A. Gran and R. Winter, editors, *Computer Safety, Reliability and Security, Proceedings of the 23nd international conference, Safecomp 2005*, pages 151–64, Fredrikstad, Norway, September 2005.
10. J. Vinter, J. Aidemark, P. Folkesson, and J. Karlsson. Reducing critical failures for control algorithms using executable assertions and best effort recovery. In *DSN 2001, International Conference on Dependable Systems and Networks, Goteborg, Sweden*, 2001.
11. H. Wasserman and M. Blum. Software reliability via run-time result-checking. *Journal of the ACM*, 44(6):826–49, 1997.

Development of an Integrated, Risk-Based Platform for Information and E-Services Security

Andrzej Białas

Institute of Control Systems, 41-506 Chorzów, Długa 1-3, Poland
abialas@iss.pl

Abstract. The paper presents a risk-based integrated platform for the information and e-services security management related to the Information Security Managements System (ISMS) concept. The current state of the work is shown, including the UML-based methodology, and the incrementally developed computer-aided tool prototype. The assumptions of the integrated platform can be specified on the basis of sampled experiences from the first deployment and case studies, an analysis of standards, legal requirements and technology, and a study of the needs and requirements of various organizations. It is assumed that the common and enhanced assets inventory will integrate information security, business continuity and IT services management processes. The paper concludes the current, initial state of the work and defines its further directions.

Keywords: information security management, risk, IT services, UML.

1 Introduction

The paper presents the work aimed at building a risk-based integrated platform for the information and e-services security management. The platform can be considered an extended version of the well known ISMS framework (*Information Security Managements System*) [1], [2], based on the PDCA (*Plan-Do-Check-Act*) scheme.

The use of today's ICT (*Information and Communication Technologies*) for the management of large businesses, critical information infrastructures, or emerging e-services, upholding e-business, e-government or e-health applications, demands technically and economically efficient solutions that should provide the right assurance for their stakeholders and users. These demands can be met by the common approach that considers the following issues:

- the needs of business processes concerning information and e-services security,
- effective use of ICT providing managed IT services for business processes,
- detailed risk characteristics, including cost/benefit aspects,
- dependable and trustworthy solutions providing the right assurance.

The security systems based on this common approach require the right management that is more and more often computer-aided. The challenge is how to build the management framework that would be an open platform integrating different methods and tools.

J. Górski (Ed.): SAFECOMP 2006, LNCS 4166, pp. 316 – 329, 2006.

For this reason, the Institute of Control Systems (ISS) and the IT Centre of the Mining Industry (COIG) have just begun the Targeted Project "The comprehensive information and e-services security system" granted by the Polish Ministry of Education and Science. The project is based on the results of the earlier project "SecFrame" [3] dealing with the ISMS implementation and computer-aided tool prototype. The concept of the integrated and risk-based information and e-services security platform (ISP) has been elaborated on the basis of:

- a study of the needs and requirements of various organizations,
- an analysis of the current state of standards, legal requirements and technology (overview of existing methodologies and tools),
- experiences sampled during the first SecFrame deployment and case studies.

For the ISP platform the following main assumptions have been taken:

- strong integration of ISMS processes, business processes, and business continuity and IT services management processes [4], [5]; it is especially important for e-services and critical information infrastructure protection;
- enhanced, three-layer, UML-model-based risk analyzer (allowing to assess the risk according to qualitative and/or quantitative measures), with a built-in *ROI* (*Return on Investment*) type mechanism;
- possibility of confronting the information of generally hypothetical nature obtained during the risk analysis with the information that presents a real situation and is gathered on-line by monitoring tools, like firewalls, IDSes, or security testers;
- consideration of implementing the selected assurance [6] methods.

The basic innovation of the ISP is its holistic approach to problem solution concerning information security, IT services management and business continuity management. So far these problems have usually been solved separately. The holistic approach allows to create a common, business-oriented and highly-integrated management system. The paper is a continuation of earlier works [7], [8], [9], that present an idea of using a UML-based approach for modelling security management systems. The paper presents first steps of the recently initiated Targeted Project, i.e.. the study of the needs and requirements of various organizations, summary of the current state of technology, experiences sampled during earlier development and deployment works, and other basic issues concerning the elaboration of the ISP platform concept. The paper concludes also the current state of the work and defines its directions for the nearest future.

2 Needs and Requirements of Organizations Concerning Information and E-Services Security Management

The information security requirements of today's organizations, which rely on ICT, depend on different factors. All these factors influence the implementation of the information security management system. The paper emphasizes the issue of e-services security. This security is of key importance for such areas as e-business, e-government and e-health. The following activities were undertaken at the beginning of the project to better specify the characteristics and needs of the organizations in which the ISP will be deployed:

- the identification of basic factors (above a hundred) influencing the information security management system, e.g. the kind and importance of business or public mission the organization carries out, its size, branch/sector, organization structure, location and environment, owned assets, legal acts, head management motivation, engaged people and their awareness, the used ICT, and business processes dependency on ICT – divided into primary and auxiliary factors;
- defining the discussed below *Organization overview criteria (OOC),* based on the primary factors, to identify the organization profile that expresses the size and character of the organization;
- refining the OOC criteria using the auxiliary factors; elaborating the *Basic security needs criteria (BSNC)* to determine numerous details needed for risk analysis and to establish the security management system.

3 Summarizing the Current State of Technology

To better position such a large project it was necessary to perform an extensive study of the current state of technology encompassing all ISP relevant and publicly available standards, recommendations, best practices, guidelines, case studies, EU Framework programmes results, concepts, methodologies, their implementations and renowned supporting tools, concerning particularly:

- information security management systems (BS-7799-2, ISO/IEC 17799 and their revised versions aiming at the elaborated ISO/IEC 2700x) as the key security standards of the ISP platform and their well-known supporting tools, including risk management tools – for the right understanding of the ISMS implementation,
- different IT security and risk management methodologies: ISO/IEC [10], US NIST publications, Canadian TRA, German IT Grundschutz as auxiliary documents – to supplement or extend the ISP platform features and facilities,
- IT services management [4], [5], [11], IT governance [12] – to better integrate them with the information security management,
- business continuity management, e.g. [13], as well as quality, environmental, occupational safety and health management systems usually co-existing in the organization – to consider their requirements in the ISP processes,
- business processes modelling – to identify their relationships with the above mentioned management systems, especially information security and IT services; "business orientation" is the key issue for the ISP platform,
- methods and tools focusing on the risk management in the information security domain – the ISP platform should be "risk-based",
- assurance methods [6], survivability, dependability, the safety approach to the risk management, large ICT infrastructures modelling and behaviour investigation – to facilitate the ISP platform implementation in large distributed applications, e.g. in critical information infrastructure protection (CIIP), and to build information security systems with better assurance,
- ICT and general technical issues (communication protocols, network equipment, cryptographic applications, physical protection) – as a context of the ISP,

- security testers and monitoring tools, including firewalls, IDSes – to allow to confront the hypothetical information concerning risk with the information that presents a real situation and is sampled on-line by these tools.

Additionally, a very exhaustive legal acts overview (above 100 acts – international, domestic, branch specific, etc.) was done to identify the ISP requirements with respect to legal compatibility, data protection and privacy, and to develop audit tools.

Basically, methods and tools are focused either on general security management or on risk analysis, and do not fully cover other issues. There are different management frameworks defined in standards but the overview concentrated on the ISMS-compliant ones, usually supported by tools, e.g. well-known Callio Secura 17799 [14] or Proteus Enterprise [15]. The frameworks focus on the security management processes, documentation management, checklists-based audit facilities, and have relatively simple risk analysis tools in comparison with others.

The second group of methods and tools, like Cobra [16], Cora [17], Coras [18], Cramm [19], Ebios [20], Ezrisk [21], Mehari (Risicare) [22], Octave [23], Riskpac [24], specialize in risk management and support, to some extent, information security management (ISMS-compatible or not). They have different advantages and gaps as well. Even if they are able to carry out the detailed risk factors analysis (Ebios), they cannot operate on monetary values during the risk analysis. Cora can perform the *ROI* analysis. Coras has the UML-based advanced model of risk implemented, incorporating the safety risk management methods (Hazop, FME(C)A, FTA) and allowing a simple causality analysis. The risk analysis methods focus rather on detailed risk analysis for the whole of ICT systems in the organization, and only [25], [8] assume to implement the combined approach [10]. During the preliminary high level risk analysis this approach allows to identify the security domains of similar security requirements, and further to perform a detailed risk analysis only for the critical domains, and to apply baseline protection for others. This approach allows to avoid a costly detailed risk analysis for the entire organization.

It should be noted that the assets inventories that focus on risk management differ from those that focus on security, business continuity or IT services management. Besides, there is no sufficient support for the central management of ISMS records.

It is very important that management systems dealing with information security [1], [2] and IT services [4], [5], and a few other systems concerning quality, environment, occupational safety and health, are based on the same PDCA scheme. They work separately but the standard [1] encourages their integration. Mehari and its Risicare risk supporting tool can identify relationships between IT service quality and risk value. The works concerning the aligning and better integration of information security management and IT services management are in progress [12], [26]. Only few of the above mentioned tools have more advanced business continuity management support implemented [15], [19], [24].

It can be useful to adopt the achievements of dependability, fault tolerance and survivability, as well as the assurance methods, for the development of the ISP, especially for a large distributed environment.

The EESA (*End To End Security Assessment*) method [27] focuses on the IT aspects of large distributed critical systems. By analyzing the information flow and the mechanisms of security services together with the risk analysis results, one can discover gaps between them and prepare a plan of actions to remove the gaps. There is an analogy between EESA and the ISP platform concerning the idea to compare the risk analysis hypotheses with the real world picture.

There are no comprehensive, scalable, modular solutions configured according to the size and character of an organization. There are no methods (except Octave-S) focused on small organizations. Built-in libraries of document patterns and process frames, checklists, predefined measures and forms support the reusability of project elements. Other advantages of the methods and tools described above can be the following: advanced reporting or documents generation and their web-site presentation, graphical visualization, statistics and measures facilities, action planning or risk workshops supporting. Looking at the current state of technology, including standards, best practices, legal acts, methods and tools, helps to select the most useful features for the ISP, achieve compliance with laws and standards, and to steer the next steps of the project. Currently, different tools for specific purposes exist but large organizations need integrated solutions for central information and service security management. Small organizations, in turn, need simple, tailored and more cost-effective security solutions.

4 Preliminary Project Results

During the ISP platform project preparation phase, the basic ISMS implementation methodology and the SecFrame tool prototype [3] were developed using the UML approach [7], [8], [9]. The general ISMS structure was expressed by class diagrams. The activity diagrams and use case diagrams were used to show the ISMS elaboration and processes specification.

The tool supports all ISMS management processes. It allows to sample the basic characteristics of an organization and its risk characteristics, and provides predefined checklists and document templates. It can perform a high-level risk analysis for the organization to identify the security needs of its particular business domains; it can also identify the assets of the organization according to the assumed asset model. Basic security roles and responsibilities are taken into account. Moreover, for each domain a detailed risk analysis can be performed allowing to order all risk scenarios by risk value with respect to the risk acceptance criteria assumed for the organization. Typical, yet exhaustive, threats and vulnerability lists are built in. The controls are selected with respect to the risk value, expressed in predefined scales or in monetary values. For each of the selected controls, a statement of applicability, implementation manner and audit records are specified. All related documents (diagrams, procedures, forms, etc.) can be attached and managed. The tool supports the audit using various types of checklists.

Currently, the tool can be considered the basic ISMS implementation, allowing to sample experiences from the first deployments and case studies. An example of an application window is presented in the Fig. 1. The risk analysis methodology and security documentation were validated during the development of the PKI project for the Polish Post which included root and operational certification authorities, registration authority, and electronic transactional application, all communicating over the corporate WAN. The tool is also used for security documentation management in an electric power plant.

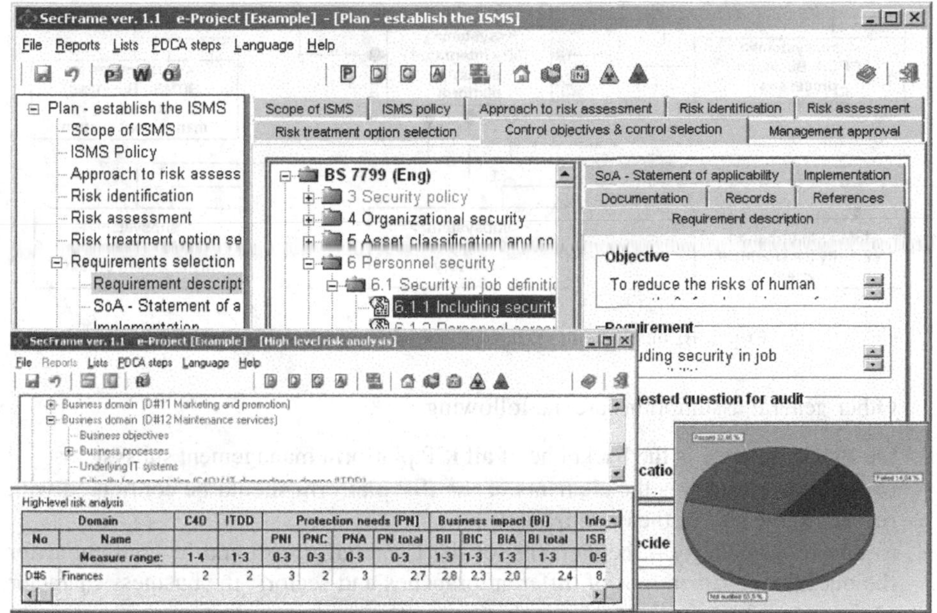

Domain		C4O	ITDD	Protection needs (PN)				Business impact (BI)				Info
No	Name			PNI	PNC	PNA	PN total	BII	BIC	BIA	BI total	ISR
	Measure range:	1-4	1-3	0-3	0-3	0-3	0-3	1-3	1-3	1-3	1-3	0-9
D#6	Finances	2	2	3	2	3	2.7	2.8	2.3	2.0	2.4	8.

Fig. 1. Information security management tool – PLAN. Based on the high-level risk analysis results (bottom left screenshot) the organization is divided into security domains of similar requirements. For each of them a detailed risk analysis can be done and, on the basis of its results, controls are selected, justified, implemented and managed by means of the PDCA processes [3]. The bottom right screenshot presents audit progress.

Currently, the tool prototype is deployed in a PKI-based management system for a wholesale coal distribution system owned by the ISP project partner, it is used in a project of a virtual consultant of public e-services, and deployed for the ISMS implementation by two consulting companies. It will be deployed shortly in a middle-size town hall. The project results are presented during trainings and workshops. All these activities should provide the ISP platform developers with important feedback and experience for the further incremental development.

5 Assumptions for the Integrated Security Platform

The results of the above mentioned preparatory works allow to define the assumptions for the ISP platform that will be refined and evaluated during the next project stages, to achieve a comprehensive information and e-services security management system, a tool supporting it, as well as the deployment and evaluation methodology.

The proposed ISP platform is shown in the Fig. 2. It has a common asset inventory (CAI) integrating: the information security management subsystem (ISMS) [1], [2] (Fig. 3), which is an enhanced version of the one previously implemented in the SecFrame tool; the IT services management subsystem (ITSMS) [4], [5]; the business continuity management system (BCMS); and the business processes communication subsystem (BPCS). The ISP platform integrates different processes co-existing with the business processes and influencing their security.

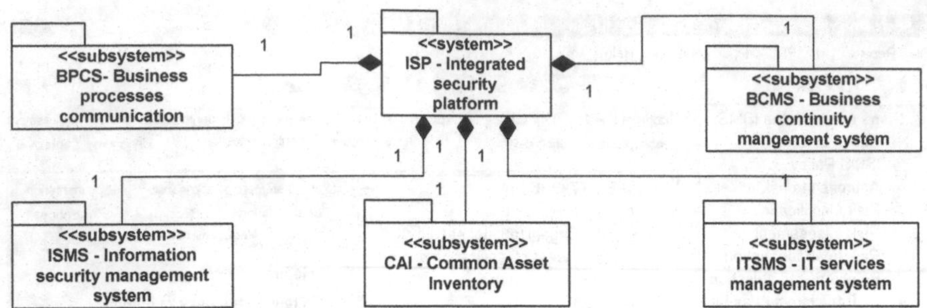

Fig. 2. Basic elements of the integrated security platform (ISP)

Other general assumptions are the following:

- the PDCA scheme is the backbone of all ISP platform management subsystems,
- to ensure scalability – the elements of the ISP platform should be configured with respect to the size of the organization;
- to ensure modularity – the elements of the ISP platform should be configured for the needs of organizations of different branches and sectors; the business character of the organization influences mainly the specific modules selection;
- to ensure openness – the ISP platform can integrate optional processes, e.g. critical information infrastructure protection processes (modelling behaviour, cascading effects simulation, survivability analysis); it will be possible thanks to CAI.

The ISP platform, encompassing ICT systems of the organization which deliver manageable IT services for business processes, should provide stakeholders and users with assurance. The assurance methods [6] can be used for the ISP platform development as well as for the ICT systems encompassed by this platform design. Rigorous development of the ISP platform processes, precise procedures, automated tools, using certified ICT components, exhaustive risk analysis, security tests or audits, evaluation and certification – all these may be considered assurance methods with respect to the information security management domain.

5.1 Applying Results of the Previous Work Concerning the ISMS Implementation

The previous works [7], [8] discuss the ISMS structure and process elaboration methodology. Every class (Fig. 3) concerns security management processes, actions, related documents and records. The refinement of these data structures allows to develop the activity diagrams expressing ISMS processes that were implemented in the SecFrame tool and the methodology related to them. The elaborated UML model can be considered as the basic implementation of the ISMS incorporated into the ISP design, which is incrementally developed and integrated with other ISP subsystems.

Currently, the development work is focusing on the following features:

- enhancing the asset inventory, as well as high- and low level risk analyzers,
- comparing the audit results (history options) and security records management,

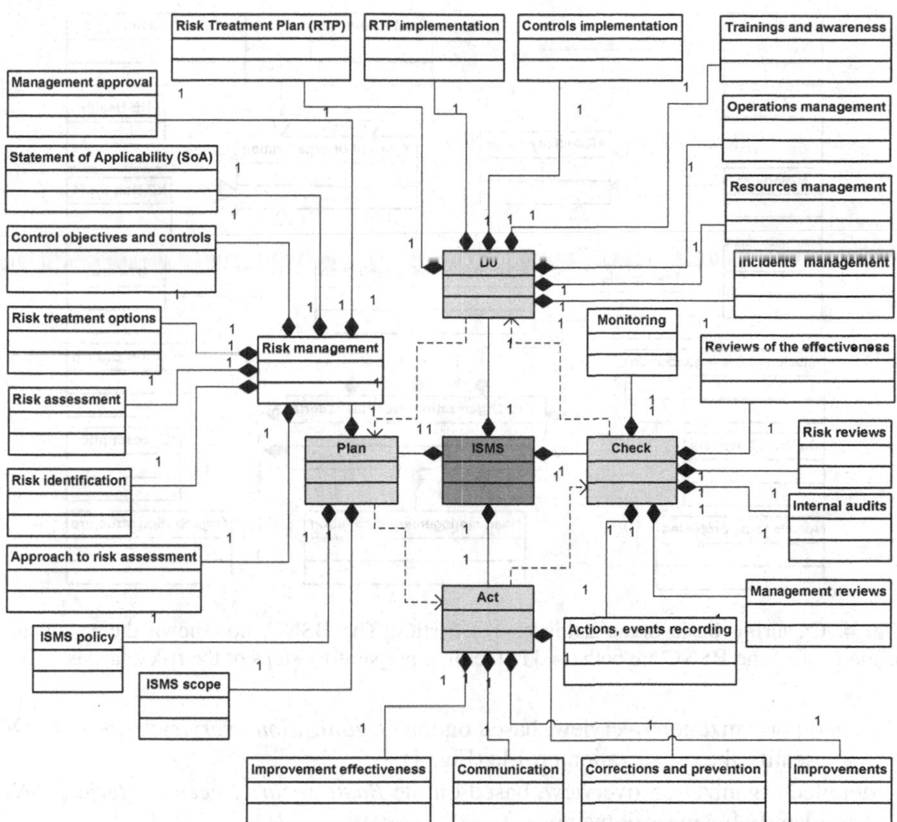

Fig. 3. Class diagram expressing the ISMS processes. Please note the ISMS hierarchical structure with PDCA classes grouping the management processes as subclasses exactly as it is presented in [1]. For this reason, its detailed description is omitted. Each class, e.g. "Incident management", expresses more detailed class diagrams presenting process details which cannot be shown there. The works [7] and [8] discuss business environment of the ISMS and the Plan stage processes elaboration with the use of activity diagrams.

- maturity model and security measures implementation,
- sampling the information from on-line monitoring systems and comparing it with the risk analysis results for the ISMS improvements.

5.2 Business Needs Orientation of the Developed Platform

The ISP does not consider business processes management though all related and synthetic business information required for the security management and for the IT services management ought to be gathered by the BPCS subsystem. It is assumed that the innovative two-step business needs analysis, continued further during the risk analysis, is performed:

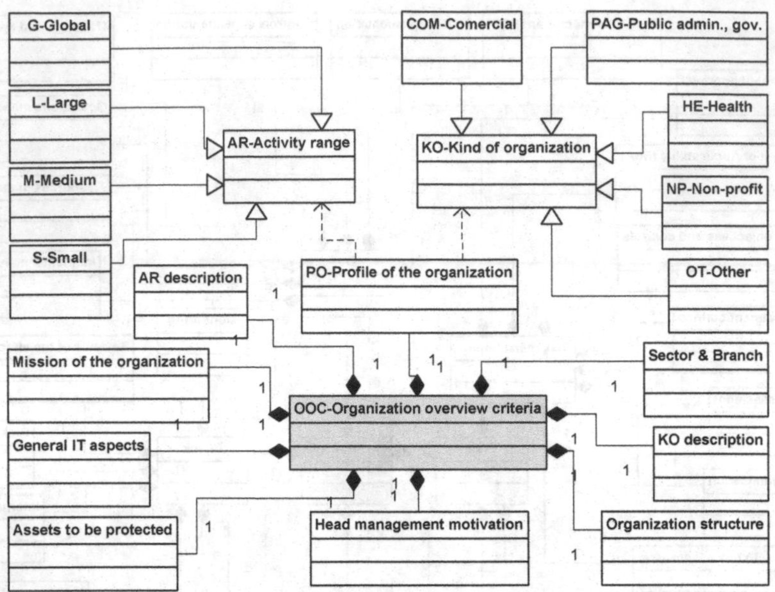

Fig. 4. Capturing basic organization characteristics. The BSNC, not shown there, are more refined. OOC and BSNC are both used in the first, preparatory steps of the risk analysis.

- general organization overview, based on the *Organization overview criteria (OOC)* – to identify the organization profile (Fig. 4),
- detailed organization overview, based on the *Basic security needs criteria (BSNC)* – to identify business domains.

The *Profile of the organization (PO)* is the combination of two basic factors: *AR (Activity range)* and *KO (Kind of organization).*

Both *OOC* and *BSNC*:

- are implemented as active questionnaires to determine, during workshops or interviews, the organization's needs and requirements with respect to the shape of the elaborated security system,
- support the ISP platform scalability (*AR*) and modularity (*KO*), and provide guidance for the risk analysis.

The *OOC* and *BSNC* case studies for different profiles are performed to refine these criteria and their implementation, e.g. *L-COM* (the distributed PKI-based system of wholesale coal distribution belonging to COIG, i.e. the project partner organization), *M-COM* (ISS – the author's organization), *M-PAG* (management of a city with 100,000 inhabitants), *S-HE* (small out-patient clinic).

To support modularity and scalability, a set of predefined processes and document templates, reference lists, checklists, measures, etc. will be proposed for every possible profile that expresses the size and kind of the organization. Then the set will be refined during the ISP deployment in the given organization.

5.3 Advanced Risk Support

The three-layer risk analysis is assumed. The *OOC* and *BSNC* analyses can be considered as the first of the three steps. On this basis, a high-level risk analysis is performed for every domain, and then a detailed (low-level) risk analysis is done within the domains.

The high-level risk analysis [10], [8] encompasses the following steps for every business domain (Fig.1):

1. Characterize business processes criticality for the organization (C4O in the Fig.1).
2. Characterize business domain dependency on ICT (ITDD in the Fig.1).
3. Identify protection needs PN concerning integrity, availability and confidentiality.
4. Determine business impact BI concerning integrity, availability and confidentiality.
5. Identify information security requirements ISR concerning integrity, availability and confidentiality.
6. Calculate high-level risk concerning integrity, availability and confidentiality.

Not only should the current organization security be under control but also the cost of achieving and maintaining this security. All activities and investments for security should improve the organization's position on the market or in the society. To reach economic efficiency, one simple rule is obeyed – only necessary and sufficient security measures can be applied. This requires the implementation of more and more efficient risk management methods and tools that are a combination of qualitative and quantitative (monetary) methods and allow simple cost/benefit analyses, including *ROI*. During the detailed risk analysis it is possible to compare:

- the annualized costs of the security maintenance (*SC* [i]), i.e. safeguard depreciation plus labour cost vs. the annualized losses (*RVC* [i]) in a given currency, derived from the risk value for a given risk case; i – current, i+1 – after reduction,
- the safeguard efficiency (*ROI*) corresponding to different safeguarding variants (Example 1).

$$ROI[i+1] = \frac{RVC[i] - RVC[i+1]}{SC[i+1] - SC[i]} \quad . \tag{1}$$

Example 1. **Simple *ROI* Interpretation for a Given Risk Scenario**
Risk reduction can be achieved by choosing 1 of 3 possible safeguard variants. The variants have different annualized costs and losses derived from the risk reduction possibility shown in the Table 1. Preliminary assessments for the organization:

SC [i] = 10,000 € current annualized safeguards cost,
RVC [i] = 136,000 € assessed annualized losses caused by risk.

Table 1. A simple *ROI* analysis example

Variant	Cost /year *SC* [i+1]	Losses /year *RVC* [i+1]	*ROI*
1	20,000 €	75,000 €	6.1
2	50,000 €	10,000 €	3.1
3	120,000 €	8,000 €	1.2

After analyzing different variants of safeguards (having different cost and risk reduction possibilities), the variant #2 was chosen for implementation. Though the variant #1 has better *ROI,* it has losses of 75,000 €/year, which was not acceptable in this organization. The variant #3, on the other hand, seems to be very expensive.

The example 1 shows that even a very simple tool can support decisions during a risk management process by simulation of different variants. Please note that ROI is especially convenient for the commercial sector where monetary values are easy to operate. The currently implemented method, based on the flat lists of triples (asset, threat, vulnerability), should be enhanced. It will allow a more efficient causality and consequence analysis, based on the UML risk model similar to the one used in [18], and the generics-based model used in the Common Criteria development [28].

5.4 ISP Asset Model and Underlying Management Systems

Strong integration of information security management with the IT services management is needed to effectively support business processes. This is achieved by:

- explicitly defined critical services, along with sensitive data, in the data assets model (Fig. 5) implemented according to the previously developed six-layer hierarchical assets model [29]; lower level assets are nested and managed by the asset of a higher level, e.g. a given business task (MISS) is performed by a given person (PERS) in a given physical environment (PHYS), by using an IT system (ITI), where the application (APPS) is responsible for data processing or IT services providing (SDCS) – to perform the above mentioned business task;

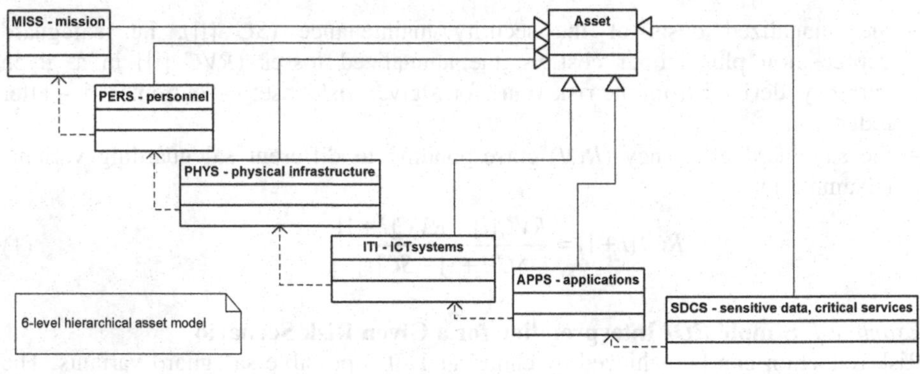

Fig. 5. Hierarchy of asset classes, representing groups of assets – a general model

- building a common assets inventory being also the configuration management database (CMDB) [4];
- building synergy between information security, business continuity and IT services processes, on the basis of their mutual relationships; all processes of both management systems should be analyzed step by step with respect to this issue.

The IT service management subsystem [4], [5], as a PDCA framework integrating management processes, is presented in the Fig. 6, but the processes used to manage these services are shown in the Fig. 7.

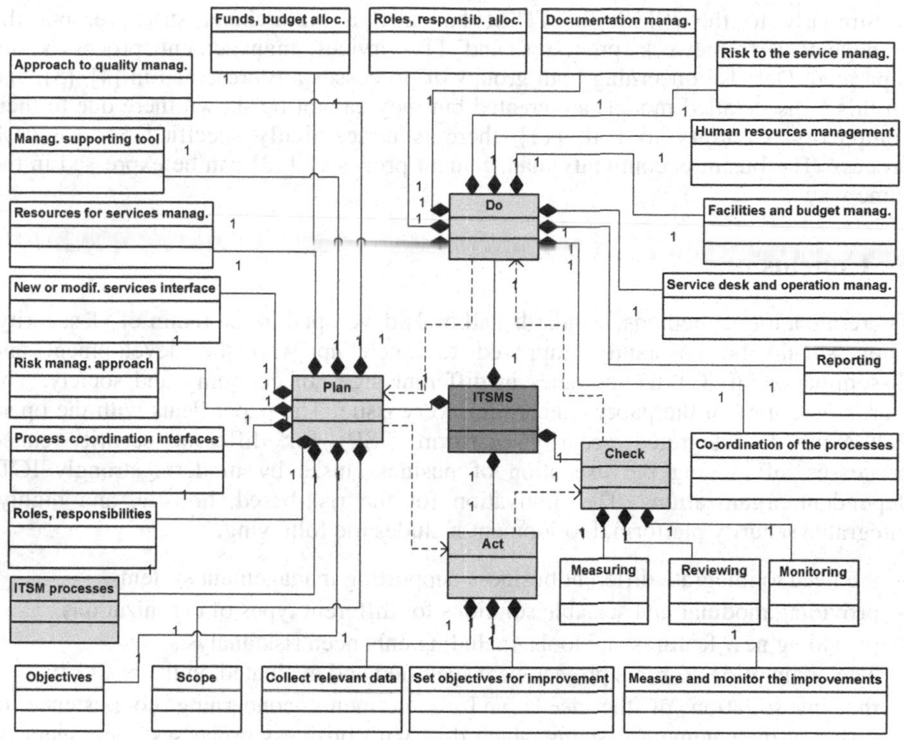

Fig. 6. IT service management framework. The ITSM processes class is shown in the Fig. 7

Please note that the ISP has a well established set of service management processes.

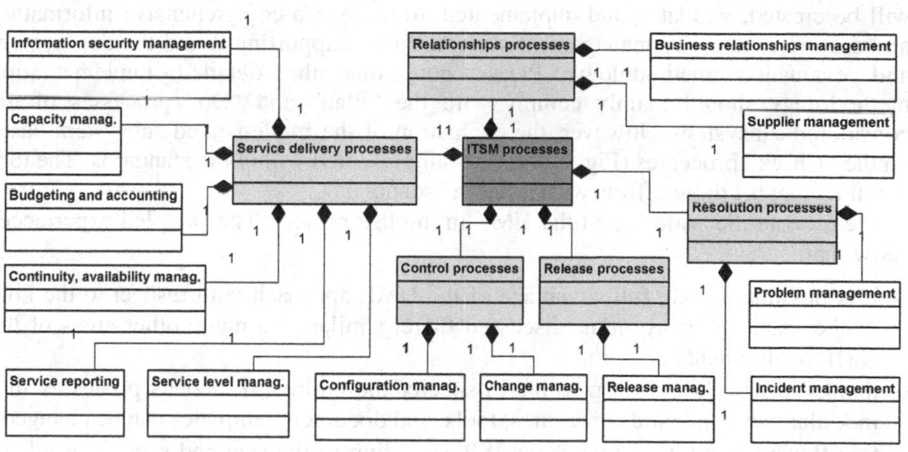

Fig. 7. IT service management processes – class diagram

Similarly to the ISMS, the ITSM has also a hierarchical structure, but the management framework processes and IT services management processes are separated. Details concerning both groups of processes are presented in [4], [5], and on this basis detailed models are created but they cannot be shown there due to their complexity. Contrary to ITIL [11], there is no explicitly specified Service desk process. The business continuity management processes [13] can be expressed in the same way .

6 Conclusions

There are a lot of methods, standards and tools developed in the realm of IT security. They should be constantly improved to catch up with the development and dissemination of ICT technologies in different areas of economy and society. The works described in the paper concern this very issue. The paper deals with the open, PDCA-based, integrated security platform (ISP) for different security-related processes influencing the execution of business tasks by modern, strongly ICT-dependent organizations. The motivation for the risk-based, holistic, and highly-integrated security platform development includes the following:

- the need to integrate different business-supporting management systems,
- providing modular and scalable solutions for different types of organizations,
- providing new features and tools, including enhanced risk analysis.

The assumptions for this project were specified and evaluated on the basis of:

- the investigation of the needs and requirements concerning co-existence of different management systems which deal with business processes, their security, continuity, IT services, quality, environment, etc.,
- the current state of technology and standards overview,
- the incrementally developed prototype used for experimentation, first deployment and case studies.

On the basis of the presented general model of the ISP platform, its detailed model will be created, validated and implemented, to achieve a comprehensive information and e-services security management system, a tool supporting it and the deployment and evaluation methodology. Please note that the detailed implementation methodology should mainly comply with the "Plan" and "Do" processes of the considered subsystem. However, the evaluation of the implemented subsystem bases on the "Check" processes (Fig. 3, Fig. 6) – all presented within the standards. The tool ought to support these efforts widely and reasonably.

Please note the wide use of the UML in the ISP project. The sampled experiences show that:

- it is possible to take full advantage of the UML approach with respect to the kind of the management systems discussed there, similarly to many other areas of the UML deployment,
- thanks to the UML it is possible to specify the entire ISP and its processes in a modular way – methods, measures, tools, and document templates can be changed,
- this flexibility allows to tailor the ISP according to the size and specific needs of the organization (document templates defined for the assumed organization profiles).

References

1. BS-7799-2. ISMS – Specification with guidance for use. British Standard Institution (2002)
2. ISO/IEC 17799. Code of practice for information security management (2000)
3. SecFrame. http://cbst.www.iss.pl
4. ISO/IEC 20000-1. IT – Service management. Specification. (2005)
5. ISO/IEC 20000-2. IT – Service management. Code of practice. (2005)
6. ISO/IEC 15443. A framework for IT security assurance (Part 1-3). (2005)
7. Białas A.: A UML approach in the ISMS implementation. In: IFIP 11.1 & 11.5 Working Conference, Fairfax (VA). Springer-Verlag (2005)
8. Białas A.: The ISMS Business Environment Elaboration Using a UML Approach. In: Zieliński K., Szmuc T. (eds.). Software Engineering: Evolution and Emerging Technologies. IOS Press Amsterdam (2005) 99-110
9. Białas A.: IT security modelling. In: Arabnia, H.R. (editor), Liwen He & Youngsong Mun (assoc. co-eds). Proc. of the 2005 International Conf. on Security and Management – SAM'05, Las Vegas. CSREA Press (2005) 502-505
10. ISO/IEC TR 13335-3, Guidelines for the management of IT Security (GMITS), Part 3
11. ITIL. http://www.itsmf.com
12. Cobit, Isaca. https://www.isaca.org
13. BSI PAS 56. Guide to Business Continuity Management (2003)
14. Callio Secura 17799. http://www.callio.com
15. Proteus Enterprise. http://www.infogov.co.uk
16. Cobra. http://www.riskworld.net
17. Cora. http://www.ist-usa.com/
18. Coras. http://coras.sourceforge.net
19. Cramm. http://www.ogc.goc.uk
20. Ebios. http://www.ssi.gouv.fr
21. Ezrisk. http://www.ezrisk.co.uk/
22. Mehari, Risicare. http://www.clusif.asso.fr; http://www.risicare.fr/
23. Octave. http://www.sei.cmu.edu
24. Riskpack. http://www.cpacsweb.com
25. IT Grundschutz. http://www.bsi.bund.de
26. Aligning Cobit, ITIL and ISO 17799 for business benefit. IT Governance, OGC, itSMF. (2005)
27. Eesa. http://www.itcon-ltd.com
28. Białas A.: IT security development – computer-aided tool supporting design and evaluation. In: Kowalik J., Gorski J., Sachenko A. (eds): Cyberspace Security and Defense. Research Issues. NATO Science Series II. Vol. 196. Springer Dordrecht (2005) 3-23
29. Białas A.: The Assets Inventory for the Information and Communication Technologies Security Management. Archiwum Informatyki Teoretycznej i Stosowanej. Polska Akademia Nauk. Vol. 16, No. 2. (2004) 93-108

Using Agent-Based Modelling Approaches to Support the Development of Safety Policy for Systems of Systems

Martin Hall-May and Tim Kelly

Department of Computer Science
University of York, York, YO10 5DD, UK
{martin.hall-may, tim.kelly}@cs.york.ac.uk

Abstract. A safety policy defines the set of rules that governs the safe interaction of agents operating together as part of a system of systems (SoS). Agent autonomy can give rise to unpredictable, and potentially undesirable, emergent behaviour. Deriving rules of safety policy requires an understanding of the capabilities of an agent as well as how its actions affect the environment and consequently the actions of others. Methods for multi-agent system design can aid in this understanding. Such approaches mention organisational rules. However, there is little discussion about how they are derived. This paper proposes modelling systems according to three viewpoints: an agent viewpoint, a causal viewpoint and a domain viewpoint. The agent viewpoint captures system capabilities and inter-relationships. The causal viewpoint describes the effect an agent's actions has on its environment as well as inter-agent influences. The domain viewpoint models assumed properties of the operating environment.

1 Introduction

1.1 Making Systems of Systems Safe

A system of systems (SoS) is a large-scale network of autonomous, heterogeneous, and often mobile entities that are individually purposeful, and yet are expected to interoperate towards a common purpose. SoS are, perhaps more than single platform systems, characterised by the interaction of feedback loops. Astonishingly complex behaviour can arise from the iteration of relatively simple cycles of behaviour. The term 'OODA' — observe, orient, decide, act — coined by Boyd [1], describes the process of relating perceptions of the environment to actions in that same environment, which allows systems to interact and operate together in a shared space. It is just this interaction of many autonomously operating cycles of behaviour that can give rise to hazards, and hence to accidents.

The authors explained in [2] that a safety policy can be used to restrict the behaviour of the component systems of a SoS such that hazards are avoided or mitigated through corrective action. As described in this paper, a safety policy decomposition proceeds from top-level safety objectives down to low-level constraints on system behaviour. However, at each step of the decomposition assumptions are inevitably made that relate to mental models of the system of systems whose behaviour the policy is intended to govern. Making these models explicit is a first step towards allowing the information that they contain to be used in a systematic policy decomposition process. Developing

J. Górski (Ed.): SAFECOMP 2006, LNCS 4166, pp. 330–343, 2006.

such models is not the principal concern of deriving a safety policy, but is a necessary precursor to a successful decomposition.

The informal role of models in policy making is well established [3]. Theoretical as well as empirical models are used by Government and other decision makers to set policies on a number of issues, ranging from health and the economy to the environment. Indeed, the defence industry uses models to guide combat decisions based on their knowledge, assumptions and best guesses of enemy capability, the anticipated operational environment as well as the configuration and inter-operation of their own forces.

In order to inform a policy decomposition we must have an understanding of the environment in which the systems are expected to operate, the type of knowledge they employ in decision-making processes, the capabilities they have and the ways in which these are used to interact with one another.

1.2 Learning from Multi-agent Systems

It has been said that "much confusion still remains about words and phrases for systems-of-systems type problems, let alone the best modeling approaches for dealing with them" [4]. There is surprisingly little consensus on appropriate modelling techniques. Is it perhaps possible to draw inspiration from related domains whose problem areas share the characteristics of SoS? Indeed, the community of research concerning the design of intelligent agents would seem to be a rich area with much to contribute to our area of research. Multi-agent systems (MAS) deal with the problem of many interacting autonomous agents, each of which may have its own goals and objectives.

Although multi-agent systems would seem germane to the problem area of SoS, it is important to recognise key differences. Often the focus of a MAS is on software agents (as opposed to embodied agents) and agents are described as 'mobile' only in the sense that they can move their code between hosts. These software agents act primarily in the 'information' world, whereas our focus is on agents that can also act in the physical world — e.g. an unmanned air vehicle (UAV). It is worth highlighting that agents are still considered embodied even if they are operating in a simulation of the real world. Contrast, for example, a simulation of a UAV agent with a meeting scheduler agent.

Pynadath and Tambe [5] sum up the agent community's very different approach to safety, as the cancellation by an agent of a meeting that a human intended to attend is considered a 'catastrophic' event. SoS and MAS share many characteristics, among them autonomous entities, local knowledge and decentralised decision-making. However, it is also necessary to recognise the primary distinction between them, namely that a SoS comprises entities that are capable of *physical*, not just computational, interaction. This capability is arguably the reason that the term SoS is much used in the military domain and is key in investigating issues of safety, since physical interaction is a prerequisite for death or injury to occur.

1.3 Structure of the Paper

Section 2 will expand on the notion of a safety policy. Sections 3–5 will introduce three viewpoints by which a SoS can be modelled. Section 6 will examine how these models can be used to inform a safety policy decomposition. Section 7 will summarise the paper.

Throughout the paper we will illustrate concepts and techniques where possible with reference to an example SoS for the military domain. Figure 1 gives a representation of the example SoS, which depicts a minimal set of systems operating together necessary to mount an attack and to clear a given region of a guerrilla enemy force. The systems communicate via a shared 'data fusion' picture, indicated by jagged lines, and include a UAV with sensors capable of target identification, long range artillery capable of launching suppressing fire on a target and infantry (carried by transport helicopters) capable of neutralising an already suppressed target.

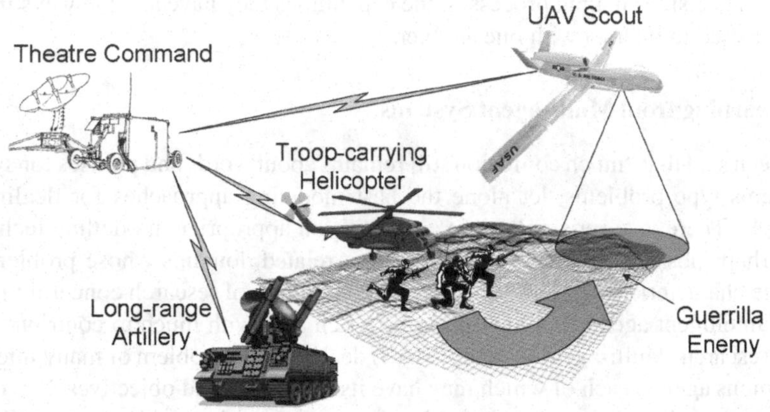

Fig. 1. A Concept View of a System of Systems for Anti-guerrilla Operations (AGO)

2 Safety Policy

Pynadath and Tambe [5] state that "it is unreasonable (if not impossible) to have humans specify sufficient safety conditions to completely determine correct agent behaviour". Quite so, the important distinction is that safety policy specifies constraints that are *orthogonal* to normal functional behaviour. A safety policy aims to circumscribe the potentially hazardous but functionally possible behaviour, in such a fashion that it leaves only that which is considered acceptably safe. It is not the job of safety policy to define functionally correct behaviour — for this is merely rigorous specification — policy is separate from the behaviour to achieve goals.

Sørby [6] describes a safety policy as being analogous to security policy in that it influences the stakeholders in a system by enforcing a number of safety requirements, which are in turn influenced by safety standards (see Figure 2). Taken together, the set of safety requirements should ensure the safety of the system.

MAS development often mentions organisational rules [7], however there is generally little explanation of how the rules are derived. This paper represents a step towards a more structured, systematic process to their derivation, which increases traceability of rules from high-level objectives and increases confidence in the completeness of the

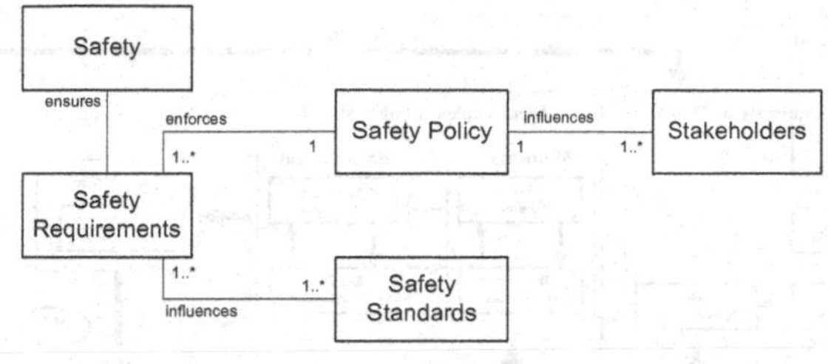

Fig. 2. Excerpt of Sørby's Safety Ontology Relating Safety Policy to Safety Requirements

rule set. Policy is a hierarchical decomposition of high-level policy objectives into constraints over agent actions and interactions. The Goal Structuring Notation (GSN) [8] — typically used to construct safety cases — can be used to represent policy decomposition structures.

To support policy decomposition, we propose modelling the SoS from three viewpoints: an agent viewpoint, a domain viewpoint and a causal viewpoint. The agent viewpoint captures the technical aspects of the SoS and its constituent component systems, including their attributes and relationships in terms of planned interactions. A domain viewpoint provides a consistent terminology and model of the SoS environmental assumptions. A causal viewpoint focuses on the way factors such as actions, states and other variables influence each other in the SoS, potentially leading to unplanned interactions. These viewpoints are the focus of this paper.

3 Agent Viewpoint

Despite the recent increase in interest in engineering systems of systems [9], there has been little consensus on a successful modelling approach. An object-oriented (OO) approach has been recommended for the specification and analysis of requirements for systems of systems [10, 11]. Caffall and Michael propose treating the SoS as a single entity comprising abstract classes, rather than decomposing the SoS into its constituent systems in a functional fashion.

Agent UML [12] extends the standard Unified Modelling Language typically used to model OO systems in various ways to enable agent-oriented design. As previously mentioned, MAS techniques often focus on software agents. Commensurately, Agent UML focuses on capabilities in terms of logical or mathematical operations and services such as 'computation', rather than capabilities for physical interaction.

The PASSI (Process for Agent Societies Specification and Implementation) methodology makes use of conventional and agent UML notation to express five different models of increasing specificity for the design of agent-based societies [13]. The process can be viewed as comprising analysis and design activities. For the purposes of this paper we concentrate on the analysis phase, including the modelling of system requirements and the agent society. Each of the five models has several phases, each of which utilises a particular (Agent) UML diagram to capture specific information.

Figure 3 shows the relationships between the models and phases of PASSI. PASSI encourages identification of agents early on in the development process. This is supported

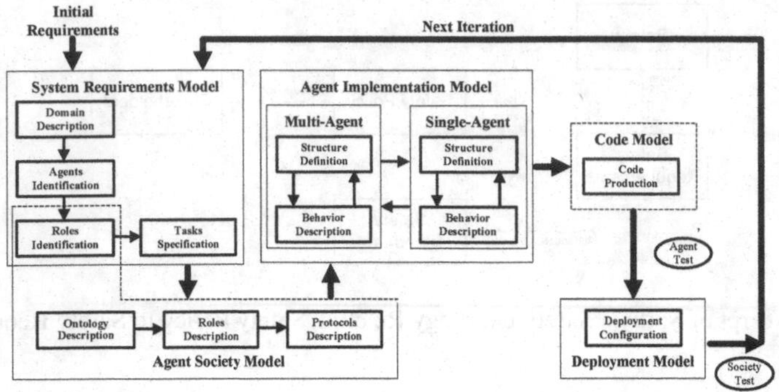

Fig. 3. The Models and Phases of the PASSI Methodology

by the claim that the types of MAS targeted by this process comprise agents that can be 'bidden' or influenced but not deterministically controlled [14]. Therefore, it is desirable to allocate required behaviours to "loci of responsibility" as soon as possible.

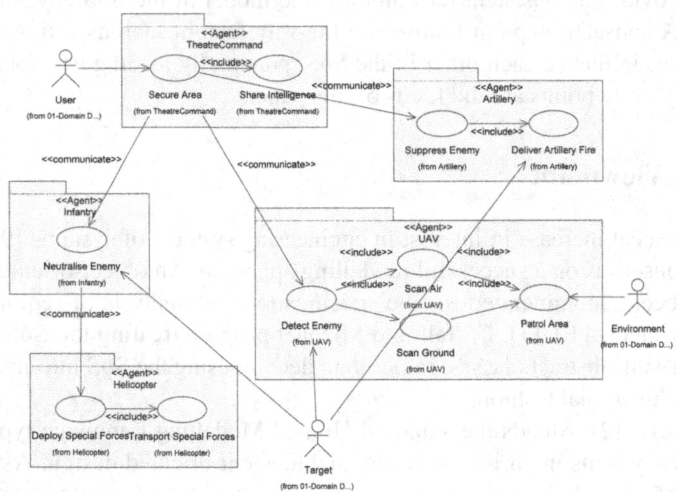

Fig. 4. An Agent Identification Diagram for the AGO System of Systems

Using the PASSI methodology the example SoS configured for anti-guerilla operations and presented in Figure 1 has been modelled. Figure 4 shows a description of the SoS in terms of use cases. The use cases represent the domain of functionality of the SoS, and external actors have been identified with which the SoS interacts. These are the user of the SoS, which is most likely to be a set of commands coming from outside of the theatre of interest, the environment and the enemy targets. Delineating what is inside the system boundary is a significant challenge even for a single platform, and respectively more difficult for a SoS [15].

In order to secure the area, the enemy must be detected (distinguished from the environment), suppressed and finally neutralised altogether. Due to the large geographical nature of the area of interest, more than one system is needed to secure it. Due to the nature of SoS, i.e. the systems are geographically dispersed, but can only act and observe locally, there is also a need to share intelligence between them. The agent identification diagram is derived from a higher level domain description diagram, which is not shown here due to space constraints. An agent is described as a package of use cases. The use cases that make up the functionality of the SoS have been assigned as the responsibility of one of five agents: artillery, infantry, UAV, helicopter or theatre command.

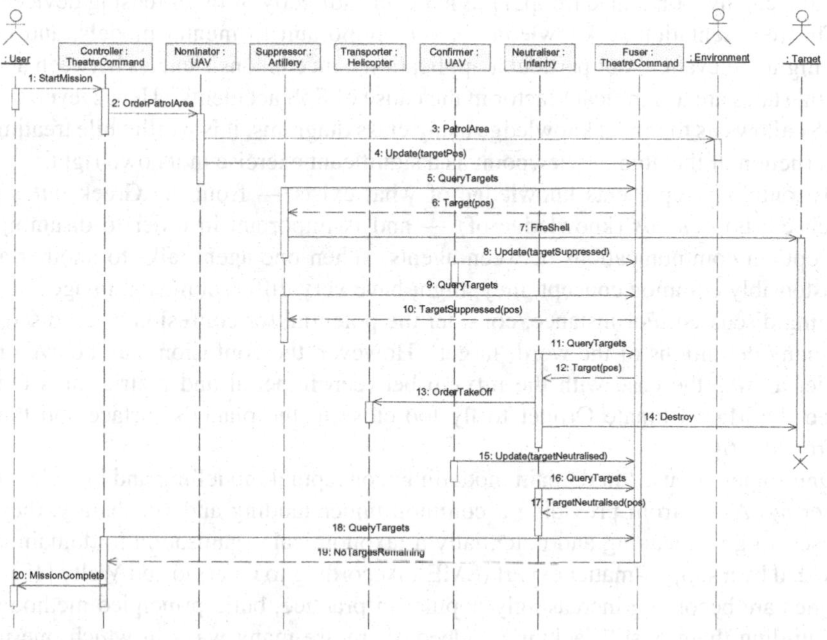

Fig. 5. A Role Identification Sequence Diagram for the AGO System of Systems

Figure 5 shows the role identification diagram, which describes an envisaged scenario. This diagram adds detail to the communicate relationships between agents in Figure 4 by identifying the role that agents play and the sequence in which messages occur. The role identification diagram is abstract, in that it does not show the reality of the interactions. An agent viewpoint is important when developing policy in order to consider the types of communications that will occur as well as which agent relies on the services or knowledge of another.

4 Domain Viewpoint

The PASSI methodology employs a knowledge-centric agent model. Agents act to achieve their objectives on the basis of local goals and knowledge, which increases through communication with other agents and exploration of the real world. It is interesting to note that PASSI eschews the use of Agent UML's extension to the class diagram in favour of the conventional notation for representing agents. Instead, knowledge is represented in the domain ontology description phase as a conventional class diagram, where each class represents a concept, a predicate or action on that concept. The communication ontology description diagram shows the agent and its ascribed knowledge attributes and the communicative relationships between them.

Communication among agents is considered different to that between agents and external 'actors'. Principally, agent communication proceeds according to certain protocols and uses a specific ontology. Communication with agents not part of the SoS (e.g. the enemy, non-squad troops) might occur indirectly through sensing devices.

The representation of knowledge is very important to mental models, and therefore highly relevant to our particular application (since inconsistencies between agents' mental states are a significant factor in the cause of SoS accidents). Hence, even though PASSI allows us to model knowledge using class diagrams, it is worthwhile treating the construction of the domain viewpoint as a significant exercise in its own right.

An ontology represents knowledge of what exists — from the Greek *ontos* (that which exists) + *logos* (knowledge of) — and is important in order to disambiguate concepts in communications between agents. When one agent talks to another about an ostensibly common concept, they might have very different mental images of what is being discussed. For instance, consider the potential for confusion when discussing the many definitions of the word 'target'. However, the confusion may be even more subtle, as was the case with the mix-up between imperial and metric units that allowed the Mars Climate Orbiter to fly too close to the planet's surface and thus be destroyed [16].

Ontologies are used in domain modelling, conceptual modelling and knowledge engineering. Aside from providing a common understanding and vocabulary, they can be used to give meaning and potentially a taxonomical organisation to domain terms provided by a subject-matter expert (SME). According to Guarino and Welty [17], "ontologies are becoming increasingly popular in practice, but a principled methodology for building them is still lacking." Indeed, there are many ways in which one might build an ontology from a data dictionary as provided by a SME. What is needed is an organising principle with which to structure the ontology.

Much work has gone into creating so-called upper ontologies. These include Cyc [18], SUMO [19] and SENSUS [20], which describe high-level terms, under which domain-specific ontologies can be organised. The upper ontology typically includes concepts such as physical, tangible and abstract entities. A mid-level ontology might include specialised versions of these concepts to do with time and space. Finally, a domain ontology is geared towards the particular application of interest. Valente et al [21] suggest for a military application the use of several ontologies including terms encompassing Communications, Organisations, Physical resources and Service descriptions.

Figure 6 shows the domain ontology diagram for the AGO system. This is necessarily simplified and could potentially be extended to include the standard terms provided by any of the above-mentioned upper ontologies. Accompanied by the communications ontology diagram, which ascribes ontologies to agents as concepts to be used in

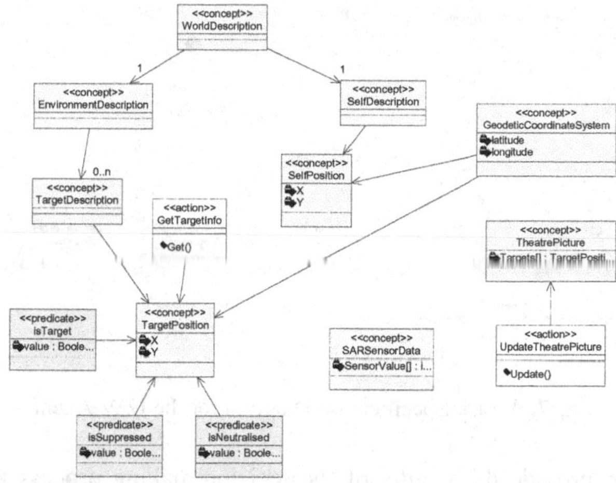

Fig. 6. A Domain Ontology Diagram for the AGO System of Systems

communications, this gives an indication of how the misinterpretation of common real-world artifacts in local mental models can occur.

5 Causal Viewpoint

The causal viewpoint recognises that accidents in a SoS arise out of, as Perrow described, dysfunctional interactions [22]. The accident model, STAMP [23], recognises the importance of this type of interaction in safety-critical applications. Similarly, we must take a more systems-theoretic approach to describing the relationships between causal factors in the lead up to an accident, rather than traditional chain-of-event failure models such as Fault Trees. As described, the behaviour of a SoS is typified by multiple interacting feedback loops. This means that it is not possible to take a mechanical approach to working through the causal chain, because many factors influence each other as well as, indirectly, themselves.

The inter- and intra-agent behaviour can be described as a feedback-based loop "observe, orient, decide, act" (OODA). Orient means updating one's mental model based on new observations, where these are interpreted through experience, training, traditions, previous observations etc. The interpreted observations allow the agent to decide among a number of alternatives and to enact the chosen one, causing some effect on the environment.

A consideration of the OODA cycle of agent behaviour can help in structuring the task specification diagram for individual agents. In Figure 7 the UAV goes through a cycle of scanning the ground for threats (observation), processing the data (orientation), deciding whether the data represents a new threat or a change to the state of an existing known target (decision) and finally passing this information to Theatre Command (action). It is only during the observation and action activities that interaction with other agents can occur. When observing, the agent not only uses its own senses to investigate the environment but can also integrate information provided by other agents.

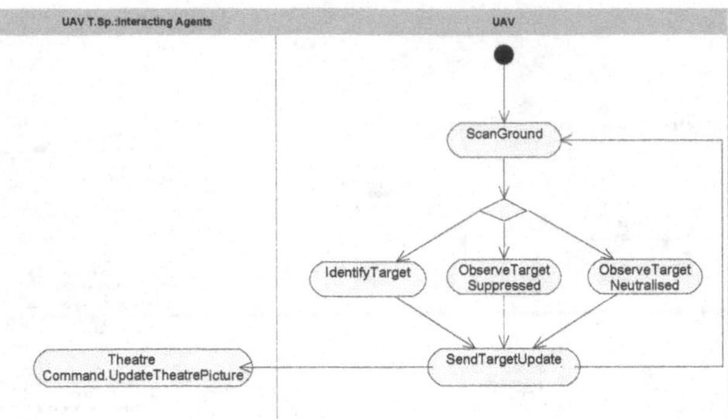

Fig. 7. A Task Specification Diagram for the UAV Agent

Similarly, it can provide the results of its decision-making process to other agents through its actions.

Figure 8 shows several loops for the Theatre Command agent, whose behaviour is more complicated than the UAV and which interacts with (influences) more agents in so doing. The sequence diagram (Figure 5) describing the interaction between roles in the AGO scenario must be consistent with the task specification diagrams. That is, the sequence of events described must be able to be generated from the interaction of all the agents' OODA cycles.

It is clear, however, that the task specification models do not capture all the unplanned interactions that are required when considering how to develop a safety policy. Planned actions are those that it is anticipated the agent will undertake in order to complete its task. We want to model agents with only local abilities and imperfect knowledge, i.e. they cannot assess the current state of the world, nor observe the effects of their actions on all other agents. The causal viewpoint needs to capture problems of failure, uncertainty and the effects of an agent's actions. For this we can take inspiration from another branch of agent theory, namely Multi-agent Influence Diagrams (MAIDs) [24].

MAIDs are an extension to Bayesian Belief Networks (BBNs) and decision networks. Using them it is possible to represent how agents' decisions are influenced by various factors. These factors include probabilistic variables (represented by circular 'chance' nodes) that are in effect 'decided' by the environment, as well as the results of other agents' decisions (rectangular nodes). Decision networks also require specifying the utility of the decisions to the agents, i.e. their preference for the result of a particular decision (represented by diamond-shaped nodes). This is not an aspect of MAIDs that is of immediate application, since we do not intend to 'solve' the MAID, i.e. calculate which combination of decisions results in the greatest utility for all the agents. Rather, we are simply using the notation to represent which variables influence which other variables and whether these variables are determined by chance or are under the control of an intelligent agent. In terms of the PASSI model, chance nodes belong to actors, i.e. the enemy, the environment, whereas decision nodes belong to the agents in the system.

The construction of a MAID also relies on a consideration of the OODA loop as it relates decisions (the choice between a number of actions) to the observations that

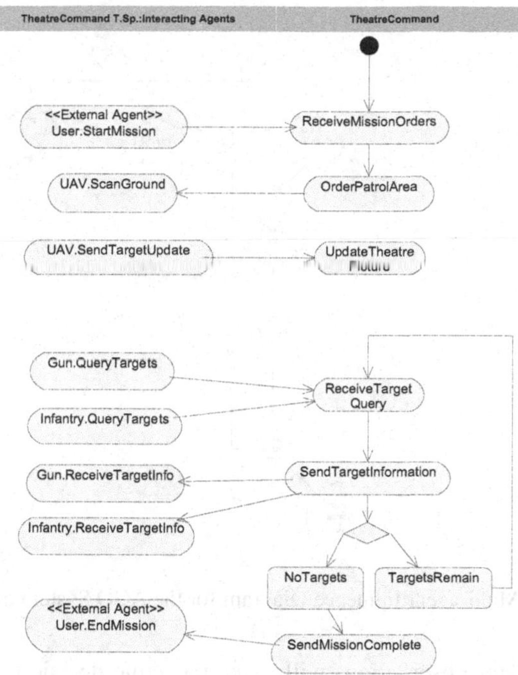

Fig. 8. A Task Specification Diagram for the Theatre Command Agent

the agent has made, i.e. the information it has available to it at the time of making the decision. Observations can be the value of probabilistic variables (the enemy has been destroyed) or actions taken by other agents, either directly or indirectly observed. An example of a direct observation might be that the artillery immediately observes the decision of the helicopters to take off. In reality, agents have limited knowledge and can only make localised observations, hence an indirect observation such as the UAV reporting that the helicopters have taken off is more likely. This observation is then subject to other factors, such as the probability of the failure of the UAV to send the message, the message getting lost or corrupted by the network, or even being misinterpreted by the recipient. All these factors combine to form the mental picture of the agent (in this case the artillery) and influence how close this picture approximates reality.

Figure 9 shows an example MAID for modelling of the artillery's decision to launch suppressing fire upon a given target. From this we can see that this decision is ultimately dependent on the result of the UAV's reconnaissance. However, there are many additional factors on which the artillery's action (or inaction) is based. These result from the fact that the artillery cannot directly observe the UAV's decision, but rather rely on the data fusion picture, which is affected by the previous state of the theatre picture, the state of the communications network, the UAV's sensor, and so on. Even in this simplified model, the number of influences are numerous.

The application of MAIDs must be judicious because they entail some rather limiting assumptions. The *common prior* assumption considers that two agents that have

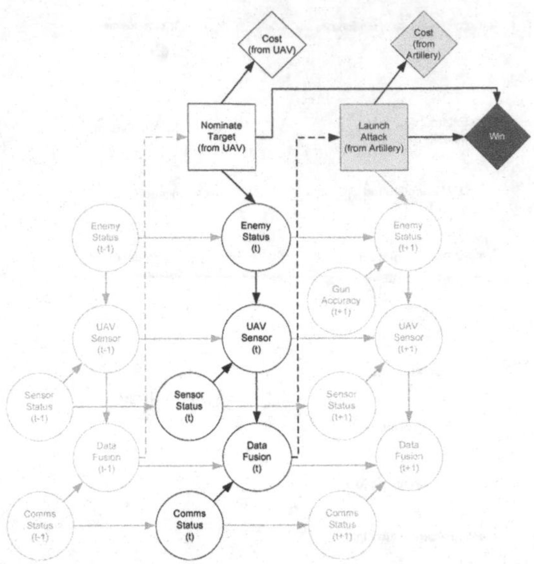

Fig. 9. A Multi-agent Influence Diagram for the AGO System of Systems

a common set of prior observations will make the same decision. The assumption of *perfect recall* does not allow for an agent to forget any observation that it has made and assumes it has all this evidence available to it when making a decision. It is important in MAIDs to explicitly represent the informational links to decision nodes, because the assumption of perfect recall only applies to each individual agent. Any particular agent may not necessarily have made the same observations as other agents, nor be able to observe the results of other agents' decisions. Therefore, informational links must be explicitly added to the graph as dashed lines.

6 Using Models in Policy Decomposition

Models serve two purposes in policy decomposition. Firstly, they aid in decomposing safety goals by, together with patterns of decomposition, providing the policy-maker with factors that should be considered in the achievement of the top-level goal. Secondly, the models provide a vocabulary for the expression of these goals. In this way, templates can be created that are more structured than the "verb-phrase noun-phrase" of traditional safety case goal statements.

6.1 Example 1

From Figure 4, it can be seen that securing the area involves both suppressing and neutralising the enemy. The former use case includes functionality that has been assigned to the artillery agent, which is capable of delivering suppressing fire onto the target. The latter use case includes functionality that has been assigned to both the helicopter and infantry agents, which brings them into proximity of the target. It is also obvious

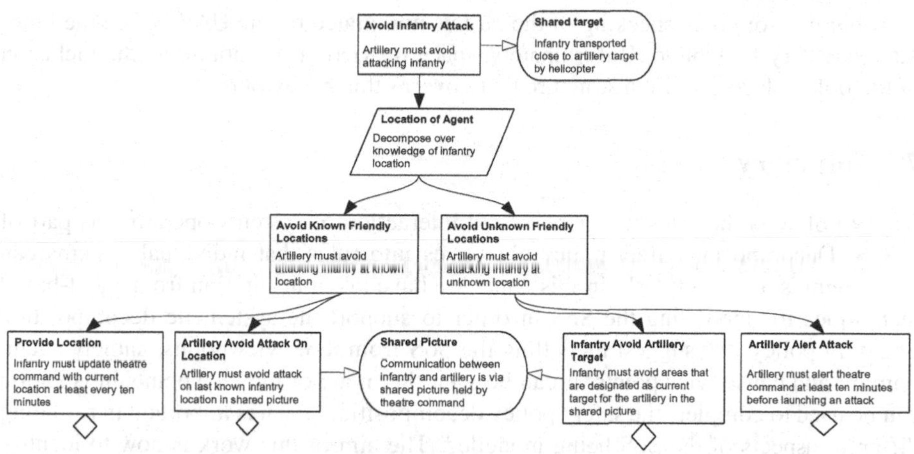

Fig. 10. An Excerpt from the Safety Policy Decomposition for the AGO SoS

that, although the helicopter and infantry communicate their efforts, there is no communication with the artillery. The hazard therefore exists that the infantry may be in the vicinity of the target at the same time as the artillery fires upon it. Given that no direct communication is possible between the two agents (nor indeed necessary to achieve the aims of the mission), a safety policy must be derived to make the artillery aware of the helicopter's movements. This leads to the policy decomposition shown in Figure 10 (represented in GSN). The left-hand side of the policy structure concentrates on informing the artillery of the infantry locations so as to avoid accidental attack, whereas the right-hand side focuses on informing the infantry to avoid an area designated as a target for the artillery.

6.2 Example 2

In understanding how an agent might misinterpret its environment we need to know additional properties about the domain in which it operates. The domain ontology (Figure 6) allows us to consider the possibility of ontology mismatches between agents when communicating. In this instance, the common ontology revolves round the location and status of a target. Due to the critical nature of these concepts, the policy governing the agents interactions should make sure that there is no chance of a mismatch between mental models, e.g. the artillery fires on a target that has already been suppressed, or the helicopters transport troops to an incorrect location due to a misunderstanding in the way target locations are represented.

6.3 Example 3

The causal model (Figure 9) prompts us to consider the other factors that influence the observations that decide an agent's actions. In this case, the artillery's decision to launch is not directly dependent on the UAV's observations, since many other factors outside of the agent's control are also involved. This must lead us to consider some level of corroboration or cross-checking of the targets nominated by the UAV before the long-range artillery fires blind. Unfortunately, space restrictions do not allow the inclusion of the policy decomposition structure that governs this behaviour.

7 Summary

Safety policy is the rules that govern safe interaction of systems operating as part of a SoS. Decomposing safety policy objectives into rules that individual systems can implement is a difficult task. In this paper we have taken inspiration from agent-based techniques for modelling the SoS in order to support the systematic decomposition of safety policy. We suggest modelling the SoS from three viewpoints, namely agent, domain and causal viewpoints. It can be seen that none of the viewpoints in isolation can be used to complete the safety policy decomposition. Each is important in revealing different aspects of the SoS being modelled. The aim of this work is now to identify and explicitly define links between the safety policy decomposition and elements of the system models.

Acknowledgement

This work is carried out under the High Integrity Real Time Systems Defence and Aerospace Research Partnership (HIRTS DARP), funded by the MoD, DTI and EPSRC. The current members of the HIRTS DARP are BAE SYSTEMS, QinetiQ, Rolls-Royce Plc and the University of York.

References

1. Boyd, J.R.: A discourse on winning and losing. Unpublished briefing, Air University Library, Maxwell AFB, Alabama, Report No. MU43947 (1987)
2. Hall-May, M., Kelly, T.P.: Defining and decomposing safety policy for systems of systems. In: Proceedings of the 24th International Conference on Computer Safety, Reliability and Security (SAFECOMP '05). Volume 3688 of LNCS., Fredrikstad, Norway, Springer-Verlag (2005) 37–51
3. Weinstein, M.C., Toy, E.L., Sandberg, E.A., Neumann, P.J., Evans, J.S., Kuntz, K.M., Graham, J.D., Hammitt, J.K.: Modeling for health care and other policy decisions: Uses, roles, and validity. Value Health **4** (2001) 348–61
4. DeLaurentis, D.A., Callaway, R.K.: A system-of-systems perspective for future public policy. Review of Policy Research **21** (2004)
5. Pynadath, D.V., Tambe, M.: Revisiting asimov's first law: A response to the call to arms. In: Proceedings of the 8th International Workshop on Agent Theories, Architectures, and Languages (Intelligent Agents VII). Volume 2333 of LNCS., Seattle, WA, Springer-Verlag GmbH (2001) 307–320
6. Sørby, K.: Relationship between security and safety in a security-safety critical system: Safety consequences of security threats. Masters thesis, Norges Teknisk-Naturvitenskapelige Universitet, Trondheim, Norway (2003)
7. Zambonelli, F., Jennings, N., Wooldridge, M.: Organizational rules as an abstraction for the analysis and design of multi-agent systems. Journal of Knowledge and Software Engineering **11** (2001) 303–328

8. Kelly, T.P.: Arguing Safety—A Systematic Approach to Managing Safety Cases. DPhil thesis, University of York, Heslington, York, YO10 5DD, UK (1998)
9. Keating, C., Rogers, R., Unal, R., Dryer, D., Sousa-Poza, A., Safford, R., Peterson, W., Rabadi, G.: System of systems engineering. Engineering Management Journal **15** (2003) 36–45
10. Caffall, D.S., Michael, J.B.: System-of-systems design from an object-oriented paradigm. In: Proceedings of the Monterey Workshop: Radical Innovations of Software and Systems Engineering in the Future, Venice, Italy, U.S. Army Research Office (2002) 146–157
11. Pfaender, H., DeLaurentis, D., Mavris, D.: An object-oriented approach for conceptual design exploration of UAV-based system-of-systems. In: Proceedings of 2nd AIAA "Unmanned Unlimited" Conference. Volume 2003-6521 of AIAA., San Diego, CA (2003)
12. Bauer, B., Müller, J.P., Odell, J.: Agent UML: A formalism for specifying multiagent software systems. In: Proceedings of the 1st International Workshop on Agent-Oriented Software Engineering. Volume 1957 of LNCS., Limerick, Ireland, Springer-Verlag (2000) 91–104
13. Cossentino, M., Potts, C.: PASSI: A process for specifying and implementing multi-agent systems using UML. (2002)
14. Jackson, M.: Problem Frames. Addison Wesley, Wokingham, England (2001)
15. Alexander, R., Hall-May, M., Despotou, G., Kelly, T.: Towards using simulation to evaluate safety policy for systems of systems. In: Proceedings of the 2nd International Workshop on Safety and Security in Multi-Agent Systems (SASEMAS '05), Utrecht, The Netherlands (2005) 5–21
16. Stephenson, A.: Mars climate orbiter mishap investigation board: Phase i report. Technical report, NASA (1999)
17. Guarino, N., Welty, C.A.: A formal ontology of properties. In: Proceedings of the 12th European Workshop on Knowledge Acquisition, Modeling and Management, Springer-Verlag (2000) 97–112
18. Guha, R.V., Lenat, D.B.: Cyc: A midterm report. AI Magazine **11** (1990) 32–59
19. Niles, I., Pease, A.: Towards a standard upper ontology. In: Proceedings of the International Conference on Formal Ontology in Information Systems, ACM Press (2001) 2–9
20. Swartout, B., Patil, R., Knight, K., Russ, T.: Toward distributed use of large-scale ontologies. In: Proceedings of the 10th Knowledge Acquisition for Knowledge-Based Systems Workshop, Banff, Alberta, Canada (1996)
21. Valente, A., Holmes, D., Alvidrez, F.C.: Using ontologies to build web service-based architecture for airspace systems. In: Proceedings of the 8th International Protégé Conference. (2005)
22. Perrow, C.: Normal Accidents: Living with High-Risk Technologies. Princeton University Press (1999)
23. Leveson, N.G.: A new accident model for engineering safer systems. Safety Science **42** (2004)
24. Koller, D., Milch, B.: Structured models for multi-agent interactions. In: Proceedings of the 8th conference on Theoretical Aspects of Rationality and Knowledge, Siena, Italy, Morgan Kaufmann Publishers Inc. (2001) 233–248

Verification of Automatic Train Protection Systems with RTCP-Nets

Marcin Szpyrka and Tomasz Szmuc

Institute of Automatics,
AGH University of Science and Technology,
Al. Mickiewicza 30, 30-059 Kraków, Poland
mszpyrka@agh.edu.pl, tsz@agh.edu.pl

Abstract. RTCP-nets are a subclass of timed coloured Petri nets. They use transitions' priorities and different time model than timed CP-nets. The subclass has been defined for modelling and analysis of embedded real-time systems and the ability of analysis of timing properties is one of the most important features of RTCP-nets. The paper discusses a formal, based on RTCP-nets, approach to verification of automatic train protection systems. Two examples of train protection systems are considered in the paper. A simple model of an automatic train stop system is used to introduce formal definition of RTCP-nets. A more complex model of automatic driver is used to present advanced aspects of modelling and verification with RTCP-nets. (*The work is carried out within KBN Research Project, Grant No. 4 T11C 035 24.*)

1 Introduction

The paper is concerned with a formal verification of safety-critical systems used to ensure railway safety. Critical systems are systems that may result in injury, loss of life or serious environmental damage upon their failure [6]. The high cost of safety-critical systems failure means that trusted methods and techniques must be used for development. For such systems, the costs of verification and validation are usually very high (more than 50% of the total system development cost). Using of formal methods can reduce the amount of testing and ensure more dependable products ([3]). A few different approaches to modelling of railway control systems have been proposed in the literature on formal methods. Some recently published papers are as follows: using of SDL language for modelling of such systems is discussed in [1], and statecharts approach is presented in [2]. A domain specific language for railway control systems modelling is discussed in [4].

The presented approach uses RTCP-nets ([7], [8]) as modelling language for safety-critical systems. RTCP-nets have been defined for modelling and analysis of embedded real-time systems. The concept is based on timed coloured Petri nets (CP-nets, [5]) but some modifications are introduced to equip Petri nets with capability of direct modelling of elements such as task priorities, timeouts, etc., but also to facilitate analysis of timing properties of high level Petri nets. Analysis of RTCP-nets may be carried out with coverability graphs. Such a graph may be used to analyse boundedness, liveness and timing properties of the corresponding RTCP-net ([8]). If the set of reachable markings of an RTCP-net is finite, it is possible to construct a finite coverability graph that represents the set of all reachable states regardless of the fact the set is finite or infinite.

J. Górski (Ed.): SAFECOMP 2006, LNCS 4166, pp. 344–357, 2006.

Trains could not run safely without signalling devices. Some automatic systems are used to transfer signal directly to a driver cab. A driver must always obey the signal, but the possibility of human error can cause serious accidents. Automatic Train Protection (ATP) systems are used to guarantee a train safety even if the driver is not capable of controlling the train. Furthermore, computer systems can drive a train without a human support. Two examples of such embedded systems are considered in the paper. A simple model of an Automatic Train Stop system is presented in section 2. A hierarchical model of an Automatic Driver System is described in section 3. Section 4 deals with verification procedures. The paper ends with a short summary in the final section.

2 RTCP-Nets

The definition of RTCP-nets is based on the definition of non-hierarchical timed CP-nets presented in [5]. For any variable v, $\mathcal{T}(v)$ will be used to denote the *type* of the variable i.e. the set of all admissible values, the variable can be associated with. Let x be an expression. $\mathcal{V}(x)$ will denote the set of all variables in the expression x, and $\mathcal{T}(x)$ will denote the *type* of the expression, i.e. the set of all possible values that can be obtained by evaluating of the expression. For any given set of variables V, the type of the set of variables is defined as follows: $\mathcal{T}(V) = \{\mathcal{T}(v) : v \in V\}$.

Let *Bool* denote the boolean type. For an arc a, $P(a)$ and $T(a)$ will be used to denote the *place node* and the *transition node* of the arc, respectively.

Definition 1. *An* RTCP-net *is a tuple* $\mathcal{N} = (\Sigma, P, T, A, C, G, I, E_M, E_S, M_0, S_0)$ *satisfying the following requirements.*

(1) Σ *is a finite set of non-empty* types *(*colour sets*).*
(2) P *is a finite set of* places.
(3) T *is a finite set of* transitions *such that* $P \cap T = \emptyset$.
(4) $A \subseteq (P \times T) \cup (T \times P)$ *is a* flow relation.
(5) $C: P \rightarrow \Sigma$ *is a* type function, *which maps each place to its type.*
(6) G *is a* guard function, *which maps each transition to an expression such that:* $\forall t \in T : \mathcal{T}(G(t)) \subseteq Bool \wedge \mathcal{T}(\mathcal{V}(G(t))) \subseteq \Sigma$.
(7) $I: T \rightarrow \mathbb{N} \cup \{0\}$ *is a* priority function, *which maps each transition to a non-negative integer called* transition priority.
(8) E_M *is an* arc expression function, *which maps each arc to a weight expression such that:* $\forall a \in A : \mathcal{T}(E_M(a)) \subseteq C(P(a)) \wedge \mathcal{T}(\mathcal{V}(E_M(a))) \subseteq \Sigma$.
(9) E_S *is an* arc time expression function, *which maps each arc to a time expression such that:* $\forall a \in A : \mathcal{T}(E_S(a)) \subseteq \mathbb{Q}^+ \cup \{0\} \wedge \mathcal{T}(\mathcal{V}(E_S(a))) \subseteq \Sigma$,
(10) M_0 *is an* initial marking, *which maps each place to a multi-set* $M_0(p) \in 2^{C(p)^*}$, *where* $2^{C(p)^*}$ *denotes the set of all multi-sets over the set* $C(p)$.
(11) $S_0: P \rightarrow \mathbb{Q}$ *is an* initial time stamp function, *which maps each place to a rational value called* initial time stamp.

A model of a simple Automatic Train Stop (ATS) system is used to introduce main features of RTCP-nets. In the ATS system, a light signal is turned on every 60 seconds to check whether the driver controls the train. If the driver fails to acknowledge the signal within 6 seconds, a sound signal is turned on. Then, if the driver does not disactivate the signals within 3 seconds, using the acknowledge button, the emergency brakes are applied automatically to stop the train. A model of such a system is shown in Fig. 1.

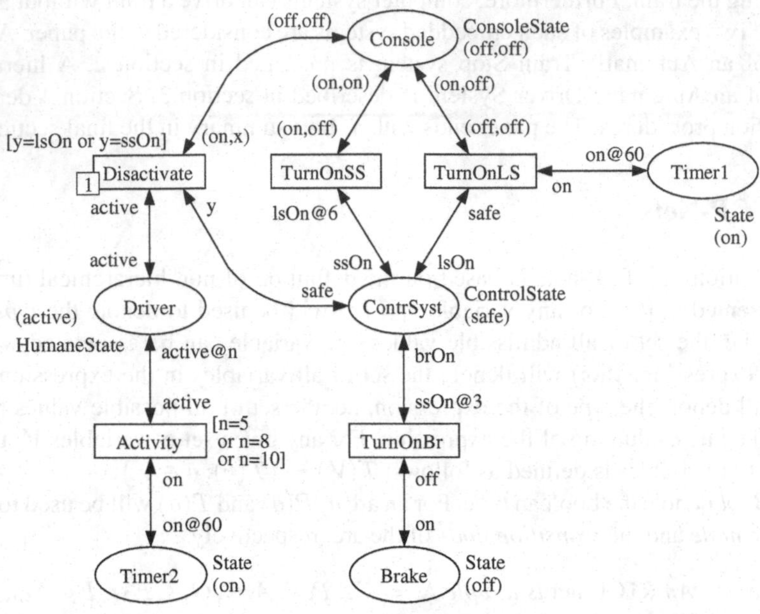

Fig. 1. Model of a simple ATS system

The RTCP-net presented in Fig. 1 contains six places: *ContrSyst* (the control element of the ATS system), *Console* (to display warning signals), *Brake*, *Driver*, *Timer1* and *Timer2*; and five transitions: *TurnOnLS* (turn on light signal), *TurnOnSS* (turn on sound signal), *TurnOnBr* (turn on brake), *Disactivate* (driver disactivates warning signals) and *Activity* (to introduce into model some delays of the driver response). Initial markings are placed into parenthesis and initial time stamps equal to 0 are omitted. The transition's *Disactivate* priority is equal to 1, while other transition's priorities are equal to 0. The weight and time expressions are separated by the @ sign. If a time expression is equal to 0 it is omitted. Each arc with double arrows stands for a pair of arcs.

A *marking* of an RTCP-net $\mathcal{N}$ is a function M defined on the set P, such that $\forall p \in P\colon M(p) \in 2^{C(p)^*}$. A *time stamp function* is a function S defined on the set P, such that $\forall p \in P\colon S(p) \in \mathbb{Q}$. A *state* is a pair (M, S), where M is a marking and S is a time stamp function. If we assume that P is ordered set, both a marking M and a time stamp function S can be represented by vectors with $|P|$ entries. Let the set of places be ordered as follows $P = \{$ *ContrSyst, Timer1, Console, Brake, Driver, Timer*$\}$. The initial state of the considered net is as follows:

$$M_0 = (safe, on, (off, off), off, active, on),$$
$$S_0 = (0, 0, 0, 0, 0, 0). \tag{1}$$

Let $X = P \cup T$ denote the set of all nodes of an RTCP-net. $In(x)$ and $Out(x)$ denote the set of *input* and *output nodes* of a node x, i.e. $In(x) = \{y \in X\colon (y,x) \in A\}$ and $Out(x) = \{y \in X\colon (x,y) \in A\}$. Let $\mathcal{V}(t)$ be the set of variables occurring in the expressions of arcs that surround the transition t and in the guard of the transition. A *binding* of a transition t is a substitution that replaces each variable of $\mathcal{V}(t)$ with a value of the corresponding type, such that the guard evaluates to $true$. The set of all bindings of a transition t is denoted by $\mathcal{B}(t)$. $G(t)_b$ denotes the evaluation of the guard expression in the binding b. Similarly, $E_M(p,t)_b$ and $E_S(p,t)_b$ denote the evaluation of the weight and the time expression in the binding b, respectively.

Definition 2. *A transition $t \in T$ is* enabled *in a state (M,S) in a binding b iff the following conditions hold:*

$$\begin{array}{l} \forall p \in In(t)\colon E_M(p,t)_b \in M(p) \wedge E_S(p,t)_b \leq -S(p), \\ \forall p \in Out(t)\colon S(p) \leq 0. \end{array} \tag{2}$$

and for any transition $t' \neq t$ that satisfies the above conditions, $I(t') \leq I(t)$ or $In(t) \cap In(t') = Out(t) \cap Out(t') = \emptyset$.

It means that a transition is enabled if all input places contain suitable tokens and have suitable time stamps, all output places are accessible and no other transition with a higher priority strives for the same input or output places. A transition $t \in T$ is enabled in a state (M,S) means that the transition t is enabled in a state (M,S) in one of its bindings. If a transition $t \in T$ is enabled in a state (M_1,S_1) in a binding b it may *fire*, changing the state (M_1,S_1) to another state (M_2,S_2) such that:

$$M_2(p) = \begin{cases} M_1(p) - \{E_M(p,t)_b\} & \text{for } p \in In(t) - Out(t), \\ M_1(p) - \{E_M(p,t)_b\} \cup \{E_M(t,p)_b\} & \text{for } p \in In(t) \cap Out(t), \\ M_1(p) \cup \{E_M(t,p)_b\} & \text{for } p \in Out(t) - In(t), \\ M_1(p) & \text{otherwise.} \end{cases} \tag{3}$$

$$S_2(p) = \begin{cases} E_S(t,p)_b & \text{for } p \in Out(t), \\ 0 & \text{for } p \in In(t) - Out(t), \\ S_1(p) & \text{otherwise.} \end{cases} \tag{4}$$

If a transition $t \in T$ is enabled in a state (M_1,S_1) in a binding b and a state (M_2,S_2) is derived from firing of the transition, then we write $(M_1,S_1) \xrightarrow{(t,b)} (M_2,S_2)$. The binding b will be omitted if it is obvious or redundant.

Two transitions *Activity* and *TurnOnLS* are enabled in the initial state. The first transition is enabled in three different bindings: $b_1 = (5/n)$ (the value of the variable n is equal to 5), $b_2 = (8/n)$ and $b_3 = (10/n)$, while the second one is enabled in the binding $b = ()$ (a trivial binding). For example, the result of firing of the transition *TurnOnLS* in the initial state is the state (M_1,S_1), where:

$$\begin{array}{l} M_1 = (lsOn, on, (on, \mathit{off}), \mathit{off}, active, on), \\ S_1 = (0, 60, 0, 0, 0, 0). \end{array} \tag{5}$$

A global clock is used to measure time. Every time the clock goes forward, all time stamps are decreased by the same value.

Definition 3. *Let* (M, S) *be a state and* $e = (1, 1, \ldots, 1)$ *a vector with* $|P|$ *entries. The state* (M, S) *is changed into a state* (M', S') *by a* passage of time $\tau \in \mathbb{Q}^{+}$, *denoted by* $(M, S) \xrightarrow{\tau} (M', S')$, *iff* $M = M'$ *and the passage of time* τ *is possible, i.e., no transition is enabled in any state* (M, S'') *such that* $S'' = S - \tau' \cdot e$, *for* $0 \leq \tau' < \tau$.

The result of firing of transitions *TurnOnLS* and *Activity* (in binding b_2) is the state (M_2, S_2), where $M_2 = M_1$ and $S_2 = (0, 60, 0, 0, 8, 60)$. None transition is enabled in the state but it is possible a passage of time $\tau = 6$ that leads to the state (M_2, S_2'), where $S_2' = (-6, 54, -6, -6, 2, 54)$. A timeout occurs in this state. A token in the place *Console* is 6 seconds old (the driver did not response within 6 seconds), so the transition *TurnOnSS* will fire.

A *firing sequence* of an RTCP-net $\mathcal{N}$ is a sequence of pairs $\alpha = (t_1, b_1), (t_2, b_2), \ldots$, such that b_i is a binding of the transition t_i, for $i = 1, 2, \ldots$ The firing sequence is *feasible* from a state (M_1, S_1) iff there exists a sequence of states such that:

$$(M_1, S_1) \xrightarrow{\tau_1} (M_1, S_1') \xrightarrow{(t_1, b_1)} (M_2, S_2) \xrightarrow{\tau_2} \ldots \xrightarrow{(t_n, b_n)} (M_{n+1}, S_{n+1}) \xrightarrow{\tau_{n+1}} \ldots \quad (6)$$

For the sake of simplicity, we will assume that there is at most one passage of time (sometimes equal to 0) between firing of two consecutive transitions. A firing sequence may be finite or infinite. The set of all firing sequences feasible from a state (M, S) is denoted by $\mathcal{L}(M, S)$. A state (M', S') is *reachable* from a state (M, S) iff there exists a finite firing sequence α feasible from the state (M, S) and leading to the state (M', S'). In such case, we can also say that the marking M' is *reachable* from the marking M. The set of all states that are reachable from (M, S) is denoted by $\mathcal{R}(M, S)$, while $\mathcal{R}(M)$ denotes the set of all markings reachable from the marking M.

3 Hierarchical Models

Hierarchical RTCP-nets are based on hierarchical CP-nets. Substitution transitions and fusion places ([5]) are used to combine pages (non-hierarchical parts of the model) but they are a mere designing convenience. The former idea allows the user to refine a transition and its surrounding arcs to a more complex net, which usually gives a more precise and detailed description of the activity represented by the substitution transition. In comparison with CP-nets general ports are not allowed in RTCP-nets. Moreover, each socket node must have only one port node assigned and vice versa. Thus, a hierarchical net can be easily "squash" to a non-hierarchical one.

A fusion of places allows users to specify a set of places that should be considered as a single one. It means, that they all represent a single conceptual place, but are drawn as separate individual places (e.g. for clarity reasons). The places participating in such a *fusion set* may belong to several different pages. They must have the same types and initial markings. Global fusion sets only are allowed in RTCP-nets.

Let's consider a model of an Automatic Driver system. A train line is divided into blocks and each block is protected by a signal. A train on a line receives two pieces of information about speed limits in the next two blocks. So we will use integer numbers to code the signals, the following pairs of signals are possible: $(0, 0)$, $(40, 0)$, $(40, 40)$ (the second number stands for 40/60 e.g. 40 or 60), $(40, 100)$, $(40, 160)$, $(160$

stands for maximum speed), $(60,0)$, $(60,40)$, $(60,100)$, $(60,160)$, $(100,0)$, $(100,40)$, $(100,100)$, $(100,160)$,$(160,0)$, $(160,40)$, $(160,100)$ and $(160,160)$.

Every time a new signals are received system uses the brake or the accelerator to adjust the speed to current limits. Moreover, it checks its speed every 10 seconds to guarantee safe and optimal train speed. A rule based system that describes the system behaviour is presented in Table 1. The symbol V stands for the train speed, $V1$ and $V2$ stand for the signals, A stands for *Accelerator* and B stands for *Brake*.

Table 1. Rule-based system for the automatic driver

V	$V1$	$V2$	A	B
$V > 0$	$V1 < V$	$V2$	off	on
V	$V1 = V$	$V2$	off	off
$V < 100$	$V1 > V$	$V2$	on	off
$V \geq 100$	$V1 > V$	$V2 > 0$	on	off
$V \geq 100$	$V1 \geq V$	$V2 = 0$	off	off

The formula $V2$ denotes that any value of the attribute $V2$ is possible. Let's consider the first rule: *If the train speed is greater than 0, but less than current block speed limit then turn on the accelerator and turn off the brake.*

Design of an RTCP-net starts by distinguishing objects that constitute the system. They are divided into subsets: *active objects*, i.e., objects performing activities, and *passive objects*, that do not perform any individual activity. State of each object is represented by marking of the corresponding place. Active objects and their activities are represented by *primary place pages*. Such a page is composed of one place that represents the object and one transition for each object activity. These pages constitute the top level of the model. Primary place pages for the considered model are shown in Fig. 2. Definitions of types and declarations of variables used in the model are as follows:

```
color Speed  = int with 0..160;
color Signal = product Speed * Speed;
color State  = bool with (off, on);
color Input  = product Speed * Speed * Speed;
color Output = product State * State;
var x1, x2 : State;
var v, v1, v2 : Speed;
```

The second level of an RTCP-net model contains *primary transition pages*. They are oriented towards activities' presentation and constitute the dynamic level of the model. Each such a page is composed of one transition that represents the activity and a few places that contains tokens necessary to execute the activity.

Some primary transition pages are presented in Fig. 3. The page *SignalReceipt* contains two passive objects: *Trigger* used to trigger off the sporadic read, and *Environment*. A marking of the second place represents all possible signals. The place *Trigger* belongs to a fusion set with the same name. Firing of the transition *SignalReceipt* changes tokens in places *AutoDriver* and *Trigger*. A token with new speed limits is placed in the

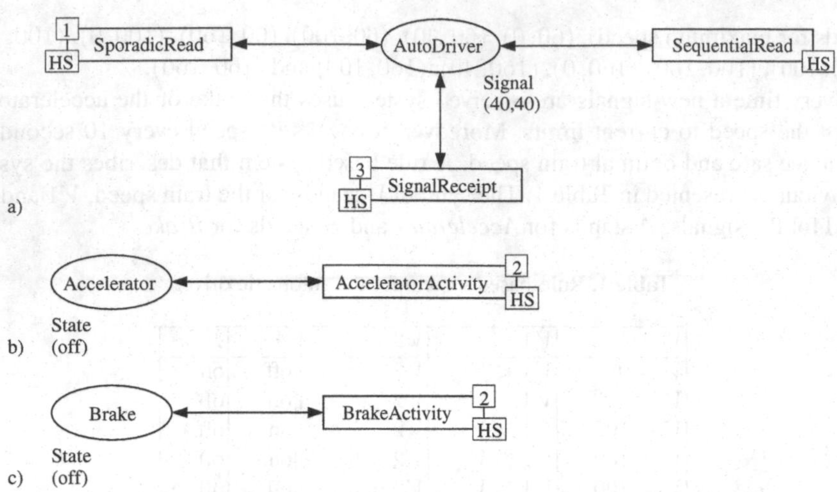

Fig. 2. Primary place pages: a) *AutoDriver*, b) *Accelerator*, c) *Brake*

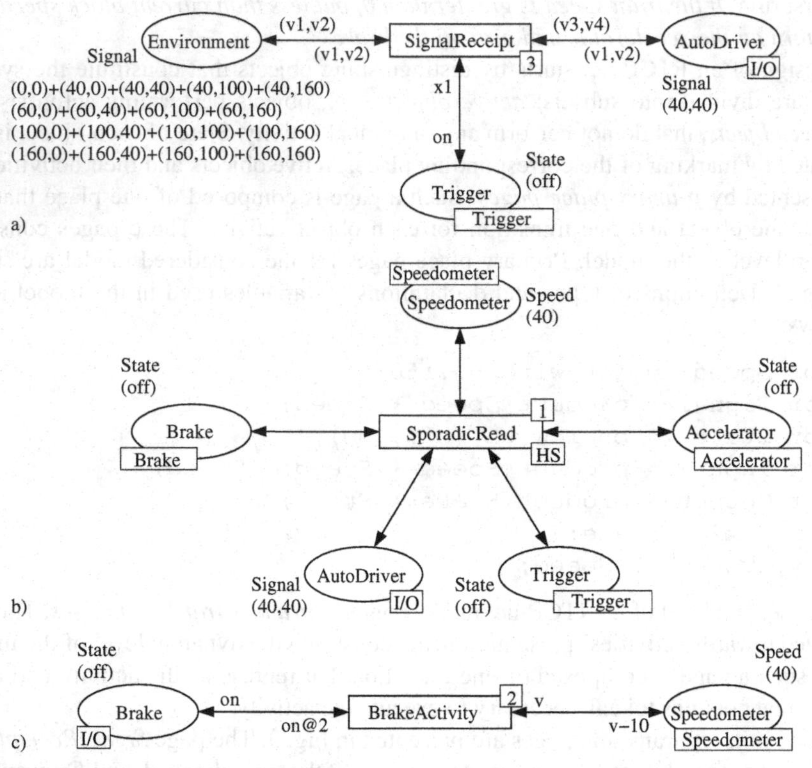

Fig. 3. Primary transition pages: a) *SignalReceipt*, b) *SporadicRead*, c) *BrakeActivity*

place *AutoDriver* and an *on* token is placed in the place *Trigger*. The page *SporadicRead* contains a passive object *Speedometer*. A token in the place represents the current train speed. The transition *SporadicRead* activity is based on the set of rules presented in the Table 1. Two more subpages are needed to represent the transition activity. The subpage for the transition *SequentialRead* is similar, but it does not contain the place *Trigger*. Moreover, the time expression of the arc going from the place *AutoDriver* to the transition *SequentialRead* is equal to 10 (the token in the place must be at least 10 seconds old to be consume by the transition). Thus, we can observe that two different activities can be model in a very simple way. The time expression guarantee that the transition *SequentialRead* will be fired every 10 seconds, while the place *Trigger* enable modelling service of sporadic events. Moreover, if the sporadic event occurs, one occurring of the transition *SequentialRead* is omitted (It is like a reseting a timer for the activity.)

The last page (Fig. 3 c) represents the *Brake* activity. If the place *Brake* contains an *on* token for at least 2 seconds, the speed decreases by 10 kph. The page *AcceleratorActivity* is constructed analogously.

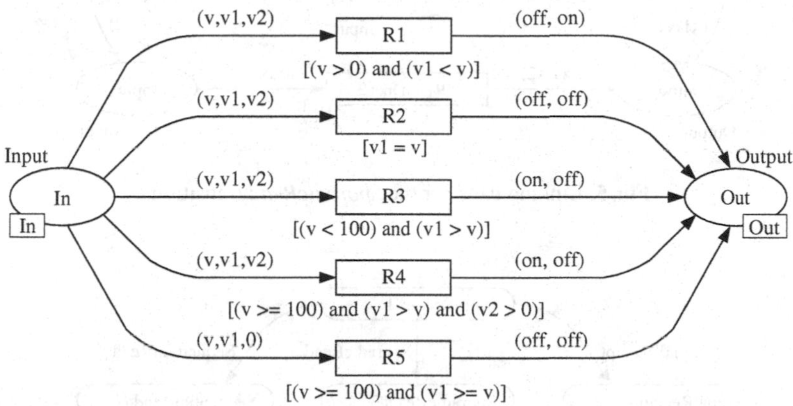

Fig. 4. D-net form of the Table 1

To be included into an RTCP-net a decision table (see Table 1) must be transformed into a D-net (see Fig. 4). Each decision rule is represented by a transition and its input and output arcs. A token placed in the *In* place denotes a sequence of values of conditional attributes. Similarly, a token placed in the *Out* place denotes a sequence of values of decision attributes.

To include the D-net into the model a linking page must be constructed. *Linking pages* are used to represent an algorithm that describes an activity in details or as an interface for gluing the corresponding D-net into a model. Such a page is used to gather all necessary information for the D-net and to distribute the results of the D-net activity. *Linking pages* and *D-nets* belong to the functional level of a model. A link page for the *SporadicRead* activity is presented in Fig. 5. A link page for the *SequentialRead* activity is constructed analogously, but it does not contain the place *Trigger*.

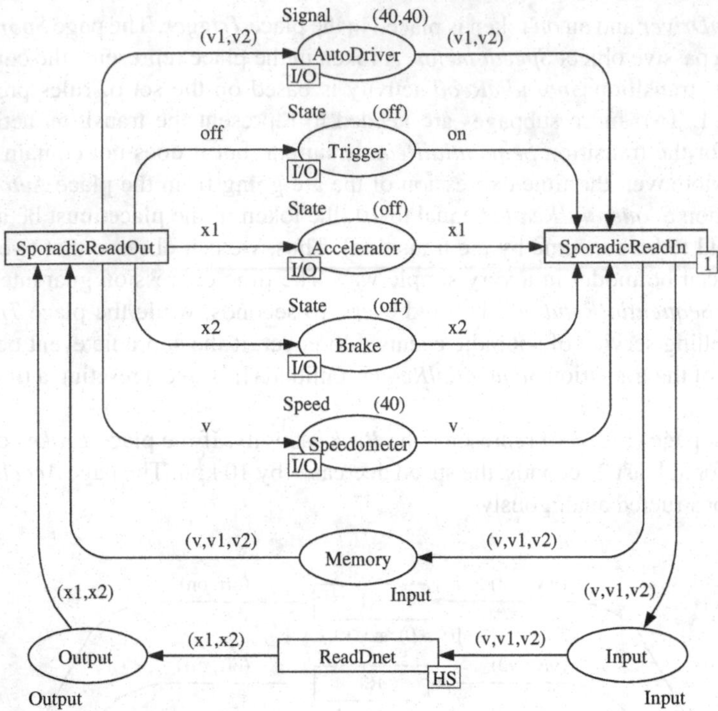

Fig. 5. Linking page for the *SporadicRead* transition

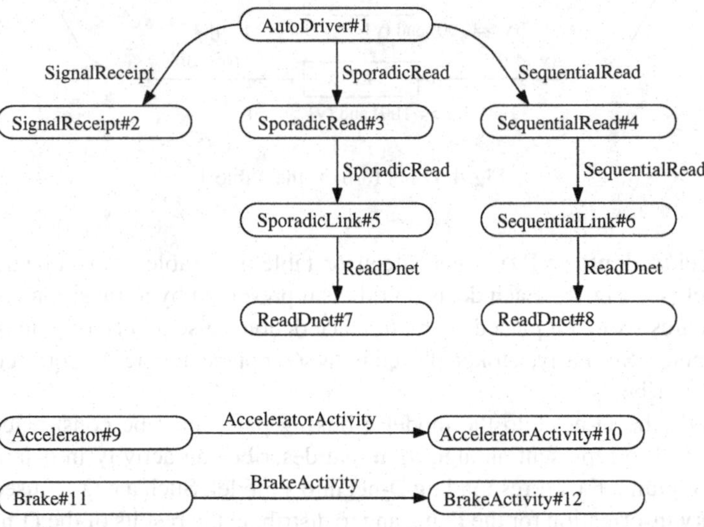

Fig. 6. Page hierarchy graph

All connections among pages are presented using a page hierarchy graph. A node in such a graph represents a single page, and an arc represents a connection between a subpage and its substitution transition. The page hierarchy graph for the considered model is shown in Fig. 6. For more details on hierarchical RTCP-nets see [7].

4 Verification

Analysis of RTCP-nets may be carried out using reachability graphs. The set of reachable states $\mathcal{R}(M_0, S_0)$ is represented as a weighted, directed graph. Each node corresponds to a unique state, consisting of a net marking and a time vector, such that the state is a result of firing of a transition. Each arc represents a change from a state (M_i, S_i) to a state (M_j, S_j) resulting from a passage of time $\tau \geq 0$ and a firing of a transition t in a binding $b \in \mathcal{B}(t)$.

Let's consider the net presented in Fig. 1. None transition is enabled in the state (M_2, S_2), but it is possible a passage of time $\tau = 6$ that leads to the state (M_2, S_2'). The transition *TurnOnSS* is enabled in the state and its firing leads to the state (M_3, S_3), where:

$$\begin{aligned} M_3 &= (ssOn, on, (on, on), \mathit{off}, active, on), \\ S_3 &= (0, 54, 0, -6, 2, 54). \end{aligned} \tag{7}$$

Thus, in the reachability graph, there will be nodes for the states (M_2, S_2) and (M_3, S_3), and an arc going from (M_2, S_2) to (M_3, S_3) with label $((TurnOnSS, ()), 6)$.

An RTCP-net $\mathcal{N}$ is said to be *bounded* if each place $p \in P$ has an upper integer bound, i.e. $\exists k \in \mathbb{N}\ \forall (M, S) \in \mathcal{R}(M_0, S_0)\colon |M(p)| \leq k$, and it is said to be *strongly bounded* if each place p has a finite upper multiset bound, i.e. $\exists X \in 2^{C(p)^*}\ \forall (M, S) \in \mathcal{R}(M_0, S_0)\colon M(p) \leq X$, and X is a finite multiset. A reachability graph for an RTCP-nets may be infinite even though the net is strongly bounded, e.g. if the time stamp of at least one place is decreasing infinitely.

Let's consider two states of the RTCP-net presented in Fig. 1, the state (M_2, S_2') and a state (M_2, S_2''), where $S_2'' = (-8, 54, -6, -6, 2, 54)$. The same transitions are enabled in both states and the same sequences of actions are feasible from the states. A token in the place *ContrSyst* is accessible for all its output transitions if its age is at least 6 time-units, i.e. the value of the time stamp is equal to or less than -6. It makes no difference whether the time stamp is equal to -6, -8, etc. The states (M_2, S_2') and (M_2, S_2'') will be said to *cover* each other and only one node in the coverability graph will be used to represent them.

Let $p \in P$ be a place of an RTCP-net $\mathcal{N}$ and let $Out_A(p)$ denote the set of output arcs of the place p. *The maximal accessibility age* of the place p is the number:

$$\delta_{max}(p) = \max_{a \in Out_A(p)} \left\{ \max_{b \in \mathcal{B}(T(a))} E_S(a)_b \right\}. \tag{8}$$

The maximal accessibility age of a place p denotes the age when tokens in the place become accessible for all output transitions of the place.

Definition 4. *Let $\mathcal{N}$ be an RTCP-net and let (M_1, S_1) and (M_2, S_2) be states of the net. The state (M_1, S_1) is said to* cover *the state (M_2, S_2) (denoted by $(M_1, S_1) \simeq (M_2, S_2)$) iff $M_1 = M_2$ and:*

$$\forall p \in P\colon (S_1(p) = S_2(p)) \vee (S_1(p) \leq -\delta_{max}(p) \wedge S_2(p) \leq -\delta_{max}(p)). \quad (9)$$

The *coverability relation* $\simeq$ is an equivalence relation on $\mathcal{R}(M_0, S_0)$. If $(M_1, S_1) \simeq (M_2, S_2)$, $(M_1, S_1) \xrightarrow{(t,b)} (M_1', S_1')$ and $(M_2, S_2) \xrightarrow{(t,b)} (M_2', S_2)'$, then also $(M_1', S_1') \simeq (M_2', S_2')$ and $\mathcal{L}(M_1, S_1) = \mathcal{L}(M_2, S_2)$.

Proposition 1. *If an RTCP-net $\mathcal{N}$ is strongly bounded and each type $\Sigma_i \in \Sigma$ is finite, then the coverability graph is also finite.*

The proof for this proposition can be found in [10].

The reachability and coverability graphs are constructed in similar way. They differ only about the way a new node is added to the graph. For the coverability graph, after calculating a new node, we check first whether there already exists a node that covers the new one. If so, we add only a new arc that goes to the found state and the new one is omitted. Otherwise, the new state is added to the coverability graph together with the corresponding arc. The coverability graph contains only one node for each equivalence class of the coverability relation.

The coverability graph for the RTCP-net presented in Fig. 1 is shown in Fig. 7. The coverability graph for an RTCP-net provides similar capabilities of analysis of the net properties as the full reachability graph. It contains all reachable markings so it is possible to check the boundedness properties – all places of the considered net are 1-bounded. The coverability graph contains the same arcs' labels as the reachability one, therefore, it is possible to check also the liveness properties – the net is not live (but it is $\mathcal{L}3$-live [8]). Each label of an arc is a pair of a transition with its binding and a passage of time. The second element of a pair can be treated as the weight of the arc. Thus, arcs' weights capture the time taken by transition from one state to the next. (We consider only states that are results of firing of transitions). Using the coverability graph, one can find the minimal and maximal times of the transition from one state to another, etc. To do this we can use typical algorithms for finding the shortest or longest paths between two nodes in a directed graph (multigraph).

To be useful RTCP-nets must be supported by computer software. A CASE tools for RTCP-nets called *Adder Tools* are being developed at AGH University of Science and Technology in Kraków. *Adder Tools* is a free software covered by the GNU Library General Public License. It is being implemented in the GNU/Linux environment by the use of the Qt Open Source Edition. The software also compiles and runs with Mac OS X and Windows. *Adder Tools* contain:

– *Adder Designer* – for design and verification of rule-based systems;
– *Adder Editor* – for design of RTCP-nets;
– *Adder Simulator* – for simulation of RTCP-nets.

Adder Tools home page, hosting information about current status of the project, is located at *http://adder.ia.agh.edu.pl*. For more details see [9].

Let's consider the model of an automatic driver presented in section 3. The state space for the model is infinite. Verification of a model usually starts by simulating it. A small part of a simulation report is presented below:

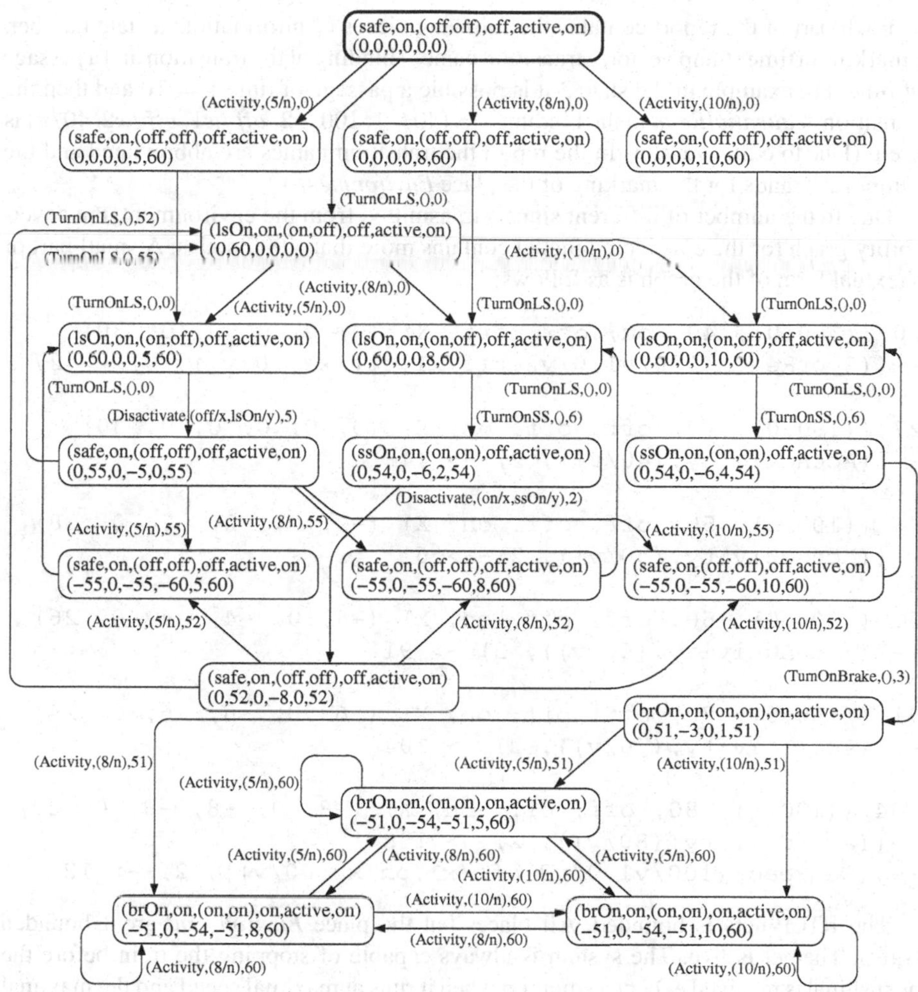

Fig. 7. Coverability graph for the RTCP-net presented in Fig. 1

```
0 ((40,40), 40, off, off, off, X) (0, 0, 0, 0, 0, 0)
--((SigReceipt,(40/v1,100/v2,40/v3,40/v4,off/x1)), 0)--> 1

1 ((40,100), 40, on, off, off, X) (0, 0, 0, 0, 0, 30)
--((SporRead,(40/v1,100/v2,off/x1,off/x2,40/v)), 0)--> 2

2 ((40,100), 40, off, off, off, X) (0, 0, 0, 0, 0, 30)
--((SeqRead,(40/v1,100/v2,off/x1,off/x2,40/v)), 10)--> 3

3 ((40,100), 40, off, off, off, X) (0, 0, -10, 0, 0, 20)
--((SeqRead,(40/v1,100/v2,off/x1,off/x2,40/v)), 10)--> 4
```

Each part of the report contains the folowing pieces of information: a state number, a marking, a time stamp vector, a transition name, a binding of the transition and a passage of time. For example in the state 2 it is possible a passage of time $\tau = 10$ and then the transition *SequentialRead* in the binding $b = (40/v1, 100/v2, \mathit{off}/x1, \mathit{off}/x2, 40/v)$ is fired. (Due to editor reasons in the report the transition names are abbreviated and the symbol X stands for the marking of the place *Environment*.)

Due to the number of different signals transmitted from the environment, the coverability graph for the considered model contains more than 4000 nodes. A small part of a textual form of the graph is as follows:

```
10 ((100,0), 40, on, off, off, X) (0, 0, 0, 0, 0, 30)
--((SporRead,(100/v1,0/v2,off/x1,off/x2,40/v)), 0)--> 27

27 ((100,0), 40, off, off, on, X) (0, 0, 0, 0, 0, 30)
--((AccActivity,(40/v)), 2)--> 44

44 ((100,0), 50, off, off, on, X) (-2, 0, -2, -2, 0, 28)
--((AccActivity,(50/v)), 2)--> 61

61 ((100,0), 60, off, off, on, X) (-4, 0, -4, -4, 0, 26)
--((AcceActivity,(60/v)), 2)--> 91

91 ((100,0), 70, off, off, on, X) (-6, 0, -6, -6, 0, 24)
--((AccActivity,(70/v)), 2)--> 104

104 ((100,0), 80, off, off, on, X) (-8, 0, -8, -8, 0, 22)
--((AccActivity,(80/v)), 2)--> 122
--((SeqRead,(100/v1,0/v2,off/x1,on/x2,80/v)), 2)--> 121
```

The RTCP-nets is bounded. All places but the place *Environment* are 1-bounded (safe). The net is live. The system is always capable of stopping the train before the next signal is received except a situation when it runs at maximal speed and the maximal speed limit is suddenly replace with the stop signal. A possible solution of this problem is to limit the maximal speed to 150 kph.

5 Summary

Some possibilities of application of RTCP-nets for modelling and verification of safety-critical systems have been presented in the paper. Two examples of models of train protection systems have been used to illustrate the approach. Due to the high cost of such systems failure using of formal methods is worth considering and it can ensure more dependable products.

RTCP-nets are based on timed coloured Petri nets but some new features introduced into the definition enhanced usefulness of them for modelling of real-time systems. The new time model and transition priorities enable users to model timeouts – system waits for an event, but if it does not occur an alternative activity is taken, and task priorities in a very simple way. RTCP-nets together with computer tools allow users to design models and manipulate its properties fast and effectively. It seams that the nets can be treated as an interesting alternative for other formal modeling languages.

References

1. Bacherini, S., Bianchi, S., Capecchi, L., Becheri, C., Felleca, A., Fantechi, A., Spinicci, E.: Modelling a railway signalling system using SDL. In: Proc. of FORMS 2003 Symposium on Formal Methods for Railway Operation and Control Systems, Budapest, Hungary (2003) 107–113
2. Banci, M., Fantechi, A., Gnesi, S.: The role of format methods in developing a distributed railway interlocking system. In: Proc. of the 5th Symposium on Formal Methods for Automation and Safety in Railway and Automotive Systems (FORMS/FORMAT 2004), Braunschweig, Germany (2004) 220–230
3. Cheng, A.M.K.: Real-time Systems. Scheduling, Analysis, and Verification. Wiley Interscience, New Jersey (2002)
4. Haxthausen, A.E., Peleska, J.: A domain specific language for railway control systems. In: Proc. of the Sixth Biennial World Conference on Integrated Design and Process Technology, IDPT2002, Pasadena, California (2002)
5. Jensen, K.: Coloured Petri Nets. Basic Concepts, Analysis Methods and Practical Use. Volume 1-3. Springer-Verlag (1992-1997)
6. Sommerville, I.: Software Engineering. Pearson Education Limited, London (2004)
7. Szpyrka, M.: Fast and flexible modelling of real-time systems with RTCP-nets. Computer Science **6** (2004) 81–94
8. Szpyrka, M., Szmuc, T.: Application of RTCP-nets for design and analysis of embedded systems. In: Proc. of Mixdes 2005, the 12th International Conference Mixed Design of Integrated Circuits and Systems, Kraków, Poland (2005) 565–570
9. Szpyrka, M..: Practical aspects of development of embedded systems with RTCP-nets and ADDER Tools. In: Proc. of Mixdes 2006, the 13th International Conference Mixed Design of Integrated Circuits and Systems, Gdynia, Poland (2006)
10. Szpyrka, M.: Analysis of RTCP-nets with reachability graphs. Fundamenta Informaticae (2006) (to appear).

Checking SCADE Models for Correct Usage of Physical Units*

Rupert Schlick[1], Wolfgang Herzner[1], and Thierry Le Sergent[2]

[1] ARC Seibersdorf research, division Information Technology
{rupert.schlick, wolfgang.herzner}@arcs.ac.at
[2] Esterel Technologies
thierry.lesergent@esterel-technologies.com

Abstract. Mismatches of units and of scales of values in physical calculations are disastrous, but rather common, in the development of embedded control systems. They can be as plain as mixing feet and metres, or as hidden as a wrong exponent in a complex calculation formula. These errors can be found by a checking algorithm, following some simple rules, if information on the units of the used variables is provided. This paper describes a developer friendly approach of providing this checking functionality in SCADE, a model-based graphical development tool for safety-critical embedded applications.

Keywords: physical units, safety, verification, error detection, dependable embedded systems, model based software development, SCADE, DECOS.

1 Introduction

Control systems usually have to deal with physical quantities like time, temperature, length, speed or electrical current. Simply using numeric standard data types like *real* or *float* paves the way for typical programming errors like mixing scales (e.g. adding seconds and milliseconds), using wrong operators (v : m*s), swapping operands (v : s/m) etc. The most well known/notorious example is the loss of the *mars climate orbiter* in 1999 [11], lost due to a unit conversion mistake not found during testing. But earth bound safety critical applications are prone to this family of errors as well.

While several methods and tools are available for various programming languages to cope with such problems (see section 5), for data-flow oriented modelling languages like Simulink [17] or SCADE [13], which are increasingly used in the domain of embedded systems, this is less the case. In particular, SCADE is especially appropriate for development of safety-critical applications, due to its strict temporal execution model, various included testing and verification tools like a model checker and a qualified C-code generator. Since in DECOS, which aims at development support of distributed embedded real-time systems of up to highest criticality, SCADE is an

* This work is partially funded by DECOS (Dependable Embedded COmponents and Systems), an integrated project funded by the EU within priority "Information Society Technologies (IST)" in the sixth EU framework programme (contract no. FP6-511 764).

J. Górski (Ed.): SAFECOMP 2006, LNCS 4166, pp. 358 – 371, 2006.

important part of the DECOS tool chain, it was decided to develop a SCADE extension which allows a developer to check its model for dimensional or physical unit errors. Since this is done at modelling time and prior to code generation, it does not affect runtime performance.

Therefore, this paper is structured as follows. The next section presents the concepts of a general approach, based on SI, the international system of physical units, and a special notation. Section 3 introduces SCADE shortly, and describes how this approach is implemented for SCADE, while section 4 gives some application examples. The last two sections address related work and draw a conclusion, respectively.

2 General Approach

This section first gives a short terminology introduction and then describes the principal rules applied in automatic unit checking at development-time.

2.1 The SI Unit System and Unit Representation

Physical *quantities* have a *dimension;* each dimension can be measured in multiple *units*. A *unit system* defines *units* for a set of mutually independent dimensions. These are the *base units*, all other units can be derived from them (giving *derived units*) by (multiple) multiplication and division of the base units.

The SI unit system [14] is the standardized unit system most widely used in engineering today. SI base units are kilograms (kg), meters (m), seconds (s), ampere (A), Kelvin (K), mole (mol) and candela (cd). The remainder of this document is based on the SI unit system unless noted otherwise.

Taking the SI units into consideration, it is fairly natural to represent a physical unit as a 7-dimensional vector, where each element denotes the exponent of the respective base unit in the given order. So, kg is denoted by [1,0,0,0,0,0,0], and s by [0,0,1,0,0,0,0]. Consequently, derived units are represented by vectors with more than one element different from 0; for instance:

$$\textbf{force: } [N]=\left[\frac{m\,kg}{s^2}\right] \quad kg^1, m^1, s^{-2}, A^0, K^0, mol^0, cd^0 \quad [1,1,\text{-}2,0,0,0,0] \tag{1}$$

In the rest of the paper, this notation will be simply referred as *unit representation*, synonymously with *unit.*

2.2 Rules for Operating on Physical Units

In scientific work and engineering, *dimensional analysis* and the *unit-factor method* are commonly used to ensure the correctness of equations and calculations.

The following rules are basically the rules for dimensional analysis, adapted for use in computer programs and extended with some issues useful in control systems.

Basic Rules. For the four basic arithmetical operations, the following rules apply:

- Addition and subtraction is allowed only for values with identical vectors.
- Multiplication gives a new unit. Base unit exponents are calculated by adding the respective base unit exponents from the multiplicands.

- Division gives a new unit. Base unit exponents are calculated by subtracting the divisors base unit exponents from the dividends exponents.

Power is derived from multiplication – base unit exponents are multiplied by the power exponent.

Root, as inverse function to power, results in the unit exponents divided by the root base. If the exponents are not divisible without remainder, the operation is not allowed. (In theory rational exponents are possible in intermediate results, but for the sake of brevity such details are not addressed here.)

More Rules. Functions like logarithm, exponentiation, or the trigonometric functions operate only on dimensionless numbers.[1] Operators typically used in programming environments should also be supported. They can be grouped as follows:

- Decision operators: all possible outputs of `if` and `case` must have the same unit.
- Comparison operators: only quantities with identical units can be compared.
- Composite data types: arithmetical operations only operate on basic data types, units of the basic data type are preserved through composition and decomposition.
- Temporal operators (SCADE specific): simply preserve the unit of their inputs.

For vector and matrix operations, similar rules to the ones for the base calculation methods apply. An important aspect is that a scalar and a vector with the same dimension definitely do not have the same dimension as a whole (see also next clause).

Exotic Rules. There are issues with units being (formally) the same for different dimensions as well as the general topic of dimensionless units and numbers.

Ambiguous Units. Due to the use of a scalar form for the notation of units, situations can occur where the same unit name applies for two or more physical quantities. One example for this situation is Newton metres. It can measure both work and torque (See formulas 2 and 3). In correct dimensional analysis, work is the scalar product of two vector quantities - force and the distance over which it moves, resulting in a scalar value; torque is the vector product of the same quantities force and the length of the lever.

The usual representation of units looses this information whether a quantity is a vector or not, therefore the dimensional analysis based on this unit check is sometimes incomplete.

$$\textbf{torque}: [Nm] = \left[\frac{m^2 \cdot \textbf{kg}}{s^2}\right] \tag{2}$$

(vector, force normal to radius, outer product of two vectors)

$$\textbf{energy/work/heat}: [J] = \left[\frac{m^2 \cdot \textbf{kg}}{s^2}\right] \tag{3}$$

(scalar, force along a way, scalar product of two vectors)

[1] These functions can be expressed as power series, where ascending powers of the argument are summed up. Adding values with different dimension exponents would break the basic rules and therefore the argument must be dimensionless.

Despite the fact that torque is formally a vector, it is often feasible and efficient to treat it as a scalar during calculation, e.g. because all relevant axes are parallel anyway.

Since energy and torque are units that are rather frequent in embedded and especially automotive applications, it seems desirable to have a means to distinguish between the two cases even when no vectors are used for calculations.

A workaround to achieve this is to introduce an additional unit "radial meter" m_r used when a radius is used in conjunction with tangential forces and other physical values. With it, the two units now become $Nm_r = m_r\ m\ kg/s^2$, and $J = m^2\ kg/s^2$.

m_r can be modelled as an additional unit in the vector and should be used consistently for all related units like angular velocity. If a lever length is used in a calculation, it must have m_r as unit. All calculation rules apply to this new unit as well as for the original seven SI units. When torque is treated as a three dimensional vector, this is not necessary, although there may be other but similar issues.

In general, dimensional analysis can be complemented by orientational analysis, checking a formula for errors in spatial orientation [15, 16]. Support for spatial dimensions and orientational analysis would address the loss of information mentioned above and possibly will be added later on, but is out of the scope of this paper

Dimensionless Units. There are two dimensionless derived SI units:

$$\textbf{angle}: [rad] = \left[\frac{m}{m}\right] = [1] \qquad \textbf{solid angle}: [sr] = \left[\frac{m^2}{m^2}\right] = [1] \tag{4}$$

In many cases, it is desirable for readability to preserve these "units". A simple solution is to make use of the "radial meter" introduced above: $rad = m/m_r$, and $sr = m^2/mr^2$.

This avoids cancelling down the unit in the fraction and still gives sensible results. For example, multiplying torque with the rotational angle it is applied for yields the accomplished work.

Dimensionless Numbers. There are a lot of dimensionless physical values in various application areas, especially in fluid dynamics. Sometimes it is helpful to keep the information about the quantity being measured by putting the same units in both the numerator and denominator as for radians above.

Generalized support for this would go beyond the scope of the drafted checking method, particularly because the technique of non-dimensionalization is especially used in number crunching and fluid dynamics, but little in the physics used in embedded control.

A group of special cases of dimensionless numbers are logarithmically scaled ratios like dB. Some of them, like decibel microvolts (dBμV), are used in technical applications. In fact, they are dimensionless and if the represented quantity is needed for calculations, the value needs to be "delogarithmized" and multiplied with the base value (e.g. 1 μV for dBμV). Then the resulting value is a dimensioned value that can be checked for consistent units use as described above.

2.3 Scaling

Along with the SI units, a set of SI prefixes is defined. They are representing factors in steps of 1000 ranging from $10^{-24} - 10^{24}$ as well as the factors 10^{-2}, 10^{-1}, 10 and 100.

The factor 10 can be modelled as an additional "unit" to represent the SI prefix in the same way as the seven SI units with the same rules for checking consistency. Only the root function behaves different, since it is valid to draw a root even if the exponent is not divisible by the root's base; for a unit exponent, this would be an error. The resulting scaling exponent would be a fractional instead of an integer number as shown in the example below:

$$\sqrt[3]{\mathbf{10^4} \cdot [m]^3} = \mathbf{10^{4/3}} \cdot [m] = \sqrt[3]{10^1} \cdot 10^1 \cdot [m] \quad (5)$$

The $\sqrt[3]{10^1}$ part must be included in a free scaling factor (see "Odd Scaling Factors" below), part of the unit information only kept for analysis.

Normalising and other conversion can be done by multiplication with dimensionless constants of a "scaled value" of 1, as 1000 milli (10^{-3}) or 1/1000 kilo (10^3).

Odd Scaling Factors

Distances, Weights, Areas and Volumes. Especially for distances, weights, areas and volumes exists a multitude of units outside of the SI system (usually old, pre-SI units) some of which are (still) widely used in some regions (e.g. US customary units) or working areas (oil barrels, gold ounces, …). All of these have in common that they are a simple factor larger or smaller than the corresponding SI units. For scaling factors, the basic calculation rules are adapted.

Angles. Angles differ from other units due to their periodicity. But since sensors may deliver angles like for torsion or rotational position in any range, it appears reasonable to allow signed values outside the circle range without any special consideration.

2.4 Absolute and Relative Values and Zero Point Translation

Most of the physical values covered above are always "relative" values. Nonetheless, at least one commonly used physical value is either relative or absolute: temperature.

A data type can be marked as "absolute". This means certain rules for calculations apply and they can have a zero point offset. At the moment, this is only aimed at temperatures but may be found useful for other units as well. In short, absolute (x_a) and relative (x_r) types of the same dimension can be combined as follows:

- $x_a \pm x_r \rightarrow x_a$: offset value stays the same
- $x_a - x_a \rightarrow x_r$: offset value must be identical, result is relative and has no offset

Other addition/subtraction expressions over absolute values are invalid.

2.5 Extended Unit Representation

According to the previous, the 7-dimensional unit representation introduced in 2.1 should be extended for

- distinction between m and m_r,
- representing the scaling exponent relative to the dimension's unit scale,
- representing an "odd" scaling factor for non SI-units or "rooting" results,
- marking of "absolute" values
- offset for absolute values .

3 Solution/Application in SCADE

After a short introduction to SCADE, this section describes how the concepts and rules discussed before are implemented in SCADE.

3.1 About SCADE

SCADE (the Safety Critical Application Development Environment) is both a notation and a toolset that was specifically developed to describe and implement safety critical systems for application domains such as aeronautics or automobile. The SCADE notation includes both block diagrams[2] and safe state machines, giving a rigorous description of the complete behaviour of the software [8]. It has been formally defined and it has the following characteristics that are key in the targeted application domain, i.e. the development of safety critical systems:

- Strong typing
- Explicit initialization of data flows
- Explicit management of time (delays, clocks, etc)
- Simple expression of concurrency (data dependencies)
- Deterministic execution

In SCADE, a node (which we can also call a "block") performs logically atomic computations, providing deterministic output values corresponding to a given set of input values, according to the previous memorized state. Nodes can use other nodes as shown in figure 5, the root node taking its inputs from the environment. Feedback loops are handled in a simple way thanks to the time operators (delay). Recursion is forbidden.

The computation is often triggered by a periodic clock (although it need not be), after inputs are sampled from the environment and hold.

The SCADE toolset supports a model-driven paradigm in which the SCADE model is the software specification. Verification activities are supported by a combination of three different tools [2, 5]:

- The SCADE Suite Simulator supports interactive or batch simulation of a SCADE model, for both data flows and safe state machines.
- The SCADE Suite Model Test Coverage (MTC) tool is used to measure the coverage of the SCADE model with respect to a given requirements-based test suite.
- The SCADE Suite Design Verifier (DV) supports corner bug detection and formal verification of safety requirements.

---

[2] Examples of block diagrams are shown in Figures 3 and 5.

The SCADE toolset also provides an API to access all the details of a model from tcl scripts. This allows in a simple way development of utilities to check for example that a model conforms to some user specific methodological rules.

The C code generator is certified with respect to DO-178B level A (avionics) [6] and IEC 61508 up to Safety Integrity Level (SIL) 4 (other industrial domains, such as automotive or railways), thus providing a guarantee that the generated code is correct with respect to the model.

3.2 Implementation

The Units-Check package for SCADE consists of:

1. The units-check function itself, fully integrated into the SCADE user interface
2. A SCADE library containing
   - predefined units (SI and non-SI)
   - conversion factor constants
   - unit related operators

This package is implemented using the following concepts:

- the unit representation (as extended in 2.5) is stored in custom annotations to the data type
- values (inputs and outputs as well as constants and internal variables) are marked with their units by use of "unit annotated" data types.
- operator effects are controlled by applying the rules described in section 2.

Units-check support for developers covers the following activities:

- Marking variables with units
- Unit conversion
- Checking a model for consistent use of units
- Extending the units library
- Extending the units system
- Integrating user-implemented operators (native SCADE and imported C functions)

Marking Variables with Units. The units-library contains a continuously expanded set of predefined aliases for the *real* data type. Wherever a variable is a physical quantity, the corresponding unit data type is to be used instead of real.

To profit from the checking script, only inputs and outputs of the root node and all used constants need to be unit-typed. However, it is good style to do the same for the inputs and outputs of all subnodes if they represent certain physical quantities.

Through the use of individual data types, unit information is documented directly in the model and improves the maintainability of the model. No changes to the program function are introduced due to SCADE's notion of the units as "compatible" data types to *real*.

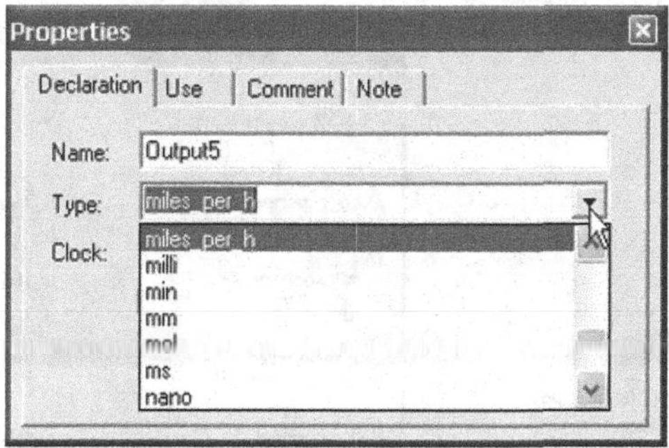

Fig. 1. Dialog window for selecting a predefined unit data type for a variable

Unit Conversion. Scaling and unit conversion is done manually by multiplication with or division by the scaling constants contained in the unit library. (See second example).

Some solutions for unit support in other languages implicitly convert units when necessary. This is not easily implemented in SCADE and would break the requirement of minimum disturbance by massively changing the executed code.

Checking a Model for Consistent Use of units. The checking function is integrated into the SCADE development environment as an analysis report for either a single node or all nodes of the project. This is quite similar to the SCADE *quickcheck* function for checking model consistency; therefore, SCADE application developers are familiar with the concept. The checking function is a tcl script using SCADE's extension mechanism.

The checking function walks through the entire model and for each operator derives the unit of the output(s) from the unit of the input(s). Conflicts for the operator inputs and conflicts between the developer defined and the derived units of the nodes outputs are reported as errors.

Extending the Units Library. Units not contained in the library can be easily added in the development model or an own library by the user.

Unit data types are defined as aliases for *real* with an added unit annotation. A dialog for unit annotations is shown in the left hand side of figure 2.

Extending the Units System. The checking script is implemented in a generic way. If a new basic unit is needed or the used unit system should be changed, the annotation type definition for units can be changed without touching the script itself.

Additional units (e.g. for memory size) can be introduced by adding fields with names in the form: *<base_unit_name>_exponent* . If wanted, but at the loss of use for the provided unit library, a unit system with completely different base units could be built by removing/renaming the existing unit exponent fields.

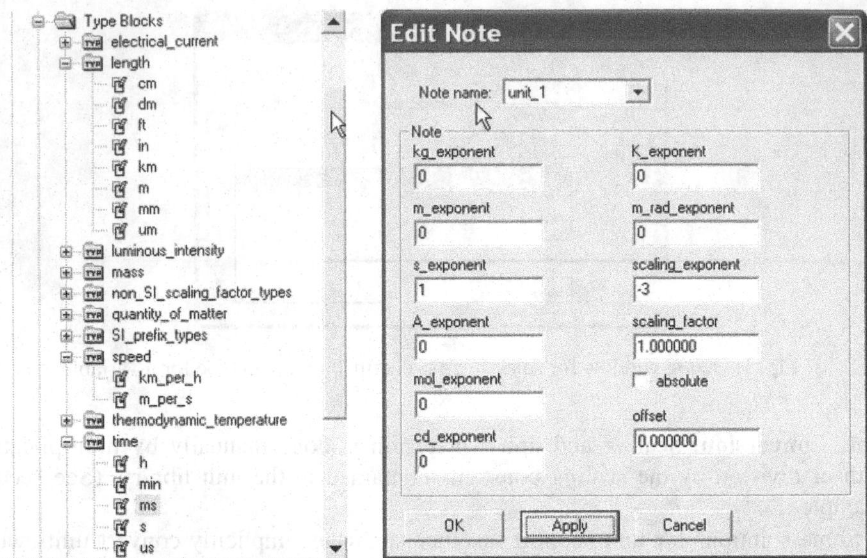

Fig. 2. View of an example units library and the unit annotation for milliseconds

Integrating User-implemented Operators. Each modelled SCADE node is itself an operator usable for the modelling of other higher level models.

Native SCADE operators. Operators (nodes) defined in SCADE are transparently traversed by the checking script.

Imported C functions, called imported operators, cannot directly be checked like normal SCADE nodes. If inputs and outputs have unit types associated, unit compatibility will be checked there. For imported operators operating on generic data types or plain reals, the developer can provide a tcl script calculating the output units from the input units and raising error messages.

4 Examples

For demonstration we use the node shown in figure 3, calculating an average *speed* in *m/s,* from a given number of wheel axle rotations per execution cycle (*ticks*). The wheel *circumference,* the execution *cycleduration* and the *cyclenumber* of the average time window are defined in constants.

As a test scenario, the units for *circumference* and *cycleduration* differ from the units assumed by the model (*cm* vs. *m* and *ms* vs. *s*).

The data type *one* represents a "dimensionless" type compatible with the other unit types. As you can see, no further unit information is given for the internal variables (the "wires") – SCADE implicitly derived the types for *_L14, _L34, _L35 and _L36* from the respective sources.

A first run of the *units-check* Data gives a result containing (among others):

unit determination error circle in type propagation for _L22 - please set manually

This is caused by back feeding the delayed value *_L22* to its own input values. The current algorithm recognizes circles; better heuristics for resolving them with less or without user interaction are possible but not implemented yet.

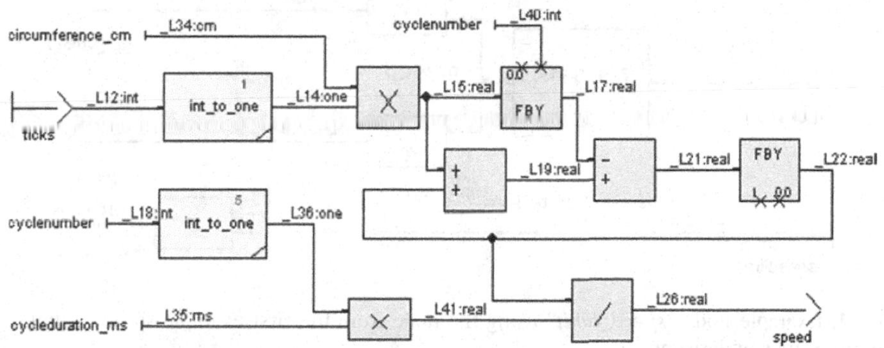

Fig. 3. SCADE node "*avg_speed*"

After manually naming *_L22* to *dist* and setting the type to meters, the *units-check* result looks as shown in table 1, containing 4 distinct error messages.

Table 1. Check result for the node "avg_speed", after manually resolving the propagation circle

eqBlock	Context	Message Type	Message
eq_avg_speed_2_1	L19 = L15 + dist	input unit mismatch	Error – units for inputs differ while they are expected to be identical
	L21 = L19 - L17	input unit mismatch	Error – units for inputs differ while they are expected to be identical
	dist = fby(L21, 1, 0.0)	unit mismatch error	Conflicting Units single {0 1 0 0 0 0 0 1.000000} and unknown
	speed = L26	unit mismatch error	Conflicting Units single {0 1 -1 0 0 0 0 1.000000} and single {0 1 -1 0 0 0 3 1.000000}

The input mismatch for the addition *_L19* = *_L15* + *dist* through the multiplication for *_L15* is caused by *circumference* having the wrong prefix (cm instead of m). This can be corrected either by changing the unit and the value of *circumference* or in the model by division of *circumference* through the scaling constant for *centi*.

The next two messages are due to error propagation. If the resulting unit cannot be determined, the unit "*unknown*" is used for further propagation. For *_L21* this means that *_L17* and *unknown* are different (message 2). The manually set unit of *dist* is in conflict with the *unknown* unit propagated from *_L21* in the third message. Solving the mismatch for *_L19* takes care of all these three error messages.

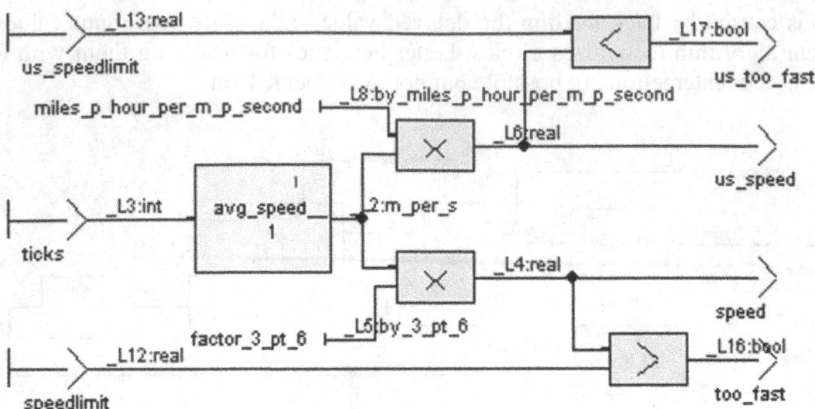

Fig. 4. Example node "*speed_limit*" using the node from the first example showing unit conversions and comparisons

The last error message tells that the derived unit for *_L26* is not the same as expected for *speed* because of its data type *m_per_s*. In a small model like this example, this error is easily traced back to the unit for *cycleduration*. In larger models, it can be helpful to explicitly set intermediate unit information as done above for *_L22* to narrow down the possible cause of a unit error.

The second example shown in figure 5 makes use of the first example as a sub-node. The calculated speed in *m/s* is converted to miles per hour and kilometres per hour; the converted values are compared to two speed_limit inputs.

In the model as shown, the speedlimit-inputs have data type real and therefore no unit information associated. This gives the *units-check* result shown in table 2, easily leading to the missing units information for the speed_limit inputs.

The used conversion factors are defined in the unit library. The *factor_3_pt_6* has an own unit data type *by_3_pt_6*, having all fields of the unit annotation except the scaling factor set to zero. The scaling factor is set to 0.2778, the reciprocal of the constants value 3.6.

Table 2. Check result for the node "speedlimit"

eqBlock	Context	Message Type	Message
eq_speedlimit_1	L16 = L4 > L12	input unit mismatch	Error – units for inputs differ while they are expected to be identical
	L17 = L13 < L6	input unit mismatch	Error – units for inputs differ while they are expected to be identical
	speedlimit : real	unit determination warning	Units information not retrievable / not given for input/hidden input
	us_speedlimit : real	unit determination warning	Units information not retrievable / not given for input/hidden input

5 Related Work

Since the problem area is well known and widespread throughout application domains, there are various tools and libraries for units support. Some theoretical work was already done in 1978 [10] and before.

Languages and tools with available, but sometimes rudimentary, unit libraries are, among others: Ada[3][9], C[4], C++ [3,18], Excel [1], Fortran-90[5][12], Java[6], Lisp[4], MatLab[7], and Visual Basic[8]. The main feature sets found are: explicit conversion, implicit conversion, documentation, runtime-check, compile-time (or other development-time) check and unit inference.

With the exception of C++ and Ada, the mentioned libraries support only runtime-evaluation (of a subset) of calculation correctness or are even limited to mere conversion helpers. In dependable embedded systems, though, unit information is usually not dynamic and therefore unit correctness can and should be treated at development time. This avoids related runtime overhead as well as the resulting runtime errors.

For C++, this can be achieved by using template metaprogramming, resulting in compile time error messages for unit errors. This usage of templates is increasingly often used as an example in the teaching of C++ templates and multiple implementations of various degrees of maturity are available, e.g. the *SIunits* library and the open source project *Quantities*[9]. [3] gives a good description of the general approach and details of implementation in the *SIunits* library.

Guo and McCamant [7] describe a different approach for C: In large (especially legacy) programs it is difficult to "annotate" each and every variable and constant with the correct unit information. To help with this problem, they propose an analysis tool that infers a set of unit types based on the usage of variables and constants in the program. This allows some consistency checks without further programmer intervention and can help a programmer annotating variables and constants. For a pre-existing open source utility with more than 50000 lines of code, they could reduce the 11000 program variables to 163 basic units requiring unit annotation.

6 Conclusion

An approach for checking SCADE models for correct usage of physical dimensions has been presented which provides the following benefits:

Development-time error recognition – and, as a result, keeping unit error discovery independent from test data and test methodology, and avoiding runtime overhead.

---

[3] http://www.dmitry-kazakov.de/ada/units.htm
[4] http://www.unidata.ucar.edu/software/udunits
[5] http://rain.aos.wisc.edu/~gpetty/physunits.html
[6] http://nanotitan.com/software/Libraries/quantity
[7] http://www.mathworks.com/matlabcentral/fileexchange/loadFile.do?objectId=10070, http://www.mathworks.com/matlabcentral/fileexchange/loadFile.do?objectId=6850
[8] http://www.entisoft.com/ESTools/Units.HTML
[9] http://www.echem.uni-tuebingen.de/~bs/AKhomepage/Quantities/quantities.html

Ease of Use – by providing libraries of predefined units, a convenient way to use them and complete integration of the toolset into the development platform.

Minimum disturbance – other SCADE features, including code generation and model checking, remain unaffected.

Retro-applicability – can be applied to existing models by only setting input, output and constant units in the model itself or a wrapper node or by simply using the model as a subnode in a unit marked model.

Extensibility and generic implementation – by allowing definition of new units and even extensions/changes to the unit system used (e.g. by adding "memory units").

Of course, it should be noted that several limitations have to be considered. There is the possibility to have ambiguity on scaling factors and exponents ($100*10^3$ vs. $1 * 10^5$) and problems with computational accuracy when scaling factors are used intensively.

Therefore, future work will address these topics, as well as trying to further improve the usability e.g. by automatically resolving unit propagation circles and showing derived units in the block diagram. Also, future extensions of SCADE like for matrix handling will be considered, possibly together with a major extension of the functionality to support orientational analysis.

Finally, it will be investigated whether the taken approach can be migrated to other platforms like e.g. Simulink.

As concluding remark, it can be stated that tools like that described in this paper are helpful for avoiding software development errors and thus important means for the verification of software.

Acknowledgements. The Authors would like to thank Esterel Technologies expert Jean-Louis Colaço for proof reading this paper.

References

1. Antoniu, T., Steckler, P., Krishnamurthi, S,.et al.: Validating the unit correctness of spreadsheet programs. In ICSE'04, Proceedings of the 26th International Conference on Software Engineering, pages 439–448, Edinburgh, Scotland (May 26–28, 2004)
2. Bouali, A., Dion, B., Konishi, K. : Using Formal Verification in Real-Time Embedded Software Development. Japan SAE, Yokohama, 2005
3. Brown, W.E.: Applied template meta-programming in SIunits: the library of unit-based computation. In: Proceedings of the Second Workshop on C++ Template Programming, Tampa Bay, FL, USA (October 14, 2001)
4. Cunis, R. 1992. A package for handling units of measure in Lisp. SIGPLAN Lisp Pointers V, 2 (Apr. 1992), 21-25.
5. Dion, B., Gartner, J.: Efficient Development of Embedded Automotive Software with IEC 61508 Objectives using SCADE Drive.
6. DO-178B: Software Considerations in Airborne Systems and Equipment Certification., RTCA/EUROCAE (1992)
7. Guo, P., McCamant, S.: Annotation-less Unit Type Inference for C. Final Project, 6.883: Program Analysis, CSAIL, MIT (December 14, 2005)
8. Halbwachs, N., Caspi, P,. Raymond, P, and Pilaud, D.: The synchronous dataflow programming language lustre. Proceedings of the IEEE, 79(9):1305–1320 (September 1991)

9. Hilfinger, P.N.: An Ada package for dimensional analysis. ACM Transactions on Programming Languages and Systems (TOPLAS), v.10 n.2, p.189-203 (April 1988)
10. Karr, M. and Loveman, D. B. 1978. Incorporation of units into programming languages. Commun. ACM 21, 5 (May. 1978), 385-391.
11. Mars Climate Orbiter Mishap Investigation Board. Phase I report (November 1999)
12. Petty, G.W. : Automated computation and consistency checking of physical dimensions and units in scientific programs. In: Software - Practice and Experience, 31, 1067-1076 (2001)
13. SCADE Suite Technical and User Manuals, Version 5.0.1, June 2005, Esterel Technologies
14. Système International d'Unités, http://www.bipm.fr/en/si/
15. Siano, D.: Orientational Analysis - A Supplement to Dimensional Analysis - I. J. Franklin Institute (320): 267. (1985)
16. Siano, D.: Orientational Analysis, Tensor Analysis and The Group Properties of the SI Supplementary Units - II. J. Franklin Institute (320): 285. (1985)
17. Using Simulink, Version 6, 2005, The MathWorks
18. Umrigar, Z. D: Fully static dimensional analysis with C++. SIGPLAN Not. 29, 9 (Sep. 1994), 135-139.

Validation and Certification of Safety-Critical Embedded Systems - The DECOS Test Bench*

Erwin Schoitsch[1], Egbert Althammer[1], Henrik Eriksson[2], Jonny Vinter[2], Laszlo Gönczy[3], Andras Pataricza[3], and György Csertan[3]

[1] ARC Seibersdorf research, Austria
{erwin.schoitsch, egbert.althammer}@arcs.ac.at
[2] SP Swedish National Testing and Research Institute
{henrik.eriksson, jonny.vinter}@sp.se
[3] Budapest University of Technology and Economics
{gonczy, pataric, csertan}@mit.bme.hu

Abstract. The integrated EU-project DECOS (Dependable Embedded Components and Systems) aims at developing an integrated architecture for embedded systems to reduce life-cycle costs and to increase dependability of embedded applications. To facilitate the certification process of DECOS-based applications, the DECOS Test Bench constitutes a framework to support Validation & Verification. By implementing a modular approach, an application safety case merely contains the application-specific issues and re-uses the safety arguments of the "generic" safety cases of the DECOS platform. The Test Bench covers the complete life cycle from the platform-independent models to deployment, including model validation and transformations. The safety cases are based on validation-plans (v-plans) comprising the steps to validate the safety requirements. The Test Bench provides a methods/tools repository, guidelines to generate and execute v-plans, and integration of tools and of remotely distributed test beds.

1 Introduction

"Smart Systems" are based on intelligent embedded control systems, which are distributed within the application systems, and often hidden to the every-day life user. E.g., more and more functions in today's cars are realized by electronics and software, 80-90% of the new innovative features are realized by distributed embedded systems. Eventually, even highly safety critical mechanical and hydraulic control systems will be replaced by electronic components. Value of electronics in cars will increase beyond 40% of the total value. Even today, upper class cars contain up to 80 ECUs, several bus systems, and about 55% of all failures are caused by electronics, software, cables and connectors [3], [11].

The DECOS project [2] aims at making a significant contribution to the safety of dependable embedded systems by facilitating the systematic design and deployment of integrated systems [1]. DECOS (Dependable Embedded Components and Systems) is a European Integrated Project in FP6, Embedded Systems area, scheduled for the

* Research supported in part by EU IST-FP6-511764 (DECOS).

J. Górski (Ed.): SAFECOMP 2006, LNCS 4166, pp. 372–385, 2006.

period 2004-2007. Co-ordinator is Austrian Research Centers Seibersdorf research (ARCS). Work is performed by 19 partners: Two research centers (ARCS, SP (Sweden)), six universities (Universities of Technology Vienna, Darmstadt, Budapest, Hamburg-Harburg, Universities of Kassel and Kiel), three technology and tool providers (TTTech Vienna, Esterel Toulouse, Infineon Munich), and eight demonstrator/application related industrial partners (Audi AEV, CR Fiat, Hella, Airbus, Thales, EADS, Liebherr Aerospace, Profactor).

In federated systems, each application subsystem is located on a dedicated processor. The federated approach provides natural separation of application functions, but causes increased weight, electric energy consumption and cost due to resource duplication and the large number of wires, buses and connectors. Integrated systems not only help to alleviate this problem, they also permit communication among application functions. A remarkable feature of the integrated DECOS architecture is that hardware nodes are capable of executing several tasks of application subsystems of different criticality. Throughout this paper, we will use the notion of a node instead of processor or component.

An integrated architecture provides a fixed number of nodes, each of which has certain properties (e.g., size of memory, computational power, I/O resources). All tasks have to be allocated such that given functional and dependability constraints are satisfied. This is discussed in detail in [4].

This paper focuses on the description of the DECOS Test Bench which supports the validation and certification process within DECOS. It has been developed within subproject 4 (validation and certification). An overview of the other subprojects is found in [5].

2 Goals of the DECOS Test Bench – Modular Certifiability

The DECOS Test Bench has the goal to facilitate *certification* of DECOS-based systems in a *modular* (component based) manner, making use of properties of the DECOS core services, high level services, and the DECOS design and development processes. Basis is the generic functional safety standard IEC 61508. A comparison and evaluation of several domain specific standards and IEC 61508 has shown, that systems conforming to higher SIL levels of IEC 61508 or related standards fulfill the major requirements of domain specific standards, such as IEC 50129 (railways), the evolving ISO 26262 automotive functional safety standard (the so-called DIN-FAKRA standard proposal) or RTCA/DO 178B for aircraft industry.

The modular certification of a DECOS-based system is based on the definition of so-called *Modular Safety Cases* and works in the following way:

- The first step is to provide *generic safety cases* for the *application independent parts of DECOS*, e.g. the core-services or the DECOS nodes. For each entity a safety case is generated. These safety cases are called generic safety cases because they provide the generic infrastructure for any DECOS application but are (per definition) independent from them (comparison: generic telephone infrastructure and applications). The generic safety cases themselves form a modular system.

- The second step is to provide the safety cases for each *application* of the system, re-using the generic safety case(s) for the DECOS infrastructure technology.

Fig. 1 shows the two approaches to establish a safety case. On the left hand side the traditional (federal) approach is shown: one large monolithic safety case for each application. On the right hand side the modular approach is illustrated: reuse of the architecture related (generic) safety cases such as the DECOS nodes, the core services and the high level services. This approach leads to a well manageable certification process and to a clearly arranged application safety case.

The modular, component-based approach to safety case generation is of utmost importance in case of re-certification of DECOS-based systems: based on the generic safety cases and the already proven properties and evidences, re-certification is considerably simplified, the process more cost-effective.

Within DECOS only certifiability will be proven: it is up to the subprojects to prove that the requirements have been met or can be met in a production process ("certifiability"). Doing so, the certifiability of the whole DECOS system is proven.

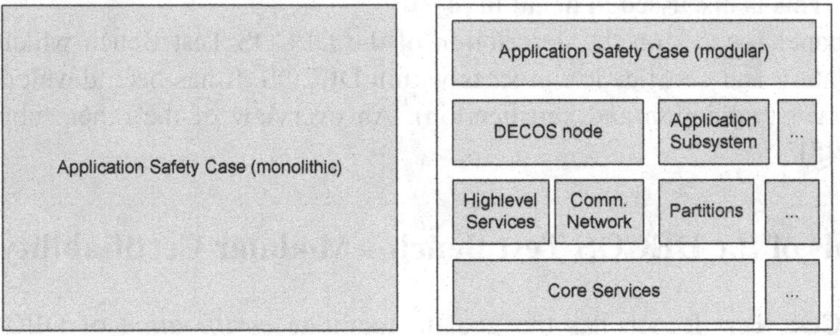

Fig. 1. Monolithic versus modular application safety case

At this stage, one "Generic Safety Case" for a safety critical part of a DECOS node has been established. It builds on the inherent assumptions and the assumed fulfillment of the requirements defined in all the subprojects for the integrated DECOS architecture and services (architecture claims, core services, high level services) [1].

The construct to be looked at is shown in Fig. 2. It consists of the safety-critical part of a DECOS node, including the SCCU (safety–critical connector unit) and the PI (Platform Interface) (for details of DECOS nodes, see [1]), but not of the application, because only the generic part is looked at. The result is an evaluation and assessment of the contribution of the DECOS architecture to the safety of application systems, which is intended to be included in the safety case of DECOS-based applications and is expected to facilitate this part of the system certification.

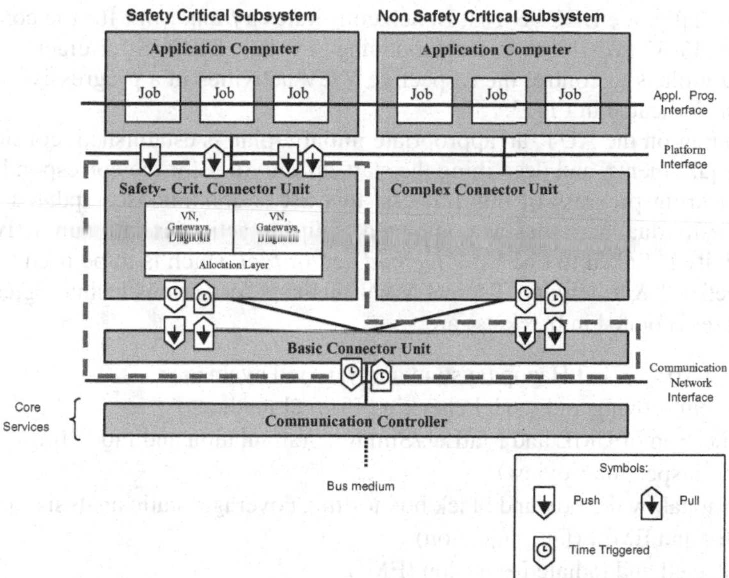

Fig. 2. DECOS node, system boundary for generic safety case

3 DECOS Test Bench Structure

The primary outputs of the DECOS Test Bench are the necessary documents to prove the certifiability of a DECOS-based system, i.e. the required (generic) safety cases. The Test Bench shall therefore allow for generating, organizing, storing and exporting the safety cases. What does this mean precisely? Typically a safety case comprises the necessary safety arguments which correspond to the *V&V activities* and the related *evidence* (for details see section 4). A V&V activity is related to one or more safety requirements and is a necessary step to prove these requirements. A V&V activity is performed either manually or by means of a V&V tool according to the selected V&V method. The evidence is the (written) proof that the V&V activity has been completed with positive results. Note that there is no evidence in case the V&V activity has failed (negative results) or been indecisive (inappropriate V&V tool).

In order to further simplify the certification process, the Test Bench provides an initial list of requirements and related V&V activities for each artefact under test (AUT, e.g. ranging from DECOS metamodels to architecture models, DECOS tools, components (hardware and software, see fig. 8), DECOS applications or DECOS application (sub) systems). The proposed V&V activities in this list are also influenced by the chosen standard and the required safety integrity level (according to IEC 61508 or related standards). The list of the V&V activities for a certain AUT is called a *validation plan* (v-plan), thus the initial list is called initial v-plan.

The DECOS Test Bench provides a number of facilities which provide guidance to generate and execute v-plans to obtain the evidence. The v-plans are explained in section 4. Among the facilities provided by the Test Bench are predefined v-plan templates and the possibility to integrate V&V tools.

Conceptually, the DECOS Test Bench constitutes a *framework* for the consolidated collective *V&V capabilities* corresponding to the DECOS artefact categories, providing v-plans to control the respective V&V activities in a progressive integrated manner, as indicated in Fig. 3.

Depending on the AUT, an appropriate initial v-plan is established, considering all related requirements, and describing the start-up activities for the corresponding V&V process. During progress of this process, this list is continuously updated by either marking individual activities as completed, splitting activities into sub-activities etc. Each activity is linked to one *V&V method* and/or *tool* which is to be used to perform the respective V&V activity. Typical V&V methods for various technologies and life cycle phases (notated in brackets) are

- FTA, FMECA and Hazop (system analysis and evaluation)
- Theorem proving and model checking (formal methods)
- Application of UML and MatLab/Simulink (simulation and modelling)
- Audit, inspection (review)
- Functional, white box and black box testing, coverage, static analysis (testing)
- SWIFI and EMFI (fault injection)
- Conducted and radiated emission (EMI)

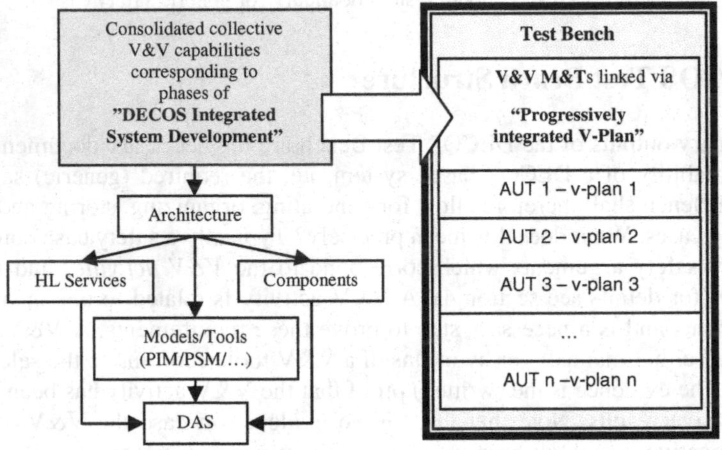

Fig. 3. Relationship between DECOS artefacts and Test Bench structure

A v-plan therefore is always specific for one AUT, comprises the list of requirements to be fulfilled for that AUT, describes the set of associated V&V activities, and contains meta-information like responsibilities and details about the AUT.

Safety cases are related to v-plans since the establishment of a safety case requires the collection of safety evidence for the claimed dependability of the respective system (or artefact), and v-plans describe how these arguments could be verified and validated.

An important aspect is that the Test Bench shall support treatment of more than one AUT at a time, illustrated in the parallelism of the various v-plans.

A top-level view of the Test Bench framework is shown in Fig. 4. Vertical alignments indicate 'uses'- or 'consists of'-relationships. So, a safety case uses a v-plan and the evidence based on positive results of V&V activity, while a v-plan essentially consists of the requirements (or claims, respectively) to be satisfied for a certain AUT, and the V&V activities performed in order to satisfy the requirements. A V&V activity is either a test case generation, or the application of a V&V method. The latter is performed by means of a certain V&V tool assigned to it.

Horizontally, major information flows are indicated. The whole process is requirements driven - requirements are derived from the DECOS artefact, relevant standards, and potentially other sources, e.g. – depending on the AUT category – from the respective domain. For instance, for an automotive brake-by-wire application, SIL3 would be a domain requirement, while for an aerospace flap-control SIL4 or equivalent would be required. In addition, requirements may also be generated internally during the V&V process, e.g. from risk analysis or by substituting general requirements, which cannot be verified as such, by more specific ones. V&V tools use the AUT in its appropriate form (specification, model, software, hardware etc.) – also called 'incarnation' – and produce results. Positive results are used to establish evidence for the validity of the stated requirements, while negative results will be reported to the developer. (Of course, also positive results will be reported to developers.) After error correction, new test cases may have to be added, and failed activities repeated. Test cases are considered to be requirements, since they have to be treated in essentially the same way; however, in addition to be entered manually, they can also be generated by means of test case generators. Finally, all collected evidence establishes the arguments for certifiability of the AUT.

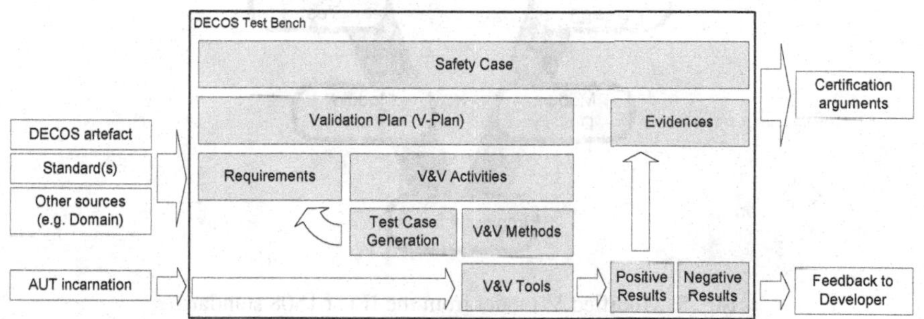

Fig. 4. Top-level structure of the DECOS Test Bench framework

Therefore, the DECOS Test Bench consists of the consolidated set of V&V tools, and a set of software services for guided use of these tools as well as management of all related documentation. These services establish the Test Bench framework, and largely coincide with the ingredients listed illustrated in Fig. 4.

In the following, specific aspects of the Test Bench framework are described: these are v-plans and evidence (section 4), execution of V&V activities (section 5), integration of external tools using model transformation (section 6) and the EMI part of the Test Bench (section 7).

4 V-Plans and Evidence

As described earlier, the v-plan describes the sequence of verification and validation activities. Within the DECOS project an example v-plan has been established for validation of the FTCOM layer. The FTCOM layer is a middleware layer of the DECOS platform which provides fault-tolerance (FT) and hardware-accelerated communication (COM) services to the application. The FTCOM layer is especially suitable as an example since it both consists of software and hardware. The hardware part is challenging due to the fact that it is an FPGA which functionality is designed using a hardware description language, i.e. software.

The DECOS platform shall be able to accommodate applications of highest safety integrity and since DECOS uses IEC 61508 as base standard, the FTCOM validation plan is consequently based on the requirements put by IEC 61508 on SIL4 safety functions. In its present form, the v-plan does not cover the complete safety life cycle of IEC 61508, instead it has been focused on the phases that have a correspondence in a development model such as the v model, see Fig. 5. In other words, concept and maintenance phases have e.g. been left out.

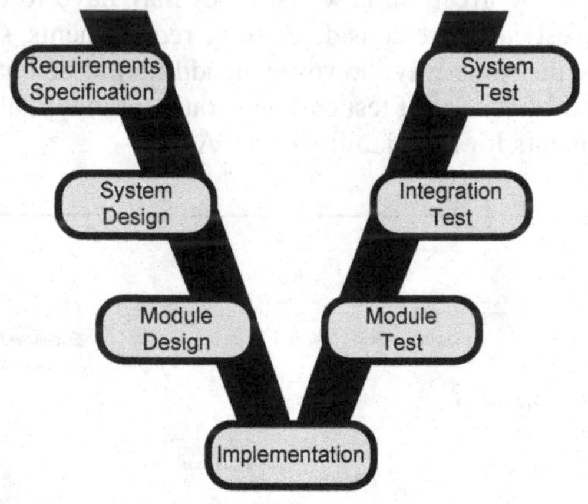

Fig. 5. Modified V-model from the IEC 61508 standard

In order to find all necessary V&V activities which will constitute the FTCOM v-plan, all methods that are highly recommended (HR), recommended (R), or mandatory for SIL4 safety functions to avoid systematic failures during the different phases of the safety lifecycle have been gathered; both for the hardware (IEC 61508-2) and the software (IEC 61508-3) parts. Additional requirements on e.g. document, configuration, and version management as well as requirement formulation have been captured in checklists.

Even though the FTCOM layer only provides 11 services, 4 hardware based and 7 software based, the vast number of V&V activities imposed by IEC 61508 makes it practically impossible (due to limited resources) to carry them all out within a three year's research development project such as DECOS, which is clearly pre-competitive and not developing a product. Instead, a few carefully selected V&V activities will be carried out as a proof-of-concept and to demonstrate certifiability. This is neither a drawback of DECOS nor of the processes implemented, and their feasibility is demonstrated by the application demonstrators in the automotive, aerospace and industrial control area. Guidelines will be provided how the processes have to be carried out in case of product certification and attention is directed to the critical issues. The selection of activities is based on the competences of the DECOS partners and the availability of a specific V&V tool. The V&V activities performed within the DECOS project range from reviews, static analyses, and formal verification to testing and fault injection. Different V&V activities apply for different DECOS artifacts. (see section 3 and 8).

5 Execution of V and V Activities

This section looks at one detail of the v-plan execution: the execution of the V&V activities. For simplicity reasons we consider the execution of only a single V&V activity in this context. Note that the Test Bench allows for parallel execution of several V&V activities due to its distributed client/server architecture[1]. As shown in Fig. 6, each V&V activity in the Test Bench has a well defined life cycle (note that the interaction with the requirements is explained below). It starts with the state "Not Ready" which means that the V&V activity has been defined but is lacking the relevant input which is necessary for execution. If the necessary input has been provided and the V&V tool has been selected, the V&V activity passes into the next state which is called "Ready". The input for the V&V activity comprises the input data requested by the tool to produce a significant output, further the definition of a deadline, and a responsible person. The Test Bench provides guidance by offering a repository of V&V methods/tools and an adequate help file. It also supports the input preparation for the selected V&V tool by offering model transformation (for details see section 6).

At this point the Test Bench offers the possibility to implicitly change to the state "Processing": an e-mail is generated which endows the responsible person with the relevant information he or she needs to execute the V&V activity. The responsible person is supposed to directly work on the Test Bench (by having installed a client on its work station). Depending on the selected V&V tool the tool execution might be automated using e. g. a message server (for details and an example see section 6) so that the results are automatically fed back into the Test Bench. In case of a manual execution of the V&V activity the Test Bench provides user guidance by offering a dialog which leads the user step-by-step through the process. An manual execution is typically required for GUI based tools or in case of distributed test sites needing specific equipment (e.g. EMI – Electromagnetic Interference – tests through a test lab, see section 7). The workflow support for the validation and certification process is designed in a manner that the Test Bench can be distributed and include remote sites

[1] Based on Telelogic DOORS®.

on both levels of integration. The Test Bench provides a distributed service for many clients and distributed test sites, based on the workflow described and a common repository for reuse of V&V results and documents.

Depending on the results of the V&V activity, there are three possibilities of the consecutive states: “Completed” if all results are positive, “Failed” if not all results are positive, in other words that there is at least one negative result and “Indecisive” if the selected V&V tool turns out to be not appropriate to cover all required aspects. In the second and third case the V&V activity shall be repeated using an updated AUT or V&V tool, respectively, setting it back to “Not Ready”. In case of a new version of the AUT the V&V activities of the associated v-plans have to be repeated as well (regression test).

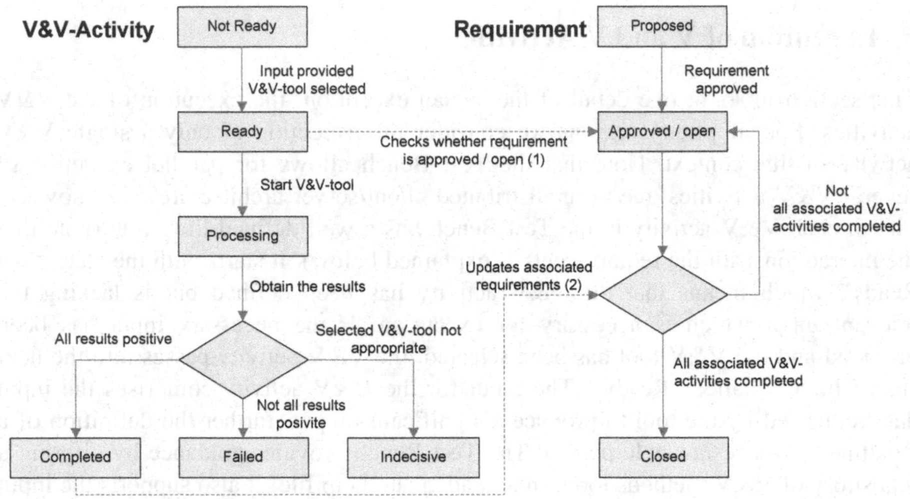

Fig. 6. Life cycle of a V&V activity and an associated requirement

Apart from this life cycle process of the V&V activities the Test Bench supports and/or automates further processes.

It automates the interaction with the associated requirements (see dashed lines in Fig. 6): (1) in the state “Ready” the associated requirements are checked whether they are already set to “Approved / open” which means that the requirement has been approved and is stable (note that the initial state “Proposed” denotes the requirements which are not approved yet). (2) In the state “Completed” the associated requirements are checked whether they have already been fully validated (i.e. all the associated V&V activities are completed). In the positive case they are set to “Closed”.

The Test Bench supports a tree-like hierarchy of V&V activities: V&V activities shall be split into sub V&V activities in case more than one V&V tools are used to perform the required task. Such V&V activities are called "compound" then, in contrast to "elementary". Also a v-plan can be seen as a compound V&V activity. The state of a compound V&V activity is automatically set to the logically lowest state of its sub V&V activities (according to Fig. 6, the order from lowest to highest corresponds to the direction from top to bottom and from left to right in the final row).

The Test Bench supports modular certifiability by allowing reference from a V&V activity to existing safety cases/arguments. It allows the reuse of modular safety cases (or successful V&V activities). Thus, the Test Bench provides a repository (or a library) of reusable safety arguments.

The Test Bench supports the generation of documents in standard format out of the database information. This allows for automating the generation of safety cases. The safety case contains the relevant evidence, but to keep the safety case slim it shall contain only the reference to the evidence which is downloaded from the document repository on request. The overall Test Bench Process as described is shown in Fig. 7.

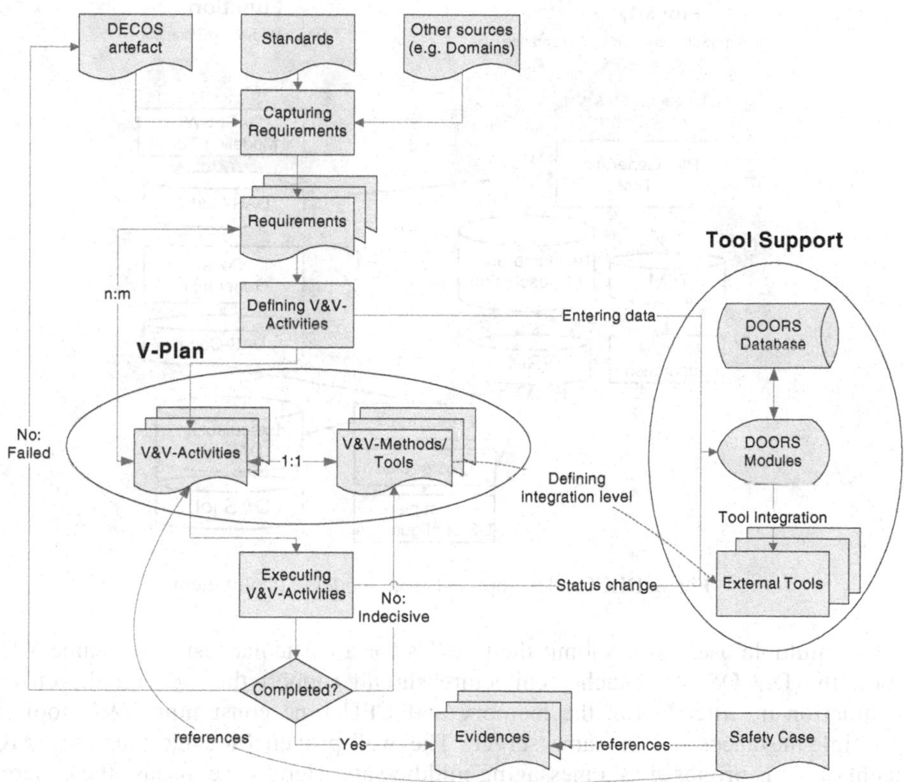

Fig. 7. The overall validation & certification process of the Test Bench

6 Integration of External Tools Using Model Transformation

One goal of the Test Bench is to provide guidance for the integration of external tools in order to facilitate the execution of the V&V activities. One part of the integration is the preparation of the input data for the V&V tools. This is done using model transformation. Hereby we describe the test bench configuration by the example of the PIM (Platform Independent Model) validation as a case study to illustrate the functioning of the Test Bench. In this step a PIM is validated against the DECOS PIM metamodel using ontology. The development process of a DECOS application is shown in Fig. 8, a part of which is the PIM generation.

In the case study, the PIM is edited by a UML modeling tool and stored in XML. Therefore, it has to be transformed into the representation format of an ontology tool and then it can be validated by posing questions against a reasoning system. The first prototype of this transformation was written in XML Schema Transformation Language [6], but a new version is also implemented in the VIATRA [7] tool by using model transformation.

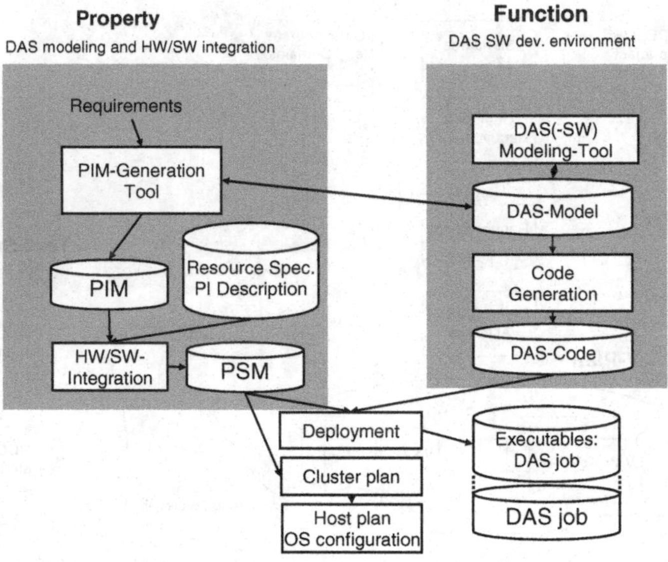

Fig. 8. DECOS development from model to deployment

As multiple users may submit their AUTs for a particular test to the same V&V tool, the DECOS test bench architecture should support the message-driven test evaluation in order to run the memory and CPU time consuming V&V tools in multiple instances on the same server. The well-proven Message Queuing (MQ) technology is proposed as a messaging middleware. Hereby we discuss the concrete implementation considerations, and present the architecture to run the test prototypes on.

The configuration of the implementation is shown in Fig. 9.

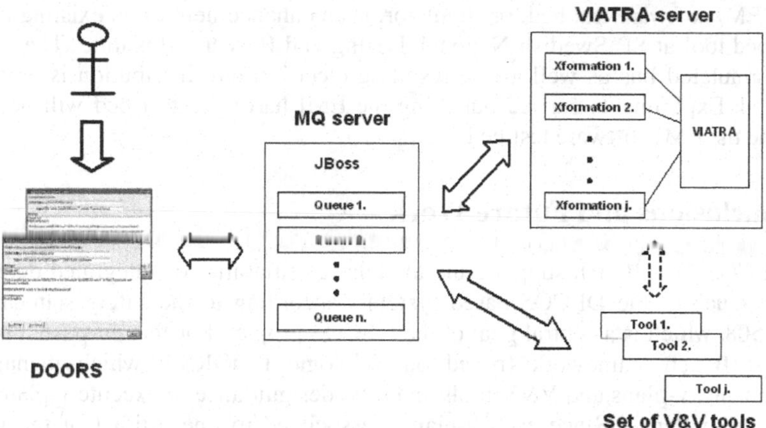

Fig. 9. Configuration of the Test Bench

The core of the basic architecture is a Java Message Service ([9]) compliant messaging server. The consumers and the receivers are the wrappers around the test bench tools sending test requests and results. We have chosen to use the JMS implementation of the JBoss [10] as it is a widespread, open product. The central messaging server and the test bench tools, such as the VIATRA framework and RACER are running on separate machines, thus the architecture is more flexible and extendable.

The requirements are stored in the DOORS tool. Sending a PIM to the test bench needs only a single Java wrapper class which takes the model, or a reference to the model stored in a repository, and sends it to a queue on the server. A concrete queue represents one test tool; in this case, VIATRA2. As the DOORS tool is able to start an executable file, this class can be instantiated from a DOORS script. Messages are extended with a unique message id to correlate response messages.

7 The EMI Part of the Test Bench

In a distributed safety-critical embedded system communication is vital. To be able to design and analyse different cable types and network topologies for the interconnection bus, a dedicated EMI test bed is developed within DECOS. The EMI test bed consists of two parts: one based on software (simulation program) and one based on hardware (measurement set-up). When designing these test beds, relevant standards from all three application areas, automotive, aerospace, and industrial control, have to be considered (e.g. MIL-Std. 461-E, DO 160D, EMC Directive 89/336/EC) . In the EMI test bed it is possible to analyse emission and susceptibility both for narrow band and wide band disturbances.

The EMI hardware test bed is set up inside an anechoic chamber of the accredited EMC test lab at ARCS where the cable under test is mounted in an adjustable fixture and driven and loaded by appropriate circuits, nodes. Three different antennas are provided to cover the targeted frequency range from 150 kHz to 1 GHz.

The EMI software test bed, or simulator, is an enhancement of an existing in-house developed tool at SP Swedish National Testing and Research Institute. The topology of the simulated bus as well as the resulting electric field distribution is graphically presented. Experiments carried out using the EMI hardware test bed will be used to fine tune the EMI software test bed.

8 Conclusions and Future Work

The DECOS Test Bench supports the modular certifiability of integrated dependable systems (such as the DECOS-based systems) according to the safety standards, e.g. IEC 61508, which is a central goal of the DECOS project. For this purpose it provides the Test Bench framework (based on Telelogic DOORS®) which manages the requirements, v-plans and V&V tools and provides guidance to execute v-plans and to obtain the evidence. Since each v-plan is associated to one artifact of the DECOS system, it is straightforward to establish a generic safety case for that artifact. An application safety case thus only contains the application-specific evidence and reuses the results of the generic safety cases.

A further strength of the DECOS Test Bench is that it supports the integration with external tools. In many cases the available input data does not fully match with the required formats of the tool. For this reason it provides a generic way of model transformation based on the tool VIATRA2. This is also true for external test sites such as the EMI Test Bed.

In the automotive application, a mixed criticality approach is demonstrated by integrating a door-control system and a critical crash warning and avoidance system demonstrator (vehicle and environment simulator with DECOS hardware in-the-loop, based on Layered FlexRay core technology).

The aerospace demonstrator is a flap control system for the Airbus outer flap control, a really critical application, with a gateway to the AFDX-bus of Airbus.

The industrial control demonstrator is control of a production- and business critical vibration control system for high-end nano-imprinting machines, controlling piezo-electric sensor and actuator networks. The long term vision of this demonstrator is critical structural control of engineering structures (helicopter cabins, aircraft wings, buildings, noise suppression etc.).

The next steps will be the following:

- Identification of a basic set of (existing) V&V tools to be integrated into the Test Bench to fulfill the major V&V requirements of the project (e.g. Item from Itemsoft for FMECA, LDRA (static and dynamic testing, coverage, top level test case generation), SCADE-MTC, a SWIFI (Software Fault Injection) tool like Propane from TU Darmstadt, a tool for PIM Validation (already explained in section 6) with the implementation of the appropriate model transformations.
- Establishment of further v-plans and evidence for the generic safety cases.
- Experiments (e.g. on quad modular redundancy by EMFI (EMI fault injection), evaluation of other basic core architectures such as Layered FlexRay and TT-Ethernet (time-triggered), evaluation of the impact of SoC (System-of-Chip) implementation of a few DECOS high level services, and a vulnerability analysis/trust case experiment) which are accomplished in the realm of DECOS.

References

[1] H. Kopetz, R. Obermaisser, P. Peti and N. Suri, "From a Federated to an Integrated Architecture for Dependable Embedded Real-Time Systems", Vienna University of Technology, Austria, and Darmstadt University of Technology, Germany, 2004

[2] DECOS: Dependable Embedded Components and Systems, Integrated Project within the EU Framework Programme 6, http://www.decos.at

[3] Association of German Car Manufacturers (VDA). HAWK2015 – Challenges for the automotive supply chain. Henrich Druck + Medien GmbH, Schwanheimer Strasse 110, D-60528 Frankfurt am Main, 2003 (in German).

[4] G. Weißenbacher, W. Herzner, E. Althammer, "Allocation of Dependable Software Modules under Consideration of Replicas", Proceedings of the ERCIM/DECOS Workshop on Dependable Software-Intensive Embedded Systems at Euromicro 2005, Aug. 31-Sept.1, 2005, Porto, Portugal. Proceedings published by ERCIM (European Research Consortium for Mathematics and Informatics), ISBN 2-912335-18-8, p. 51-58.

[5] E. Schoitsch, "The Integrated Project DECOS, From a Federated to an Integrated Architecture for Dependable Safety-Critical Embedded Systems – an Overview", Proceedings of the ERCIM/DECOS Workshop on Dependable Software-Intensive Embedded Systems at Euromicro 2005, Aug. 31-Sept.1, 2005, Porto, Portugal, Proceedings published by ERCIM (European Research Consortium for Mathematics and Informatics), ISBN 2-912335-18-8, p. 9-14. www.ercim.org

[6] XSL Transformations (XSLT) Version 1.0 W3C Recommendation 16 November 1999 http://www.w3.org/TR/xslt

[7] The VIATRA2 Model Transformation Framework, Generative Model Transformer Project, The Eclipse Foundation. http://eclipse.org/gmt/

[8] Volker Haarslev, Ralf Möller, Michael Wessel: RACER User's Guide and Reference Manual Version 1.7.19

[9] Java Message Service Spec. Version 1.1 http://java.sun.com/products/jms/docs.html

[10] JBoss Application Server. JBoss Inc.. http://labs.jboss.com/portal/jbossas/index.html

[11] E. Schoitsch, "Design for Safety AND Security of Complex Embedded Systems: A Unified Approach"; invited presentation des NATO Advanced Research Workshops, TU Gdansk, Springer, "Cyberspace Security and Defense: Research Issues", p. 161-174, ISBN-10 1-4020-3380-X, Springer Dordrecht, Berlin, Heidelberg, New York.

Encapsulating Application Subsystems Using the DECOS Core OS

Martin Schlager[1], Wolfgang Herzner[2], Andreas Wolf[1], Oliver Gründonner[1], Maximilian Rosenblattl[1], and Erwin Erkinger[1]

[1] TTTech Computertechnik AG
Schoenbrunner Strasse 7, 1040 Vienna, Austria
Tel.: +43 1 5853434 0; Fax: +43 1 5853434 90
martin.schlager@tttech.com
[2] Austrian Research Centers GmbH
Software Systems TechGate
Donau-City-Str. 1, 1220 Vienna, Austria
wolfgang.herzner@arcs.ac.at

Abstract. This paper presents an approach to structured integration of different application subsystems on the same embedded hardware, as currently developed in DECOS (Dependable Embedded Components and Systems), an integrated project within the Sixth Framework Programme of the European Commission. Those application subsystems can have different criticality levels and vendors. Furthermore, reliable communication among application subsystems is a major concern.

Focusing on the Encapsulated Execution Environment (EEE), which separates application subsystems in the space AND the time domain, this approach outlines the concepts and principles of an exokernel operating system, of partitioning, and of virtualization. The Core Operating System (COS) is described as a case study, including the hardware used, the current feature set, and benchmark values of central COS operations.

This paper also presents a model for a platform-independent application interface layer. Parts of this interface layer are generated from task specification to provide tasks with tailored communication services.

Keywords: Embedded Systems, Dependability, Virtualization.

1 Introduction

The development of electronic architectures in domains like the automotive, aerospace, or industrial control domain calls for a steadily increasing integration density of independent application subsystems. As mentioned in [1], it is expected that in the near future application subsystems from different vendors are seamlessly integrated in the same hardware platform. A study of A.D. Little [2], for example, states that currently about 70 ECUs are used in cars and in the next decade, a significant reduction to about 20 ECUs is expected. Application subsystems may have different levels of criticality and must be protected against

J. Górski (Ed.): SAFECOMP 2006, LNCS 4166, pp. 386–397, 2006.

each other in space and time. Otherwise, each module on the common hardware has to be developed to fulfill the highest safety requirements.

This paper presents an approach to the integration of mixed criticality subsystems that are executed on the same embedded hardware. This approach is currently under development in DECOS (Dependable Embedded Components and Systems), an integrated project within the Sixth Framework Programme of the European Commission. The Core Operating System (COS) of the DECOS Encapsulated Execution Environment (EEE), an exokernel [3] operating system, separates application subsystems in the space and the time domain. In order to minimize dependency of application software from specific implementations of the underlying DECOS services, a so-called platform interface layer (PIL) realizes the interface between the application subsystems and the COS.

The remainder of the paper is structured as follows: Subsequent to this introduction, section 2 describes the concepts and technology of the EEE. Section 3 outlines the experiences that have been gained through the implementation of the COS of the EEE, including the hardware used, the current feature set, and benchmark values of central COS operations. Section 4 starts with the conceptual DECOS node architecture from the viewpoint of an application and thereafter elaborates the implementation of the PIL on the EEE. Section 5 gives a short summary of the paper.

2 Concepts and Technology

In contrast to the federated architecture of traditional systems, the integrated architecture of the DECOS EEE provides means to support applications of different safety criticality levels to be executed in parallel on top of the same physical hardware, without any undesired interference between those applications. The architecture addresses the concept of modular certification, i. e., a safety-relevant application that is certified to a higher certification level can be executed together with a non-safety-relevant application that is certified to a lower certification level or is even not certified at all. Non-safety-relevant applications shall not inherit the criticality level of safety-relevant applications. This requirement is the reason why system resources (time and space) have to be shared among the applications, without any undesired interactions. Especially errors of one application shall not interfere with other applications. This *fault containment* is one of the main features of the DECOS EEE, where unspecified behavior of an application is recognized and its propagation prevented by the EEE.

Fault containment is achieved due to a strong and reliable *encapsulation* of every application which prevents undefined (unwanted) interaction to or from other applications. The encapsulation is achieved by separating the applications into *independent partitions* and arranging the protection in the space and time domain based on these partitions (refer to figure 1). The system resources are statically distributed to the partitions by the EEE.

The protection in the *space domain* prevents undefined accesses and manipulation of data in the memory of the system. Every partition is associated to a

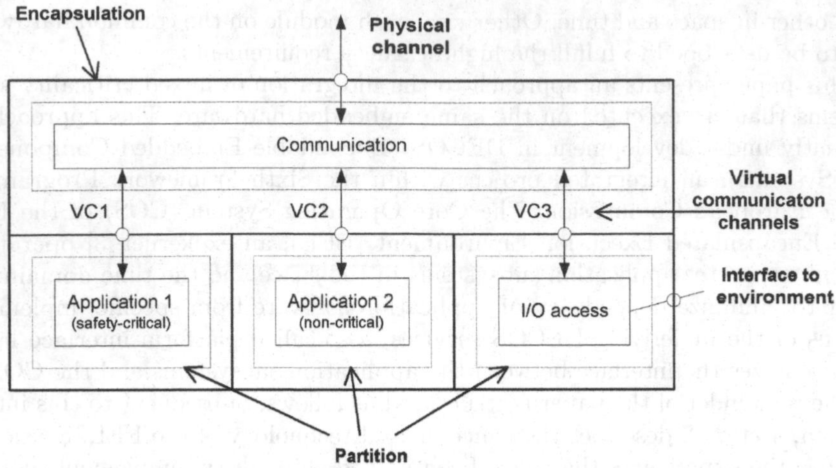

Fig. 1. A DECOS Node (Example)

(private) list of memory regions with read, write and execute rights. In addition the access to system I/O resources is also controlled by the space protection.

The protection in the *time domain* provides a guaranteed time window, where the CPU exclusively executes the program (i. e., the application) of the partition. Every partition is associated to a time window within a periodic schedule where every partition is activated at least once per (core) cycle (refer to figure 2). The EEE activates the partition at the start of the defined time window, and deactivates the partition at the end of the time window. The EEE prevents any exceptions to this schedule. Asynchronous events (like interrupts) are associated with at least one partition and are activated only in this partition.

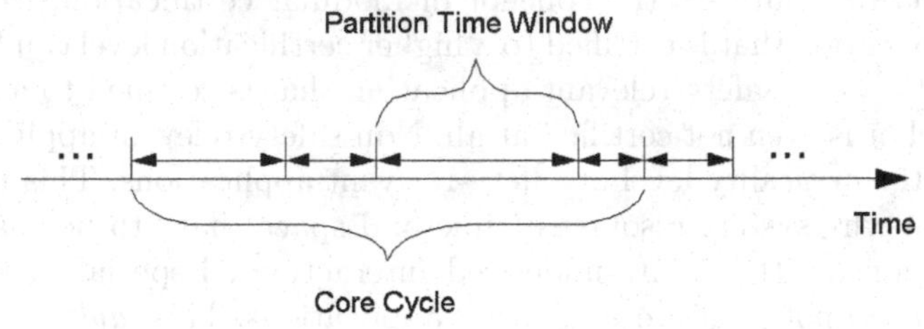

Fig. 2. Core Schedule (Example)

The strong protection mechanisms of the DECOS EEE enable the integration of safety-relevant tasks with non-safety-relevant tasks in separate partitions without compromising dependability properties of the safety-relevant task. However, every exchange of data between partitions requires additional means of the EEE. For this purpose *virtual communication channels* can be set up as a high-level service on top of the EEE, which can be used to transport information, without violating the encapsulation properties of the partitions.

Within an encapsulated partition a separate operating system could be realized. In case a separate operating system runs within a partition, the EEE offers virtualization of the resources that are bound to a partition. That means that resources within a partition can be further (sub-)managed without interference of other partitions.

The DECOS EEE consists of the core operating system (COS), which provides means for partition handling and protection, error handling and health monitoring, and inter-partition communication. A partition interfaces the services of the COS via the *system interface (SI)* (refer to figure 3).

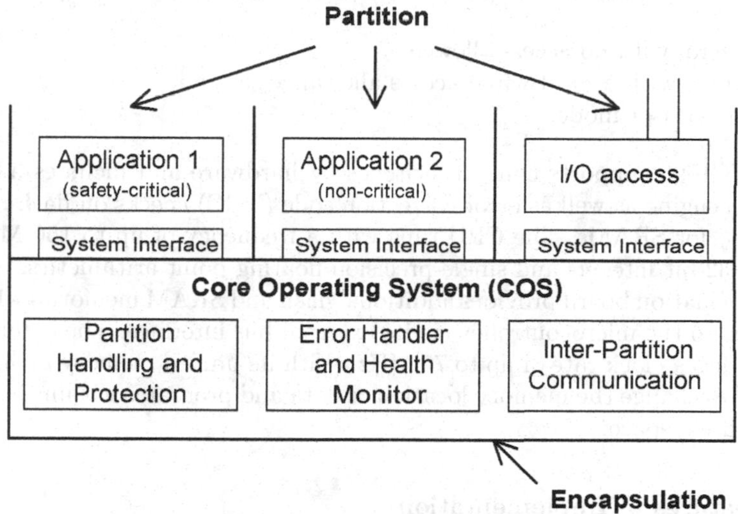

Fig. 3. Core Operating System and Partitions

The COS is implemented as an exokernel [3] that limits its functionality exclusively to the management (dispersal and protection) of shared resources – in our case memory and CPU time management. This leads to a slim kernel which can be tested more easily than a bigger kernel approach.

Memory protection is supported by a hardware/software mechanism as described in [1]. This ensures a maximum of flexibility without the cost of reduced reliability. Inter-partition communication can be realized either by message channels that are explicitly provided by the COS, or by the use of a statically defined shared memory.

For interrupt handling, the COS kernel is responsible for ensuring that a partition is only interrupted if it wants to receive the interrupt. So interrupts may be ignored and multiple occurrences may get lost if they are not handled in time.

A partition could contain a local operating system which we call *partition operating system (POS)*. The purpose of a POS is to enhance the services that are offered via the SI of the COS. In section 4 the DECOS platform interface layer (PIL) is introduced, which can be regarded as a basic POS.

3 Implementation of COS

A prototype implementation of the EEE COS has been implemented using an Infineon TriCore TC1796B [4]. This 32-bit microcontroller provides sophisticated memory protection over the unified data and program address space as well as several internal and external flash and SRAM memories. Additionally, it provides three levels of input/output space access protection:

- level zero, with no access allowed,
- level one, with a hard-wired access allowance set and
- the supervisor mode.

The TC1796 supports context switches by hardware and includes a CRC32 checksum engine as well as error correction code (ECC) checks on flash memory and parity for SRAMs. The CPU runs with a frequency of up to 150 MHz and provides 32-bit integer- and single-precision floating point arithmetics.

The evaluation board provides additional flash and SRAM memories which are connected to the microcontroller via its external bus interface. The external bus interface has a clock rate of up to 75 MHz. With its unified memory architecture it is easy to change the memory location of data and programs within the virtual 4 GB address space.

3.1 Features of Implementation

To provide clear distinction between the COS and the partitions, the COS was implemented to run as handler for every interrupt or hardware exception. Every service of the COS is executed after a context switch. Thereby the context of the currently active partition is saved by hardware in a context save area. After that, the COS service is executed. COS services are for instance timer events, interrupts, and service requests by partitions. The context save areas are an ingenious concept of the TC1796 to store the context, i.e., the current register set, in a linked list instead of pushing it on the stack. This concept allows manipulating the partition contexts in an easy way, especially when adding additional context save areas for function invocation.

Protection in space has been realized through the memory protection unit of the microcontroller. Furthermore, extensive checking of memory addresses (with respect to read and write operations) that originate from the partition via a system call must be performed. This is necessary because the COS runs in supervisor mode and has read and write access to the whole memory. Without that, a partition could provide an illegal pointer to a COS service that reads or manipulates data of another partition.

The Protection in Time paradigm was implemented using an interrupt provided by a free running hardware clock timer with compare match functionality. This timer interrupt has the highest priority and preempts the active partition after a statically defined time period.

Several OS services like message channels, health checks, error reporting and logging can be configured through the system interface which interacts with the COS via system calls.

Flexibility is limited by the number of objects of each type in the COS, which must be predefined. There is no dynamic allocation of memory at all, so all objects needed at runtime must be defined at design time. Nevertheless most of them can be enabled, disabled or reconfigured at runtime. This design not only prevents typical problems when using dynamic memory allocation but also enables direct access for most objects.

As COS objects may be manipulated at runtime it is necessary to ensure data consistency. A central design decision is that COS operations must be atomic and cannot be interrupted. This affects static COS operations like scheduling as well as dynamic operations like system calls via the system interface, which are initiated by the partitions dynamically. To enforce the protection in time, system calls must not happen shortly before the deactivation of the partition. For that, the COS checks at the begin of a system call if there is enough time left to perform the request. Otherwise, the call is suspended and performed the next time the partition is activated and there is enough time to execute the request.

Synchronization to a global time source is done within the time space of a designated synchronization partition which needs to be scheduled for this task. Within this partition's time space, a "virtual time jump" is performed by manipulating the local system time, i.e., synchronizing the local clock to the global time source. The synchronization is established by varying durations of the sync partition. This ensures that no timer event of a partition gets lost as well as execution time for each partition can be guaranteed, regardless of time synchronization. Each partition is granted the execution time (number of CPU ticks) defined at design time [5].

3.2 Performance

Although not a driving factor of this prototype implementation, performance is a central concern. Starting with non-optimized code and deactivated caching, using either optimized code or caching improves COS performance by 25 to 37 percent. Optimized code and enabling of caching boosts the overall performance by about 80(!) percent. It seems that optimized code is specifically tailored to the use of the instruction cache. Using different memory locations for code and data can also have massive impact. For that, all performance values depicted in table 1 are only valid for the specific configuration and not worst case execution times (WCET).

As outlined in table 1, partition switching, i.e., partition activation plus partition deactivation, and COS services, like for instance the sending of a message,

Table 1. Performance of COS

Operation	40 MHz CPU and Sys	150 MHz CPU, 75 MHz Sys
Startup	35,600 ticks, 890 μs	29,500 ticks, 393 μs
Partition activation	6,000 ticks, 150 μs	4,800 ticks, 64 μs
Partition deactivation	6,750 ticks, 169 μs	4,900 ticks, 66 μs
Send message (1 word)	3,400 ticks, 85 μs	2,150 ticks, 29 μs
Receive message (1 word)	3,700 ticks, 93 μs	2,350 ticks, 32 μs

create significant overhead. This is due to massive switching overhead and because of the need for extensive checking of access rights. There is only a small difference between sending/receiving one single word and several words. The copy operation itself needs only a few ticks per word.

3.3 Issues

The existence (or non-existence) of several properties of the selected microcontroller may potentially ease or constrain the implementation of the above mentioned concepts of partitioning and protection. During the implementation of the COS for the TC1796 it turned out that all important features of the COS could be realized. However, we found several restrictions that have been introduced by the selection of the TC1796. In the following, we will discuss our experiences during the implementation of the COS:

- The memory protection system of the TriCore family provides up to four memory protection register sets (PRSs) (see [4], chap. 8.1), but the TC1796 only supports two ([6], chap. 2.4.5).

  Since the COS is the handler for every interrupt and trap, one PRS is needed for the COS, and so only one is left for all partitions. That's why the memory protection must be virtualized for the partitions.

  For the TC1796 one PRS contains 4 data segment protection register pairs, 1 mode register for read and write access, 2 code segment protection register pairs, and 1 mode register for execute access. From this it follows that up to 14 registers must be set before every partition switch.
- The memory protection, as briefly described in the previous paragraph, works excellently for read-, write-, and execute-protection, but not for I/O-protection. For I/O there are only three access modes ([4], chap. 1.3), with predefined access rights: User-0 Mode, which has no access to peripheral devices, User-1 Mode, which has access to a set of the peripheral devices and additionally can also disable and enable interrupts globally, and Supervisor Mode, with full access.

  Hence a partition that is not trusted could only be executed in User-0 Mode, and two possibilities exist for all other partitions that need I/O access:

  - The partition must be certified to the same level as the COS. However, this approach would contradict the basic idea of DECOS.

- The I/O code of the partition will be moved into a separate I/O partition, and only the I/O partition has to be certified to the same (high) level as the COS. However, this approach introduces an overhead for the communication between application partition and I/O partition as well as additional partition switches.

If neither of the two concepts is realized, it is possible that a partition could affect the peripheral of another partition, or that partitions could affect the COS by disabling interrupts globally, and so the protection in time is disabled. Even the use of the HW watchdog ([6], chap. 16) cannot fully avoid the violation of the protection in time. However, if acceptable for a certain system, the HW watchdog could at least shut down a partition that disables the interrupts and thus, limits such an error to a unique event.

– While debugging a program with the On-Chip Debug Support, OCDS, of the TC1796 ([6], chap. 17), it is not possible to use PRSs, because the on-chip breakpoints are realized through the PRSs. This means that the memory protection system must be disabled during debugging, and so it is hardly possible to debug problems regarding the protection system and to test the protection settings with the OCDS respectively.
– State of the art microcontrollers use sophisticated buffering methods such as caching and prefetch buffers to improve average execution time. The TC1796 has several caches and instruction buffers to minimize latency effects. To maximize safety, the program code of the COS resides in flash memory, where ECC can correct single bit failures and detect up to two bit failures. Using burstmode and buffering improves performance dramatically, especially when using the external flash ROM. But caching and using buffers makes execution time indeterministic. Particularly, a special buffer within the TriCore CPU which cannot be disabled and is not controllable makes WCET analysis very hard. When not using caches, execution time of simple loops may vary by two orders of magnitude. With caches, the impact of the buffer is attenuated to a variation of about plus-minus 30 percent. It is hard to say if the measured execution times are worst case, even if a specific call was measured several thousand times. Even after several thousand measurements, additional execution time measurements of the same code with identical call parameters would sometimes yield new maximum values. So performance values given in the table above are not WCET, but maximum execution times measured after several hundred thousand calls (average execution time was mostly about half the maximum execution time).
– A central design decision was the atomicity of COS operations to ensure data integrity. To guarantee partition execution times, COS operations may not be requested if they are too close to the preemption of the current partition. So the COS has to check if the time left is sufficient. Therefore, a table of WCET values of all system calls is needed. However, the measurement of the WCETs turned out to be very tricky because of the above mentioned buffering methods.

4 PIL and Architectural Services

As already addressed briefly in the introduction, the primary goal of DECOS is the provision of a uniform platform for integration of embedded distributed (real-time) applications of mixed (up to highest) criticality. As described in the previous sections, the EEE strongly supports this goal by allowing the integration of various application subsystems on a single node without the risk of affecting other subsystems by a faulty one thanks to its strong partitioning in both space (memory protection) and time (time windows). Due to that, it provides fault isolation on subsystem level.

A further important goal of DECOS is to minimize dependency of application software from specific implementations of the underlying DECOS services, as well as to put minimal restrictions on the form of how these services are realized. Although the described approach is a major achievement of the DECOS project, other node implementations are possible, and have actually been carried out within DECOS.

In order to explain how this will be realized on the platform described before, a short outline of basic corresponding DECOS concepts is given in [7], which may also help to put EEE into the greater context established by DECOS.

4.1 Conceptual DECOS Node Architecture

In the conceptual DECOS view, an application is a distributed embedded (real-time) system, consisting of a set of so-called *Distributed Application Subsystems* or DASs. Each DAS consists of a set of (application) *jobs*, which exchange information by either state or event messages. Note that *job* in this diction corresponds to *subsystem* used in this paper, and to avoid confusion, we will use that term rather than *job*. State messages realize sample semantics, i.e. the latest transmitted value is always valid and overwrites any previous transmitted value; they always have to be transmitted in a time-triggered style with required periodicity. In contrast, event messages carry event information, where each message must not overwrite previous messages of the same event type, und must therefore be queued. Event messaging not only bears the risk of queue overflow but it is also more difficult to implement than state messaging (due to the need for queue handling). It was therefore decided that safety-critical subsystems must not use event messages, and all system services needed to support safety-critical subsystems must be as simple as possible in order to ease their certification up to SIL 4 (safety integrity level 4, [8,9]). Consequently, a conceptual architecture of a DECOS-conformant system node has been defined, which is depicted in figure 4.

Evidently, DECOS takes a layered architecture approach. On top, applications access DECOS services solely through the API of the Platform Interface Layer (PIL). Among other functionalities, PIL provides services for sending and receiving state and event messages in a platform-independent way. Below PIL, the Secondary Connector Units (SCU) provide so-called *DECOS architectural services* like virtualization of physical bandwidth of the communication network

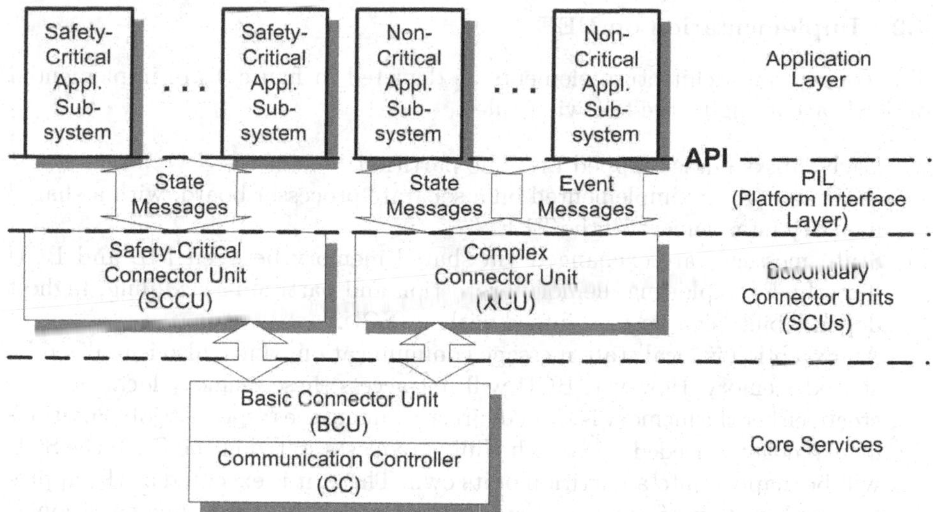

Fig. 4. Conceptual Architecture of a DECOS Node

shared by all DASs, such that each DAS operates as it would own a physical network, or gateways for a controlled information exchange between different DASs. At bottom, the communication with other nodes is realized, together with core services like deterministic message transport and global fault-tolerant clock synchronization. In particular, the Basic Connector Unit (BCU) interfaces between the communication network and the SCUs by splitting bandwidth between them.

Using concepts of model-based system engineering (MBSE), with OMG's MDA as prominent representative [10], for each DAS a so-called PIM (Platform Independent Model) is specified, which describes its jobs (or subsystems, respectively), the exchanged messages, and all further performance- and dependability-related requirements. From such DAS-PIMs, the allocation of jobs to computing nodes, the schedules for message transmissions and job executions, as well as platform interface and middleware services are finally generated (configured).

For instance, if a job X receives a state message S of type t_S and may send event messages E of type t_E, then essentially the following C-API will be generated for it:

```
DCS_RetCode DCS_get_S
            (t_S *out_S, DCS_bool *out_validityIndicator);

DCS_RetCode DCS_queue_E
            (const t_E * in_E, const DCS_Time* in_timeout);
```

('DCS' stands for DECOS.) Some more functions are generated for allowing different access styles, but according to the same principle. In addition, domain-specific services like for CAN support are possible and envisaged. However, these will largely use the native PIL-API, and will therefore not further be addressed here.

4.2 Implementation on EEE

The conceptual architecture elements as depicted in figure 4 are implemented on EEE according to the following rules:

- Each subsystem is mapped into one partition.
- BCU and CC are implemented on a separate processor board, with a shared memory interconnect to the EEE.
- State messages are exchanged via shared memory between PIL and BCU directly. By exploiting memory protection and partition scheduling, highest dependability can be guaranteed without SCU.
- An exception is local state message communication, which also is realized by shared memory. However, BCU will not access these memory locations. Instead, either the memory is shared directly among the respective job partitions or, if a delay is needed due to scheduling requests stated in the PIM, the SCU will be mapped into a partition of its own. There, it is executed at the appropriate phase to perform a copy operation from writing to reading partition.
- This "SCU partition" will also comprise gateways between safety-critical subsystems and from safety- to non-critical subsystems of different DASs.
- Event messages are handled by PIL. In each partition, a queue of its own is established for each event, both outgoing and incoming. For each event message, a buffer for one message is defined in the memory shared with BCU.
- Whenever a queue for outgoing messages is not empty and that BCU buffer is marked as free, PIL moves the oldest message from its queue into that buffer. At next opportunity, the BCU will transmit the message and mark the buffer as free.
- Symmetrically, whenever the BCU buffer of an incoming message is marked as filled, PIL moves it into the local receive queue of each recipient, as long as this is not filled completely. In the latter case, an input overflow occurred, and that message is lost for the respective receiving partition. In any case, the BCU buffer is marked as free. This avoids back propagation of a faulty receiver to the sender or other receivers: if the input channel of a receiver overflows, only that receiver will lose the message.
- An explicit XCU partition will be used if gateways between non-critical subsystems of different DASs are needed.

5 Conclusion

Integrating applications with different levels of safety relevance (and possibly from different vendors) on the same hardware requires protection mechanisms that guarantee that no malicious interference between the applications can take place. The Core Operating System (COS) that is currently under development in the European research project DECOS offers the required level of encapsulation. The COS is an exokernel operating system that offers mechanisms for protection and virtualization of hardware resources and thus allows the integration of mixed criticality applications on the same hardware.

After elaborating the concepts of encapsulation and virtualization, we presented the intermediate (performance) results of our COS implementation, as well as implications of the chosen microcontroller (an Infineon TC1796). Furthermore, the concept of a platform interface layer (PIL) has been introduced that offers an abstraction layer for the application software. The implementation of the PIL has been briefly outlined.

Acknowledgments

We would like to thank our colleagues Georg Stöger, Bernhard Wenzl and the anonymous reviewers for their comments on earlier versions of this paper. This work was supported by the European IST project DECOS under contract No. IST-511764.

References

1. Martin Schlager, Erwin Erkinger, Wilfried Elmenreich, and Thomas Losert. Benefits and Implications of the DECOS Encapsulation Approach. In *Proceedings of the 8th International IEEE Conference on Intelligent Transportation Systems*, pages 13–18, September 2005.
2. Wolfgang Bernhart and Hans-Peter Erl. Markt- und Technologiestudie Leistungselektronik Automotive, A.D.Little, September 2005.
3. Dawson R. Engler, M. Frans Kaashoek, and James OToole Jr. Exokernel: an operating system architecture for application-level resource management. M.I.T. Laboratory for Computer Science. Cambridge, MA 02139, March 1995.
4. Infineon Technologies AG. TriCore 1 32-Bit Unified Processor Core Volume 1 (of 2): V1.3 Core Architecture, User's Manual. `http://www.infineon.com/upload/Document/TriCore_1_um_vol1_Core_Architecture.pdf`, October 2005. V1.3.6.
5. Hermann Kopetz. Real-Time Systems: Design Principles for Distributed Embedded Applications. Springer-Verlag GmbH, The International Series in Engineering and Computer Science Vol. 395, 1997.
6. Infineon Technologies AG. TC1796 32-Bit Single-Chip Microcontroller Volume 1 (of 2): System Units, User's Manual. `http://www.infineon.com/upload/Document/cmc_upload/documents/011/9544/tc1796_um_v1.0_2005_06_sys.pdf`, June 2005. V1.0.
7. Hermann Kopetz, Roman Obermaisser, Philipp Peti, and Neeraj Suri. From a federated to an integrated architecture for dependable embedded real-time systems. Technical report, Vienna University of Technology, Austria, and Darmstadt University of Technology, Germany, 2004.
8. Vivien Hamilton and Ceri Rees. Safety integrity levels: An industrial viewpoint, towards system safety. In *Proceedings of the Seventh Safety-critical Systems Symposium*, page 111 126. Springer, 1999.
9. Wolfgang Herzner, Egbert Althammer, Georg Weißenbacher, and Erwin Schoitsch. From Requirements to Deployment – Verify That the Right Things Are Done Correctly – The DECOS Test Bench. In *Proceedings of the 8th International IEEE Conference on Intelligent Transportation Systems*, volume IEEE (2002, ISBN: 07803-9216-7), pages 7–12, September 2005.
10. Anneke Kleppe, Jos Warmer, and Wim Bast. *MDA Explained – The Model Driven Architecture: Practices and Promises.* Addison Wesley, 2003.

Modeling the Railway Control Domain Rigorously with a UML 2.0 Profile

Kirsten Berkenkötter and Ulrich Hannemann

University of Bremen,
P.O. Box 330 440
28334 Bremen, Germany
{kirsten, ulrichh}@informatik.uni-bremen.de

Abstract. We introduce the Railway Control Systems Domain (RCSD) profile of the Unified Modeling Language UML 2.0 as a domain specific modeling language for railway and tramway control systems. The RCSD profile covers the segments of the rail network, sensors, and control elements like signals and switches. Using these terms of the railway domain, it facilitates the communication between domain experts and specialists for embedded control system development. Defined as a profile for UML 2.0, the development of precise RCSD descriptions is supported by standard UML tools, visualizing railway networks in the same way as domain experts are used to. The static description of networks is complemented by the characterization of the dynamics within the network with trains running on predefined routes. This behaviour is provided by the semantics of a state transition system derived from the object diagram of a particular network model. This rigorous semantic approach constitutes a prerequisite for further tool-supported analysis of safety requirements, and generation of the actual control system.

1 Introduction

With the present paper we contribute to the *model driven development* process of railway control systems. With emphasis on a modeling language and its formal semantics, we support the foundation of the widely automated generation of controller components in the railway domain. As we provide a means to capture the requirements of these control components thoroughly and unambiguously, the focus within the development process shifts towards the modeling phase, i.e. the formalization of the application users' view onto the system.

We demonstrate our approach of utilizing a UML 2.0 profile as a *domain specific language* for a problem in the railway control system domain. The *domain of control* – also called *physical model* – consists of a railway network composed of track segments, points, signals, and sensors. Trains enter the domain of control at distinguished entry segments and request to take pre-defined routes through the network. Detection of trains is possible only via sensor observations. A *controller* monitors state changes within the network, derives train locations, and governs signals and points to enable the correct passage of trains through the network.

J. Górski (Ed.): SAFECOMP 2006, LNCS 4166, pp. 398–411, 2006.

With all activities, the controller must ensure that no hazardous situation arises, formulated by requiring compliance with a specific set of *safety conditions.*

The railway control domain is a perfect candidate to apply a domain specific language as it contains a rather limited amount of different entities. The specialized objects involved may exhibit only a limited variation of behavior, and the high safety requirements already established in the railway domain have resulted in a decent formalization of component descriptions. Part of the challenge of formulating a domain theory of railways [Rai] lies in the long history of the domain where domain experts gathered a respectable amount of knowledge which is hard to contain in a computing science formalism. Thus, an approach to deal with critical railway control applications has to carefully connect the expertise in railway engineering with the development techniques of safety critical software.

Among the various proposed solutions, we observe a number of characteristics that we deem desirable: (1) The UniSpec language within the EURIS method [FKvV98] provides a domain specific language with *graphical elements* to reflect the topology of a railway network. (2) In order to support the development process with *standard tools* the wide-spectrum Unified Modeling Language UML [RJB04] is used in the SafeUML project [Hun06] which specifically aims at generating code conforming to safety standards. The use of UML is restricted here by guidelines to ensure maintenance of safety requirements which still allow sufficiently expressiveness for the modeling process. (3) In [PBH00, HP02, HP03a] the domain analysis concentrates on the relevant issues for formal treatment of the control problem using a presentation form of tables and lists as foundation for a *formal model.*

Based on these experiences, we propose to use the *profile* mechanism for UML 2.0 [OMG04, OMG05b] to create a *domain-specific* description formalism for requirements modeling in the railway control systems domain (RCSD). This approach allows us to use a graphical representation of the domain elements with domain specific icons in order to facilitate the communication between domain experts and specialists for embedded control systems development. As the profile mechanism is part of the UML standard, the wide-spread variety of existing tools can be adapted within the very spirit of the UML using UML-inherent concepts. Since a profile allows to introduce new semantics for the elements of the profile we can attach a rigorous mathematical model to the descriptions of the domain model. Timed state transition system semantics form the base for formal transformations towards code generation for the controller as well as for the verification task that guarantees conformance to the safety requirements. Consequently, the RCSD profile [BHP] constitutes the first and founding step in a development process for the automatic generation and verification of controllers derived from a domain model as outlined in [HP03a, HPG+04].

The next section gives a brief introduction to the railway control domain terminology as background for the development of a profile. Section 3 explains first the basic concepts and techniques for the construction of a UML 2.0 profile, followed by selected examples of the RCSD profile. An example in Section 4 demonstrates the successful connection between the typical domain notation and the conceptual view of the profile. In Section 5, we sketch the underlying mathematical model induced by a RCSD description of the physical model and give an overview on the development of the associated controller. We also indicated how this semantic model can be used for tool-supported verification and code generation.

2 Elements of the Railway Domain

Creating a domain specific profile requires identifying the elements of this domain and their properties as e.g. described in [Pac02]. We focus on the modeling of main tracks. All elements that are not allowed on main tracks as e.g. track locks are discarded. The further elements are divided into track elements, sensors, signals, automatic train runnings, and routes. Elements in the domain that come in different but similar shapes like signals are modeled as one element with different characteristics. In this way, we can abstract the railway domain to eight main modeling elements. These are described in the following:

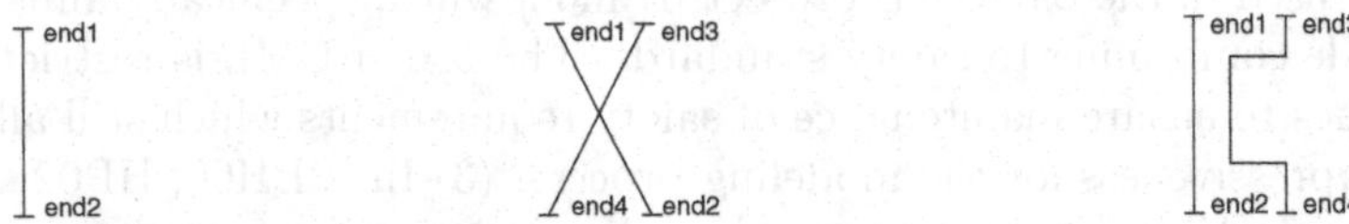

Fig. 1. Segment **Fig. 2.** Crossing **Fig. 3.** Interlaced segments

Track Elements. The track network consists of segments, crossings, and points. Segments are rails with two ends (see Fig. 1), while crossings consist of either two crossing segments or two interlaced segments (see Fig. 2 and Fig. 3). In general, the number of trains on a crossing is restricted to one to ensure safety. Points allow a changeover from one segment to another one. We use single points with a stem and a branch (see Fig. 4). There is no explicit model element for double points, as these are seldom used in practice. If needed, they can be modeled by two single points. Single slip points and double slip points are crossings with one, respectively two, changeover possibilities from one of the crossing segments to the other one (see Fig. 5 and Fig. 6). All points have in common that the number of trains at each point in time is restricted to one.

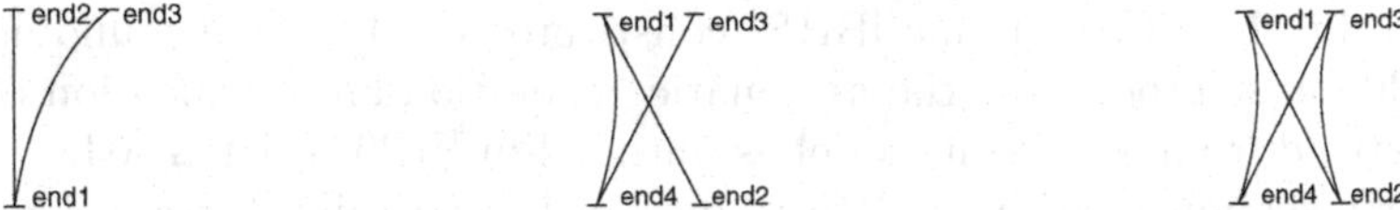

Fig. 4. Single point **Fig. 5.** Single slip point **Fig. 6.** Double slip point

Sensors. Sensors are used to identify the position of trains on the track network, i.e. the current track element. To achieve this goal, track elements have entry and exit sensors located at each end. The number of sensors depends on the allowed driving directions, i.e. the uni- or bidirectional usage of the track element. Each sensor is the exit sensor of one track element and the entry sensor of the following one. If the track elements can be used bidirectionally, another sensor is needed that works vice versa.

Signals. Signals come in various ways. In general, they indicate if a train may go or if it has to stop. The permission to go may be constrained, e.g. by speed limits or by obligatory directions in case of points. As it is significant to know if a train moves according to signaling, signals are always located at sensors.

Automatic Train Running. Automatic train running systems are used to enforce braking of trains, usually in safety-critical situations. The brake enforcement may be permanent or controlled, i.e. it can be switched on and off. Automatic train running systems are also located at sensors.

Route Definition. As sensors are used as connection between track elements, routes of a track network are defined by sequences of sensors. They can be entered if the required signal setting of the first signal of the route is set. This can only be done if all points are in the correct position needed for this route. Conflicting routes cannot be released at the same time. Some conflicts occur as the required point positions or signal settings are incompatible. Another problem are routes that cross and are potentially safety-critical.

3 The UML 2.0 RCSD Profile

The next step is tailoring the UML 2.0 to the railway domain to provide the previously identified elements of the domain. There are two approaches to achieve this goal. The first one is using the UML 2.0 profile mechanism described in [OMG04] and [OMG05b] that allows for: (1) introducing new terminology, (2) introducing new syntax/notation, (3) introducing new constraints, (4) introducing new semantics, and (5) introducing further information like transformation rules.

Changing the existing metamodel itself e.g. by introducing semantics contrary to the existing ones or removing elements is not allowed. Consequently, each model that uses profiles is a valid UML model. The second approach is adapting the UML 2.0 metamodel to the needs of the railway domain by using MOF 2.0 (see [OMG06]). This approach offers more possibilities as elements can be added to or removed from the metamodel, syntax can be changed, etc. In fact, a new metamodel is created that is based on UML but is not UML anymore.

We have chosen the first approach - defining a UML 2.0 profile - as this supports exactly the features we need: the elements of the railway domain are new terminology that we want to use as modeling elements. To simplify communication between domain specialists and system developers, the usual notation of the railway domain should be used in a defined way. Therefore, constraints are needed to determine the meaning of the new elements. Track networks described with the new profile are transfered to transition systems. This is done by transformation rules. Also, we have valid UML models and therefore various tool support.

A UML 2.0 profile mainly consists of stereotypes, i.e. extensions of already existing UML modeling elements. You have to choose which element should be extended and define the add-ons. The RCSD profile uses either *Class*, *Association*, or *InstanceSpecification* as basis of stereotypes. In addition, new primitive datatypes and enumerations can be defined as necessary.

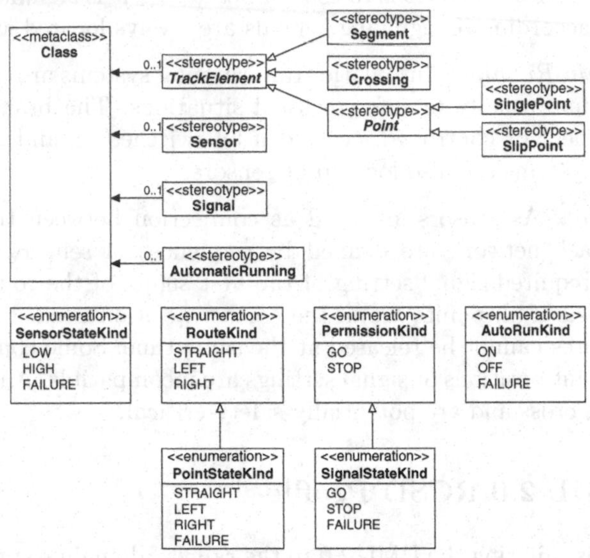

Fig. 7. Network elements part of the RCSD profile

Unfortunately, defining eight stereotypes as suggested by the domain analysis in Sec. 2 is not sufficient. New primitive datatypes and enumerations are needed to model attributes adequately. Special kinds of association are needed to model interrelationships between stereotypes. Furthermore, UML supports two modeling layers, i.e. the model layer itself (class diagrams) and the instances layer (e.g. object diagrams). In the RCSD profile, both layers are needed: class diagrams are used to model specific parts of the railway domain, e.g. tramways or railroad models. They consist of the same components but with different characteristics. Second, object diagrams show explicit track layouts for such a model. Here, the symbols of the railway domain have to be used. We need stereotypes on the object level to define these features. For these reasons, the RCSD profile is structured in six parts: the definition of primitive datatypes, network elements on class level, associations between these elements, network elements and associations on object level, routes, and top-level constraints.

Defining new primitive types is the easiest part. New datatypes must be identified and their range of values specified. In our case, these are identifiers for all controllable elements, identifiers for routes (e.g. to specify conflicting ones), time

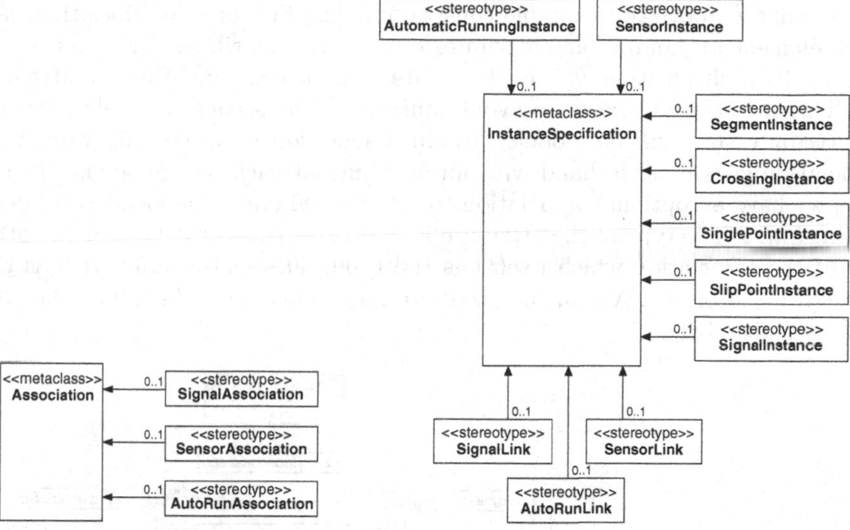

Fig. 8. Associations part of the RCSD profile

Fig. 9. Instances of network elements and associations part of the RCSD profile

instants and durations. All of them have in common that the value domain is $\mathbb{N}$. Nevertheless, defining different datatypes is important as we have to consider constraints like: all signal identifiers are unique, all point identifiers are unique and so on.

The next part of the profile defines all track network elements, i.e. segments, crossing, points, signals, sensors, and automatic train runnings (see Fig. 7). *Segment*, *Crossing*, and *Point* have in common that they form the track network itself, therefore they are all subclasses of the abstract *TrackElement*. Similarly, *SinglePoint* and *SlipPoint* are specializations of *Point*. All elements are equipped with a set of constraints that define which properties each element must support and how it is related to other elements.

To give an example, each *TrackElement* has at least two ends that are connected to at most two *Sensors*, one entry sensor and one exit sensor. The number of sensors depends on the function of the track element, i.e. if it is used uni- or bidirectionally or if it is a sink or source of the track network. As properties, the maximal number of trains allowed on the element at one point in time and - optional - fixed speed limits are needed. These features are defined by OCL 2.0 (see [OMG05a]) constraints that each *TrackElement* in a model must fulfill.

```
(ownedAttribute->one(a1 |
  a1.name='limit' and
  a1.oclIsTypeOf(Integer) and
  a1.upperBound()=1 and
  a1.lowerBound()≥0 and
  a1.isReadOnly=true)) or
(not ownedAttribute->exists(a2 |
  a2.name='limit'))
```

```
(ownedAttribute->one(a1 |
  a1.name='e1Entry' and
  a1.oclIsTypeOf(Sensor) and
  a1.upperBound()=1 and
  a1.lowerBound()≥0 and
  a1.isReadOnly=true and
  a1.association.oclIsTypeOf
    (SensorAssociation))) or
(not ownedAttribute->exists(a2 |
  a2.name='e1Entry'))
```

We can see above two example constraints. The first one describes that each track element has an optional attribute *limit*. If this attribute exists, its type is *Integer*, its multiplicity is *0..1* or *1*, and its value is constant. Else, no attribute at all with this name exists to avoid confusion. The second example describes an attribute that will be modeled by an association in a class diagram. Each association goes hand in hand with an attribute at each navigable end. In this case, we have an optional association to a sensor where the associated property is *end1Entry*. The type of the attribute is *Sensor* as this is the type at the other end of the association which itself has the type *SensorAssociation* that is also defined in the profile. Again, the attribute has a constant value and either *0..1* or *1* as multiplicity.

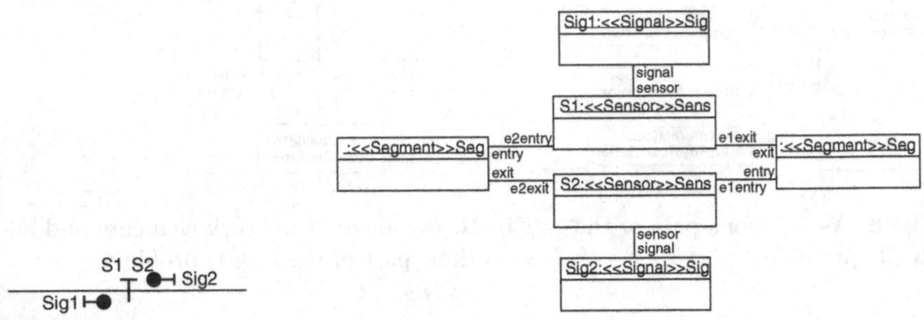

Fig. 10. RCSD notation

Fig. 11. UML notation

Such constraints describe the appearance of each stereotype. To give another example, *Points* have at least three ends with associated sensors and are not sinks or sources of the track network. They also have more attributes, i.e. *pointId*, *actualState*, *requestedState*, *requestTime* and *delta_p*. These are their identification number as points are controllable, the actual state that is either *STRAIGHT*, *LEFT*, *RIGHT*, or *FAILURE*, the requested state that is either *STRAIGHT*, *LEFT*, or *RIGHT*, the time of the last request, and the duration needed to switch the point after a request has been received. The possible values for the requested and actual state of the point are defined by *RouteKind* and *PointStateKind* as shown in Fig. 7. Other elements have similar required attributes and associations. An example model is shown in Sec. 4.

As associations *SensorAssociation* that connect track elements and sensors, *SignalAssociations* that connect signals and sensors, and *AutoRunAssociations* that connect automatic train runnings and sensors are used as shown in Fig. 8. Here, constraints are needed to determine the kind of stereotype at the ends of each association. Most important, two constraints of *SensorAssociation* describe that each sensor is the exit sensor of one track element and the entry sensor of the following one. In that way, routes can be defined as sequences of sensors.

For each non-abstract modeling element and each association, there exists a corresponding instance stereotype (see Fig. 9). Most important is the definition of domain-specific notation. Of course, usual UML notation can be used but is

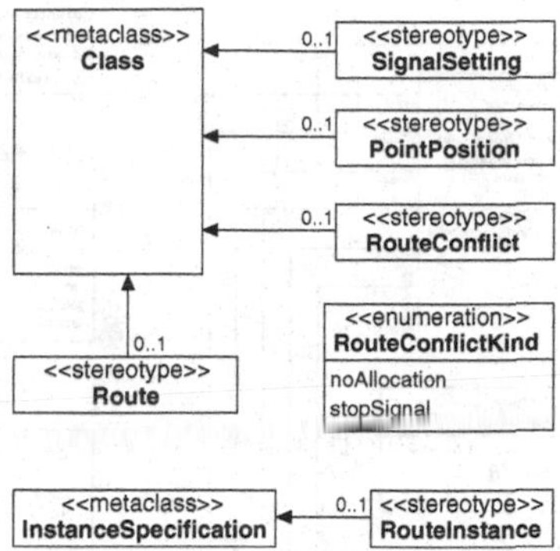

Fig. 12. Route definition part of the RCSD profile

infeasible as we can see in the direct comparison. In Fig. 10, two bidirectional segments connected by two sensors *S1* and *S2* are shown. Signal *Sig1* is associated to *S1*, signal *Sig2* is associated to *S2*. For comparison, the same constellation in object notation is given in Fig. 11.

Furthermore, the profile defines routes and their instances. Each *Route* is defined by an ordered sequence of sensors. Also, the signal setting for entering the route is given. Other properties are ordered sets of required point positions and of conflicts with other routes. The stereotypes to describe this information are given in Fig. 12. Again, constraints are used for unambiguous and strict definitions of attributes and suchlike.

The last part of the profile is a set of top-level constraints that describe interrelationships between stereotypes. The first example states that all point ids have to be unique. The second example describes that all sensors in route definitions really exists:

```
SinglePointInstance::allInstances()->
  collect(slots)->union
    (SlipPointInstance::allInstances()->
      collect(slots))->
select(s1 |
  s1.definingFeature.name='pointId'
  or
  s1.definingFeature.name='pointIdOpp')->
isUnique(s2 | s2.value)
```

```
def: r1:RouteInstance::allInstances()->
  collect(slots)->
    select(s2 |
      s2.definingFeature='routeDefinition')

def: r2:SensorInstance::allInstances()->
   collect(slots)->
    select(s1 |
      s1.definingFeature.name='sensorId')->
        collect(value)

r1.forAll(s3 | r2->including(s3.value))
```

4 Modeling with the RCSD Profile

The stereotypes and data types defined in the profile are used in UML diagrams. A class diagram is used to model a concrete problem in the railway domain, e.g. trams. The concrete track networks are object diagrams related to the class diagram.

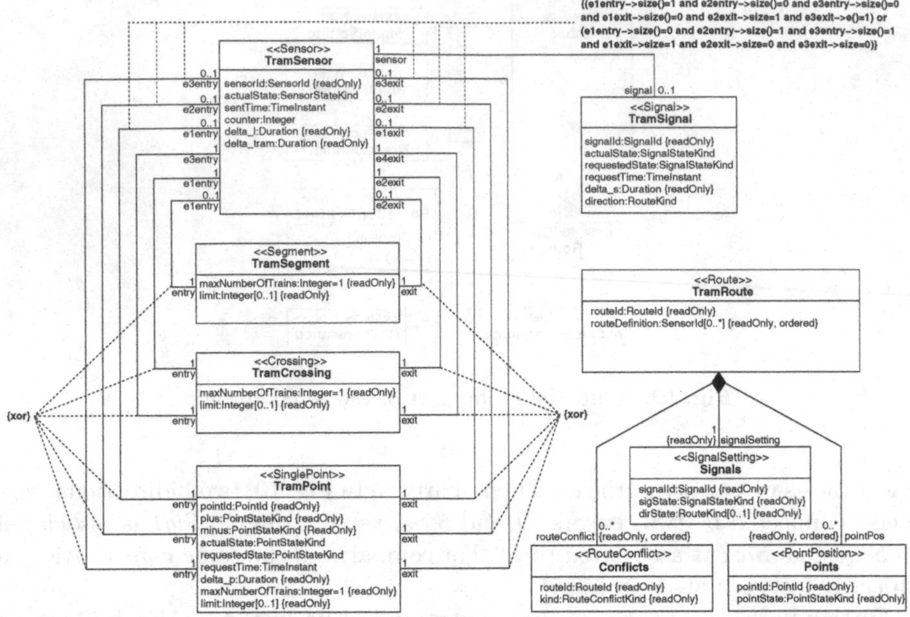

Fig. 13. Generic tram network

In our example, a tram track network is given in a class diagram as shown in Fig. 13. The interrelationships between the different stereotypes from RCSD are concretized for trams: there are no automatic running systems and no slip points, all segments are used unidirectionally, and signals do not use speed limits. The maximal number of trains allowed on each segment is 1. The network description of a concrete tram track network to be controlled is an *object diagram* that is based on the class diagram given above. An object diagram in RCSD profile notation is shown in Fig. 14.

In Fig. 15, a fragment of the same track network is shown in usual UML notation, i.e. an object diagram. Comparing the two figures, it is obvious that the RCSD profile notation is more comprehensible and therefore preferable in the communication process between domain experts and software designers.

5 Semantics

In this section we describe the behavior of the physical model – as captured in a RCSD object diagram – as a *Timed State Transition System* (TSTS). We extend this view by incorporating the behavior of a controller which has to guarantee safety conditions for the running system. The operations of this controller are given as generic patterns independent from the particular physical model. The composition of the controller and the individual domain of control should then allow only sequences of transitions which never violate a safety condition. Since

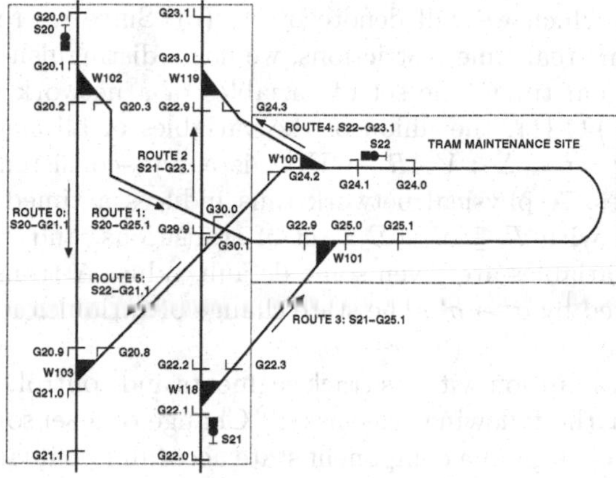

Fig. 14. Concrete tram network in profile notation

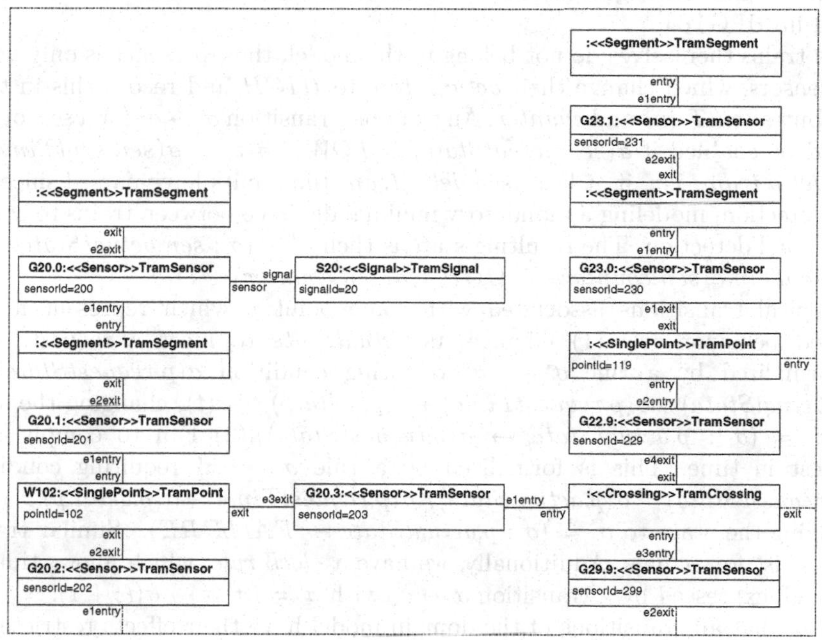

Fig. 15. Fragment of a concrete tram network in usual UML notation

we give a strict mathematical model of this composition, it can be proven by *bounded model checking* techniques.

As listed in Section 2, a physical rail network consists of a set of segments, a set of signals, and a set of sensors. Among the segments, the set of points and the set of crossings are of special interest for the formulation of safety conditions. Each element e in one of these sets owns some attributes according to the profile definition, which we will denote by $var(e)$. Since we require that components fulfill some real-time restrictions, we use a distinguished variable $t \in \mathbb{N}$ to denote the actual time. The set of variables of a network is thus given by $VAR = \bigcup_e var(e) \cup \{t\}$, the union of the variables of all elements and t. As customary, a *state* $\sigma \in \Sigma : VAR \mapsto VAL$ is a type-consistent mapping from variables to values. A physical network thus induces a timed state transition system (Σ, σ_0, T) with $T \subseteq \Sigma \times \Sigma$ a set of transitions, and $\sigma_0 \in \Sigma$ an initial state, where all variables are given some default value. A transition $t = (\sigma, \sigma')$ will also be denoted by $\sigma \rightarrow \sigma'$. The state change of variables $\bar{x}$ to values $\bar{v}$ from σ to σ' is expressed by $\sigma' = (\sigma : \bar{x} \mapsto \bar{v})$[1].

The network description with its track segments and control elements exhibits some behavior for the following reasons: (1) Change of a sensor status due to a train passing. (2) Change of a component state according to its normal individual behavior, e.g. setting the state of a signal to the requested state (3) Changes due to decisions of the control component. We give some examples for the first two groups of state changes, an extended selection with in-depth explanations is listed in [HPG+04].

As trains themselves do not belong to the model, their presence is only noted via sensors, which change their *actualState* to $HIGH$ and record this in their attributes *sentTime* and *counter*. An example transition $\sigma \rightarrow \sigma'$ for a sensor *sen* would be enabled if $\sigma(sen.actualState) = LOW \wedge \sigma(t) > \sigma(sen.sentTime) + sen.delta\_tram$, i.e., if at least *sen.delta_tram* time units have passed since the last detection, modeling a mandatory minimal distance between trains to ensure individual detection. The resulting state is then $\sigma' = (\sigma : sen.actualState, sen.sentTime, sen.counter \mapsto HIGH, t, \sigma(sen.counter) + 1)$.

Typical transitions associated with some point p which represent its intended behavior are: (1) Change its *actualState* to meet a request. This is formalized by a rule $\sigma \rightarrow \sigma'$ requiring condition $\sigma(p.requestState) \neq \sigma(p.actualState) \wedge \sigma(p.requestTime) + \sigma(p.delta\_p) \leq \sigma(t)$, changing the state to $\sigma' = (\sigma : p.actualState \mapsto \sigma(p.requestState))$.(2) Fail to comply to a request in time. This is formalized by a rule $\sigma \rightarrow \sigma'$ requiring condition $\sigma(p.requestState) \neq \sigma(p.actualState) \wedge \sigma(p.requestTime) + \sigma(p.delta\_p) > \sigma(t)$, changing the state to $\sigma' = (\sigma : p.actualState \mapsto FAILURE)$. Similar transitions exist for signals. Additionally, we have a *clock rule*, which allows time to proceed, expressed by a transition $\sigma \rightarrow \sigma'$ with $\sigma' = (\sigma : t \mapsto \sigma(t) + 1)$.

Note that all transitions of the domain model have their effects restricted to the variables of one object, allowing to model the network in a compositional fashion as parallel composition of its constituents as illustrated in [HP03b]. Yet, all changes of the physical network, i.e. point positions, signal positions, and sensor states are covered by these transitions only.

The *controller* observes sensor state changes, deriving the current train locations within the network from them. Trains may issue requests to pass through the network on pre-defined routes. The controller issues commands to switch

[1] For brevity, we use a *simultaneous assignment* notation here which coincides with a reasonable granularity of operations which should be uninterruptible.

signal and point states and monitors the correct state of these track elements. The architectural model of the controller consists of three components [HP02]: (1) a *route dispatcher* which registers the requests of individual trains for specific routes and administers the allocation of these routes, (2) a *route controller* responsible for setting points and signals for active routes, and (3) a *safety monitor* checking for deviations of the actual from the expected state and subsequently ensuring a safe state.

These separated tasks of the controller are executed by sets of transition *patterns*, i.e. generic transitions which abstract from the concrete physical model. As an example, we have for each route r a transition for the route dispatcher component which checks whether r is requested, r is not yet scheduled for activation, and no conflicting routes are active or scheduled.

The state space Σ' of the controller is an extension of the state space Σ of the domain model as additional variables are needed, e.g. for the administration of routes some data structure is needed to store the current state of a route reservation. The controller model together with the domain model (Σ, σ_0, T) induces a TSTS (Σ', σ'_0, T') where σ'_0 is the extension of σ_0 by assigning appropriate initial values to the additional variables of Σ'. The set of transitions T' contains the set T and the set of transitions generated from the controller model and the domain data. As demonstrated in [HPG+04], the concrete transitions are derived by instantiating the generic rules according to the physical layout of the network and the route definitions.

In an independent derivation, we formulate a set of safety conditions out of the physical model. These safety requirements are informally listed as: (1) No trains are driving in opposite directions on the same segment. (2) No trains are moving in opposite direction towards the same sensor. (3) The number of trains approaching a point from stem and branches at the same time is at most 1. (4) On each segment the number of trains passing in one direction is less than a predefined maximum. (5) There are no trains residing simultaneously on crossings. Observe that these requirements are formulated generically in terms of track elements only and that each condition involves only a very limited part of the network. Within the physical model, these requirements are instantiated to a set of constraints. As an example from Fig. 14, we take a closer look on the crossing between sensors $G20.3$ and $G30.0$, and respectively, between $G29.9$ and $G22.9$. Clearly, requirement (5) has to be satisfied for this track element. The fact that a train is present in a segment, can be deduced from a comparison of the counters of its entry and exit sensors: Assuming the default settings that no train is present in a segment and both sensors have the same value of their respective *counter* attribute, the predicate $\sigma(G20.3.counter) > \sigma(G30.0.counter)$ models the fact that at least one train is still located between the sensors $G20.3$ and $G30.0$. Consequently, requirement (5) can be formalized for this instance of a crossing as $\neg(\sigma(G20.3.counter) > \sigma(G30.0.counter) \wedge \sigma(G29.9.counter) > \sigma(G22.9.counter))$.

For a given network, we can thus automatically derive a TSTS as model which exhibits the behavior of this network under supervision of the controller and a set of constraints which have to hold throughout all executions within our model. Analyzing whether a violation of safety requirements is possible amounts to a check whether some state is reachable that does not satisfy all constraints.

While we present a rather abstract mathematical model here, it is an easy task to come up with an equivalent model which encodes all transitions as guarded commands. Representation of timed state transition systems in a special programming language suited for further analysis then boils down to encode states and transitions into this language. This has been worked out in [HPG+04] for SystemC [GLMS02, MRR03], as input language for a proof by bounded model-checking that the safety requirements are satisfied. The SystemC code can be compiled into C/C++ code, leading to the generation of executable code for the controller. In a similar fashion, it is even possible to take the generated machine code and verify its correctness w.r.t. the requirements on the domain model by comparing the TSTS model of the network/controller model to a TSTS model of the machine code. This comparison is feasible, as the abstraction function from the data structures of the machine code to the data model of the domain description is total, and for all transition patterns of the above model a correct refinement in machine code exists.

6 Conclusions

We have presented the RCSD profile for UML 2.0 as suitable formalism to capture the domain specific requirements of the railway control systems domain. In particular, the feature to use a domain specific graphical notation for the domain description helps to bridge the gap between domain experts and developers of controller systems. As any model denoted in the RCSD profile formalism is still a UML model, standard tools which support the profile mechanisms can be used in the development process. Existing UML tools support the analysis of RCSD models as textual representations of a model serve as input for the generation of the TSTS model or the SystemC model. Another example would be the application of graph transformations to the RCSD object instance diagram for simulation purposes [GZ04].

We associate a formal behavioral model with RCSD descriptions as any object diagram induces a timed state transition system, which covers the behavior of the domain of control. Together with the utilization of design patterns for the controller component, we generate a model which serves as foundation for the formal verification of this model w.r.t. a set of safety requirements. In addition, the TSTS model serves as reference for the verification of executable code for the controller. A major advantage of using the transition system model as the semantical model of a RCSD description lies in the fact that various concrete programming languages as well as other formal specification languages can use the transition system model as reference.

References

[BHP] K. Berkenkötter, U. Hannemann, and J. Peleska. The Railway Control System Domain. Draft, http://www.informatik.uni-bremen.de/agbs/research/RCSD/.

[FKvV98] W. J. Fokkink, G. P. Kolk, and S. F. M. van Vlijmen. EURIS, a specification method for distributed interlockings. In *Proceedings of SAFECOMP '98*, LNCS, volume 1516, pp. 296–305. Springer-Verlag, 1998.

[GLMS02] T. Grötker, S. Liao, G. Martin, and S. Swan. *System Design with SystemC*. Kluwer Academic Publishers, 2002.

[GZ04] M. Gogolla and P. Ziemann. Checking BART Test Scenarios with UML's Object Constraint Language. Formal Methods for Embedded Distributed Systems - How to master the complexity. F. Kordon, M. Lemoine (Eds.), Kluwer, Boston. pp. 133-170, 2004.

[HP02] A.E. Haxthausen and J. Peleska. A Domain Specific Language for Railway Control Systems. In *Proceedings of the Sixth Biennial World Conference on Integrated Design and Process Technology, (IDPT2002), Pasadena, California*, June 23-28 2002.

[HP03a] A. E. Haxthausen and J. Peleska. Automatic Verification, Validation and Test for Railway Control Systems based on Domain-Specific Descriptions. In *Proceedings of the 10th IFAC Symposium on Control in Transportation Systems*. Elsevier Science Ltd, Oxford, 2003.

[HP03b] A. E. Haxthausen and J. Peleska. Generation of Executable Railway Control Components from Domain-Specific Descriptions. In *Proceedings of the Symposium on Formal Methods for Railway Operation and Control Systems (FORMS'2003), Budapest/Hungary*, pp. 83–90. May 15-16 2003.

[HPG+04] A.E. Haxthausen, J. Peleska, D. Große and R. Drechsler. Automated Verification for Train Control Systems. Proceedings of Symposium FORMS/FORMAT 2004, Braunschweig, Germany, 2nd and 3rd Dec. 2004.

[Hun06] H. Hungar. UML-basierte Entwicklung sicherheitskritische Systeme im bahnbereich. In *Dagstuhl Workshop MBEES - Modellbasierte Entwicklung eingebetteter Systeme*, Informatik Bericht, pp. 63–64, TU Braunschweig, Jan 2006.

[MRR03] W. Müller, J. Ruf, and W. Rosenstiel. *SystemC – Methodologies and Applications*, chapter 4, pp. 97–126. Kluwer Academic Publishers, 2003.

[OMG04] Object Management Group. Unified Modeling Language (UML) Specification: Infrastructure, version 2.0. http://www.omg.org/docs/ptc/04-10-14.pdf, October 2004.

[OMG05a] Object Management Group. OCL 2.0 Specification, version 2.0. http://www.omg.org/docs/ptc/05-06-06.pdf, June 2005.

[OMG05b] Object Management Group. Unified Modeling Language: Superstructure, version 2.0. http://www.omg.org/docs/formal/05-07-04.pdf, July 2005.

[OMG06] Object Management Group. Meta Object Facility (MOF) 2.0 Core Specification. http://www.omg.org/docs/formal/06-01-01.pdf, January 2006.

[Pac02] Joern Pachl. *Railway Operation and Control*. VTD Rail Publishing, Mountlake Terrace (USA), 2002. ISBN 0-9719915-1-0.

[PBH00] J. Peleska, A. Baer, and A. E. Haxthausen. Towards Domain-Specific Formal Specification Languages for Railway Control Systems. In *Proceedings of the 9th IFAC Symposium on Control in Transportation Systems 2000, June 13-15, 2000, Braunschweig, Germany*, pp. 147–152, 2000.

[Rai] A grand challenge for computing science: Towards a domain theory of railways. http://www.railwaydomain.org.

[RJB04] J. Rumbaugh, I. Jacobson, and G. Booch. *The Unified Modeling Language – Reference Manual, 2nd edition*. Addison-Wesley, July 2004.

Access Control Coherence of Information Systems Based on Security Constraints

Aneta Poniszewska-Marańda

Institute of Computer Science, Technical University of Lodz, Poland
anetap@ics.p.lodz.pl

Abstract. Security administration in an information system is a complex task. In order to be defined properly, the security policy requires formulation of a large number of security constraints. Moreover, the information system used in an enterprise should be coherent, which means that all its element, including relations between them as well as their constraints should posses this property.

The objective of this paper is to present security constraints of a security schema in an information system based on the RBAC model and the methods to assure the coherence of global security schema. Starting from the global schema of the coherent security, any insertion of a new application should respect the global coherence of the new security schema being the consequence of the fusion of these two schemas.

1 Introduction

In an information system, data protection against improper disclosure or modification is an important requirement. The access control regulates what a user can do directly and what the programs executed on behalf of the user are allowed to do. The system administrators have to implement access control mechanisms to protect the confidentiality and integrity of applications and its data. In the past, the user access was granted by adding necessary permissions to each individual application, which made the administration, involving many users and several different applications, complicated and ineffective.

The alternative is not to assign users directly to permissions for each application but to assign users to roles and the permissions to roles for each application. Then any change in the user's position or their needs can be solved by the administrator simply by assigning the user to another role. Since roles contain appropriate permissions, the administrator does not have to update authorizations for each user application. Such situation can be solved by using the role-based access control (RBAC) model as an access control model in the security processes of an information system. The RBAC model is an interesting alternative to the traditional access control models, like MAC (Mandatory Access Control, [1]) or DAC (Discretionary Access Control, [1]). The RBAC model was defined in the nineties of the 20th century [2,3]. The most important idea of the RBAC model is the concept of role, which facilitates the access control management performed by the security administrator as users and permissions can be assigned to roles.

J. Górski (Ed.): SAFECOMP 2006, LNCS 4166, pp. 412–425, 2006.

Each user has a utilization profile that defines his roles in the enterprise. The role is the set of permissions that allow execution of the system functions and the access to data used by these functions. The user playing a given role is allowed to execute all accesses to which the role is authorized.

The actual complexity of organizations gave rise to the idea of extending the standard RBAC model to ensure a finer decomposition of responsibilities in an enterprise [10]. To this aim, the notion of a function has been introduced. Since a person employed in an enterprise may have many responsibilities in it, he may be attached to an entire set of roles. Each role defined in the extended RBAC model makes it possible to realize a specific task associated with the enterprise process. At the same time, every role can contain many functions that a user can take, and therefore it is possible to choose functions in the system that are necessary for a given role. Consequently, a role can be presented as a set of functions that this role can take and realize. As each function can have one or more permissions, a function can be defined as a set of permissions. If an access to an object is required, then the necessary permissions can be assigned to the function to complete the desired job.

The security administration in an information system is a complex task. Numerous security constraints should be formulated in order to define the security policy in a proper way. The security constraints specified for an application give the possibility to manage its complexity. The application developer can define the security constraints associated with this application. On the other hand, with his good knowledge of the global security policy, the security administrator can set up the constraints on the global level. The main difficulty is to assure the global coherence of all elements (applicative and organizational) when a new application with new elements, i.e. roles, functions, permissions is added into the existing information system.

The objective of this paper is to present security constraints of a security schema in an information system basing on the RBAC model. The first part of the paper deals with the partition of responsibilities between the application developer and the security administrator in the design and creation of the information system security. The next part describes classification of the security constraints. The last part presents the global coherence maintenance based on the security constraints: the integration chain of constraints in a coherent system, the definition of the system coherence and the verification of the security system coherence while a new application is being added to an existing information system. This verification is realized using a proposed algorithm to assure the system coherence.

2 Partition of Responsibilities in Creation of Information System

Two types of actors cooperate at the conception stage of creation of an information system (IS) and a security schema associeted with it [9,11]: the information system developer, who knows specifications of an information system that need to be realized and the security administrator who has the knowledge of the general security constraints that should be respected on the enterprise level. Fig. 1 presents the partition of responsibilities between these two actors and their cooperation to establish the global access control (i.e. security schema) using the extended RBAC model.

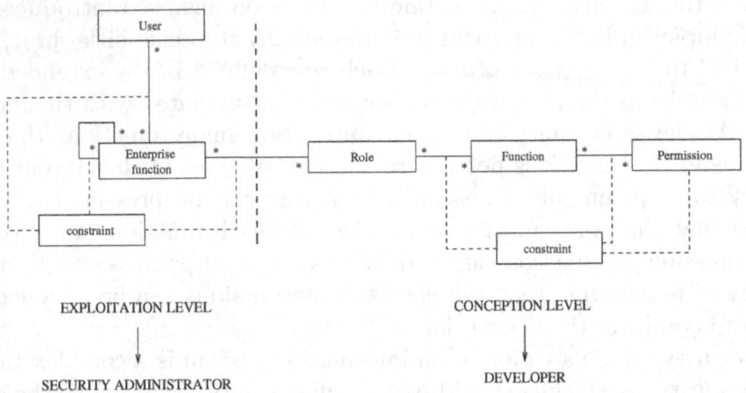

Fig. 1. Responsibilty areas of application developer and security administrator

The tasks of the application developer are: definition and assignment of elements (permissions to functions and functions to roles) and setting up the constraints associated with this application. The security administrator should manage the set of applications assuring the global coherence of a system. The tasks of the security administrator are: assignment of elements (roles to enterprise functions and users to enterprise functions) and setting up the constraints on the relations between thses elements. The security administrator should also verify whether these new constraints remain in agreement with the constraints of the existing information system in order to guarantee coherence of the new information system.

3 Security Constraints

A **security constraint** is an information assigned to the system elements that specifies the conditions to be satisfied so that the security rules and global coherence be guaranteed.

The security constraints can be classified into two groups. On one hand, it is possible to distinguish the constraints expressed in the application context (i.e. application constraints). They are verified on the conception level by the application developer. For example, taking the information system of a university and, particularly, one of its applications - management of student grades - a student can access this application only on the level of his own grades. On the other hand, we can distinguish the global constraints or, in other words, organization constraints that determine the global security policy of an information system. They are proposed on the organization level by the global security administrator [4,5,6]. For example, only the teacher responsible for a group of students gains access to the school dossiers of the students in this group.

The differences between the two types of actors in our approach led to the choice of two languages to express the constraints:

- OCL language [7,8], proposed as the most suitable language for the formulation of the developer's constraints because it was created to allow constraint definitions in different UML diagrams.
- RCL 2000 language [4,5], created to support the constraints of RBAC model, seems to be the best to express the administrator's constraints.

3.1 Classification of Security Constraints

Our classification of constraints reflects the cycle of application life: *analysis-development* and *exploitation-maintenance*. In the *analysis-development* phase, the application developer composes utilization constraints that guarantee confidentiality and integrity of the data manipulated by this application. In the *exploitation-maintenance* phase, the application is inserted in the existing information system. This insertion should respect the global coherence of the system using the global security constraints. Therefore, the first classification level of constraints is proposed as follows:

- constraints from the developer's point of view - constraints on the application level, specified to create a complex application,
- constraints from the administrator's point of view - organization constraints defined on the global security level of an enterprise.

The second classification level of constraints represents the constraints associated with an extended RBAC model:

- constraints imposed on a permission - limit the set of objects accessible for a permission.
- separation of duty (SOD) constraints - represent the concept of mutually exclusive roles and mutually exclusive permissions [6]
- prerequisite constraints - based on the concept of prerequisite roles or prerequisite permissions: e.g. a user can be assigned to role Teacher only if he has been assigned to role Employee; or a permission p can be assigned to a function only if this function has a permission q (e.g. the permission of "read" some file asks the permission of "read" the directory in which this file is situated),
- cardinality constraints - numerical limitation on classes in role-based system or numerical limitation on application elements; e.g. the number of users authorized to be assigned to a role is limited (in application example there is only one person who can be assigned to role Dean), or the permission of "read" the file with confidential information about the system users can be given only to one specific role.

– session constraints and role hierarchy constraints in the RBAC model,
– administration constraints - associated with the ARBAC model [2].

The last level of the classification of constraints comprises:

– static constraints that exist before different types of data access in a system is executed, e.g. the constraints on the value domain taken by the data,
– dynamic constraints that appear during the session and are responsible for the necessity to possess certain types of access to the data in a system.

Basing on these three classification types of constraints and on the responsibilities of both the application developer and the security administrator presented in the previous section, constraints of a global classification in the information system security have been built as shown in Fig. 2. This classification does not allow for the constraints connected with temporal or spatial aspects that are necessary in the workflow process.

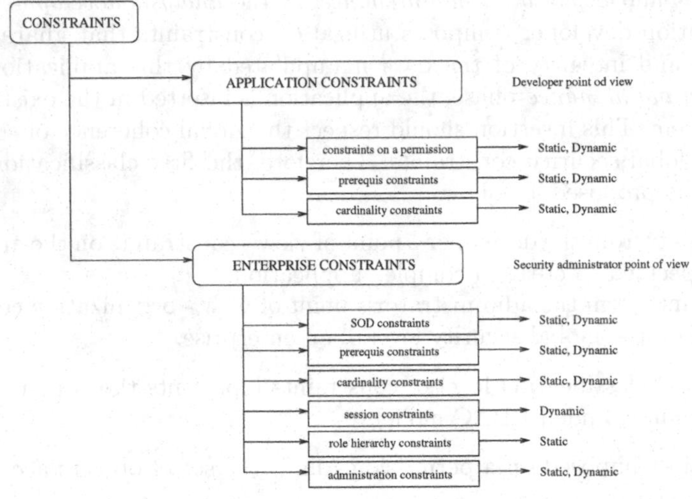

Fig. 2. Classification of security constraints

4 Coherence of Information System Security - Confrontation of Two Viewpoints

The responsibilities of the application developer are different from those of the security administrator. The developer is expected to meet the needs of his client as well as of future system users. Moreover, he must ensure that the set of roles and the set of permissions in the system should be in agreement with the application constraints. The security administrator is responsible for the coherence of constraints as well as the coherence in the assignment of users to roles. He works on the elements received from the developer in agreement with the security policy.

The confrontation of the two points of view consists in verification that the developer's work does not contain incoherences with regard to the work of the security administrator. Confrontation of the two points of view makes it possible to find out possible problems that can be caused by:

- addition of a new enterprise function to the system by the security administrator,
- addition of a new application that uses elements of another application existing in the system, e.g. the data stored in the system,
- addition of a new application with new roles, functions or/and permissions whose elements will be included in the role hierarchy of the system,
- addition of new elements, e.g. roles or functions, and new relations between these elements and the elements already existing in the system,
- removal of elements from the system, e.g. an application, enterprise functions, roles, etc. by the security administrator.

These problems have to be resolved either on the conception level and/or the security administration level. The confrontation of the two points of view can reveal possible incoherences between these two levels and then enable their solution. As the security administrator bases his work on the results produced by the developer, the coherence rules should be obeyed on both levels.

For example, an application "Management of students" that already exists in the university information system, contains information about students (name, surname, address, birth date, year of study, chosen courses, etc.). A new application "Management of grades", that manages the grades of students, added to the system uses certain data of the application "Management of students", for example: name, surname of a student. In this situation, the security administrator should eliminate possible incoherences, by determining the data (i.e. objects) of the first application that can be used by the second application, i.e. by defining the constraints specifying the set of objects of the first application accessible by the second one.

4.1 Integration Chain of Constraints in Coherent System

The verification of coherence is to guarantee that addition of a new application to an information system will not cause incoherences and this verification should be executed before its integration in the existing security system. It might be interesting to see how the addition of a new application in an information system can be automated and how the administrator can be assisted in detecting the incoherences or/and determining new relations between the elements already existing in a system [9,11].

Fig. 3 presents the flow diagram of verification of the two points of view under consideration. The first part allows generation of the model specification. The parser analyses the UML model of an application from the conception viewpoint and preserves the concepts that can be used to make this verification. The model representation is given according to the UML meta-model. The security administrator, on the other hand, provides the extended RBAC Model of an application with the constraints expressed in the extended RCL 2000 language.

The second part is the stage of verification and correction of the elements and constraints defined by the developer and by the security administrator. It is necessary to compare these two groups of constraints and eventually apply the changes if they are not coherent. The constraints on the developer level are expressed in OCL. We propose to translate the constraints expressed in the OCL language into the RCL 2000 language on the security administrator level. It is also necessary to iterate the previous stages up to the final validation made by the security administrator. It can be realized at the moment of integration of the new application in the existing global system.

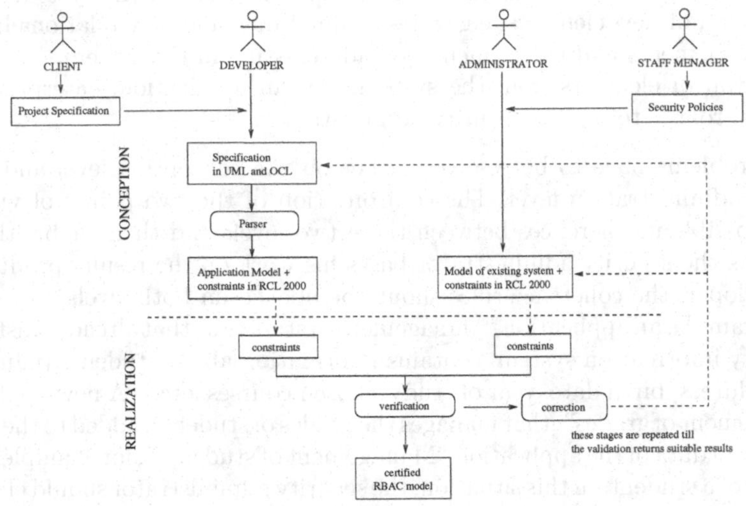

Fig. 3. Validation chain of modifications for global security schema

Validation of the two levels presented above is as follows:

- translation of UML Model performed by the developer into the model comprehensible to the security administrator, followed by
- integration of new elements according to the constraints defined by the developer (on the application level) and by the security administrator (on the system level that will contain the new application).

It is necessary to unify the concepts used by the developer and the security administrator if the developer's work is to be validated more or less automatically and the security administrator to be assisted in finding possible conflicts.

4.2 Definition of Coherence

The purpose of Model validation is to guarantee that the addition of a new application to an information system will not produce incoherences. It is necessary to verify whether the set of elements (users, roles, functions, etc.) of a new application has common elements with the set of the system elements.

Let E be a set of system elements and contains the following subsets: users, sessions, roles, functions, permissions, methods and objects

$$E = \{U,\ R,\ F,\ P,\ M,\ O\}\,,\ E_i \in E \textit{ and } e_{ij} \in E_i\ -\ \textit{an element } j \textit{ of set } E_i$$

The definitions (including the definitions of constraints) for an element $e_{ij} \in E_i$ in the information system limit the set of elements accessible on the system level. Let: $E_s(e_{ij})_i$ be a set of the elements related to element e_{ij} by the constraint associations in the system;

$$E_{S_k}(e_{ij}) \in E_S(e_{ij})\,,\ E_{S_k}(e_{ij}) ::= \\ \{U_S(e_{ij}) \mid S_S(e_{ij}) \mid R_S(e_{ij}) \mid F_S(e_{ij}) \mid P_S(e_{ij}) \mid M_S(e_{ij}) \mid O_S(e_{ij})\}$$

The following definition of coherence is proposed:

Definition. The extended RBAC model is coherent if and only if each element $e_{ij} \in E_i$ (user, role, function, permission, method or object) satisfies the following condition: for each element $e_{ij} \in E_i$ the set of elements in relation with e_{ij} should be different than the empty set, i.e.

$$\forall e_{ij} \in E_i,\ \forall k\ \left(E_{S_k}(e_{ij}) \in E_S(e_{ij})\ \wedge\ E_{S_k}(e_{ij}) \neq \emptyset\right) \tag{1}$$

in particular:

$$\forall\, u_j \in U,\ (E_{Sk}(u_j) ::= R_S(u_j) \wedge \forall k\ E_{Sk}(u_j) \neq \emptyset)$$

$$\forall\, r_j \in R,\ (E_{Sk}(r_j) ::= U_S(r_j) \mid F_S(r_j) \wedge \forall k\ E_{Sk}(r_j) \neq \emptyset)$$

$$\forall\, f_j \in F,\ (E_{Sk}(f_j) ::= R_S(f_j) \mid P_S(f_j) \wedge \forall k\ E_{Sk}(f_j) \neq \emptyset)$$

$$\forall\, p_j \in P,\ (E_{Sk}(p_j) ::= F_S(p_j) \mid M_S(p_j) \mid O_S(p_j) \wedge \forall k\ E_{Sk}(p_j) \neq \emptyset)$$

$$\forall\, m_j \in M,\ (E_{Sk}(m_j) ::= P_S(m_j) \wedge E_{Sk}(m_j) \neq \emptyset)$$

$$\forall\, o_j \in O,\ (E_{Sk}(o_j) ::= P_S(o_j) \wedge E_{Sk}(o_j) \neq \emptyset)$$

The concepts of role inheritance and function inheritance (reflexive associations) are not taken into consideration. There are roles in the set of roles that do not inherit other roles, therefore the set of roles $R_S(e_{ij})$ for $e_{ij} \in R$ can be empty. Analogously, there are functions in the set of functions that do not inherit other functions, therefore the set of functions $F_S(e_{ij})$ for $e_{ij} \in F$ can be empty. In consequence, the verification of role inheritance or function inheritance is not necessary for the verification of the model coherence.

Moreover, the session concept is not considered either, because it represents the dynamic aspect of the model. A session becomes opened in the system by a user who is in contact with it. Therefore, the analysis cannot be made for U-S or S-R relations.

4.3 Verification of Security System Coherence During Addition of an Application

To prove that the system remains coherent after new elements have been added, the definition of coherence should continue to be satisfied. The case that is going to be considered is the addition of a new application as involves addition of new elements, new relations and new constraints, which may give rise to incoherences. To find possible incoherences it is necessary to verify whether the set of elements (roles, functions, etc.) of the new application has any common elements with the set of the existing elements. These common elements, their relations with other elements and their constraints can lead to incoherences. Therefore, the conditions of coherence should be verified for each common element.

Let E_A be a set of elements of the new application that contains the subsets: users (U_A), sessions (S_A), roles (R_A), functions (F_A), permissions (P_A), methods (M_A) and objects (O_A) of the new application

$$E_A = \{U_A,\ R_A,\ F_A,\ P_A,\ M_A,\ O_A\}\ and\ E_{A_i} \in E_A$$

It must be checked whether $E' = E \cap E_A$ contains any elements or not, that is to say it is necessary to verify whether the new application has any elements common with the elements already existing in the system. The verification of coherence should be executed for each subset in the following way:

$$U' = U \cap U_A,\ R' = R \cap R_A,\ F' = F \cap F_A,\ P' = P \cap P_A,$$
$$M' = M \cap M_A\ and\ O' = O \cap O_A$$

Let: $E'_i \in E'\ and\ E'_i ::= \{U' \mid S' \mid R' \mid F' \mid P' \mid M' \mid O'\}$, $ec_{ij} \in E'_i$ be an element of set E'_i. The calculation of set intersection E' can yield one of the following two results:

- $E' = \emptyset$, i.e. $E \cap E_A = \emptyset$ - there are no common elements in the set of system elements and the set of elements of the new application; consequently, there are no incoherences between the new application and the existing system (between the conception and administration levels),
- $E' \neq \emptyset$, i.e. $E \cap E_A \neq \emptyset$ - the common elements exist, and consequently, they should be studied to identify and eliminate possible incoherences.

The constraints defined for a common element $ec_{ij} \in E'_i$ determine a set of elements accessible for it on both the application level and the global system level. Let: $E_S(ec_{ij})$ be a set of elements related to a common element ec_{ij} by constrained associations in the existing system, and let $E_A(ec_{ij})$ be a set of elements being in relations with a common element ec_{ij} by constrained associations in the new application.

$$E_{Sk}(ec_{ij}) \in E_S(ec_{ij})\ and$$
$$E_{Sk}(ec_{ij}) ::= U_S(ec_{ij}) \mid R_S(ec_{ij}) \mid F_S(ec_{ij}) \mid P_S(ec_{ij}) \mid M_S(ec_{ij}) \mid O_S(ec_{ij})$$

$$E_{Ak}(ec_{ij}) \in E_A(ec_{ij})\ and$$
$$E_{Ak}(ec_{ij}) ::= U_A(ec_{ij}) \mid R_A(ec_{ij}) \mid F_A(ec_{ij}) \mid P_A(ec_{ij}) \mid M_A(ec_{ij}) \mid O_A(ec_{ij})$$

The coherence is verified if equation (1) is verified, if $E_S(ec_{ij}) \cap E_A(ec_{ij}) \neq \emptyset$.

4.4 Verification Algorithm of System Coherence

If a new application is added to the system, it can have common elements with this system. It must be verified that the constraints defined on these common elements do not provoke incoherences. To eliminate possible incoherences, the following stages of verification algorithm are proposed ([9]): (1) find all common elements of each type, (2) identify the constraints for each common element, (3) verify the global coherence of the common elements, (4) identify the constraints that provoke the incoherences, and (5) propose and realize the necessary modifications in the definitions of the constraints that have provoked the incoherences.

Find all common elements of each type means to find common users (U'), common roles (R'), common functions (F'), common permissions (P'), common methods (M') or/and common objects (O') in the new application and the actual system.

Identify the constraints for each common element is carried out as follows: for an element $ec_{ij} \in E_i'$ the set of constraints contains the set of constraints already defined in the system and the set of constraints defined in the new application:

$$\forall\, ec_{ij} \in E_i',\ C\left(ec_{ij}\right) = C_S\left(ec_{ij}\right) \cup C_A\left(ec_{ij}\right)$$

$$C\left(ec_{ij}\right) - set\ of\ constraints\ of\ an\ element\ ec_{ij}$$
$$C_S\left(ec_{ij}\right) - set\ of\ constraints\ of\ element\ ec_{ij}\ that\ exists\ in\ the\ system$$
$$C_A\left(ec_{ij}\right) - set\ of\ constraints\ of\ element\ ec_{ij}\ in\ a\ new\ application$$

In particular, the set of constraints for common role $r_j \in R'$ is defined by:

$$\forall\, r_j \in R',\ C\left(r_j\right) = C_S\left(r_j\right) \cup C_A\left(r_j\right)$$

and, analogously, for the elements of the other types:

$$\forall\, f_j \in F',\ C\left(f_j\right) = C_S\left(f_j\right) \cup C_A\left(f_j\right)$$

$$\forall\, p_j \in P',\ C\left(p_j\right) = C_S\left(p_j\right) \cup C_A\left(p_j\right)$$

$$\forall\, m_j \in M',\ C\left(m_j\right) = C_S\left(m_j\right) \cup C_A\left(m_j\right)$$

$$\forall\, o_j \in O',\ C\left(o_j\right) = C_S\left(o_j\right) \cup C_A\left(o_j\right)$$

$$\forall\, u_j \in U',\ C\left(u_j\right) = C_S\left(u_j\right) \cup C_A\left(u_j\right)$$

Verify the global coherence of the common elements - verify whether these constraints do not provoke incoherences, it signifies to verify if the common elements with their constraints satisfy the definition of coherence:

$$\forall\, ec_{ij} \in E_i' \wedge \forall k,\ \left(E_{Sk}\left(ec_{ij}\right) \in E_S\left(ec_{ij}\right) \wedge E_{Sk}\left(ec_{ij}\right) \neq \emptyset\right)$$

If the common elements are coherent, it is not necessary to make changes in the new application; otherwies the constraints provoking incoherences should be identified for each common element.

Identify the constraints that provoke the incoherences - it is necessary to find the constraints of the common element that are responsible for the incoherences on this element. It should be determined which sets of constraints $C_S\left(ec_{ij}\right)$ and/or $C_A\left(ec_{ij}\right)$ do not satisfy the definition of coherence:

$\forall\ ec_{ij} \in E'_i$ for which the incoherences are identified, find the sets of constraints that are responsible for these incoherences, i.e. the sets $C_S(ec_{ij})$ and/or $C_A(ec_{ij})$.

Propose and realize the necessary modifications in the definitions of the constraints that provoke the incoherences. This stage is realized manually by the security administrator and/or application developer. These modifications can be carried out on the security administration level according to the constraints defined in the system and in the considered application. If this is not possible, the application developer should also perform the modifications on the level of the new application.

The algorithm 1 shows the stages of verification of the system coherence after the addition of a new application.

Table 1. The verification of system coherence after the addition of a new application

```
VerificationCoherence (E, E_A)
Begin
  for each (E_i ∈ E and E_Ai ∈ E_A) do
    E'_i = E_i ∩ E_Ai
    if E'_i ≠ ∅ then
      for each ec_ij ∈ E'_i do
        C_S (ec_ij) = identifyConstraints (ec_ij)
        C_A (ec_ij) = identifyConstraints (ec_ij)
        coherence = verifyCoherence (ec_ij, C_S (ec_ij), C_A (ec_ij))
        if (! coherence) then
          CI (ec_ij) = findConstraintsIncoherent (ec_ij, C_S (ec_ij), C_A (ec_ij))
          show (CI (ec_ij))
          return coherence
        endIf
      done
    endIf
  done
  return true
End
```

The first stage, i.e. identification of common elements in the system and the new application consists in the passage of sets of elements of the same type from the system and from the application, i.e. U with U_A, R with R_A, etc. and then the determination of their common elements:

$$U' = U \cap U_A,\ R' = R \cap R_A,\ F' = F \cap F_A,\ P' = P \cap P_A,\ M' = M \cap M_A \text{ and } O' = O \cap O_A$$

The set of users U_A of the new application will be empty because the application developer does not define the users who will use this application. The task of determination of future users of the application is realized by the security administrator. Therefore, the next section takes into consideration the following sets of common elements:

$R' = R \cap R_A,\ F' = F \cap F_A,\ P' = P \cap P_A,\ M' = M \cap M_A \textit{ and } O' = O \cap O_A$

Stage of Identification of Constraints for Common Elements. This stage requires identification of constraints defined for a common element $ec_{ij} \in E'_i$, i.e. a set $C(ec_{ij}) = C_S(ec_{ij}) \cup C_A(ec_{ij})$. For each element $ec_{ij} \in E'_i$, it is possible to find two groups of constraints on the system level and on the new application level:

- the constraints attached "directly" to an element ec_{ij}, i.e. the constraints applied exactly to this element,
- the constraints attached "indirectly" to an element ec_{ij}, i.e. the constraints defined on the elements that are joined to an element ec_{ij} by the relations of the RBAC model.

The process of identification of constraints for common elements is realized by the passage of graph of constraints defined for these elements. This passage creates the set of constraints defined for a common element $ec_{ij} \in E'_i$ as follows:

$$C_S(ec_{ij}) = c_S(ec_{ij}) \cup \bigcup C_S(el_{ij})$$

$$C_A(ec_{ij}) = c_A(ec_{ij}) \cup \bigcup C_A(el_{ij})$$

$c_S(ec_{ij})$ - *set of constraints defined on element* ec_{ij} *in the system*
$c_A(ec_{ij})$ - *set of constraints defined on element* ec_{ij} *in the new application*
$el_{ij} \in E_i$ - *an element attached to element* ec_{ij}*, for example: for* $ec_{ij} = f$ *(function) element* $el_{ij} = p$ *(permission) or* $el_{ij} = r$ *(role)*
$C_S(el_{ij})$ - *set of constraints defined on* el_{ij}*, attached directly or indirectly to* ec_{ij} *in the system*
$C_A(el_{ij})$ - *set of constraints defined on* el_{ij}*, attached directly or indirectly to* ec_{ij} *in the new application*

In particular, the constraints defined for a role r_j:

$C_S(r_j) = c_S(r_j) \cup \bigcup C_S(el_j)$ *and* $C_A(r_j) = c_A(r_j) \cup \bigcup C_A(el_j)$
where $C_S(el_j) ::= C_S(u_j) \mid C_S(f_j)$ and $C_A(el_j) ::= C_A(u_j) \mid C_A(f_j)$

$$C(r_j) = C_S(r_j) \cup C_A(r_j)$$

The identified set of constraints, defined for a common element $ec_{ij} \in E'$, limits the elements accessible for this element.

Stage of Verification of Coherence for Common Elements. This stage of algorithm verifies the coherence of the common elements of both the system and the new application, i.e. it checks whether the definition of coherence is still satisfied after addition of the new application. Therefore, to verify the coherence of the common elements it is necessary:

- to determine the elements accessible for each common element, i.e. to identify the set $E_S(ec_{ij})$ - the elements limited by the constraints defined on the system level (i.e. $C_S(ec_{ij})$) and on the new application level (i.e. $C_A(ec_{ij})$),

– to verify that the definition of coherence is still satisfied for each common element in the set of accessible elements $E_S(ec_{ij})$.

The identification of elements accessible for each common element ec_{ij} should be realized with the passage of graph of relations (i.e. associations) of the common element with the other elements according to the constraints identified on the system level $C_S(ec_{ij})$ and on the new application level $C_A(ec_{ij})$.

If the definition of coherence is satisfied for each common element, then the system after the addition of the new application is still coherent. In the opposite case, it is necessary to eliminate the incoherences introducing changes in the constraints. Therefore, the constraints responsible for any possible incoherences in the system should be identified.

Stage of Searching for Responsible Constraints. It is of use to receive a list of the constraints that produce incoherences if the system turns out to be incoherent after a new application has been added. Thus, it is necessary to verify which sets of constraints $C_S(ec_{ij})$ and/or $C_A(ec_{ij})$ provoke the situations in which the definition of coherence is not satisfied: *for each common element $ec_{ij} \in E'_i$ for which the incoherences are identified, the sets of constraints that are responsible for these incoherences, i.e. the set that belongs to sets $C_S(ec_{ij})$ and $C_A(ec_{ij})$* should be found.

For element $ec_{ij} \in E'_i$ the identification of constraints that produce incoherences involves identification of sets $E_{Sk}(ec_{ij}) \in E_S(ec_{ij})$ such as: $E_{Sk}(ec_{ij}) = \emptyset$.

In view of numerous solutions that can be applied the final choice of constraints to eliminate or modify should be made by the security administrator and/or the application developer. The security administrator should choose the level on which the modifications of constraints can be realized taking into consideration: the simplicity of modifications, the facility of verification of the system coherence and future profits on the global system level.

After the modifications have been introduced, the stages of coherence verification should be executed once again to obtain the new definitely coherent system.

5 Conclusions

The paper discusses security constraints of a security schema in an information system of an enterprise based on the extended RBAC model. The proposed classification of security constraints is carried out on three levels depending on different aspects of creating the security in the information system. The main classification divides the constraints into two groups: constraints defined by the application/system developer and constraints determined by the security administrator of an enterprise information system.

The discussed approach requires collaboration of the system developer and the global security administrator since both of them define security elements and constraints for the system, though each one on a different level. The issues of their activities have to be confronted and verified. The confrontation of the two viewpoints consists of the verification that the developer's work does not cause incoherences in the global security of the information system through identification of the problems that may have appeared between these two levels.

Starting from the global schema of coherent security, any insertion of a new application should respect the global coherence of new security schema. The information system used in an enterprise should be coherent, which means all the elements defined in the system, their relations and their constraints should be coherent. After the definition of the system coherence is given the integration of a new application in the existing security system can be performed taking into consideration the coherence of the entire system. The paper proposes the algorithm for the verification of system coherence after addition of a new application. This algorithm helps to introduce desired modifications into the information system, e.g. addition of a new application with preserving the coherence of information system security.

References

1. S. Castano, M. Fugini, G. Martella and P. Samarati, Database Security, ACM Press, Addison-Wesley, 1994
2. R. S. Sandhu, E. J. Coyne, H. L. Feinstein and C. E. Youman, Role-Based Access Control Models, IEEE Computer, vol 29, number 2, 1996
3. D. Ferraiolo, R. S. Sandhu, S. Gavrila, D. R. Kuhn and R. Chandramouli, Proposed NIST Role-Based Access Control, ACM, TISSEC, 2001
4. G.-J. Ahn, The RCL 2000 Language for Specifying Role-Based Authorization Constraints, 1999
5. G.-J. Ahn and R.S. Sandhu, The RSL99 Language for Role-Based Separation of Duty Constraints, ACM Transactions on RBAC, 1999
6. G.-J. Ahn and R. S. Sandhu, Role-based Authorization Constraints Specification, ACM Transactions on Information and Systems Security, 2000
7. G. Booch, J. Rumbaugh and I. Jacobson, The Unified Modeling Language User Guide, Addison Wesley, 1998
8. J. B. Warmer and A. G. Kleppe, The Object Constraint Language. Precise modeling with UML, Addison-Wesley, 1999
9. G. Goncalves, F. Hemery and A. Poniszewska, Verification of Access Control Coherence in Information System during Modifications, Proceedings of 12th IEEE International WETICE, Austria, 2003
10. A. Poniszewska-Maranda, G. Goncalves and F. Hemery, Representation of Extended RBAC Model Using UML Language, Proceedings of SOFSEM 2005: Theory and Practice of Computer Science, Springer-Verlag, 2005
11. A. Poniszewska-Maranda, Role Engineering of Information System Using Extended RBAC Model, Proceedings of 14th IEEE International WETICE, Sweden, 2005

Automatic Test Data Generation by Multi-objective Optimisation

Norbert Oster and Francesca Saglietti

Department of Software Engineering
University of Erlangen-Nuremberg, Germany
oster@informatik.uni-erlangen.de
saglietti@informatik.uni-erlangen.de
http://www11.informatik.uni-erlangen.de/

Abstract. This paper presents a technique for automated test data generation applicable to both procedural and object-oriented programs. During the generation, the test cases are optimised such as to maximise structural code coverage by minimising at the same time the number of test cases required. To cope with these two inherently conflicting goals, hybrid self-adaptive and multi-objective evolutionary algorithms are applied. Our approach is based on a preliminary activity that provides support for the automatic instrumentation of source code in order to record the relevant data flow information at runtime. By exclusively utilising the insight gained hereby, test data sets are successively enhanced towards the goals mentioned above. Finally, the efficiency of the test set generated is evaluated in terms of its fault detection capability by means of mutation testing. In addition, the actual coverage percentage achieved is determined by taking into account the results of a static data flow analysis of the system under test. Thanks to the dramatic decrease of effort required for generating and verifying test cases, the technique presented here allows to substantially improve the V&V-phase of complex, safety-relevant software. Preliminary experimental results gained so far are reported in the paper.

Keywords: testing, data flow, evolutionary algorithms, automated test data generation, object-oriented software, mutation testing.

1 Introduction and Related Work

In spite of considerable advances in the field of software engineering contributing to support the software development on the base of sound engineering knowledge, the number and criticality of software faults still represents a major challenge, due to the growing complexity of today's software systems and to their increasing safety relevance. In order to ensure the required level of reliability and availability demanded by the application envisaged, testing still represents an essential phase, certainly not replaceable by other techniques, be they conceived to support design or verification activities, by formal or informal methods. Average estimates of quality assurance effort amount to ca. 37% of the total development and to ca. 60% of the total software life-cycle costs [1]. Such figures clearly reflect the impressive role and decisive importance of software testing with regard to both the underlying safety and business risks.

J. Górski (Ed.): SAFECOMP 2006, LNCS 4166, pp. 426–438, 2006.

The main reason why testing requires a substantial amount of time and money - in particular when done according to control flow or data flow oriented strategies - lies in the fact that considerable work still has to be carried out by hand. Already the identification of test cases for the purpose of fulfilling a given testing criterion usually requires an elaborate, tiresome and error-prone task. Moreover, after execution of the test data identified, the results of the test runs are to be analysed in terms of their compliance with the specification or with the behaviour envisaged resp. needed. This step has to be iterated as long as the target coverage criterion is not completely achieved.

What is usually referred to *test automation* today, mostly relates and is restricted to the automatic support of the process of running the test cases identified. On the other hand, determining whether a particular coverage criterion is fulfilled by a given set of test cases still represents a task poorly supported, as soon as criteria going beyond basic control flow testing (typically statement and branch coverage) are concerned. Actually, the most ungrateful task to be carried out by testing personnel consists of extending the present test set by new test cases allowing to increase coverage up to the target level. As widely known, uncontrolled random generation of input data is of limited usefulness, since runs already tested tend to repeat themselves, while the random generation of data covering the few paths still missing becomes increasingly improbable. Additionally, all the test runs have to be validated one by one; therefore, the smaller the set of test cases achieving the testing target, the lesser the effort spent on validation.

Recently, evolutionary algorithms have become popular in the field of test case generation and several approaches to software testing have been published [2,3,4,5,6,7,8]. For instance, genetic algorithms were successfully applied to approximate upper and lower bounds of execution time in real-time applications [2]. Within a project led by automotive industry, test cases were generated by evolutionary optimisation such as to reveal specific critical defects [7], like the overrunning of parking spots by an automatic car parking system. Evolutionary techniques were also used to generate test cases for statement and branch coverage of programs written in C [6], where for each statement resp. branch still uncovered, one individual test case is searched such as to cover it. Data flow oriented testing of functional block diagrams was recently addressed in [8]; the approach presented there, however, is constrained to quite simple functional blocks without loops.

The novelty of our technique, which will be presented in the rest of the article, concerns different aspects. It provides a fully automatic generation and evaluation of test cases for object-oriented programs, allowing for the complete Java language without any restrictions, and thus including programs written in classical paradigms. Moreover, the key issue of this technique in comparison to related ones concerns the fact that the optimisation simultaneously addresses the following two objectives:

- the maximisation of the coverage achieved by the test set and
- the minimisation of the number of test cases required to do so.

2 Data Flow Based Testing

The approach presented here was originally developed for data flow based testing. It soon turned out that the technique is universally applicable to most other structural testing strategies. For example, an extension of this method in order to include condition coverage criteria is in progress within our current research project. The classical theory of data flow based testing, as was originally introduced by Rapps and Weyuker [9] is well-known to scientists working in the field. This theory was extended by Ntafos [10] as well as Laski and Korel [11] towards more sophisticated coverage concepts and adapted to the peculiarities of modern object-oriented programming languages. The testing concept is based on the control flow of the program annotated by relevant data flow information, as shortly summarized in the following.

The goal of data flow based testing is to execute inputs allowing each assignment of a value to a variable (so-called *definition*, or *def* in short) to reach instructions requiring to read that value. Reading a value may be carried out for different purposes, or *uses*: they may be *computational uses* (*c-uses*), if the value of a variable is read in order to perform a computation, or *predicative uses* (in short *p-uses*), if the value of a variable is used within a conditional statement in order to come to a decision. According to this semantic, c-uses are associated to control flow nodes containing a computation, whereas p-uses related to a conditional statement are associated to edges leaving the control flow node containing that condition.

More than 10 different testing criteria based on data flow coverage were defined and hierarchically organized in [9,10,11]; most of them subsume classical branch coverage. Among them is the widely known *all-uses* criterion, which requires the execution of *at least one* sub-path from *any* definition of any variable to *any* reachable use of that variable, where no further definition of the variable under consideration occurs along the sub-paths considered.

Thanks to the enrichment of the underlying control flow by additional data flow information, in general such testing strategies are superior to simple control flow strategies in terms of their fault detection capability. For example, the obvious fault in figure 1 may remain undetected after a test conceived to achieve statement or branch coverage, e.g. covering the following two paths of instructions: 1,2,3,4,5,6,7,9,10,11 and 1,2,3,5,6,7,8,9,10,11. In fact, none of these paths allows the assignment of variable c (def in line 4) to reach its use (c-use in line 8), as required by data flow testing of variable c.

Faults and anomalies usually discovered by data flow testing include, but are not limited to the following classes:

1. faults/anomalies detectable by static analysis:
   - dead code
   - endless loops
   - non-initialised variables
   - misplaced statements, like definitions without reachable uses
2. faults/anomalies detectable by dynamic execution:
   - faults in the context of conditions, especially concerning their antecedent data flow
   - def/use-pairs, which, though associated with respect to control flow, cannot actually be covered by any input data
   - anomalous conversions or type-inconsistent uses
   - in the particular case of object-oriented programs: incorrect call sequences that manifest themselves by messages reaching an object in an improper state

```
public int f(int a, int b, String c) {
    ... // any statements
    if (a > 0) {
        c = null;
    }
    ... // contains no def of c
    if (b < 0) {
        b = c.length();
    }
    return b;
}
```

Fig. 1. Example source code

In spite of the superiority of data flow testing, its practical application to industrial systems is still limited, mainly due to the effort required until recently and which fortunately is starting to become affordable, thanks to the evolutionary approach described in the following.

3 Static and Dynamic Data Flow Analysis of Java Programs

In order to discover as many of the faults described in section 2 as possible, test cases must be identified such as to cover all the data flow entities requested by the criterion under consideration; this set of entities can be determined by static analysis prior to testing. In order to evaluate how many entities were covered and especially which ones were not yet, the execution of each test case must be traced by dynamic analysis.

3.1 Static Analysis

The static analyser implemented in our project is based on symbolic execution. For reasons of simplicity we preferred to analyse Java byte code instead of the original source code. This choice offers different advantages: it allows us to avoid carrying out type inference, which is already taken over by the compiler; in addition, it permits to perform testing activities based on a level close to the real behaviour of the underlying machine.

For the entire program under consideration, the analyser represents each method as a data flow annotated Interprocedural Control Flow Graph. After selecting a starting method (typically `public static void main(String[])`), each subsequent statement is virtually interpreted by symbolic execution. In order to cope with pointer-aliasing [12], a points-to-set is constructed to be considered during the further symbolic execution, as proposed in [13,14]. The interprocedural control flow considered is limited to the system under test only, excluding external code (e.g. libraries) in order to avoid redundant verification activities. Since loops might influence the points-to-set of certain variables, an optimised fixed point iteration strategy is applied, such that superfluous reconsideration of sub-paths is avoided. For example, when the points-to-set at a node is expected to change due to reconsideration of one of its ancestors, the analysis of the respective node is postponed until the ancestors have been analysed. This yields a safe set of def/use-pairs (possibly including uncoverable pairs) as well as all the loop-free sub-paths (so-called *DU-paths*) connecting them.

3.2 Dynamic Analysis

For the sake of automatic generation of data flow based test cases by means of evolutionary algorithms, the static analysis mentioned above can be omitted when replaced by dynamic analysis. This is crucial since such a static analysis turned out to be very time-consuming, requiring hours of computation, even for moderately sized systems. In order to gain an objective measure of the number of data flow pairs covered by a given test case (see section 4), the source code of the system under test is instrumented [15] by using ANTLR[1], where the source of each class is transformed into an *abstract syntax tree* (AST) first. This tree is then modified at dedicated locations by inserting additional nodes, representing calls to a logging facility. At this step, all available information concerning the instrumentation is stored in a so-called *instrumentation log* in order to keep the runtime overhead as small as possible. The instrumentation phase is concluded by converting the modified AST back to Java source code. In such a way, during the execution of a test case, the logging facility efficiently receives data flow related messages from the running system and stores them in a *runtime log*. After resolving the data of the runtime log based on the instrumentation log, the complete data flow of the underlying test case is reproduced, resulting in an objective measure of the number of data flow pairs actually covered. Since each instance of a class can easily be distinguished at runtime, pointer-aliasing is accurately resolved at very low cost.

3.3 Overall Process

The complexity of static analysis varies depending on the criterion under consideration. For relatively simple criteria like *branch*- and *all-defs*-coverage [9], the instrumentation log yielded by the dynamic analysis as described in section 3.2 is sufficient to statically determine the number of entities to be covered, as in such cases no detailed analysis concerning all *def/use-pairs* is required. The upper half of figure 2 shows the results of a static analysis performed for *branch*- and *all-defs*-coverage based on the instrumentation log of the dynamic analysis tool at source code level.

For more complex criteria like *all-uses* resp. *all-DU-paths* on the other hand, all *def/use-pairs* resp. all loop-free sub-paths between each *def* and its *uses* have to be identified. For this reason, an explicit and detailed static analysis as described in section 3.1 is needed. The results from the static analysis of byte code executed for the *all-uses*- and *all-DU-paths*-criteria is shown in the lower part of figure 2.

4 Multi-objective Test Set Generation and Optimisation

At first glance, classical random test case generators might be helpful, but when applied to structural testing, they usually spawn a lot of superfluous data. This is due to the fact

[1] ANother Tool for Language Recognition, see `http://www.antlr.org/`

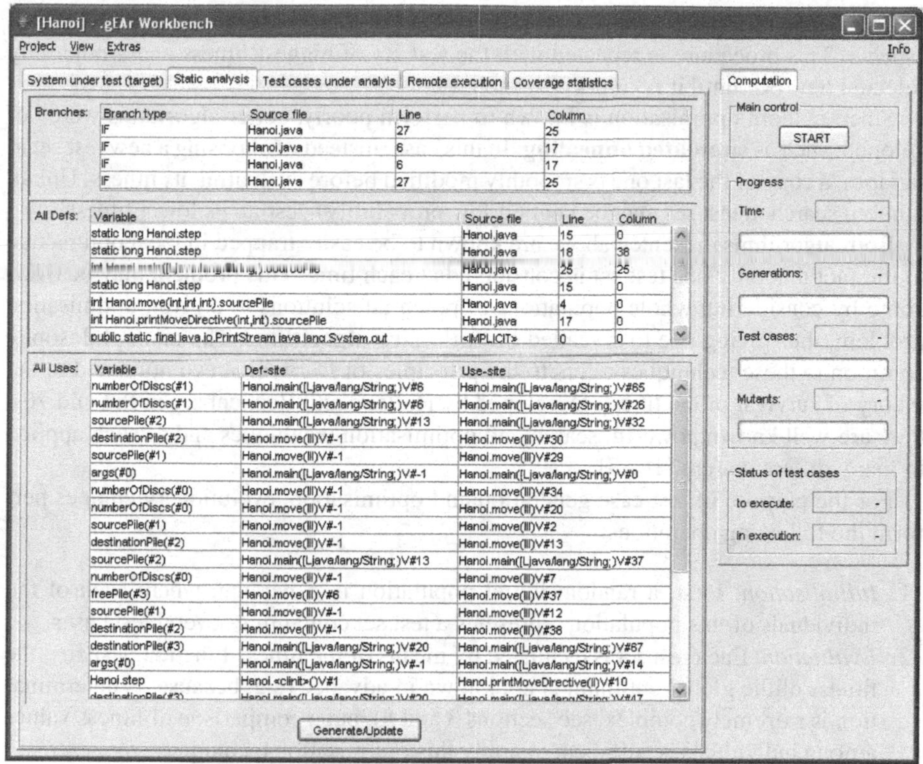

Fig. 2. Static analysis output

that they create many similar test cases covering the same paths many times while possibly not executing others at all. The problem that arises here is that all those test cases have to be validated individually. Therefore, the smaller the set of generated test cases fulfilling the testing goal, the lesser the effort spent on validation. In order to cope with this conflicting task, so-called multi-objective optimisation can be applied. Many different techniques for general multi-objective optimisation problems were proposed in the literature, four of which were adopted and compared in our research project. A principal item that has to be addressed first is the definition of the optimisation goal, expressed in terms of the so-called *fitness function*. Multi-objective optimisation strategies keep track of at least two such *objectives*. In our case, one objective is the number of entities (e.g. *branches* or *def/use-pairs*) to be covered and the other is the size of the test set. A solution consists of combining both objectives into one fitness function by means of a weighted sum, considering that one fitness value has to be maximised while the other must be minimised.

For the purpose of comparing the performance of different optimisation strategies, different algorithms were implemented. The simplest approach among them is based on a **multi-objective random search**, where first two sets of test cases, are chosen at random. The sizes of both test sets and the number of entities covered by each are then determined. The overall fitness of each test set is evaluated by a weighted sum of its values, once these values were normalised in order to avoid overruling of single aspects. This procedure is repeated with the test set of highest fitness and a randomly selected new one until it is stopped by the tester.

Since random optimisation is known to perform poorly, better algorithms were developed, such as **simulated annealing**. In this case, instead of choosing a new test set at random, a copy of the last one is smoothly modified before evaluating its fitness. Unlike random search, a test set may be kept (at low probability) despite its lower fitness.

Both algorithms presented above are known to be easily trapped in local optima due to the fact that only one test set is considered at each time. This problem may be overcome by considering whole populations of potential solutions to a given optimisation problem, thus giving rise to so-called **evolutionary algorithms**. The main philosophy common to these techniques refers to the principles of Darwinian evolution and to the theory of survival of the fittest. Developed by Holland and Rechenberg in the mid 70s, they are well known powerful search and optimisation techniques and as such applied in many different areas [16,17].

For the purpose of test case generation and optimisation, evolutionary engines perform the following operations:

1. *Initialisation*: First, a random initial population is generated, where each of the individuals of this population represents a test set containing several test cases.
2. *Evaluation*: Each test set is evaluated by means of the fitness function. Usually, the fitness of the global optimum is not known in advance (e.g. because its determination is extremely complex, see sections 3 and 5), but a comparison of fitness values among individuals is sufficient to apply this optimisation technique.
3. A new generation is constructed by repeatedly applying the following two steps:
   - *Selection*: Two test sets are randomly selected from the old generation with probability proportional to the size of their fitness values (several selection criteria exist [16]).
   - *Crossover*: The test sets selected are merged in such a way as to form two new individuals (again, different crossover strategies may be applied), which are successively added to the population.
4. *Mutation*: Each test set of the new population is subjected to mutation, i.e. to slight modification by adding, removing or modifying some of their test cases. This is done in order to introduce new genetic material such that the search procedure is not limited to mere combinations of initial values.
5. At this point steps 2 - 4 are repeated for the new generation. In order to reduce execution time, unmodified test cases are not re-executed.
6. The whole optimisation process is stopped as soon as a solution can be found to be optimal or after a predetermined number of iterations, thus yielding at least a sub-optimal solution.

Within our research project, we decided to implement two different variants of genetic algorithms: the **Multi-Objective Aggregation (MOA)** makes use of the weighted sum as described for the non-evolutionary algorithms above. This approach suffers from crucial problems, like the determination of appropriate weights. For this reason, alternatives like the *Vector Evaluated Genetic Algorithm (VEGA)*, the *Niched Pareto Genetic*

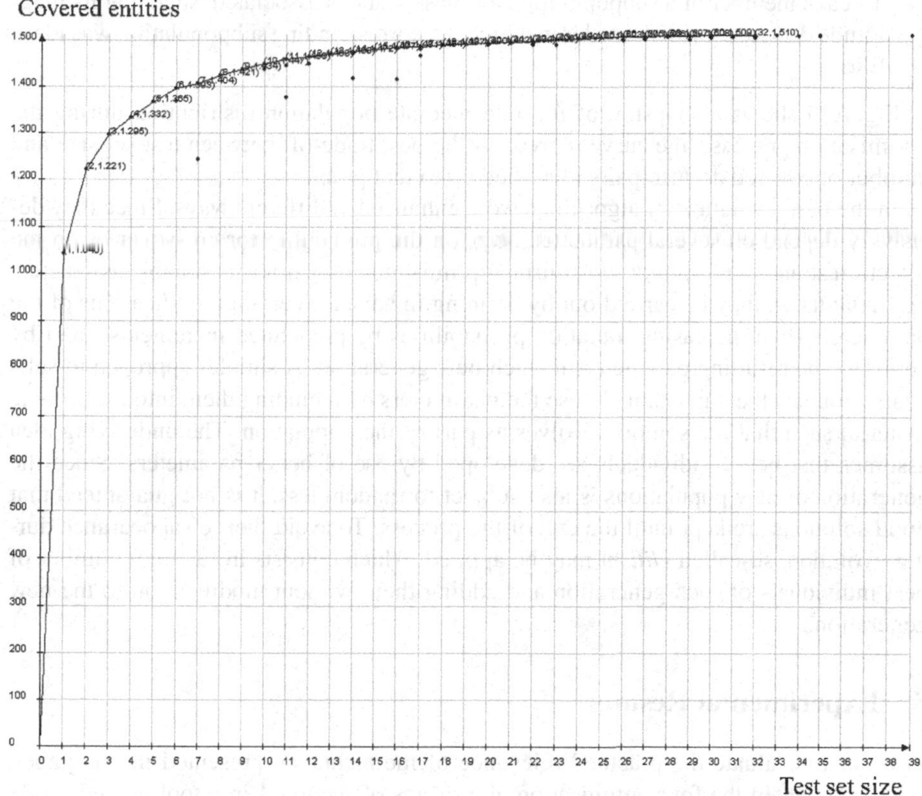

Fig. 3. Pareto-optimal front of test cases

Algorithm (NPGA) and the *Non-dominated Sorting Genetic Algorithm (NSGA)* [18,19] were considered, which avoid requiring weights by evaluating the fitness of step 2 considering the domination relation. A solution is said to be non-dominated, if it is optimal in the sense that no other known solution is better with respect to all objectives at the same time. Proceeding this way, the three alternative algorithms mentioned above offer several optimal results aligned up the so-called Pareto-front, hereby reflecting the trade-off between the objectives.

Different experimental investigations showed that the **Non-dominated Sorting Genetic Algorithm** is generally outperforming VEGA and NPGA. Therefore, we choose this algorithm as our fourth alternative. In NSGA, step 2 of the outline above is carried out in three steps:

1. Each objective is evaluated on its own.
2. The population is partitioned into sub-populations by identifying one maximal non-dominated subpopulation and repeating this step for the remaining population until a non-dominated subpopulation is left.

3. To each member of a subpopulation a fitness value is associated, such that its magnitude decreases with the order in which the corresponding subpopulation was identified.

Figure 3 shows a snapshot of the intermediate population distribution during the optimisation process - the curve represents the best trade-off between test set size and number of covered def/use-pairs identified up to that point.

In the past, evolutionary algorithms were enhanced in different ways. Since they decisively depend on several parameters, e.g. on the probability for crossover or on the selection strategy, *self-adaptation* during optimisation may offer reasonable assistance. Self-adaptation may be carried out by defining in advance certain modifications of the parameters (like increasing mutation probabilities by predefined increments), and by applying the resulting parameters to each new generation. A simpler approach to self-adaptation lets the algorithm choose the parameters by including them into the genetic material such that the solution evolves as part of the population. The underlying idea assumes that better individuals are developed by use of better parameters. Since the generation of new populations is also subject to randomness, it is not guaranteed that good solutions are kept until the end of the process. To avoid their disappearance during evolution, so-called *elitism* may be applied, which consists in saving a number of best individuals of each generation and adding them without modification to the new generation.

5 Experimental Results

In order to evaluate the practical relevance of the technique presented in this paper, we implemented the four optimisation algorithms of section 4 in a tool named *.gEAr* (DOTgEAr: Data flow Oriented Test case generation with Evolutionary Algorithms). It automatically generates test cases for most basic data flow criteria as well as branch coverage and is now being extended to include condition coverage and equivalence class testing.

In order to speed up the test set generation and optimisation, .gEAr makes use of distributed, fault tolerant test case execution. This is achieved by executing hidden daemon processes on simple networked PCs which receive the executable system under test and a test case, run the program in the background (unperceived by the actual user) and send back the coverage data. In our experimental setup, we used between 10 and 45 of such "execution servers", depending on their availability. Because of varying workload on and availability of the PCs, a comparison based on the actual runtime required would be quite complex and of limited significance. For this reason, we opted for a comparison of performance of the different optimisation algorithms based on the number of test runs required. In figure 4, the x-axis represents the total number of test cases executed and thus provides a "relative indicator" of runtime. On the other hand, the y-axis shows the number of def/use-pairs covered by the optimal test set as was identified after processing the corresponding amount of test cases.

We applied .gEAr to a number of projects ranging from 38 lines of code (LOC) in 1 class up to 5439 LOC in 27 classes. Two of them (projects 5 and 6 in table 1) were extracted without any modifications from the Java™ source repository. In most cases,

Simulated Annealing outperformed *Multi-objective Aggregation* and *Random testing*, e.g. in case of project BigFloat as shown in figure 4. As expected, Random testing soon got stuck in a local optimum. Even if *Non-dominated Sorting Genetic Algorithm (NSGA)* did not surpass the simulated annealing in terms of performance, it offers a higher flexibility as described in section 4, because it does not just return a single optimal result, but a complete front of trade-offs. In figure 4 the line labelled NSGA was chosen to reflect the test set of highest coverage within each corresponding Pareto front.

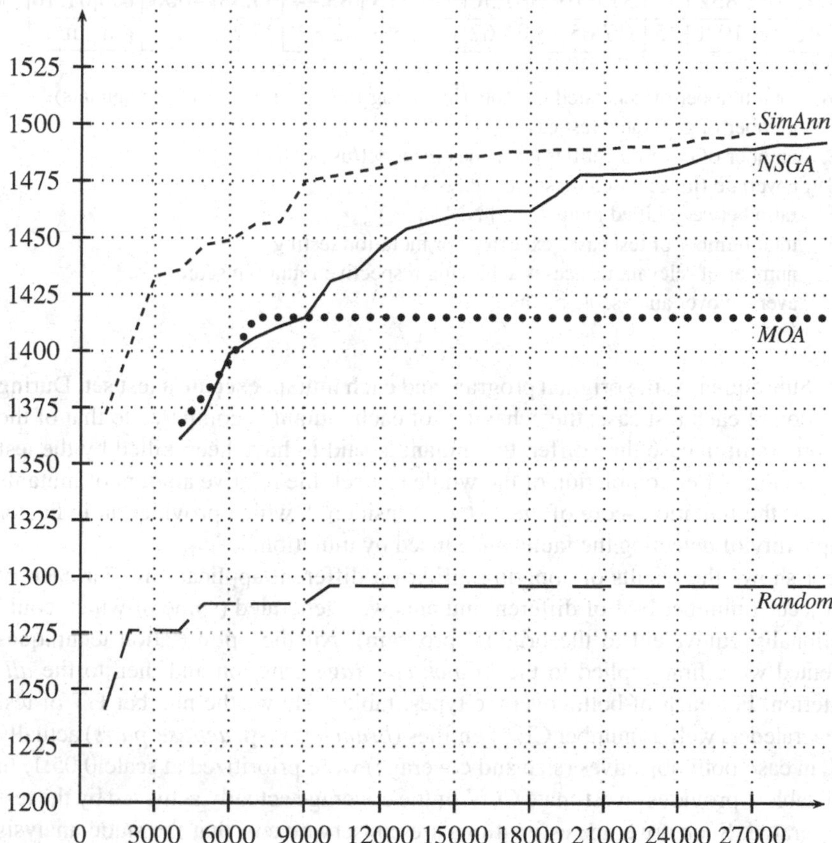

Fig. 4. Comparison of the performance of different optimisation techniques (*BigFloat*), units on the axis are specified in the running text

As coverage criteria measure how exhaustively a system under test was explored in terms of its structure, some correlation between testing coverage and fault detection capability might be expected, as was also revealed by a number of experimental investigations. In order to analyse more rigorously this correlation, we decided to use a more objective indicator of fault detection by test cases generated by .gEAr, namely the so-called *mutation score*. The key idea consists of introducing small modifications into the system under test, each representing a typical fault and resulting in a particular mutant

Table 1. Experimental results

			branch coverage				all-uses coverage				mutation testing		
ID	Project	NM	GT	CE	COV	MS	GT	CE	COV	MS	ET	RT	MS
1	BigFloat	1528	5	144	98,63	69,18	17	1511	82,83*	75,85	3000	232	95,75
2	Dijkstra	220	1	26	100	70,45	2	168	93,75*	71,82	10000	8	75,91
3	Hanoi	227	2	4	100	74,89	2	42	96,67	76,65	1000	11	85,90
4	Huffman	623	3	61	100	74,32	3	353	92,86*	75,44	n/a	6	100
5	JDK sort	852	1	37	100	61,50	2	315	83,44	65,38	4000	108	81,46
6	JDK log	1970	35	317	65,23	24,62	61	1599	82,82*	25,23	n/a	n/a	n/a

NM: total number of generated mutants (including functionally equivalent mutants)
GT: number of generated test cases
CE: number of covered entities (branches resp. def/use-pairs)
COV: coverage (in %; based on static analysis)
MS: ratio between killed mutants and NM (in %)
ET: total number of test cases executed for mutation testing
RT: number of relevant test cases achieving respective mutation score
* average over analysable methods

program. Subsequently, the original program and each mutant execute a test set. During the execution of each test case, the behaviour of each mutant is compared to that of the original program; in case they differ, the mutant is said to have been killed by the test case in question. After completion of the whole test set, the relative amount of mutants killed yields the mutation score of the test set considered, which provides an indicator of its capability of detecting the faults introduced by mutation.

Table 1 shows the results of applying .gEAr on different applications. For each of the 6 projects a number NM of different mutants was generated (some of which could be functionally equivalent to the original program). All the optimisation techniques implemented were first applied to the *branch coverage*-criterion and then to the *all-uses*-criterion. For each of both coverage types, table 1 shows the number GT of test cases generated as well as number CE of entities (*branches* resp. *def/use-pairs*) actually covered, in case both objectives (size and coverage) were prioritized at scale 0.05:1. In addition, table 1 provides an estimate COV of the coverage actually achieved by the test cases generated. Such coverage estimations are conservative in that the static analysis counts *all* entities which should be covered, not just those which actually can be covered during operation.

The columns MS indicate the ratio between the number of mutants killed and the total number NM of mutants generated. To determine the exact mutation score, this ratio must be adjusted by considering functionally equivalent mutants. Unfortunately, an analysis of functional equivalence between original program and mutants cannot be carried out automatically; on the other hand, a manual check is prohibitive due to the substantial amount of mutants generated. In order to estimate the number of equivalent mutants, we availed ourselves of statistical sampling theory by uniform random generation of a high number ET of inputs on which to execute original program and mutants. Mutants surviving all ET inputs generated can be assumed to be functionally equivalent to the original program at a high confidence level. The number of test cases killing the remaining mutants is given in column RT of table 1.

In the light of these considerations, the results of table 1 evidently show that the fault detection capability per test case is several orders of magnitude higher when test cases are generated and optimised by .gEAr as presented in this paper rather than by classical random generation.

6 Conclusion and Outlook

This article has presented an approach supporting the automatic generation of test data for object-oriented programs implemented in Java with respect to control flow and data flow based criteria. The technique proposed is based on evolutionary algorithms aiming at maximizing data flow coverage and minimizing the size of the test set, and thus the effort for validation.

Different search and optimization methods have been implemented for several data flow criteria and validated by practical examples. The preliminary results achieved confirm the efficiency and ease of use of the approach adopted. Nevertheless, both results and performance can be enhanced by extending the evolutionary algorithms presented, e.g. by *hybridisation*. A possible hybridisation approach consists in interleaving the global optimisation phase with a local test case generation.

Method and tool described in this article have found the interest of a major German industrial company involved in the development of software for medical devices. In cooperation with this industrial partner we intend to apply the process on large-scale industrial applications, thus helping to reduce verification costs and to enhance the effectiveness of test activities at the same time.

References

1. Liggesmeyer, P.: Software-Qualität – Testen, Analysieren und Verifizieren von Software. Spektrum - Akademischer Verlag, Heidelberg; Berlin (2002)
2. O'Sullivan, M., Vössner, S., Wegener, J.: Testing temporal correctness of real-time systems - a new approach using genetic algorithms and cluster analysis. In: EuroSTAR98 Software Testing Analysis & Review. Number 6 in EuroSTAR, Munich Park Hilton (1998) 397–418
3. Hutchins, M., Foster, H., Goradia, T., Ostrand, T.: Experiments on the effectiveness of dataflow- and controlflow-based test adequacy criteria. In: Proceedings of the 16th International Conference on Software Engineering. Number 16 in ICSE, IEEE (1994) 191–200
4. Michael, C.C., McGraw, G.: Automated software test data generation for complex programs. In: Automated Software Engineering. Thirteenth IEEE Conference on Automated Software Engineering, IEEE (1998) 136–146
5. Baresel, A.: Automatisierung von Strukturtests mit evolutionären Algorithmen. Diplomarbeit, Lehr- und Forschungsgebiet Softwaretechnik, Humboldt-Universität Berlin, Berlin (2000)
6. Wegener, J., Buhr, K., Pohlheim, H.: Automatic test data generation for structural testing of embedded software systems by evolutionary testing. In Langdon, W.B., et al, E.C.P., eds.: GECCO 2002: Proceedings of the Genetic and Evolutionary Computation Conference, New York, Morgan Kaufmann Publishers (2002) 1233–1240

7. Baresel, A., Sthamer, H., Wegener, J.: Applying evolutionary testing to search for critical defects. In Deb, K., et al, R.P., eds.: Genetic and Evolutionary Computation – GECCO-2004, Part II. Volume 3103 of Lecture Notes in Computer Science., Heidelberg, ISGEC, Springer-Verlag (2004) 1427–1428
8. Jee, E., Yoo, J., Cha, S.: Control and data flow testing on function block diagramms. In Winther, R., Gran, B.A., Dahll, G., eds.: Computer Safety, Reliability, and Security: 24th International Conference, SAFECOMP 2005. Volume 3688 / 2005 of Lecture Notes in Computer Science (LNCS)., Berlin Heidelberg, Springer Verlag GmbH (2005) 67–80
9. Rapps, S., Weyuker, E.J.: Selecting software test data using data flow information. IEEE Transactions on Software Engineering **SE-11**(4) (1985) 367–375
10. Ntafos, S.C.: On testing with required elements. In: Proceedings of COMPSAC '81, Chicago, IEEE Computer Society (1981) 132–139
11. Laski, J.W., Korel, B.: A data flow oriented program testing strategy. IEEE Transactions on Software Engineering **9**(3) (1983) 347–354
12. Ostrand, T.J., Weyuker, E.J.: Data flow-based test adequacy analysis for languages with pointers. In: Proceedings of the Symposium on Testing, Analysis, and Verification, New York, ACM, ACM Press (1991) 74–86
13. Chatterjee, R., Ryder, B.G., Landi, W.A.: Relevant context inference. In: Proceedings of the 26th ACM SIGPLAN-SIGACT symposium on Principles of programming languages, New York, ACM, ACM Press (1999) 133–146
14. Chatterjee, R., Ryder, B.G.: Data-flow-based testing of object-oriented libraries. Technical Report DCS-TR-433, Department of Computer Science, Rutgers University, New Jersey (2001)
15. Oster, N., Dorn, R.D.: A data flow approach to testing object-oriented java-programs. In Spitzer, C., Schmocker, U., Dang, V.N., eds.: Probabilistic Safety Assessment and Management (PSAM7/ESREL'04). Volume 2., Berlin, Springer-Verlag London (2004) 1114–1119
16. Goldberg, D.E.: Genetic Algorithms in Search, Optimization and Machine Learning. Addison-Wesley (1989)
17. Wilke, P., Gröbner, M., Oster, N.: A hybrid genetic algorithm for school timetabling. In McKay, B., Slaney, J., eds.: AI 2002: Advances in Artificial Intelligence. Volume 2557 / 2002 of Lecture Notes in Computer Science., Heidelberg, Springer-Verlag (2002) 455–464
18. Srinivas, N., Deb, K.: Multiobjective optimization using nondominated sorting in genetic algorithms. Evolutionary Computation **2**(3) (1994) 221–248
19. Zitzler, E., Thiele, L.: Multiobjective optimization using evolutionary algorithms – a comparative case study. Technical report, Swiss Federal Institute of Technology Zurich, Computer Engineering and Communication Networks Laboratory (TIK), Gloriastrasse 35, CH-8092 Zurich, Switzerland (1998)

Author Index

Lecture Notes in Computer Science

For information about Vols. 1–4116

please contact your bookseller or Springer

Vol. 4228: D.E. Lightfoot, C.A. Szyperski (Eds.), Modular Programming Languages. X, 415 pages. 2006.

Vol. 4224: E. Corchado, H. Yin, V. Botti, C. Fyfe (Eds.), Intelligent, Data Engineering and, Automated Learning - IDEAL 2006. XXVII, 1447 pages. 2006.

Vol. 4219: D. Zamboni, C. Kruegel (Eds.), Recent Advances in Intrusion Detection. XII, 331 pages. 2006.

Vol. 4217: P. Cuenca, L. Orozco-Barbosa (Eds.), Personal Wireless Communications. XV, 532 pages. 2006.

Vol. 4213: J. Fürnkranz, T. Scheffer, M. Spiliopoulou (Eds.), Knowledge Discovery in Databases: PKDD 2006. XXII, 660 pages. 2006. (Sublibrary LNAI).

Vol. 4212: J. Fürnkranz, T. Scheffer, M. Spiliopoulou (Eds.), Machine Learning: ECML 2006. XXIII, 851 pages. 2006. (Sublibrary LNAI).

Vol. 4208: M. Gerndt, D. Kranzlmüller (Eds.), High Performance Computing and Communications. XXII, 938 pages. 2006.

Vol. 4207: Z. Ésik (Ed.), Computer Science Logic. XII, 627 pages. 2006.

Vol. 4206: P. Dourish, A. Friday (Eds.), UbiComp 2006: Ubiquitous Computing. XIX, 526 pages. 2006.

Vol. 4205: G. Bourque, N. El-Mabrouk (Eds.), Comparative Genomics. X, 231 pages. 2006. (Sublibrary LNBI).

Vol. 4203: F. Esposito, Z.W. Ras, D. Malerba, G. Semeraro (Eds.), Foundations of Intelligent Systems. XVIII, 767 pages. 2006. (Sublibrary LNAI).

Vol. 4202: E. Asarin, P. Bouyer (Eds.), Formal Modeling and Analysis of Timed Systems. XI, 369 pages. 2006.

Vol. 4201: Y. Sakakibara, S. Kobayashi, K. Sato, T. Nishino, E. Tomita (Eds.), Grammatical Inference: Algorithms and Applications. XII, 359 pages. 2006. (Sublibrary LNAI).

Vol. 4197: M. Raubal, H.J. Miller, A.U. Frank, M.F. Goodchild (Eds.), Geographic, Information Science. XIII, 419 pages. 2006.

Vol. 4196: K. Fischer, E. André, I.J. Timm, N. Zhong (Eds.), Multiagent System Technologies. X, 185 pages. 2006. (Sublibrary LNAI).

Vol. 4194: V.G. Ganzha, E.W. Mayr, E.V. Vorozhtsov (Eds.), Computer Algebra in Scientific Computing. XI, 313 pages. 2006.

Vol. 4193: T.P. Runarsson, H.-G. Beyer, E. Burke, J.J. Merelo-Guervós, L. D. Whitley, X. Yao (Eds.), Parallel Problem Solving from Nature - PPSN IX. XIX, 1061 pages. 2006.

Vol. 4192: B. Mohr, J.L. Träff, J. Worringen, J. Dongarra (Eds.), Recent Advances in Parallel Virtual Machine and Message Passing Interface. XVI, 414 pages. 2006.

Vol. 4191: R. Larsen, M. Nielsen, J. Sporring (Eds.), Medical Image Computing and Computer-Assisted Intervention - MICCAI 2006, Part II. XXXVIII, 981 pages. 2006.

Vol. 4190: R. Larsen, M. Nielsen, J. Sporring (Eds.), Medical Image Computing and Computer-Assisted Intervention - MICCAI 2006, Part I. XXXVVIII, 949 pages. 2006.

Vol. 4189: D. Gollmann, J. Meier, A. Sabelfeld (Eds.), Computer Security - ESORICS 2006. XI, 548 pages. 2006.

Vol. 4188: P. Sojka, I. Kopeček, K. Pala (Eds.), Text, Speech and Dialogue. XIV, 721 pages. 2006. (Sublibrary LNAI).

Vol. 4187: J.J. Alferes, J. Bailey, W. May, U. Schwertel (Eds.), Principles and Practice of Semantic Web Reasoning. XI, 277 pages. 2006.

Vol. 4186: C. Jesshope, C. Egan (Eds.), Advances in Computer Systems Architecture. XIV, 605 pages. 2006.

Vol. 4185: R. Mizoguchi, Z. Shi, F. Giunchiglia (Eds.), The Semantic Web - ASWC 2006. XX, 778 pages. 2006.

Vol. 4184: M. Bravetti, M. Núñez, G. Zavattaro (Eds.), Web Services and Formal Methods. X, 289 pages. 2006.

Vol. 4183: J. Euzenat, J. Domingue (Eds.), Artificial Intelligence: Methodology, Systems, and Applications. XIII, 291 pages. 2006. (Sublibrary LNAI).

Vol. 4182: H.T. Ng, M.-K. Leong, M.-Y. Kan, D. Ji (Eds.), Information Retrieval Technology. XVI, 684 pages. 2006.

Vol. 4180: M. Kohlhase, OMDoc - An Open Markup Format for Mathematical Documents [version 1.2]. XIX, 428 pages. 2006. (Sublibrary LNAI).

Vol. 4179: J. Blanc-Talon, W. Philips, D. Popescu, P. Scheunders (Eds.), Advanced Concepts for Intelligent Vision Systems. XXIV, 1224 pages. 2006.

Vol. 4178: A. Corradini, H. Ehrig, U. Montanari, L. Ribeiro, G. Rozenberg (Eds.), Graph Transformations. XII, 473 pages. 2006.

Vol. 4176: S.K. Katsikas, J. Lopez, M. Backes, S. Gritzalis, B. Preneel (Eds.), Information Security. XIV, 548 pages. 2006.

Vol. 4175: P. Bücher, B.M.E. Moret (Eds.), Algorithms in Bioinformatics. XII, 402 pages. 2006. (Sublibrary LNBI).

Vol. 4174: K. Franke, K.-R. Müller, B. Nickolay, R. Schäfer (Eds.), Pattern Recognition. XX, 773 pages. 2006.

Vol. 4173: S. El Yacoubi, B. Chopard, S. Bandini (Eds.), Cellular Automata. XV, 734 pages. 2006.

Vol. 4172: J. Gonzalo, C. Thanos, M. F. Verdejo, R.C. Carrasco (Eds.), Research and Advanced Technology for Digital Libraries. XVII, 569 pages. 2006.

Vol. 4169: H.L. Bodlaender, M.A. Langston (Eds.), Parameterized and Exact Computation. XI, 279 pages. 2006.

Vol. 4168: Y. Azar, T. Erlebach (Eds.), Algorithms – ESA 2006. XVIII, 843 pages. 2006.

Vol. 4167: S. Dolev (Ed.), Distributed Computing. XV, 576 pages. 2006.

Vol. 4166: J. Górski (Ed.), Computer Safety, Reliability, and Security. XIV, 440 pages. 2006.

Vol. 4165: W. Jonker, M. Petković (Eds.), Secure, Data Management. X, 185 pages. 2006.

Vol. 4163: H. Bersini, J. Carneiro (Eds.), Artificial Immune Systems. XII, 460 pages. 2006.

Vol. 4162: R. Královič, P. Urzyczyn (Eds.), Mathematical Foundations of Computer Science 2006. XV, 814 pages. 2006.

Vol. 4161: R. Harper, M. Rauterberg, M. Combetto (Eds.), Entertainment Computing - ICEC 2006. XXVII, 417 pages. 2006.

Vol. 4160: M. Fisher, W.v.d. Hoek, B. Konev, A. Lisitsa (Eds.), Logics in Artificial Intelligence. XII, 516 pages. 2006. (Sublibrary LNAI).

Vol. 4159: J. Ma, H. Jin, L.T. Yang, J.J.-P. Tsai (Eds.), Ubiquitous Intelligence and Computing. XXII, 1190 pages. 2006.

Vol. 4158: L.T. Yang, H. Jin, J. Ma, T. Ungerer (Eds.), Autonomic and Trusted Computing. XIV, 613 pages. 2006.

Vol. 4156: S. Amer-Yahia, Z. Bellahsène, E. Hunt, R. Unland, J.X. Yu (Eds.), Database and XML Technologies. IX, 123 pages. 2006.

Vol. 4155: O. Stock, M. Schaerf (Eds.), Reasoning, Action and Interaction in AI Theories and Systems. XVIII, 343 pages. 2006. (Sublibrary LNAI).

Vol. 4154: Y.A. Dimitriadis, I. Zigurs, E. Gómez-Sánchez (Eds.), Groupware: Design, Implementation, and Use. XIV, 438 pages. 2006.

Vol. 4153: N. Zheng, X. Jiang, X. Lan (Eds.), Advances in Machine Vision, Image Processing, and Pattern Analysis. XIII, 506 pages. 2006.

Vol. 4152: Y. Manolopoulos, J. Pokorný, T. Sellis (Eds.), Advances in Databases and Information Systems. XV, 448 pages. 2006.

Vol. 4151: A. Iglesias, N. Takayama (Eds.), Mathematical Software - ICMS 2006. XVII, 452 pages. 2006.

Vol. 4150: M. Dorigo, L.M. Gambardella, M. Birattari, A. Martinoli, R. Poli, T. Stützle (Eds.), Ant Colony Optimization and Swarm Intelligence. XVI, 526 pages. 2006.

Vol. 4149: M. Klusch, M. Rovatsos, T.R. Payne (Eds.), Cooperative Information Agents X. XII, 477 pages. 2006. (Sublibrary LNAI).

Vol. 4148: J. Vounckx, N. Azemard, P. Maurine (Eds.), Integrated Circuit and System Design. XVI, 677 pages. 2006.

Vol. 4146: J.C. Rajapakse, L. Wong, R. Acharya (Eds.), Pattern Recognition in Bioinformatics. XIV, 186 pages. 2006. (Sublibrary LNBI).

Vol. 4144: T. Ball, R.B. Jones (Eds.), Computer Aided Verification. XV, 564 pages. 2006.

Vol. 4142: A. Campilho, M. Kamel (Eds.), Image Analysis and Recognition, Part II. XXVII, 923 pages. 2006.

Vol. 4141: A. Campilho, M. Kamel (Eds.), Image Analysis and Recognition, Part I. XXVIII, 939 pages. 2006.

Vol. 4139: T. Salakoski, F. Ginter, S. Pyysalo, T. Pahikkala, Advances in Natural Language Processing. XVI, 771 pages. 2006. (Sublibrary LNAI).

Vol. 4138: X. Cheng, W. Li, T. Znati (Eds.), Wireless Algorithms, Systems, and Applications. XVI, 709 pages. 2006.

Vol. 4137: C. Baier, H. Hermanns (Eds.), CONCUR 2006 – Concurrency Theory. XIII, 525 pages. 2006.

Vol. 4136: R.A. Schmidt (Ed.), Relations and Kleene Algebra in Computer Science. XI, 433 pages. 2006.

Vol. 4135: C.S. Calude, M.J. Dinneen, G. Păun, G. Rozenberg, S. Stepney (Eds.), Unconventional Computation. X, 267 pages. 2006.

Vol. 4134: K. Yi (Ed.), Static Analysis. XIII, 443 pages. 2006.

Vol. 4133: J. Gratch, M. Young, R. Aylett, D. Ballin, P. Olivier (Eds.), Intelligent Virtual Agents. XIV, 472 pages. 2006. (Sublibrary LNAI).

Vol. 4132: S. Kollias, A. Stafylopatis, W. Duch, E. Oja (Eds.), Artificial Neural Networks – ICANN 2006, Part II. XXXIV, 1028 pages. 2006.

Vol. 4131: S. Kollias, A. Stafylopatis, W. Duch, E. Oja (Eds.), Artificial Neural Networks – ICANN 2006, Part I. XXXIV, 1008 pages. 2006.

Vol. 4130: U. Furbach, N. Shankar (Eds.), Automated Reasoning. XV, 680 pages. 2006. (Sublibrary LNAI).

Vol. 4129: D. McGookin, S. Brewster (Eds.), Haptic and Audio Interaction Design. XII, 167 pages. 2006.

Vol. 4128: W.E. Nagel, W.V. Walter, W. Lehner (Eds.), Euro-Par 2006 Parallel Processing. XXXIII, 1221 pages. 2006.

Vol. 4127: E. Damiani, P. Liu (Eds.), Data and Applications Security XX. X, 319 pages. 2006.

Vol. 4126: P. Barahona, F. Bry, E. Franconi, N. Henze, U. Sattler, Reasoning Web. XII, 269 pages. 2006.

Vol. 4124: H. de Meer, J.P. G. Sterbenz (Eds.), Self-Organizing Systems. XIV, 261 pages. 2006.

Vol. 4121: A. Biere, C.P. Gomes (Eds.), Theory and Applications of Satisfiability Testing - SAT 2006. XII, 438 pages. 2006.

Vol. 4120: J. Calmet, T. Ida, D. Wang (Eds.), Artificial Intelligence and Symbolic Computation. XIII, 269 pages. 2006. (Sublibrary LNAI).

Vol. 4119: C. Dony, J.L. Knudsen, A. Romanovsky, A. Tripathi (Eds.), Advanced Topics in Exception Handling Components. X, 302 pages. 2006.

Vol. 4117: C. Dwork (Ed.), Advances in Cryptology - CRYPTO 2006. XIII, 621 pages. 2006.